Fundamentals of
Management

Fundamentals of
Management
Sixth Edition

James H. Donnelly, Jr.
Professor of Business Administration and
  Ashland Oil Faculty Fellow
University of Kentucky

James L. Gibson
Professor of Business Administration
University of Kentucky

John M. Ivancevich
Hugh Roy and Lillie Cranz Cullen Chair and
Professor of Organizational Behavior and
Management
University of Houston

1987

BUSINESS PUBLICATIONS, INC.

Plano, Texas 75075

© BUSINESS PUBLICATIONS, INC., 1971, 1975, 1978, 1981, 1984, and 1987

ISBN 0-256-03682-9
Library of Congress Catalog Card No. 86–71879
Printed in the United States of America
1 2 3 4 5 6 7 8 9 0 K 4 3 2 1 0 9 8 7

to
Helene S. Donnelly, Jeanne M. Servais, Connie Vick
Dianne Gibson
Anne and Mike Ivancevich

Preface

Recognition of Fundamentals of Management

Recently the *Academy of Management Review* published a review of the 10 leading management textbooks.* The results of the study established *Fundamentals of Management* as among the best of the books studied. In addition, the supplementary resources that accompany the text received very high ratings.

This gratifying recognition of our efforts has provided us with additional incentive to continue to improve our book. The rationale for this edition remains the same as for previous editions. Management, we believe, is practiced best by individuals who have had some access to high-quality, challenging textbooks.

Objectives For This Edition

Every textbook must serve two constituencies well in order to be effective: (1) *academicians* who teach the course and (2) *students* who take the course. With this in mind, we established specific objectives for each of these groups.

Objective for our colleagues. It is our belief that a high-quality textbook never compromises the integrity of the field it explores. Therefore, in this edition, our objective has been *to establish our text in every respect as a quality work of management scholarship that we as academicians could be proud of.*

Objective for student readers. We believe that a high-quality textbook never loses sight of its ultimate purpose—to help students learn. In this edition our objective has been *to continue striving to make our textbook the most contemporary, comprehensive, challenging, readable, and exciting management textbook available in America today.*

Key Characteristics

A high-quality textbook possesses several key characteristics. It is comprehensive, systematic, scientific, practical—and exciting.

---

* Allen C. Bluedorn, "Resources for the Introductory Management Course," *Academy of Management Review,* July 1986, pp. 684–91.

Comprehensive.   This text is comprehensive because it covers the major management topics affecting students, teachers, and practitioners. The study cited above found that our book is being used to cover American Assembly of Collegiate Schools of Business (AACSB) common body of knowledge requirements for both Organizational Behavior/Organization Theory and Production/Operations Management. The materials selected for this book reflect our extensive contacts with teaching colleagues, students, practicing managers, accrediting agencies such as AACSB, and professional societies such as the Academy of Management and the American Management Association.

Systematic.   In studying management, a beginning student can easily be overwhelmed by the vast number of concepts, theories, and topics. The systematic approach of *Fundamentals of Management* helps overcome this tendency. In each chapter's subject matter, readers are able to see where they have been, where they are, and where they will be going.

This book is divided into five parts. And each part is structured around three fundamental managerial tasks common to all organizations: managing work and organizations, managing people, and managing production and operations.

Part I, Management and the Managerial Environment, introduces the reader to the job of management, the study of management, the environment in which a manager must perform, and the important national concern for productivity.

Part II, Managing Work and Organizations, examines the classical foundations of the field and the three primary management functions of planning, organizing, and controlling. It includes a new chapter on human resource management.

Part III, Managing People, focuses on the behavioral contributions to such important management issues as motivation, group behavior, leadership, communications, and organizational development.

Part IV, Managing Production and Operations, explains management science's contributions to production and operations management, decision-support systems, and techniques for routine and nonroutine production and operations decisions.

Part V, Emerging Management Issues, examines management's social and ethical responsibilities, multinational management, the changing world of management, and management as a career.

Scientific.   *Fundamentals of Management* presents concepts and theories that have been subjected to extensive research. However, our textbook does not attempt to teach social or behavioral science, or operations management. It provides bases for applying to management many relevant contributions from numerous scientific disciplines. In this edition, *every* chapter has been revised to include the most up-to-date thinking and research.

Practical. To become an effective manager, the student must learn to analyze management problems and solve them by applying relevant management theory. *Fundamentals of Management* stresses a practical approach to learning these vital skills. Subject matter is reinforced with descriptions of how actual managers in real organizations have applied the concepts to solve problems. In addition, there are 65 case applications and experiential exercises to bring the chapter material to life in real-world situations.

Exciting. The practice of management is exciting, and a management textbook should be too. We try to convey this excitement to our readers. Every chapter, except for the opening one, begins with an account of an organization or individual manager facing a particular management problem or real-life situation that will be discussed in the following pages. In addition, each chapter contains at least three contemporary examples of real-world applications of concepts discussed in the chapter. Important points are illustrated and summarized in each chapter.

A LEARNING-ORIENTED TEXTBOOK

In addition to the features retained and updated from previous editions, several new features that encourage learning have been recently added.

Learning objectives. Clear, attainable goals are spelled out at the start of each chapter. In each chapter, the student learns to *define, describe, discuss, compare,* and *identify* essential issues affecting modern management.

Management in action. To arouse reader interest, we have added all new and more exciting chapter-opening vignettes taken from real-life situations to orient students to concepts and problems discussed in the text.

Figures and tables. Important points are illustrated with well-crafted visuals, including key concepts to reiterate essential material.

Management FOCUS. A series of all new, timely, real-life examples is drawn from over 60 of America's leading companies. These examples illustrate problems modern managers confront daily, and they appear at exact points in the discussion where the concept or theory is being discussed.

Cases. Throughout the text, cases have either been added and/or updated:

End of chapter. There are now a total of 42 cases. New ones have been added to this edition, and old ones have been updated and revised. These cases feature familiar organizations and current issues to show practical applications of concepts in the chapters.

End of part. Three "Comprehensive" real-world cases appear at the end of Part II, Managing Work and Organizations, Part III, Managing People, and Part IV, Managing Production and Operations. Analysis of these cases requires comprehension of relevant aspects of the entire part.

End of text. This book concludes with two issue-oriented "Integrative" cases. The cases tie together all relevant aspects of all chapters.

Summary of key points. Every chapter concludes with a concise, point-by-point summary of key topics.

Discussion and review questions. Every chapter concludes with relevant questions addressing the major issues explored.

Additional references. Every chapter concludes with 15 to 20 additional references to give students initial sources for writing projects. Except for classic works, these references have been totally updated for all chapters and include the latest available work.

Glossary. Every key term in the book is included in an extensive glossary.

Indexes. To help students locate information, the book contains three indexes: a comprehensive author index, a detailed subject index, and a new company index that is used to relate concepts to actual firms discussed in the chapters.

Experiential exercises. Twelve "Experiential Exercises" are included where appropriate. We included these learning methods in the previous edition, and several new ones have been added here. We have received positive reactions to these exercises. They move the material from "seeing" and "listening" to "doing." The understanding of management concepts is greatly enhanced when students can actively join in the learning process. More and more contemporary students seek out courses that include opportunities to learn from experience.

THE FUNDAMENTALS OF MANAGEMENT INSTRUCTIONAL SUPPORT SYSTEM

With this edition we introduce our Instructional Support System, a coordinated and integrated complete system of instructional support for both teacher and student. As mentioned earlier, the supplementary materials available with our text have been rated the best available. The goal for our new Instructional Support System is to make them even better for the present edition.

Instructional Support for Instructors

Teaching resource guide.   We believe that even the most experienced and dedicated teacher will find useful hints and insightful ideas in this unique guide. From a pedagogical perspective, we believe this is the real strength of the *Fundamentals of Management* Instructional Support System. We encourage those interested in *teaching* management to examine this element of the system because we believe there is nothing available that approaches its quality and innovativeness. Over 250 sources were used to develop the material. A special feature of the guide provides four series on topics that are particularly relevant to management today: American Entrepreneurship, The Japanese Challenge, Group Think, and Career Issues.

Instructor's manual.   Far more than the traditional instructor's manual, ours is organized to follow each chapter in the text and includes: chapter objectives, chapter synopsis, chapter outline with tips and ideas, suggested films to supplement class discussion, 10 additional end-of-chapter questions along with answers per chapter, exciting "mindbenders" that can be used for class discussion, suggested transparencies, term paper topics, end-of-chapter practical exercises, additional experiential exercises, transparency masters, suggested class projects and speakers, and suggested readings. It is a complete manual in every respect.

Transparencies.   A complete set of quality four-color transparencies has been developed specifically for our Instructional Support System. These transparencies are a separate element in addition to the over 100 transparency masters of text illustrations included in the Instructor's Manual, and the additional ones included in the Teaching Resource Guide.

Test bank.   This examination resource contains a wide variety of materials such as true/false, multiple choice, and essay questions. Items are categorized by type of question.

Automated test service.   A complete, high-quality testing service is provided.

A management experience.   This PC-compatible management game is both exciting and challenging. It was designed specifically as an element for our Instructional Support System to provide management students with a truly interactive learning experience.

Instructional Support for Students

Study guide.   This innovative supplement is far more than a review for students. It includes articles from *The Wall Street Journal* and *Barron's* related to each chapter, experiential exercises, and a reference guide showing how to write to key people in corporations and other organizations. It is truly instructional support for students. Also included is standard fare for such supplements: chapter previews; key terms; chapter outlines; study questions, including true/false, multiple choice, short answer, and discussion questions. We have found that because of the innovative content of the guide, many instructors use it as an active part of the class rather than as something students use alone to help them prepare for examinations. In fact, many instructors have commented that it is as much a workbook or "practice set" as it is a study guide.

Perspectives on management. This supplement contains over 30 articles from a cross-section of current management literature. They are all timely and less theoretical than in previous editions. The articles are those that are currently influencing the practicing manager. The articles do not have to be read in sequence; however, they follow the same organization as the text and are carefully balanced so that each subject area receives the same amount of emphasis.

In conclusion, the *Fundamentals of Management* Instructional Support System has been developed to provide instructors and students with a complete set of integrated support elements to make possible a challenging and rewarding management course. Suggestions for improvement from instructors and students are encouraged.

ACKNOWLEDGMENTS

The authors wish to acknowledge the contributions of reviewers of previous editions. They have contributed much to the success of *Fundamentals of Management* because their ideas and suggestions are reflected throughout our book. For this edition we are especially indebted to Stan Guzell of Youngstown State University, James R. Necessary of Ball State University, James Pesek of Clarion State College, John Pierce of the University of Minnesota, and Lawrence Podell of Baruch College of the City University of New York and William Patterson College.

Finally, Richard W. Furst, Dean of the College of Business and Economics, University of Kentucky, and James W. McFarland, Dean of the College of Business Administration, University of Houston, provided much support for our efforts. Dianne Gibson, Margaret Ivancevich, Judy Haywood, and Karen Lytwyn provided tremendous assistance in preparing the manuscript.

James H. Donnelly, Jr.
James L. Gibson
John M. Ivancevich

Contents

PART I
MANAGEMENT AND THE MANAGERIAL ENVIRONMENT

PART III
MANAGING PEOPLE

Fundamentals of
Management

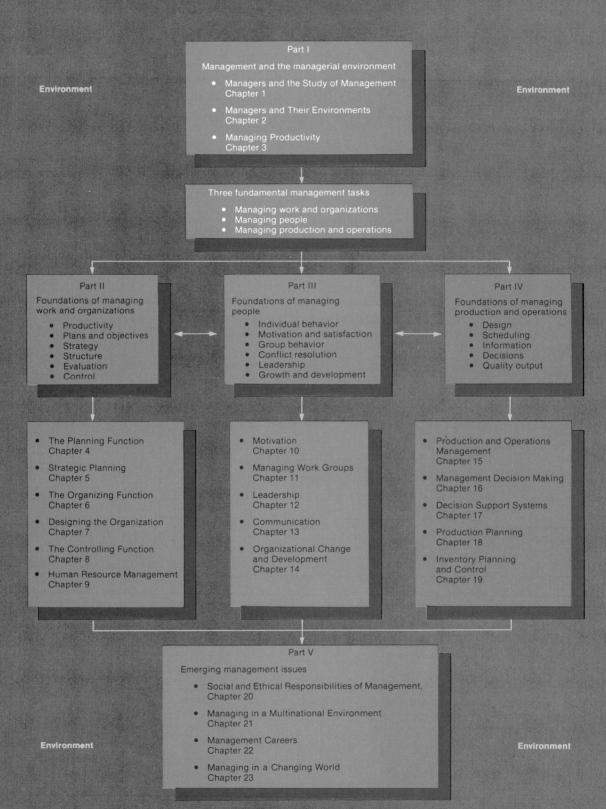

Environment

Part I

Management and the managerial environment

- Managers and the Study of Management
  Chapter 1

- Managers and Their Environments
  Chapter 2

- Managing Productivity
  Chapter 3

Environment

Three fundamental management tasks

- Managing work and organizations
- Managing people
- Managing production and operations

Part II

Foundations of managing
work and organizations

- Productivity
- Plans and objectives
- Strategy
- Structure
- Evaluation
- Control

Part III

Foundations of managing
people

- Individual behavior
- Motivation and satisfaction
- Group behavior
- Conflict resolution
- Leadership
- Growth and development

Part IV

Foundations of managing
production and operations

- Design
- Scheduling
- Information
- Decisions
- Quality output

- The Planning Function
  Chapter 4

- Strategic Planning
  Chapter 5

- The Organizing Function
  Chapter 6

- Designing the Organization
  Chapter 7

- The Controlling Function
  Chapter 8

- Human Resource Management
  Chapter 9

- Motivation
  Chapter 10

- Managing Work Groups
  Chapter 11

- Leadership
  Chapter 12

- Communication
  Chapter 13

- Organizational Change
  and Development
  Chapter 14

- Production and Operations
  Management
  Chapter 15

- Management Decision Making
  Chapter 16

- Decision Support Systems
  Chapter 17

- Production Planning
  Chapter 18

- Inventory Planning
  and Control
  Chapter 19

Part V

Emerging management issues

- Social and Ethical Responsibilities of Management,
  Chapter 20

- Managing in a Multinational Environment
  Chapter 21

- Management Careers
  Chapter 22

- Managing in a Changing World
  Chapter 23

Environment

Environment

MANAGEMENT AND THE MANAGERIAL ENVIRONMENT

Chapter 1

MANAGERS AND THE STUDY OF MANAGEMENT

LEARNING OBJECTIVES

After completing Chapter 1, you should be able to:

■ **Define**
the terms *manager* and *management*.

■ **Describe**
the evolution of management as a field of study.

■ **Discuss**
why the study of management can be important to almost anyone.

■ **Compare**
the three approaches to management.

■ **Identify**
the work of management.

Almost everyone reading this book is, has been, or someday will be a manager. Most of the accomplishments of our society happen because groups of people get involved in joint efforts. Every time you participate in an organized effort or receive the benefits of an organized effort, a manager of some sort is responsible for achieving results. *Managers are ultimately responsible for the achievement of results through the specialized efforts of other people, whether individually, in groups, or in organizations.* The program director of a campus club is a manager, as are a bank's chief executive, a college dean, a governor, and a football coach. What these individuals have in common is that they all manage. *Management is the process undertaken by one or more individuals to coordinate the activities of others to achieve results not achievable by one individual acting alone.* And the process of management should be studied by anyone planning to become a successful manager.

The purpose of this chapter is to briefly examine management as a field of study and to explain the work of management. The chapter concludes by outlining the plan for this book.

WHY STUDY MANAGEMENT?

The study of management is important for two reasons. First, our society depends on specialized institutions and organizations to provide the goods and services we desire. These organizations are guided and directed by the decisions of one or more individuals designated as "managers." It is America's managers who allocate society's resources to various and often competing ends. Managers have the authority and responsibility to build safe or unsafe products, seek war or peace, build or destroy cities, clean up or pollute the environment. Managers establish the conditions under which we are provided jobs, incomes, lifestyles, products, services, protection, health care, and knowledge. It would be very difficult to find anyone in our nation who is neither a manager nor affected by the decisions of a manager.

Second, individuals not trained as managers often find themselves in managerial positions. Many individuals presently being trained to be teachers, accountants, musicians, salespersons, artists, physicians, or lawyers will one day earn their living as managers. They will manage schools, accounting firms, orchestras, sales organizations, museums, hospitals, and government agencies. The United States is an organizational society, and its organizations must have managers.

THE EVOLUTION OF MANAGEMENT AS A FIELD OF STUDY

Because the growth in the number and size of organizations is relatively new in history, the study of management is relatively new. Many of the first individuals to study and write about management were practicing managers. They described their own experiences and tried to generalize the principles they believed could be applied in similar situations. Even today, a great deal of what we know about management comes from the autobiographies and memoirs of men and women who are or have been practicing managers.

Now, however, other individuals also are interested in management for scientific reasons. Social and behavioral scientists view the management of organizations as an extremely important social phenomenon worthy of study through scientific inquiry. As scientists, these men and women make no value judgments regarding good or bad management practices. Their objective is to understand and explain the practice of management.

Between the two extremes of management practice and management science, there are many individuals who have contributed to the study of management. They include engineers, sociologists, psychologists, anthropologists, lawyers, economists, accountants, mathematicians, political scientists, and philosophers.

Such differing perspectives on the same subject cannot be neatly classified. Thus, as a manager, you will have at your disposal many ways of looking at management's tasks. Each may be more useful for some problems than for others. For example, a management theory that emphasizes employee satisfaction may be more helpful in dealing with a problem of high employee turnover than with delays in production. Because there is no single, universally accepted management theory, you should be familiar with the various major theories.

There are three well-established approaches to management thought: the *classical approach,* the *behavioral approach,* and the *management science approach.* Although these approaches evolved in historical sequence, later ideas have not always replaced earlier ones. Rather, each new approach has added to the knowledge of the previous ones. At the same time, each approach has continued to develop on its own. And at last, some merging did occur as later theorists attempted to integrate the accumulated knowledge. Two of these attempts to integrate theories—the *systems approach* and the *contingency approach*—will be discussed later in this section.

The Classical Approach

The classical approach was the first attempt to study modern management. Today, it remains a core knowledge area of the modern manager. Management began to be studied seriously at the beginning of this century. Managers were seeking answers to basic, practical questions, such as how to increase the efficiency and productivity of a rapidly expanding work force. The technological insights of engineers became increasingly significant as leaders of business sought to expand the productivity of workers during World War I.

These efforts led to an extensive body of knowledge concerning plant design, job design, work methods, and other aspects of the *management of work*.

At about the same time, many small, single-product companies were expanding into large multiproduct organizations. The individuals who managed these organizations recognized that the *management of organizations* was quite different from the management of work. Thus, men and women began to study the problems of managing large, complex organizations. They viewed management much as it is viewed in this book: as the process of coordinating group effort toward group goals. It was in this period that *planning, organizing,* and *controlling* were identified as the functions that comprise the management process.

Let us briefly examine each management function:

Planning: The planning function helps an organization define and meet its objectives. Managers, through their plans, outline what an organization must do to be successful.

Organizing: After managers establish objectives and draw up plans to achieve them, they must design and develop an organization able to achieve their goals. Organizing means turning plans into action with the help of leadership and motivation.

Controlling: A manager must make sure the actual performance of the organization conforms to the performance planned for the organization.

The important contributions of the classical approach will be covered in greater detail in Part II of the book.

The Behavioral Approach

The behavioral approach developed partly because practicing managers found that the ideas of the classical approach did not always achieve total efficiency and workplace harmony. Managers encountered problems because subordinates did not always behave as the classical approach said they were supposed to. Thus, increased interest developed in helping managers become more effective at *managing people.* The behavioral approach uses the concepts of psychology, sociology, anthropology, and other behavioral sciences to assist managers in understanding human behavior in the work environment. The emphasis of the behavioral approach focuses on the interrelationships between people, work, and organizations. It concentrates on such topics as motivation, communications, leadership, and work group formation, which can assist managers with the people aspects of their job.

The important contributions of the behavioral approach will be covered in greater detail in Part III of the book.

The Management Science Approach

In one sense, the management science approach is a modern version of the early emphasis on the management of work by the classical approach. Its essential feature is the use of mathematics and statistics as aids in *managing operations*. Its management literature focuses on solving technical rather than behavioral problems. It concentrates on concepts and tools useful to managers in solving problems related to what the organization produces. The computer contributed greatly to the growth of this approach, because it can analyze complex production and operations problems in a way not previously possible.

The important contributions of the management science approach will be covered in greater detail in Part IV of the book.

Attempts to Integrate the Three Approaches

During the last 20 years, there have been attempts to achieve integration of the three approaches to management. One of these attempts, the *systems approach*, stresses that organizations must be viewed as total systems, with each part linked to every other part. Another, the *contingency approach*, stresses that the correctness of a managerial practice is contingent upon how it fits the particular situation in which it is applied. Let us briefly examine each.

The systems approach.   The systems approach to management is really a way of thinking about management problems. It views an organization as a group of interrelated parts with a single purpose. The action of one part will influence the others, and managers cannot deal separately with individual parts. For example, it is incorrect to think that if a production problem exists, the solution to the problem will not have an impact in the marketing area. In solving problems, managers using the systems approach must view the organization as a dynamic whole and must try to anticipate the intended as well as unintended impacts of their decisions. Such managers do not solve individual problems. Rather, they intervene in a total system of interrelated parts, using the management functions of planning, organizing, and controlling.

The age-old confrontation between production costs and the marketing objective of a broad product line is one example of the interrelated nature of management problems. Each objective conflicts with the other. For production costs to be their lowest, the firm would produce one color and one style. To achieve the marketing objective, several models and several colors would be required but at higher costs. In this situation, a compromise is necessary for the overall system to achieve its objective. The objectives of the individual parts must be compromised to meet the objective of the entire firm.

Using the systems approach, individual managers must adopt a broad perspective of their jobs. With a systems perspective, they can more easily achieve coordination between the objectives of the various parts of the organization and the objectives of the organization as a whole.[1]

The contingency approach.   The systems approach forces managers to recognize that organizations are systems made up of interdependent parts and that a change in one part will affect other parts. It seeks to identify the characteristics of jobs, people, and organizations, allowing managers to see the interdependence between the various segments of an organization. The basic idea of the contingency approach is that there is no best way to plan, organize, or control. Rather, managers must find different ways to fit different situations. A method highly effective in one situation may not work in other situations. The contingency approach seeks to match different situations with different management methods.

Actually, the idea of contingency, or situational, thinking is not new. An early writer in the classical approach spoke during the 1920s of the "law of the situation." Mary Parker Follett noted that "different situations require different kinds of knowledge, and the man possessing the knowledge demanded by a certain situation tends in the best managed businesses, other things being equal, to become the leader of the moment."[2]

The contingency approach has grown in popularity over the last two decades because some research has found that, given certain characteristics of a job and certain characteristics of people doing the job, specific management practices tend to work better than others. For example, rigid plans, clearly defined jobs, autocratic leadership, and tight controls have at times resulted in high productivity and satisfied workers. At other times, just the opposite (general plans, loosely defined jobs, democratic leadership, and loose controls) has produced the same results.[3]

If, for instance, productivity needs to be increased, the manager will not

---

[1] For earlier discussions of the systems approach see Seymour Tilles, "The Manager's Job—A Systems Approach," *Harvard Business Review,* January–February 1963, pp. 73–81; Fremont E. Kast and James E. Rosenzweig, "General Systems Theory: Applications in Organizations and Management," *Academy of Management Journal,* December 1972, pp. 447–65. For a recent discussion, see M. L. Markus, *Systems in Organizations* (Marshfield, Mass.: Pitman Publishing, 1984).

[2] The many contributions of Mary Parker Follett are collected in Henry C. Metcalf and Lyndall Urwick, eds., *Dynamic Administration* (New York: Harper & Row, 1941).

[3] Henry L. Tosi and John W. Slocum, Jr., "Contingency Theory: Some Suggested Directions," *Journal of Management,* Spring 1984, pp. 9–26; A. Grandori, "A Prescriptive Contingency View of Organizational Decision Making," *Administrative Science Quarterly,* June 1984, pp. 192–209.

automatically assume a new work method is needed (a classical solution) or that a new motivational approach needs to be tried (a behavioral solution). Instead, the manager will study the characteristics of the workers, the nature of the job, and his or her own leadership approach before deciding on a solution.[4]

Both the systems approach and the contingency approach can provide valuable insights for students of management.

THE WORK OF MANAGEMENT

In introducing the three approaches to management, we have established that all modern managers essentially face three managerial tasks:

1. Managing work and organizations.
2. Managing people.
3. Managing production and operations.

No matter what an organization engages in, its manager will face these three tasks. Thus, managing is more than solving behavioral problems; it is more than solving technical problems; it is more than managing individual work; it is more than planning a department's future. The work of management is all of these. Learning to be a manager requires knowledge and skills relevant to each of these three tasks, which provide a point of departure for the study of management and also provide the structure and organization of this book.

Managing Work and Organizations

Whether the organization is small or large, private or public, management must make sure the work of the organization gets done and the organization itself is managed. For example, a college dean must make sure the work of the school gets done. Programs must be planned and classes scheduled; students must be advised; classes must be taught; faculty must be hired and evaluated. However, the college as an organization or entity also must be managed. Decisions must be made regarding the organization of the college, the number of departments, the development of job descriptions, and the assignment of tasks and authority. Decisions also must be made regarding changing educational needs and their impact on the present work of the college. Enrollments must be projected, new buildings planned, and funding

---

[4] For critiques of the contingency approach, see Justin G. Longenecker and Charles D. Pringle, "The Illusion of Contingency Theory as a General Theory," *Academy of Management Review,* July 1978, pp. 679–82; Harold Koontz, "The Management Theory Jungle Revisited," *Academy of Management Review,* April 1980, pp. 175–87.

needs identified. In all kinds of organizations, both the work and the organization itself must be managed.

Managing People

The popular saying that management is "getting work done through other people," although an oversimplification, underscores the importance of the managerial task of managing people. There are no "peopleless" organizations, so managers must know how to motivate, lead, and communicate, and they must understand interpersonal relations and the behavior of groups of people.

The organizations in our society are far more than instruments for providing each of us with goods and services. They also create the settings in which the majority of us spend our lives. In this respect, they have profound influence on our behavior. We are just becoming aware of some of the psychological effects of this type of involvement.

Managing Production and Operations

Every organization does something. It may manufacture automobiles, cure the ill, educate, protect, govern, or entertain. The process used to produce the organization's output also must be managed. The term *production* focuses on manufacturing technology and on the flow of materials in a manufacturing plant. In fact, the production function in a manufacturing organization is specifically concerned with the activity of producing goods: the design and operation of a system of people, materials, equipment, money, and information to produce a product or group of products.

The term *operations* is broader in scope and is used for the production activity in any organization—goods-producing, service-producing, public, private, profit, or nonprofit. Operations management is similar to production management except that it focuses on a wider class of problems. It includes organizations whose technologies may be quite different from those of a manufacturing firm.

There are many similarities between the flow of materials in a manufacturing firm, the processing of claims in an insurance company, student registration in a college, and the delivery of health care in a hospital. So an important focus of any managerial work is the task of managing operations.

Figure 1–1 illustrates that while each of the three managerial tasks can be discussed separately, they are very much interrelated. The figure also provides us with a framework that we will build upon throughout this book.

Figure 1–2 summarizes the challenges a modern manager faces and the wide knowledge necessary to plan, organize, and control. Managers must rely primarily on information based on the classical approach to manage work and organizations. To manage people, they need behavioral information. To control operations, they must have a management science perspective.

FIGURE   1–1   The Work of Management

*The work of
management involves
three interrelated tasks;
managing work and
organizations,
managing people, and
managing production
and operations.*

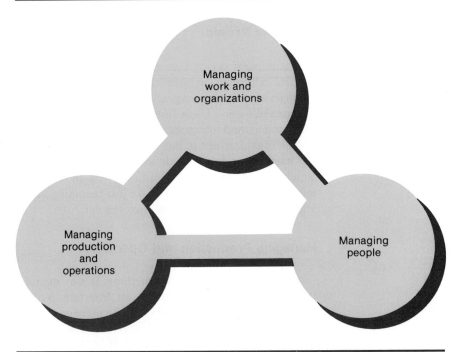

PLAN FOR THE BOOK

The purpose of this book is to prepare managers for the future—leaders well versed in all traditions of management. Managers must be well grounded in the techniques of planning, organizing, and controlling; they must understand the role of human behavior in organizations; and they must be skilled in the various ways to manage operations. Figure 1–3 illustrates the framework that will be followed in the book.

The three main managerial tasks serve as focal points for the three major sections of this textbook:

- Part II, "Managing Work and Organizations," contains six chapters devoted to various aspects of the three primary management functions: planning, organizing, and controlling.
- Part III, "Managing People," concentrates on the behavioral foundations of effective management. This section contains five chapters that discuss such important management topics as motivation, group behavior, leadership, communications, and development of the organization and its members.

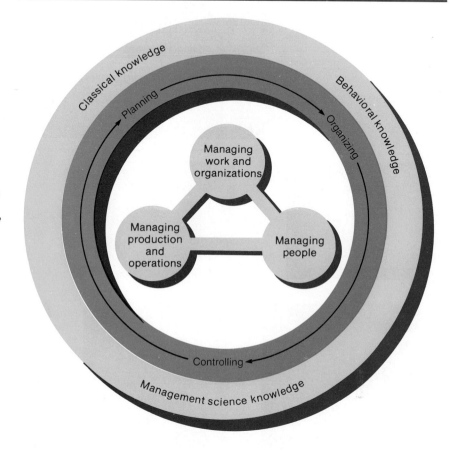

This figure illustrates the management tasks, the management functions, and the three approaches to management.

- Part IV focuses on the managerial task, "Managing Production and Operations." Its five chapters include discussions of production and operations management, decision making, management information systems, and introductory discussions of several tools useful in planning and controlling production and operations.

The book concludes with "Emerging Management Issues," important topics such as the social and ethical responsibilities of management, international management, the manager's changing world, and a chapter devoted to the career of management.

The remaining two chapters in this introductory section addresses the

FIGURE 1–3 Plan for the Book

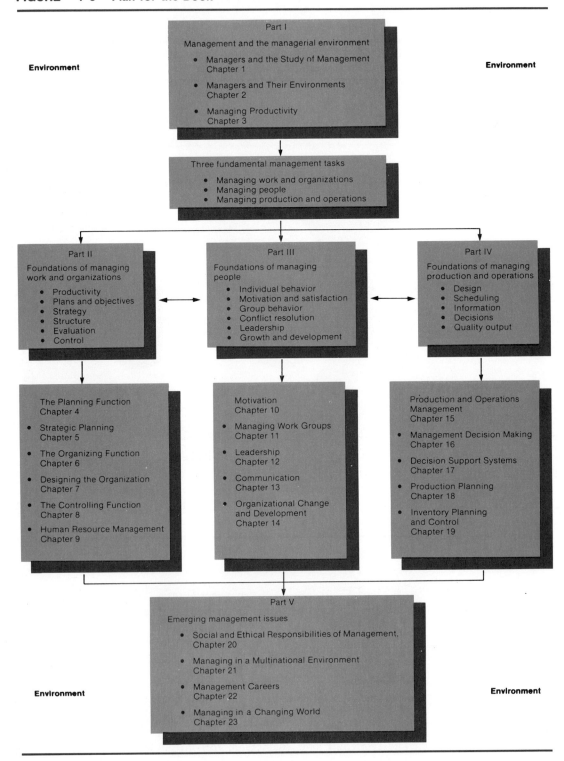

environments in which managers must manage and the important contemporary issue of productivity and the quality of work life.

SUMMARY OF KEY POINTS

- Our society depends on specialized institutions and organizations to provide the goods and services we desire. Thus, management is important to the workings of society.

- Managers are ultimately responsible for the achievement of results through the specialized efforts of other people, whether individually, in groups, or in organizations.

- Management is the process undertaken by one or more individuals to coordinate the activities of others to achieve results not possible by one individual acting alone.

- Three fundamental tasks comprise managerial work: managing work and organizations, managing people, and managing production and operations. These three tasks are generally applicable to managers in all types of organizations.

- Management literature offers a variety of viewpoints and emphasis. We have sought to introduce some clarity by identifying three mutually supportive approaches to management: classical, which focuses on the task of managing work and organizations; behavioral, focusing on the task of managing people; and management science, which focuses on the task of managing production and operations.

- Figure 1–2 outlines the practical challenges and required knowledge of a modern manager. It relates the three management functions of planning, organizing, and controlling to the three fundamental managerial tasks and the three approaches to the study of management. It serves as a summary of this introductory chapter.

- In the study of management, future managers cannot ignore the contributions of any of the three approaches. Each deals with an important task future managers will face. With this in mind, review Figure 1–3, the plan for our book.

DISCUSSION AND REVIEW QUESTIONS

1. Did any management decisions influence you today? Outline and discuss at least one.
2. Explain why management is required to coordinate group effort.
3. Some people believe that managers are an important social resource in our nation. Do you agree? Discuss.
4. What is the significance of the fact that our nation is "an organizational society"?

5. Evaluate the statement: "Management is getting work done through people."

6. Choose any management job with which you are familiar. Outline how the work and organization, people, and operations are managed.

7. What are the important differences between the three approaches to management as you now know them?

8. Have you ever managed anything—for example, as part of a job or in a social or civic organization? If so, did you perform the management functions of planning, organizing, and controlling without being aware of it? Discuss your managerial experience and relate it to the functions of management.

9. One writer has stated: "People who don't manage are either too young, too old, or found in institutions for the incompetent." What is this writer trying to say? Do you agree? Why?

10. Would a basketball coach be likely to use a contingency approach to managing? Explain.

ADDITIONAL REFERENCES

Cummings, L. L. "The Logics of Management." *Academy of Management Review,* October 1983, pp. 532–36.

Dubno, P. "Attitudes toward Women Executives: A Longitudinal Approach." *Academy of Management Journal.* December 1985, pp. 235–39.

Kantrow, A. M. "Why Read Peter Drucker?" *Harvard Business Review,* January–February 1980, pp. 74–82.

Koontz, H. *Toward a Unified Theory of Management.* New York: McGraw-Hill, 1964.

Koprowski, E. J. "Exploring the Meaning of 'Good' Management." *Academy of Management Review,* July 1981, pp. 459–68.

Maitland, I.; J. Bryson; and A. Van De Ven. "Sociologists, Economists, and Opportunism." *Academy of Management Review,* January 1985, pp. 59–65.

Prein, H. "A Contingency Approach for Conflict Intervention." *Groups and Organization Studies,* March 1984, pp. 81–102.

Presthus, R. *The Organizational Society.* New York: Alfred A. Knopf, 1962.

Smith, K. G., T. R. Mitchell, and C. E. Summer. "Top Level Management Priorities in Different Stages of the Organizational Life Cycle." *Academy of Management Journal,* December 1985, pp. 799–820.

Stewart, R. "A Model for Understanding Managerial Jobs and Behavior." *Academy of Management Review,* January 1982, pp. 7–13.

Urwick, L. "That Word 'Organization,'" *Academy of Management Review,* January 1976, pp. 89–91.

Walton, C. C. *Ethos and the Executive.* Englewood Cliffs, N.J.: Prentice-Hall, 1969.

Whitely, W. "Managerial Work Behavior: An Integration of Results from Two Major Approaches." *Academy of Management Journal,* June 1985, pp. 344–62.

Yorks, L., and D. A. Whitsett. "Hawthorne, Topeka, and the Issue of Science versus Advocacy." *Academy of Management Review,* January 1985, pp. 59–65.

Selected Management and Related Periodicals

The vast majority of reports and writings on management are contained in the periodicals listed below. Some of these, such as the *Academy of Management Review,* are devoted entirely to topics in management, while *Organizational Behavior and Human Performance,* and *Management Science* are directed toward specialists trained in these areas. Others such as *Harvard Business Review, Business Horizons,* and *California Management Review* are general-interest journals, while *Business Week, Forbes, Fortune,* and *The Wall Street Journal* report current events and practices.

Academy of Management Journal
Academy of Management Review
Administration and Society
Administrative Science Quarterly
Advanced Management Journal
Business and Society Review
Business Horizons
Business Management
Business Week
California Management Review
Canadian Manager
Columbia Journal of World Business
Decision Sciences
Forbes
Fortune
Group and Organization Studies
Harvard Business Review
Human Resource Management
Industrial Engineering
Industrial and Labor Relations Review
Industrial Management Review
Information and Management
Interfaces
International Management
Journal of Applied Behavioral Science

Journal of Applied Psychology
Journal of Business
Journal of Human Resources
Journal of Management
Journal of Management Studies
Journal of Systems Management
Long Range Planning
Management International Review
Management Review
Management Science
Managerial Planning
Michigan Business Review
Operations Research
Organizational Behavior and Human Decision Processes
Organizational Dynamics
P & IM Review
Personnel
Personnel Journal
Personnel Psychology
Public Administration Review
Sloan Management Review
Strategic Management Journal
Training and Development Journal
The Wall Street Journal

EXPERIENTIAL EXERCISE

ATTITUDES ABOUT BUSINESS ORGANIZATIONS

Purpose

The purpose of this exercise is to identify attitudes that students have about business and various industries.

The Exercise in Class

1. Individually, each student is to complete the surveys about business and various industries (see Exhibits 1 and 2).
2. After individuals complete the surveys, the instructor will form five- to seven-person groups to discuss the individual ratings.
3. Each group will calculate an average group score for each item (adding the individual scores and dividing by the number of individuals in the group to arrive at an average).
4. The average scores will be placed by the group on the board or a flip chart for the class to discuss.

The Learning Message

Differences in student opinions exist. This exercise will display these differences and may also point out why they exist (e.g., backgrounds, pessimism, optimism, values).

Survey of Business

In your opinion, have business organizations in general been supportive in each of the following areas? Use the following scale to indicate how supportive you believe business has been, placing the appropriate number in the space after each area of concern.

> 5—significant support
> 4—some support
> 3—undecided
> 2—little, if any, support
> 1—no support

Area of concern:

Energy conservation _____
Improving quality of worker's life _____
Controlling environmental pollution _____
Fighting inflation _____
Helping higher education _____
Retraining obsolete employees _____
Developing urban areas _____
Hiring the handicapped _____
Hiring minorities _____
Promoting ethical behavior _____
Technological advancement _____
Rewarding good performance _____
Maintaining fair profit margins _____
A strong government _____

Survey of Industries

Please provide a rating for the industries listed below. In other words, what are your general impressions of these industries? Why do you feel this way? Use values of 1 to 5 according to the scale below. Place the number you choose for the industry in the appropriate blank space.

5—very good
4—generally good
3—unsure
2—generally poor
1—very poor

Industry:

Automobile	_____	Television	_____
Steel	_____	Aerospace	_____
Tobacco	_____	Health care	_____
Food processing	_____	Education	_____
Banking	_____	Fast food	_____
Publishing	_____	Computer	_____
Religion	_____	Paper	_____
Oil	_____	Insurance	_____
Chemicals	_____	Car repair	_____
Electronics	_____	Prescription drugs	_____
Tire and rubber	_____		

MANAGERS AND THEIR ENVIRONMENTS

LEARNING OBJECTIVES

After completing Chapter 2, you should be able to:

■ **Define**
an organization in terms of a system.

■ **Describe**
the organizational environment as a system.

■ **Discuss**
the internal and external environments in which a manager must function.

■ **Compare**
the skills necessary for effective managerial performance.

■ **Identify**
the various roles managers must perform.

☐ MANAGEMENT IN ACTION

What Does an Old Jukebox Maker Do When Its Environment Changes*

Back in the days when Elvis was king, so was the Seeburg Phonograph Corp. At one time, its name was on half of the 550,000 jukeboxes in soda fountains, bars, and diners across the nation. But certain changes occurred:

1. As population moved to the suburbs, city soda fountains shut down.
2. Interstate highways and fast-food outlets siphoned customers away from small-town diners and juke joints.
3. Video games competed for young people's quarters.

For Seeburg, these environmental changes added up to disaster. The company was sold twice, declared bankruptcy twice, and was finally dissolved by Stern Electronics in 1982.

Seeburg's encore started in 1984, when two former managers paid Stern $2 million for the rights to the Seeburg name and its assets. Now, with its old-time management back in place, a new Seeburg hopes to ride new technology to new heights. Its new jukebox plays compact disks, the recordings read by laser beams that are the sensation of the audio business. Management believes the high-quality, digital-audio sound of compact disks will revitalize the industry. One executive stated, "It's hard to call something as fancy and as sophisticated as this a jukebox."

When Seeburg ships its first compact-disk jukebox in the spring of 1986, it hopes to pull off a repeat of the company's 1948 success: the first jukebox that offered a menu of 100 selections. That system catapulted the company, which started out in 1902 as a piano manufacturer, to the industry's number 1 spot, which it held for nearly 30 years. The upcoming machines will shuffle only 60 disks. But because these are compact-disk albums containing 10 or more tunes that can be played individually, the new jukes will offer 600 selections—triple the number available on the latest conventional systems.

Many factors in a firm's external environment influence managerial performance. Seeburg's management is seeking to respond and adapt to technological as well as cultural and social changes. Technological, cultural, and social change are some of the forces this chapter will discuss. We will not only discuss the various environments in which managers must exist but also describe the skills necessary to deal with these environments.

---

* Source: "Can High Tech Put Seeburg Back in the Groove?" *Business Week,* December 2, 1985, p. 89.

Many different forces inside and outside an organization influence a manager's performance. So the management functions of planning, organizing, and controlling often must be accomplished under constantly changing conditions. A manager must deal with two environments: the organization's *internal environment,* which usually can be controlled, and the often unpredictable and uncontrollable whims of the outside world, the *external environment.*

THE ORGANIZATION

Organizations vary in purpose and in technology. Schools, hospitals, banks, telephone companies, civic groups, and restaurants are all examples of organizations with differing goals and needs. But they and any other organization have one element in common: managers.

The basic concepts of systems theory can help managers simplify and deal with the complex interactions of internal and external environments.[1] An organization can be viewed as simply one element in a number of elements that depend on each other. The organization takes resources (input) from the larger system (the external environment), processes these resources within its internal environment, and returns them to the outside in changed form (output). Figure 2–1 displays the fundamental elements of the organization as a system.

A business firm has two major inputs: human and nonhuman resources. Human inputs come from the people who work in the firm. They contribute their time and energy to the organization in exchange for wages and other tangible and intangible rewards. Nonhuman resources consist of raw materials and information. These are transformed or used in combination with human resources to provide other resources. A steel mill employs people and blast furnaces, plus other tools and machinery, to transform iron ore into steel and steel products. General Motors takes steel, rubber, plastic, fabrics, and—in combination with people, tools, and equipment—makes automobiles. A university uses resources to teach students, do research, and to provide information to society through the educational process. The inputs are students, faculty, and money. A hospital's inputs are its staff, supplies, and patients. The patients are processed through the application of medical knowledge and treatment. The output is patients restored to a level of health consistent with the severity of the disease.

It is the manager who must coordinate the activities of the entire system (organization) or one of the many subsystems (departments) within the organization. For the manager, the systems concept emphasizes that (1) the ultimate

---

[1] For further discussion, see M. L. Markus, *Systems in Organizations* (Marshfield, Mass.: Pitman Publishing, 1984).

FIGURE   2–1   The Organizational Environment as a System

Every organization interacts with a larger system by taking resources and providing outputs.

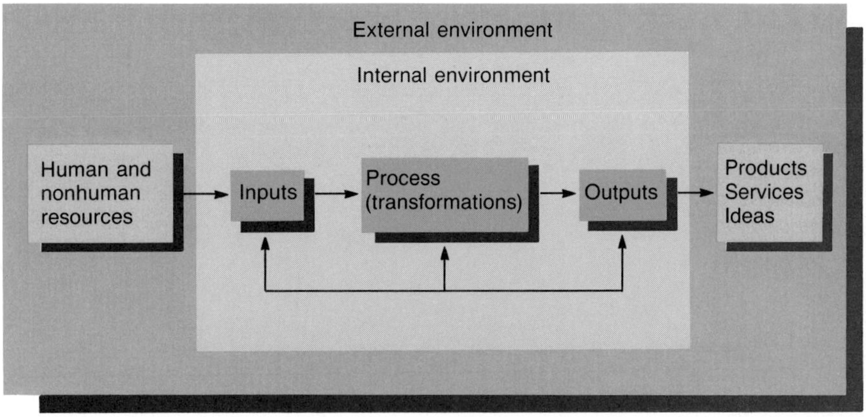

survival of the organization depends upon its ability to *adapt to the demands of the environment* and (2) in meeting these demands, *the total input-process-output cycle must be the focus of managerial attention.*

THE INTERNAL ENVIRONMENT

This section examines the environment inside the organization in which a manager must function. It includes discussions of the settings where managers work, the day-to-day activities that utilize much of their time, and some generalized skills necessary to cope with the internal environment. We shall begin by looking at the various *levels* of management, then focus on managerial *skills* and *roles.*

Three Management Levels

Most organizations function on at least three distinct but overlapping levels, each requiring a different managerial focus and emphasis.[2] They include the *operations level,* the *managerial level,* and the *strategic level.* These are illustrated in Figure 2–2.

---

[2] The classic works in this area are Henry Mintzberg, *The Nature of Managerial Work* (New York: Harper & Row, 1973); Henry Mintzberg, "The Manager's Job, Folklore and Fact," *Harvard Business Review,* July–August 1975, pp. 49–61.

FIGURE   2–2   The Levels of Management

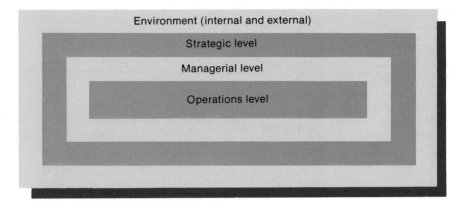

*Three overlapping
levels constitute most
organizations, each
with its own focus and
emphasis.*

The operations level.   We know from Chapter 1 that every organization, whether it produces a physical product or a service, has an operations function.[3] In any organization, therefore, there is an operations level that focuses on performing effectively, whatever it is that the organization produces or does. In the case of a physical product, there is the flow of materials and the supervision of the operations. Colleges must be sure their students are properly processed, registered, scheduled, and taught and their records are maintained. Banks must see that checks are processed and financial transactions are recorded accurately and quickly.

As Figure 2–2 shows, an operations function is at the core of every organization. The managerial task here is to develop the best allocation of resources that will produce the desired output.

The managerial level.   As an organization increases in size, someone must coordinate the activities at the operations level as well as decide which products or services to produce. These problems are the focus of the managerial level. A dissatisfied student complains to the dean of the college. A sales manager mediates disagreement between customers and salespeople. Production schedules and amounts to be produced must be planned for an automobile manufacturer.

At this level, the managerial task is really twofold: (1) managing the operations function and (2) serving as a liaison between those who produce the

---

[3] For a discussion of technology in service organizations, see Karl Albrecht and Ron Zemke, *Service America* (Homewood, Ill.: Dow Jones–Irwin, 1985); Peter K. Mills and Dennis Moberg, "Perspectives on the Technology of Service Organizations," *Academy of Management Review.* July 1982, pp. 467–78.

FIGURE   2–3   Managers and the Levels of Management

The primary focus of managers' activities depends on their level in the organization.

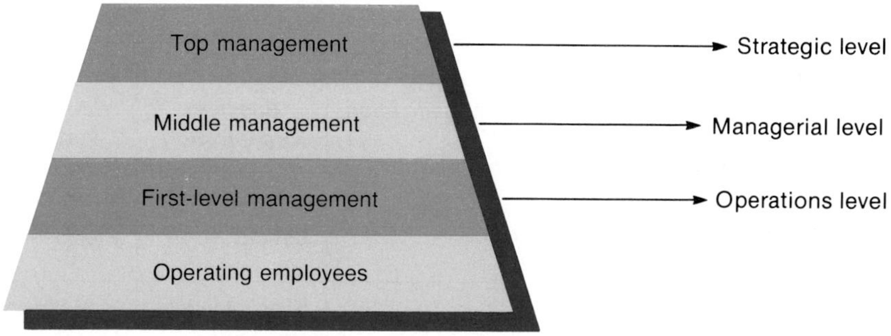

Top management	→ Strategic level
Middle management	→ Managerial level
First-level management	→ Operations level
Operating employees	

---

product or service and those who use the output. In other words, for the operations level to do its work, a manager must make sure it has the correct materials and also must see that the output gets sold or used.

The strategic level.   Every organization operates in a broad social environment. As a part of the environment, an organization also is responsible to the environment. The strategic level must make sure the managerial level operates within the bounds of society. Since the ultimate source of authority in any organization comes from society, the organization must provide goods and services to society in a manner approved by society. Thus, the strategic level determines the long-range objectives and direction for the organization—in other words, how the organization will interact with its environment.[4] The organization also may seek to influence its environment through lobbying efforts, advertising efforts, or educational programs aimed at members of society.

Types of Managers and Levels of Management

Understanding the three levels of management can be helpful in determining the primary focus of managers' activities at different levels in an organization. For example, a set of terms widely used in organizations includes *top management, middle management,* and *first-level management.* These are illustrated in Figure 2–3. The figure indicates that top management corresponds to the strategic level in Figure 2–2. Middle management corresponds

---

[4] George S. Day, *Analysis for Strategic Market Decisions* (St. Paul, Minn.: West Publishing, 1986).

FIGURE   2–4   Managers at Different Organizational Levels in Three Types of Organizations

Type of Organization / Level of Management	Business Organization	Educational Institution	Government Organization
Top	Director	President	Cabinet secretary
Middle	Superintendent Manager	Vice president Dean	Commissioner Division director
First	Supervisor	Department chairperson	Program manager

Different organizations use various terms to identify managers at different organizational levels.

to the managerial level, and first-level management corresponds to the operating level.

While the terms *top, middle,* and *first-level management* may not always correspond exactly to the three levels outlined in Figure 2–2, they do provide an understanding of what managers do at each level. The term *manager* covers all three levels, from the chief executive officer to the first-level supervisor. All are managers, but the focus of their activities varies.

The actual terms used to identify managers at various organizational levels differ from organization to organization. Figure 2–4 compares terms typically used in three types of organizations: business, education, and government.

Generally speaking, the activities of supervisors, chairpersons, and program managers are similar despite the different terms used to identify them. A chairperson of a department in a college could be expected to spend most of the time dealing with the faculty as individuals. Similarly, managers, presidents, and cabinet secretaries spend much of their time being concerned about the work that their organization is doing in terms of the expectations of owners, customers, and taxpayers. While we can identify similarities in managerial jobs as a function of their level in the organization, we must also recognize that dissimilarities will also exist. These dissimilarities arise from the uniqueness of each organization and the environments in which they exist.[5]

---

[5] M. Nash, *Managing Organization Performance* (San Francisco: Jossey-Bass, 1983); R. Stewart, "A Model for Understanding Managerial Jobs and Behavior," *Academy of Management Review,* January 1982, pp. 7–13.

FIGURE   2–5   The Skills of Managers

Top
management

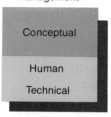

Middle
management

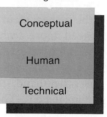

First-level
management

*The mix of managerial
skills will vary by
organizational level.*

The Skills of Managers

Certain general skills are needed for effective managerial performance,
regardless of the level of the manager in the hierarchy of the organization.
However, the mix of skills will differ depending on the level of the manager
in the organization. These skills and the necessary mix are illustrated in
Figure 2–5.[6] The figure indicates that there are three basic skills—technical,
human, and conceptual—needed by all managers.

---

[6] These managerial skills were first described in Robert L. Katz, "Skills of an Effective
Administrator," *Harvard Business Review,* September–October 1974, pp. 90–102.

Technical skill is the ability to use the tools, procedures, or techniques of a specialized field. Accountants, engineers, nurses, physicians, and musicians each have specific technical skills in their fields of specialization. Managers must possess sufficient technical skill to accomplish the jobs for which they are responsible. *Human skill* is the ability to work with and understand people. To manage people effectively, managers must participate effectively with others. *Conceptual skill* is the ability to comprehend all activities and interests of the organization. This skill involves understanding how the organization functions as a whole and how the parts depend upon or relate to one another.

While all three of these skills are essential for effective managerial performance, Figure 2–5 indicates that their relative importance to a specific manager depends on his or her level in the organization. Technical skill is critical at the lower levels of management but becomes less so as one moves up through the management ranks. A production foreman and a nursing supervisor will need more technical skill than the president of a company or a hospital administrator, because they deal with the day-to-day problems in manufacturing and nursing.

On the other hand, the importance of conceptual skill increases as one rises in management. The higher one is in the hierarchy, the more involved one becomes in longer-term decisions that can influence many parts of the organization or the entire organization. Thus, conceptual skill is most critical for top managers.

While human skill is critical at every level in management, it probably is most important at the lowest level. The greatest number of manager-subordinate interactions are likely to occur at this level.

The Roles of Managers

Recently it has been determined that managers perform 10 different but closely related roles. These are illustrated in Figure 2–6. The figure shows that the 10 roles can be separated into three different groupings: interpersonal roles, informational roles, and decisional roles.[7]

Interpersonal roles.   These roles focus on interpersonal relationships. The three roles of figurehead, leader, and liaison result from formal authority. By assuming them, the manager is able to move into the informational roles that in turn lead directly to the decisional roles.

All managerial jobs require some duties that are symbolic or ceremonial in nature. A college dean will hand out diplomas at graduation, a shop

---

[7] These managerial roles were first identified and described in Mintzberg, "The Manager's Job;" Jay W. Lorsch, James P. Baughman, James Reece, and Henry Mintzberg, *Understanding Management* (New York: Harper & Row, 1978).

FIGURE   2–6   The Overlapping Roles of Managers

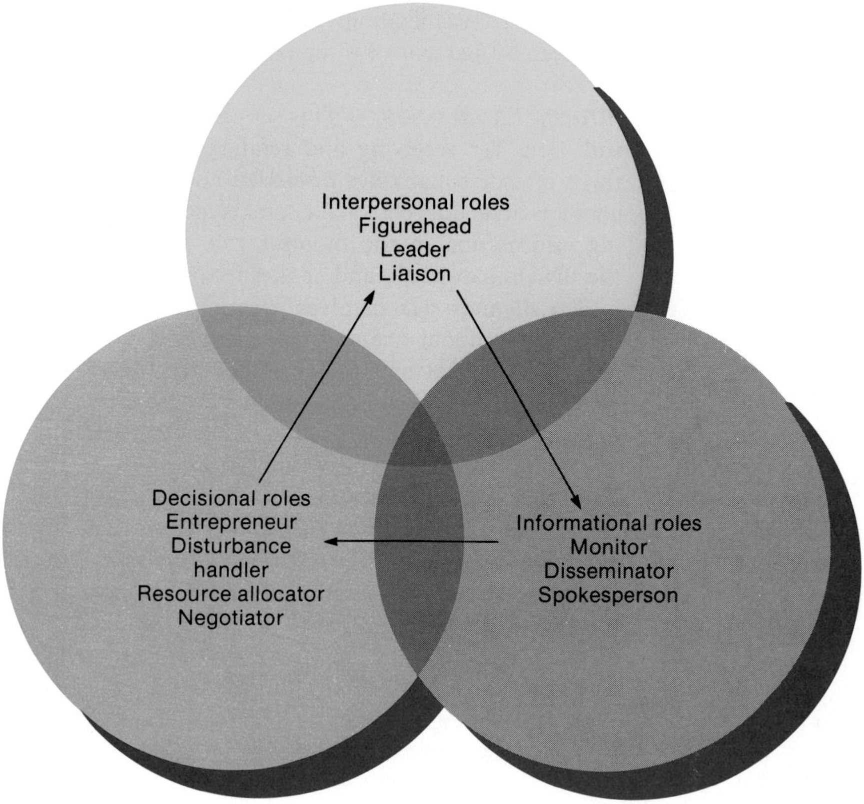

Managers perform many overlapping roles.

Interpersonal roles
Figurehead
Leader
Liaison

Decisional roles
Entrepreneur
Disturbance
handler
Resource allocator
Negotiator

Informational roles
Monitor
Disseminator
Spokesperson

foreman attends the wedding of a subordinate's daughter, the mayor of New York City gives the key to the city to an astronaut. These are examples of the *figurehead role.*

The manager's *leadership role* involves directing and coordinating the activities of subordinates. This may involve staffing (hiring, training, promoting, dismissing) and motivating subordinates. The leadership role also involves controlling—making sure that things are going according to plan.

The *liaison role* gets managers involved in interpersonal relationships outside of their area of command. This may involve contacts both within and outside the organization. Within the organization, managers must interact with numerous other managers and individuals. They must maintain good relations with the managers who send work to the unit as well as those who receive work from the unit. For example, a college dean must interact with individuals all over the campus; a supervisory nurse in an operating room must interact with supervisors of various other groups of nurses; a production supervisor must interact with engineering supervisors and sales managers. Finally, managers often have interactions with important people outside the organization. It is easy to see that the liaison role often can consume 50 percent of a manager's time.

Informational roles.   This set of roles establishes the manager as the central focus for receiving and sending nonroutine information. Through the three interpersonal roles discussed above, the manager builds a network of contacts. The interpersonal contacts aid the manager in gathering and receiving information in the monitor role and transmitting that information in the disseminator role and spokesperson role.

The *monitor role* involves examining the environment in order to gather information about changes, opportunities, and problems that may affect the unit. The formal and informal contacts developed in the liaison role are often useful here. The information may concern competitive moves that could influence the entire organization or knowing whom to call if the usual supplier of an important part cannot fill an order.

The *disseminator role* involves providing important or privileged information to subordinates that they might not ordinarily know about or be able to obtain. In a lunch conversation, the president of a firm hears that a large customer of the firm is on the verge of bankruptcy. Upon returning to the office, the president contacts the vice president of marketing, who in turn instructs the sales force not to sell anything on credit to the troubled company.

In the *spokesperson role,* the manager represents the unit to other people. This representation may be internal, when a manager makes the case for salary increases for members of the unit to top management. The representation also may be external, when an executive speaks for the organization on a particular issue of public interest to a local civic organization.

Decisional roles.   While developing interpersonal relationships and gathering information are important, these two activities are not ends in themselves. They serve as the basic inputs to the process of decision making. In fact, some people believe that these decisional roles—entrepreneur, disturbance handler, resource allocator, and negotiator—are a manager's most important duties.

The purpose of the *entrepreneur* role is to bring about changes for the better in the unit. The effective first-line supervisor is looking continually for new ideas or new methods to improve the unit's performance. The effective college dean constantly plans changes that will result in higher-quality education. The effective marketing manager diligently seeks new product ideas.

In the *disturbance-handler role,* managers make decisions or take corrective action in response to pressure that is beyond their control. Because there are disturbances, the decisions usually must be made quickly, which means that this role will take priority over other roles. The immediate goal is to bring about stability. When an emergency room supervisor responds quickly to a local disaster, a plant supervisor reacts to a strike, or a first-line manager responds to a breakdown in a key piece of equipment, each is dealing with disturbances in the environment. These responses must be quick and must result in a return to stability.

The *resource-allocator role* places a manager in the position of deciding who will get what resources, including money, people, time, and equipment. There are never enough resources to go around; the manager must allocate the scarce resources toward numerous possible ends. Resource allocation, therefore, is one of the most critical of the manager's decisional roles. A first-line supervisor must decide whether an overtime schedule should be established or whether part-time workers should be hired. A college dean must decide, based on available faculty, which courses to offer next semester. The president of the United States must decide whether to allocate more to defense and less to social programs, or vice versa.

In the *negotiator role,* managers must bargain with other units and individuals to obtain advantages for their own units. The negotiations may be over work, performance, objectives, resources, or anything influencing the unit. A sales manager may negotiate with the production department over a special order for a large customer. A first-line supervisor may negotiate for new typewriters; a top manager may negotiate with a labor union representative.

Management level and management roles.   A manager's level in the organization influences which managerial roles are emphasized. Obviously, top managers spend much more time in the figurehead role than first-line supervisors do. The liaison role of top and middle managers involve individuals and groups outside the organization, while the liaison role at the first-line level is outside the unit but inside the organization. Top managers monitor the environment for changes that can influence the entire organization. Middle managers monitor the environment for changes likely to influence the particular function that they manage (for example, marketing). And the first-line supervisor is concerned about what will influence his or her unit. However, while both the amount of time in the various roles and the activities performed in each role may differ, all managers perform interpersonal, informational, and decisional roles.

THE EXTERNAL ENVIRONMENT

No organization is self-sufficient. Whether profit or nonprofit, each organization provides something to the outside environment and in turn depends on the environment for survival. We shall classify the numerous components of the external environment into two categories: *direct-action components,* which have a direct influence on the performance of the organization, and *indirect-action components,* which influence the climate in which the organization operates and may (under some conditions) become direct-action components.

Direct-Action Components of the External Environment

The major direct-action components of a manager's external environment are the organization's clients that it must satisfy, its competitors, and the organizations and individuals that supply resources. Figure 2–7 illustrates the direct-action components.

Clients.   A business organization's customers are critical, and managers constantly must be aware of the present needs and emerging needs of clients. This may involve altering present products or services, developing new ones, or even entering new businesses.

Competitors.   The actions of competitors that directly impact on managers are of two basic types. *Intratype competition* occurs between institutions en-

---

FIGURE   2–7   Direct-Action Components of the External Environment

---

The performance of an organization is influenced directly by several factors.

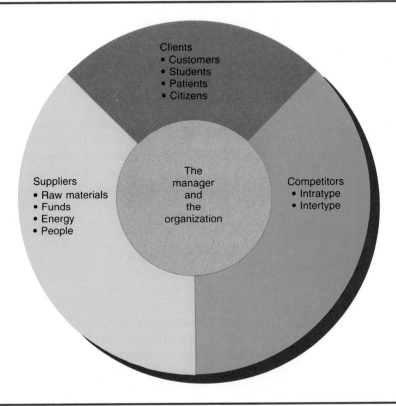

gaged in the same basic activity. General Motors competes with Ford for automobile purchasers. Kellogg competes with Post for cereal customers. One college competes with other colleges for undergraduate and graduate students, faculty members, and athletes. Your bank competes with the bank down the street for savings customers and loan business. *Intertype competition* arises between different types of organizations. For example, hospitals compete with health maintenance organizations for patients and medical practitioners. Recently, banks have been forced to compete for savings customers with such organizations as American Express and Sears, Roebuck and Co. Finally, some colleges and universities have faced competition from professional teams for high school athletes.

Suppliers: Every organization requires input from the environment in the form of raw materials, services, energy, equipment, labor, and funds. They use these inputs to produce outputs. Thus, organizations depend on those who supply the resources.

Our nation's recurring problems with oil have underscored the reality that the ability of an organization to compete for and attract resources is critical. The availability of resources determines the organization's capacity to respond to the threats and opportunities presented to it. Depending on the type of organization, some suppliers will be more critical than others. Public colleges, for example, need alumni backing, faculty, and backing of state legislators who influence budget allocations. A hospital needs funds and qualified staff. A business organization needs money, labor, and equipment. The suppliers of all of these resources have a direct-action impact on management.

Indirect-Action Components of the External Environment

The indirect-action components of the external environment can affect managers in at least two ways. First, outside organizations can have a direct influence on an organization or an indirect influence through a direct-action component. For example, a consumer activist group may lobby for certain causes, such as equal credit opportunities for women or product safety. Local media may pressure to keep open a plant that management planned to close down. Legislation may force managers to alter the way they report certain information concerning hiring practices.

Second, certain indirect-action components can influence the climate in which the organization must function. For example, the economy may expand or decline, requiring responses from management. New technological breakthroughs may alter the entire way an organization does business. Imagine the impact of digital watches on traditional watch manufacturers.

How management perceives its role in relation to the environment will affect greatly its reaction to the environment.[8] For example, some managers regard the environmental changes confronting them as beyond their control and influence. Such managers are likely to take a *passive* approach. They are likely to plan and program their future to fit the prevailing and forcasted conditions. In such a case, their success will depend on a predictable environment. Other managers, however, do not view environmental forces as fixed but rather as flexible and able to be molded to the organization's best interests, at least over the long run. Such *aggressive* managers view external change as less formidable. In fact, many believe change to be responsive to varying degrees of influence by their firms. These organizations are likely to be vigorous in pursuing their objectives. Such companies as Renault in France, Sony in Japan, and Sears, Roebuck and Co. and Citicorp in the United States are aggressive organizations. These and other organizations apparently have little difficulty responding to change and meet little resistance in getting such changes accepted throughout their organizations.[9] Some of the more important components of the indirect-action environment follow.

Technological.   Changes in technology can influence the destiny of an organization. (The impact of technology on traditional jukeboxes has forever changed the Seeburg Corporation.) Technology may be a constraint when opportunities exist but the necessary equipment is not present. However, technological innovations can create opportunities for entirely new industries or vastly alter existing industries. Think of the impact of teaching machines on education, video games on the toy industry, automated teller equipment on banking, and synthetic fibers on the apparel and carpeting industries. Technology has vastly altered educational instruction in many fields. Instructors have had to learn new ways of teaching, and students have been exposed to new learning methods. Electronic banking has reduced operating costs for bankers and has made banking services more widely and conveniently available to customers.

To appreciate the pace of technological achievement, examine Figure 2–8. Science and technology will be compelling forces for change in the future. In fact, a relatively new field, "technological forecasting," is attempting to predict what technological developments can occur within a specified period of time with a given level of resource allocation. In many organizations, managers will be forced to be alert and to plan to react to technological changes. In other organizations, a prime managerial responsibility will be to instigate such changes. The Management Focus on staying ahead of the pack illustrates the necessity of responding to technological changes and offers some useful guidelines.

[8] S. M. Schmidt and D. Kipnis, "Managers' Pursuit of Individual and Organizational Goals," *Human Relations,* October 1984, pp. 781–94.

[9] Peter F. Drucker, *Managing in Turbulent Times* (New York: Harper & Row, 1980); Peter F. Drucker, "Entrepreneurial Strategies," *California Management Review,* Winter 1985, pp. 9–25.

MANAGEMENT FOCUS
How Do You Stay ahead of the Pack?

Some companies seem to have done everything right, yet they lost competitive leadership because they failed to respond to technological and other environmental changes. Du Pont was beaten by Celanese when bias-ply tire cords changed from nylon to polyester. B. F. Goodrich was beaten by Michelin when the radial overtook the bias-ply tire. NCR wrote off $139 million in electromechanical inventory (and the equipment to make it) when solid-state, point-of-sale terminals entered the market.

These companies lost even though they were low-cost producers. They lost even though they were market leaders. They lost even though they were profitable. They lost because they failed to identify environmental signs of change and because they failed to make an effective transition from old to new technology—management response to change was too slow.

Such judgments, of course, are easy to make in hindsight. It's much more difficult to predict today what technologies will dominate the environment 5 or 10 years from now. Even so, some companies (such as IBM, Dow, and Eli Lilly) have persistently stayed ahead of change in their industries over the years. These organizations appear to have managers who recognize the realities of managing in changing environments:

1. They recognize that all products and processes have performance limits. So they support research in order to understand the limits of the product or process. When these limits are uncovered, other opportunities or products are then more aggressively supported.
2. They take all competition seriously. Each competitor is watched closely and respected.
3. If there is substantial potential in a new technology, they pursue it aggressively. They train people to use the technology, and they devise strategies to protect their position.
4. The aggressive effort begins early. Technological changes may proceed slowly, then explode—rarely in a predictable fashion. Managers simply cannot wait until after the explosion.

Source: Adapted from Richard N. Foster, "To Exploit Technology, Know When to Junk the Old," in *The Wall Street Journal on Management.* (Homewood, Ill.: Dow Jones–Irwin, 1985), pp. 64–67.

Rapid technological change can vastly alter the destiny of an organization.

FIGURE   2–8   Some Technological Advances Expected by the Year 2000

Undersea farming and mining.
Mechanical devices to replace human organs.
Reliable weather forecasts.
Extensive use of robots and machine slaves.
Centralization of business information and high-speed data processes.
Human hibernation for fairly extensive time periods.
Increased mastery of energy.
New rapid-transit systems.

Economic.   Economic changes pose both opportunities and problems for managers. An expanding economy has an effect on the demand for a company's product or service; it also facilitates the establishment of new enterprises. A major slowdown in economic growth can bring failure to some organizations, as was common in the early 1970s and early 1980s.

The impact of the economic environment on management practices is almost certain to be unpredictable. There will be many shifts and changes in inflation rates, productivity, savings patterns, unemployment rates, and energy use. Managers must continually monitor changes in economic factors in order to minimize threats and capitalize on opportunities.

Political, legal, and regulatory.   Numerous laws and a multitude of authorities characterize the political, legal, and regulatory environment faced by most managers. This indirect-action component of the external environment may act as both constraint and opportunity.[10] For example, when government action to combat inflation constrains builders of single-unit houses, it provides opportunities for apartment builders. The Vocational Education Act provides opportunities for certain types of educational institutions while acting as a constraint for others. Some groups of organizations, such as insurance companies, view medicare as a constraint; yet nursing homes capitalize on the opportunities it provides. And antipollution laws stimulated the growth of the pollution control industry.

Most observers believe government involvement in profit and nonprofit organizations will continue. This can be expected as people continue to call upon government to protect the consumer, preserve the environment, and push for an end to discrimination in employment, education, and housing. Even here, however, constraints for some organizations provide opportunities for others. As the Office of Economic Opportunity (OEO) enforces its antidis-

---

[10] See David W. Fisher, "Strategies toward Political Pressures: A Typology of Firm Responses," *Academy of Management Review,* January 1983, pp. 71–78.

crimination regulations, it creates opportunities for other organizations offering consulting services and training.

Cultural and social.   Change appears to be a constant element in our social system. All of us are part of a cultural and social fabric that affects our behavior. Traditions, customs, and beliefs influence all people and organizations. We all contribute to it, influence it, and in turn are affected by it. Managers must identify the changing cultural and social conditions that will influence their organizations. Yet many organizations either have not considered the impact of such changes or have underestimated their impact.

The importance of cultural and social changes can be readily seen from the impact of the ecology movement on numerous industries, the consumerism impact on the automobile and supermarket industries, and the general societal demand for more social responsibility on the part of both public and private organizations. These changes, coupled with the more specific problems of equal rights for women and minority groups, make cultural and social change an indirect-action component that cannot be ignored. Societal values must eventually be reflected in what organizations do. This indirect-action component of a manager's environment very often can become a direct-action component. This is especially true if society's expectations are unmet.[11]

International.   For many organizations, this indirect-action component presents a great challenge. It provides managers with both opportunities and threats. For some who are dependent on foreign resources, the international component could be a problem. For some, it will provide foreign competition in American markets. For others, it will provide opportunities to sell their products in new markets.[12]

When a business firm decides to leave its national borders and do business in other countries, it becomes a multinational company (MNC). With the decision to become an MNC, the international-environment component takes on an increasingly important and complex role. The organization becomes subject to the perils of different cultures, economies, and political whims. Why then are so many American business organizations becoming directly involved in international business? There usually are two major factors. First, the firm might be forced into it by weakening opportunities at home. Economic

---

[11] Ralph Nader, "Reforming Corporate Governance," *California Management Review,* Summer 1984, pp. 126–32.

[12] Much has been written during the last few years concerning the international challenge for U.S. business, particularly from the Japanese. For representative examples, see W. Ouchi, *Theory Z: How American Business Can Meet the Japanese Challenge* (Reading, Mass.: Addison-Wesley Publishing, 1981); R. T. Pascale and A. G. Athos, *The Art of Japanese management: Applications for American Executives* (New York: Simon & Schuster, 1981); Lester M. Thurow, *The Management Challenge: Japanese Views* (Cambridge, Mass.: MIT Press, 1985).

growth may decline, taxes may increase, or legislation may become too burdensome. Second, the firm might be drawn overseas by outstanding opportunities to market its products in other nations while continuing to do business at home. Whatever the reasons, once a firm makes the decision to do business abroad, it confronts a whole new set of circumstances.

Thus, whether competition from abroad, opportunity abroad, or dependency on foreign resources is involved, the international component of the indirect-action environment will increase in importance in the next decade. In fact, it will be extremely difficult to find a manager who will not be influenced in some way by this environmental component.

International competition has had a drastic impact on the American automobile industry. The Management Focus on Japan's luxury cars indicates what impact it will likely have in the future.

MANAGEMENT FOCUS
What Will Happen When Japan Sells Luxury Cars?

American automakers were hurt but not devastated when Japan grabbed control of the small-car market a few years ago. Detroit maintained a strong hold on the luxury car market. But the Japanese are planning to attack the top of the line, and that may pose a serious threat to the long-term health of the U.S. auto industry.

The first new Japanese imports will most likely be Honda's "executive luxury" car, Legend, which will be introduced at about $18,000. Mazda Motor Corp. is expected to introduce a big car, the 929, in 1988. Also in 1988, Nissan Motor Co. and Mitsubishi Motors Corp. will introduce upscale automobiles. Competition in the U.S. car market is expected to be very intense.

The mix of cars arriving from Japan has been shifting strongly toward the more expensive models since quotas began in 1981. The proportion of low-priced Japanese models sold in the U.S. dropped from 52 percent to 45 percent in 1985 alone.

This hurts Detroit, which has been relying more and more heavily on luxury cars for its profits. While accounting for only about 10 percent of cars sold, they account for about one third of the profit. U.S. automakers clear $5,000 on each luxury car that sells for $27,000 or more, while they barely break even on small cars. It is safe to say that U.S. automakers have not seen or heard the last from the Japanese.

Source: "Detroit Beware: Japan Is Ready to Sell Luxury," *Business Week*, December 9, 1985, pp. 114–118.

FIGURE   2–9   Direct-Action and Indirect-Action Components of the Manager's External Environment

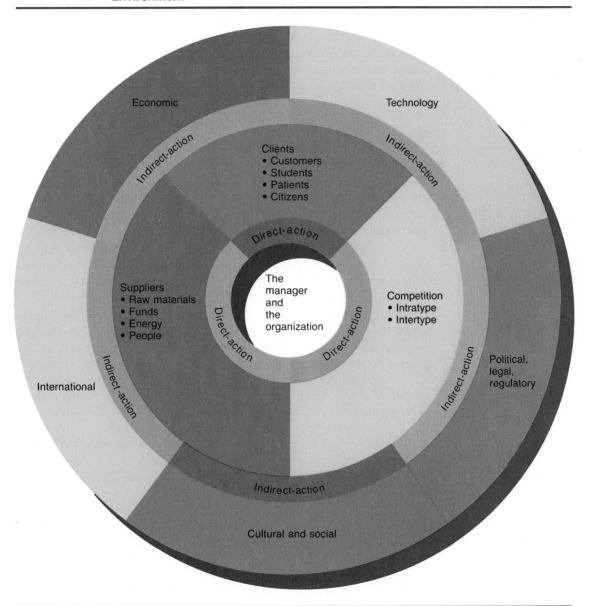

A manager's external environment consists of both direct-action and indirect-action components.

Figure 2–9 illustrates the direct-action and indirect-action components of the external environment and also serves as a summary of our discussion of management's external environment. It illustrates the many forces that influence organizational performance. Obviously, some organizations will survive more easily than others will in turbulent and uncertain environments. In any case, a major challenge to management is to anticipate and adapt to change that is beyond the control of the organization, in order to initiate change that is within its control.

SUMMARY OF KEY POINTS

- In systems theory, the organization is viewed as one of a number of elements that depend on each other. An organization takes resources (inputs) from the larger system (the environment), processes these resources, and returns them in changed form (output). Figure 2–1 presents the organization as a system.

- For the manager, the system concept emphasizes that *(a)* the ultimate survival of the organization depends on its ability to adapt to the demands of the environment and *(b)* in meeting these demands, the total sequence of input-process-output must be the focus of managerial attention.

- Most organizations function on at least three distinct but overlapping levels. The *operations level* focuses on effective performance, whether the organization produces something or performs a service; the task at this level is to develop the best allocation of resources in order to produce the desired output. The *managerial level* focuses on coordinating the activities at the operations level and serves as a liaison between those who produce the product or service and those who use the output. The *strategic level* determines the long-range objectives and direction of the organization—that is, how the organization will interact with the environment.

- The terms *top, middle,* and *first-level* managers are closely associated with the strategic, managerial, and operations levels. Together (see Figure 2–3), they are useful in understanding the different activities of managers.

- Certain skills are required for effective managerial performance. Technical skill, human skill, and conceptual skill are all necessary managerial skills. However, as Figure 2–5 indicates, a different mix is required depending upon the level of the manager in the organization.

- Managers at all levels perform a variety of tasks. Specifically, they perform 10 different but closely related roles. The 10 roles can be separated into three different groupings: *interpersonal roles* (figurehead, leader, liaison), *decisional roles* (entrepreneur, disturbance handler, resource allocator, negotiator), and *informational roles* (monitor, disseminator, spokesperson).

■ A manager's external environment can be visualized as consisting of *direct-action components* and *indirect-action components*. Direct-action components include the organization's clients, competitors, and suppliers. Indirect-action components include technology; the economy; the political, legal, and regulatory environment; cultural and social changes; and the international situation. Direct-action components directly influence the manager and the organization. Indirect-action components influence the climate in which the manager has to perform and often have the potential of becoming direct-action components.

DISCUSSION AND REVIEW QUESTIONS

1. In your own words, describe an organization as a system. Do you believe this approach is useful? Why?

2. Managers feel that the systems approach has little practical value. Do you agree or disagree?

3. Describe your management class, using the concept of a system. Must your instructor adapt the management class to the demands of the environment? Can you describe your management class, using the input-process-output cycle?

4. If you were trying to identify top managers at the school you attend, what titles would you look for? If you had to identify them based on what they do, what would you look for?

5. Discuss technical, human, and conceptual skills in relation to a college instructor. What, in your opinion, would be a good mix? Why?

6. Describe an encounter you recently had with a manager. It could be in a business, civic, school, hospital, or government organization. What managerial role or roles do you believe the person was performing?

7. Clearly describe the external environment your school presently faces. Use the direct-action and indirect-action categories to discuss the important environmental components.

8. Consult a recent business periodical such as *Business Week, Fortune,* or *Forbes.* Locate a report of an environmental component (either direct- or indirect-action) and its impact on an organization.

9. "Anyone can manage; all it takes is common sense." What do you think of that statement?

ADDITIONAL REFERENCES

Andrew, C. G., and G. A. Johnson, "The Crucial Importance of Production and Operations Management." *Academy of Management Review,* January 1982, pp. 143–47.

Arlow, P., and M. Gannon. "Social Responsiveness, Corporate Structure, and Economic Performance." *Academy of Management Review,* April 1982, pp. 235–41.

Asmen, D., and A. Meyerson, eds. *The Wall Street Journal on Management.* Homewood, Ill.: Dow Jones–Irwin, 1985.

Chusmir, L. H. "Job Commitment and Organizational Women." *Academy of Management Review,* October 1985, pp. 595–602.

Dalton-Mia, R. R., and J. J. Sullivan. "The Effects of Manager's Sex on the Assignment to a Challenging or Dull Task and Reasons for the Choice." *Academy of Management Journal,* September 1981, pp. 603–12.

Davis, K.; W. C. Frederick; and R. L. Blomstrom. *Business and Society: Concepts and Policy Issues.* New York: McGraw-Hill, 1980.

Naisbitt, J. *Megatrends: Ten New Directions Transforming Our Lives.* New York: Warner Books, 1982.

Peters, T. J., and R. H. Waterman, Jr. *In Search of Excellence.* New York: Harper & Row, 1982.

Pritchett, P. *After the Merger: Managing the Shockwaves.* Homewood, Ill.: Dow Jones–Irwin, 1985.

Sathe, V. "Some Implications of Corporate Cultures: A Manager's Guide to Action." *Organizational Dynamics,* August 1983, pp. 4–23.

MANAGING PRODUCTIVITY

LEARNING OBJECTIVES

After completing Chapter 3, you should be able to:

■ **Define**
productivity.

■ **Describe**
attributes common to organizations with successful productivity records.

■ **Discuss**
how sagging productivity can diminish the standard of living in a society.

■ **Compare**
productivity measurement in white-collar and blue-collar occupations.

■ **Identify**
some companies that have improved productivity through effective management of work, people, and operations.

■ MANAGEMENT IN ACTION

At Honda, Productivity Is Achieved through High-Quality Cars*

Today, the fourth-biggest maker of American cars isn't an American firm. It's Japan's Honda, which will turn out more American cars in 1985 than American Motors. Demand for Hondas has been strong and is growing; Their appeal centers on consistently high quality.

Customer satisfaction is extremely important to Honda management. Aware of Volkswagon's American experience, the company decreed that maintaining quality would be its main productivity goal. Lists of the world's best-produced cars almost always include the Honda Accord. (*Road & Track* magazine compared the Accord SE-i with the Mercedes Benz 190E. In a rating of 21 attributes, the Mercedes scored 166 points, the Accord 163. The Mercedes' list price is about $10,000 above the Honda's— $23,000 versus $13,000). Because Honda has been so concerned about the quality part of productivity, the American public now equates Honda with quality.

How did Honda transport its productivity interest in quality to the U.S. operations in Marysville, Ohio? The company flew 200 American workers representing all areas of the Ohio plant to its facilities in Sayama, Japan. The workers, traveling in groups of 8 to 20, stayed for two weeks to three months, working with the Japanese and closely observing their work habits and practices. When they returned to Marysville, the Americans served as teachers and trainers of the Sayama method. The emphasis in producing Hondas of high quality at low cost is an important reason why the firm has been successful in Ohio.

Even though costs are maintained at lower than competitive costs, the Marysville car still cost about $500 more than equivalent models made in Japan and shipped to the U.S. Labor costs 50 percent more in Marysville than in Japan, and productivity is 10 percent lower. Honda, however, is betting that productivity will improve at Marysville as the Americans learn and become more comfortable with the firm's productivity practices. For the Japanese corporation, productivity is so embedded in costs, quality, efficiency, and sales issues that it is given top priority. At the same time, an important criterion in productivity measurement at Honda is quality. They believe that quality leads to customer satisfaction, which in turns leads to more sales. What do you think?

---

* Source: Adapted from Faye Rice, "America's New No. 4 Automaker—Honda," *Fortune*, October 28, 1985, pp. 30–33.

In this chapter, managing productivity is presented as a process that must be managed properly. Managers that understand how productivity is tied to sales, standard of living, prices, and other factors are able to initiate planning, organizing, and controlling practices that can aid in the accomplishment of goals. As will be seen, it is important for managers to not only understand but also to measure productivity.

Productivity has become a day-to-day concern for managers because productivity indicates the overall efficiency of their firms. Also, it is the key that opens the door to management action and reward programs. Productivity gains mean a higher standard of living, shorter working hours, longer vacations, bigger paychecks, and more fringe benefits. Very concerned about productivity, the U.S. government even sponsored a White House conference in September 1983 to examine how productivity influences the lives of Americans.[1]

This chapter presents a straightforward, nontechnical view of productivity from the perspective of managers, with special emphasis on managing productivity in organizational settings. After all, it is managers at Frito-Lay, Hewlett-Packard, Beatrice Foods, and other organizations who must cope with productivity problems, trends, and issues. And management can be the single most important reason why productivity goals are achieved—unless, of course, the fundamentals of management are not properly performed, in which case managers can be the single greatest obstacle to productivity growth. In essence, this chapter will contend that managers need to apply the fundamentals of management to improve productivity.

THE PRODUCTIVITY CONCEPT

Everyone has a handy definition for productivity, and no two are quite the same. Some of the more popular definitions of the term include:

> *Productivity* is the relationship between the outputs generated from a system and the inputs provided to create those outputs.[2]
> *Productivity* is doing more with less.[3]
> *Productivity* designates how efficiently a business uses its resources.[4]

For the purposes of this book, productivity can be defined in simple terms as any ratio of output to one or more corresponding inputs. The unit of

---

[1] *Productivity Growth: A Better Life for Americans,* White House Conference Report, April 1984.

[2] D. Scott Sink, *Productivity Management: Planning, Measurement and Evaluation, Control, and Improvement* (New York: John Wiley, 1985), p. 3.

[3] Michael Le Boeuf, *The Productivity Challenge* (New York: McGraw-Hill, 1982), p. 8.

[4] Charles R. Day, Jr., "Solving the Mystery of Productivity Measurement," *Industry Week,* January 26, 1981, p. 87.

output can be anything: dollars, BTUs, units of product, customers served, patients treated, or whatever is meaningful to the job or organization.

What managers attempt to do is to produce more output with less input. This means that productivity is concerned with the overall effectiveness and efficiency of getting things done. It means making more from what you have and working smarter rather than harder. Thus, when productivity is increasing, the value of output is rising faster than the costs of production; the organization, the individual, or society is doing more with less.

Let's look at the productivity definition and examine how inputs and output are interrelated. In the case of Mom's apple pie,[5] the labor input is Mom. Her efficiency could be increased if she attended a cooking school that taught her how to bake more pies in less time. Or we could buy her a better grade of apples, which produces a better-quality pie and reduces the time Mom has to take to cut out brown, soft spots. Mom's productivity could also be increased if she had a more energy-efficient oven or a food processor. Another improvement in her efficiency would be to rearrange her kitchen. The rearrangement could enable Mom to produce more pies in the same time or the same number of pies in less time. All of these steps could improve Mom's apple pie productivity.

If Mom's productivity improves, she may decide to produce the pies needed in less time than it usually takes—and enjoy her improvement by taking in a movie. Or, she may wish to make more pies in the same amount of time, sell the extras, and treat herself to the vacation in Canada she always wanted. Mom can enjoy the benefits of the productivity gain by increasing her standard of living.

In the United States today, employees and managers are Mom. However, they are not enjoying sufficient productivity gains. Instead, there is a sense of uncertainty, a loss of confidence, and a feeling that working harder and smarter is needed to turn things around. To improve productivity, management functions will have to be efficiently practiced. The productivity management process will necessitate directing attention to productivity planning and action. That is, planning, organizing, and controlling will need to focus on the relationship of quantities of outputs and quantities of input.[6]

The United States versus Other Nations

For the most part, U.S. productivity has shown little growth since 1977. And while productivity has stood still, costs have risen steadily. Consider, for example, the number of Oldsmobiles produced. The compensation to

---

[5] This example is adapted from Le Boeuf, *Productivity Challenge,* pp. 9–10.

[6] D. J. Sumanth, *Productivity Management and Engineering* (New York: McGraw-Hill, 1984), p. 78

FIGURE   3–1   United States versus Other Nations: Productivity Levels

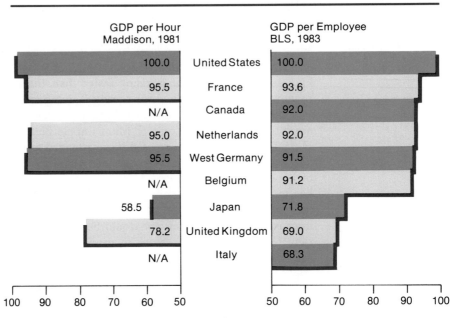

Source: Angus Maddison; Bureau of Labor Statistics.

autoworkers for generating that output has increased significantly; and when wage increases, salary adjustments, cost-of-living increases, and fringe-benefit improvements are given without corresponding increases in productivity, businesses such as General Motors make up the difference by raising prices. This difference, by definition, is inflation. It hurts every person because costs are increasing faster than productivity, and prices are raised to compensate for the difference.

Traditionally, the United States has had the most productive work force in the world. However, this country has come face-to-face with a declining growth rate,[7] while other nations such as France, the Netherlands, and West Germany have made significant gains. Actually, few consistent statistics are available to compare productivity growth rates and levels among nations. A picture of relative performance among nations is presented in Figure 3–1. The gross domestic product (GDP) per hour is used because employees in different countries work different numbers of hours. The U.S. work force is still in the lead. However, the lead is in part a function of the way in which the various gross domestic products are translated into dollars for

[7] John A. Patton, "No One to Blame but Themselves," *Management Review,* October 1982, pp. 13–18.

comparison with the United States. In Figure 3–1, both GDP per hour and GDP per employee shows that France, the Netherlands, and West Germany are leading competitors in the productivity race. Japanese performance depends heavily on whether the input factor of the ratio is hours or employees, since the Japanese work substantially longer hours. Procedures, values, and philosophies vary from country to country. Yet examples of these many differences give American managers valuable insight into methods of improving productivity, especially useful because no single factor is to blame for the current U.S. slump.

Three Exceptions to Declining Productivity

While U.S. productivity in general has not been growing at a significant rate in recent years, some notable exceptions exist, and important managerial lessons can be learned from such examples.[8]

Texas Instruments (TI) began to formalize an approach to productivity as early as 1948[9] A work simplification team was established to better *manage the work* activities of employees; managing work in the simplest and most efficient manner became the objective of training programs for all TI employees. From 1968 through 1978, TI's productivity growth averaged 15 percent per year. During this same time period, the U.S. manufacturing sector as a whole averaged annual productivity gains of a scant 1.9 precent. Also, the manufacturing sector increased prices by about 7.2 percent per year, while Texas Instruments reduced average prices for its products and services each year.

Delta Airlines is one of a handful of organizations that has survived government deregulation of the airline industry with good financial performance. Their management has a reputation of being extremely dedicated to *managing people* with care, fairness, and sensitivity through its numerous programs. The company advertises "The Delta Family Feeling," promotes from within, pays better than most airlines, and works extremely hard to avoid laying off workers.[10] Due to its open-door policy, ex-president William Beebe explains, "My rug has to be cleaned once a month. Mechanics, pilots, flight attendants—they all come in to see me. If they really want to tell us something, we'll give them the time."[11]

---

[8] Leonard M. Apcar, "Productivity Gains at Slow 1% Pace, Reflecting Sluggishness in Economy," *The Wall Street Journal,* August 28, 1985, p. 7.

[9] Mark Shepard, Jr., and J. Fred Bucy, "Innovation at Texas Instruments," *Computer,* September 1979, pp. 83–88.

[10] Thomas J. Peters and Robert T. Waterman, Jr., *In Search of Excellence* (New York: Harper & Row, 1982), pp. 253–54.

[11] Ibid.

Another exception to declining productivity is the Rubbermaid Company.[12] This firm pays particular attention to *managing production and operations* to assure quality products and services. Rubbermaid has introduced more than 500 products in the past five years.

Texas Instruments, Delta, and Rubbermaid demonstrate that progress in productivity can be achieved through effective management. The managerial emphasis in each company is slightly different: TI concentrates on managing work, Delta focuses on managing people, and Rubbermaid emphasizes managing production and operations to assure quality. In each case, management plays a significant and ongoing role. Instead of pointing a finger of blame at some event, situation, or condition when there are productivity problems, the managers in these three organizations are motivated to take steps that will lead to productivity gains.

FACTORS AFFECTING PRODUCTIVITY

Diverse views abound about the overall productivity problem in the United States. Here is one observation from an anonymous expert in nonsense:

> The population of the United States is 225 million, but there are 63 million retired, leaving 162 million to do the work. Those too young to work total 86 million, leaving 76 million to do the work. Then there are 36 million employed by the Federal government, and that leaves 40 million to do the work. The number in the armed forces is 13 million, which leaves 27 million to do the work. Deduct 25,765,000, the number employed by state and local government, and the 520,000 in hospitals and the like and you have 715,000 left to do the work. But of these, 462,000 are bums and vagrants who won't work. So that leaves 253,000. Now it may interest you to know that there are 252,998 in jail so that leaves two (2) people to carry the load. That's you and I, and I'm taking a week's vacation effective tomorrow. So carry on. You will be absolutely terrific!

When it comes to productivity problems, everyone has a pet scapegoat: Some managers blame government regulations. The government blames OPEC. Labor leaders blame foreign competition. In one survey, 80 percent of 221 managers polled blamed "poor management.[13] One management consultant estimates that, on the average, workers are productive only 55 percent of the time they are on the job. About 15 percent of their effort is lost to normal personal time, but 30 percent is lost through scheduling problems, unclear assignments, improper staffing, and poor discipline.[14]

---

[12] Cynthia Hutton, "America's Most Admired Corporations," *Fortune,* January 6, 1986, pp. 16–27.

[13] Le Boeuf, *Productivity Challenge,* p. 12.

[14] "Workers Held Working Only 55% of Shift," *Los Angeles Times,* October 1, 1979.

Actually, the productivity problem is a combination of many problems. The following collection, although incomplete, illustrates situations that managers must be aware of and understand. Productivity improvement does not just happen. Competent, hard-working, and knowledgeable managers make it happen.

Conditions that Detract from Productivity

Management inattention.   C. Jackson Grayson, founder of the Houston-based American Productivity Center, believes that one of the biggest impediments to productivity growth lies in management's lap. He asserts that management has neglected productivity improvement strategies in favor of such goals as increasing market shares, mergers, and acquisitions.[15] A related managerial shortcoming is suggested by Jerome Rosow, president of the Work In America Institute. He believes that the widely used military heirarchical organization structure gets in the way of increasing productivity. It is too rigid, too inflexible, and too unresponsive to worker needs, because managers believe that the structure, once in place, can do the job without further attention.[16]

Productivity is the topic of much public discussion by managers. However, there are still too many managers who are talking but not doing anything in the workplace. According to Grayson, neglect is still too widespread; and unless there is more understanding of—and action on—managing productivity by managers, problems will remain and become even greater.

Lack of managerial focus.   Those immortal words of the comic strip character Pogo, "We have seen the enemy and he is us," capture the essence of the meaning of "lack of focus." Many managers have not yet accepted and put into practice the theme that management involves managing work and organizations, people, and production and operations. The neglect of any one of these three legs on the "management stool" results in more problems. For years, managers have tended to focus on the management of work and organizations, production and operations, while only dabbling in the exercise of managing people.

Excessive layers of management.   Many organizations have fostered excessive red tape by establishing layer upon layer of management, creating an expensive bureaucratic burden of meetings, memos, computer printouts, and paperwork. At Ford Motor Co., 11 levels of management separate the

---

[15] Frank Gibney, "U.S., Japanese Free Enterprise as Different as Dollars and Yen," *Houston Chronicle,* April 3, 1983, p. 30.

[16] Joel E. Ross, *Productivity, People, and Profits* (Reston, Va.: Reston Publishing, 1981). p. 7.

factory worker and the chief executive officer. In contrast, Toyota has six levels, significantly fewer. Sears Roebuck & Co. adds executives to its corporate headquarters rather than placing them in its stores.[17] Sears has one of the highest profit-to-cost ratios of any retailer.

Cumbersome organizational structures block internal communication, eliminate singleness of purpose, and prevent the achievement of results. The more levels of management, the greater the cost. While excess cost shows up in payroll and fringe benefits, the real costs are hidden in the organization's delayed response to change. In these times of rapid changes in the environment, an organization that is streamlined can maximize opportunities by responding quickly while at the same time minimizing costs.[18]

Some examples of what firms are doing to reduce layers of management are provided in the Management Focus entitled "Small Staff = Higher Productivity."

MANAGEMENT FOCUS
Small Staff = Higher Productivity

Companies, by eliminating many staff overseer jobs and getting rid of layers of approvers, are decentralizing authority as well as responsibility, with an eye toward inducing efficiency, effectiveness, and substantially improved productivity. When Ian MacGregor took over British Shell, one of his first decisions was to cut the corporate staff from 1,000 to 175. Jack Reichert, when he chaired the Brunswick Corporation, pared his corporate staff from 600 down to 200. General Motors is setting up its new Saturn division along the lines of fewer layers. The list grows each day as General Electric, U.S. Steel, and others chip away at management layers, improving productivity by removing redundant and unnecessary managers.

A. T. Kearney, Inc., a consulting firm, studied 41 companies—26 superior performers and 15 also-rans. The top performers averaged 500 fewer staff people per $1 billion in sales than did the sluggish companies. The top 26 also had an average of 7 levels of management, while the 15 poorer performers averaged about 11 layers.

Some executives will reduce staff and get little productivity benefit. Others will reduce staff and prime the productivity pump. John Harvey Jones of Imperial Chemical Industries is cutting staff, decentralizing authority, and selling the firm's lavish headquarters building. People Express's managing officers have no secretaries, few layers

[17] Peters and Waterman, *In Search of Excellence,* p. 303.

[18] Frederick Horbush, Jr., *Raising Productivity* (New York: McGraw-Hill, 1977), p. 196.

MANAGEMENT FOCUS (*continued*)

of management, and an obsession with providing quality service. The presiding officer of People, Don Burr, believes that this tone and commitment will be translated into more productivity per worker. Staff reductions are what more and more executives believe are needed to energize a firm in terms of productivity growth.

Source: Adapted from Thomas J. Peters, "Why Smaller Staffs Do Better," *New York Times,* April 21, 1985, pp. 1, 14F.

Managerial focus on short-term results.   Managers are pressured to generate immediate productivity so that they can be rewarded. Because this year's profit or this quarter's market share is the basis for pay increases or bonuses, the emphasis is on the short-term. Such a perspective results in tunnel vision: Managers focus on short-term financial results at the expense of total productivity gains over the longer term, and the long-range consequences of management decisions are too often given little or no priority. Research and development and capital investment for the future are not rewarded in the present.

A short-term emphasis also delays plant and equipment maintenance and improvement, reduces training and development for employees, and creates a pressure-packed, crisis-oriented work environment. Each of these factors can contribute to the productivity problem. Unless more attention is paid to intermediate and long-term results, future productivity gains will not be attainable.

The changing work force.   Another culprit in the productivity decline is the changing nature of the American work force. Three specific changes are relevant:[19]

First, there has been a slowdown in movement from the farms to the factories. From 1948 to 1966, large numbers of individuals moved from farms to factories, which greatly improved the output per labor hour and resulted in an increase in national productivity. However, since 1966, the migration from farms to factories has slowed. Today, less than 4 percent of our labor force works on farms, and there is little migration from farms to factories.

Second, during the same period, large numbers of inexperienced workers entered the labor force. The number of new workers soared as more women entered organizations and children from the post-World War II baby boom came of age. Productivity was affected in two ways. One, because of inexperience, the new workers were less productive. (Fortunately, inexperienced work-

_____

[19] These three changes are presented by Le Boeuf, *Productivity Challenge,* pp. 19–20.

ers eventually become experienced. As they do, their productivity contributions increase.) A second effect was that many experienced and productive workers were lured into early retirement with lucrative pension plans.

Finally, the overall economy is changing the nature of its output from manufacturing to information. American workers used to spend about 70 of every 100 work hours producing tangible products, such as cars, steel billets, toasters, or rugs. But today's work force devotes only about 40 hours to manufacturing. The other 60 hours go to completing forms, filing reports, processing payrolls, and exchanging information.

Measurement difficulties.   The American work force has shifted from predominantly blue collar to predominantly white collar before managers have learned how to accurately quantify results and achievements of white-collar jobholders. The manufacturing sector has measures for direct labor, material standards, and overhead, necessary for financial planning and reporting. But they do not meet the requirement for all jobs nor take into account the salary of a service worker. Measurement experts haven't devised a uniform way to measure the output of clerks, managers, accountants, and other service-oriented occupations. Thus, typically, the impact on profit is not measured. In the absence of proper productivity measurements, managerial evaluation cannot take place.

Lack of productivity goals.   There is an old axiom that "If you don't know where you're going, there's no way to get there." Goals are necessary for a number of reasons: It's a basic tenet of psychology that most behavior is goal directed. It is natural for a person to seek goals. Goals provide a vehicle for channeling time and effort. Also, the exercise of setting organizational and productivity goals forces individuals to spend time thinking seriously about their jobs and deciding how better to accomplish the work.

Unfortunately, goal setting often is taken for granted. It seems simple to set goals and let things naturally occur. Remember, however, that productivity improvement doesn't just happen. For goals in productivity improvement to generate positive benefits, they must meet a number of criteria.[20] They need to be:

Realistic: Productivity goals must be realistic and challenging but not too difficult to achieve.
Specific: Productivity improvement goals must be stated in specific terms and with a specific timetable. "To reduce production cost" is not definitive. "To reduce production cost by 4 percent within the next

[20] For a discussion of goal setting, see Gary P. Latham and Edward A. Locke, "Goal Setting—A Motivational Technique that Works," *Organizational Dynamics,* Autumn 1979, pp. 68–80; John M. Ivancevich and Samuel V. Smith, "Goal Setting Interview Skills: Simulated and On-the-Job Analysis," *Journal of Applied Psychology,* December 1982, pp. 697–705.

six months without an increase in wage and fringe-benefit costs"
is a more specific goal statement.

Comprehensive: Productivity improvement goals must be generated for
all elements within an organization, including both white-collar and
blue-collar jobs. A complete picture of results and effectiveness is
needed.

Meaningful: Productivity improvement goals must be meaningful to the
individual employee and the organization. Individual goals that are
either incompatible or make no contribution toward fulfilling an
organization's goals can be disruptive.

Formalized: Productivity improvement goals should be formally documented. Writing tends to crystallize thought, and thinking motivates
action. Self-evaluations are also made easier if the goals are stated
on paper.

Productivity improvement goals, when they meet these criteria, can bring
management and employees together. Goals provide a common base of discussion, attention, and motivation. They also channel the work force's efforts
toward accomplishment of productivity growth.

Government regulations.   Many managers blame government regulations—especially in health, safety, equal employment quotas, energy, and the
environment—for slowing our productivity growth. They complain that such
regulations require large expenditures for nonproductive compliance and re-
tard productivity growth.[21] No perfectly accurate estimates are available,
but some assume that the cost of government regulations amounts to about
$100 billion annually in lost productivity.[22]

In some instances, government regulations distract managers. Instead of
concentrating on improving products and operating efficiency, managers have
been forced to spend more time worrying about what the government might
do next. An example of diverting attention is found at Goodyear Tire and
Rubber Company. In one week, the company's computer center cranked
out 345,000 pages of paper, weighing 3,200 pounds, to meet *one* government
safety regulation.[23]

Most would agree, however, that government regulations have not all
been bad. Employee health and safety regulations and those opening up jobs
to minorities and women are designed to produce a healthier, more productive
work force in the future. Other regulations, such as environmental curbs,
may be worth some sacrifice in productivity. For instance, from 1948 to

---

[21] Robert E. McGarrah, "The Productivity Crisis: Illusions and Realities," *Management
World,* May 1982, pp. 8–11.

[22] Ross, *Productivity,* p. 8.

[23] Ralph E. Winter, "Many Businesses Blame Governmental Policies for Productivity Lag,"
The Wall Street Journal, October 28, 1980, p. 1.

1965, when productivity was rising about 3.2 percent a year, chemical companies buried toxic wastes in Love Canal near Niagara Falls, New York. The dumping probably required fewer labor-hours than other disposal methods. But the wastes now have been implicated for health problems and birth defects among local residents.

This list of eight factors is certainly not exhaustive. Other factors often cited—such as aging plants and equipment, foreign competition, increasing energy prices, a decrease in research and development expenditures, and labor-management conflicts—also are contributors to the productivity decline.

Keys to Improved Productivity

Out of the lists of causes, several clear pictures emerge. First, a key to greater productivity lies in better management of three elements: work and organizations, people, and production and operations. We are all aware of the bandwagon adoption of such popular approaches as Japanese management, piecework incentives, robotics, and decision support systems.[24] None of these approaches is inherently wrong—in fact, some have been successful in various situations.[25] (Some of these successes will be presented and discussed later in the book.) Yet, when a management approach to improving productivity is chosen at random, or because some other firm is using it, or because a top manager had a whim, the results are not always so positive.

Second, productivity must be measured carefully. To establish a system of measurements, is a prerequisite to any productivity improvement program. Through a measurement-tracking system, an organization and its management can determine any productivity improvement and compare it to past performance. Measures form the basis upon which progress can be analyzed and sustained through management action. Unfortunately, measuring productivity is easier said than done. Today, many organizations do not have individual- and group-productivity measures.

Third, any program of productivity improvement must be planned, organized, and controlled.[26] These three management functions, applied to productivity improvement, aid in communicating the message about the importance of productivity.

Since productivity is the lifeblood of our economy and the key to our high standard of living, productivity growth is important for the well-being of future generations. Only by productivity improvement can the real national

---

[24] Lynda C. McDermott, "The Productivity Bandwagon—The Hottest Game in Town?" *Training and Development Journal,* April 1982, pp. 68–73.

[25] Peter F. Drucker, *Managing in Turbulent Times* (New York: Harper & Row, 1980).

[26] James O'Toole, *Making America Work: Productivity and Responsibility* (New York: Continuum, 1981).

wealth of a country increase. More productive use of resources (e.g., human talent, raw materials, technology) can help conserve scarce or expensive resources and reduce waste. Without productivity gains to match them, all increases in wages and salaries, in other operations costs, and in prices contribute to inflation. Problems of inflation, unemployment, an increasing foreign trade deficit, and an unstable dollar in the money markets around the world can be attacked through productivity improvement. Of course, in addition to the nation, individuals can also acquire benefits from productivity growth, such as improvement in the real standard of living.

PRODUCTIVITY AND MANAGEMENT

Managers today must make some important choices. On the one hand, they are faced with bad news about foreign competition, increased costs of energy and raw materials, increasing government regulation, and the changing nature of the labor force. On the other hand, technology, capital investment, and other substitutes for labor are not always the optimal solutions to productivity problems. This means that better management may be the key to improved productivity.

People Are the Key

Productivity can be boosted through new equipment and new job designs, but people are also extremely important. In most recent reports on how to improve productivity, a major theme is the importance of always respecting people.[27] But the orientation toward people in some companies started years ago—full-employment policies in times of recession, training (when little training was usually done), knowing employees on a first-name basis.

It sounds elementary; but in the hustle and bustle of everyday business, people too often receive less attention than they should. Also, paying lip service to people and using gimmicks to show concern are not tolerated in productive firms: Action and real concern are the rule. Some companies, such as Mary Kay Cosmetics, Daly & Co., NCR, and IBM, have demonstrated that people are the key to productivity gains. For example, at Texas Instruments, outstanding productivity teams are recognized by being invited to describe their successes to the board of directors. At Dana Corporation, the president Rene McPherson insists on face-to-face manager-employee communication and on discussing the operating results (for example, profits, costs, return on investments) with all employees.

---

[27] Thomas J. Peters and Nancy Austin, *A Passion for Excellence* (New York: Random House, 1985), pp. 107–11.

The Customer Connection

Have you ever bought a bag of stale Frito-Lay corn chips? Probably not. Frito-Lay wants no customer to bite into a stale chip. It provides quality and service to prevent both the stale chip and the lost customer. Highly productive companies learn from the people to whom they provide products and services: They provide unparalleled quality, service, and reliability—products that work, last, and can be serviced. They begin their search for new products and ideas by talking with their customers. Top managers at IBM and Digital Equipment spend at least 30 days per year conferring with key customers, and both companies compensate their managers partially based on customer-satisfaction surveys. The "customer connection" means that managers listen to, work with, and want to please customers.

Building on Strengths

Productive organizations seem to have a golden rule: "Never acquire a business you don't know anything about." McDonald's sticks with fast food, Delta is an airline, and Frito-Lay is a food business. The knowledge one acquires in a business is cumulative and takes time to become useful. Temptations to move into unfamiliar areas usually are resisted by successful companies.

Keeping the Structure Simple and the Staff Lean

Bureaucracy is to be avoided if at all possible. An example of simplicity in structure, despite its size, is Johnson & Johnson. The company is a $5 billion firm structured into 150 independent divisions, each an average size of just over $30 million. Each division is called a company and is headed by a chairperson of the board. The companies are aggregated into eight groups of up to 20 companies each, and the companies have either a geographic or product similarity.

There also is a tendency today to keep the number of staff people to a minimum. The philosophy is fewer administrators (managerial staff especially) and more operators (workers). Some examples of lean staffs are:

- Emerson Electric, with 54,000 employees, has fewer than 100 people in corporate headquarters.
- Dana employs 35,000 people and has a staff of around 100.
- Schlumberger, a $6 billion diversified oil service company, operates with a staff of 90.
- ROLM, a $200 million business, runs with about 15 people in corporate headquarters.

Controls Must Exist but Not Suffocate

In productive organizations, firm central control systems and direction coexist with maximum individual autonomy. For example, when Rene McPherson became president of Dana, he threw out all of the company's policy manuals. In their place, he substituted a one-page philosophy statement and a control system that requires divisions to report costs and revenues each day. Rules and controls in too many organizations have a negative tone. They intimidate; they suppress creativity; and they result in monitoring every action of employees. Such controls suffocate the creative and self-motivation spark in employees. Although the productive companies definitely have rules and procedures, they have a positive tone and deal with quality, service, innovation, and experimentation.

Such attributes of productive companies illustrate the importance and the role of management in managing productivity. Too many managers and citizens seem to have given up hope for improving productivity. Giving up, passing the buck, and not accepting responsibility are not attributes of productive companies. On the contrary, managing work and organizations, people, and production and operations is accepted as the responsibility of managers.

PRODUCTIVITY MEASUREMENT

Productivity was defined earlier as "any ratio of output to one or more inputs." It is a relative measure in the sense that its meaning is based on comparing the present ratio with the ratio for a previous period called a *base period.* Despite the importance of productivity measurement, useful measures are not widely available and are often misunderstood. The reasons for having productivity measures can be stated simply: they make possible the better management of work and organizations, people, and production and operations. The use of good productivity measures allows managers to facilitate worker achievement and productive work.

Some specific uses for productivity measures are outlined in Figure 3–2. They point to three main reasons why productivity measures are important. First, the measures help managers answer the question "How well did we (I) do?" Problems and opportunities are isolated by measures, especially when a trend or deviation can be spotted. Second, measurement is important for managerial planning: "What should we do?" Analyzing results of past attempts to improve productivity provides a true basis for future plans. Third, measurement creates awareness and directs future managerial action.

An interesting approach to measurement is the "gross corporate product," which is described in the Management Focus on "Measuring Productivity."

MANAGEMENT FOCUS
Measuring Productivity Contributions of Employees

As already mentioned, U.S. managers are now aggressively pursuing a policy of productivity catch-up in competition with the Japanese, West Germans, French, and Canadians. Economist Christos Athanasopoulos, has proposed an easy way for any business to track and measure its productivity. Take the firm's annual net sales, then subtract the cost of outside purchases. The result is the "gross corporate product" (GCP). The GCP measures the business's contribution to the national economy.

Now divide the calculated GCP by the number of employees. This provides management with an indicator of the average employee's contribution to the company—individual productivity.

Suppose a firm has 100 employees. If its GCP in 1986 was $5 million, the individual contribution was $50,000. That is, each worker contributed $50,000 to the company. If the GCP is $7 million in 1987 (with the same number of employees), each worker would contribute $70,000. Productivity will have increased 40 percent. The "human productivity" index is then 140, according to Athanasopoulos's approach.

The productivity index can then be used to link productivity and wages. This is done by subtracting the rate of inflation from the rise in productivity. The result is the average pay increase the company can give without raising prices. If inflation in 1987 is 4 percent, the imaginary company can afford to hike wages 36 percent (40 − 4).

The linkage of productivity and wages provides workers with a concrete incentive to increase personal productivity. If workers can produce more, they can earn more. Of course, the linkage works in the other direction. When productivity gains are not achieved and inflation exists, there will have to be a cut in wages and benefits.

Adapted from "What's Your Company's 'GCP,'" *Management Review,* March 1985, pp. 4–6.

Comparing Productivity: Some Problems

The official source of statistics for productivity within the United States is the Bureau of Labor Statistics (BLS) of the Department of Labor. The BLS publishes quarterly indexes of output per work hour for the overall private sector in the United States, and for the nonfarm and manufacturing

---

FIGURE   3–2   Uses of Productivity Measures

Managing Work and Organizations

Establish goals.	Allow industry comparisons.
Call attention to the management process.	Permit comparisons with baseline.
Aid in decision making.	Serve as planning tool.
Justify expenditures.	Serve as organizing tool.
Communicate efficiency.	Provide early warning about problems.

Managing People

Place emphasis on results.	Help motivate.
Introduce short- and long-term perspective.	Show career progress.
Provide feedback.	Involve people.
Identify training and development needs.	Serve as compensation factor.

Managing Production and Operations

Illustrate sales, expense, profit relationship.	Use to emphasize quality.
Improve budgeting and decision making.	Equate quality with customer satisfaction.
Establish standards.	Improve scheduling.
Aid in workplace design decisions.	Facilitate comparisons across time periods.

The value of productivity measures in managing work and organizations, people, and production and operations.

and corporate sectors.[28] The BLS also publishes indexes for additional sectors such as mining, transportation and utilities, and trade at irregular intervals. Indexes for other sectors, such as services, construction, finance, real estate, and government, are not published due to deficiencies in the available data. Thus, information available for industry comparisons pertains to some industries but not to others.

The comparative data used in the BLS measures are based on outputs derived from total measures such as gross national product, which refers to the total goods and services produced in the economy. This perspective can help a firm compare itself with others in the industry. However, such a broad perspective has minimal value to any single organization and little value to the individual manager. Generalized measures are not oriented enough toward the organization or individual to satisfy managers. Also, the BLS statistics exclude the service and government sectors of the economy.

---

[28] William A. Ruch, "The Measurement of White-Collar Productivity," *National Productivity Review,* Autumn 1982, pp. 416–26.

FIGURE   3–3   Five Ways to Increase a Productivity Ratio in White-Collar Workers

---

$$\text{Productivity} = \frac{\text{OUTPUT}}{\text{INPUT}}$$

1. $\dfrac{+}{+}$ Output increases faster than input; "managed growth."

2. $\dfrac{-}{-}$ Input decreases more than output (for example, phasing out an old product, closing an inefficient plant); "managed decline."

The output/input manipulation and the positive results.

3. $\dfrac{0}{-}$ Producing the same output with fewer inputs; cost reductions and greater efficiency.

4. $\dfrac{+}{0}$ More outputs from the same inputs; "working smarter."

5. $\dfrac{+}{-}$ The ideal; maximum increase in the ratio by a combination of the above.

Key: $0 =$ No change in factor. $+ =$ Increase in factor. $- =$ Decrease in factor.

Source: Adapted from William A. Ruch, "The Measurement of White-Collar Productivity," *National Productivity Review,* Autumn 1982, pp. 416–26. © Executive Enterprises Publications Co., Inc., 33 West 60th Street, New York, NY 10023. Reprinted with permission.

White-Collar Measurements

The term *white-collar* designates any employee from secretaries, clerks, engineers, scientists, first-line supervisors, keypunch operators, and salespersons to the chief executive officer.[29] Although there are no easy ways to measure white-collar productivity, a few points seem important.

Guidelines. The purpose of the measurement system must fit the needs of the organization. Figure 3–3 summarizes five organizational methods to increase productivity: managing growth, managing decline, efficiency, working smarter, and a combination.

As most analyses of productive organizations illustrate, people are an important key to success. If the efforts, work, and output of employees are to be measured, their involvement in the measurement process is important. Who knows more about the job than the worker? The use of group discussions,

---

[29] Thomas C. Tuttle and John J. Romanowski, "Assessing Performance and Productivity in White-Collar Organizations," *National Productivity Review,* Summer 1985, pp. 211–24.

brainstorming, or team meetings can help identify and may even produce acceptable white-collar productivity measures.

Clearly defining output is important. First, output measures that are meaningful, specific, and comprehensive should be established. It is also important to recognize that white-collar output cannot always be stated in quantitative terms. Some white-collar contributions, such as goodwill and improved subordinate job satisfaction, can only be assessed in subjective terms.

After the output measures are defined, input measures should be established. Some examples of white-collar input are number of hours worked, total compensation, number of employees managed, and computer time utilized. Whichever input measures are used, they should fit the job and the purpose of the measurement.

A final guideline is to not become bogged down in efforts to develop the perfect, most comprehensive measurement system. Keep it short and simple—KISS—is the common practice in effective organizations.

Designing situation-specific assessments.   Once these few measures are used and refined, more sophistication can be built into assessments. Measurement experts are not suggesting the use of oversimplified measures that exclude important input factors. On the contrary, the type of productivity measures needed are ones that relate output to all associated inputs.[30]

Suppose for example, that management is interested in the ratio of output per hours to profit for an H & R Block part-time accountant. If, when developing a measure of productivity, the managers fail to include the rate of pay, the results will be a misleading or incomplete productivity gauge. Assume that last year an accountant at H & R Block completed 200 forms requiring one hour each and the compensation received was $10 per form. This year, the same accountant completed 250 forms that required about one hour each, but was paid $15 per form. Now examine the calculations in Table 3–1. When labor costs are excluded, the index is 100.0. However, when increased labor costs are included, the index of productivity for this year—using last year as the base period—is 60.0 (.06 divided by .10 × 100 = 60.0). This hypothetical example points out the care that must be exercised. All relevant input factors are necessary to acquire a valid picture of white-collar productivity.

To determine how much one group or individual contributes to output (product or service) requires time, patience, and organization. *Time* is needed to think about and discuss what should be measured, how it should be measured, what should be included as input measures, and how output should be specified. *Patience* is needed to experiment with the measurement program.

---

[30] D. S. Sink, T. C. Tuttle, and S. J. DeVries, "Productivity Measurement and Evaluation: What Is Available?" *National Productivity Review,* Summer 1984, pp. 265–87.

TABLE   3–1   Accountant Output per Input

	Labor Cost Excluded	Labor Cost Included
Last year	$\dfrac{200 \text{ forms}}{200 \text{ labor hours}}$ or 1 per hour	$\dfrac{200 \text{ forms}}{200 \text{ labor hours} \times \$10 \text{ per form}}$ or .10 forms per labor dollar
This year	$\dfrac{250 \text{ forms}}{250 \text{ labor hours}}$ or 1 per hour	$\dfrac{250 \text{ forms}}{250 \text{ labor hours} \times \$15 \text{ per form}}$ or .06 forms per labor dollar
Productivity ratio this year	100.0	60.0

A complete versus a partial productivity calculation.

Some of the initial ideas and measures may not be valid, meaningful, or comparable. Modification, refinement, and redoing measures take a lot of patience. In some cases, the process has taken a few years. *Organization* is needed to provide a central point of responsibility. Some organizations, such as Tenneco, now have a director of productivity, and Baltimore Gas & Electric Company has a corporate performance analyst. The buck must stop some-where, and some type of organizational arrangement is one way to provide the needed structure.[31]

Time, patience, and organization require resources: people, money, sup-plies, and computer time to design, implement, and evaluate a productivity program. Another important resource is top management support for pro-ductivity measurement. When top management commitment is clear, noticea-ble, and sustained, there is a greater chance that those involved in the difficult task of measurement will expend the time and have the patience to accomplish the job.[32]

The need to measure and improve productivity is found in every work activity and organization. Comparing past and present productivity levels is a way for organizations to determine progress, decline, and lack of change. Certainly obstacles to productivity measurement exist, including the need to make comparisons, the problem of measuring white-collar productivity, and the fact that resources must be provided. Resources cost money, but they can help organizations and their employees, both managers and nonman-agers, realize their potential to improve productivity.

---

[31] Marta Mooney, "Organizing for Productivity Management," *National Productivity Review,* Spring 1982, pp. 141–51.

[32] Paul S. Goodman, "Social Comparison Processes in Organizations," in *New Directions in Organizational Behavior,* B. M. Staw and G. R. Salancik eds. (Chicago: St. Clair Press, 1977), p. 103.

APPLYING THE FUNCTIONS OF MANAGEMENT TO PRODUCTIVITY

The importance of managing work and organizations, people, and production and operations is emphasized whenever the functions of management are highlighted. Three important management functions that will be covered in Part II of this book are planning, organizing, and controlling. However, a brief description here of each function and its relationship to productivity will provide a foundation for the remainder of the book.

Planning and Productivity

Planning is the most basic of the management functions because it involves the determination of organizational mission, strategies, and objectives. Since productivity is a major objective for most organizations, it is logical to suggest that this goal is a part of the organization's planning strategy. More organizations realize this every day and are making efforts to integrate productivity improvement into strategic plans.

Hershey, the chocolate company, is among the growing number of firms that have integrated productivity into their strategic plans, and today productivity objectives are a key target area there. Managers incorporate productivity objectives into decision making every day. After all, Hershey must compete head-on with firms like Mars in the $8 billion-a-year U.S. candy market. Both Hershey and Mars, although they have distinct corporate styles and cultures, believe that productivity improvement is a must if they are to remain competitive.[33]

Organizing and Productivity

The importance of organization in bringing about productivity improvement has already been noted. Assignment of tasks, responsibilities, authority to make decisions, and the involvement of people all require organization. The duties of chief executive officers, steering committees, managers, operating employees, and union leaders (if unionized) need to be integrated through organizational efforts. A challenge to managers is to decide which form of organization can best stimulate employee cooperation and achieve productivity gains. Teams, brainstorming groups, quality circles, and troubleshooting units are all examples of ways to attack productivity problems.

One firm that has paid particular attention to organizational arrangements is Texas Instruments. TI uses an organizational arrangement called productivity improvement teams (PITS), teams of 8 to 10 workers that set their own

---

[33] Steve Lawrence, "Bar Wars: Hershey Bites Mars," *Fortune,* July 8, 1985, pp. 52–57.

improvement goals and measure their progress. PITS have been major contributors to productivity improvements at TI.

There is no one best organizational arrangement that always will improve productivity. What works at Texas Instruments might fail miserably at Hughes Aircraft or Chase Manhattan Bank. What is needed are managers who understand the specifics of organizing and who are willing to experiment and take risks in solving their unique productivity problems.

Controlling and Productivity

Productivity improvement is no different than any managerial effort; it must be controlled. Developing standards, reviewing progress to meet the standards, and correcting deficiencies uncovered in the review are steps in the productivity control process. To have an effective productivity control system, an organization needs to have valid measures. The measures must be integrated into existing reporting and reward systems, then used to trace progress, correct any deviations, and reward individuals and groups. Employees, both managers and nonmanagers, need information about productivity so that they can be aware and informed before taking any action.[34]

Acceptance and commitment to the goal of productivity improvement hinge on being aware and informed. Most employees will accept the need for productivity improvement if management delivers the message tactfully. Control systems permit managers to show employees how productivity is linked to their standard of living, national and industry unemployment levels, organizational competitive advantages, return on investment, individual job security, career progress, and job satisfaction. By tracking, comparing, and analyzing productivity in employee terms, a control system can be a very powerful communication and motivational device.

One control issue to be considered is whether productivity improvements can be brought about without significant costs. The Management Focus on computerization costs (opposite page) stresses that productivity gains stimulated by a computer can spawn employee ailments that are costly.

LOOKING AHEAD

This chapter has attempted to improve your understanding of productivity. Because the manager's job is to influence what happens within organizations, the theme throughout *Fundamentals of Management* is that by managing work and organizations, people, and production and operations, managers play a vital role in improving productivity. However, this important and

---

[34] Aubrey C. Daniels, "Performance Management: The Behavioral Approach to Productivity Improvement," *National Productivity Review,* Summer 1985, pp. 225–36.

MANAGEMENT FOCUS
Costs of Computerizing

Thousands of times a day, Jane Scarfo rolled cans and cartons across the electronic scanning window at her checkout station in a Vancouver supermarket. For items the scanner wouldn't read, she manually punched 11-digit codes into the computerized register. After 16 months of pulling and punching, her right palm went numb and her fingers began tingling. Pain gradually shot through her wrist to her elbow. A physician diagnosed carpal tunnel syndrome, a wrist disease linked to jobs requiring rapid repetitive motions. Her disorder was judged to be work related, and she won a small disability settlement. But at age 31, she finds it difficult to write or to grip a coffee cup with her unstable right hand.

Computers have changed millions of jobs but not always for the better. While they have raised productivity and increased efficiency, they have also spawned new strains. Computers, in some ways, have become the electronic equivalent of the assembly line.

Increasingly, computer workers are winning disability claims, causing companies concern about soaring insurance costs. Organizations are starting to redesign workspaces to reduce computer stress, and states are considering new laws to deal with computer health and safety.

In the United States, three fourths of all jobs will involve some use of video display terminals (VDTs) by the end of the century. Fifteen million, or 14 percent, already do. As the use of VDTs increases, so do workers' complaints, ranging from eyestrain and muscular aches to worries that low-level radiation may cause miscarriages and birth defects.

Unions and medical experts are pushing for more research. The unions are also lobbying the states for laws and regulations to govern VDT use and design. New Mexico's governor recently set health and safety guidelines for VDT workers by executive order. One price of the computer and the productivity growth it allows may be the occupational ailments that have to be addressed by management.

Source: Adapted from Cathy Trost, "The Price of Progress" (Special Report—Technology in the Workplace), *The Wall Street Journal,* September 16, 1985, pp. 34, 36.

crucial job can be achieved only through knowledge, hard work, and increased effort. A crucial and challenging opportunity of the next two decades is to apply the fundamentals of management to improving productivity. The future well-being of our society depends largely on our managers' ability to effect an improvement in productivity among blue-collar and white-collar employees. Managerial work on such a major goal is not easy or simple, but it certainly will be challenging and stimulating.

SUMMARY OF KEY POINTS

- Productivity is concisely defined as any ratio of output to one or more corresponding inputs.
- Any list of reasons for the productivity decline problem is endless. Some of the more manager-oriented reasons are:

    Management inattention.
    Lack of focus.
    Excessive layers of managers.
    Focusing too much on short-term results.
    Changing work force.
    Measurement difficulties.
    Lack of productivity goals.
    Government regulations.

- Before attempting to correct productivity problems or sluggishness, it is important for a manager to have realistic, specific, comprehensive, meaningful, and formalized goals.
- Some organizations are exceptions to the productivity decline in the United States. A number of successful firms seem to have some common attributes:

    A special emphasis on people.
    The customer or client is the center of attention.
    They build on strengths.
    They keep the structure simple and the staff lean.
    Controls exist but are not too tight.

- Despite the importance of productivity measurement, useful measures are not widely available and are often misunderstood. Measures make possible better management of work and organizations, people, and production and operations.
- A number of obstacles must be overcome in measuring white-collar productivity. They include a tendency to measure activities rather than results, difficulty in matching inputs and outputs within a time period, and resistance, fear, and misunderstanding among white-collar employees.

DISCUSSION AND REVIEW QUESTIONS

1. How could a manager measure the productivity of registered nurses working in the emergency room of a big-city hospital?

2. What responsibility does the union movement have in improving productivity in U.S. firms?

3. The following statement was made: "Defining and counting output generally is much more difficult than determining input in the measurement of white-collar productivity." Do you agree? Why?

4. Explain, in your words, why an increase in output and a decrease in input would be ideal as far as productivity is concerned.

5. Why are people such an important element in improving the present state of productivity in the United States?

6. Explain in your own words how productivity decline can influence your standard of living.

7. McDonald's is considered to be a successful firm. What productivity attributes does McDonald's clearly have that help maintain its success?

8. The chapter focused to some extent on measurement. Why would not only the measurement of quantity but also of quality be important in efforts to improve productivity?

9. A manager states: "My job defies measurement. It is too abstract for outsiders to understand." Is this a reasonable statement? How should this manager be compensated if this statement is true?

10. Why would it be difficult to solve an organization's productivity problems with a quick-fix solution such as some extra pay, changing the structure a little, redesigning jobs a little bit?

ADDITIONAL REFERENCES

Bohman, L. G., and T. E. Deal. *Modern Approaches to Understanding and Managing Organizations.* San Francisco: Jossey-Bass, 1984.

Crosby, P. B. *Quality without Tears: The Art of Hassle-Free Management.* New York: McGraw-Hill, 1984.

Kendrick, J. M. *Improving Company Productivity: Handbook with Case Studies.* Baltimore: The Johns Hopkins Press, 1984.

Lynch, J., and D. Orne. "The Next Elite: Manufacturing Supermanagers." *Management Review,* April 1985, pp. 49–51.

Midas, M. T., Jr., and W. B. Werther, Jr. "Productivity: The Missing Link in Corporate Strategy." *Management Review,* March 1985, pp. 44–47.

"The Revival of Productivity." *Business Week,* February 13, 1984, pp. 92–100.

Schwarz, J. E., and T. I. Volgy. "The Myth of America's Productivity Decline." *Harvard Business Review,* September–October 1985, pp. 98–107.

Werther, W. B., Jr.; W. A. Ruch; and L. McClure. *Productivity through People.* St. Paul, Minn.: West Publishing, 1986.

CASES

APPLICATION I
MANAGING THE BIG EIGHT*

The "Big Eight"—the premier American CPA firms—collectively audit virtually all of the *Fortune* 500 companies. Counted among the largest partnerships in the world, several of the Big Eight recently hit an historical landmark: In 1982, revenues of the top three of these firms cascaded over the billion dollar mark. At that point, Peat, Marwick, Mitchell was in first place, followed closely by Arthur Andersen and Coopers & Lybrand. In 1983, Arthur Andersen edged into the lead by a nose, and five of the eight firms exceeded a billion dollars in revenues.

That these firms continue to grow at rates approaching 10 percent each year is remarkable, considering that they are dealing to some extent with a finite audit market (particularly with respect to large clients) and an essentially nondifferentiable product (the audit report). The generic nature of this product, at least in the public's eye, is further attested to by the fact that these eight firms are usually referred to collectively and their individual names are not even known by most of the public.

The Big Eight, much as any exemplary industrial firm, have been successful in that they have reacted to environmental forces in an appropriate and enterprising manner. Hence, understanding their success should lead to managerial insights, not only for professional accounting partnerships and service firms in general but for all competitive businesses. Specifically, the following characteristics, policies, and actions seem to have contributed heavily to their success:

A unique organizational structure.

Partner involvement in developing client relationships.

Support of higher-education programs from which the firms draw their highly qualified staffs.

Use of technological advances to increase effectiveness and efficiency.

Identifying new areas of business that are close enough to their areas of expertise to give them a competitive advantage over other service firms.

Responding to changes in the environment in a manner consistent with the public images the firms wish to present.

---

* Source: Adapted from Mary T. Washington and Theodore J. Mack, "Managing the Big Eight," *New Management,* Fall 1985, pp. 47–52.

As an example of how policies and actions have resulted in productivity gains, let's take a closer look at how technological advances were used to improve productivity.

Even though constant employee turnover increases the profitability of a Big Eight firm, pressures to reduce audit fees also have increased dramatically, and clients frequently expect their fees to decline as the firm gains knowledge of the client's business. Consequently, the Big Eight firms have shown an interest in increasing the efficiency of their audit procedures in recent years, primarily through the use of statistical auditing packages, minicomputers, and other emerging technologies.

Peat, Marwick, Mitchell recently introduced a minicomputer-based audit package that improves audit efficiency in a number of ways. Because many audit tasks that were previously performed manually are now automated, the auditor is freed to spend more time on the complex features of the audit, such as solving involved accounting problems. This tool assists the auditor with:

1. Financial statement preparation (manually prepared statements and adjustments that previously took hours are now done very rapidly.
2. Detailed workpaper preparation.
3. Audit confirmation preparation and analysis.
4. Statistical sampling (the firm previously used a time-sharing network or manual procedures).
5. Retrieving relevant information on industry statistics from public data bases.
6. Financial modeling and analytical review.
7. Managing the engagement.
8. Word processing. Although this computer tool may not be usable for all clients, it represents a remarkable step toward automating the audit process.

To varying degrees, all of the Big Eight firms are developing such computer packages and analytical tools aimed at more efficient and effective auditing. Following medical applications of "expert systems," the Big Eight have shown an increased interest in developing these knowledge-based computer programs that simulate the judgmental process of an expert auditor. Both Arthur Andersen and Price Waterhouse are involved in developing expert systems to handle problems that do not lend themselves to typical algorithmic solutions. Price Waterhouse is in the process of utilizing a currently available PC-based expert system to accumulate and distribute case histories to their Computer Assisted Tax Service Group. Although the interest in and development of expert systems is still in its infancy, the use of such systems could feasibly help less knowledgeable auditors in making complex decisions.

Collectively, the Big Eight firms have responded admirably both to competitive pressures and environmental changes, but there is some evidence that these same pressures may cause a radical restructuring of the industry in the future. In 1985 merger talks (which later fell through) between Deloitte Haskins & Sells and Price Waterhouse raised discussion about the possibility of the Big Eight becoming the "Big Four." It is significant that increased competition and management consulting were cited as the reasons for these merger talks (both firms were characteristically closemouthed about the actual reasons).

Although the merger did not occur, the fact that it was being considered at all is good evidence of the pressures Big Eight firms have been under in trying to maintain and expand their market shares. The resulting firm would certainly have been the largest in market share.

Accounting firms, like manufacturers, are searching for innovative and effective ways to increase productivity, differentiate their products, and serve their customers. We may yet see the day when the Big Eight becomes the Big Four as these mammoth public accounting firms continue to cope with changes in their environment.

Questions for Analysis

1. How is productivity measured in an accounting firm?
2. How could the productivity of an accounting firm like Deloitte Haskins & Sells increase its productivity?
3. Why would it be more difficult to monitor productivity data in a service firm like Price Waterhouse than in an automobile company like General Motors?

APPLICATION II

PRODUCTIVITY GAINS AT ANY COST—THE MANAGER'S DILEMMA*

A public-opinion report issued by Opinion Research Corporation (ORC), Princeton, New Jersey, discussed productivity and automation in the United States. The vast majority of the respondents to the survey believed that American-made products would be more competitive in world markets if new technologies such as automation were increased. They also believed that increased automation would result in higher productivity rates. Likewise, the respondents linked automation to improved standards of living as a result of productivity gains.

---

* Source: Adapted from Alice M. Green, "Factory of the Future: The Love/Hate Response to Automation," *Iron Age,* February 25, 1983, pp. 45–56.

An improved standard of living and productivity gains would be music to the ears of everyone. However, the ORC survey identified among respondents a nagging fear of losing jobs to increased automation. Many citizens expressed despair and fear over the possibility of retraining for new skills.

Figures issued by the Bureau of Labor Statistics lend some credence to the public's fear of job loss. There has been a decrease in the manufacturing segment from 30 percent of the work force in 1960 to less than 25 percent in 1986, and this trend is expected to continue. The declining birthrate, the shift of jobs into the service sector, and the unpleasantness of many factory jobs are some of the reasons for this shift, in addition to the advent of new technologies.

The shock of technological changes will come gradually to some, suddenly to others. The transition eventually will produce a better work environment and productivity gains, but semiskilled and unskilled workers will face the full force of the shift to more automated and computerized factories. There will be fewer workers in the factory, fewer people assembling parts, and fewer people doing the individual processes. Also, the need for workers is going to switch from one of performing work to one of providing the maintenance and upkeep of the systems and machines that are actually doing the work.

One of the most formidable tasks facing management as organizations increase use of automation, robots, and computers is the retraining of the work force. Some organizations already have moved fast to prepare their employees. For example, at General Motors, workers are trained to install, repair, maintain, and monitor the new technologies—robots, and automated assembly lines. Training is designed to help the workers be a part of and understand the change.

Introduction of new methods to improve productivity also is under way at Honeywell, Inc. Honeywell's Modern Technology Concepts training program gives managers and scientists course work on microprocessors, optical systems, and computer graphics. They also receive training in employee counseling, career planning, and communication. These courses are designed to make the transition from the old technologies to the new technologies easier, to minimize resistance to change, and to reduce fear among managers and scientists.

Productivity improvement is an important goal of introducing new technologies. But managers have important planning, organizing, and controlling work to be done. In addition, many workers have to be convinced that the workplace of the future will be exciting, challenging, and more productive. Today, there are many workers who believe that the more productive workplace will be devoid of human interchange, loaded with gadgets, and have an elite corps of technologists who will run around in white coats taking orders from talking machines. The question being asked is whether productivity improvement is worth putting up with if it leads to a faceless work environment.

Questions for Analysis

1. What are some of the productivity promises and pitfalls of increased automation in the workplace?
2. Are white-collar workers immune from job displacement caused by shifts to new technologies such as robots, automated lines, and computers? Why?
3. What must General Motors and Honeywell do to determine if their training programs are having a positive impact on participants?
4. Some people state that training for the organization of the future should actually begin long before an individual enters the labor force. What would be the value of preparing individuals for organizational life while they are elementary or high school students?

EXPERIENTIAL EXERCISE

MEASURING PRODUCTIVITY FOR JOBS WITH INTANGIBLE OUTPUTS

Purpose

The purpose of this exercise is to encourage participants to think about the issues and difficulties associated with developing measures of productivity for intangible output.

The Exercise in Class

Measuring production output when you can count products is relatively simple, but the same measurement methods cannot be applied to groups such as corporate planners, research scientists, lawyers, and accountants. Because of the difficulty of measuring such outputs, researchers now are beginning to learn how to incorporate subjective assessments when analyzing productivity.

Productivity measures are difficult to construct for these groups:

Lawyer.	Surgeon (cardiovascular).
Teacher (college).	Judge.
Accountant.	Politician.
Engineer (electrical).	Personnel manager.

1. Establish groups of four to six students who will develop lists of possible productivity measures for the occupations listed above. Each student group will be assigned a different occupation.
2. The student groups should select a spokesperson to present the list to the class.
3. As each list is presented, the class should discuss what the student group has come up with. Particular attention should be paid to whether the measures being presented are realistic, specific, comprehensive, meaningful, and formalized.

The Learning Message

Since productivity improvement is such an important goal, groundwork must be done for measuring and analyzing it in all types of jobs. Productivity is most difficult to measure in jobs associated with intangible outputs. This exercise should identify some of the problems encountered in these kinds of jobs.

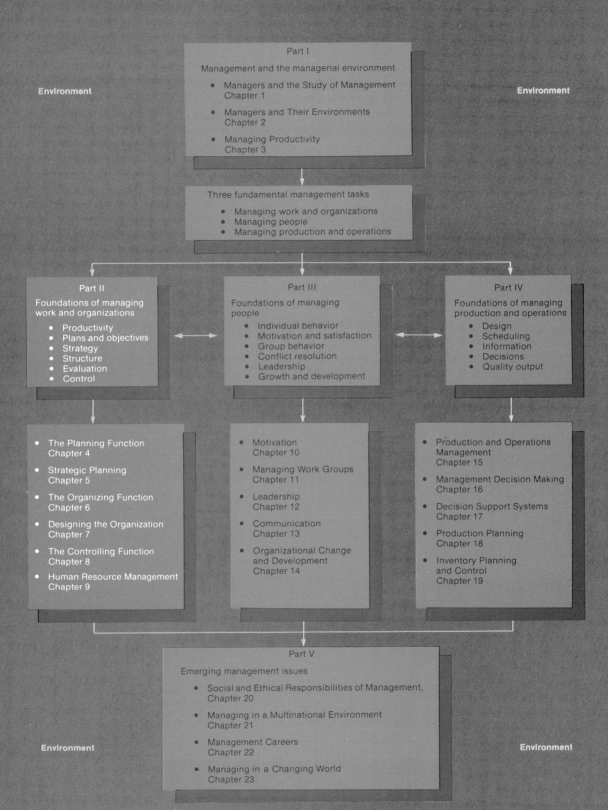

Environment

Part I

Management and the managerial environment

- Managers and the Study of Management
  Chapter 1
- Managers and Their Environments
  Chapter 2
- Managing Productivity
  Chapter 3

Environment

Three fundamental management tasks

- Managing work and organizations
- Managing people
- Managing production and operations

Part II

Foundations of managing work and organizations

- Productivity
- Plans and objectives
- Strategy
- Structure
- Evaluation
- Control

Part III

Foundations of managing people

- Individual behavior
- Motivation and satisfaction
- Group behavior
- Conflict resolution
- Leadership
- Growth and development

Part IV

Foundations of managing production and operations

- Design
- Scheduling
- Information
- Decisions
- Quality output

- The Planning Function
  Chapter 4
- Strategic Planning
  Chapter 5
- The Organizing Function
  Chapter 6
- Designing the Organization
  Chapter 7
- The Controlling Function
  Chapter 8
- Human Resource Management
  Chapter 9

- Motivation
  Chapter 10
- Managing Work Groups
  Chapter 11
- Leadership
  Chapter 12
- Communication
  Chapter 13
- Organizational Change
  and Development
  Chapter 14

- Production and Operations
  Management
  Chapter 15
- Management Decision Making
  Chapter 16
- Decision Support Systems
  Chapter 17
- Production Planning
  Chapter 18
- Inventory Planning
  and Control
  Chapter 19

Part V

Emerging management issues

- Social and Ethical Responsibilities of Management,
  Chapter 20
- Managing in a Multinational Environment
  Chapter 21
- Management Careers
  Chapter 22
- Managing in a Changing World
  Chapter 23

Environment

Environment

MANAGING WORK AND ORGANIZATIONS

PART II

■ FOUNDATIONS OF MANAGING WORK AND ORGANIZATIONS

As the 20th century began, certain managers and others who wanted to improve the practice of management began to put their ideas in writing. These managers were particularly concerned with two issues: (1) increasing the productivity of individuals performing *work* and (2) increasing the productivity of *organizations* within which work is performed. Directing their attention and energies to determining ways to manage work and organizations so that higher levels of output would be produced at lower costs, they created a body of management literature known as the classical approach.

The classicial approach still has modern-day applications because of its central concern for increasing productivity. For example, its early ideas on how to manage the work of individuals have come to be known as scientific management. The first proponents of scientific management were practicing engineers and managers who believed and demonstrated that work could be done more efficiently and thus more productively. They urged managers to systematically study the actual performance of work and to collect objective data on their observations, believing that through analysis of the data, the most efficient—the "best"—way to do a job could be determined.

Scientific management proponents felt that managers, not workers, should determine the manner and methods by which work is done. This point of view was in sharp contrast to the traditional craft system, where each worker learned a job and then taught it to apprentices. The craft system encouraged individuals to develop a sense of ownership of their jobs. Scientific management, however, discouraged that notion.

While scientific management ideas were being shaped, classical organization theory began to evolve. Those who developed classical organization theory believed that organizations are the settings within which individuals perform jobs—that the organization is a collection of individual jobs—so the organization should be designed and managed according to principles and practices that stress efficiency and productivity.

The two issues—jobs and productivity—addressed in the classical approach are critical for the modern manager. Achieving high levels of productivity in the performance of individual and organizational work is as much a concern today as it was at the turn of the century. Figure 1 identifies some of the important contributors to classical management thought.[1]

THE MANAGEMENT OF WORK

In modern manufacturing, the first-level manager is concerned with

[1] This designation is consistent with the usage in Daniel A. Wren, *The Evolution of Management Thought* (New York: John Wiley & Sons, 1979).

FIGURE   1   Primary Contributors to Classical Management Thought

Scientific Management *(management of work)*	*Classical Organization* *Theory* *(management of organizations)*
H. E. Emerson (1853–1931)	H. Fayol (1841–1925)
H. L. Gantt (1861–1919)	J. D. Mooney (1884–1957)
F. B. Gilbreth (1868–1924)	L. Urwick (1891–)
L. M. Gilbreth (1878–1972)	
F. W. Taylor (1856–1915)	

---

the day-to-day routine of coordinating the work of specialized labor. Each specialized worker does a job according to a set of rules and procedures designed to assure efficient completion of the job. The rules and procedures result from analysis of the technical and human requirements of the job and of its relationship to other jobs.

While the techniques for managing the work of individuals are now highly developed, they were still being formalized in the early years of the 20th century. Scientific management's proponents contended that the work individuals do can be analyzed from a scientific point of view. Industrial engineers believed that objective analyses of facts and data collected in experiments should reveal the best way to do the work. They analyzed the work performed at lower levels in the organization—shoveling, pig-iron handling, and sheet-metal cutting, for example. Although these types of jobs were relatively mundane, they were crucial to the industrial development of America.

Scientific management ideas are based upon an assumption that a cause of conflict between management and labor is inefficient use of scarce resources.[2] Management and labor were seen as continually in conflict, each believing that its share of the economic pie could be increased only at the expense of the other. For example, management was viewed as believing that wages could increase only at the expense of profit. But this is the case only if the total size of the economic pie is fixed. When the entire supply of economic goods and services is increased through more efficient use of resources, then the shares of both groups can increase.

The proponents of scientific management argued that the economic causes of labor-management disagreements could be eliminated by applying certain physiological and engineering principles to the jobs of blue-collar workers. Thus, at a time of serious concern for economic growth and resource conservation, scientific management became an important social and economic doctrine. Contained within that doctrine were

---

[2] For a discussion of the historical setting and ideology of scientific management, see Samuel Haber, *Efficiency and Uplift* (Chicago: University of Chicago Press, 1964).

certain assumptions about human beings. Specifically, scientific management adopted an assumption of classical economic theory: that people basically are motivated by the desire for economic betterment.[3] So if managers and workers were shown new methods that increased their chances for economic well-being, they would adopt them. The major and lasting changes wrought by scientific management were intended to be in the ways that workers historically had done manual work. The suggested changes in the manager's job were minor in comparison.

To appreciate fully the importance of scientific management as a philosophy and practice, you must understand its major contributions. These contributions were in the areas of (1) work management, (2) work simplification, (3) work scheduling, and (4) efficiency.

Principles of Work Management: Taylor

As the 20th century opened, business was expanding. New products and new markets were being created, but labor was in short supply. To offset labor shortages, two alternative solutions were possible: (1) substitute capital for labor or (2) use labor more efficiently. Both approaches reduce labor cost per unit of output and, ordinarily, the average total cost of the output. A leading proponent of using labor more efficiently was an engineer whose ideas initiated scientific management: Frederick W. Taylor.

As a supervisor at the Philadelphia Midvale Steel Company in the late 1800s, Taylor became interested in ways to improve lathe work. He began gathering facts and applying an objective analysis that was to typify his entire career.[4] He studied the work of individual lathe workers to discover exactly how they performed their jobs; he identified each aspect of each job and measured everything measurable. His goal was to provide the lathe operator with scientifically based, objective standards that would define *a fair day's work.*

Later, Taylor undertook a series of studies to determine objective work standards. In some cases, he dealt with physical factors of work. He found, for example, that the optimum weight of a shovel load is 22 pounds and that there is an appropriately shaped shovel for each kind of task.

In other instances, Taylor and his associates dealt with the human factor of work. For example, he trained a pig-iron handler to increase his tonnage load from 12½ to 47½ long tons per day.

The culmination of Taylor's efforts was four principles for managing work:

---

[3] William F. Whyte, *Money and Motivation* (New York: Harper & Row, 1955), pp. 2–3; James L. Gibson, "Organization Theory and the Nature of Man," *Academy of Management Journal,* September 1966, pp. 233–45.

---

[4] Lyndall Urwick, *The Golden Book of Management* (London: Newman Neame Ltd., 1956), pp. 72–79, outlines Taylor's career and personal life. Also see Lyndall Urwick and E. F. L. Brech, *The Making of Scientific Management* (London: Sir Isaac Pitman & Sons, 1951).

1. For each element of a man's work, develop a science that replaces the old rule-of-thumb method.
2. Scientifically select, train, teach, and develop the worker. (In the past, workers chose their own work and trained themselves as best they could.)
3. Cooperate with the workers so as to ensure that all of the work is done in accordance with the principles of the science that has been developed.
4. Recognize that there is almost an equal division of work and responsibility between management and workers. Managers take over all work for which they are better fitted than the workers. (In the past, almost all of the work and the greater part of the responsibility were thrown upon the workers.[5])

These four principles became the basic guidelines for managing the work of individuals.

Taylor was the first individual to study work in a serious manner.[6] His experiments with stopwatch studies and work methods inspired others to undertake similar studies in other work contexts. One result of the efforts of those who followed was the discovery of ways to simplify work.

Principles of Work Simplification: The Gilbreths

Frank and Lillian Gilbreth, a husband-and-wife team, combined their talents to produce important breakthroughs in work simplification. An untrained but insightful engineer, Frank Gilbreth was an apprentice bricklayer in his first job. His observations of skilled bricklayers' motions convinced him that many of their body movements (bending, reaching, stooping, troweling) could be combined or eliminated. Bricklaying could be simplified, and production could be increased. By combining and eliminating body movements and increasing the number of bricks laid in a given time period, resources (bricklayer's time) are reduced and output (bricks laid) is increased. The consequence is a marked increase in labor productivity.

Gilbreth's analysis of the sequence and path of basic body movements enabled him to reduce the number of motions required to lay brick from 18 to 4½. Bricklayers who used Gilbreth's method increased their production by 200 percent. Economy in the use of human energy, combined with technological improvements such as an adjustable stand to eliminate stooping for the brick and a mortar of proper consistency to eliminate "tapping," resulted in a science of the craft of masonry.[7] Gilbreth's work was quite compatible and consistent with that of Taylor's, since each

[5] Frederick W. Taylor, *Principles of Scientific Management* (New York: Harper & Row, 1911), pp. 36–37.

[6] Edwin A. Locke, "The Ideas of Frederick W. Taylor," *Academy of Management Journal,* January 1982, pp. 14–24, reviews Taylor's influence on contemporary management and concludes that it is substantial and pervasive.

[7] Claude S. George, Jr., *The History of Management Thought* (Englewood Cliffs, N.J.: Prentice-Hall, 1968), p. 97.

sought the elusive "one best way" to do a job.

Principles of Work Scheduling: Gantt

A close associate of Taylor at Midvale and Bethlehem Steel was a young graduate engineer named Henry L. Gantt. Like Taylor and the Gilbreths, Gantt was concerned with problems of productivity at the shop-floor level. Gantt's major contribution to scientific management is a chart showing the relationship between work planned and completed on one axis and time elapsed on the other. The *Gantt Chart* is still used in industry as a method for scheduling work.

While Taylor and the Gilbreths focused on the workers, Gantt believed that the way managers did their work could be improved and made more productive. He stated that expertise should be the sole criterion for the exercise of authority and that managers, as the recipients of authority, have the moral obligation to make decisions by scientific methods, not by opinion. Thus, Gantt broadened the scope of scientific management by including the work of managers as appropriate for analysis and change.

Principles of Efficiency: Emerson

The public became aware of Harrington Emerson in 1910, when he testified as an expert witness before the Interstate Commerce Commission that the railroads could save $1 million per day by using the methods

and philosophy of scientific management. Emerson's ideas are embodied in a set of principles that define the manner in which the efficient use of resources is to be accomplished. His principles encompass the basic elements of the scientific management approach. In summary, they contend that a manager should: (1) use scientific, objective, and factually based analyses; (2) define the aims of the undertaking; (3) relate each part to the whole; (4) provide standardized procedures and methods; and (5) reward individuals for successful execution of the task.

Emerson's contributions go beyond his principles of efficiency, though they and his testimony before the ICC would have assured his place in management history. He also recognized the positive lessons to be learned from the military's use of formalized staff and advisory positions. In his capacity as one of the first management consultants, he proposed the creation of a strict organization whose activities would be defined by clear statements of goals and purposes.[8]

Scientific management had had only minimal impact on management practice at the time that Taylor and his colleagues were writing. Although some firms adopted some of its methods and practices, scientific management's alternatives to waste, inefficiency, and industrial disharmony were largely ignored.

One cause of the seeming failure

---

[8] William F. Muhs, "Worker Participation in the Progressive Era: An Assessment by Harrington Emerson," *Academy of Management Review,* January 1982, p. 101.

of scientific management can be found in the failure of its proponents to understand fully the psychological and sociological aspects of work. Throughout Taylor's writing, one finds the implicit assumption that people are motivated basically by economic considerations and that when given adequate information, they will choose rationally the alternative that maximizes their economic well-being. In the context of the times, such an assumption was credible. Factory workers were, by and large, first-generation immigrants, ignorant of their surroundings and laboring for subsistence wages.

A significant and lasting contribution of scientific management, however, has been the identification of management's responsibilities for managing work. According to Taylor and his colleagues, management is responsible for:

- *Planning* the work by predetermining the expected quantity and quality of output for each job.
- *Organizing* the work by specifying the appropriate ways and means to perform each task.
- *Controlling* the work by *(a)* selecting and training qualified individuals, *(b)* overseeing the actual job performance, and *(c)* verifying that actual quantity and quality of output meet expectations.

At the work level, the responsibilities of management were defined in terms of functions: planning, organizing, and controlling. The stage was now set for considering management's responsibilities for managing organizations.

THE MANAGEMENT OF ORGANIZATIONS

Practicing managers were the first contributors to the literature on classical organization theory. They brought their practical orientations to bear on the problem of coordinating large-scale organizations.

The two lasting contributions of classical organization theory are (1) the principles of management and (2) the principles of organization. Through the application of these principles, the supporters of the theory argued, managers can manage *organizations* on the same basis that they manage *work*. The primary emphasis of these principles is to increase the probability that managerial action will result in efficiently performing organizations.

Principles of Management

Many early writers sought to define the principles of management. Chief among them was a Frenchman named Henri Fayol,[9] manager of a large coal company, who sought to discover principles of management that determine the "soundness and good working order" of the firm.

---

[9] Henry Fayol, *General and Industrial Management,* trans. J. A. Conbrough (Geneva: International Management Institute, 1929). All subsequent references in this text are to the more widely available translation by Constance Storrs (London: Pitman Publishing, 1949).

Such principles are flexible and adaptable to circumstances and events. Fayol was not seeking fixed rules of conduct; rather he sought guidelines to thinking. Deciding upon the appropriateness of a principle for a particular situation was, in his view, the "art" of management. Fayol believed that any number of principles might exist, but he described only those he most frequently applied in his own experience.

Fayol's chief desire was to elevate the status of management practice by supplying a framework for analysis. His framework included a statement of management functions and principles.

Management functions. Fayol identified five functions in which managers must engage:

1. *Planning:* Includes all those activities of a manager that result in predetermined courses of action. The manager should make the best possible forecast of future events that affect the firm and draw up plans that guide future decisions.

2. *Organizing:* Includes all activities that result in a structure of tasks and authority. This managerial function determines the appropriate machines, material, and human mix necessary to accomplish the planned courses of action.

3. *Commanding:* To be successful, the manager should set a good example and know thoroughly the personnel and the agreements made between personnel and the firm. Managers should have direct, two-way communcation with subordinates. Furthermore, managers continually

should evaluate the organizational structure and subordinates. They should not hesitate to change the structure if they consider it faulty or to fire subordinates who are incompetent.

4. *Coordinating:* Includes activities that bind together all individual efforts and direct them toward a common objective. Thus, Fayol saw coordinating as simply another element of the total managerial process. (The concept of management used in this textbook, on the other hand, suggests that coordination is the fundamental purpose of management.)

5. *Controlling:* This means assuring that actual activities are consistent with plans. Fayol did not expand the concept beyond stating that everything should be "subject to control."

These five functions describe the jobs of managers in organizations. Until the time of the classical organization theorists, the work of managers had been as much ignored as the work of blue-collar workers. Fayol and others sought to define the work of managers in terms of categories of activities, or functions, that they themselves had performed in their management careers.

Management principles. Fayol proposed 14 principles to guide the thinking of managers in resolving concrete problems. He did not believe in blind obedience to fixed rules of conduct, relying instead on managers' "experience and sense of proportion" to guide the degree of application of any principle in any situation. These principles are presented in Table 1.

TABLE 1 Classical Principles of Management

---

1. *Division of labor.* Work should be divided and subdivided into the smallest feasible elements, to take advantage of gains from specialization.
2. *Parity of authority and responsibility.* Each jobholder should be delegated sufficient authority to carry out assigned job responsibilities.
3. *Discipline.* Employees should obey whatever clearly stated agreements exist between them and the organization; managers should fairly sanction all instances of breached discipline.
4. *Unity of command.* Employees should receive orders from and be accountable to only one superior.
5. *Unity of direction.* Activities that have the same purpose should be grouped together and operate under the same plan.
6. *Subordination of individual to general interests.* The interests of the organization take precedence over the interests of the individual.
7. *Fair remuneration.* Pay should be based on achievement of assigned job objectives.
8. *Centralization.* Authority should be delegated in proportion to responsibility.
9. *Scalar chain.* An unbroken chain of command should exist through which all directives and communications flow.
10. *Order.* Each job should be defined so that the jobholder clearly understands it and its relationship to other jobs.
11. *Equity.* Established rules and agreements should be enforced fairly.
12. *Stability of personnel.* Employees should be encouraged to establish loyalty to the organization and to make a long-term commitment.
13. *Initiative.* Employees should be encouraged to exercise independent judgment within the bounds of their delegated authority and defined jobs.
14. *Esprit de corps.* Employees should be encouraged to define their interests with those of the organization and thereby achieve unity of effort.

Classical principles can serve as guidelines for managerial decision making.

The principles do not answer questions of degree of specificity, but Fayol did not suggest that they would relieve management from the responsibility for determining what he called "the appropriate balance." Indeed, he emphasized time and again that the moral character of the managers determines the quality of their decisions.

Principles of Organization

In 1931, James D. Mooney and Alan C. Reiley authored *Onward Industry,* which was revised in 1947 by Mooney and entitled *The Principles of Organization.* [10] This book is a vital part of the literature of classical management thought. It complements Fayol's work and adds a new dimension.

Mooney viewed management as the technique, or art, of directing and inspiring other people. Organization, on the other hand, is the technique of relating specific duties or functions in a coordinated whole. The primary purpose of management, according to

---

[10] James D. Mooney, *The Principles of Organization* (New York: Harper & Row, 1947).

Mooney, is to devise an appropriate organization.

Mooney's personal experience and his examination of organization in governmental, church, military, and industrial institutions formed the basis for a framework of concepts describing the essential nature of organizations. These experiences led him to believe that natural laws of organizing existed, and it was these natural laws, or principles, that he sought to discover through logic. The principles of organization, according to Mooney, are as follows:

1. *Coordination.* Coordination is the primary reason for organizing. Since organizations are natural outgrowths of specialization and division of labor, their purpose must be to achieve coordinated performance of all the jobs within the organization.

2. *Authority.* The necessity for organization sets into motion other activities, which in turn are guided by other principles. The first essential activity of authority is the definition of each managerial job in terms of its duties and responsibilities. The creation of managerial jobs results in the creation of a chain of command, or hierarchy, in which each successive job up the chain has greater authority than the one preceding it. The inevitability of the chain of command in organizations led Mooney to see that an underlying principle must be in effect: the principle of authority.

3. *Leadership.* The delegation of authority is guided by the principle of leadership, which (in Mooney's terms) is the personification of authority. Through the delegation of authority, leaders confer authority on subordinates, and so on down the chain.

4. *Specialization.* Parallel to the process of delegating is the process of defining tasks. The principle of specialization underlies this function. Regardless of the type of organization, the necessity exists (as Fayol, Taylor, and other classical writers had observed) for people to do different jobs at different times.

MANAGING WORK AND ORGANIZATIONS: A SYNTHESIS

The various perspectives of the classical approach can be synthesized. One such synthesis is provided by Lyndall Urwick, who contends that management's fundamental responsibility is to define the individual jobs to be done (work) and to develop ways to coordinate the jobs (organization).[11] Work and organization are central managerial concerns. Moreover, the classicial approach emphasizes that managers should discharge this responsibility through the application of rigorous and objective analysis. Arbitrary, subjective opinions about the way work should be done and managed are to be avoided.

Once work is organized into an ongoing entity, the responsibility of management is to direct it toward specific purposes. Classical thought stresses the importance of recognizing that organizations exist in societies to provide economic goods, health

---

[11] Lyndall Urwick, *The Elements of Administration* (New York: Harper & Row, 1944).

care, education, and government. That is, all organizations have purposes, and it is management's job to achieve those purposes. Through planning, organizing, and controlling activities, managers perform their jobs.

The ideas of scientific management and classical organization theory are compatible and can be viewed as an integral set. Taken together, the two perspectives define not only the first historical concerns of management but what may be the central concerns of managers in all times and places.

This synthesis of scientific management and classical organization theory reflects the essence of classical management theory: "that all management principles fit together in a balanced and interrelated framework."[12] Yet it is recognized that much remains to be done in the routine management of day-to-day operations. Even though the organization structure and jobs are designed and individuals are selected and trained, there is room for managerial interpretation of appropriate behavior. The principles of management also must take into account the variable nature of human behavior.

MANAGING WORK AND ORGANIZATIONS: CLASSICAL PERSPECTIVE

The first and foremost contribution of the classical approach was that of identifying management as a distinct element of organized society. The classical writers believed that management—like law, medicine, and other occupations—should be practiced according to principles that managers can learn. Moreover, they argued, these principles can be discovered by the application of scientific methods. As Taylor pointed out, manual tasks could be studied and subsequently managed by applying the basic laws of physiology and physics. Mooney made a strong case that the organizing function can be analyzed by applying the fundamentals of deductive logic.

The identification of the planning, organizing, and controlling functions provides a basis for training managers. Many contemporary management textbooks, including this one, are based upon these functions. The manner in which management functions are presented and explained often differs, depending upon the particular point of view of the author. Yet, the essence of any listing of management functions is acknowledging that managers are concerned with *what* the organization is to be doing, *how* it is to be done, and *whether* it is achieved.

Contemporary business firms, hospitals, universities, and government agencies recognize the need to perform these functions. Planning offices, organizational-analysis units, and quality-control sections can be found in many large organizations. Smaller organizations implement these functions in more general, nonspecialized ways, primarily through the efforts of top manage-

---

[12] Joseph L. Massie, "Management Theory," in *Handbook of Organizations,* ed. James H. March (Skokie, Ill.: Rand McNally, 1965), p. 413.

ment. The essential point is that the classical approach makes a strong case that someone, either managers or their subordinates, must perform these functions.

The contributions of the classical approach go beyond the important work of identifying the management field, its functions, and principles. Many modern management techniques are direct outgrowths of its endeavors. For example, time and motion analysis, work simplification, incentive wage systems, production scheduling, personnel testing, and budgeting are modern management techniques derived directly from the classical approach. The classical approach emphasizes the *rational, logical,* and *integrated* nature of management's responsibilities.[13]

---

[13] Daniel Nelson, *Frederick W. Taylor and the Rise of Scientific Management* (Madison: University of Wisconsin Press, 1980).

THE PLANNING FUNCTION

LEARNING OBJECTIVES

After completing Chapter 4, you should be able to:

■ **Define**
the planning function in terms of managerial responsibilities and decisions.

■ **Describe**
the planning function in terms of its four principal elements.

■ **Discuss**
why the planning function must begin with the determination of objectives.

■ **Compare**
arguments for and against the alternative means for implementing a plan.

■ **Identify**
the most useful forecasting technique for a particular set of circumstances.

☐ MANAGEMENT IN ACTION

New Planners and New Plans for Coors Beer*

The fourth generation of the Coors family has taken over active management of the family brewery. Peter Coors and his brother Jeffrey are now in charge and are trying to inject some life into the stagnating brewery. "My father and uncle had to concentrate on getting beer out the door," says Jeff. "We're in an era where volume, success, and the bottom line do not come automatically."

That may be a profound understatement. Few other major brewers have been hurt as badly by their own blunders or by such giant competitors as Anheuser-Busch, Inc. and Miller Brewing Co. Coors' share of the key California market, for example, has fallen from 44 percent in 1976 to just over 14 percent in 1985.

Observers say the brothers are likely to speed up diversification into new businesses such as biotechnology and packaging and also introduce new products at the brewery. But the biggest change they see is that for the first time, *formalized planning* is taking place at Coors. Planning was one management function previous generations didn't bother with.

The two brothers have been responsible for planning major changes in Coors' advertising theme and in new-product development. Their changes in advertising have been highly praised, but the jury is still out on several new products. Their Coors Light accounts for nearly 50 percent of Coors volume and is second only to Miller's Lite in light-beer sales. George Killian's Irish Red Ale, sold in New England, is doing well; but sales of Herman Joseph's, sold in only six states, have been lackluster. Colorado Chiller, designed for the wine cooler market, failed in test markets in 1985 and was sent back to the drawing board. The brothers have high hopes for Coors Extra Gold, a heartier premium beer currently being tested.

By introducing formal planning into the company, Pete and Jeff Coors have recognized the critical importance of this management function. At Coors and elsewhere, planning involves setting objectives, determining ways to achieve those objectives, evaluating resource constraints, and implementing the plan. These elements are the central topics of this chapter.

---

*Source: "Can Pete and Jeff Coors Brew Up a Comeback," *Business Week,* December 16, 1985, pp. 86–88.

Managers have a primary responsibility for planning. In fact, some managers see planning as the primary management function and think that organizing and controlling are secondary. Whatever its relative importance to other management functions, planning is essential if organizations are to achieve effective levels of performance. As the experience at Coors indicates, the ability or inability of a firm to adapt to change is linked directly to its planning system.

THE FOCUS OF PLANNING

Planning focuses on the future: what is to be accomplished and how. In essence, *the planning function includes those managerial activities that determine objectives for the future and the appropriate means for achieving those objectives.* The outcome of the planning function is a plan, a written document that specifies the predetermined courses of action.

THE ELEMENTS OF PLANNING

The planning function requires managers to make decisions about four fundamental elements of plans. They are:

1. Objectives.
2. Actions.
3. Resources.
4. Implementation.

Objectives are integral to plans because they specify future conditions that the planner deems satisfactory. For example, the statement "The firm's objective is to achieve a 12 percent rate of return on invested capital by the end of 1988" refers to future, satisfactory condition.

Actions are the specified, preferred means to achieve the objectives. The preferred course of action to lead to a 12 percent return might be to engage in a product development effort so that five new products are introduced in 1988.

Resources are constraints on the courses of action. For example: "The total cost to be incurred in the development of five new products must not exceed $10 million." A plan should specify the kinds and amounts of resources required, as well as the potential sources and allocations of those resources. Specifying resource constraints also involves *budgeting*—identifying the sources and levels of resources that can be committed to planned courses of action.

Finally, a plant must include ways and means to implement the intended actions. *Implementation* involves the assignment and direction of personnel to carry out the plan.

Establishing objectives and prescribing actions also require *forecasting* the

---

FIGURE   4–1   The Planning Function

The planning function is a complex set of interrelated steps that predetermines the use of resources to undertake actions to achieve performance-relevant objectives.

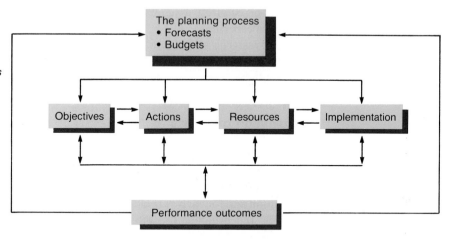

---

future. A manager cannot plan without explicit consideration of future events and contingencies that could affect what will be possible to accomplish.

Although the four elements of the planning function are discussed separately, they are in fact intertwined. As will be seen, objectives must be set according to what is possible, given the forecasts of the future *and* the budgets of resources. Moreover, availability of resources can be affected by the very actions that management plans. In the previous example, if a 12 percent return is not achieved, $10 million may not be available, because stockholders, bondholders, or other sources of capital will not invest the funds. Then, other action may not be feasible.

In some organizations, planning is the combined effort of managers and staff personnel. In other organizations, planning is done by the top management group. In still others, it is done by one individual. Planning activities can range from complex, formal procedures to simple and informal ones. Although the *form* of planning activities varies from organization to organization, the *substance* is the same. Plans and planning inherently involve objectives, actions, resources and implementation directed toward improving an organization's performance in the future. Figure 4–1 outlines the planning function.

THE IMPORTANCE OF PLANNING

Planning can occur at all levels in an organization. Supervisors who identify standard output and direct subordinates in using standard procedures are engaged in planning. Sales managers who define sales quotas and assign sales-persons to particular territories are engaged in planning. In both instances, these managers determine objectives (standard output, sales quotas), actions (standard procedures, assignment to territories), and resources (production workers, salespersons).

The pervasiveness of planning is ample evidence of its importance in management. But we can identify some rather specific benefits—[1] the kind the Coors brothers surely hope will accrue from their planning efforts:

Coordination of efforts

Management exists because the work of individuals and groups in organizations must be coordinated, and planning is one important technique for achieving coordinated effort. An effective plan specifies objectives both for the total organization and for each part of the organization. By working toward planned objectives, the behavior of each part will contribute to and be compatible with goals for the total organization.

Preparedness for change

An effective plan of action allows room for change. The longer the time between completion of a plan and accomplishment of an objective, the greater the necessity to include contingency plans. Yet if management has considered the potential effect of the change, it can be better prepared to deal with it. History provides some vivid examples of what results from failure to be prepared for change. The collapse of Penn Central Railroad, W. T. Grant, and the A&P grocery chain are due in large part to management's lack of preparedness. Through the use of formalized planning, the Coors brothers hope to avoid a similar fate.

Development of performance standards

Plans define expected behaviors; and in management terms, expected behaviors are performance standards. As plans are implemented throughout an organization, the objectives and courses of action assigned to each individual and group are the bases for standards. These standards can be used to assess actual performance. In some instances, the objectives provide the standards: Performance of a manager can be assessed in terms of how close that manager's

---

[1] See A. A. Thompson, Jr., and A. J. Strickland III, *Strategic Management: Concepts and Cases,* 3rd ed. (Plano, Tex.: Business Publications, 1984), chaps. 1 and 2.

unit comes to accomplishing its objective. In other instances, the courses of action are the standards: A production worker can be held accountable for doing his or her job in the prescribed manner. Through planning, management derives a rational, objective basis for performance standards. Without planning, performance standards are likely to be nonrational and subjective.

Management development

The act of planning involves high levels of intellectual activity. Those who plan must be able to deal with abstract and uncertain ideas and information. Planners must think systematically about the present and the future. Through planning, the *future* state of the organization can be improved if its managers take an *active* role in moving the organization toward that future. Planning, then, implies that managers should be *proactive* and *make* things happen rather than *reactive* and *let* things happen. Through the act of planning, managers not only develop their ability to think futuristically but, to the extent that their plans are effective, their motivation to plan is reinforced. Also, the *act* of planning sharpens managers' ability to think as they consider abstract ideas and possibilities for the future. Thus, both the result *and* the act of planning benefit both the organization and its managers.

SETTING OBJECTIVES AND PRIORITIES

The planning function begins with the determination of future objectives, and those objectives must satisfy expectations from its environment. Whether the organization is a business, a university, or a government agency, the environment supplies the resources that sustain it. In exchange for these resources, the organization must supply the environment with goods and services at an acceptable price and quality. The increasing interdependence between organizations and their environments has caused corporate managers to turn more and more to formal planning techniques. Moreover, the evidence is clear that organizations using formal approaches to planning are more profitable than those that do not.[2]

Management initiates planning to determine the *priority* and *timing* of objectives. In addition, management must also resolve *conflict* between objectives and provide *measurement* of objectives so that results can be evaluated.[3]

---

[2] See Milton Moskowitz, "Lessons from the Best Companies to Work For," *California Management Review,* Winter 1985, pp. 42–47.

[3] Max D. Richards, *Setting Strategic Goals and Objectives,* 2nd ed. (St. Paul, Minn.: West Publishing, 1985).

Priority of Objectives

The phrase "priority of objectives" implies that at a given time, accomplishing one objective is more important than accomplishing others. For example, the objective of maintaining a minimum cash balance may be more important than achieving minimum profitability to a firm having difficulty meeting payrolls and due dates on accounts. Priority of objectives also reflects the relative importance of certain objectives regardless of time. For example, survival of the organization is a necessary condition for the realization of all other objectives.

Managers must establish priorities if they want to allocate resources in a rational manner. Managers always face alternative objectives that must be evaluated and ranked. Managers of nonbusiness organizations are particularly concerned with the ranking of seemingly interdependent objectives. For example, a university president must determine the relative importance of teaching, research, and community service. Because determining objectives and priorities is inherently a judgmental decision, it is an inherently difficult process.

Time Frame of Objectives

Time dimensions imply that an organization's activities are guided by different objectives, depending upon the duration of the action that is being planned. Managers usually identify short-run, intermediate, and long-run objectives. Short-run objectives can be accomplished in less than a year; intermediate objectives require one to five years; and long-run objectives extend beyond five years. The relationship between priority and timing is quite close, since long-run objectives are those that must be accomplished to assure the long-term survival of the organization.

The time dimension is reflected in the practice by many organizations of developing different plans for different periods of time. The long-run objective of a business firm could be stated in terms of a desired rate of return on capital, with intermediate and short-run plans stated in terms of objectives that must be accomplished to realize the ultimate goal. Management is then in a position to know the effectiveness of each year's activities in terms of achieving not only short-run but also long-run objectives.

In some instances, short-run objectives and long-run objectives may appear antagonistic. Many observers of contemporary business management argue that the emphasis on short-run profitability detracts from efforts to make commitments to such long-run objectives as improving productivity or growth. The Management Focus describes the efforts of Taft Broadcasting to stress the importance of long-run objectives.

MANAGEMENT FOCUS
Short-Run Profit or Long-Run Growth

Early in 1985, Taft Broadcasting Co. was just another media company with a cozy broadcast group. Shortly thereafter, it moved into the big time with the announcement that it would pay $760 million for Gulf Broadcast Co.'s five television and seven radio stations.

Although the long-term results of the strategy remain unclear, the acquisition should give Taft an immediate lift. All the new stations are in the expanding Sun Belt, all are established entities, and three of the five TV stations finished strongly in recent ratings. And with stations reaching 15 percent of U.S. TV households, Taft has a lock on a large audience for its own programming, which includes animation by its Hanna-Barbera Productions, Inc. as well as live-action shows.

The deal has altered the way others regard Cincinnati-based Taft. As one industry expert stated, "The significance of the Gulf acquisition was to solidify Taft's image as a dynamic, modern broadcaster." Making money—which they have always done well—is fine. But Taft has decided that long-run growth is better.

Source: "Taft Hits the Big Time, but Raiders May Lie in Wait," *Business Week*, October 21, 1985, p. 66.

In recent years, the increasing pace of environmental change has prompted many organizations to adopt *strategic planning,* which focuses on all the activities that lead to the definition of long-term objectives and strategies to achieve those objectives. This is in contrast with *functional* or *operational planning,* which is done in the individual units within the organization and focuses on more immediate objectives and problems. Because of its growing importance, strategic planning will be the focus of Chapter 5.

Conflicts among Objectives

At any point in time, stockholders (owners), employees (including unions), customers, suppliers, creditors, and governmental agencies are all concerned with the operation of the firm. The process of setting objectives must not overlook these interest groups, and plans must incorporate and integrate their interests. The form and weight to be given to any particular interest group precisely illustrates the nature of management's dilemma. Yet management's responsibility is to make these kinds of judgments. Some of the most common planning trade-offs faced by managers in business organizations are:

1. Short-term profits versus long-term growth.
2. Profit margin versus competitive position.
3. Direct sales effort versus development effort.
4. Greater penetration of present markets versus developing new markets.
5. Achieving long-term growth through related businesses versus unrelated businesses.
6. Profit objectives versus nonprofit objectives (that is, social responsibilities).
7. Growth versus stability.
8. Low-risk environment versus high-risk environment.

Management must consider the expectations of diverse groups on whom the firm's ultimate success depends. For example, present and potential customers hold ultimate power over the firm. If they are not happy with the price and quality of the firm's product, they withdraw their support (stop buying), and the firm fails because of lack of funds. Suppliers can disrupt the flow of materials to express disagreement with the firm's activities. Government agencies have the power to enforce the firm's compliance with regulations. The existence of these interest groups and their power to affect the objectives of the firm must be recognized by managers. The business firm will exist only as long as it satisfies the larger society.[4]

Studies of objectives that business managers have set for their organizations affirm the difficulty of balancing the concerns of interest groups. These studies also suggest that the more-successful firms consistently emphasize profit-seeking activities that maximize the stockholder's wealth. This is not to say that successful firms seek only profit-oriented objectives but rather that such objectives are dominant. Evidently, such firms are managed by persons who value pragmatic, dynamic, and achievement-oriented behavior. These persons, at the same time, recognize that businesses have an increasing responsibility to do what is best for society.[5] The interrelationship among the managers' values, society's needs, and organizational objectives has been aptly summarized: *"What to make, what to charge,* and *how to market the wares* are questions that embrace moral as well as economic questions. The answers are conditioned by the personal value system of the decision maker and

---

[4] D. Quinn Mills, "Planning with People in Mind," *Harvard Business Review,* July–August 1985, pp. 97–105.

[5] See M. L. Gimpl and S. R. Daken, "Management and Magic," *California Management Review,* Fall 1984, pp. 125–36; R. T. Pascale, "The Paradox of Corporate Culture: Reconciling Ourselves to Socialization," *California Management Review,* Winter 1985, pp. 26–41; Frederick D. Sturdivant, *Business and Society: A Managerial Approach,* 3rd ed. (Homewood, Ill.: Richard D. Irwin, 1985), for relevant discussions of these and related management problems.

the institutional values which affect the relationships of the individual to the community."[6]

Measurement of Objectives

Objectives must be understandable and acceptable to those who will help to achieve them. In fact, many people believe that specific, measurable objectives increase performance of both employees and organizations, and that difficult objectives, if accepted by employees, result in better performance than do easier objectives. In practice, effective managerial performance requires establishing objectives in every area that contributes to overall organizational performance. Management expert Peter Drucker has stated that objectives should be established in at least eight areas of organizational performance: (1) market standing, (2) innovations, (3) productivity, (4) physical and financial resources, (5) profitability, (6) manager performance and responsibility, (7) worker performance and attitude, and (8) social responsibility.[7] This classification in no way implies relative importance nor is it the only such classification system available.

Drucker has observed that "the real difficulty lies indeed not in determining what objectives we need, but in deciding how to set them."[8] This involves determining *what* should be measured in each area and *how* it should be measured. Immediately, one can recognize the difficulty of measuring performance in certain areas. For example, how can a manager measure employee attitudes and social responsibility? The more abstract the objective, the more difficult it is to measure performance.

Nevertheless, effective planning requires measurement of objectives. A variety of measurements exist to quantify objectives in the eight areas that Drucker suggests.

Profitability objectives. These include the ratios of (1) profits to sales, (2) profits to total assets, and (3) profits to capital (net worth). The tendency in recent years has been to emphasize the ratio of profits to sales as an important measure of profitability. Both quantities required to calculate this measure are taken from the income statement, which management generally regards as a better test of performance than the balance sheet.

---

[6] Clarence C. Walton, *Ethos and the Executive* (Englewood Cliffs, N.J.: Prentice-Hall, 1969), p. 192.

[7] Peter Drucker, *The Practice of Management* (New York: Harper & Row, 1954); reemphasized in Peter Drucker, *Management: Tasks, Responsibilities, Practices* (New York: Harper & Row, 1974). For recent work by this reknowned management writer, see *Managing in Turbulent Times* (New York: Harper & Row, 1980); and *Innovation and Entrepreneurship* (New York: Harper & Row, 1985).

[8] Drucker, *Practice of Management* p. 64.

However, other managers believe that the true test of profitability must combine the income statement and the balance sheet. These managers, therefore, would use either the profit:total-asset ratio or the profit:net-worth ratio. Which of these two measures is preferred depends on whether the *source* of capital is an important consideration. The profit:total-asset ratio measures management's use of all resources, regardless of origin (that is, creditors or owners). The profit:net-worth ratio measures how management used the owner's contribution. The measures are not mutually exclusive. All three ratios can be used as profitability objectives, because each measures and therefore evaluates different yet important aspects of profitability.

The purposes of profit are to measure efficiency, recover one cost element of being in business (return on invested capital), and provide funds for future expansion and innovation. The minimum profitability is that which assures the continuous stream of capital into the organization, given the inherent risks of the industry in which the organization operates.

Marketing objectives.   These measure performance relating to products, markets, distribution, and customer-service objectives. They concern prospects for long-run profitability. Thus, well-managed organizations measure performance relating to market share, sales volume, number of outlets carrying the product, and number of new products developed.

Productivity objectives.   Productivity is measured with ratios of output to input. Other factors being equal, the higher the ratio, the more efficient is the use of inputs.

Drucker has long proposed that the *ratios of value added to sales and to profit* are the superior measures of productivity.[9] He believes that a business's objective should be to increase these ratios and that departments in the firm should be evaluated on the basis of these increases. The argument for value added is that it measures the increase in value of the purchased materials due to the combined efforts of the firm, since value added is equal to the difference between the purchase price and the market value of materials and supplies. In this way, the efficiency of the firm's efforts is measured directly. This measure of productivity also could be used for comparisons among the individual departments in the firm.

Physical and financial objectives.   These measures reflect the firm's capacity to acquire resources sufficient to achieve its objectives. The measurement of physical and financial objectives is comparatively easy since numerous accounting measures can be used. Liquidity measures such as the current ratio, working-capital turnover, the acid-test ratio, debt-to-equity ratio, and accounts receivable and inventory turnover can be used in establishing objectives and evaluating performance in financial planning.

---

[9] Ibid., pp. 71–73.

TABLE   4–1   Selected Measures of Objectives

Objective	*Possible Measures*
Profitability	1. Ratio of profit to sales.
	2. Ratio of profit to total assets.
	3. Ratio of profit to capital.
Marketing	1. Market share.
	2. Sales volume.
	3. Rate of new-product development.
	4. Number of outlets.
Productivity	1. Ratio of output to labor costs.
	2. Ratio of output to capital costs.
	3. Ratio of value added to sales.
	4. Ratio of value added to profit.
Physical and financial	1. Current ratio.
	2. Working-capital turnover.
	3. Ratio of debt to equity.
	4. Accounts receivable turnover.
	5. Inventory turnover.

Management must determine which measures are appropriate to reflect the extent to which objectives are achieved.

Other objectives.   Objectives for profitability, market standing, productivity, and physical and financial resources are amenable to measurement. Objectives for innovation, employee attitudes, manager behavior, and social responsibility are, however, not so easily identifiable or measurable in concrete terms. This is important because, without measurement, any subsequent evaluation will be inconclusive. For example, a vaguely stated objective such as "to become more socially responsible" will be virtually impossible to evaluate whether or not it is accomplished. Selected measures of objectives are summarized in Table 4–1.

An Example of Objectives in Planning

Stating objectives clearly is a critical element of planning. Our discussion of objective setting is summarized in Table 4–2, based on an organization's actual experience in establishing objectives. This organization established seven objectives that management ranked in the order of priority shown in the table.

Clear objectives can be converted into specific targets and actions. Note that management also stated each objective in Table 4–2 in more specific secondary objectives, which can become goals for individual departments. For example, the secondary objective associated with Objective 1 can serve as a financial management objective. Those associated with Objective 2 can be marketing objectives. And those associated with Objective 3 can be the goals of the personnel department.

TABLE   4–2   The Development of Objectives

Objective	Possible Secondary Objectives	Possible Indicators
1. Achieve a 15 percent return on investment.	a. Earn maximum return on idle funds.	a. Interest income.
2. Maintain a share of the market of 40 percent.	a. Retain 75 percent of old customers. b. Obtain 25 percent of first-time customers.	a. Percent replacement purchases. b. Percent initial purchases.
3. Develop middle managers for executive positions.	a. Develop a merit review system by year-end. b. Select 10 managers to attend industry-sponsored executive school.	a. Report submitted on November 1. b. Number selected by January 1.
4. Help to ensure that clean air is maintained in all geographical areas in which the firm has plant locations.	a. Reduce air pollution by 15 percent.	a. By April 1, pollutants to be 125 pounds/hour measured at stack by electrostatic.
5. Provide working conditions that constantly exceed industrywide safety levels.	a. Automate loading process in Plant B. b. Reduce in-plant injuries by 10 percent by year-end.	a. Installation to be 50 percent complete by January 1. b. Ratio of labor-days lost to total labor-days.
6. Manufacture all products as efficiently as possible.	a. Increase productivity by 5 percent through installation of new punching machine.	a. Installed by August 1. b. Ratio of output to total labor-hours.
7. Maintain and improve employee satisfaction to levels consistent with our own and similar industries.	a. Improve employee satisfaction levels in all functional areas by 15 percent by year-end.	a. Ratio of quits to total employees. b. Attitude survey questionnaires administered to all employees.

Management can subdivide objectives and develop relatively precise indicators of achievement.

COURSES OF ACTION

Action is the catalyst that can determine success or failure in meeting objectives. Planned courses of action are called *strategies* and *tactics*. The difference between the two usually implies the scope and magnitude of the action. Whatever the name, a planned action is directed toward changing a future condition—that is, achieving an objective. For example, if an objective is to increase productivity from five units of output per labor hour to six units per labor hour, a course of action has to be identified and implemented. In some instances, managers simply do not know what action to take. When President Kennedy stated as a national objective the placing of an American on the moon by 1970, no one knew exactly what was necessary to accomplish that objective.

Other instances can present numerous alternative courses of action. In such cases, managers must select the alternative that is least costly but most effective. For example, productivity increases can be achieved through a variety of means, including improved technology, employee training, management training, reward systems, and improved working conditions. Often several viable courses of action do exist for top managers who are planning for the total organization. As the plan becomes more localized to a single unit in the organization, the number of alternatives tends to become smaller yet more familiar.

Management often can change its primary strategy to take advantage of apparent opportunities. The Management Focus on Frontier Airlines describes how a company changed its basic course of action in response to a change in its competitive environment. Unfortunately the changes were too late in this case.

MANAGEMENT FOCUS
Frontier Airlines Is Too Late with Its Change of Plans

Before airline fare deregulation in 1978, Frontier Airlines, Inc. was a well-established regional airline. It had a strong competitive position as Denver's favorite air carrier. After deregulation, Frontier extended its route structure to Los Angeles, Seattle, and San Diego and dropped flights to 41 smaller cities. These moves met with early success because Frontier could compete with the major airlines for fares on these more lucrative routes.

But the recession and airfare competition caused Frontier's top management to reconsider its earlier moves. Its 1982 profit, $9.2 million, was a sharp drop from the 1981 profit of $50.9 million. The feeling among some industry analysts was that Frontier Airlines had lost sight of its niche in the industry. Instead of remaining a profitable, Denver-based regional airline, it chose to compete with the larger airlines—United, American, and Delta.

Major airlines have technological and marketing advantages not usually available to the smaller carriers. For example, travel agents sell 6 percent of Frontier's tickets, and Frontier is making strong efforts to increase agency sales. But United has a computerized reservation system that makes it easier to book a passenger on a United flight than on a Frontier flight.

In early 1983, Frontier launched a major effort to regain its position as Denver's favorite airline. Unfortunately the changes were too late. The airline lost $44.9 million during 1983 and 1984. In 1985,

MANAGEMENT FOCUS *(continued)*

Frontier Airlines was purchased by People Express Airlines for $300 million.

Source: Adapted from "Where Frontier Lost Its Way," *Business Week,* February 7, 1983, p. 120; "People Express Wins the Duel for Frontier Airlines," *Business Week,* October 21, 1985, p. 42.

The important point is that courses of action and objectives are causally related; that is, the objective is caused to occur by the courses of action. The intellectual effort required in planning involves not only knowing *what* alternatives will accomplish an objective but also *which* one is most efficient. In some instances, managers can test the effects of a course of action by forecasting. Forecasting is *the process of using past and current information to predict future events.*

A typical objective in business planning is to maintain or increase sales volume. Sales volume is a primary source of liquid resources such as cash, accounts receivable, and notes receivable, which managers can use to finance the firm's activities. Courses of action that affect sales include price changes, marketing and sales activities, and new-product development. Factors beyond the control of management also affect sales. Such external factors include the price of competing and substitute products, competitors' marketing/sales activities, and general economic conditions (expansion, recession, inflation). Although managers cannot control many of the factors that determine sales volume, forecasting remains a valuable managerial tool.

Forecasting Sales Volume

Four methods currently are used to forecast future events. Here, they are presented in the context of forecasting sales volume, although the methods generally are applicable to forecasting other events.

1. *Hunches:* Estimates of future sales can be based upon past sales data, comments by salespersons and customers, and instinctive reaction to the "general state of affairs." This approach is relatively cheap and usually effective in firms whose market is stable or at least changing at a predictable rate.

2. *Market Survey:* Estimates of future sales can be based upon the opinions customers express to the organization's salespeople. More sophisticated statistical sampling techniques yield more refined information. The forecaster can specify both the range of projected sales and the degree of confidence in the estimates.

3. *Time-Series Analysis:* Estimates of future sales can be based upon the relationship between sales and time. The movement of sales over time is

affected by at least three types of factors: seasonal, cyclical, and trend. That means a firm's sales can vary in response to seasonal factors, in response to cycles common to business activity generally, and to trends of long duration.

The management of a brewery knows that peak sales occur during the summer months. But it also is aware of the cyclical nature of beer consumption, as beer drinkers shift to liquor when their incomes increase and shift back when their incomes decline. For long-term planning, the manager also must know something about the trend in beer consumption. Consumer preferences change with time and with the introduction of new products.

4. *Econometric Models:* These allow systematic evaluation of the impact of a number of variables on sales. Estimates of future sales can be based upon the relationship between past sales and a number of independent variables. These techniques are the most sophisticated of the methods, yet they offer no hope for the elimination of *all* uncertainty; management judgment is still needed. The econometric approach begins with the identification of those variables that affect the sales of the firm's product. Among the obvious variables are price, competing products, and complementary products. Variables such as the age of existing stocks of the goods, availability of credit, and consumer tastes are less obvious. Measurements of these variables are obtained for previous years and matched with sales of the product for the same years.

No perfect method exists for forecasting future sales. Hunches, market surveys, time-series analysis, and econometric models provide estimates that may or may not be reasonable. They can be no better than the information that goes into them. As technological breakthroughs in information processing occur, we can expect sales forecasts to become more accurate and consequently be better guides for planning. At present, however, forecasting requires a great deal of managerial judgment.

RESOURCES

The sales forecast presumes that a firm has a product to sell, so managers must first utilize resources to acquire or produce that product. And just as managers use forecasts to approximate income from sales, they must also forecast the future availability of major resources including personnel, raw materials, and capital. Techniques for forecasting resources are the same as those employed to forecast sales: hunches, market surveys, time-series analysis, and econometric models. The only difference is that the analyst is seeking to know the quantities and prices of goods that can be purchased rather than those to be sold.

The sales forecast, whether for 1 or for 10 years, predicts the firm's level of activity. At the same time, the prediction is conditioned by the availability of resources, by economic and social events beyond the province and control of management, and by the predetermined objectives. Given an adequate supply of resources, the manager's next task is *the allocation of resources necessary to implement a plan.* The principal technique management uses in this phase of the planning function is the *budget.*

Budgeting Resources

The third phase of the planning function is budgeting resources for each important part of the plan. A very close relationship exists between budgeting

---

FIGURE   4–2   The Budgeting Process

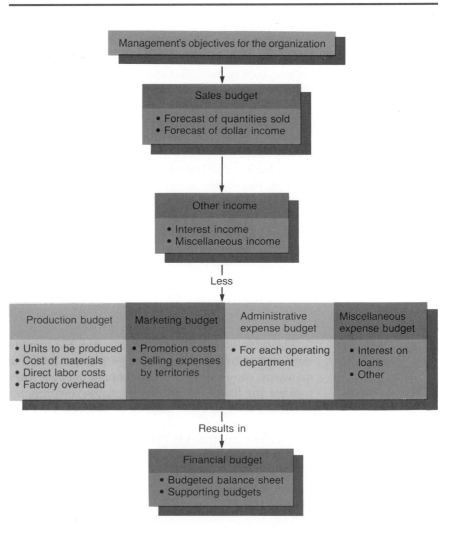

The budgeting process consists of actions, decisions, and documents that affect the entire organization.

Management's objectives for the organization

Sales budget
- Forecast of quantities sold
- Forecast of dollar income

Other income
- Interest income
- Miscellaneous income

Less

Production budget	Marketing budget	Administrative expense budget	Miscellaneous expense budget
• Units to be produced • Cost of materials • Direct labor costs • Factory overhead	• Promotion costs • Selling expenses by territories	• For each operating department	• Interest on loans • Other

Results in

Financial budget
- Budgeted balance sheet
- Supporting budgets

as a planning technique and budgeting as a control technique. But this section is concerned only with the preparation of budgets prior to operations, as a part of planning. However, after the organization has been engaged in activities for a time, actual results are compared with the budgeted (planned) results, and analysis may lead to corrective action. This, as we shall see later, is the essence of controlling.

The complexity of the budget phase is shown in Figure 4–2. The sales forecast plays a key role, as is evident in the placement of the sales budget; all other budgets are related to it either directly or indirectly. The production budget, for example, must specify the materials, labor, and other manufacturing expenses required to support the projected sales level. Similarly, the marketing expense budget details the costs associated with the level of sales activity projected for each product in each sales region. Administrative expenses also must be related to the predicted sales volume. The projected sales and expenses are combined in the financial budgets, which consist of pro forma financial statements, inventory budgets, and the capital additions budget.

Forecast data are based upon assumptions about the future. If these assumptions prove wrong, the budgets are inadequate. So the usefulness of financial budgets depends mainly on the degree to which they are flexible to changes in conditions. Two principle means exist to provide flexibility: variable budgeting and moving budgeting.

Variable budgeting provides for the possibility that actual output deviates from planned output. It recognizes that certain costs are related to output (variable costs), while others are unrelated to output (fixed costs). Thus, if actual output is 20 percent less than planned output, it does not follow that actual profit will be 20 percent less than that planned. Rather, the actual profit will vary, depending upon the complex relationship between costs and output. Table 4–3 shows a variable budget that allows for output variations. It demonstrates the behavior of costs and profits as output varies.

Variable budgeting requires adjustments in all supporting budgets for completeness. The production, marketing, and administrative budgets must likewise allow for the impact of output variation.

TABLE   4–3   A Hypothetical Variable Budget

Output (units)	1,000	1,200	1,400	1,600
Sales (at $5.00 per unit)	$5,000	$6,000	$7,000	$8,000
Variable costs (at $3.00 per unit)	3,000	3,600	4,200	4,800
Fixed costs	1,000	1,000	1,000	1,000
Total costs	4,000	4,600	5,200	5,800
Planned profit	$1,000	$1,400	$1,800	$2,200

A variable budget reflects the fact that planned profit and total costs do not vary proportionately with planned sales.

Moving budgeting is the preparation of a budget for a fixed period (say, one year) with periodic updating at fixed intervals such as one month. For one year) with periodic updating at fixed intervals such as one month. For example, a budget is prepared in December for the next 12 months, January through December. At the end of January, the budget is revised and projected for the next 12 months, February through January. In this manner, the most recent information is included in the budgeting process. Premises and assumptions constantly are being revised as management learns from experience.

Moving budgets have the advantage of systematic reexamination; they have the disadvantage of being costly to maintain. Budgets are important instruments for implementing the objectives of the firm, yet they must be viewed in perspective as one item on a long list of demands for a manager's time.

IMPLEMENTATION OF PLANS

All the planning in the world will not help an organization realize objectives if plans cannot be implemented. (Implementation of plans involves resources and actions as shown in Figure 4–1.) In some instances, the manager can take all the necessary steps to apply resources in planned actions to achieve objectives. In most instances, the manager must implement plans through *other people,* motivating them to accept and carry out the plan. *Authority, persuasion,* and *policy* are the manager's means of implementing plans.

Authority

Authority is a legitimate form of power, in the sense that it accompanies the position not the person. That is, the nature of authority in organizations is the right to make decisions and to expect compliance to the implications of these decisions. Thus, a manager can reasonably expect subordinates to carry out a plan so long as it does not require illegal, immoral, or unethical behavior. Authority is often sufficient to implement relatively simple plans that involve no significant change in the status quo. But a complex and comprehensive plan can seldom be implemented through authority alone. Persuasion is another important managerial tool.

Persuasion

Persuasion is a process of selling a plan to those who must implement it, communicating relevant information so individuals understand all implications. In this sense, it requires convincing others to base acceptance of the plan upon its merits rather than upon the authority of the managers.

Persuasion does present a hazard. What happens if the plan is not implemented after all persuasive efforts have been exhausted? If the plan is crucial and must be implemented, management must resort to authority. Consequently a manager who has failed once at the use of persuasion must limit use of the technique in the future. Individuals who were the objects of unsuccessful attempts at persuasion and who had thought they had the choice of accepting or rejecting a plan would be skeptical of future persuasive efforts.

Policy

When plans are intended to be rather permanent fixtures in an organization, management develops policies to implement them. Policies usually are written statements that reflect the basic objectives of the plan and provide guidelines for selecting actions to achieve the objectives. Once plans have been accepted by those who must carry them out, policies become important management tools for implementing them. Effective policies have these characteristics:

1. *Flexibility.* A policy must strike a reasonable balance between stability and flexibility. Conditions change, and policies must change accordingly. On the other hand, some degree of stability must prevail if order and a the exact degree of requisite flexibility; only the judgment of management can determine the appropriate balance.

2. *Comprehensiveness.* A policy must be comprehensive enough to cover any contingency if plans are to be followed. The degree depends upon the scope of action controlled by the policy itself. If the policy is directed toward very narrow ranges of activity—for example, hiring policies—it need not be as comprehensive as a policy concerned with public relations.

3. *Coordination.* A policy must provide for coordination of the various subunits whose actions are interrelated. Without coordinative direction provided by policies, each subunit is tempted to pursue its own objectives. The ultimate test of any subunit's activity should be its relationship to the policy statement.

4. *Ethical.* A policy must conform to the canons of ethical behavior that prevail in society. The increasingly complex and interdependent nature of contemporary society has resulted in a great number of problems involving ethical dimensions that are only vaguely understood. The manager is ultimately responsible for the resolution of issues which involve ethical principles.

5. *Clarity.* A policy must be written clearly and logically. It must specify the intended aim of the action it governs, define the appropriate methods and action, and delineate the limits of freedom of action permitted to those whose actions are to be guided by it.

The ultimate test of the effectiveness of a policy is whether or not the intended objective is attained. If the policy does not lead to the objective, it should be revised. Policies must be subjected to reexamination on a continual basis.

KEY PLANNING ISSUES

We have seen that planning, a fundamental activity of managers, can cover any time span from the short run to the long run. We also have surveyed some of the more important forecasting and budgeting techniques. These do not encompass the entire range of problems and issues associated with planning. Our discussion has, however, underscored the fact that planning is the essence of management; all other managerial functions stem from planning.

How does a manager begin the planning process? Many professionals agree that much of the task consists of asking the appropriate questions. Table 4–4 suggests the basic ones. Other, more specific questions might well be posed. Yet the fundamental questions are appropriate regardless of the type and size of the organization.

TABLE   4–4   Key Managerial Planning Issues

Planning Element	Key Managerial Decisions
Objectives	1. What objectives will be sought?
	2. What is the relative importance of each objective?
	3. What are the relationships among the objectives?
	4. When should each objective be achieved?
	5. How can each objective be measured?
	6. What person or organizational unit should be accountable for achieving the objective?
Actions	1. What are the important actions that bear on the successful achievement of objectives?
	2. What information exists regarding each action?
	3. What is the appropriate technique for forecasting the future state of each important action?
	4. What person or organizational unit should be accountable for the action?
Resources	1. What resources should be included in the plan?
	2. What are the interrelationships among the various resources?
	3. What budgeting technique should be used?
	4. Which person or organizational unit should be accountable for the preparation of the budget?
Implementation	1. Can the plan be implemented through authority or persuasion?
	2. What policy statements are necessary to implement the overall plan?
	3. To what extent are the policy statements comprehensive, flexible, coordinative, ethical, and clearly written?
	4. Who or what organizational units would be affected by the policy statements?

Effective managerial planning involves identifying the appropriate questions for each planning element.

SUMMARY OF KEY POINTS

- The planning function includes those managerial activities that result in predetermined courses of action. Planning necessarily focuses on the future, and management's responsibility is to prepare the organization for the future.

- Planning requires managers to make decisions about objectives, actions, resources, and implementation. These four factors are essential to effective planning.

- Through planning, management coordinates efforts, prepares for change, develops performance standards, and manages development.

- Objectives are statements of future conditions that, if realized, are deemed satisfactory or optimal by the planner. All sets of objectives have three characteristics: priority, timing, and measurement. How management responds to priority, timing, and measurement issues in setting objectives reflects individual values and economic considerations.

- To be useful in planning, objectives should be stated in measurable terms and should relate to significant organizational performance determinants. In particular, objectives should be set for profitability, marketing, productivity, physical and financial resources, innovation, manager behavior, employee attitudes, and social responsibility.

- Courses of action to achieve objectives must be specified. Terms such as strategies and tactics refer to planned courses of action. An important activity in specifying courses of action is that of forecasting future demand for the organization's output and future availability of resources.

- Resource requirements of a plan must be forecast and specified by budgets. Management can select the type of budget that best suits the planning needs of the organization.

- The fourth part of planning is implementation, a phase that takes account of the fact that plans usually are carried out by other people.

- The three approaches to implementation are authority, persuasion, and policy. Approaches can be used individually or in combination.

- Implementation by policy has the advantage of continuously reinforcing the plan for those who must implement it. Effective policies are those that produce the planned course of action.

DISCUSSION AND REVIEW QUESTIONS

1. What is the basis for saying that planning is the essential management function? Discuss.
2. A manager is overheard saying, "Plan? I never have time to plan. I live from day to day just trying to survive." Comment.

3. Is it accurate to say that since it involves value judgments, planning is the implementation of the manager's value system?

4. Three primary areas for setting objectives in universities are teaching, research, and public service. Discuss potential conflict that a professor might encounter between these objectives.

5. Describe potential conflicts between the objectives of a production department and the objectives of a marketing department in a business.

6. Is it true that the planning function is only as good as the underlying forecasts?

7. How would you measure the results of policies designed to meet a firm's social requirements?

8. Consult your school's catalog. Select any school policy statement and evaluate it based on the criteria for a good policy statement discussed in this chapter. What is your conclusion?

9. Explain why planning systems should be revised.

10. Discuss the issues that management would take into account when determining whether to use authority or persuasion to implement a plan.

ADDITIONAL REFERENCES

Ackoff, L. R. *A Concept of Corporate Planning.* New York: John Wiley & Sons, 1970.

Allen, L. A. "Managerial Planning: Back to the Basics." *Management Review,* April 1981, pp. 15–20.

Buzzell, R. D., and M. Chussil. "Managing for Tomorrow." *Sloan Management Review.* Summer 1985, pp. 3–13.

Christopher, W. F. "Is the Annual Planning Cycle Really Necessary?" *Management Review,* August 1981, pp. 38–42.

Felix, G. H., and J. L. Riggs. "Productivity Measurement by Objectives." *National Productivity Review,* Autumn 1983, pp. 386–93.

Kantrow, A. M. "Why Read Peter Drucker?" *Harvard Business Review,* January–February 1980, pp. 74–82.

Lachman, R. "Public and Private Sector Differences: CEOs' Perceptions of Their Role Environments." *Academy of Management Journal,* September 1985, pp. 671–79.

Liao, W. M. "Simulating Learning Curve Parameters for Managerial Planning and Control." *Accounting and Business Research,* Spring 1982, pp. 141–47.

Luksus, E. J. "Strategic Budgeting: How to Turn Financial Records into a Strategic Asset." *Management Review,* March 1981, pp. 57–61.

Makridakis, S.; S. Wheelwright; and V. McGee. *Forecasting Methods and Applications.* New York: John Wiley & Sons, 1983.

Pearce, J. S. "Company Mission as a Strategic Tool." *Sloan Management Review,* Spring 1982, pp. 15–24.

Pekar, P. P. "Setting Goals in the Non-Profit Environment." *Managerial Planning,* March–April, 1982, pp. 43–46.

Schick, A. G. "University Budgeting: Administrative Perspective, Budget Structure, and Budget Process." *Academy of Management Review,* October 1985, pp. 794–802.

Shim, J. K., and R. McGlade. "Current Trends in the Use of Corporate Planning Models." *Journal of Systems Management.* September 1984, pp. 24–31.

Skandera, S. "Planning in the Age of Robotics." *International Management Review* 24, no. 2 (1984), pp. 46–52.

Valenta, J. R. "Planning-Budgeting Balance." *Managerial Planning,* May–June 1982, pp. 16–18.

Wyman, J. "Technological Myopia: The Need to Think Strategically about Technology." *Sloan Management Review,* Summer 1985, pp. 59–64.

CASES

APPLICATION I

IBM'S APPROACH TO PLANNING

In the mid-1980s, International Business Machines Corp. made headline news by announcing that it would invest $350 million in its Lexington, Kentucky, plant. The Lexington plant manufactures typewriters, keyboards, and printers and employs 6,200 people. IBM is the largest private employer in the city, and city officials welcomed the firm's commitment to the plant's future.

John Opel, president and chief executive officer of IBM, said the $350 million investment would be used to purchase and install automated equipment that will increase the plant's productivity by 30 percent and make the Lexington plant "the most advanced typewriter manufacturing facility anywhere."

IBM's investment in automated manufacturing methods is but one aspect of the company's plan for the 1980s. According to published reports, IBM's plan is based on four primary objectives: (1) achieve low-cost production through investment in automated manufacturing facilities; (2) achieve low-cost distribution by selling small computers and office products through independent distributors, mail orders, catalogs, and company-owned retail stores; (3) position the organization and its products to attack the marketplace, segment by segment; and (4) pursue growth and profit opportunities in every area of the computer business from mainframe computers to home computers. These four objects reflect IBM's transformation to a high-volume, mass-market business from a one-at-a-time, custom-built, custom-marketed operation.

IBM's plan for the 1980s and its steps to implement the plan result from a sophisticated planning system that enables IBM to react to changes in technology and the marketplace. IBM *expects* change and attempts to stay abreast of it by requiring both line managers and staff specialists to "scan the environment." When they detect a change in technology, competitors' actions, government policy, or economic activity, they alert the management, and a plan of action is initiated. IBM's planning system has two separate, yet interrelated types of plans: program plans and period plans.

Program planning involves efforts to develop a new product, improve an existing product, or improve the performance of a unit within the organization. A program plan usually has a single objective to be accomplished in a brief time span—for example, the decision to upgrade the productivity of the Lexington typewriter plant. When program planning is directed toward product development and improvement, planners first determine customer requirements for information and information processing, then translate those needs into products. If the product is one that IBM has never attempted to produce, planners will rely upon the marketing staff for specifications of the customer's needs.

IBM relies on information obtained from its own econometric model to forecast demand for its products as well as to forecast the U.S. economy. Other sources of forecast data are (1) analysis of growth and replacement patterns for existing and new products, (2) extrapolations of historical information, (3) interviews and questionnaire data obtained from customers, and (4) analysis of backlog for existing products. These forecasts are combined for projections of future product demand, and projections are translated into product targets and plans of action.

Period planning involves the total organization and each unit within the organization. Each unit may have several program plans in various stages of implementation, but only one period plan is in effect at any one moment. The period plan has two components: (1) a long-range corporate plan and (2) short-range unit plans.

The long-range corporate plan covers a five-year period. It results from considerable interaction between line, field, and corporate staff under the direction of the Corporate Management Committee (CMC). The plan specifies corporate and operating-unit profit targets, which then are implemented by specifying corporate and unit strategies that reflect best estimates of economic conditions, competitors' moves, and product development. The corporate plan is the master plan, the basis for action taken throughout the corporation during the five-year period. Four basic objectives—low-cost production, low-cost distribution, product positioning, and wide-spectrum competitive effort—are included in IBM's corporate plan.

The short-range unit plans cover two years and are based upon the corporate plan. Each unit prepares a plan that focuses on budget and implementation issues. The unit's responsibility is to achieve its assigned target by taking appropriate action within the parameters of its operation. (The Office Products Division, for instance, must pursue action that reduces production costs.

Investing in automated equipment is appropriate action to take to achieve the corporate objective.) Each unit submits its plan to the CMC, where it is reviewed for compatibility with the corporate plan. When approved, the unit proceeds with implementation.

Questions for Analysis

1.   Evaluate IBM's approach to planning in terms of the four fundamental parts of plans.
2.   In what ways does IBM attempt to react to environmental changes in its planning system?
3.   Some critics say that IBM moved too slowly into the personal-computer market. If that criticism is valid, can the fault be IBM's planning system? Explain.

APPLICATION II

PROBLEM IDENTIFICATION IN A CONSUMER PRODUCTS FIRM

The top management of a large consumer products company was preparing for its annual planning session. Typically at these sessions, management identified the company's significant problems, set priorities, and provided guidelines and policies for the preparation of detailed plans.

The seven functional departments of the company were production, personnel, sales, staff development and training, finance, legal counsel, and engineering. Each of these functions consisted of subunits and operated on annual plans that developed from the planning session. Managers of each of the functional departments had been instructed, in advance of the sessions, to define the single significant problem facing the company from the perspective of that function. Top managers would devise a set of company problems from those enumerated by the functional managers. Problems were ranked in order of priority. The problems presented for discussion are summarized in the following paragraphs.

Excessive downtime of machine-paced operations was the major concern of the production manager; downtime had increased by 20 percent over the previous year. The problem was blamed on the need for more intensive preventive maintenance to stay within quality-control tolerances imposed by new, more restrictive state consumer protection laws.

The manager of the personnel department perceived things differently, seeing the major company problem as the excessive number of grievances that went to the departmental level for arbitration. The personnel manager indicated that the settlement of grievances at that level was usually inappropriate and reflected the inability of first-line managers to deal with problems.

The sales manager said that the major problem was the spiraling cost of product distribution. The company's distribution system was based upon regional warehouses linked to production facilities by a fleet of trucks. The rising cost of fuel was driving up the delivered cost of products and disrupting delivery schedules—all of which indicated the necessity for increasing the delivered price to customers who already were disgruntled by previous price increases.

The manager of staff development and training cited the inability of first-line supervisors to deal effectively with their subordinates as the firm's major problem. The problem grew out of the company's affirmative response to equal opportunity laws that required employment of persons formerly considered marginal. For the most part, these new employees required intensive skill training and close supervision. Moreover, they tended to be sensitive to criticism. The problem resulted in significant expense to train supervisors to manage with greater sensitivity.

To the finance department, the company's primary goal must be to reduce reliance on short-term debt to meet current obligations. The financial manager observed that the company's cash flow was seriously unbalanced, the major cause being the company's liberal credit terms and, subsequently, unpredictable collections from customers.

The chief legal officer said the company must either meet the recently legislated air quality standards or be brought under injunction. The company's principal source of power was coal. The air quality standards required the removal of air pollutants through the use of filter mechanisms, but at heavy expense to the company.

The engineering department's manager considered the company's most significant problem to be the high turnover of engineers who left for better-paying jobs with other companies. He stated that salaries must be upgraded or the company would face a continued drain of engineering talent.

Questions for Analysis

1. In what order of priority would you place these problems?
2. Is there any basis for interrelating the problems, or is each a separate, unrelated problem? Explain.
3. Once problems are identified, what information is needed for subsequent planning decisions?

STRATEGIC PLANNING

LEARNING OBJECTIVES

After completing Chapter 5, you should be able to:

◼ **Define**
strategic planning in terms of the direction it gives to the entire organization.

◼ **Describe**
how the mission and strategies of an organization should mesh.

◼ **Discuss**
why strategic planning has grown in importance in recent years.

◼ **Compare**
organizational objectives and operational objectives.

◼ **Identify**
appropriate strategies for each business type identified in a portfolio matrix.

■ MANAGEMENT IN ACTION

"Swatches" Are Strategic Hope for the Swiss Watch Industry*

It was a lack of appreciation of electronics that almost doomed the Swiss watch industry. Twenty years ago, the Swiss were engaged in a $2.5 million research program to develop an all-electronic quartz watch. But having designed the technology, they worried about putting it into large-scale production. As has happened with so many other technologies, the Japanese recognized its promise and ran with it. With the extreme accuracy and high reliability at a reasonable cost that quartz offers, the Japanese soon cut deeply into Switzerland's market share.

Rather than recognize the inevitable and shift into quartz, the stubborn Swiss dug in, insisting on the virtues of mechanical movements. By the early 1980s, Switzerland's worldwide market share for watches had nosedived to 10 percent from more than 40 percent in the early 1970s. The two largest watchmakers in the country collapsed, and Swiss banks saw no choice but to mount a rescue operation. The banks forced a merger of the two companies in 1983 and currently have loans outstanding of $250 million.

In 1984, signs of a turnaround began to emerge. Total industry exports rose by 13 percent, and the new, merged company reported sales of $650 million, the breakeven point. Switzerland's share of the worldwide watch market meanwhile climbed gradually upward, reaching about 12 percent compared to 10 percent in 1983.

Largely to thank for this revival is the Swatch—a product opposite to the hand-crafted, genteel image the Swiss have traditionally sought for their watches. Since its introduction in late 1982, Swatch has achieved household-word status in many countries. Smart, sassy, novel, and available in seemingly limitless colors, designs, and even scent combinations, Swatch has breathed new life into the Swiss watch industry.

"It is a first step to new success," says a Swiss bank official who sees it as evidence that the local industry can come up with new strategies, radically new products, and address new markets. There is a renewed push into electronics; diversification is expected into instruments, lasers, robots, batteries, and industrial jewels.

Defining and redefining the purpose and direction of a business is vital. This chapter will describe how managers develop strategic plans.

---

*Source: "Can New Management Team Keep Swiss Watches Ticking?" *International Management,* June 1985, pp. 57–58; Russell Miller, "A Switch in Time: The Success of Swatches," *Management Review,* October 1985, pp. 41–45.

The preceding chapter examined the four phases of planning and introduced important planning terminology. However, before a production manager, marketing manager, or personnel manager can develop plans for their individual departments, a larger plan—a blueprint—for the entire organization must be developed. Otherwise, on what would the individual departments' plans be based?

In other words, for the various planning activities, there is a larger context that we would like to consider in this chapter. A large business organization usually has several business divisions and several product lines within each division (such as General Electric or Philip Morris). Before any planning can be done by individual divisions or departments, a plan must be developed for the entire organization. Then, objectives and strategies established at the top level provide the planning context for each of the divisions and departments. Finally, divisional and departmental managers develop their plans within the constraints developed at the higher levels.[1]

THE GROWTH OF STRATEGIC PLANNING

Many of today's most successful business organizations continue to survive because many years ago they offered the right product at the right time; the same can be said for nonprofit and government organizations. Many critical decisions of the past were made without the benefit of strategic thinking or planning. Whether these decisions were based on wisdom or luck is not important. They resulted in momentum that has carried these organizations to where they are today. However, present-day managers increasingly recognize that wisdom and intuition alone are not sufficient to guide the destinies of large organizations in today's ever-changing environment. These managers are turning to strategic planning.[2]

In earlier, less dynamic periods in our society, the planning systems utilized by most organizations extrapolated current-year sales and environmental trends for 5 and 10 years. Based on these, they made plant, product, and investment decisions. In most instances, the decisions were fairly accurate because the factors influencing sales were more predictable and the environment was more stable.

In the years after World War II, many of the factors on which earlier planners counted could no longer be taken for granted. Uncertainty, instability, and changing environments became the rule rather than the exception.

---

[1] John H. Grant and William R. King, *The Logic of Strategic Planning* (Boston: Little, Brown, 1982), chap. 1.

[2] L. Rosenberg and C. D. Schewe, "Strategic Planning: Fulfilling the Promise," *Business Horizons,* July–August 1985, pp. 54–63.

FIGURE   5–1   The Strategic Planning Process

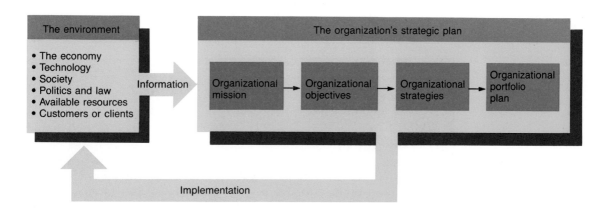

Strategic planning emphasizes the impact of the organization's environment.

Managers faced increased inflation and increased foreign competition, techno-logical obsolescence, and changing market and population characteristics.

Because changes are occurring so rapidly, there is increased pressure on top management to respond. In order to respond more accurately, on a more timely schedule, and with a direction or course of action in mind, managers are increasingly turning to the use of strategic planning. *Strategic planning is a process that involves the review of market conditions; customer needs; competitive strengths and weaknesses; sociopolitical, legal, and economic con-ditions; technological developments; and the availability of resources that lead to the specific opportunities or threats facing the organization.* In practice, *the development of strategic plans involves taking information from the environ-ment and deciding upon an organizational mission and upon objectives, strate-gies, and a portfolio plan.* The strategic planning process is depicted in Figure 5–1.

As indicated, to develop a unity of purpose across the organization, the strategic planning process must be tied to objectives and goals at all levels of management. At Matsushita, for example, department managers provide three plans every six months: (1) a five-year plan that incorporates technologi-cal and environmental changes; (2) a two-year plan that translates strategies into new products; (3) a six-month operating plan, developed by department managers, that addresses monthly projections for production, sales, profits, inventories, quality control, and personnel requirements.

The basic questions that must be answered when an organization decides to examine and restate its mission are "What is our business?" and "What should it be?" While the questions may appear simple, they are in fact such difficult and critical ones that the major responsibility for answering them must be with top management.[3] The Management Focus "What Is Our Mission?" tells how a few well-known firms present their mission to employees and other constituents.

MANAGEMENT FOCUS
What Is Our Mission?

Polaroid

Polaroid manufactures and sells photographic products utilizing company inventions in the field of one-step instant photography and light polarizing products. The company considers itself to be engaged in one line of business.

General Motors

General Motors is a highly integrated business engaged primarily in the manufacture, assembly, and sale of automobiles, trucks, and related parts and accessories classified as automotive products. Substantially all of GM's products are marketed through retail dealers, distributors, and jobbers in the United States and Canada and through distributors and dealers overseas. To assist in the merchandising of GM products, General Motors Acceptance Corporation and its subsidiaries offer financial services and certain types of automobile insurance to dealers and customers.

PepsiCo, Inc.

PepsiCo operates in five business segments: beverages, food products, food service, transportation, and sporting goods. Each division develops its own plans and goals consonant with its operating environment and PepsiCo's corporate objectives.

The corporation's steady growth record is based upon high perfor-

---

[3] Lewis W. Walker, "The CEO and Corporate Strategy in the Eighties: Back to Basics," *Interfaces,* January–February 1984, pp. 3–9; Peter Drucker, *Management: Tasks, Responsibilities, Practices* (New York: Harper & Row, 1974), chap. 7.

mance standards, a flexible approach to marketing challenges, and the integrity of its products, people, and business practices. Also, the premium placed on results has helped to make PepsiCo products and services leaders in the fields in which they compete. Known around the world, PepsiCo is synonymous with leisure-time activity. Its marketing and service divisions, all in growth fields, are synchronized to the popular basics of everyday life.

THE STRATEGIC PLANNING PROCESS

The output of the strategic planning process is the development of a strategic plan. Figure 5–1 indicates that there are four components to such plans: mission, objectives, strategies, and portfolio plan. Let us examine each one.

Organizational Mission

The organization's environment supplies the resources that sustain the organization, whether it is a business organization, a college or university, or a governmental agency. In exchange for these resources, the organization must supply the environment with goods and services at an acceptable price and quality. In other words, every organization exists to accomplish something in the larger environment, and that purpose or mission usually is clear at the start. As time passes, however, the organization expands, the environment changes, and managerial personnel change. And one or more things are likely to occur. First, the original purpose may become irrelevant as the organization expands into new products, new markets, and even new industries. Second, the original mission may remain relevant, but some managers begin to lose interest in it. Finally, changes in the environment may make the original mission inappropriate. The result of any or all of these three conditions is a "drifting" organization, without a clear mission or purpose to guide critical decisions. When this occurs, management must renew the search for purpose or restate the original purpose.

The mission statement should be a long-run vision of what the organization is trying to become—the unique aim that differentiates it from similar organizations. The need is not for a stated purpose (such as "to fulfill all the cosmetic needs of women") that would enable stockholders and managers to feel good or to promote public relations. Rather, the need is for a stated *mission* that provides direction and significance to all members of the organization, regardless of their level.

Developing a statement: key elements.   In developing a statement of mission, management must take into account three key elements: the organization's history, its distinctive competencies, and its environment.[4]

1. *History.* Every organization, large or small, profit or nonprofit, has a history of objectives, accomplishments, mistakes, and policies. In formulating a mission, the critical characteristics and events of the past must be considered. It would not make sense for McDonald's to become a chain of gourmet restaurants or for Yale University to become a community college, even if such moves were opportunities for growth in the future.

2. *Distinctive competencies.* While there are many things an organization may be able to do, it should seek to do that which it can do best. Distinctive competencies arc thc things that an organization does well—so well, in fact, that they are an advantage over similar organizations. Proctor & Gamble probably could enter the synthetic fuel business, but such a decision certainly would not take advantage of its major distinctive competence: knowledge of the market for low-priced, repetitively purchased consumer products. No matter how appealing an opportunity may be, the organization must have the competencies to capitalize on it. An opportunity without the competence to capture it is not really an opportunity for the organization.[5]

3. *Environment.* The organization's environment dictates the opportunities, constraints, and threats that must be identified before a mission statement is developed.[6] For example, technological developments in the communications field (such as long-range picture transmission, closed-circuit television, and the television phone) may have a negative impact on business travel and certainly should be considered in the mission statement of a large motel chain.[7]

Characteristics of a mission statement.   Needless to say, it is extremely difficult to write a useful and effective mission statement. It is not unlikely for an organization to spend a year or two developing a useful mission.

---

[4] Philip Kotler, *Marketing Management: Analysis, Planning, and Control,* 5th ed. (Englewood Cliffs, N.J.: Prentice-Hall, 1985), chap. 2.

[5] For a study of the relationship between corporate distinctive competencies and firm performance in 185 industrial firms, see M. A. Hitt and R. D. Ireland, "Corporate Distinctive Competence, Strategy and Performance," *Strategic Management Journal,* July–September 1985, pp. 273–93.

[6] See C. Smart and I. Vertinsky, "Strategy and the Environment: A Study of Corporate Responses to Crises," *Strategic Management Journal,* April–June 1984, pp. 199–214. This study of the largest U.S. and Canadian companies examines the relationship between a firm's external environment and its repertoire of strategic responses to cope with crises. For a different view of the environment, see L. Smirich and C. Stubbart, "Strategic Management in an Enacted World," *Academy of Management Review,* October 1985, pp. 724–36.

[7] For a related discussion, see Carl P. Zeithaml and Louis W. Fry, "Contextual and Strategic Differences among Mature Businesses in Four Dynamic Performance Situations," *Academy of Management Journal,* December 1984, pp. 841–60.

When completed, an effective mission statement will *focus on markets rather than products; it will also be achievable, motivating,* and *specific.* [8]

1. *Market Rather than Product Focus:* The customers or clients of an organization are critical in determining its mission. Traditionally, many organizations defined their business in terms of what they made ("our business is glass") and, in many cases, named the organization after the product or products (for example, National Cash Register, Harbor View Savings and Loan Association). Often these organizations have found that when products and technologies become obsolete, their mission is no longer relevant and the name of the organization may no longer describe what it does. Thus, a more enduring way of defining the mission is needed. In recent years, a key feature of mission statements has been an *external* rather than *internal* focus. In other words, the mission statement should focus on the broad class of needs that the organization is seeking to satisfy (external focus), not on the physical product or service that the organization is offering at present (internal focus). This has been clearly stated by Peter Drucker:

> A business is not defined by the company's name, statutes, or articles of incorporation. It is defined by the want the customer satisfies when he buys a product or service. To satisfy the customer is the mission and purpose of every business. The question "What is our business?" can, therefore, be answered only by looking at the business from the outside, from the point of view of customer and market. [9]

While Drucker was referring to business organizations, the same necessity exists for both nonprofit and governmental organizations. [10] That necessity is to state the mission in terms of serving a particular group of clients or customers and/or meeting a particular class of need.

2. *Achievable:* While the mission statement should "stretch" the organization toward more effective performance, it should at the same time be realistic and achievable. In other words, it should open a vision of new opportunities but should not lead the organization into unrealistic ventures far beyond its competencies. Examples would be a pen manufacturer stating it is in the communications business or an antique car restorer viewing its mission in terms of transportation.

3. *Motivational:* One of the side (but very important) benefits of a well-defined mission is the guidance it provides employees and managers working either in geographically dispersed units or on independent tasks. A well-defined mission provides a shared sense of purpose *outside* of the various activities taking place within the organization. [11] Therefore, end results (such

---

[8] Drucker, *Management,* pp. 77–89; Kotler, *Marketing Management,* chap. 2.

[9] Drucker, *Management,* p. 79.

[10] See Paul C. Nutt, "A Strategic Planning Network for Nonprofit Organizations," *Strategic Management Journal,* January–March 1984, pp. 57–76; Peter Smith Ring and James L. Perry, "Strategic Management in Public and Private Organizations: Implications of Distinctive Contexts and Constraints." *Academy of Management Review,* April 1985, pp. 276–86.

FIGURE   5–2   Some Actual Mission Statements

Organization	Mission
1. Office equipment manufacturer	We are in the business of problem solving. Our business is to help solve administrative, scientific, and human problems.
2. Credit union	To produce a selected range of quality services to organizations and individuals to fulfill their continuing financial needs.
3. Large conglomerate	Translating new technologies into commercially salable products.
4. Consumer-products paper company	The development and marketing of inedible products for food stores.
5. State department of health	Administering all provisions of law relating to public health laws and regulations of the state board of health, supervising and assisting county and regional boards and departments of health, and doing all other things reasonably necessary to protect and improve the health of the people.
6. Appliance manufacturer	A willingness to invest in any area of suitable profit and growth potential in which the organization has or can acquire the capabilities.

Mission statements reflect the different roles that organizations play in society.

as sales, patients cared for, reduction in violent crimes) can be viewed as the result of careful pursuit and accomplishment of the mission and not as the mission itself.

4. *Specific:* As we mentioned earlier, public relations should not be the primary purpose of a statement of mission, which must be specific and provide direction and guidelines to management when it chooses between alternative courses of action. In other words, "to produce the highest-quality products at the lowest possible cost" sounds very good, but it does not provide direction for management.

Figure 5–2 presents actual mission statements of various types of organizations. While some have been abbreviated, they illustrate clearly the purpose of each as defined by management. Review each one with respect to the four criteria just discussed.

The questions related to the mission statement need to be asked and answered at the inception of an organization and whenever it is experiencing serious problems. However, a successful organization should also ask them from time to time.[12] The reason for this should be clear: Because of the ever-changing environment, even the most successful definition of purpose will sooner or later become obsolete. Thus, the process of periodically address-

---

[11] W. Graham Astley, "Toward an Appreciation of Collective Strategy," *Academy of Management Review,* July 1984, pp. 526–35.

[12] Drucker, *Management,* p. 87.

ing the issue will force management to anticipate the impact of environmental changes on the organization's mission, objectives, markets, and products.

The Management Focus on Family Dollar Stores demonstrates how a clear statement of mission serves as the basis for supporting strategies. The company remained true to its mission even as other discounters were moving away from theirs.

MANAGEMENT FOCUS
Family Dollar Stores' Mission

Family Dollar Stores, Inc. has been more than "just average" in sales and earnings during a period of distress for other discount merchandisers. Although the company's success is due to many factors, its management believes that much can be attributed to the firm's mission and supportive strategies. Family Dollar sells only low-priced merchandise (apparel, housewares, and automotive goods) through outlets located in blue-collar neighborhoods. Other discount merchandisers have moved away from their discount images by offering items such as Izod shirts and home computers. Family Dollar Stores, however, remains true to its mission: 95 percent of the merchandise carried in its stores sells for less than $15. Other policies that complement the mission include self-service operations, cash only (no credit), centralized purchasing to acquire quantity discounts, and locating stores in small towns (to avoid big-city advertising costs). With 579 stores located throughout the Southeast, Family Dollar Stores' management is looking forward to prosperous times.

Source: Adapted from "Family Dollar Stores: As Rivals Fall, the Discounter Keeps Growing," *Business Week,* January 24, 1983, pp. 89–90.

Finally, the mission statement of organizations whose strategic planning process is very sophisticated also will include major policies they plan to adhere to in the pursuit of their mission. Such policies establish the ground rules for the organization in its relationships with government, customers or clients, suppliers, distributors, and creditors. An example of such a document is shown in Figure 5–3.

Organizational Objectives

In the previous chapter, we saw that a critical phase of planning is the determination of future outcomes that, if achieved, enable the organization

---

FIGURE   5–3   Example of a Mission Statement and Supporting Organizational Policies

---

It is the basic purpose of this organization, in all of its decisions and actions, to attain and maintain the following:
1. A continuous, high level of profits, which places it in the top bracket of industry in its rate of return on invested capital.
2. Steady growth in profits and sales volume, and investment at rates exceeding those of the national economy as a whole.
3. Equitable distribution of the fruits of continuously increasing productivity of management, capital, and labor among stockholders, employees, and the public.
4. Design, production, and marketing, on a worldwide basis, of products and services that are useful and beneficial to its customers, to society, and to mankind.
5. Continuous responsiveness to the needs of its customers and of the public, creating a current product line that is "first in performance" and a steady flow of product improvements, new products, and new services that increase customer satisfaction.
6. A vital, dynamic product line, by continuous addition of new products and businesses and prompt termination of old products and businesses when their economic worth, as measured by their profit performance, becomes substandard.
7. The highest ethical standards in the conduct of all its affairs.
8. An environment in which all employees are enabled, encouraged, and stimulated to perform continuously at their highest potential of output and creativity and to attain the highest possible level of job satisfaction in the spirit of the Westinghouse Creed.

Mission and policy statements reflect an organization's highest standards of conduct.

Source: D. C. Rogers, *Business Policy and Planning* (Englewood Cliffs, N.J.: Prentice-Hall, 1977), p. 84.

to satisfy the expectations of its relevant environment. These desired future outcomes are objectives. Organizational objectives are the end points of an organization's mission and are what it seeks through the ongoing, long-run operations of the organization. The organizational mission is defined into a finer set of specific and achievable organizational objectives.

As with the statement of mission, organizational objectives are more than good intentions. In fact, if formulated properly, they will accomplish the following:

1. They will be capable of being converted into specific actions.
2. They will provide direction. That is, they serve as a starting point for more specific and detailed objectives at lower levels in the organization. Each manager will then know how his or her objectives relate to those at higher levels.
3. They will establish long-run priorities for the organization.
4. They will facilitate management control, because they will serve as standards against which overall organizational performance can be evaluated.

Organizational objectives are necessary in any and all areas that may influence the performance and long-run survival of the organization. These were identified in the previous chapter as market standing, innovations, pro-

FIGURE   5–4   Sample Organizational Objectives

Manufacturing firm

Area of Performance	Possible Objective
1. Market standing	To make our brands number one in their field in terms of market share.
2. Innovations	To be a leader in introducing new products by spending no less than 7 percent of sales for research and development.
3. Productivity	To manufacture all products efficiently as measured by the productivity of the work force.
4. Physical and financial resources	To protect and maintain all resources—equipment, buildings, inventory, and funds.
5. Profitability	To achieve an annual rate of return on investment of at least 15 percent.
6. Manager performance and responsibility	To identify critical areas of management depth and succession.
7. Worker performance and attitude	Maintain levels of employee satisfaction consistent with our own and similar industries.
8. Social responsibility	To respond appropriately whenever possible to societal expectations and environmental needs.

Objectives at the organizational level tend to be broadly stated.

ductivity, physical and financial resources, profitability, manager performance and responsibility, worker performance and attitude, and social responsibility.

The above objectives are by no means exhaustive. An organization may very well have additional ones. The important point is that management must translate the organizational mission into specific objectives that will support the realization of the mission. The objectives may flow directly from the mission or be considered subordinate necessities for carrying out the mission of the organization. Figure 5–4 presents some examples of organizational objectives. Note that they are broad statements that serve as guides and that they are of a continuing nature. They specify the end points of an organization's mission and the results that it seeks in the long run, both externally and internally. Most importantly, however, the objectives in Figure 5–4 are all capable of being converted into specific targets and actions for *operational plans* at lower levels in the organization.

Organizational Strategies

When an organization has formulated its mission and developed its objectives, it knows where it wants to go. The next management task is to develop

---

FIGURE   5–5   Product-Market Matrix

A firm's basic strategy involves decisions regarding customers and markets.

Products / Markets	Present Products	New Products
Present Customers	Market penetration	Product development
New Customers	Market development	Diversification

---

a "grand design" to get there.[13] This grand design constitutes the organizational strategies. The role of strategy in strategic planning is to identify the general approaches that the organization will utilize to achieve its organizational objectives. It involves the choice of major directions the organization will take in pursuing its objectives.[14]

Achieving organizational objectives comes about in two ways. They are accomplished by better managing what the organization is presently doing and/or finding new things to do. In choosing either or both of these paths, it then must decide whether to concentrate on present customers, to seek new ones, or both. Figure 5–5 presents the available strategic choices. Known as a product-market matrix, it shows the strategic alternatives available to an organization for achieving its objectives. It indicates that an organization can grow in a variety of ways by concentrating on present or new products and on present or new customers.

Market penetration strategies.   These organizational strategies focus on improving the position of the organization's present products with its present customers. For example:

1. A brewer concentrates on getting its present customers to purchase more of its product.
2. A charity seeks ways to increase contributions from present contributors.
3. A bank concentrates on getting present depositors to use additional services.

---

[13] See Ellen Earle Chaffee, "Three Models of Strategy," *Academy of Management Review,* January 1985, pp. 89–98.

[14] Ari Ginsberg, "Operationalizing Organizational Strategy: Toward an Integrated Framework," *Academy of Management Review,* July 1984, pp. 548–57.

Such a strategy may involve devising a marketing plan to encourage present customers to purchase more of the product or a production plan to produce the present product more efficiently. In other words, it concentrates on improving the efficiency of various functional areas in the organization.

Market development strategies.   Following this strategy, an organization would seek to find new customers for its present products. For example:

1. A manufacturer of industrial products may decide to develop products for entrance into the consumer market.
2. A governmental social service agency may seek individuals and families who have never utilized the agencies' services.
3. A manufacturer of children's hair care products decides to enter the adult market because of the declining birthrate.

Product development strategies.   In choosing either of the remaining two strategies, the organization in effect seeks new things to do. With this particular strategy, the new products developed would be directed to present customers. For example:

1. A cigarette manufacturer may decide to offer a low-tar cigarette.
2. A social service agency may offer additional services to present client families.
3. A college or university may develop graduate programs for minority students.

Diversification.   An organization diversifies when it seeks new products for customers it is not serving at present.[15] Some examples include:

1. A discount store puchases a savings and loan association.
2. A cigarette manufacturer diversifies into real estate development.
3. A college or university establishes a corporation to find commercial uses for the results of faculty research efforts.

On what basis does an organization choose one (or all) strategies? The answer lies in the organization's mission and its distinctive competencies. This underscores the critical role the mission statement plays in the direction(s) the organization takes. Management will select those strategies that capitalize on the organization's distinctive competencies and are consistent with its mission.[16]

---

[15] See Jeffrey L. Kerr, "Diversification Strategies and Managerial Rewards: An Empirical Study," *Academy of Management Journal,* March 1985, pp. 155–79, for a study of the relationship between diversification and the design of managerial reward systems in 20 large industrial firms.

[16] N. Venkatramen and J. C. Camillus, "Exploring the Concept of 'Fit' in Strategic Management," *Academy of Management Review,* July 1984, pp. 513–25; H. Mintzberg and J. A. Waters, "Of Strategies, Deliberate and Emergent," *Strategic Management Journal,* July–September 1985, pp. 257–72.

Organizational Portfolio Plan

The final phase of the strategic planning process is the formulation of the organizational portfolio plan. In reality, most organizations at a particular time are a portfolio of businesses. For example, an appliance manufacturer may have several product lines (such as televisions, washers and dryers, refrigerators, stereos) as well as two divisions, (consumer appliances and industrial appliances). A college or university will have numerous schools (e.g., education, business, law, architecture) and several programs within each school. The YMCA has hotels, camps, spas, and schools. Some widely diversified organizations such as Philip Morris are in numerous unrelated businesses, such as cigarettes, land development, industrial paper products, and breweries.

Managing such groups of businesses is made a little easier if resources and cash are plentiful and each group is experiencing growth and profits. Unfortunately, providing larger and larger budgets each year to all businesses is no longer feasible. Many are not experiencing growth, and profits and/or resources (financial and nonfinancial) are becoming more and more scarce. In such a situation, choices must be made; and some method is necessary to help management make the choices. Management must decide which businesses to build, maintain, or eliminate or which new businesses to add. One of the best known and widely used methods to accomplish this is the *business portfolio matrix* developed by the Boston Consulting Group.[17]

The business portfolio matrix.   Obviously, the first step in this approach is to identify the various divisions, product lines, and so forth, that can be considered a business. When identified, these are referred to as *strategic business units* (SBUs) and have the following characteristics:

They have a distinct mission.
They have their own competitors.
They are a single business or collection of related businesses.
They can be planned for independently from the other businesses of the total organization.

Thus, depending on the type of organization, an SBU could be a single product, product line, division, a department of business administration, or a state mental health agency. Once the managers have identified and classified all of the SBUs, some means is then necessary to determine how resources should be allocated among the various SBUs. This is the important contribution of the Boston Consulting Group's approach.

---

[17] There are other portfolio models; each has its supporters and detractors. The one presented here, while one of the most popular, is also not without critics. The important point is the concept of viewing an organization as a "portfolio" of businesses or activities, each competing for resources. The interested reader should consult Day, *Analysis,* chaps. 5–7; Richard G. Hammermesh and Roderick E. White, "Manage beyond Portfolio Analysis," *Harvard Business Review,* January–February 1984, pp. 103–9; J. A. Seeger, "Revising the Images of BCG's Growth/ Share matrix," *Strategic Management Journal,* January–March 1984, pp. 93–97.

FIGURE   5–6   Business Portfolio Matrix

Each business can be classified according to projected market growth rate and estimated market share.

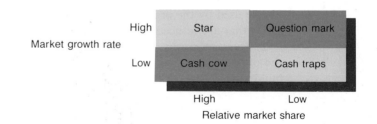

Using this approach, the organization would classify all of its SBUs in the business portfolio matrix. (An example is shown in Figure 5–6.) Its basic purpose is to assist management in deciding how much resource support should be budgeted to each SBU.

The business portfolio matrix illustrates two business indicators of great strategic importance. The vertical indicator, *market growth rate,* refers to the annual rate of growth of the market in which the product, division, or department is located. For example, the number of individuals of college age is declining, and the impact on enrollments has been felt. However, enrollments in some fields of study have been increasing. Thus, certain departments in a college would have different market growth rates.

The horizontal indicator, *relative market share,* illustrates an SBU's market share compared to that of the most successful competition. This indicator ranges from high to low share of the market. As illustrated, four classifications of SBUs can be identified by dividing the business portfolio matrix in the ways indicated:

1. *Stars.* An SBU that has a high share of a high-growth market is considered a star. Examples might include an electronics firm with a high share of the video recorder market or a university with an outstanding, nationally recognized master's degree program in business administration (enrollments in most business schools are growing, in contrast to declining enrollments across most university departments). Obviously, stars need a great deal of financial resources because of their rapid growth. When growth slows down, they become cash cows and become important generators of cash for the organization.[18]

2. *Cash cows.* An SBU that has a high share of a low-growth market is labeled a cash cow. A bank that has a large share of passbook savings depositors in a community that is not growing or a state university with the largest number of elementary education majors in the state would be examples of

---

[18] See David A. Aaker and George S. Day, "The Perils of High Growth Markets," *Strategic Management Journal,* October–December 1985, pp. 24–32.

such SBUs. They produce a great amount of cash for the organization but, since the market is not growing, do not require a great amount of financial resources for growth and expansion. As a result, the cash they generate can be used by the organization to satisfy current debt and to support other SBUs that are in need of cash.

3. *Question marks.* When an SBU has a low share of a high-growth market, the organization must decide whether to spend more financial resources to build it into a star, or to phase it down or eliminate it all together. Elimination was the decision made by General Electric with its computer business and line of vacuum cleaners. Many times, such SBUs require high amounts of resources just to maintain their share, let along increase it.

4. *Cash traps.* When an SBU has a low share of a low-growth markct, it may generate enough cash to maintain itself or may drain money from other SBUs. The only certainty is that cash traps are not great sources of cash. A men's cosmetics firm that still sells a traditional oily liquid hair tonic or the Slavic language department in a college or university might be examples of cash traps.

Strategic choices   Thus, depending on whether the SBUs are products, product lines, entire divisions, or departments, an organization may have one star, three cash cows, two question marks, and two cash traps. After classifying each SBU according to the business portfolio matrix, management must then decide which of four alternative strategies should be pursued for each.[19]

1. *Build:* If an organization has an SBU that it believes has the potential to be a star (probably a question mark at present), this would be an appropriate objective. Thus, the organization may even decide to give up short-term profits in order to provide the necessary financial resources to achieve this objective.

2. *Hold:* If an SBU is a very successful cash cow, a key objective would certainly be to hold or preserve the market share so that the organization can take advantage of the very positive cash flow. The opportunity to use cash cow businesses to generate resources for diversification was recognized by Pennzoil. This firm's strategy of diversification is described in the Management Focus.

3. *Harvest:* This objective is appropriate for all SBUs except those classified as stars. The basic objective is to increase the short-term cash return without too much concern for the long-run impact. It is especially worthwhile when more cash is needed for a cash cow whose long-run prospects are not good because of a low market growth rate.

4. *Divest:* Getting rid of SBUs with low shares of low growth markets is often appropriate. Question marks and cash traps are particularly suited for this objective.

---

[19] Stephen C. Burnett, "The Ecology of Building, Harvesting, and Holding Market Share," Report #6, *Research in Marketing* (1983), pp. 1–63.

The Management Focus on Pennzoil describes their strategy of diversification.

MANAGEMENT FOCUS
Pennzoil's Cash Cow

Pennzoil sold over 130 million gallons of lubricating oil last year, 550 percent more than in 1962. But despite this impressive sales increase, J. Hugh Liedtke, CEO of Pennzoil, believes that the lubricating oil business is a source of cash to be used to develop other lines of business. The cash that the oil business generated enabled Liedtke to develop a strong portfolio of businesses in potentially high-growth industries.

Favoring natural-resource industries, Liedtke has directed Pennzoil's investments in oil and gas exploration and in metals and minerals mining. His strategy's success is based upon his assumption that, in the long run, metals and minerals will be in short supply and Pennzoil will be in a position to profit from that shortage.

Meanwhile, Pennzoil's lubricating oil business continues to prosper and to increase its market share. It now has a 20 percent market share, right behind the leader Quaker State. The increase in Pennzoil's share is due largely to innovative promotion and distribution approaches. In a typical year, Pennzoil spends $25 million on ads featuring race car driver Jim Hill and Johnny Rutherford. Also important to its growth has been the development of sales outlets in K mart, Target stores, and other large, mass merchants. Over half of all car motor oil is sold through these outlets. Despite the relatively slow growth of the industry, Pennzoil continues to prosper by being aggressively competitive. The success of its Pennzoil business, in turn, provides the cash for its diversification into long-term growth industries.

Source: Adapted from "Pennzoil: Squeezing Out Lube-Oil Profits to Keep Gambling on Natural Resources," *Business Week,* February 21, 1983, pp. 118–19.

SBUs will change their positions in the business portfolio matrix. As time goes by, question marks may become stars, stars may become cash cows, and cash cows may become cash traps. In fact, one SBU can move through each category as the market growth rate declines; how quickly these changes occur is influenced by the technology and competitiveness of the industry. This underscores the importance and usefulness of viewing an organization in terms of SBUs, and the necessity of constantly seeking new ventures as well as managing existing ones.[20]

STRATEGIC PLANNING: USING THE PROCESS

We have completed our discussion of the elements and process of strategic planning. The Management FOCUS on 3M illustrates how an already successful organization utilized this process to become even more effective.

MANAGEMENT FOCUS
3M Company's Strategic Planning System

The experience of 3M Company illustrates how an already effective organization uses strategic planning. In 1981, when 3M management began to revamp their strategic planning system, the company had achieved sales of $6.5 billion from over 45,000 products. Most of these products were rooted in the original technologies for coated abrasives or pressure-sensitive tape. Since then, their planning efforts have taken the company into new products and markets as diverse as recording equipment, medical products, and pharmaceuticals.

The strategic planning system developed during 1982 and 1983 was consistent with the history of the firm in keeping responsibility for strategic decisions with the operating-unit managers. The key principles of the system are:

1. *Characterizing the industry.* Each operating unit must characterize its industry. Managers must identify the factors, such as size and growth of the industry, that will influence the strategies they choose. Key external influences such as new technology, regulatory changes, key competitors, and competitor market shares and strategies must be analyzed.

2. *Determination of key success factors.* Each operating unit must understand the key factors that will influence success in their particular industry. The essential question managers must ask and answer is: "Where do I get the competitive edge for long-term success in my industry?"

3. *Selection of a business strategy.* The stage of the business in the industry life cycle strongly influences strategy selection at

---

[20] Anil K. Gupta and V. Govindarajan, "Business Unit Strategy, Managerial Characteristics, and Business Unit Effectiveness at Strategy Implementation," *Academy of Management Journal,* March 1984, pp. 25–41.

MANAGEMENT FOCUS (*continued*)

3M. For example, in a new industry, strategies will emphasize market penetration and market development. Mature businesses will likely emphasize improved efficiency and product innovation and development. Each strategy must be backed up by appropriate operational plans that identify the costs and expected results and establish schedules and responsibilities.

　　4. *Measuring strategic performance.* Management seeks to estimate the financial consequences of various strategies. Effective monitoring of performance is based on financial and nonfinancial strategy measurements.

Source: Michael Tita and Robert Allio, "3M's Strategy System—Planning in an Innovative Corporation," *Planning Review*, September 1984, pp. 10–15.

Strategic planning provides direction for an organization's mission, objectives, and strategies, facilitating the development of plans for each of the organization's functional areas. A completed strategic plan guides each area in the direction the organization wishes to go and allows each area to develop objectives, strategies, and programs consistent with those goals. The relationship between strategic planning and operational planning is an important concern of managers.

Relating the Strategic Plan and Operational Plans

Most managers in an organization will not directly develop the organization's strategic plan. However, they may be involved in this process in two important ways: (1) They usually influence the strategic planning process by providing inputs in the form of information and suggestions relating to their particular areas of responsibility. (2) They must be completely aware of what the process of strategic planning involves as well as the results, because everything their respective departments do, the objectives they establish for their areas of responsibility, should all be derived from the strategic plan.

In well-managed organizations, therefore, there is a direct relationship between strategic planning and the planning done by managers at all levels. The focus of the planning and the time perspectives will, of course, differ. Figure 5–7 illustrates the relationship between the strategic plan and operational plans. It indicates very clearly that all plans should be derived from the strategic plan while at the same time contributing to the achievement of the strategic plan.

FIGURE   5–7   **The Relationship between the Organization's Strategic Plan and Operational Plans**

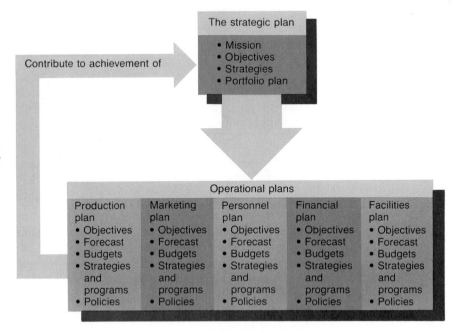

Strategic plans provide direction to operational plans of organizational subunits.

Relating Organizational Objectives and Strategies and Operational Objectives and Strategies

If planning is done properly, it will result in a clearly defined blueprint for management action *at all levels* in the organization. Figure 5–8 illustrates the *hierarchy of objectives and strategies,* using only one objective from the strategic plan and two strategies from the strategic plan. In the figure, all objectives are related to other objectives at higher and lower levels in the organization. We have illustrated only four possible operational objectives. Obviously many others could be developed, but our purpose is that the reader clearly understand how objectives and strategies from the strategic plan for the entire organization (above the dotted line) relate to objectives and strategies that are part of operational plans for individual departments (below the dotted line). As we move down from the top of the organization to lower levels in terms of who does the planning, we increase the detail and specificity of the objectives, and we decrease their time span. However, although the scope, time span, and issues confronted by operational plans differ, they are all derived from those in the strategic plan.

FIGURE 5–8   Relating Organizational Objectives and Strategies and Operational Objectives and Strategies

One organizational objective, (the profitability objective) from Figure 5-4

Achieve an annual rate of return on investment of at least 15 percent

Two possible organizational strategies from the product/market matrix, Figure 5-5

1. Market penetration

Improve position of present products with present customers

2. Market development

Find new customers for present products

Four possible operational objectives derived from strategic plan

1. Marketing department objective

Increase rate of purchase by existing customers by 10 percent by year-end.

2. Production department objective

Design additional features into product that will induce new uses by existing buyers.

3. Marketing department objective

Increase market share by 5 percent by attracting new market segments for existing use by year-end.

4. Production department objective

Design additional features into product that will open additional markets with new uses.

Specific course of action undertaken by departments designed to achieve the operational objective

Marketing strategies and programs

Production strategies and programs

Marketing strategies and programs

Production strategies and programs

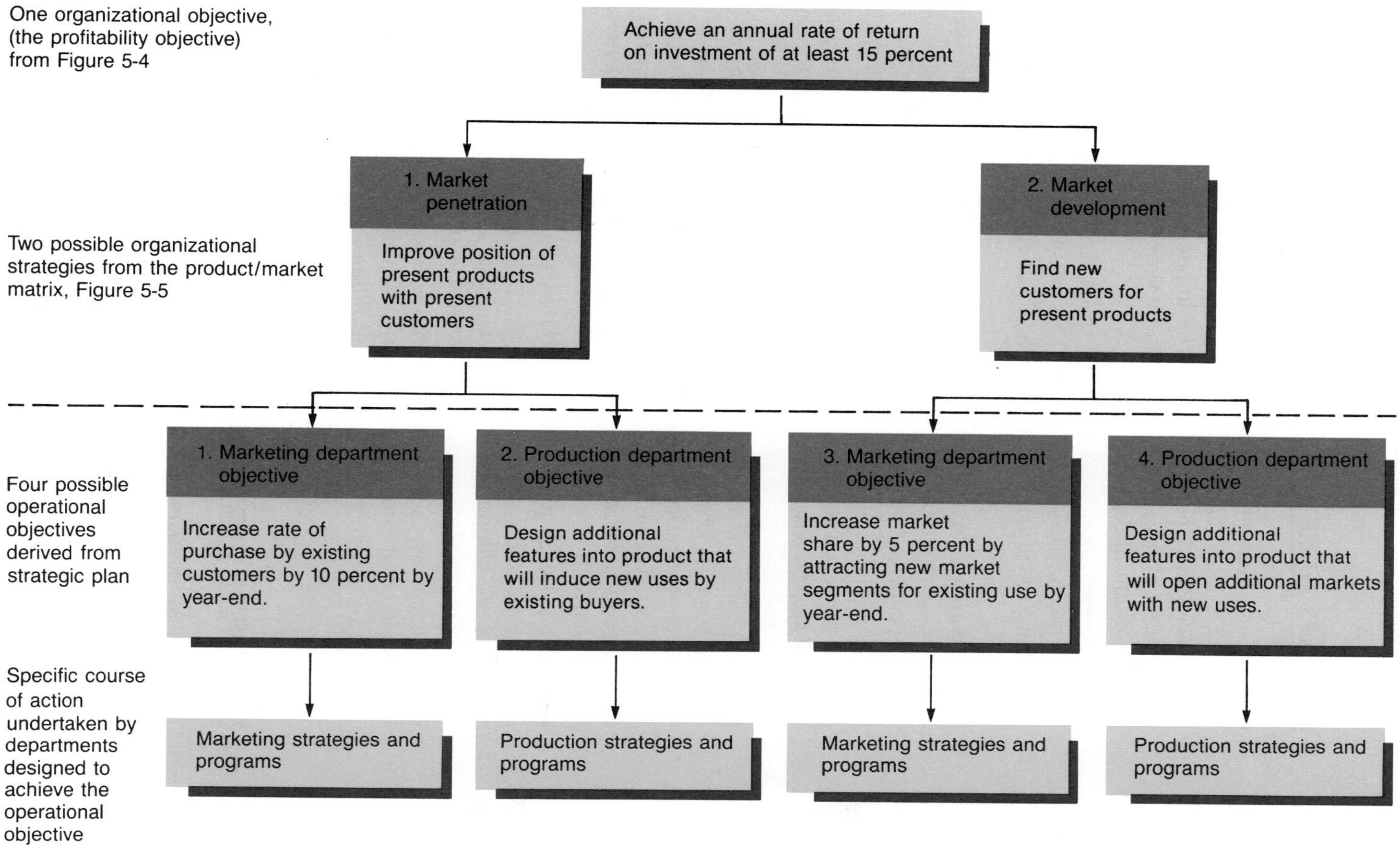

Effective planning requires that all subobjectives be compatible with organizational objectives.

SUMMARY OF KEY POINTS

- Strategic planning involves the total organization in that it specifies the organization's relation to its environment in terms of mission, objectives, strategies, and portfolio plan. The importance of strategic planning has increased as organizations seek more rational responses to environmental change and uncertainty.

- The organization's mission is a specification of the organization's basic purpose, its reason for being. The mission statement should take into account the organization's history, distinctive competencies, and environment.

- To be useful, the mission statement should be focused on markets (clients) rather than products (services), and should be achievable, motivational, and specific.

- Organizational objectives are derived from the mission. They are guideposts for assessing the degree of movement toward achieving the mission. They are the bases for establishing operational objectives for the subunits and departments of the organization.

- Organization strategies are the broad approaches the organization takes to achieve its objectives. Business firms can follow four basic strategies: market penetration, market development, product development, and diversification. The strategies selected by the organization must not only contribute to the achievement of objectives but also be compatible with the mission.

- Organizational portfolios depict the relative strength of each strategic business and the relative growth rate of the industry in which the business competes. The portfolio analysis suggests corporate strategies based upon the positioning of strategic businesses in the portfolio matrix.

- The corporate objectives and strategies contained in the strategic plan are converted into operational objectives and strategies. Through strategic planning, organizations can achieve unity and continuity of action.

DISCUSSION AND REVIEW QUESTIONS

1. Discuss the following statement: "In well-managed organizations, operational planning must be based on a strategic plan."

2. Explain why you agree or disagree with the following statements: *(a)* Planning is the easiest where environmental change is minimal. *(b)* Planning is most valuable where environmental change is great.

3. "All managers plan in one way or another." Evaluate this statement.

4. Hospital costs are soaring, leading to daily room rates of $300 or more in

some hospitals, while other hospitals are experiencing underutilization, particularly in the maternity and pediatrics sections. Some experts predict that 1,400 hospitals will close in the next 10 years. Could strategic planning be of any assistance to a hospital? Discuss.

5. Are you familiar with any organizations whose missions became obsolete or irrelevant? What happened to the organization? Discuss.

6. The text has stated that an effective mission statement will focus on markets rather than products and be achievable, motivating, and specific. Select three of the actual mission statements presented in Figure 5–2 and evaluate them based on these criteria.

7. What is the relationship between organizational mission, organizational objectives, and organizational strategies?

8. Could your college or university make any use of the product-market matrix (Figure 5–5) in its long-range planning? Discuss.

9. Most colleges, universities, hospitals, and churches are facing financial problems. Could any of these organizations make use of the business portfolio plan approach developed by the Boston Consulting Group? Explain.

10. If planning is done properly, how will the operational plans developed by different units of an organization be related to the strategic plan? Explain.

ADDITIONAL REFERENCES

Anderson, C., and C. P. Zeithaml. "Stage of the Product Life Cycle, Business Strategy, and Business Performance." *Academy of Management Journal,* March 1984, pp. 5–24.

Chanin, M. N., and H. J. Shapiero. "Dialectical Inquiry in Strategic Planning: Extending the Boundaries." *Academy of Management Review,* October 1985, pp. 663–75.

Chussil, M. J. "Responses to PIMS: Fact or Folklore." *Journal of Business Strategy,* Spring 1984, pp. 93–96.

David, F. R. "Computer Assisted Strategic Planning in Small Businesses." *Journal of Systems Management,* July 1985, pp. 24–33.

Dutton, J., and A. Thomas. "Treating Progress Functions as a Managerial Opportunity." *Academy of Management Review,* April 1984, pp. 235–47.

Galbraith, C., and D. Schendel. "An Empirical Analysis of Strategy Types." *Strategic Management Journal,* April–June 1983, pp. 153–73.

Ghemawat, P. "Building Strategy on the Experience Curve." *Harvard Business Review,* March–April 1985, pp. 143–49.

Ghosh, B. C., and A. Y. Nee. "Strategic Planning—A Contingency Approach: Part I." *Long Range Planning,* April 1983, pp. 93–103.

————. "Strategic Planning—A Contingency Approach: Part II." *Long Range Planning.* December 1983, pp. 46–58.

Grey, B., and S. S. Ariss. "Politics and Strategic Change across Organizational Life Cycles." *Academy of Management Review,* October 1985, pp. 707–23.

Gupta, A. K, "Contingency Linkages between Strategy and General Manager Characteristics: A Conceptual Examination." *Academy of Management Review,* July 1984, pp. 399–412.

Hambrick, D. C. "High Profit Strategies in Mature Capital Goods Industries." *Academy of Management Journal,* December 1983, pp. 687–707.

————. "Taxonomic Approaches to Studying Strategy: Some Conceptual and Methodological Issues." *Journal of Management,* Spring 1984, pp. 27–41.

Harrigan, K. R. "Vertical Integration and Corporate Strategy." *Academy of Management Journal,* June 1985, pp. 397–425.

Haspeslagh, P. "Portfolio Planning: Uses and Limits." *Harvard Business Review,* January–February 1982, pp. 58–73.

Henderson, B. D. "The Application and Misapplication of the Experience Curve." *Journal of Business Strategy,* Winter 1984, pp. 3–9.

Lang, J. R. "Behavioral Science Concepts in Strategic Management." Paper presented at the 10th Annual Convention, American Institute of Decision Sciences, St. Louis, Missouri, October 31, 1978.

Linneman, R. A., and H. E. Klein. "Using Scenarios in Strategic Decision Making." *Business Horizons,* January–February 1985, pp. 64–74.

MacMillan, Ian C.; Donald C. Hambrick; and Diana L. Day. "Strategic Attributes and Performance in the BCG Matrix—A PIMS–Based Analysis of Industrial-Product Businesses." *Academy of Management Journal,* September 1982, pp. 510–31.

————. "The Product Portfolio and Profitability—A PIMS–Based Analysis of Industrial-Product Businesses." *Academy of Management Journal,* December 1982, pp. 733–55.

Miller, H. J., and H. L. Smith. "Retrenchment Strategies and Tactics for Healthcare Executives." *Hospital and Health Services Administration,* May–June 1985, pp. 31–43.

Nagel, A. "Strategy Formulation in the Smaller Firm." *Long Range Planning,* August 1981, pp. 115–20.

Pappas, C. "Strategic Management of Technology." *Journal of Product Innovation Management,* January 1984, pp. 30–31.

Porter, M. E. "Contributions of Industrial Organization to Strategic Management." *Academy of Management Review,* October 1981, pp. 609–20.

Preble, J. F. "The Selection of Delphi Panels for Strategic Planning Purposes." *Strategic Management Journal,* April–June 1984, pp. 157–70.

Ramaprasad, A., and I. I. Mitroff. "On Formulating Strategic Problems." *Academy of Management Review,* October 1984, pp. 597–605.

Szilagyi, A. D., and D. M. Schweiger. "Matching Managers to Strategies: A Review and Suggested Framework." *Academy of Management Review,* October 1984, pp. 626–37.

Thompson, A., and A. Strickland. *Strategy Formulation and Implementation.* Plano, Tex.: Business Publications, 1984.

"Who's Excellent Now." *Business Week,* November 5, 1984, pp. 76–88.

CASES

APPLICATION I
CITIBANK'S DIVERSIFICATION STRATEGY

Citibank, a subsidiary of Citicorp, was facing heavy competition in its traditional lines of business. Savings banks, savings and loan associations, credit unions, and brokerage houses were competing effectively with banks by moving into such typical banking activities as interest-bearing checking accounts and by offering higher interest rates for deposits. Because of the squeeze on profit, the bank had to consider other sources of earnings.

Citibank decided to enter the computer services industry, using its considerable expertise and experience in data processing. It identified three distinct business units to be developed:

1. *Systems.* The bank combines its own programs and software with someone else's hardware and markets the system to end-users.
2. *Remote computing.* The bank sells time on its own computers to outside customers.
3. *Software.* The bank sells its software packages to other firms with similar applications.

These three businesses were mutually supportive but were aimed at different customer needs.

The foundation for the move into computer services began in the early 1970s, when Citicorp decided to streamline its own data processing capability. The program moved away from reliance on a central mainframe computer to small minicomputers that could be located near the spot where processing was required. The program encountered numerous problems. But when it was finally going, the effect was to enable one person to handle work that previously would have taken six people.

Many of the products that Citibank now markets were developed as a result of the streamlining program. These products enable other banks to streamline their own "back office" processing and turn a potential cost center into a potential profit center. Citibank not only sells the system but also offers continuing educational and consultative support services. This capability distinguishes Citibank from other suppliers of computer services.

At the present time, Citibank has set its sights on selling computer services to 20 percent of the nation's 50,000 financial institutions. That objective's potential profit of $250 million by 1990 would be equivalent to 10 percent of Citicorp's net income. The diversification into computer services represents an important potential source of earnings to Citicorp.

Citicorp's entry into computer services has met considerable opposition from both banking and computer service competitors. Banking competitors believe that Citicorp's data processing relationships with other banks put it in a better position to acquire them. This concern is particularly telling if laws regulating interstate banking are changed so that banks can branch across state lines. Computer service competitors charge that Citicorp is violating the National Bank Act and the Bank Holding Company Act. These acts limit banks and their holding companies from offering services unrelated to their basic banking business.

Other observers note that some customers might well purchase Citibank's computer services with the expectation that their loan applications would receive more favorable treatment. The bank is in the position of playing two different roles but is able to combine the two roles and thereby confuse the customer. For example, Citibank might "persuade" the customer that it should subscribe to the bank's computer services.

Despite these criticisms, Citibank is now well entrenched in the computer services industry. To reverse its decision to enter the industry would involve a complete overhaul of the long-term corporate strategy.

Questions for Analysis

1. What environmental forces caused Citicorp to move into the computer service industry?
2. Is the computer service business consistent with Citicorp's mission? Its distinctive competence?
3. Where would Citicorp's computer service business show up on a portfolio matrix? Explain.

APPLICATION II

STRATEGIC PLANNING AT THE FAMILY STORE

In 1894, John Jacobi opened a small dry-goods store in a small mountain town in a southeastern state. In addition, he traveled by wagon to larger communities in the state to sell his clothing and other dry goods. By 1916, Jacobi's Dry Goods Store had outgrown its small quarters, moved to a larger facility, and expanded its line to become what would be known today as a small department store. Since the store now carried almost everything a typical family would need, John decided to change the name of the store to *The Family Store*. This he thought was a better description of what the store sold and, in addition, was better for promotional purposes. However, he still traveled the state (in a small truck this time) to sell to other stores.

Despite the depression in the late 1920s and the early 1930s, The Family Store and John Jacobi continued to thrive because of their good service, wide selection, and reasonable prices; business was so good that by 1936 there were seven stores located throughout the state. John had expanded to 12 stores before he passed away in 1952 at the age of 81 and management of the organization was turned over to the oldest son John, Jr. Because of the growing economy, the business continued to thrive during the 1950s and into the 1960s, mainly because of its excellent reputation and little competition from national chains in the rural state.

In the mid-60s, however, business began to decline as some large shopping malls began to be built throughout the state and regional department store chains entered the state. This, coupled with the entrance of several discount chains (e.g., K mart) into the state, caused sales to decline in many of the Family Stores located in large communities. John's response to these environmental changes was to open five *Family Discount Stores* in the more populated regions of the state. Thus, as the 70s came to a close, there were 12 Family Stores and 5 Family Discount Stores in the state.

Early in 1980, as he reviewed the organization's performance for 1979, it became painfully evident to John that something needed to be done regarding the direction of the organization. With the exception of two, all Family Stores had slowly declining sales each year from 1974 to 1979; the other two had experienced declines during the last three years. The Family Discount Stores unfortunately had not done much better. None of the five had ever achieved the levels of sales and profits originally expected, and two actually lost money during the last two years. On his desk, John had a copy of a list of several social and economic trends that were expected to influence retail businesses in the next decade. These are shown in Exhibit 1.

EXHIBIT   1   Trends Impacting on Retail Businesses

- The nation's economy will continue to grow despite a recession at the beginning of the 1980s.
- The post-World War II baby boom generation will be moving into middle age, and the demand for homes will increase.
- Real wages will grow.
- As baby boomers start families, they will buy homes, furnishings, and durable goods.
- Family incomes will grow, and the number of employed wives will increase, especially among college-educated women.
- The demand for home-oriented goods and services will expand more rapidly than the demand for goods and services consumed by individuals.
- A much higher proportion of total personal income will represent earnings of women.
- The young (25–44) and affluent segment will be the most important. Households aged 45 and over will become less important since their number will be growing slowly. The younger segment will consist of both spouses educated and working.

The way John saw it, it was time to make some critical long-range decisions regarding the organization. For example: Should they concentrate on smaller communities where regional and national chains do not have outlets? Should they compete aggressively with the chains and, if so, on what basis? Should they seek a unique direction for their organization distinct from any other? What kind of organization is The Family Store?

"Who says we have to be a retailer?" John thought as he left the office. "I can see it now, The Family Record Store, The Family Bookstore, The Family Inn Motel. Who am I kidding? We are a chain of department stores. Maybe we have outworn our purpose and should just sell out to some national chain. Maybe I'm going crazy?"

Questions for Analysis

1. Why is Jacobi facing the problems he is now facing? Were they inevitable? Discuss in detail.
2. Assume you are hired as a consultant by Jacobi. What, if anything, could you do to help him?

EXPERIENTIAL EXERCISE

THE IMPORTANCE OF THE PLANNING FUNCTION

Purpose

The purpose of this exercise is to emphasize the importance of planning in organizations in various industries.

The Exercise in Class

1. Every person in the class should be assigned the same organization from the list below and answer the following questions:

   a. What events in this organization's environment should be considered in developing a strategic plan for the successful achievement of objectives?

   b. How likely are important events to occur? That is, what is the probability of an event (e.g., energy shortage, shortage of qualified job candidates, increase or decrease in demand, increase or decrease in competition)?

c. How can managerial planning improve the organization's chances of surviving the occurrence of positive and/or negative events cited in your answer to *b.*

The organizations for the exercise:

General Motors	Del Taco	Wells Fargo Bank
Standard Brands	Pacific Stereo	Revlon
Walt Disney	Levi Strauss	Honeywell
General Mills	Sears	Volvo

2. After completing the first part of the exercise individually, the instructor will form groups of four to six students. The groups will each be assigned one of the remaining organizations. Each group will have a different organization. Each group should answer questions *a, b,* and *c* and report its answers to the class.

The Learning Message

This exercise, requiring some out-of-class homework to prepare the answers, will show that some organizations need planning more than others because of the events they must deal with in the environment.

6

THE ORGANIZING FUNCTION

LEARNING OBJECTIVES

After completing Chapter 6, you should be able to:

■ **Define**
the organizing function in terms of required management decisions.

■ **Describe**
the effects of the span of control on the manager and the organization.

■ **Discuss**
the relationships between the planning and organizing functions.

■ **Identify**
the ways to describe differences among jobs.

■ **Compare**
two organizations using the dimensions of structure as the bases for the comparison.

▢ MANAGEMENT IN ACTION

Marine Midland Bank's Revised Organization

Marine Midland Bank has assets of $18.7 billion and ranks as the 14th largest bank in the United States, its growth largely the result of a series of acquisitions of local and regional banks in upstate New York. But even with its relatively large size, Marine Midland has lagged behind its competition in profitability. It has had little success in attracting the kinds of customers that are the sources of improved profitability: large corporations and wealthy individuals. Prior to 1980, Marine Midland was organized on a regional basis. The organization structure was the result of the acquisition program that has helped the bank prosper. The acquired banks were left largely intact as operating entities, resulting in considerable duplicaion of specialized and costly activities.

Marine has embarked upon a campaign to become more profitable by a combination of personnel, strategic, and organizational changes. The group planning Marine's future believed that its organizational structure would have to be changed if its personnel and strategic changes were to be successful. The group believed that the regional structure was inconsistent with its strategic decision to concentrate on the most profitable banking functions. Consequently the bank reorganized along functional lines.

The planning group eventually settled upon seven main functional categories: retail banking, corporate banking, international banking, trust banking, financial market services, commercial middle-market banking (serving customers with sales of $1 million to $125 million) and commercial asset-based financing (mortgages and equipment leases). The new structure facilitates the development and implementation of corporatewide strategy and policy. For example, Marine has set a minimum trust fund level and charges a fee for servicing small savings accounts. It also has centralized such activities as data processing and accounting. The emphasis on banking functions and customers is reinforced by the organization structure. The anticipated outcome is increased profitability, made possible in part by a more rational organizational structure.

The issue that Marine Midland's management faced—the issue of appropriate organization structure—recurs in all types of organizations and is complex and difficult to analyze. But the importance of organization structure to profitability and productivity cannot be stressed enough. Organizing is a major management function.

The purpose of the organizing function is to *achieve coordinated effort through the design of a structure of task and authority relationships.* The two key concepts are design and structure. Design, in this context, implies that managers make a conscious effort to predetermine the way in which work is done by employees. Structure refers to relatively stable relationships and aspects of the organization. Organizational structure, considered by many to be the anatomy of the organization, provides a foundation within which the organization functions. Thus, the structure of an organization, similar to the anatomy of a living organism, can be viewed as a framework. In this context, the purpose of structure is to regulate or at least reduce the uncertainty regarding the behavior of individual employees.

When viewed in rather abstract terms, the organizing function is the process of breaking down the overall task into individual assignments and then putting them back together in units, or departments, along with a delegation of authority to a unit manager. We can describe the organizing function in terms of dividing tasks into jobs, departmentalizing jobs, and delegating authority.

Dividing tasks involves determining the scope and content of individual jobs. Jobs are the building blocks of organizations. But to be manageable, jobs must be combined into departments. *Departmentalization* involves determining both the basis by which individual jobs will be combined into departments and the optimal number of jobs assigned in a department. Finally, *delegating authority* involves the distribution of the right to make decisions among jobs, particularly managerial jobs.

Organizational structures can vary widely, depending upon the decisions of managers regarding division of tasks, departmentalizing jobs, and delegating authority. Tasks can be more or less specialized, jobs can be grouped into departments according to different bases, and authority can be centralized or decentralized. As described in the Management in Action, Marine Midland Bank changed its organization structure by redefining jobs and redepartmentalizing. Modern management theory is based upon the principle that there is no one best structure. The appropriate structure varies from situation to situation.[1] The challenge to management is to design the appropriate structure.

In this chapter, the discussion focuses on structure. Attention is paid to the three important *parts* of all organization structures: jobs, departments, and authority. Chapter 7 examines the issues associated with *designing* the appropriate framework.

DIVIDING TASKS

The most important consideration in dividing tasks is specialization of labor. The gains derived from such specialization can be calculated in purely

---

[1] See Jeffrey D. Ford and W. Harvey Hegarty, "Decision Makers Beliefs about the Causes and Effects of Structure," *Academy of Management Journal,* June 1984, pp. 271–91.

FIGURE   6–1   The Economics of Specialization

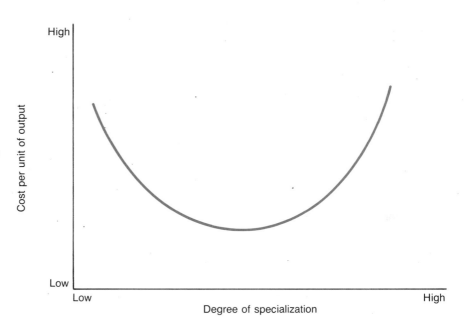

There are limits on the
gains to be attained
from specialization.

---

economic terms. Figure 6–1 shows this relationship. As the job is divided into ever-smaller elements, additional output is obtained. But more people and capital must be employed to do the smaller jobs. At some point, the costs of specialization (labor and capital) begin to outweigh the increased efficiency of specialization (output), and the cost per unit of output begins to rise.

The problem of determining the appropriate degree of specialization becomes increasingly difficult as the task becomes more abstract. For example, managerial work is more abstract than blue-collar work. Managers do not produce tangible products that can be weighed or measured in some way. Managers seldom use tools or equipment. They get their work done by communicating, thinking, and acting. Blue-collar work, on the other hand, is repetitive, involves definite sequences of actions, and produces tangible products. Nevertheless, the principle of specialization states that one must investigate the potential for gains through specialization.

The classical approach attempted to determine the optimal application of specialization of labor to blue-collar jobs. According to the classical writers, the work of lathe operators, assemblers, ironworkers, bricklayers, and similar employees can be broken down into separable and discrete hand, eye, and body movements. These movements are shown in Table 6–1.

TABLE   6–1   The Basic Movements of Manual Work

	Movement	Objective
1.	Grasp	To gain control of an object.
2.	Position	To line up, orient, or change position of a part.
3.	Pre-position	To line up part or tool for use in another place.
4.	Use	To apply tool.
5.	Assemble	To assemble parts or objects.
6.	Disassemble	To separate objects.
7.	Release load	To release a part or object.
8.	Transport empty	To reach for something.
9.	Transport loaded	To change location of an object.
10.	Search	To seek to find an object.
11.	Select	To locate an object from a group of objects.
12.	Hold	To hold object in fixed position and location.
13.	Unavoidable delay	To wait for other body member or machine as a part of the work movement.
14.	Avoidable delay	To wait for other body member or machine not a part of the work movement.
15.	Rest for fatigue	To remain idle as a part of the cycle to overcome fatigue.
16.	Plan	To determine course of action.
17.	Inspect	To determine quality of item.

Manual work consists of specific and identifiable body movements.

Through the application of motion and time studies, the manager can identify for each job the preferred basic movements: those that minimize effort but result in the completion of the assigned tasks. For example, a typist must reach for blank paper (transport empty), take hold of the blank paper (grasp), carry the blank paper to the typewriter (transport loaded), arrange the blank paper in the typewriter (position), and type the required message (use). The design of the typist job would attempt to increase the output (typed messages) by (1) simplifying the job requirements to the fewest possible movements and (2) eliminating unnecessary movements. The typist then would need to be trained to do the relatively fewer preferred basic movements.

Individual jobs can be defined in terms of the required movements. But there are other ways to describe jobs—for example, *depth* and *scope*. Job depth refers to the relative freedom that the jobholder has in performing assigned tasks. Ordinarily, one expects the depth of a job to increase as one moves up in the levels of the organization. The job of the chief executive would have more depth than the job of an assembly-line worker. But there also can be differences in job depth among persons at the same level. For example, a maintenance person has considerably more job depth than does a lathe worker, even though the two jobs usually are at the same level in an organization. The maintenance employee typically can select the methods to be used in maintaining and repairing equipment. By contrast, the lathe worker has little discretion in the selection of work methods.

The scope of a job refers to the length of time of the job cycle. The more often the job is repeated in a given time period, the more limited is its scope. We can expect to find differences in job scope among jobs at the same level and at different levels in the organization. Generally, the more specialized a job, the narrower its scope. Thus, depth and scope reflect two outcomes of specialization: (1) relative freedom of choice in selecting the means to do a job and (2) relative "size" of the job. Highly specialized jobs have relatively little depth and scope.

In recent years, there has been growing interest in defining jobs in terms of the perceptions of those who perform them. The researchers and practitioners who pioneered this perspective believe that jobs can be described in terms of five "core dimensions":[2]

1. *Variety.* Individuals can perceive their jobs to have variety. They usually are engaged in work requiring them to perform many different operations and procedures. People who have highly specialized jobs usually perceive little variety in their assignments.

2. *Task identity.* The perception of task identity depends upon whether or not the individual's job results in a complete piece of work. Generally, highly specialized jobs produce perceptions of reduced task identity.

3. *Task significance.* Individuals have perceptions of the relative significance of their jobs to other people. The perception of task significance is inversely related to specialization.

4. *Autonomy.* The perception of autonomy reflects the individual's sense of personal control over key aspects of the job. The perception of autonomy is directly related to job depth.

5. *Feedback.* The perception of feedback reflects the amount of information that the individual obtains upon completing the task. Feedback is usually provided by supervisors. In some instances, feedback is a result of doing the work.

Whether one thinks in terms of job movements, job depth and scope, or job core dimensions, it is evident that jobs are different. But how are they different? And how different should they be? These questions are fundamental and far from simple. Here, we are concerned only with describing the way jobs are different. The following chapter will provide some guidelines in determining the degree and kind of those differences.

---

[2] For earlier work, see J. Richard Hackman, Greg Oldham, Robert Janson, and Kenneth Purdy, "A New Strategy for Job Enrichment," *California Management Review,* Summer 1975, pp. 57–71. Also see Greg R. Oldham and J. Richard Hackman, "Relationships between Organizational Structure and Employee Reactions: Comparing Alternative Frameworks," *Administrative Science Quarterly,* March 1981, pp. 66–83.

DEPARTMENTALIZING JOBS

Once the total task of the organization is divided into individual jobs, those jobs must be combined into groups, or departments. Departmentalizing jobs involves two considerations: (1) the bases for classifying jobs into departments and (2) the size of each department.

Departmental Bases

Managerial problems associated with departmentalization are directly related to the degree that individual jobs have been specialized. That is, the number of ways to group jobs increases with the number of different (specialized) jobs. Thus, the owner-manager of a small-town clothing store specializing in men's clothing and employing three persons has little difficulty determining the way jobs should be grouped, as compared to the management of Sears, Roebuck & Co. In general, jobs are grouped into two major categories: *outputs* and *internal operations.*

Output-oriented bases.   The three commonly used output-oriented bases are *product, client,* and *geographic.*

1. *Product departmentalization* involves grouping together all activities necessary to manufacture a product or product line. The grouping of activities along product lines permits the utilization of the specialized skills of those people affiliated with a particular product or product line. An example of this type of departmentalization is presented as a partial organization chart in Figure 6–2A.

2. *Customer departmentalization* is the grouping of activities based upon the customers served. For example, a company may have two sales departments that deal with two major groups of customers. One department may service the general public, while the other may be designed to provide goods to an industrial group of customers. Customer departmentalization is shown in Figure 6–2B.

3. *Geographical departmentalization* groups activities according to physical location or spatial location. Marine Midland Bank was organized by geographic location prior to its reorganization. This departmental basis was a convenient choice, given the growth strategy of the bank. Figure 6–2C illustrates an example of geographical departmentalization.

These three bases for grouping work—product, customer, and geography—are oriented toward factors external to the actual operations of the firm. For example, the customer is a factor "out there" in the market. The geographical territory is also "out there," as is the distribution of the product.

Internal operations-oriented bases.   Two bases for grouping jobs in this category are *function* and *process.*

FIGURE   6–2   Output-Oriented Departmentalization

A.   Product lines

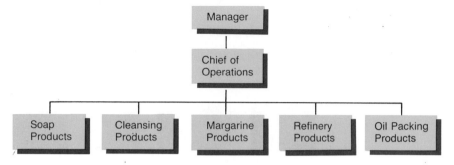

Each of the five product departments produces and sells a specific product.

Output-oriented departments reflect outputs, customers, or locations.

B.   Customer lines

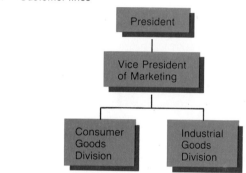

Each of the two customer departments meets the product and service needs of a specific group of customers.

C.   Geographic lines

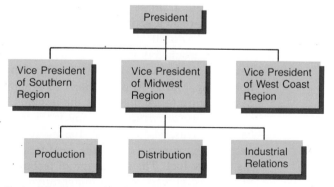

Each of the three regional departments produces and sells products in the assigned geographic area.

FIGURE   6–3   Departmentalization Based on Internal Operations

A.   Functional lines

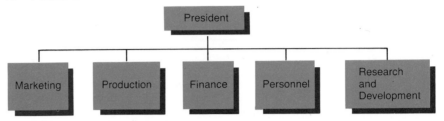

Each of the five functional departments carries out its assigned part of the total business.

Internal operations-oriented departments reflect functions or processes.

B.   Process lines

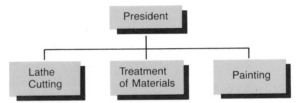

Each of the three process departments carries out its
assigned part of the total production process.

---

1. *Functional departmentalization* is used when organizations are designed on the basis of the operations performed by a unit. For example, in a food-processing firm, all job-related activities involved in recruiting and selecting management trainees might be assigned to the personnel department. All marketing-related activities would be the responsibility of the marketing department. And all activities concerned with the actual production of goods would be grouped in the production department. The functional organization design is used extensively in manufacturing firms. But it also is applicable in banking. Marine Midland Bank reorganized along functional departmental bases. Figure 6–3A illustrates the design.

2. *Process departmentalization* is the grouping of jobs according to technical operations. For example, the manufacturing of a product may include cutting the materials on a lathe, heat-treating the materials, and finally painting the product. The same type of technical division of work may be found in an office of a business administration department at a college. A number of typists may be assigned specific duties to perform. One types manuscripts; another typist is concerned with correspondence; and the third handles the

---

**TABLE   6–2   Comparison of Departmental Bases in Four
                Organizational Settings**

		Organizational Settings			
The specific departmental bases vary according to type of organization.	**Basis**	**Business**	**Hospital**	**University**	**Public Health**
	Function	Manufacturing	Surgery	Teaching	Engineering
	Process	Assembly	Diagnosis	Evaluation	Inspector
	Product	Truck	Patient care	Degree	Safe drinking water
	Customer	Military	Children	Graduate student	Residential

---

telephone and the typing of classroom materials. In Figure 6–3B, the division of work along process lines is presented.

The bases for departmentalization are generally identifiable in any organizational setting. In Table 6–2, four bases are identified in four organizational settings. There we see, for example, that the equivalent to the Truck Division of General Motors (product bases) are patient care in hospitals, degrees in universities, and safe drinking water in a public health agency. The only basis not shown is geographic, which becomes relevant only if the organization is dispersed, with offices and facilities in different locations.

Multiple departmental bases.   Large corporations use different bases at different levels. For example, corporations such as General Motors and General Electric use product as the basis for departmentalizing at the highest level. Each product department, usually termed a division, will have all the resources to act as an independent business unit. The departmental basis at the next level down is typically function. Note in Figure 6–4 that the vice president of Product B, has three functional departments: marketing, production, and personnel. The next level is departmentalized by geography (West Coast and East Coast reporting to marketing), process (manufacturing and finishing reporting to production) and clientele (Managerial-Related and Non-managerial-Related reporting to Personnel). Thus, at each level, different bases can exist both among and within departments.

Selecting appropriate departmental bases: The principle of departmentalization specifies the guidelines to be followed in grouping activities. But the basis actually chosen is a matter of balancing advantages and disadvantages. For example, departmentalizing on the basis of customers or products brings together, under the control of a single manager, all the resources necessary to make the product and/or service for the customers. Additionally, the specification of objective is considerably easier when the emphasis is on the final product. At the same time, the ease of objective identification and

FIGURE   6–4   Organizational Design Using Mixed Departmentalization

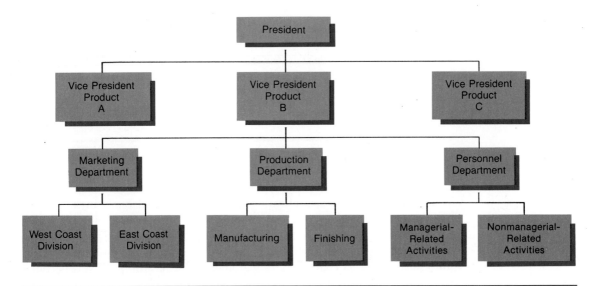

Most organizations use different departmental bases at each level of the organization.

measurement can encourage the individual departments to pursue their own objectives at the expense of company objectives. A second disadvantage of product and customer departmentalization is that the task of coordinating the activities tends to be more complex. Reporting to the unit manager are the managers of the various functions (production, marketing, and personnel, for example), whose diverse but interdependent activities must be coordinated.

Departmentalization based upon internal operations (function and process departments) has advantages as well as disadvantages. The primary advantage is that these departments are based upon specific skills and training. And activities assigned to a department emphasize the skills that individual members bring to the job. The managerial task of coordinating the activities of process departments is considerably less complex than in the product department. This is due to the similarity of the subordinates' tasks. At the same time, the disadvantages of process departments must be recognized, principally the difficulty of providing job depth for the managers of such groups. Since process departmentalization involves breaking up a natural work flow and assigning parts of this flow to different departments, each departmental manager must coordinate the task with those of other departmental managers. As shown in Figure 6–3B, the president must limit the freedom of the managers of each of the three process departments in order to coordinate their activites.

The relative advantages of the alternative departmentalization bases can be evaluated in terms of three criteria:

1. Which approach (basis) permits the maximum use of special technical knowledge?
2. Which provides the most efficient utilization of machinery and equipment?
3. Which provides the best hope of obtaining the required control and coordination?

These three criteria, taken together, identify the important issues when determining departmental bases.[3] After the managers of Marine Midland Bank reviewed these three issues, they concluded that functional departmentalization was more advantageous than geographical departmentalization. Accordingly, the bank changed its structure to incorporate the functional basis.

Departmental Size

Departmental bases determine the *composition* of the jobs assigned in a particular department. The second decision regarding departments is to determine the *number* of jobs assigned to a particular department. This decision involves determining the departmental size.

The size of a department determines the number of subordinates who report to a supervisor, which has two important implications. First, the total is influential in determining the complexity of individual managers' jobs. All things equal, it is easier to manage 6 persons rather than 10. Second, the span of control determines the shape, or configuration, of the organization; the fewer the number of people reporting to a supervisor, the larger the number of managers required.

For example, assume that a company has 48 nonmanagers and the span of control is 8. There would be six supervisors. This type of structure is illustrated in Figure 6–5A, where there are three levels of management: president, senior supervisor, and supervisor.

If the same number of workers (48) were supervised by two superiors, an organization with only two managerial levels could be structured. The organizational design resulting from widening the span of control to 24 is presented in Figure 6–5B. By increasing the span of control from 8 to 24, one level of management and six managerial positions are eliminated from the organization.

The relatively flat organization that results from wide spans of control

---

[3] For a discussion of issues of departmentalization in a nonbusiness setting, see Peggy Leatt and Rodney Schneck, "Criteria for Grouping Nursing Subunits in Hospitals," *Academy of Management Journal,* March 1984, pp. 150–64.

FIGURE   6–5   The Relationship of Span of Control to Organizational Structure

A.   Narrow span of control

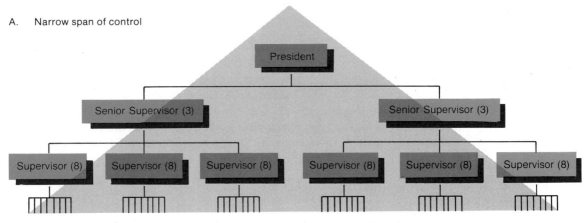

Changing the average span of control changes the shape of an organization.

B.   Wide span of control

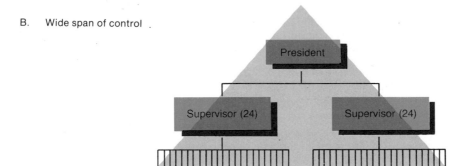

shortens the communication channel from top to bottom. It also fosters more general supervision, since (as noted earlier) managers with a wide span of control will not be able to devote as much time to each individual employee. In contrast, narrow spans of control foster close supervision but at the cost of lengthened communication channels and increased cost of management.

The cost of excessive supervision does not go unnoticed in organizations experiencing economic hardship. As the Management Focus on the Dana

Corporation indicates, some firms have attempted to reduce the number of managerial levels.

MANAGEMENT FOCUS
Increasing Spans of Control at Dana Corporation

In recent years, the Dana Corporation of Toledo, Ohio, has undergone some changes in its organization structure. One of the objectives of Dana's top management is to reduce the total number of managerial jobs. A promising approach to achieving that goal is to increase spans of control. Thus, top management is encouraging plant managers to organize according to how many people a manager can supervise rather than by what functions coincide with a manager's title. Plant managers evaluate the supervisory skills of each manager, who is then assigned a correspondingly appropriate number of individuals. For example, a quality-control manager may supervise people involved in maintenance and shipping instead of only six quality-control inspectors. The people who do the maintenance and shipping are assigned to the quality-control manager because of his or her supervisory skill. The concept underlying Dana's approach is that management should be defined in terms of control rather than as boxes on an organization chart.

The determination of span of control is far from a trivial decision. As we have seen, the number of people reporting to a manager has direct implication for both the manager and the organization itself.[4] As is the case in most important managerial decisions, no formula specifies the optimal span of control. At best, managers can utilize the following guidelines:

1. The more competent the manager and subordinate, the wider the span of control can be.
2. The fewer nonmanagerial responsibilities assigned to the manager, the wider the span of control can be.
3. The more alike the jobs being supervised, the wider the span of contol can be.
4. The more routine the jobs and overall work of the department, the wider the span of control can be.

---

[4] John B. Cullen and Douglas D. Baker, "Administration Size and Organization Size: An Examination of the Lag Structure," *Academy of Management Journal,* September 1984, pp. 644–53.

5. The closer the physical proximity of the jobs, the wider the span of control can be.

Spans of control can differ for managers at the same level. A manager with demonstrated competence can, for example, manager more jobs than an inexperienced one can or managers with similar competence can have different spans of control, depending upon the nature of the jobs they manage. Thus, the factors that bear on the optimal span of control relate (1) to characteristics of the *manager* and (2) to characteristics of the *jobs* to be managed.

The process of dividing the tasks into jobs and departmentalizing the jobs into groups creates a framework for accomplishing the organization work. And this framework gives rise to managerial jobs.

The third consideration in organizing is to delegate authority to each managerial job.

DELEGATING AUTHORITY

Authority generally is defined as the legally or organizationally sanctioned right to make a decision without approval by a higher-ranking manager.[5] The issue of delegating authority involves balancing the advantages and disadvantages of decentralization of authority. And it has implications for the creation of a chain of command and the use of staff personnel. The usual practical concern is the extent to which authority will be delegated downward—that is, decentralization. Although the exact degree of decentralization cannot be determined precisely, relative advantages and disadvantages can be identified.

Pros and Cons of Decentralization

Advantages.   The first advantage of decentralized authority is that it encourages managers to develop their decision-making ability. As authority is pushed down within the organization, managers must adapt and prove themselves if they are to advance. That is, they must become generalists who know something about the numerous job-related factors that they cope with in the decentralized arrangement. Because managers in a decentralized structure often have to adapt to and deal with difficult decisions, they are trained for promotion into positions of greater authority and responsibility. In a decentralized structure, managers readily can be compared with their peers

---

[5] For an interesting perspective on the concept of authority, see Trudy Heller, "Changing Authority Patterns: A Cultural Perspective," *Academy of Management Review,* July 1985, pp. 488–95.

on the basis of actual decision-making performance. In effect, the decentralized authority can lead to a more satisfied group of managers, because under this arrangement managers can be evaluated on the basis of results, not personalities.

Second, decentralized authority leads to a competitive climate within the organization. The managers are motivated to contribute in this competitive atmosphere since they are compared with their peers on various performance criteria.

The third advantage of decentralization is that managers are able to exercise more autonomy, and this increased job depth satisfies the desire to participate in problem-solving. Such freedom is assumed to lead to managerial creativity and ingenuity, which contribute to the flexibility and profitability of the organization.

Disadvantages.   The major disadvantages of decentralization are readily identified. First, decentralization of authority usually requires more intensive and expensive management training. The cost of training increases because managers often must be retrained to make decisions formerly made at higher levels. Even if additional training is not necessary, costs will increase because of the necessity to employ more highly skilled and, therefore, more expensive individuals to fill the positions.

A second disadvantage is that decentralization requires more sophisticated planning and reporting methods than does centralization. Delegating the right to make a decision without approval necessitates establishing methods to measure overall accountability for the use of authority. Consequently there will be an increase in the upward flow of information to upper management. Even though authority is delegated, upper management cannot delegate its responsibility for achieving the organization's mission and objectives. Therefore, upper management must implement more extensive planning and reporting procedures when authority is decentralized.

A third disadvantage applies primarily to instances of change from centralized to decentralized authority. Such a change requires top managers to delegate a portion of their decision-making authority to middle and first-level managers. In some instances, top management may be unwilling or unable to delegate further. These managers may equate authority with power and, therefore, view delegation as undermining their power and influence in the organization. These attitudes can limit if not defeat any effort to decentralize and could be highly resistant to change.

The relative advantages and disadvantages of decentralization also reflect the stage of business development. For example, a rapidly growing firm often can benefit from decentralization. But as growth begins to slow, decentralization can be a liability. The Management Focus describes such a circumstance in Warner Communications.

MANAGEMENT FOCUS
Warner Communications' Decentralization

Warner Communications had become a $3 billion-a-year music and entertainment conglomerate prior to 1976. That year, it bought Atari for $28 million. By the end of 1981, Atari had captured 75 percent of the home video game market on annual sales of $1 billion. Warner Communications never looked better, and investors agreed by bidding its stock from $1.87 to $58.50 a share in just six years.

The problems began when the 1982 profits increased only 15 percent, after a disastrous fourth quarter with sales and profits far below projections. The primary cause was disappointing sales of Atari during the Christmas season. But there was other disturbing news. A former Warner executive claimed that top management should have known sooner that the fourth quarter was not up to expectations.

The explanation for top management's slow reaction is that the company's organization structure is too decentralized. The impression is that the company is out of control. The decentralized structure seemed appropriate for the company when it was growing rapidly. The structure also is compatible with Warner's philosophy of giving artists considerable freedom. But at some point, decentralization can become its own worst enemy. At Warner Communications, top management is now beginning to analyze the steps required to recentralize authority.

Source: Adapted from Anne B. Pillsbury, "Warner's Fall from Grace," *Fortune,* January 10, 1983, pp. 82–83.

The issue of delegation of authority is linked closely to the issues of chain of command and the role of staff personnel.

Chain of Command

The chain-of-command relationship is a series of superior-subordinate relationships. Starting at the top of the organization with the president and progressing down to the unskilled employee, the managerial chain of command is a hierarchy of jobs, differentiated by authority. Figure 6–6 depicts the chain of command in a hypothetical managerial hierarchy.

FIGURE   6–6   Chain of Command

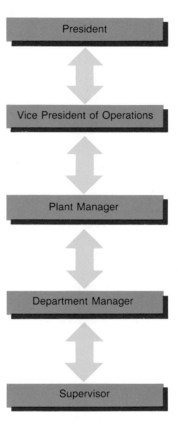

A chain of command routes orders, directives, and information.

The chain of command is the formal channel that determines authority, responsibility, and communications. Because of the complexity of these relationships, no individual ordinarily should be subject to the direct command of more than one superior. Receiving commands from two or more superiors is likely to bring about confusion and frustration.

Managers provide an unbroken chain of command from top to bottom. At the same time, they must recognize the need for providing the opportunity to bypass the chain when conditions warrant. A subordinate should be empowered to communicate directly with a peer outside the chain, provided that the appropriate superiors approve beforehand the circumstances that permit the crossovers. Figure 6–7 shows a bridge between F and G, that D and E have approved. Under special circumstances, F and G may communicate directly without going through channels, yet neither F nor G would be ac-

---

FIGURE   6–7   Fayol's Bridge

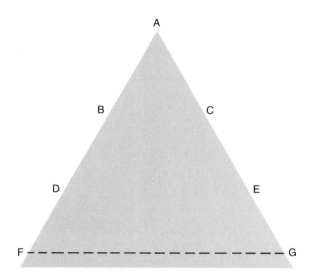

A chain of command can be "broken" with prior approval.

countable to anyone but their immediate superiors—in this case, D and E, respectively.

Staff Personnel

Delegation of authority has implications for the way staff personnel contribute to organizations. An important point in examining organization structure is to distinguish between *line* and *staff*. Many different definitions of line and staff can be found in management literature. Perhaps the most concise and least confusing definition is one that defines line as deriving from operational activities in a direct sense—creating, financing, and distributing a good or service—while staff is viewed as an advisory and facilitative function for the line. The crux of this viewpoint of line and staff is the degree to which the function contributes directly to the attainment of organizational objectives. The *line functions* contribute directly to accomplishing the firm's objectives, while *staff functions* facilitate the accomplishments of the major organizational objectives in an indirect manner.

Figure 6–8 illustrates a line-and-staff orgnizational design. Using the criterion that the line function contributes directly to the firm's objectives leads to the conclusion that the marketing and production departments perform activities directly related to the attainment of a most important organizational objective: placing an acceptable product on the market. The activities of

FIGURE   6–8   A Line-and-Staff Structure

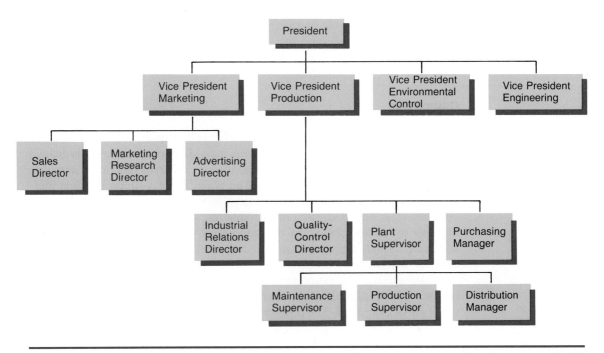

Line-and-staff organizations that take advantage of specialized staff personnel must guard against undermining the authority of line personnel.

the managers of environmental control and engineering are advisory in nature. That is, they are helpful in enabling the firm to produce and market its product but do not directly contribute to the process. Thus, they are considered to be staff departments in this particular firm.

The unbroken-chain-of-command idea quite clearly defines the appropriate role of the staff specialist in the organization: The staff specialist advises and provides information but has no authority over the work of a particular line manager's subordinates. To place a subordinate under the jurisdiction of a staff official as well as a line manager would violate and weaken the chain of command. Thus, the delegation-of-authority issue focuses not only on who makes what decisions but also on with whom one communicates, whom one directs and is directed by, and where one is located in a hierarchy of authority.

DIMENSIONS OF ORGANIZATION STRUCTURE

The effects of division of tasks, departmentalization, and delegation of authority are "policies and activities occurring within organizations that prescribe or restrict behavior of organizational members."[6] To describe these policies and activities, many different terms have been used by those who research and theorize about organization structure. These labels for *the dimensions of structure* enable us to compare organization structures and identify similarities and differences.[7] In recent years it has become customary to use three dimensions: *complexity, formality,* and *centralization.*

Complexity

Complexity is a direct consequence of dividing tasks. When referring to the organization structure rather than the individual job, complexity is defined as the number of different occupational titles or different functional activities pursued within an organization. Thus, an organization with production, marketing, and finance departments reporting to top management would be more complex than one that has only production and marketing. Specialization of tasks by dividing work at the same level of an organization is termed *horizontal complexity.* Organization structures differ in the degree to which they are horizontally complex.

A second way to view complexity in organizations is in terms of the number of managerial levels; that is, the number of different positions in the chain of command. The positions in the chain of command reflect specialization of the managerial functions of planning, organizing and controlling. Thus, organizations can have more or less horizontal complexity and more or less *vertical complexity.*

The managerial implications of horizontal and vertical complexity are straightforward: it is easier to manage similarities than differences. Accordingly, the more complex an organization or unit, the more difficult its managerial jobs. Complex organizations are difficult to manage, because of the dissimilarities in both the tasks of the units and the jobs of individuals. But the cost of increased complexity can be offset by the increased productivity that results from specialization.

Formalization

Formalization refers to the extent to which job expectations, rules, procedures, policies, and other sources that describe expected behavior have been put in written form. A term often used to describe this dimension is *standardization,* although standardization most often refers to written statements that

---

[6] Dan R. Dalton, William D. Toder, Michael J. Spendolini, Gordon J. Fielding, and Lyman W. Porter, "Organization Structure and Performance: A Critical Review," *Academy of Management Review,* January 1980, p. 57.

[7] Ibid., for a review of these dimensions.

define the exact procedures and methods a jobholder will use to accomplish a job outcome.

Organizations differ in degree of formalization. Generally speaking, however, complexity and formalization are correlated: An organization that is highly complex also will be highly formalized. Complexity most often occurs when tasks have well-established methods for accomplishing recognizable and measurable outcomes. To reduce the possibility of incorrect or inappropriate behavior in such circumstances, it is practical to put into writing the preferred methods and outcomes. Simple and routine production and administrative tasks lend themselves to extensive formalization; complicated and nonroutine scientific and research tasks are not amenable to formalization.

Centralization

As noted earlier, *centralization* refers to the degree of distribution of decision-making authority throughout the organization. Other terms often used to refer to the idea include *autonomy* and *participation.* As a practical matter, it is relatively more difficult to identify the degree of centralization than the degree of complexity or formalization. In a sense, everyone in an organization makes decisions. Even the lowliest laborer can decide where to place the shovel to remove the dirt from a ditch. And to complicate matters further, decisions often are the result of groups and consultation with other individuals.

The extremes of centralization are identifiable. At one extreme is an organization in which *all* decisions are made by *one* individual, the top manager. At the other extreme is an organization in which *all* decisions are made by *all* members of the organization. Because decision making is a primary source of power in organizations, political terms often are used to describe the two extremes: "all decisions, one individual" is autocratic; "all decisions, all individuals" is democratic. These terms are value laden and not very useful to describe work organizations, despite the tendency to use them.

In actuality, organizations lie between the extremes. They are more or less centralized but never absolutely centralized or decentralized. The relevant consideration is to ascertain the locus of authority for deciding the objectives of the organization. All other decisions are subordinate to the decision regarding what the organization is seeking to accomplish. To the extent that that decision is widely shared, the organization is less centralized.

SUMMARY OF KEY POINTS

- The organizing function involves designing or redesigning a structure of task and authority relationships to achieve coordinated effort. The organizing function includes all managerial activities required to specify the means to accomplish the work of individuals, groups, and organizations.

- The three key decisions of the organizing function are *(a)* the appropriate *division* of tasks, *(b)* the appropriate basis and size of *departments,* and *(c)* the appropriate degree of *delegated authority.* The organization structure takes on a specific form depending upon management's response to each of these decisions.

- Dividing tasks involves determining the depth and scope of each job. Although the principle of specialization of labor indicates that economic gains can be derived from specialized (low depth and scope) jobs, at some point the gains of specialization are less than its costs. The managerial decision is to identify the optimal level of specialization for each general class of jobs.

- Departmentalizing jobs involves recombining jobs in departments according to some basis and of some size. The bases for departments include product, customer, geographic (external bases), and functional and process (internal bases). The selection of appropriate departmental bases for each level in the organization requires managers to balance the advantages and disadvantages of each basis.

- The size of departments (the span of control) has *managerial* and *organizational* implications. The managerial implications are that as the manager becomes responsible for more and more subordinates, the number of potential relationships increases at an exponential rate; the manager is less and less able to give attention to each subordinate and to each possible group of subordinates. The organization implications are that as the span of control decreases, the number of managerial levels increases; the chain of command lengthens through which directives and communications flow.

- Delegating authority involves determining how much decision-making latitude should be given to each managerial job. This involves determining the appropriate authority commensurate with the responsibility of the job. In practical terms, delegating authority involves balancing the advantages and disadvantages of decentralization.

- Delegating authority creates a chain of command—a graded chain of jobs that vary by degrees of decision-making authority. Generally the chain of command should be the official channel for all manangement directives and communicatives. Moreover, it should be "unbroken" from top to bottom in the sense that each individual reports to one, and only one, boss.

- The three organizing parts—jobs, departments, and authority—can be combined in a variety of structural configurations. Differences in organization structures are the result of differences in the three parts: jobs can be more or less specialized; departments can be more or less homogenous; authority can be more or less centralized.

- Differences in organization structures can be described by noting differences in the *dimensions* of structure. It has become customary to use three dimensions to describe differences in structure: *(a)* complexity, *(b)* formalization, and *(c)* centralization.

■   Complexity refers to degree of specialization; formalization refers to degree of written rules, procedures, and policies; centralization refers to degree of delegation of authority. Although there are unusual cases, the usual situation is for organizations to tend to be either complex, formal, and centralized or simple, informal, and decentralized. These two extremes are the basic models of organization design.

DISCUSSION AND REVIEW QUESTIONS

1.   What general objectives do managers attempt to achieve through the organizing function? How do they know whether the objectives are in fact achieved?

2.   Describe an organization to which you belong, in terms of division of tasks, departmentalization, and delegation of authority.

3.   Identify the bases for departmentalization in the college where you are enrolled. What alternative bases could be used? And what would be the relative advantages of each alternative?

4.   What would be some of the symptoms of problems that could be caused by a malfunctioning organization structure?

5.   What are the appropriate terms to be used in describing individual jobs? Should depth and scope be the terms used? Or should variety, task identity, task significance, autonomy, and feedback be used?

6.   What are the important factors to be taken into account when determining the optimal span of control for a particular manager? Explain how you could develop a single scale that would recognize the relative importance of each factor.

7.   Obtain information regarding the spans of control of the chairpersons in the college you attend. Chances are, no two chairpersons will have the same span of control. What accounts for these differences? Should the differences exist?

8.   Using the same set of departmental heads studied above, determine the degree of decentralization of authority by documenting the decisions that each can make without checking first with the dean (or other appropriate official). Then determine whether some have more or less authority in comparison to their peers. What accounts for differences in authority among chairpersons?

9.   Explain how the idea of an unbroken chain of command is created by the process of delegating authority.

10.   Can all the causes of line-staff conflict be eliminated by explicit definition of authority and responsibility? Explain.

ADDITIONAL REFERENCES

Allen, R. W., and L. W. Porter. *Organizational Influence Processes.* Glenview, Ill.: Scott, Foresman, 1983.

Astley, W. G., and P. S. Sachdeva. "Structural Sources of Intraorganizational Power: A Theoretical Synthesis." *Academy of Management Review,* January 1984, pp. 104–13.

Blackburn, R. S. "Dimensions of Structures: A Review and Reappraisal." *Academy of Management Review,* January 1982, pp. 59–66.

Daft, R. L. *Organization Theory.* St. Paul, Minn.: West Publishing, 1983.

Dalton, D. R., and I. F. Kesner. "Organizational Growth: Big Is Beautiful." *Journal of Business Strategy,* Summer 1985, pp. 38–48.

Miller, D. "Evolution and Revolution: A Quantum View of Structural Change in Organizations." *Journal of Management Studies,* April 1982, pp. 131–51.

Miners, H. "How Staff Jobs Weaken Line Management." *Management Today.* June 1982, pp. 33–35.

Mintzberg, H. *Structure Fives: Designing Effective Organizations.* Englewood Cliffs, N.J.: Prentice-Hall, 1983.

Nystrom, P. C., and W. H. Starbuck. *Handbook of Organizational Design,* vols. 1 and 2. New York: Oxford University Press, 1983.

Pavett, C. M., and A. W. Lau. "Managerial Work: The Influence of Hierarchical Level and Functional Specialty." *Academy of Management Journal,* March 1983, pp. 170–77.

Perkins, D. N. T.; V. F. Nieva; and E. E. Lawler III. *Managing Creation: The Challenge of Building a New Organization.* New York: John Wiley & Sons, 1983.

Tosi, H. L. *Theories of Organization.* New York: John Wiley & Sons, 1984.

CASES

APPLICATION I

ORGANIZATION STRUCTURE OF SAXE REALTY COMPANY

Saxe Realty Company, Inc., located in the San Francisco Bay area, was founded in 1938 by Jules and Marion Saxe. For most of its history, the company was a single-office agency run by its founders. But over time, the company grew in size and sales revenue, which increased from $1 million in 1973 to over $10 million in 1979. Rather than a single office, the company had six branches located in the San Francisco and Marin County area.

The firm grew for many reasons. An important reason was the founders' ability to do certain things very well. They knew how to select locations, time moves, and design offices. They recruited and hired people with above-average ability and trained them to be effective salespersons. The rewards of growth were enjoyed by the Saxe family and employees of their firm.

But with growth came problems stemming from the mismatch between the firm's organization structure, management practices, and the requirements of a large firm compared to a small one. In the early days, Saxe Realty could handle its business matters in simple and informal ways. After all, it was a family corporation, and family members ran it as a family, not as a business.

Some of the problems that surfaced with growth included the absence of clearly defined roles and areas of responsibility. People were in jobs because of family relationships rather than skills. Important decisions were made by relatively few people, who often did not have knowledge of all available information. The firm, moreover, had no strategic plan. It responded and reacted to opportunities rather than being proactive. In a sense, the firm's success had simply outgrown its organization.

Saxe consequently had to make many changes in its operations and organization structure, the overriding goal being to move Saxe away from an entrepreneurial-style firm to a professionally managed one. The change itself involved a process of preparation and implementation. Significant changes do not just come about; they must be planned and managed. But only the end results of the change are of interest here.

The organization structure that Saxe adopted relies upon geography as the basis for departmentalization. There is a central office, and the branch offices report to it. Geographic departmentalization encourages decentralization, one of the outcomes sought by Saxe's top management. Branch managers are responsible for the day-to-day activities of their offices. The central office maintains overall direction through planning and controlling processes. For example, all branch offices participate in the annual planning process, during which objectives for each branch are developed. These objectives are then the targets and the responsibility of branch managers.

Saxe's top management developed formal descriptions for all key positions, defining the responsibilities of each job with special attention to avoiding overlap and duplication of effort. The company's experience during its entrepreneurial stage was that things were often left undone because everyone assumed that someone else was doing them. In other instances, several people would assume responsibility for a task when it required the attention of only one person. A key consideration in the new organization structure was to define explicitly and formally the work expected from each individual job.

The new structure provides for reporting channels from each branch associate to the chief executive officer. The chain of command is the channel for progress reports on planned objectives, financial and sales reports, and other informational needs. In comparison to the previous organization, the chain of command is much more explicit and formal. Individuals are encouraged to go through channels.

The entire change at Saxe has been both extensive and time consuming. Nearly every aspect of the firm's operations has been affected. And the changes took two years or more to fully implement.

Questions for Analysis

1. Draw an organization chart that depicts the structure being implemented at Saxe.
2. What alternative structures could Saxe have implemented, and what would be the advantages of each in comparison to the one Saxe did implement?
3. What are the relationships between the planning function and the organizing function as depicted in the Saxe case?

APPLICATION II

IVY UNIVERSITY—EVENING BUSINESS PROGRAM*

Dr. John Sherman, the undergraduate coordinator for the evening business program, finished his brief letter of resignation. He had served as coordinator for two years, his first two at Ivy University. He contemplated the fact that no one else would want the position, but he had paid his dues. The work was important to the university, but he had experienced endless frustration in trying to staff and schedule the evening class program. In his view, some new faculty member could take it on, and he could devote more time to his research and teaching.

Ivy University, a small, private, suburban university, started the evening program with only modest enrollment and course offerings. Full-time faculty were encouraged to teach and given some additional compensation for each course on an extra-load basis. Usually, the lower-paid junior faculty accepted the additional courses. The university also ran a reasonably successful evening M.B.A. program as a complement to a small, day (full-time) M.B.A. program. Enrollment in both programs has grown over the years, and staffing of the evening courses has become a considerable chore, particularly with the undergraduate offerings. The regular faculty preferred to teach the evening M.B.A. courses rather than other evening courses.

Dr. Sherman utilized a large number of adjunct (part-time) faculty for the 15 courses offered each term in the evening. Adjunct faculty usually consisted of area residents with "appropriate" educational and experiential credentials, as well as doctoral students from a nearby university. While some adjuncts had taught for several years, most would teach for only one or two terms. Thus, a number of new adjuncts had to be recruited each year. Pay for the instructors amounted to a per-course stipend well below

---

* Source: Case written by Dr. Gail L. Miller, Westminster College, New Wilmington, Pennsylvania. Used with permission.

what a full-time faculty member would receive. Because of the usual financial uncertainties facing the university, the administration was very insistent on continuing this policy. As a coordinator, Sherman had teaching responsibilities in his field of expertise (finance), and he received a lighter teaching load. As with other members of the Department of Business, his "immediate" supervisor was the departmental chairperson. Each of the college's two other departments, Accounting and Economics, also had an undergraduate evening coordinator. However, very few courses were offered from those subject areas. The department heads were responsible to the dean of the College of Business.

The actual advising and enrolling of evening students was carried out through the Evening Programs Office, and Sherman would consult with the director periodically. This office was separate from the College of Business and scheduled programs from other colleges within the university, such as Nursing, Education, and a few from the Arts and Sciences' College. The dean of the College of Business had given Sherman considerable latitude in determining the course offerings and in working with the Evening Programs Office in establishing the schedule. The other coordinators worked with this office as well. However, the evening M.B.A. program was handled by the College of Business. Minor problems arose, naturally, but student and administrative complaints about the program had intensified lately. Administrative concerns were voiced over the following:

Heavy dropout and low continuation in a particular instructor's accounting sequence.

Reports that two faculty members hired by Sherman did not have the minimum educational credential required by the university.

Concern by the dean over salary levels established by Sherman in negotiations with adjunct faculty.

An immediate response to an incident to be described later.

Student concerns ranged from excessive absences of certain instructors to complaints on instructor availability and advising. Surprisingly, Sherman did not hear many complaints about the quality of instruction. But his reponsibility resided more with staffing the evening program and teaching his load of day courses. Sherman also felt that because of the low pay and the need for instructors, the department should not bother adjunct faculty with evaluations, meetings, or other reports required of full-time faculty. The evening M.B.A. program, in contrast, had fewer complaints. Regular faculty and the dean usually taught one or two night courses per year, and seldom were outside faculty employed. Most regular faculty, at times, expressed concern over the "low quality" of the undergraduate evening program and were reluctant to allocate departmental money to it—if they were able to make such judgments.

Because of an unfortunate incident, the dean announced that stronger controls must be placed on the operation of the evening program immediately, and Dr. Sherman was to propose them by the end of the week. Apparently, a daughter of one of the university's trustees complained about the casual teaching attitude exhibited by an instructor and discussed this with her father. To the extent that Dr. Sherman could recall, no previous complaints had been lodged concerning this faculty member, who was one of the longer-term adjunct faculty.

Sherman, while feeling some responsibility to the program, knew that his resignation of the coordinator position would have little impact on his evaluation, since his publication record was better than his peers'. And, he had served longer than the two previous coordinators, one of whom now serves as the M.B.A. coordinator.

Questions for Analysis

1. Is there a problem that requires reorganization?
2. What would be your recommendations? Explain.
3. How would you implement your recommendations?

EXPERIENTIAL EXERCISE

DESIGNING THE NEW VENTURE

Purpose

The purpose of this exercise is to provide students with first-hand experience in organizing a new business venture.

The Exercise in Class

A few years ago, George Ballas got so frustrated trying to keep his lawn neatly trimmed around the roots of oak trees that he developed what is now called the Weed Eater. The original Weed Eater was made from a popcorn can that had holes in it and was threaded with nylon fishing line. Weed Eater sales in 1972 totaled $568,000; but by 1978, sales were in excess of $100 million. There are now 20 or so similar devices on the market.

Two brothers from Pittsburgh, George and Jim Gammons, are starting a new venture called Lawn Trimmers, Inc. They are attempting to develop an organization that makes a profit by selling Lawn Trimmers that do not wear out for over 2,000 trimming applications. The Weed Eater and similar products often have breaks in the nylon lines that require the user to turn off the trimmer and readjust the line. The Gammons have developed a new type of cutting fabric that is not physically harmful and cuts for over 2,000 applications.

In order to sell the Lawn Trimmers, the Gammons brothers will have to market their products through retail establishments. They will make the products in their shop in Pittsburgh and ship them to the retail establishments. The profits will come entirely from the sales of the Lawn Trimmers to retail establishments. The price of the product is already set, and it appears that there will be sufficient market demand to sell at least 6,000 Lawn Trimmers annually.

1. The instructor will set up teams of five to eight students to serve as organizational design experts who will provide the Gammons brothers with the best structure for their new venture. The groups should meet and establish a design that would be feasible for the Gammons at this stage in their venture.
2. Each group should select a spokesperson to make a short presentation of the group's organizational design for the Gammons.
3. The class should compare the various designs and discuss why there are similarities and differences in what is presented.

The Learning Message

This exercise will show that organizational design necessitates making assumptions about the market, competition, labor resources, scheduling, and profit margins, to name just a few areas. There is no one best design that should be regarded as a final answer.

DESIGNING THE ORGANIZATION

LEARNING OBJECTIVES

After completing Chapter 7, you should be able to:

■ **Define**
organization design in terms of the universalistic and contingency viewpoints.

■ **Describe**
the implications of technology, environmental uncertainty, and strategy for the design of organization structure.

■ **Discuss**
the fundamental differences between classical and neoclassical organization design.

■ **Compare**
the alternative arguments that conclude there is no "one best" organization design.

■ **Identify**
criticisms of the universalistic viewpoints made by those who support the contingency viewpoint.

■ MANAGEMENT IN ACTION

McDonald's: The Design Story*

McDonald's Corporation, a giant selling billions of hamburgers, has experienced a history of growth and profits. In spite of its huge size, McDonald's success is based on product consistency and uniformity. A customer can also expect the same level of quality from one purchase to the next at the local McDonald's store.

To achieve this uniformity, each store must be stamped from the same mold. McDonald's mold was designed and maintained through the use of an extensive bureaucracy. The company has taken advantage of size and bureaucracy without succumbing to organizational rigidity or employee dissatisfaction.

Rules and regulations are the gospel at McDonald's. The company's operating manual has 385 pages describing the most minute activities in each outlet. The manual prescribes that certain equipment—cigarette, candy, and pinball machines—is not permitted in the stores. It also prescribes strict standards for personal grooming. Men must keep their hair short and their shoes black and highly polished. Women are expected to wear hair nets and to use only very light makeup. The store manager is even provided with a maintenance reminder for each day of the year, such as "Lubricate and adjust potato-peeler belt."

McDonald's uses a well-defined hierarchy. Field service managers visit each store regularly. An inspector will observe each store for three days, timing the counter and drive-through operations, and checking cooking procedures. Grades of A through F are given for cleanliness, quality, and service.

Each store has a refined division of labor and qualified personnel. Assistant managers are assigned to cover each shift, and crew leaders are responsible for specific periods, such as breakfast or lunch. Cooks and waitresses know exactly what to do. Trainers teach new employees the exact procedure for greeting customers and taking orders. Hostesses are assigned the task of helping young children and old people, and they coordinate birthday parties and make sure customers are comfortable.

McDonald's uses the bureaucratic design approach that will be presented in more detail in the chapter. In McDonald's case, bureaucracy is not associated with the negative consequences often portrayed in discussing this form of design.

---

* Source: Robert Levering, Milton Moskowitz, and Michael Katz, *The 100 Best Companies to Work For in America* (Reading, Mass: Addison-Wesley Publishing, 1984), pp. 365–66; Richard L. Daft, *Organization Theory and Design* (St. Paul, Minn.: West Publishing, 1986), pp. 177–78.

By 1980, top managers at General Motors knew that the organizational structure that had served them so well for years had to be changed. Increased foreign competition, the fuel crunch, the recession, poor-quality problems with faulty brakes, diesel engine problems, and front-wheel-drive delays were all major concerns. As a result of problems and environmental conditions, General Motors embarked on the most extensive structure redesign ever undertaken. The plan was based on previous experiences, anticipated market conditions, and present-day knowledge about how to structure an organization. In this chapter, the choices made by management to change structure will be introduced.

Contemporary organization design theory can be divided into two categories. One is based upon the premise that there is one "best way" to design an organization *regardless of the situation.* This is termed the *universalistic* approach. The second category states that the best way to organize *depends upon the situation.* This category is termed the *contingency* approach. Within these two categories, however, are differences of opinion. Disagreements occur over what precisely is the one best way to organize and over which factors in a situation must be taken into account.

UNIVERSALISTIC APPROACH

In reality, there is no universal design. Instead, two quite different designs have been proposed by researchers and practitioners. They are the *classical design* and the *neoclassical design.*

Classical Organization Design

The characteristics of classical organization design include high complexity, high formalization, and high centralization. The arguments that support classical design have been very influential in the development of modern management theory.

The writers of the scientific management and classical approaches to management made forceful cases for the superiority of classical organization design over any alternative design. They reasoned that classical design is a natural extension of specialization of labor to the organizational level.

Organization structures with high levels of complexity (e.g., the number of activities or subsystems within the organization), formalization (e.g., the extent to which rules, procedures, and instructions are written), and centralization (e.g., the hierarchal level that has authority to make a decision) reflect the assumption that *the design of jobs determines the design of organizations.* Figure 7–1 diagrams this assumption and its consequences.

The use of classical designs in organization structure was widespread during the late 1800s, when industrialization of Western civilization was at its height.

FIGURE   7–1   The Classical Design Assumption

Classical design theory assumes that job design is the principal determinant of organization design.

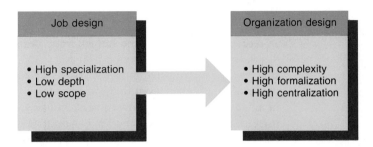

A primary social and managerial concern was efficient use of resources with maximum production. Out of these times came two different yet compatible sets of ideas. One set, put forth by German political economist Max Weber, has come to be associated with *bureaucracy* as an ideal type of organization. The other set of ideas have come to be associated with the classical approach.

Bureaucratic-approach to organization design.   Bureaucracy refers to the form of organization first described in the literature of public administration as government by bureaus—that is, unelected civil servants. Bureaucracy usually is associated with the negative consequences of large organizations, such as red tape, unexplained delays, and general frustrations. However, the term also describes an organizational design that its proponents believed to be "superior to any other form in precision, in stability, in the stringency of its discipline, and its reliability. It thus makes possible a high degree of measurement of results for the heads of the organization and for those acting in relation to it."[1]

The characteristics of a bureaucracy are:

1. It has a clear division of labor, with each job well defined, understood, and routine.
2. Each manager has a clearly defined relationship with other managers and subordinates through a formal hierarchy.
3. Each employee relies on specific rules, policies, and procedures to guide behaviors.
4. Favoritism is minimized through the impersonal application of rules, policies, discipline, and rewards.
5. Rigid and equitable selection criteria are used to hire candidates for vacant jobs.

---

[1] Max Weber, *The Theory of Social and Economic Organization,* trans. A. M. Henderson and Talcott Parsons (New York: Oxford University Press, 1947), p. 334.

An organization structure high in each of these five characteristics is an ideal type of bureaucracy. That is, such an organization would be ideally suited to achieving efficient results. An organization that scores low on any one or all of these characteristics would be less than ideal and, therefore, less efficient than it could be.

According to Weber, the bureaucratic design compares to other designs "as does the machine with nonmechanical modes of production,"[2] a conclusion based on extensive analyses of the Prussian civil service and military organizations. He believed that the advantages of bureaucracy were applicable in any context, whether government, military, or business. The bureaucratic organization approach provides a workable set of guidelines. A manager can design and redesign structures by comparing the proposed (or actual) bureaucracy with the ideal type.

Classical approach to organization design.   The classical approach to organization design, developed in the early 1900s, proposes that managers designing organization structures should be guided by certain *principles of organization.*[3] Managers following these principles can design a *classical* type of organization structure.

The important principles of organization in the classical approach are:

1. *Division of labor.* Work should be divided and subdivided to the highest possible degree consistent with economic efficiency.
2. *Unity of direction.* Jobs should be grouped according to function or process, and jobs that are alike should be grouped in departments.
3. *Centralization of authority.* Accountability for the use of authority is retained at the executive, or top management, level.
4. *Authority and responsibility.* A jobholder must have authority commensurate with job responsibility.
5. *Unity of command.* Each jobholder should report to one, and only one, superior.

Applying these principles creates organizations where jobs are highly specialized, departments are based upon function and process, spans of control are narrow, and authority is centralized. Such organizations tend to be relatively "tall," with several layers of management through which communications and directions must pass. Together the bureaucratic and classical design theories describe the essential features of classical organization design.

---

[2] Max Weber, *From Max Weber: Essays in Sociology,* trans. H. H. Gerth and C. W. Mills (New York: Oxford University Press, 1946), p. 214.

[3] For the original statement of classical principles, see Henri Fayol, *General and Industrial Management,* trans. C. Storrs (London: Pitman Publishing, 1949). pp. 19–42.

Characteristics common to classical and bureaucratic approaches. The five classical principles are comparable to the five bureaucratic characteristics. Each set of guidelines stresses specialization of labor and centralized authority. Each attempts to design a structure of jobs that minimizes the impact of those who hold the jobs.

Proponents of classical organization design stress the importance of achieving predictable, reliable human behavior. The effects of high complexity, formalization, and centralization include not only predictable human behavior but high levels of efficiency and productivity as well.

An example of a classical approach is illustrated in the Management Focus on United Parcel's organization design.

MANAGEMENT FOCUS
Organization Design at United Parcel

United Parcel Service (UPS) is in direct competition with the U.S. Postal Service in the delivery of small packages. Even though the postal service is subsidized and pays no taxes, UPS has been able to compete successfully by stressing efficiency of operations. It apparently achieves great efficiencies through a combination of automation and organizational design.

Specialization and formalization are highly visible characteristics of the UPS structure, making use of clearly defined jobs and an explicit chain of command. Jobs are arranged in a hierarchy of authority consisting of eight managerial levels. The high degree of specialization enables management to use many forms of written reports such as daily worksheets that record each employee's work quotas and performance. Company policies and practices are in written form and are routinely consulted in hiring and promotion decisions. Apparently UPS has found that a classical organization design is well suited to its purposes.

Source: Richard L. Daft, *Organization Theory and Design* (St. Paul, Minn.: West Publishing, 1983), pp. 126–27.

Neoclassical Organization

In a historical sense, neoclassical organization design is a reaction to classical design. Its characterics include low complexity, low formalization, and

---

FIGURE   7–2   The Neoclassical Design Assumptions

Neoclassical design theory assumes that individual differences and situational characteristics are the principal determinants of organizational design.

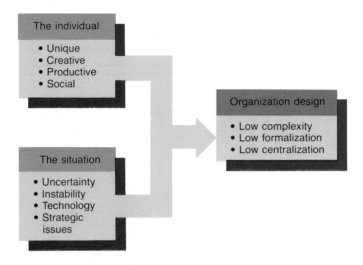

low centralization. These characteristics describe organization structures in which jobs are relatively despecialized, departments contain a heterogeneous mix of jobs, spans of control are wide, and authority is decentralized. Thus, neoclassical design can be viewed as the opposite of classical design.

The arguments supporting neoclassical design are based on two assumptions: (1) The uniqueness of individuals cannot be ignored. (2) The demands of situations cannot be ignored. Figure 7–2 outlines the neoclassical approach to organization design.

The uniqueness of individuals.   Individuals' impact on and importance to organization design were first noted in the famous Hawthorne studies, a series of experiments carried out at the Hawthorne Western Electric plant in Cicero, Illinois. These studies served as the basis for the contention that high specialization of labor and centralized authority underestimate the capabilities of employees. Rather than being passive and inert beings who dumbly perform assigned tasks, employees are unique, multifaceted persons seeking more than monetary rewards from work. The researchers at the Hawthorne plant found that workers were members of friendship groups and that these groups defined the level of output considered fair and equitable. The groups seemed to exert far greater influence on employees than their managers did, even though the groups had no authority to back up their influence.

Subsequent studies have supported the Hawthorne findings that classical organization design contains inherent flaws. For example, a very early study analyzed the relationship between rules and job behavior.[4] The results show that the extensive use of rules encourages the individual to follow rules in robot-like fashion. Such behavior eventually leads to confusion and uncertainty because rules cannot cover all circumstances. A later study supported the idea that rules define minimum levels of expectations and that extensive use of rules discourages innovative behavior.[5]

Chris Argyris, an early proponent of neoclassical ideas, believes that classical design suppresses the development and growth of employees.[6] In his view, domination through the use of formal rules and centralized authority can cause subordinates to become passive, dependent, and noncreative. Such conditions are not congruent with the human needs for autonomy, self-expression, accomplishment, and advancement. Consequently the organization forfeits a considerable portion of its human resources through the use of classical design.

The demands of situations.   The assumption that the situation makes a difference is based on considerable research. As noted earlier, classical designs gained in popularity during the early periods of industrialization and economic development (the late 1800s and early 1900s). That period of relative stability and predictable change, however, eventually gave way to one of instability and uncertainty. Today, advanced technology in communications, transportation, manufacturing processes, and medicine creates the necessity for organizations to be *adaptable* and *flexible* so that new ways of doing work can be quickly utilized.

A leading advocate of neoclassical design is Rensis Likert.[7] After considerable study, he proposed that in contemporary society, neoclassical organizations utilize human and technical resources more fully than those with classical design. Because neoclassical design emphasizes the importance of decentralized authority, nondirective and participative management behavior is encouraged. Relatively wide spans of control and heterogeneous departments facilitate the interaction of multiple and diverse points of view. Consequently, as circumstance and technology change, the organization is able to respond because of the diverse perspectives that can be brought to bear on any issue or problem it confronts.

---

[4] Robert K. Merton, "Bureaucratic Structure and Personality," *Social Forces* 18 (1940), pp. 560–68.

[5] Alvin W. Gouldner, *Patterns of Industrial Bureaucracy* (New York: Free Press, 1954).

[6] Chris Argyris, *Personality and Organization* (New York: Harper & Row, 1975); Chris Argyris, "Personality and Organization Revisited," *Administrative Science Quarterly,* 1973, pp. 141–67.

[7] Two classic works are Rensis Likert, *New Patterns of Management* (New York: McGraw-Hill, 1961); Rensis Likert, *The Human Organization* (New York: McGraw-Hill, 1967).

Ardent proponents of neoclassical design believe that even if the organization exists in a relatively stable environment, the neoclassical way is best. They contend that individuals have fuller and more satisfying worklives in neoclassical organizations and that neoclassical organization design is *universally applicable* and the best way to organize in modern society. Therefore, it is the superior alternative to classical design.

CONTINGENCY ORGANIZATION DESIGN

An important alternative point of view, termed the *contingency approach,* is that either classical or neoclassical can be the best way to organize, depending upon the nature of underlying factors such as the organization's strategy, environment, and technology. This approach to organization design is based on the idea that different organization designs facilitate different purposes.[8] Classical organizations are somewhat more efficient and productive but somewhat less adaptive and flexible than neoclassical organizations.

A particular organization—whether it is a business firm, government agency, hospital, university, or one unit within an organization—should be structured on the basis of whether it must be (1) relatively efficient and productive—best suited for classical design—or (2) adaptive and flexible, making it more suited to neoclassical design. The critical issue is to determine the circumstances that create the need to be relatively efficient and productive or adaptive and flexible.

Researchers and practitioners who have contributed to the ideas of contingency design have suggested a number of circumstances, or variables, that influence the design decision. Among these variables are age of the organization, size of the organization, form of ownership, technology, environmental uncertainty, strategic choice, member (employee) needs, and current fashion.[9] There is evidence that older organizations are more complex, formalized, and centralized than newer ones. Also, researchers have noted the tendency of large organizations to be designed more along classical than neoclassical lines. No attempt will be made here to discuss all the evidence related to each of these variables. Rather, the three variables with the most important implications for management are analyzed: technology, environment, and strategic choice.

---

[8] W. Alan Randolph and Gregory G. Dess, "The Congruence Perspective of Organizational Design: A Conceptual Model and Multivariate Research Approach," *Academy of Management Review,* January 1984, pp. 114–27.

[9] Jeffrey D. Ford and W. Harvey Hegarty, "Decision Makers' Beliefs about the Causes and Effects of Structure," *Academy of Management Journal,* June 1984, pp. 271–91; Louis W. Fry and John W. Slocum, Jr., "Technology, Structure, and Workgroup Effectiveness: A Test of a Contingency Model," *Academy of Management Journal,* June 1984, pp. 221–46.

FIGURE   7–3   Technology and Organization Design

Technology affects organization design through its impact on job design.

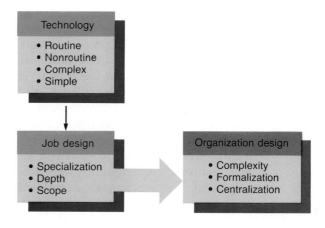

Technology

Technology is often defined as the processes employed by manufacturing firms to convert inputs into outputs. In a broader sense, it can be thought of as all of the equipment, material, knowledge, and experience used to perform tasks in an organization. Using this broader view, it is easy to see that any kind of work—making cars, shoes, or computers or serving clients, patients, customers, or students—involves technology. The technology can be either machines or knowledge.

The role of technology as a contingency variable is shown in Figure 7–3. Technology affects the design of jobs, and these in turn affect the design of organizations.[10] Organization design, then, is contingent upon the state of technology that management incorporates in the design of individual jobs.

Interest in the relationship between technology and structure was originally stimulated by the studies of Joan Woodward.[11] In one study, Woodward classified technologies as unit, mass, or process production. *Unit production* refers to production to meet a customer's specific order. Here, the product is developed after an order is received. The manufacture of custom-made

[10] Nancy M. Carter, "Computerization as a Predominate Technology: Its Influence on the Structure of Newspaper Organizations," *Academy of Management Journal,* June 1984, pp. 247–70; J. Child, "New Technology and Developments in Management Organization," *Omega,* no. 3 (1984), pp. 203–10; Gareth Jones, "Task Visibility, Free Riding and Shirking: Explaining the Effect of Structure and Technology on Employee Behavior," *Academy of Management Review,* October 1984, pp. 684–95.

[11] Joan Woodward, *Industrial Organization: Theory and Practice* (London: Oxford University Press, 1965).

shirts is an example of unit-production technology. *Mass production* refers to the production of large quantities, such as on an assembly line. Zenith Corporation uses mass-production technology to make television picture tubes. *Process production* refers to producing materials or goods on the basis of weight or volume. Processing 3 million barrels of oil or producing vats of paint are examples of process production.

Woodward found a strong relationship between performance and both organizational design and technology. The highest-performing organizations with unit and process technologies used neoclassical design. However, the highest-performing organizations with mass-production technologies used a classical design. These findings are summarized in Figures 7–4 and 7–5. The effects of unit and process manufacturing technology are jobs with low specialization, high depth, and scope. These jobs are best organized in a structure with relatively low complexity, formalization, and centralization. The rationale is that employees must have considerable latitude, discretion, and freedom of choice in the use of such technologies. Mass production, on the other hand, requires little latitude on the part of employees.

Woodward's findings are evidence that managers need to consider the effects of technology on organization design. She encouraged managers to consider the role that technology plays in influencing work behavior and to recognize that appropriate design decisions require consideration of technological complexities.

Three principles that resulted from Woodward's research suggest how technology influences organizational design:

1. The more complex the technology—going from a unit system to a process system—the greater the number of managerial personnel and levels of management.

FIGURE   7–4   Unit and Process Technology and Organization Design

Complex technology (unit and process) requires complex jobs that must be managed through neoclassical organization designs.

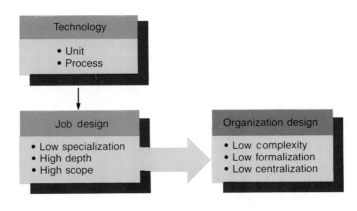

FIGURE   7–5   Mass-Production Technology and Organization Design

Simple technology (mass) requires simple jobs that must be managed through classical organization designs.

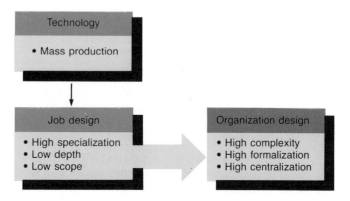

2. The more complex the technology, the larger the number of clerical and administrative personnel.
3. The span of control of first-line managers increases from unit-production systems to mass-production systems and then decreases from mass-production systems to process-production systems.

Successful firms in each technology category seem to employ the design characteristics suggested by these three principles. The idea that an organization design must be compatible with the technology it uses to achieve optimal performance is termed organization "fit." An effective organization fits its technological requirements.

It is intuitively appealing to expect that routine technology (such as mass-production techniques) is most efficiently used in organizations adhering to classical design. Likewise, nonroutine technology (such as unit and process techniques) should be compatible with neoclassical organization design. Yet, to demonstrate the validity of what seems obvious is often a difficult task. Woodward's research stimulated a great number of follow-up studies examining the relationship between technology and structure in a variety of settings. The researchers have used a variety of definitions and measurements; therefore, their findings are inconsistent.

The problem of verifying the exact relationship has been complicated by inconsistency (1) in definition and measurement of the two key concepts—technology and structure—and (2) in selecting the level of analysis—individual, group, and organizational. Details of these rather technical issues are beyond the scope of this discussion, but it is important to acknowledge that conclusions drawn from one survey of the technology-structure literature agree with the expectations mentioned above. Louis W. Fry contends that routine technology (mass production, assembly lines for example) is associated with classical design, while nonroutine technology (unit, small batch, and process) is associated with neoclassical design.[12]

Environment

Every organization must operate within an environment. There are competitors, suppliers, customers, creditors, and the government, each making demands on the organization. Any of these external forces can have a significant effect on the organization's design.

The environment can be *stable*—one in which there is little unpredictable change and customer tastes remain relatively steady. New technology is rare, and the need for innovative research to stay ahead of competition is minimal. There has been little change in the environments affecting the manufacturers of such items as accordions, zippers, and book covers.

In a *changing* environment, however, there are changes in the competition's strategy, market demands, advertising, personnel practices, and technology. The changes are usually frequent and expected. Automobile manufacturers operate in a changing environment.

A *turbulent* environment exists when changes are unexpected and unpredictable. New competitive strategies, new laws, and new technology can create a turbulent condition. Electronic firms such as IBM, Hewlett-Packard, and Honeywell face unexpected environmental forces.

Matching an organizational design to the environment requires accurate managerial assessment of the environmental forces. Over 20 years ago, a British group interested in organizational design studied 20 English and Scottish firms and concluded that two types of organizational systems exist. These were labeled *mechanistic* and *organic.*[13] Mechanistic structures have the same characteristics as classical designs; organic structures have the characteristics of neoclassical designs.

The group concluded that classical designs are optimal in stable environments and neoclassical designs are most suited to turbulent environments. The relationship between environmental characteristics and organization design is summarized in Figure 7–6. Employees of organizations that deal in stable and placid environments will not confront unexpected events. Consequently their jobs can be designed to include minimal depth and scope and maximum specialization. But changing, turbulent environments create unexpected events and circumstances that cannot be anticipated. Jobs must be designed that give employees considerable scope and depth. The compatible

[12] Louis W. Fry, "Technology-Structure Research: Three Critical Issues," *Academy of Management Journal,* September 1982, pp. 532–52.

[13] Tom Burns and G. M. Stalker, *The Management of Innovation* (London: Tavistock Publications, 1961).

FIGURE   7–6   Environmental Characteristics and Organization Design

---

Environmental characteristics affect organization design through their impact on job design.

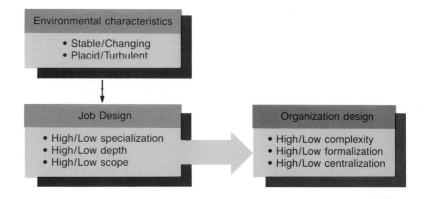

organization design for such jobs is one with low complexity, formalism, and centralization—neoclassical design. Organizations need to align their structures with their environments.

Following the lead of the English study group, an American team studied 10 companies in three industries: plastics, consumer foods, and standardized containers. The team was concerned about how to design departments in organizations faced with distinct environments.[14] Unlike other analysts of organization design, they believed that the organization design decision could be made less complicated if managers considered it in terms of parts of the organization.

Designing organizational subunits.   The American team proposed that organizations should be designed with an emphasis on the different subunits, or departments, of the organization. Those departments facing highly uncertain and turbulent environments should follow neoclassical design prescriptions; they should be relatively despecialized, informal, and decentralized. On the other hand, a department facing certain and predictable environments should follow classical design ideas and be specialized, formalized, and centralized. The contingency viewpoint is reflected in the researchers' conclusion that "the internal functioning of organizations must be consistent with the organization task, technology, external environment, and the needs of its members if the organization is to be effective."[15]

---

[14] Paul R. Lawrence and Jay W. Lorsch, *Organization and Environment* (Homewood, Ill.: Richard D. Irwin, 1967). Also see Paul R. Lawrence, "The Harvard Organization and Environment Research Program," in *Perspectives on Organization Design and Behavior,* ed. Andrew H. Van de Van and William Joyce (New York: John Wiley & Sons, 1981), pp. 311–37.

[15] Ibid., p. 85.

The impact of the environment at the overall organizational level is shown in Figure 7–6. The environmental effect holds true at the subunit, or departmental, level as well. Environmental characteristics such as uncertainty, change, turbulence, and volatility affect the design of organizational subunits by defining the characteristics of the jobs.[16] The managerial implications of this effect include having a diverse range of organizational designs among departments within the same organization.

For example, a manufacturing firm typically must deal with three critical subenvironments, one of which is the *market* for its products. This subenvironment is the source of pressure to compete for customers through pricing, promotion, product development, and other marketing activities. The dominant characteristic of the market subenvironment can range from highly uncertain to highly certain. The degree of certainty would be influenced by (1) the reliability of available information on customer preferences and competitors' actions and (2) the rate of change in those preferences and actions. A relatively certain market subenvironment is one for which reliable information exists regarding stable customer preferences and competitors' actions. An uncertain market subenvironment is the opposite: unreliable information and changing preferences and actions. Firms in plastics and computer manufacturing face relatively uncertain market subenvironments. Public utilities and container manufacturers face relatively certain market environments.

The environmental-contingency model specifies that the organization design of departments "fit" the demands of the department's subenvironment.[17] Accordingly, the organization design of the marketing departments facing uncertain environments would take on characteristics of the neoclassical approach. Those facing certain environments would organize according to the classical approach.

Most manufacturing firms face two other important subenvironments in addition to the market subenvironment. The *technical-economic subenvironment* refers to the external sources of information and resources required in the production of the firm's product. This subenvironment can be certain or uncertain depending upon knowledge and rates of change in the technology of production and sources, types, and supplies of human, physical, and natural resources. Production departments must be organized to reflect the state of this subenvironment.

---

[16] For example, see J. Daniel Sherman and Howard L. Smith, "The Influence of Organizational Structure on Intrinsic versus Extrinsic Motivation," *Academy of Management Journal,* December 1984, pp. 877–84.

[17] For related research in a nonbusiness setting, see G. H. Gaertner, K. N. Gaertner, and D. M. Akinnusi, "Environment, Strategy, and the Implementation of Strategic Change: The Case of Civil Service Reform," *Academy of Management Journal,* September 1984, pp. 525–43.

The other key subenvironment is the *scientific* knowledge that firms use in their research and development departments. Research and development units are typically closer to neoclassical structures than are any other department, because of the relatively high degree of uncertainty in the scientific subenvironment compared to market and technical-economic subenvironments. After all, the fundamental characteristic of research is to reveal the unknown. But in some industries, the scientific subenvironment can be relatively stable and certain in comparison to those of other industries. For example, the container industry's scientific subenvironment is far less uncertain than the personal-computer industry's.

The process of designing organization structure on a department-by-department basis can result in considerable diversity of designs within the same organization. The environmental perspective emphasizes fitting departments to subenvironments, then designing methods to coordinate the departments toward organizational objectives. The methods can range from strict applications of rules and procedures to the use of cross-departmental groups and individuals.

An organization with departments predominantly designed along classical lines could achieve interdepartmental coordination through rules, procedures, and policy. But an organization made up of departments designed according to neoclassical guidelines could achieve coordinated effort only through cross-departmental teams and individuals.

Matrix organization design.   Organizations facing environmental uncertainty often cope by using a *matrix* organization design. A matrix design usually is a classical organization design that adopts some features of a neoclassical design. Matrix designs are found in organizations that need both high efficiency and high responsiveness to environmental changes. They often are found in technical organizations where technical, engineering, scientific, and other specialists are grouped together to work on complex projects.[18] The projects may be long run or short run, with the needed specialists being borrowed from various departments of the organization. The critical point is that a rapid response to a changed circumstance is required.

Assume an organization has just found out that its competition has introduced a new product far superior to the company's products. Management considers it critical that the firm respond immediately with a similar or better product; otherwise the firm will suffer irreversible adverse consequences. It has formed a new-product development team whose sole responsibility is to develop this product.

---

[18] W. C. Wall, Jr., "Integrated Management in Matrix Organization," *IEEE Transactions on Engineering Management,* February 1984, pp. 30–36.

FIGURE   7–7   Matrix Organization Design

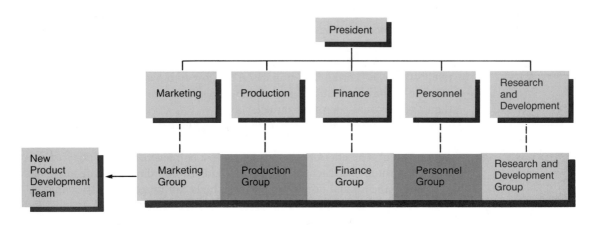

Matrix design attempts to obtain the advantages but not the disadvantages of both the classical and neoclassical designs.

In Figure 7–7, the organization has changed a traditional organizational structure into a matrix organization to facilitate completion of the critical new product. A manager is appointed to head the project and is provided personnel with the necessary skills from each functional area to complete the job. The manager has authority over the personnel assigned to the team and is accountable for their performance. In many cases, when a project is completed, the personnel will return to their respective functional units. In some organizations, especially those in highly skilled industries, there may be several project teams working on different tasks.

In a matrix organization, it is possible for an individual to have two managers. However, proponents believe it provides the flexibility to work on critical projects.[19] Matrix organization brings together the specialized talent that often is necessary to complete a project. It preserves the strengths of the classical design while adding the strengths of the neoclassical design.[20]

Although matrix organization designs are appropriate in some instances,

---

[19] M. H. Wright, Jr., "The Dynamics of Matrix Management," *Manage,* October 1984, pp. 29–32.

[20] See Ralph Katz and Thomas J. Allen, "Project Performance and the Locus of Influence in the R&D Matrix," *Academy of Management Journal,* March 1985, pp. 67–87, for a study that examines the relationship between project performance and the relative influence of project and functional managers in 86 research and development teams in nine technology-based organizations.

they may fail in others. As the Management Focus on Intel illustrates, matrix design loses its appeal once the need for rapid response no longer exists.

MANAGEMENT FOCUS
Intel, No Growth, and Matrix Organization Design

Intel Corporation has been a technology leader in the semiconductor industry. But even an industry that has enjoyed phenomenal success runs into difficulty during periods of economic downturn, and the leading firms in those industries suffer along with the rest. Throughout the 1970s, Intel's sales growth averaged 60 percent per year. Then, when sales plummeted, so did profits. The company began experiencing problems created by the necessity to conserve resources and attain efficiencies. Included in the attempts to achieve greater efficiency were pay cuts and longer working hours. Consequently Intel began to lose key people and to experience lower morale.

The company's organization structure also came under attack. During its period of rapid growth, Intel was organized as a matrix structure. As a result, managers reported to multiple bosses, each of whom provided technical and functional direction. Conflicts often arose, and managers were uncertain whose direction took precedence. One observer stated that the structure had become so complex that people spent more time in meetings than working on projects. One of the questions that Intel's top management was evaluating was whether matrix is an appropriate structure for a firm that has reached the size of Intel and requires greater top management control.

Strategic Choice

As noted in the discussion of the planning function, strategy involves the selection of missions, objectives, and the appropriate courses of action to achieve these objectives. Logically, several courses of action could be identified for any given objective; and for each strategy, an alternative organization design exists. Thus, the specific organization design should follow from a specified strategy. The Management Focus on Porsche reports an example of how a new chief executive changed organization design to implement a new strategy.

MANAGEMENT FOCUS
New Strategy and Structure at Porsche

Porsche makes expensive, high-performance automobiles. It doesn't produce many—less than one 10th as many as BMW and Mercedes-Benz. The company's primary appeal is to the conspicuous-consumption segment of the automobile market. As such, Porsche is especially vulnerable to world attitudes. Conspicuous consumption during economic decline is simply not fashionable.

Against such a backdrop, Peter W. Schutz (an American) took over the presidency of Porsche in the early 1980s. The fact that the company was in financial difficulty was problem enough for Schutz; being an American managing in a conservative German company compounded his challenge.

Schutz began his efforts to revive Porsche by redefining its basic business. In his view, Porsche is not really in the car business but in the leisure-time business. Owners of Porsches substitute them for summer homes, yachts, and other diversions. Schutz encouraged his marketing and promotion managers to develop and communicate the leisure-time theme.

But there were other changes to be made: organizational structure changes. Porsche's organization structure at the time Schutz took over was highly formalized and centralized. The company was unable to react quickly to environmental changes, because communications were stifled. In addition, a production orientation rather than market orientation dominated decision making. Schutz believed the company needed to be "opened up." He began an effort to restructure the company to break down communication barriers among units, to decentralize authority, and to develop a greater awareness of marketing. What Schutz attempted to do was to redesign the organization structure to "fit" the purposes and strategies that he believed were appropriate for Porsche.

Porter's views. An influential writer in the field of corporate strategy, Michael E. Porter states that corporations can adopt one of three general strategies:[21] (1) cost leadership, (2) differentiation, and (3) focus.

Cost leadership implies that the firm will outstrip its competition by being the low-cost producer. The firm will build efficiently scaled facilities, pursue cost control policies, avoid marginal customers, and generally be cost conscious in all areas of the business. In other words, the firm will emphasize

---

[21] Michael E. Porter, *Competitive Strategy* (New York: Free Press, 1980), pp. 34–46.

efficiency and productivity. With lower costs, the firm can afford lower prices. And with lower prices, it can generate large sales volumes. Two firms that have achieved notable success by striving for cost leadership are Briggs & Stratton and Lincoln Electric.

The organization design that facilitates overall cost leadership must be one that encourages efficiency and productivity. The classical design, with its emphasis on complexity, formalization, and centralization, fits this strategy.

Differentiation suggests that the firm will create products that are perceived to be unique. The perception of uniqueness (differentiation) can be based on a variety of factors, such as brand image, product features, customer service, or a dealer network. To be effective, differentiation requires creativity, basic research skill, strong marketing, and a reputation for quality. Firms such as Mercedes, Jenn-Air, Coleman, and Caterpillar have pursued differentiation successfully. Differentiation strategy does not imply that cost control is ignored. It is simply not the primary strategic consideration.

The emphasis on differentiation requires flexible response to changing customer preferences and perceptions. Organization designs that facilitate differentiation tend to have neoclassical characteristics. Neoclassical designs—with their emphasis on low specialization, low formality, and decentralized authority—encourage the freedom of action required for differentiation.

Focus, the third general strategy, involves achieving either cost leadership or differentiation, or both, in a particular segment of the market. Rather than competing throughout the market, the firm focuses on one segment. For example, Porter Paint attempts to serve the needs of the professional painter rather than the do-it-yourself customer. Thus, the focus strategy implies a trade-off between market share and profitability. The compatible organization design implies a mix of classical and neoclassical characteristics, because the firm can attempt both cost leadership and differentiation aimed at its segment.

The point here is not the relative benefits of any of the three generic strategies. Nor are we concerned with whether these are in fact *the* generic strategies. Rather, the point is to demonstrate the relationship between *strategy* and *structure.* [22] Although Porter's ideas have been widely received, they rest on ideas previously developed.

Chandler's views.   The contemporary impetus for the idea that structure should reflect strategy is the work of Alfred D. Chandler. [23] After studying the history of some of America's largest firms, Chandler concluded that

---

[22] Gregory G. Dess and P. S. Davis, "Porter's (1980) Generic Strategies as Determinants of Strategic Group Membership and Organizational Performance," *Academy of Management Journal,* Stptember 1984, pp. 489–510. For another discussion of the relationship between strategy and structure, see Thomas J. Peters, "Strategy Follows Structure: Developing Distinctive Skills," *California Management Review,* Spring 1984, pp. 17–25.

[23] Alfred D. Chandler, *Stratety and Structure* (Cambridge, Mass.: MIT Press, 1962).

organization structures follow the growth strategies of firms. He also found that growth strategies tend to follow a certain pattern. In their initial stage, firms are typically plants, sales offices, or warehouses in a single industry, at a single location, performing a single function such as manufacturing, sales, or warehousing. As they grow, their growth follows a fairly standard path through four stages of growth:

1. *Volume expansion.* Firms manufacture, sell, or distribute more of their product or service to existing customers.
2. *Geographic expansion.* The firm continues to do what it has been doing but in a larger geographic area by means of field units.
3. *Vertical integration.* The firm either buys or creates other production or distribution functions. For example, manufacturers integrate backward by acquiring or creating sources of supply; they integrate forward by acquiring or creating sales and distribution functions.
4. *Product diversification.* The firm becomes involved in new industries through merger, acquisition, or creation (product development).

As a firm moves through each stage, it must change its organization structure. Initially, classical design is appropriate because volume expansion of a single product or service in a single industry stresses low unit cost (efficiency) and maximum resource utilization (production). There is relatively little concern for response to change and uncertainty. But as the firm moves through the growth steps from geographic expansion ultimately to product diversification, it becomes increasingly concerned with adaptability and flexibility, because it now faces diverse and complex environments. Thus, the organization

---

FIGURE   7–8   Strategic Choices and Organization Design

Managers' choices of corporate strategy influence organization design through their effects on job design.

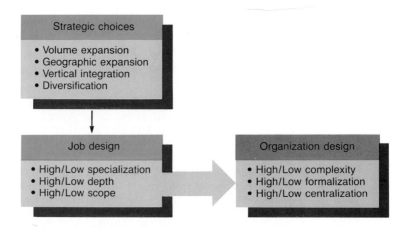

structures of highly diversified firms are characterized by product-based divisions and departments, decentralized authority, and relatively wide spans of control. The strategic-choice contingency approach is diagrammed in Figure 7–8. Implicit in this approach is the assumption that managers know that they should alter the organization design as they change the firm's strategy from volume expansion to product diversification.

The idea that organization design should change to reflect the organization's strategic choice implies growth-oriented strategy and that managers will know the need for changing the structure is termed a *process approach* to organization design. A process approach places its emphasis on how and why an organization moves from one design to another.

But the same could be said for other approaches to organization design. Both the technology and uncertainty approaches assume that managers know what design to use in a particular situation. The simpler one-best-way approaches also recognize the importance of competent managers. Nevertheless, the proponents of contingency approaches often present their ideas without giving explicit attention to the role of the organization's management, particularly how managers think and behave in specific situations.

SUMMARY OF KEY POINTS

- The decision to design or redesign an organization involves choosing from among a number of alternatives. These alternative designs can be classified as either *universalistic* or *contingency.*

- Universalistic designs are based upon the assumption that there is one best way to organize, *regardless* of the situation. The best way can be either a classical or a neoclassical design.

- Classical design, with its high degree of specialization (complexity), written rules and policies (formalism), and low delegation of authority (centralization), places emphasis on obtaining maximum production and efficiency.

- Neoclassical design, with its low degree of specialization (simplicity), unwritten but implicit rules and policies (informalism), and high delegation of authority (decentralization), places emphasis on obtaining maximum flexibility and adaptability and on employee satisfaction.

- The alternative to the universalistic approach is the contingency approach. Contingency designs are based upon the assumption that the best way to organize depends on the situation or setting. The best design can tend toward either the classical or the neoclassical.

- The contingency approach is more widely accepted in contemporary management theory and practice. However, there is little consensus among its proponents as to what specific factor or set of factors determines the correct organization design.

- One factor many believe to be important is technology. They feel that firms using either job-order or process technology will be more effective and productive if their designs tend toward neoclassical characteristics. Firms using mass-production technology will benefit from classical characteristics.

- A second factor often linked to organization design is environmental uncertainty. This body of opinion notes that organizations facing uncertain environments require flexibility and adaptability to survive and therefore should use neoclassical designs. In contrast, firms that face certain environments must seek high levels of production and efficiency. Here, the classical design is appropriate.

- A third influential factor is the environmental-contingency approach. It encourages managers to design the total organization in terms of departmental structures. In this perspective, the organization's environment actually consists of subenvironments. And managers must design departments to deal with the demands and conditions inherent to those subenvironments.

- A final influential contingency factor is strategic choice. According to this perspective, a firm's organization design should correspond to the requirements of its overall strategy. Cost leadership strategy, for example, calls for the classical design; production differentiation and/or diversification require neoclassical design.

DISCUSSION AND REVIEW QUESTIONS

1. Contrast the main arguments of universalistic and contingency approaches to organization design. Which of the two approaches is easier to implement in practice? Explain.

2. Contrast the main features of the classical and neoclassical organization designs.

3. Compare what you believe to be the popular meaning of the term *bureaucracy* with the meaning in management literature. Why do *bureaucracy* and *bureaucratic* have negative connotations?

4. Explain why an organization with classical design characteristics is likely to be more efficient and productive but less flexible and adaptable than an organization with neoclassical design characteristics.

5. Compare two organizations that you know either through employment or membership. Describe them in terms of classical and neoclassical design characteristics. What explains the difference you find in the two organizations?

6. What are the bases for the opinion that technology is an important contingency variable? Do you believe that technology is the *primary* factor to be considered when management designs a structure? Explain.

7. What are the bases for the opinion that environmental uncertainty is an important contingency variable? Do you believe that environmental uncertainty is

the *primary* factor to be considered when management designs a structure? Explain.

8. What are the relevant subenvironments of business firms? Of hospitals? Of universities? What subunits, or departments, exist in typical business firms, hospitals, and universities to deal with those subenvironments?

9. What are the bases for the opinion that strategy is an important contingency variable? Do you believe that strategy is the *primary* factor to be considered when management designs a structure? Explain.

10. Develop an explanation of the important contingency variables that would integrate the technology, environment, and strategy points of view.

ADDITIONAL REFERENCES

Brenneman, D. S., and L. D. Kittredge. "Matching Management Systems to Organizational Realities of Large Scale Agencies." *Public Productivity Review,* December 1983, pp. 354–77.

Burgelman, R. A. "A Model of the Interaction of Strategic Behavior, Corporate Context, and the Concept of Strategy." *Academy of Management Review,* January 1983, pp. 61–70.

Burns, T., and G. M. Stalker. *The Management of Innovation.* London: Tavistock Publications, 1961.

Galbraith, J. R. "Designing the Innovating Organization." *Organizational Dynamics.* Winter 1982, pp. 5–25.

Jelinek, M., and M. C. Burstein. "Production Administrative Structure: A Paradigm for Strategic Fit." *Academy of Management Review,* April 1982, pp. 242–52.

Mahmoudi, H., and G. Miller. "A Causal Model of Hospital Structure." *Group and Organization Studies,* June 1985, pp. 209–23.

Nystrom, P. C., and W. H. Starbuck, eds. *Handbook of Organizational Design. Vol. I: Adapting Organizations to Their Environment.* New York: Oxford University Press, 1981.

Pitts, R. A. "Toward a Contingency Theory of Multibusiness Organization Design," *Academy of Management Review,* April 1980, pp. 203–10.

Timm, M. M., and M. G. Wanetik. "Matrix Organization: Design and Development for a Hospital Organization." *Hospital and Health Services Administration,* November–December 1983, pp. 46–58.

Warner, M. "New Technology, Work Organization and Industrial Relations." *Omega,* no. 3 (1984), pp. 203–10.

Woodward, S. N. "Performance in Planning a Large Project." *Journal of Management Studies,* April 1982, pp. 183–98.

CASES

APPLICATION I

ORGANIZATION DESIGN OF B. F. GOODRICH'S R&D

The research and development (R&D) effort at B. F. Goodrich is vital for the long-run survival of the firm, just as it is in most industrial organizations. B. F. Goodrich believes that the traditional role of R&D has been to develop *new* products and processes but that the role is changing to one of protecting and improving the *current* products and lines of business. R&D effort is directed toward cutting product costs, improving productivity, and responding to safety, health, and environmental problems.

The orientation away from "blue-sky" research to "applied" research requires the research, scientific, and technical personnel in R&D units to be very much involved in the company. To obtain commitment and involvement from its R&D staff, B. F. Goodrich has adopted a number of organization design practices. The practices are intended to provide a maximally productive internal organization for R&D and to assure that R&D is properly integrated with the remainder of the organization.

The organization design of R&D units stresses the development of explicit objectives for each unit and for each individual. Once the objectives are developed, individuals have considerable freedom to select how they will achieve those objectives. The job design provides considerable depth and scope for scientists to pursue objectives, using the research and technical methods they desire.

A second organization design feature is open communication channels, both upward and downward. Managers and subordinates alike discuss issues and problems prior to selecting a solution. These channels stress informal discussions that are issue-directed. The units confront and resolve many nagging personnel and procedural problems before they become major issues. B. F. Goodrich believes that open communications are essential for maintaining the creative environment necessary for fruitful R&D work.

The relationship between R&D and other corporate units also must be designed. The company refers to these relationships as "interfaces" and is strongly concerned about designing organizational practices that reduce conflict between R&D and other units. For example, conflict exists between R&D and manufacturing. One cause of the conflict is the purposes of the two units. Manufacturing's primary objective is to establish a production line that produces continuously a product with specified quality and quantity. Once that line is in place and fine-tuned, manufacturing personnel resist efforts to change it. But it is the purpose of R&D to do precisely that: to change the line when a technical breakthrough is developed. Changing the line to adopt a potentially unsuccessful technology is bound to cause disruption, and manufacturing managers will resist R&D efforts.

To understand B. F. Goodrich's approach to integrating R&D into the line organization, one must understand its overall organization. The company consists of three groups: the Chemical Group, an Engineered Systems Group, and the Tire Group. In addition, there are corporate staff units, including a corporate R&D unit. The company's first integrative practice is to appoint in each of these groups a senior vice president for operations. Reporting to this official are managers of production, manufacturing services, technical, and quality-control units. Thus, within each group, there is *one* executive who is responsible for all production-related issues, including the application of new manufacturing methods developed by research efforts.

The second practice involves the reporting relationship of R&D staff. For example, tire development engineers at the plant level *and* tire research personnel at the corporate-level units all report to the vice president for tire R&D (who in turn reports to the senior vice president for tire operations). This organization design practice focuses all research and development activities for tires under one manager. The arrangement not only accelerates the adoption of new technology but avoids some of the conflict between tire research and tire development, as well. The former is concerned with developing prototypes of new tire design; the latter is responsible for getting them into production.

Questions for Analysis

1. Which approach to organization design does B. F. Goodrich seem to be following in managing its R&D effort? Explain.
2. What other organizational units are likely to have conflicting objectives, and how can organization design practices minimize these conflicts?
3. What alternative design practices could B. F. Goodrich consider?

APPLICATION II

ORGANIZATION PROBLEMS IN AN ELECTRONIC PRODUCTS COMPANY

The plant superintendent and the personnel manager of a large electronic products manufacturing facility were discussing current problems. It was their practice to meet at least twice a month to "review the situation," particularly with respect to personnel. The plant had been opened less than a year ago, and management had spent the better part of its time recruiting and training employees. The superintendent believed that sufficient time had been spent in gearing up the plant and that it was now time to begin to expect that problems would be the exception rather than the rule. He specifically was concerned with the high levels of downtime, scrappage, labor cost, and absenteeism.

The personnel manager argued for more patience. She stated that the new employees had not had sufficient time to develop the basis for understanding and relating to one another. "Nonsense," replied the plant manager. "We have organization charts, job descriptions, and policy manuals. There is no reason for the work to go undone or half done if the people are trained to do it. And they *are* trained, because you trained them!"

The personnel manager could agree with most of the superintendent's comments. The employees had been trained. But she went on to suggest that the existence of a formal structure does not assure that employees will behave in the correct manner. She persuaded the superintendent of the wisdom of using an employee opinion questionnaire to determine the extent to which employees understood the organization.

The opinion questionnaire was completed by all 600 employees, managers and nonmanagers alike, on company time. It included approximately 100 questions dealing with a variety of issues concerning the organization structure. The responses to the questionnaire were tabulated by the personnel manager's staff, and a summary was prepared for discussion with the plant superintendent. Some highlights of the summary are as follows:

1. Of the nonmanagerial employees, 35 percent stated that they very often felt that there is day-to-day uncertainty concerning the goals of their job.
2. Twenty percent of the nonmanagerial employees stated that they often had difficulty getting necessary job-related information from their supervisors.
3. Of the managerial personnel, 20 percent believed that there was seldom enough communication between their units and those with which they came in contact.
4. Forty percent of the nonmanagerial personnel believed that strict enforcement of rules and procedures usually prevented appropriate action.
5. Thirty percent of management believed that they seldom had authority commensurate with their responsibility.
6. Twenty percent of management believed that coordination was rarely achieved through planning.

The plant superintendent read the summary report and stated: "How is it possible for people to believe these ways? After all, we have all kinds of documents, procedures, and policies that define our organization structure. The only explanation I can accept is that they simply haven't been told."

Questions for Analysis

1. What would be your response to the superintendent if you were the personnel manager?
2. Do you, as the personnel manager, believe that the evidence from the opinion survey warrants a critical analysis of the organization structure? Why?
3. How would the superintendent know that the organization structure of the plant is the best one?

THE CONTROLLING FUNCTION

LEARNING OBJECTIVES

After completing Chapter 8, you should be able to:

■ **Define**
the controlling function in terms of the three attributes of effective control.

■ **Describe**
representative standards, information, and corrective action for general methods of control.

■ **Discuss**
the bases for distinguishing among preliminary, concurrent, and feedback control methods.

■ **Compare**
the control techniques designed to maintain quality of inputs and those designed to maintain quality of outputs.

■ **Identify**
the different standards that can be used to assess potential profitability of capital investments.

☐ MANAGEMENT IN ACTION

Quality Is Important in Service Too*

Controlling product quality is obviously very important in organizations that produce goods. However, as the U.S. economy becomes more and more a service economy, the issue of quality control in service companies such as airlines, hotels, health care organizations, and financial institutions is receiving a great deal of attention. This account is about one individual who decided to do something about service quality control in his organization.

In 1981, Scandinavian Airlines System (SAS) was struggling with a severe downturn in business, mainly caused by the worldwide recession. The board of directors of SAS was concerned. The company president resigned, and the board promoted a young "superstar," 39-year-old Jan Carlzon.

What followed was a spectacularly successful turnaround in which SAS went from an $8 million loss to a gross profit of $71 million on sales of $2 billion in a little over a year. SAS was voted "airline of the year" and laid claim to being the most profitable airline in Europe. All of this happened in a remarkably short span of time, while the rest of the airline industry was losing a combined $1.7 billion per year.

How did Carlzon achieve such a turnaround? His most obvious approach was attention to controlling the quality of the customer experience. Carlzon has said many times that "we have 50,000 moments of truth every day." A moment of truth, by Carlzon's definition, is an episode in which a customer comes into contact with any aspect of the company, however remote, and thereby has an opportunity to form an impression. Just as manufacturers instill quality-control systems that set standards and compare performance with the standards, Carlzon believes that service firms must do the same. He believes that if the moments of truth go unmanaged, the quality of service will regress to mediocrity. Backed by Carlzon's quality-control system for service, SAS became the most punctual airline in Europe. Quality is important in services too.

Carlzon's efforts to improve service quality required managers to pay attention to all the attributes of effective control. They had to set *standards* (customer expectations), obtain *information* (market research), and take *corrective action* (delegated authority for quality improvement to line managers). This chapter reviews a number of control methods in terms of these three attributes.

---

* Source: Karl Albrecht and Ron Zemke, *Service America: Doing Business in the New Economy* (Homewood, Ill.: Dow Jones–Irwin, 1985), chap. 2.

The third management function, *controlling,* includes *all activities the manager undertakes in attempting to assure that actual results conform to planned results.* Here, the controlling function is presented in terms of three primary topics. First, this chapter describes the conditions that determine the effectiveness of the controlling function. Managerial control is effective when *standards* can be established for the variables that are to be controlled, when *information* is available to measure the established standards, and when managers can take *corrective action* whenever the variable deviates from its desired, or standard, state. Second, this chapter will provide a basis for classifying and understanding managerial control procedures. This classification scheme then is used to discuss the third topic: managerial control procedures. Contemporary management practice utilizes a number of control procedures, and it is these *practical* applications that should receive extended attention.

Standards are derived from—and have many characteristics of—objectives. Standards are targets. To be effective, they must be stated clearly and related logically to the objectives of the unit. Standards are the criteria against which future, current, or past actions are compared. They are measured in a variety of ways, including physical, monetary, quantitative, and qualitative terms. The various forms that standards can take will be made clear in subsequent discussions of control methods.

Information must be provided that reports actual performance and permits appraisal of the performance against standards. Such information is most easily acquired for activities that produce specific and concrete results; for example, production and sales activities have end products that are easily identifiable and for which information is readily obtainable. The performance of legal departments, research and development (R&D) units, and personnel departments is quite difficult to appraise, because the outcomes of such activities are hard to measure.

Managerial actions to correct deviations are stimulated by the discovery of the need for action and from the ability to implement the desired action. People responsible for taking the corrective steps must know that they are indeed responsible and that they have the assigned authority to take action. Unless the job and position descriptions include specific statements clearly delineating these two requirements, the control function surely will fall short of its objective.

In many contemporary organizations, the responsibility and authority for corrective action often are ambiguous. Contemporary organizations consist of so many interdependent units that corrective action often must be taken by individuals who do not have the delegated authority but who must nonetheless influence others to accept solutions.

Finding solutions and influencing acceptance of new ideas and solutions often require creativity on the part of a manager. The Management Focus on managers' creativity indicates that some well-known organizations believe creativity to be so important that they seek ways to teach it and nurture it in their employees.

MANAGEMENT FOCUS
Making Managers More Creative

In 1985, more than 20,000 executives will attend workshops that they hope will help them find newer and better solutions, develop new products, and more effectively influence subordinates. Many large corporations realize that creativity is not such an elusive quality after all. And most important, research is proving that creativity can be taught.

General Electric Co. dishwashers now sport self-diagnostic control systems that were developed in a creativity session. Mead Corp. says creativity training has helped speed its new carbonless copypaper from lab to market. "People like to ooh and ah about creativity," says Herbert A. Simon, professor of psychology and computer science at Carnegie-Mellon University. "We think the creative process can be explained."

Many companies now see creativity training as a long-term commitment that should pervade the corporate structure all the way from the R&D lab to the executive suite. In particular, companies are looking for ways to prevent employees' creative flashes from being discouraged by corporate bureaucracy. One solution is so-called idea teams that bring together about seven people from different disciplines and levels in the company. They work with a senior manager who does not know the technical aspects of the problems and has no vested interest in the project's success or failure but who has the clout to see that ideas get a hearing at higher corporate levels.

Other companies are setting up what they call innovation centers. Eastman Kodak's seven-year-old Office of Innovation—commissioned by top management to ensure that good ideas generated by anyone get heard—helped develop the company's instant Trimprint film. In 1986, Hallmark Cards, Inc. will open its $20 million Technology and Innovation Center as a greenhouse for creative thinking.

Source: "Are You Creative?" *Business Week,* September 30, 1985, pp. 80–84.

The control function, then, involves the implementation of methods that provide answers to three basic questions: What are the planned and expected results? By what means can the actual results be compared to planned results? What corrective action is appropriate from which authorized person?

FIGURE   8–1   The Controlling Function

Control methods relate to specific system elements: inputs, processing, and outputs.

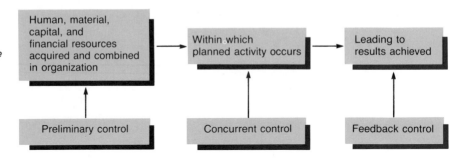

THREE TYPES OF CONTROL

The control function can be broken down into three types on the basis of the focus of control activity.[1] Figure 8–1 describes the three types.

Preliminary control focuses on the problem of preventing deviations in the quality and quantity of resources used in the organization. Human resources must meet the job requirements as defined by the organization structure; employees must have the capability, physical and intellectual, to perform the assigned tasks. The materials must meet acceptable levels of quality and must be available at the proper time and place. In addition, capital must be on hand to assure the adequate supply of plant and equipment. Finally, financial resources must be available in the right amounts and at the right times. Methods exist that enable management to implement preliminary control. Some are described later in this chapter.

Concurrent control monitors ongoing operations to ensure that objectives are pursued. Principally, concurrent control is implemented by the directing or supervisory activities of managers. Through personal, on-the-spot observation, managers determine whether the work of others is proceeding in the manner defined by policies and procedures. The delegation of authority provides managers with the power to use financial and nonfinancial incentives to affect concurrent control. The standards guiding ongoing activity are derived from job descriptions and from policies resulting from the planning function.

Feedback control methods focus on end results. Corrective action is directed at improving either the resource acquisition process or the actual

---

[1] In this section, we identify feedback control as a separate type. Many students will recognize that feedback also can be viewed as part of the broader concept of control insofar as it refers to the information reported to the manager. Also see P. Lorange, M. F. S. Morton, and S. Goshal, *Strategic Control* (St. Paul, Minn.: West Publishing, 1985).

FIGURE   8–2   A Simple Feedback Control System

Feedback control systems are self-correcting.

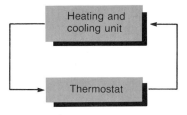

---

operations. This type of control derives its name from the fact that *historical* results guide *future* actions. An illustration of feedback control (see Figure 8–2) is a thermostat, which automatically regulates the temperature of a room. Since the thermostat maintains the preset temperature by constantly monitoring the actual temperature, future results (temperature) are directly and continually determined by historical results (again, temperature). The feedback methods employed in business include budgets, standard costs, financial statements, quality control, and performance evaluation.

In the three types of control, examine the *focus* of corrective action. As shown in Figure 8–3, preliminary control methods are based on information that measures some attribute or characteristic of resources; the focus of corrective action is in turn directed at the resources. That is, the variable measured is the variable acted upon. Similarly, concurrent control methods are based upon information related to activity, and it is activity that is acted upon.

FIGURE   8–3   The Three Types of Control as Distinguished by Focus of Corrective Action

---

The corrective action of a control method does not always affect the variable that is measured.

Resources	Activity	Results
Preliminary control methods	Concurrent control methods	Feedback control methods

⟶ Information

– – ⟶ Corrective action

TABLE   8–1   Control Types and Techniques

Managers can use
many different control
techniques.

Types of Control	Control Techniques
Preliminary control	Selection and placement. Staffing. Materials inspection. Capital budgeting. Financial budgeting.
Concurrent control	Direction.
Feedback control	Financial statement analysis. Standard cost analysis. Quality-control procedures. Employee performance evaluation.

However, the focus of corrective action associated with feedback control is not that which is measured—results. Rather, resources and activity are acted upon.

This distinction between preliminary, concurrent, and feedback permits classification of some of the more widely used control techniques, as shown in Table 8–1. The 10 techniques are presented in the remainder of this chapter, and the emphasis will be on standards, information, and corrective action as appropriate for each technique.

PRELIMINARY CONTROL

Preliminary control procedures include all managerial efforts to increase the probability that actual results will compare favorably with planned results. From this perspective, policies are important means for implementing preliminary control, since policies are guidelines for future action. Yet, it is vital to distinguish between *setting* policies and *implementing* them. Setting policy is included in the planning function, whereas implementing policy is a part of the control function. Similarly, job descriptions are aspects of the control function, since they predetermine the activity of the jobholder. At the same time, however, it is necessary to distinguish between *defining* and *staffing* the task structure. The former is a part of the organizing function; the latter, part of the controlling function.

Preliminary Control of Human Resources

The organizing function defines the job requirements and predetermines the skill requirements of the jobholders. These requirements vary in degree of specificity, depending upon the nature of the task. At the shop level, the skill requirements can be specified in terms of physical attributes and manual dexterity. On the other hand, the job requirements of management and staff personnel are more difficult to define in terms of concrete measurements.

Preliminary control is achieved through procedures that include the selection and placement of managerial and nonmanagerial personnel.[2] We should distinguish between procedures designed to obtain qualified subordinate managers (staffing) and those designed to obtain qualified nonmanagers and operatives (selection and placement). Although basic procedures and objectives are essentially the same, the distinction is important because managerial competence is the fundamental determinant of the organization's success.

Candidates for positions must be recruited from inside or outside the firm, and the most promising applicants must be selected from the list of contenders. The selection decision is based upon the congruence of an applicant's skills and personal characteristics, and the job requirements. The successful candidate must be trained in methods and procedures appropriate for the job. Most modern organizations have elaborate procedures for providing training on a continual basis.

Preliminary Control of Materials

The raw material that is converted into a finished product must conform to standards of quality.[3] At the same time, a sufficient inventory must be maintained to ensure a continuous flow to meet customer demands. The techniques of inventory control are discussed in a later chapter; at this point, we should only be concerned with the quality of incoming materials.

In recent years, numerous methods to control the quality of materials have been devised to use statistical sampling—inspection of samples rather than of the entire lot. These methods are less costly in terms of inspection time, but there is the risk of accepting defective material if the sample does not happen to contain any of the defectives.

A complete discussion of statistical sampling is beyond the scope of this text, but the essence of the procedure can be explained easily. Suppose, for example, that management sets a standard 3 percent level of defective items as the maximum that it will accept from the supplier. The material is inspected

---

[2] This phase of preliminary control is an aspect of personnel management. See R. L. Mathis and J. A. Jackson, *Personnel: Human Resource Management* (St. Paul, Minn.: West Publishing, 1985).

[3] As the chapter-opening Management in Action illustrated, quality is important in services as well as products. See Charles D. Zimmerman, "Quality: Key to Service Productivity," *Quality Progress,* June 1985, pp. 32–35; Carol A. King, "Service Quality Assurance Is Different," *Quality Progress,* June 1985, pp. 14–18.

by selecting a random sample and calculating the percentage of defective items in that sample. The decision that must then be made, based on the sample, is whether to accept or reject the entire order or to take another sample. Errors can be made in sampling, so that a lot is accepted when it contains more than 3 percent defectives or is rejected when it contains less than 3 percent defectives. The control system will be constructed based upon a careful balancing of the relative costs of these two types of errors.

The characteristics of preliminary control of materials are illustrative of control systems that are quite routine. The decision to accept or reject materials recurs frequently and must be made on a fairly regular basis. The standard is easily measured, and information (the sample) is readily available. The decision to accept or reject (or take another sample) is based upon straightforward instructions; given the sample results, the decision is automatic. The inspector's instructions may read: "If sample defectives are equal to or less than 3 percent, accept the lot; if sample defectives are equal to or more than 5 percent, reject the lot; if sample defectives are between 3 and 5 percent, take another sample." If a second sample is required, the inspector's actions will be determined by another set of instructions.

Preliminary Control of Capital

The acquisition of capital reflects the need to replace existing equipment or to expand the firm's productive capacity. Capital acquisitions are controlled by establishing criteria of potential profitability that must be met before the proposal is authorized. Such acquisitions ordinarily are included in the *capital budget,* an intermediate and long-run planning document that details the alternative sources and uses of funds. Decisions made by the manager that involve the commitment of present funds in exchange for future funds are termed *investment decisions.* And the methods that serve to screen investment proposals derive from economic analysis.

In this section, a number of methods in widespread practice will be discussed. Each involves the formulation of a standard that must be met in order to accept the prospective capital acquisition.

The payback method: The simplest and apparently most widely used method is the payback method. This approach calculates the number of years needed for the proposed capital acquisition to repay its original cost out of future cash earnings. For example, a manager is considering a machine that will reduce labor costs by $4,000 per year for each of the four years of its estimated life. The cost of the machine is $8,000, and the tax rate is 50 percent. The additional aftertax cash inflow from which the machine's cost must be paid is calculated as follows:

Additional cash inflow before taxes (labor cost savings)		$4,000
Less additional taxes		
Additional income	$4,000	
depreciation ($8,000 ÷ 4)	2,000	
Additional taxable income	$2,000	
Tax rate	.5	
Additional tax payment		1,000
Additional cash inflow after taxes		$3,000

After additional taxes are deducted from the labor savings, the payback period can be calculated as follows:

$$\frac{\$8,000}{\$3,000} = 2.67 \text{ years}$$

The proposed machine will repay its original cost in two and two-thirds years; if the standard requires a payback of, at most, three years, the machine would be deemed an appropriate investment.

The payback method suffers many limitations as a standard for evaluating capital resources. It does not produce a measurement of profitability. More importantly, it does not take into account the time value of money; that is, it does not recognize that a dollar today is worth more than a dollar at a future date. Other methods can be employed that include these important considerations.

Rate of return on investment.   One alternative measure of profitability, consistent with methods ordinarily employed in accounting, is the simple rate of return. Using the above example, the calculation would be as follows:

Additional gross income		$4,000
Less depreciation ($8,000 ÷ 4)	$2,000	
Less taxes	1,000	
Total additional expenses		3,000
Additional net income after taxes		$1,000

The rate of return is the ratio of additional net income to the original cost:

$$\frac{\$1,000}{\$8,000} = 12.5 \text{ percent}$$

The calculated rate of return would then be compared to some standard of minimum acceptability, and the decision to accept or reject would depend upon that comparison. The measurement of the simple rate of return has the advantage of being easily understood. It has the disadvantage, however, of not including the time value of money. The discounted rate of return method overcomes this deficiency.

Discounted rate of return.   The discounted rate of return is a measurement of profitability useful as a standard for screening potential capital acquisitions. It takes into account the time value of money. This method is similar to the payback method in that only cash inflows and outflows are considered. The method is widely used because it is considered the "correct" method for calculating the rate of return. Based upon the above example:

$$\$8,000 = \frac{\$3,000}{(1+r)} + \frac{\$3,000}{(1+r)^2} + \frac{\$3,000}{(1+r)^3} + \frac{\$3,000}{(1+r)^4}$$
$$r = 18 \text{ percent}$$

The discounted rate of return (r) is 18 percent, which is interpreted to mean that an \$8,000 investment repaying \$3,000 in cash at the end of each of four years yields a return of 18 percent.

The rationale of the method can be understood by thinking of \$3,000 inflows as cash payments received by the firm. In exchange for each of these four payments of \$3,000, the firm must pay \$8,000. The rate of return, 18 percent, is the factor equating cash inflows and present cash outflow.[4]

Preliminary Control of Financial Resources

An adequate supply of financial resources must be available to assure payment of obligations arising from current operations. Materials must be purchased, wages paid, interest charges and due dates met. The principal means of controlling the availability and cost of financial resources is budgeting—particularly cash and working-capital budgets.

---

[4] The time value of money is explicitly considered in the method in the following way: If we remember that 18 percent is the rate of return and that there are four distinct and separate future receipts of \$3,000, we can see that \$8,000 is the *present value* of the future proceeds.

$\$2,542$ = Present value of \$3,000 to be received in 1 year
     or $\$2,542 \times (1.18) = \$3,000$
$2,155$ = Present value of \$3,000 to be received in 2 years
     or $\$2,155 \times (1.18)^2 = \$3,000$
$1,826$ = Present value of \$3,000 to be received in 3 years
     or $\$1,826 \times (1.18)^3 = \$3,000$
$\underline{1,547}$ = Present value of \$3,000 to be received in 4 years
     or $\$1,547 \times (1.18)^4 = \$3,000$
$\$8,070$ = Total present value; error due to rounding.

FIGURE   8–4   Simple Relationships between Cash and Inventory

---

Managing cash flows requires understanding of basic business operations.

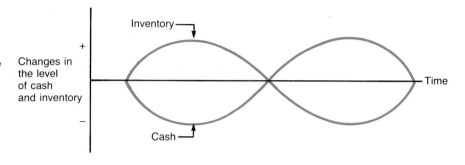

These budgets anticipate the ebb and flow of business activity when materials are purchased, finished goods are produced and inventoried, goods are sold, and cash received. This operating cycle results in a problem of *timing* the availability of cash to meet the obligations. The simple relationship between cash and inventory is shown in Figure 8–4. As inventories of finished goods increase, the supply of cash decreases as materials, labor, and other expenses are incurred and paid. As inventory is depleted through sales, cash increases. Preliminary control of cash requires that cash be available during the period of inventory buildup and be used wisely during periods of abundance. This requires the careful consideration of alternative sources of short-term financing during inventory buildup and of alternative short-run investment opportunities during periods of inventory depletion.

To aid in the process, attention is given by managers to certain financial ratios. For example, the standard may be in terms of the current ratio (the ratio of current assets to current liabilities), and a minimum and a maximum are set. The minimum ratio could be set at 2:1 and the maximum at 3:1, a practice recognizing the cost of both too little and too much investment in liquid assets. The control would be in terms of corrective action when the actual current ratio deviates from the standard. Other financial ratios contributing to control of financial resources include the acid-test ratio, inventory turnover, and average collection period. These ratios are discussed in greater detail in the section on feedback control methods.

CONCURRENT CONTROL

Concurrent control consists primarily of actions of supervisors who direct the work of their subordinates. *Direction* refers to the acts of managers when they undertake (1) to instruct subordinates in the proper methods and procedures and (2) to oversee subordinates' work to assure that it is done properly.

Direction follows the formal chain of command, since the responsibility of each superior is to interpret for subordinates the orders received from higher echelons. The relative importance of direction depends almost entirely upon the nature of the tasks performed by subordinates. The supervisor of an assembly line that produces a component part requiring relatively simple manual operations may seldom engage in direction. On the other hand, the manager of an R&D unit must devote considerable time to direction. Research work is inherently more complex and varied than manual work. So it requires more interpretation and instruction.

Directing is the primary function of the first-line supervisor; but as with the universal management functions, every manager in an organization engages at some time in directing employees.[5] Directing employees is guided by the stated goals and policies of the organization as reflected in the planning function. It is apparent that as a manager moves up the hierarchy, the relative importance of directing diminishes as other functions become relatively more important. For example, the chief executive officer will devote considerably more time to the planning and organizing functions.

The scope and content of the direction phase varies according to the nature of work being supervised, as noted above.[6] Also, a number of other factors determine differences in the form of direction. For example, since direction is basically the process of personal communication, the amount and clarity of information are important factors. Subordinates must receive sufficient information to carry out the task and must understand the information that they receive. On the other hand, too much information and too much detail can be damaging. The manager's mode and tone of expression also greatly influence the effectiveness of direction.

The tests of effective direction are related to the characteristics of effective communication. To be effective, a directive must be reasonable, intelligible, appropriately worded, and consistent with the overall goals of the organization. Whether these criteria are met is not the manager's decision to make. Rather, it is the subordinate who decides. Many managers have assumed that their directives were straightforward and to the point, only to discover that their subordinates failed to understand or to accept them as legitimate.

The process of direction includes not only the manner in which directives are communicated but also the mannerisms of the person who directs. Whether the supervisor is autocratic or democratic, permissive or directive, considerate or inconsiderate has implications for the effectiveness of direction

[5] Lawrence Steinmetz and H. Ralph Todd, Jr., *First-Line Management,* 3rd ed. (Plano, Tex.: Business Publications, 1983).

[6] For a related discussion of problems in managing professional employees, see Joseph A. Raelin, "The Basis for the Professional's Resistance to Managerial Control," *Human Resource Management,* Summer 1985, pp. 147–75.

as a concurrent control technique.[7] A later chapter delves deeply into leadership behavior as related to performance of individuals and groups.

Direction involves day-to-day oversight of the subordinates' work. As deviations from standards are identified, managers take immediate corrective action through demonstrating and coaching their subordinates to perform their assigned tasks appropriately.

FEEDBACK CONTROL

The distinguishing feature of feedback control methods is a focus on *historical* outcomes as the bases for correcting *future* actions. For example, the financial statements of a firm are used to evaluate the acceptability of historical results and to determine the desirability of making changes in future resource acquisitions or operational activities. In this section, four feedback control methods widely used in business are outlined: financial statement analysis, standard cost analysis, quality control, and employee performance evaluation. Our objective is to demonstrate the general features of feedback control techniques through these four examples.

Financial Statement Analysis

A firm's accounting system is a principal source of information from which managers can evaluate historical results. Periodically the manager receives a set of financial statements that usually includes a balance sheet, an income statement, and a sources-and-uses-of-funds statement. These statements summarize and classify the effects of transactions in terms of assets, liabilities, equity, revenues, and expenses—the principal components of the firm's financial structure.

A detailed analysis of the information contained in the financial statements enables management to determine the adequacy of the firm's earning power and its ability to meet current and long-term obligations. Managers must have measures of and standards for profitability, liquidity, and solvency. Whether a manager prefers the rate of return on sales, on owner's equity, on total assets, or a combination of all three, it is important to establish a meaningful norm—one that is appropriate to the particular firm, given its industry and stage of growth. An inadequate rate of return will negatively affect the firm's ability to attract funds for expansion, particularly if a downward trend over time is evident.

---

[7] Barry Waldon, "The Human Side of Control," *Supervisory Management,* June 1985, pp. 34–39.

The measures of liquidity reflect the firm's ability to meet current obligations as they become due. The widest known and most often used measure is the ratio of current assets to current liabilities. The standard of acceptability depends on the particular firm's own operating characteristics. Bases for comparison are available from trade associations that publish industry averages. A more rigorous test of liquidity is the acid-test ratio. It relates only cash and near-cash items (current assets excluding inventories and prepaid expenses) to current liabilities.

The relationship between current assets and current liabilities is an important determinate of liquidity. Equally important is the *composition* of current assets. Two measures that indicate composition and rely upon information found in both the balance sheet and income statement are the accounts receivable turnover and the inventory turnover. The accounts receivable turnover is the ratio of credit sales to average accounts receivable. The higher the turnover, the more rapid is the conversion of accounts receivable to cash. A low turnover would indicate a time lag in the collection of receivables, which in turn could strain the firm's ability to meet its own obligations. The appropriate corrective action might be a tightening of credit standards or a more vigorous effort to collect outstanding accounts. The inventory turnover also facilitates the analysis of appropriate balances in current assets. It is calculated as the ratio of cost of goods sold to average inventory. A high ratio could indicate a dangerously low inventory balance in relation to sales, with the possibility of missed sales or production slowdowns. Conversely, a low ratio might indicate an overinvestment in inventory to the exclusion of other, more profitable assets. Whatever the case, the appropriate ratio must be established by the manager, based upon the firm's experience within its industry and market.

Another financial measure is solvency, the ability of the firm to meet its long-term obligations—its fixed commitments. The solvency measure relates the claims of creditors and owners on the assets of the firm. An appropriate balance must be maintained—a balance that protects the interests of the owners yet does not ignore the advantages of long-term debt as a source of funds. A commonly used measure of solvency is the ratio of net income before interest and taxes to interest expense. This indicates the margin of safety, and ordinarily a high ratio is preferred. However, a very high ratio combined with a low debt-to-equity ratio could indicate that management has not taken advantage of debt as a source of funds. The appropriate balance between debt and equity depends upon a great number of factors; and the issue is an important topic in financial management. But as a general rule, one can say that the proportion of debt should vary directly with the *stability* of the firm's earnings.

The ratios discussed above are only suggestive of the great number and variety of methods used to evaluate the financial results of the firm. Accounting as a tool of analysis in business management has a long history predating scientific management.[8] The point here is that financial statement analysis as a part of the management process is clearly a feedback control method.

Standard Cost Analysis

Standard cost accounting systems date from and are considered a major contribution of the scientific management era. A standard cost system provides information that enables management to compare actual costs with predetermined (standard) costs. Management then can take appropriate corrective action or assign the authority to take action to others. The first use of standard costing was to control manufacturing costs. But in recent years, standard costing has been applied to selling, general, and administrative expenses. Here we discuss standard manufacturing costs.

The three elements of manufacturing costs are direct labor, direct materials, and overhead. For each of these, an estimate must be made of cost per unit of output. For example, the direct labor cost per unit of output consists of the standard usage of labor and the standard price of labor. The standard usage derives from time studies that fix the expected output per labor-hour; the standard price of labor will be fixed by the salary schedule appropriate for the kind of work necessary to produce the output. A similar determination is made for direct materials. Thus, the standard labor and standard materials costs might be as follows:

Standard labor usage per unit	2 hours
Standard wage rate per hour	$3.00
Standard labor cost (2 × $3.00)	$6.00
Standard material usage per unit	6 pounds
Standard material price per pound	$ .30
Standard material cost (6 × $.30)	$1.80

The accounting system enables the manager to compare incurred costs and standard costs. If during the period covered by the report, for example, 200 units of output were produced, the standard labor cost is $1,200 (200 × $6.00) and the standard material is $360 (200 × $1.80). If the actual payroll cost for that same time period was $1,500 and the actual material cost was $400, there was an *unfavorable labor variance* of $300 and an *unfavorable material variance* of $40. Management must determine the reasons for the variances and decide what corrective action is appropriate.

---

[8] A. C. Littleton, *Accounting Evolution to 1900* (New York: Russell & Russell, 1966).

Assuming that the standards are correct, the manager must analyze the variance and fix the responsibility for restoring the balance between standard and actual costs. It is obvious that if actual labor cost exceeds standard labor cost, the reason for the difference is found in labor usage and labor wage rates. Either actual labor usage exceeded standard labor usage or actual wage rates exceeded standard wage rates, or some combination of both. Suppose that, in this example, the accountant reports the actual payroll consisted of 450 actual hours at an average wage rate of $3.33. The questions management must resolve are now narrowed to two: What happened during the period to cause output per labor-hour to go down (to produce 200 units of output should require 400 labor hours)? And why was the average wage rate more than the standard wage rate? The answers to these questions are found in the resources and activity stages of the cycle (see Figure 8–3).

Similar analyses are made to discover the causes for the unfavorable material variance. The first step is discovering the relationship between actual and standard usage and between actual and standard price. As with the labor, the manager may find actual material usage exceeded that specified by standard and/or the actual price exceeds the standard price. Once the cause is isolated, the analysis must proceed to fix responsibility for corrective action.

The analysis of manufacturing-overhead variance is considerably more complicated than that for labor and material.[9] Suffice it to say that it is necessary to isolate the causes through comparisons with standards and budgets.

Quality-Control Analysis

Quality control uses information regarding attributes and characteristics of output to ascertain whether the manufacturing process is "in control" (that is, producing acceptable output). To make this determination, the manager must specify the crucial product characteristic. It may be weight, length, consistency, or defects. A major development in the last 10 years or so has been the emergence of concern for product quality, perhaps due mostly to the influx of Japanese imports with a reputation for quality.[10] American

---

[9] The reader can consult any text in cost accounting and management accounting for discussions of standard cost analysis. For example, see E. A. Deakin and M. W. Maher, *Cost Accounting* (Homewood, Ill.: Richard D. Irwin, 1984; J. O. Cherrington, E. D. Hubbard, and D. Luthy, *Cost and Managerial Accounting* (Dubuque, Iowa: W. C. Brown, 1985).

[10] Sang Lee and M. Ebrahimpour, "An Analysis of Japanese Quality Control Systems: Implications for American Manufacturing Firms," *Advanced Management Journal,* Spring 1985, pp. 24–31.

business managers have responded by instituting quality-improvement programs, just as Jan Carlzon is determined to control service quality at SAS. Many manufacturing firms have implemented these methods, as described in the Management Focus on Roper Appliance.

MANAGEMENT FOCUS
Quality Control at Roper Appliance

Roper Appliance manufactures gas and electric cooking appliances. The firm, based in Kankakee, Illinois, depends on numerous suppliers of component parts for its own products. In response to increased consumer concern and demand for product quality, Roper began a program of quality control that has some unusual features.

G. James Alaback, director of quality assurance at Roper, initiated the program. The central idea is that Roper can increase the quality of its product only if its suppliers increase the quality of their products—the component parts of Roper's appliances. To carry forward this idea, Roper's managers began meetings with key suppliers to share with them their quality-improvement concepts and information. The suppliers and Roper began cooperative efforts of testing and evaluation of part reliability and safety. The cooperative relationship is the essence of Roper's program, and it is the basis for a number of other features.

For example, Roper conducts training programs for top management of key suppliers. These programs stress techniques of quality improvement and quality assurance. Roper's own quality-assurance staff assist suppliers who wish to set up quality-improvement programs. The program is firmly established in Roper and, according to Alaback, "We feel that the quality-improvement effort will be a permanent, ongoing activity."

Management must often be concerned with consistent *quantity* as well as quality. For example, a manufacturer of peanut butter must maintain a minimum quantity of peanut butter in each container of 12 ounces. The company could weigh each container when it is filled—that is, 100 percent of the output could be inspected. An alternative is to inspect samples of output to make inferences about the process based upon the sample information. This latter approach is termed *statistical quality control*. This method makes use of statistical sampling theory; and since the amount of time devoted to inspection is reduced, the cost of inspection also is reduced. Moreover, the acceptable standard of 12 ounces is achieved.

TABLE   8–2   Summary of the Controlling Function

Technique	Standards	Information	Corrective Action
1. Job description	Job specifications—skills, experience, education bearing on job success.	Test scores, credentials, background data.	Hire/no hire; remedial training.
2. Selection	Job specifications—skills, experience, education bearing on job success.	Test scores, credentials, background data.	Place/no place; remedial training.
3. Materials inspection	Percent or number defective within tolerance limits.	Sampling of inputs.	Accept, reject, or retest.
4. Capital budgeting	Simple rate of return; payback period; discounted rate of return.	Projected cost, revenue, and engineering data.	Accept, reject.
5. Financial budgeting	Requirements arising out of the forecasting step of planning.	Projected cost, revenue, and engineering data.	Accept, reject; revise.
6. Direction	Required job behavior in terms of end results.	Plans and job specifications.	Change plans and/or job specifications; train, fire people.
7. Financial statement analysis	Relevant data found in trade, banking, and rule-of-thumb sources.	Balance sheet, income statement.	Revise inputs; revise direction.
8. Standard cost analysis	Standard times/usage from engineering studies.	Cost accounting system.	Revise inputs; revise direction.
9. Quality control	Percent or number defective consistent with marketing strategy.	Sampling procedures.	Revise inputs; revise direction.
10. Employee performance evaluation	Job-related performance criteria.	Managerial observation; self-reports.	Retrain, replace personnel; change assigned jobs.

Standards, information, and corrective action are necessary for each control technique.

Employee Performance Evaluation

No doubt, the most important and difficult feedback control technique is performance evaluation. It is so important because people are the most crucial resource in any organization. As is so often said, "People make the difference."[11] Effective business firms, hospitals, universities, and governments are staffed by people effectively discharging their assigned duties. Evaluation

[11] Richard E. Walton, "From Control to Commitment in the Workplace," *Harvard Business Review,* March–April 1985, pp. 76–84.

is difficult because the standards for performance are seldom objective and straightforward; many managerial and nonmanagerial jobs do not produce outputs that can be counted, weighed, and evaluated in objective terms. Because of the importance of employee performance evaluation, the next chapter will present an in-depth discussion of the topic.

The discussion of the controlling function is conveniently summarized in Table 8–2. There, the techniques are compared in terms of standards, information, and corrective action relevant for each one. The table also brings into focus the relationship between the planning function as a source of standards and the organizing function as a source of information. The overriding managerial responsibility is to integrate the three functions into a coherent management process that enables the organization to achieve the levels of performance expected by the elements of society that sustain it.

SUMMARY OF KEY POINTS

- The controlling function includes activities undertaken by managers to ensure that actual results conform to planned results. The controlling function logically follows the planning and organizing functions.
- The three necessary requirements for effective control are predetermined standards, information, and corrective action.
- Three types of control can be identified that are based on the focus of corrective action. Preliminary control focuses on inputs; concurrent control focuses on ongoing operations; feedback control focuses on inputs *and* ongoing operations.
- Preliminary control methods require standards of acceptable quality and quantity of inputs, such as materials, financial, capital, and human resources. Information permitting managers to determine whether resources meet standards is the basis for corrective action.
- Concurrent control methods require standards of acceptable behavior, activity, and execution of ongoing operations. The primary source of concurrent control is observations of supervisors; the corrective action is directed toward improving the quality and quantity of resources and improving the operations.
- Feedback control methods require standards of acceptable quality and quantity of outputs. The information must reflect the desired characteristics of the ouput. But unlike preliminary and concurrent control, the focus of corrective action is not that for which the standard is set—output. Rather, managers take corrective action to improve inputs and operations.
- The controlling function is highly developed in management practice. A great number of methods and systems allow managers to attain high levels of performance in the controlling function.

- New developments in information and data processing will bring about profound changes in the methods and systems of management control.

DISCUSSION AND REVIEW QUESTIONS

1. It is said by some management experts that the term *control* should not be used in the management literature. These experts argue that control implies some loss of freedom and individuality and that such implications should be avoided. Do you agree with these experts? What is your reasoning?

2. Illustrate the relationship between goals, policies, and standards in the context of an organization of which you are a member.

3. Why are preliminary and concurrent control procedures so widely used in universities, hospitals, governmental agencies, and other nonmarket institutions?

4. The term *cybernetics* was coined by modern systems theorists such as Norbert Wiener. As an extraclassroom exercise, research this term and relate it to the chapter discussion of feedback control procedures.

5. Some management writers have argued that the creation of organization structures is basically a form of the controlling function and not a separate managerial function. What would be your response to this argument?

6. A number of standards have been discussed as measures of investment profitability. These measures include the payback period, the rate of return, and the discounted rate of return. If only one measure is "correct," why do others exist in management practice?

7. Financial managers state that financial ratios are similar to other statistical data in the way that they can be used, or misused, to prove a point. How can the nonfinancial expert, such as a plant superintendent, know whether the financial expert is misusing such ratios to press for a certain point of view in an executive decision?

8. Under what circumstances would the use of feedback control procedures be inappropriate?

9. The concept of "responsibility accounting" has received much attention in the accounting literature. Research this concept in terms of its relationship to the chapter discussion of necessary conditions for effective managerial control.

10. "Performance evaluation would be a simple task if it weren't for the fact that people are involved." Comment on this statement.

11. Directing is a crucial aspect of control; and information received (the perceived performance of subordinates) and sent (orders and instructions) are key elements of directing. What abilities and traits do you believe are associated with effective directing?

ADDITIONAL REFERENCES

Beyer, J. M., and H. M. Trice. "A Field Study of the Use and Perceived Effects of Discipline in Controlling Work Performance." *Academy of Management Journal,* December 1984, pp. 743–64.

Carson, R. L. "Recognizing and Correcting Financial Fallacies." *Management Review,* August 1982, pp. 17–22.

Chow, C. W., and W. S. Waller. "Management Accounting and Organizational Control." *Management Accounting,* April 1982, pp. 36–41.

Dreher, G. F., and P. R. Sackett. *Employee Staffing and Selection.* Homewood, Ill.: Richard D. Irwin, 1983.

Ferry, M. J. "Quality Assurance." *Journal of Information Management,* Winter 1985, pp. 25–27.

Giglioni, G. B., and A. G. Bedian. "A Consensus of Management Control Theory: 1900–1972." *Academy of Management Journal,* June 1974, pp. 292–305.

Gray, H. J. "A New Synthesis—Blending Control with Creativity." *Management World,* October 1984, p. 1.

Harrington, D. R., and B. D. Wilson. *Corporate Financial Analysis.* Plano, Tex.: Business Publications, 1983.

Jaeger, A. M., and B. R. Baliga. "Control Systems and Strategic Adaptation: Lessons from the Japanese Experience." *Strategic Management Journal,* April–June 1985, pp. 115–34.

Logan, G. M. "Loyalty and a Sense of Purpose." *California Management Review,* Fall 1984, pp. 149–56.

Michael, S. R. "Feedforward versus Feedback Control." *Managerial Planning,* November–December 1980, pp. 34–38.

Muczyk, J. P., and R. E. Hastings. "In Defense of Enlightened Hardball Management." *Business Horizons,* July–August 1985, pp. 23–29.

Rockart, J. F., and M. E. Tracy. "The CEO Goes on Line." *Harvard Business Review,* January–February 1982, pp. 82–88.

Weiss, J. A., and J. E. Gruber. "Using Knowledge for Control in Fragmented Policy Arenas." *Journal of Policy Analysis and Management,* Winter 1984, pp. 225–47.

CASES

APPLICATION I

CONTROLLING THE QUALITY OF CUSTOMER SERVICE AT AMERICAN EXPRESS

The Card Division of American Express recognizes how important it is to develop and maintain high quality in customer service. Customer service is not only related to customer goodwill but to profits, as well. The company estimates that it gains 33 cents of extra sales revenue for each day earlier a card is mailed to a customer. On an annual basis, that 33 cents per day per card turns into $1.4 million in net profit. Getting new and replaced cards into the hands of customers in a timely manner is an important aspect of customer-service quality. But when American Express began to delve more deeply, it discovered considerable ambiguity surrounding the concept.

The decision to control the quality of customer service reflected the importance of the concept. But the initiative had to be provided by a key manager. Ruth C. Finley, a regional vice president of the Card Division, was the prime mover behind the effort. She stated: "For some time, we had been dissatisfied with the traditional approach for evaluating customer service. Reports to management were biased because they seldom included customers who had problems but did not complain, or those who were only marginally satisfied with the company's service." She believed that the true measure of customer service must be based on the perceptions of cardholders and service establishments and that standards must reflect those perceptions.

The decision to base customer-service quality on the perceptions of those who receive the service meant a major overhaul in the firm's control procedures. The company began by determining what customers expected from American Express. Analyses of letters of complaint indicated three important attributes of customer service: timeliness, accuracy, and responsiveness. Cardholders expected bills to be received on time, address changes processed quickly, and complaints acted upon.

Once customer expectations were identified, the company's quality-assurance staff began to develop standards for the delivery of customer services. Eventually, the staff identified more than 180 standards to measure customer quality. These standards reflected acceptable performance of service elements such as processing applications, issuing cards, responding to billing inquiries, and authorizing charges on accounts. The standards were based upon customers' expectations of what constituted timely, accurate, and responsive service.

Other factors also were considered. In addition to customers' perceptions, the performance standards reflected competitive, capability, and economic factors. For example, some standards are *imposed* by competition; others are influenced by the organization's current processing *capability;* while yet other standards must reflect the *economic* trade-off potential. As each of these factors was considered, the appropriate standards began to take shape, and the program was implemented.

The program had impact. The time required to process personal card applications was reduced from 35 days to 15 days, the time required to replace cards from 15 days to 2 days, the time needed to respond to customer inquiries from 16 days to 10 days. The profit potential of these improvements was quite large. For example, the reduction in the delivery time for new and replaced cards yielded an estimated additional revenue of $17.5 million. Also, when cards were received in a timely manner, the customer did not have to use a competitor's card.

The revenue and profit potential of the quality-control program had side benefits. The program focused the attention of the entire company on customer expectations. Departments pride themselves on their record of rendering customer service. Moreover, employee morale increased because every employee has a stake in and makes contributions to improve customer service. Each employee feels more a part of the company and representative of the company when serving customers.

The success of the program in controlling customer service in the card division stimulated similar efforts in other company divisions. The company's Travel and Travelers Cheque division began to implement a similar procedure. American Express is convinced that standards can be set for any quantity that is vital to profitability, regardless of the ambiguity and subjectiveness of the quantity itself.

Questions for Analysis

1. Is the American Express program for controlling the quality of customer service a form of precontrol, concurrent, or feedback control?
2. Identify the three elements of effective control in the American Express program.
3. For what reasons should American Express set standards at the "economically feasible" level rather than at the highest possible level?

APPLICATION II

DEVELOPING A NEW PRODUCT

The plant manager of a major electronics manufacturer called a meeting with his immediate subordinates to decide whether to go into full-scale production and marketing of a new product, a miniature thermostat. The miniature thermostat MT had been in the developmental process for the past three years, and the manager believed that it was time to make a decision. The meeting was to be attended by the marketing manager, the production superintendent, the purchasing manager, and the plant cost accountant. The plant manager instructed each official to bring appropriate information and be prepared to make a final decision regarding the MT.

Prior to the meeting, the plant manager noted the following facts concerning the MT:

1. Developmental efforts had been undertaken two years ago in response to the introduction of a similar product by a major competitor.
2. Initial manufacturing studies had indicated that much of the technology

and know-how to produce the MT already existed in the plant and its work force.

3. A prototype model had been approved by Underwriter's Laboratory.
4. A pilot production line had been designed and installed. Several thousand thermostats already had been produced and tested.
5. Market projections indicated that the trend toward miniaturization of components such as thermostats was likely to continue.
6. The competitor who had introduced the product was successfully marketing it at a price of 80 cents each.
7. The cost estimates derived by the cost accountant over the past two years consistently indicated that the firm could not meet the competitor's price and at the same time follow its policy of marking up all products 14 percent to the selling price.

Because of the plant manager's concern for the cost of the MT, the cost accountant was asked to brief the group at the outset of its meeting. The accountant's data are shown in Exhibit 1.

The accountant noted that the firm would not be able to manufacture and sell the MT for less than 80.5 cents each, given present actual costs. In fact, to meet their markup objective would require a selling price of approximately 94 cents each, impossible since the competitor was selling the same product for 80 cents. She explained that if the MT could be manufactured at standard costs, the product could compete successfully with the competitor's thermostat.

The marketing manager stated that the MT was an important product and that it was critical for the firm to have an entry in the market. He maintained that in a few years, the MT would be used by all major customers; he also stated that competition already had moved into the area with a

---

EXHIBIT 1

	Actual Costs	Standard Costs
Direct labor	5.9¢	5.2¢
Direct material	34.0	19.4
Manufacturing overhead (438 percent of standard direct labor)	22.8	22.8
Total manufacturing cost	62.7	47.4
Spoilage (10 percent)	6.3	4.7
Selling and administrative costs (40 percent of direct labor and overhead)	11.5	11.2
Total cost per MT	80.5	63.3
Required price to achieve 14 percent markup in selling price	93.6¢	73.6¢

strong sales program. He added that he personally did not place too much reliance on the cost estimates, because the plant had so little experience with full-scale production of the MT.

The manufacturing superintendent stated that he was working with engineers to develop a new method for welding contacts and that if the technique proved successful, direct labor cost would be reduced significantly. This would have a cumulative effect on cost, since overhead, spoilage, and selling and administrative expenses are based on direct labor. He also believed that with a little more experience, the workers could reach standard times on the assembly operations. He stated that much progress in this direction had been made in the past four weeks.

The purchasing manager stated that material costs were high because the plant did not procure materials in sufficient quantity. She stated that with full-scale production, material costs should reduce to standard.

Questions for Analysis

1. If you were the plant manager, what would be your decision regarding the MT?
2. If you decided to manufacture the MT, would your decision indicate that the standard of 14 percent markup is not valid?

EXPERIENTIAL EXERCISE

PAPER PLANE CORPORATION

Purpose

To work on a task that requires planning, organizing, and controlling.

The Exercise in Class

Unlimited groups of six participants each are used in this exercise. These groups may be directed simultaneously in the same room. Approximately a full class period is needed to complete the exercise. Each person should have assembly instructions (Exhibit 1) and a summary sheet (Exhibit 2) plus ample stacks of paper (8½ by 11 inches). The physical setting should be a room large enough so individual groups of six can work without interference from other groups. A working space should be provided for each group.

EXHIBIT   1   Instructions for Aircraft Assembly

Instructions for aircraft assembly

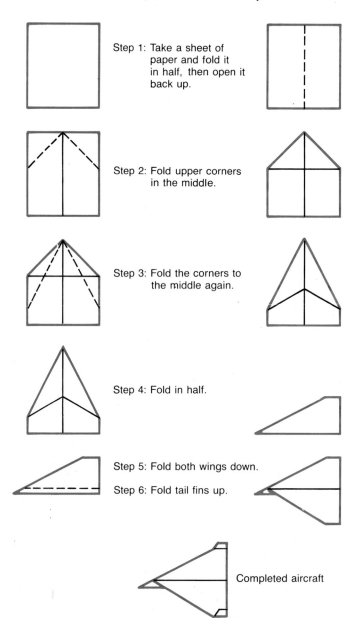

Step 1: Take a sheet of
paper and fold it
in half, then open it
back up.

Step 2: Fold upper corners
in the middle.

Step 3: Fold the corners to
the middle again.

Step 4: Fold in half.

Step 5: Fold both wings down.

Step 6: Fold tail fins up.

Completed aircraft

EXHIBIT   2   Summary Sheet

Round 1:
Bid: _____ Aircraft @ $20,000.00 per aircraft
= _____
Results: _____ Aircraft @ $20,000.00 per
aircraft = _____
Less: $300,000.00 overhead
_____ × $3,000 cost of raw materials
_____ × $25,000 penalty
Profit: _____
Round 2:
Bid: _____ Aircraft @ $20,000.00 per aircraft
= _____
Results: Aircraft @ $20,000.00 per
aircraft = _____
Less: $300,000.00 overhead
_____ × $3,000 cost of raw materials
_____ × $25,000 penalty
Profit: _____
Round 3:
Bid: _____ Aircraft @ $20,000.00 per aircraft
= _____
Results: _____ Aircraft @ $20,000.00 per
aircraft = _____
Less: $300,000.00 overhead
_____ × $30,000 cost of raw materials
_____ × $25,000 penalty
Profit: _____

The participants are doing an exercise in production methodology. Each group must work independently of the other groups. The objective is to make paper airplanes in the most profitable manner possible.

Paper Plane Corporation: Data sheet

1. Each group will choose a manager and an inspector, and the remaining participants will be employees.
2. The facilitator will give the signal to start. This is a 10-minute, timed event utilizing competition among the groups.
3. After the first round, each group should report its production and profits to the entire class. Each group reports the manner in which it planned, organized, and controlled for the production of the paper airplanes.
4. This same procedure is followed for as many rounds as there is time.

Your group is the complete work force for Paper Plane Corporation. Established in 1943, Paper Plane has led the market in paper plane production.

Presently under new management, the company is contracting to make aircraft for the U.S. Air Force. You must establish a plan and organization to produce these aircraft. You must make your contract with the Air Force under the following conditions:

a. The Air Force will pay $20,000 per airplane.
b. The aircraft must pass a strict inspection.
c. A penalty of $25,000 per airplane will be imposed for failure to meet the production requirements.
d. Labor and other overhead will be computed in $300,000.
e. Cost of materials will be $3,000 per bid plane. If you bid for 10 but only make 8, you must pay the cost of materials for those you failed to make or that did not pass inspection.

The Learning Message

This exercise is an application of the planning, organizing, and controlling management functions. It will illustrate how these functions, if applied, can improve the end result or performance.

9

HUMAN RESOURCE MANAGEMENT

LEARNING OBJECTIVES

After completing Chapter 9, you should be able to:

■ **Define**
human resource management (HRM).

■ **Describe**
the activities conducted by various divisions of a human resource department: employment, training and development, wage and salary management, and employee benefits and services.

■ **Discuss**
the view that HRM is both a staff function and a line responsibility.

■ **Compare**
HRM activities in large and small business organizations.

■ **Identify**
the roles that the government plays in each phase of HRM.

MANAGEMENT IN ACTION

Companies That Understand How to Manage Human Resources*

American companies are rarely viewed from the perspective of their employees—that is, how well or badly are the human resources treated? The book *100 Best Companies to Work For in America* is a unique guide to excellence that rates America's top companies from an employee's perspective: pay, benefits, ambience, job security, training opportunities, and chances for advancement. In this Management in Action, we attempt to portray a few of the companies that are paying particular attention to human resource management issues and concerns.

Hewlett-Packard Company   (high technology; Palo Alto, California). Work units are kept small. There are no time clocks. You can work any eight-hour shift you want, beginning at 6 A.M., 7 A.M., or 8 A.M. The typical H–P office layout is a network of open partitions. Everyone is accessible. Concepts central to the H–P spirit are:

- Respect and dignity: individual self-esteem.
- Insurance: personal work protection.
- Training and education: a must for everyone.
- Performance: let's do it with enthusiasm.

Hallmark Cards, Inc.   (social-expression products; Kansas City, Missouri): Employees can receive interest-free loans of up to $1,000; free refreshments during breaks; a physical-fitness building at corporate headquarters; automatic, low-interest $2,500-a-year college loans for children of employees, with no payback until after graduation.

Publix Supermarkets, Inc.   (food markets; Lakeland, Florida). A new employee knows that dress codes are followed, profanity is frowned upon, and enthusiasm when interacting with customers is the way of doing business. Publix tells job applicants that if they are hired, they must devote themselves to making shopping a pleasure for customers. Employees share in a major benefit: they are the only shareholders. If Publix succeeds, the employees' wages and benefits grow and grow.

Managing work and organizations is made easier in firms like Hewlett-Packard, Hallmark Cards, and Publix because managers have accepted the responsibility for optimizing the use of employee skills and talents.

---

*Adapted from "15 Great Companies to Work For," *Management Review,* August 1985, pp. 39–43.

To meet the challenges of managing work and organizations, managers must understand the potential of human resources and then secure, retain, and develop these resources. This is the foundation of what is now called human resource management (HRM).

The management of any organizational unit or department—marketing, finance, accounting, personnel—involves the accomplishment of objectives through use of the skills and talents of people. Thus, HRM is considered both a line management responsibility and a staff function.[1]

In organizations of any size—large, medium, or small—human resources must be recruited, compensated, developed, and motivated. The small organization typically cannot afford to have a separate HRM department (also called personnel or industrial relations) that continually follows the progress of individuals and reviews the accomplishment of goals. Instead each manager is responsible for using the skills and talents of employees. Larger firms usually have a HRM department that can be a source of help to line managers. In either case, much of the work in recruitment, compensation, and performance appraisal must be finalized and implemented by managers.

HUMAN RESOURCE MANAGEMENT FUNCTION

The HRM program at General Mills serves the needs of that organization and facilitates the accomplishment of its objectives. But without modifications, their program would probably not be well suited for Burger King or Eli Lilly. Each company develops its own HRM program after considering such factors as size, type of skills needed, number of employees required, unionization, clients and customers, financial posture, and geographic location.

The successful HRM program also requires the cooperation of managers, because it is they who must interpret and implement policies and procedures. Line managers must translate into action what a HRM department provides. Without managerial support at the top, middle, and lower levels, HRM programs cannot succeed. Therefore, it is important that managers clearly understand how to mesh their responsibilities with those of the HRM department.

Human resource management can be defined as the process of accomplishing organizational objectives by acquiring, retaining, terminating, developing, and properly using the human resources in an organization. The notion of accomplishing objectives is a major part of any form of management. Unless objectives are regularly accomplished, the organization ceases to exist.

The *acquisition* of skilled, talented, and motivated employees is an important part of HRM. The acquisition phase involves recruiting, screening, selecting, and properly placing personnel.

---

[1] John M. Ivancevich and William Glueck, *Foundations of Personnel,* 3rd ed. (Plano, Tex.: Business Publications, 1986), p. 7.

Retaining competent individuals is important to any organization. If qualified individuals regularly leave a company, it becomes continually necessary to seek new personnel. This costs money and is time consuming.

The opposite of retention is, of course, *termination,* which is an unpleasant part of any manager's job. Employees occasionally must be terminated for breaking rules, failing to perform adequately, or job cutbacks. The procedures for such terminations usually are specified by an HRM staff expert or are covered in a labor-management contract.

FIGURE   9–1   An Example of a Personnel/Human Resource Management Department

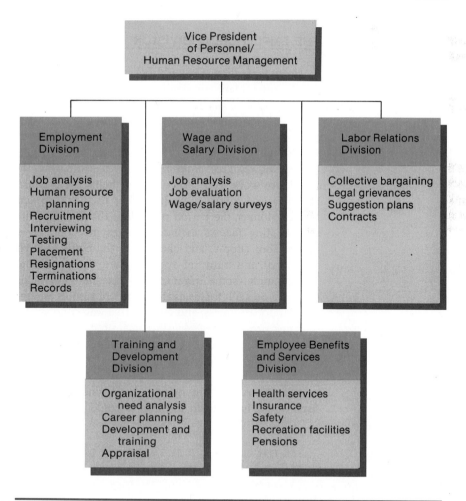

HRDs are organized according to each company's needs and objectives.

Developing personnel involves training, educating, appraising, and generally preparing personnel for present or future jobs. These activities are important for the economic and psychological growth of employees. Self-realization needs cannot be satisifed in an organization that does not have an efficient set of development activities.

The *proper use of people* involves understanding both individual and organizational needs so that the full potential of human resources can be employed. This part of human resource management suggests that it is important to match individuals over time to shifts in organizational and human needs.

HRM in larger organizations such as Alcoa, Bausch & Lomb, Polaroid, and Marriott is performed in a staff department like the one shown in Figure 9–1. Remember, however, that each company organizes its department according to its own set of needs and objectives.

THE EMPLOYMENT DIVISION

An organization can only be as effective as the people who operate the office, store, plant, or equipment. Thus, acquiring the necessary people is the first phase of any HRM program. This phase is carried out by the employment division.[2] Recruitment, selection, placement, and other employment activities of the employment division stem from the human resource plans established by managers throughout the organization.

Human resource planning involves estimating the size and makeup of the future work force. This process helps the organization acquire the right numbers and kinds of people when they are needed. Experience indicates that the longer the period predicted, the less accurate the prediction. Other complicating factors include changes in economic conditions, fluctuations in the labor supply, and changes in the political environment.[3]

Formal and informal approaches to human resource planning are used. For example, some organizations use mathematical projections. Data are collected on such topics as the supply of resources, labor market composition, demand for products, and competitive wage and salary programs. From these data and previous records, statistical procedures are used to make predictions. Of course, unpredictable events can alter past trends, but somewhat reliable forecasts can be made.

Suppose that the president of Lifter, Inc. didn't know that they would receive contracts from Boeing, Ford, and Republic Steel. In this case, the firm would have to do the best it could to meet the increased demand for

---

[2] M. Beer, B. Spector, P. R. Lawrence, D. Q. Mills, and R. Walton, *Managing Human Assets* (New York: Free Press, 1982), p. 12.

[3] L. James Harvey, "Effective Planning for Human Resource Development," *Personnel Administrator,* October 1983, pp. 45–52, 112.

its products. The president is faced with not having enough people to fulfill the contracts.

Estimating from experience is a more informal forecasting procedure.[4] For example, simply asking department managers for opinions about future human resource needs is an informal procedure. Some managers are confident in planning, whereas others are reluctant to offer an opinion or are just not reliable forecasters.

The J. C. Penney Company, a large retail merchandiser, plans its human resource needs from information supplied by each retail store. Penney's develops five-year consumer-demand projections for each position in the organization. Personnel needs in management are supplied primarily through promotion, because experienced employees have low turnover and clearly defined career paths. The company recruits recent college graduates for lower-level managerial and staff positions. All J. C. Penney managerial employees are called associates to give them a stronger sense of commitment to the organization, and each employee is evaluated on potential for being promoted. These evaluations give the company a readily available companywide inventory of human resources. A computer is used to match present and anticipated vacancies with available associates.

Recruitment

Recruitment is an essential step in staffing an organization. Its primary objective is to acquire the best-qualified applicants to fill vacancies.[5] However, even before acquiring applicants, it is necessary to understand clearly the job that needs to be filled. The methods and procedures used to acquire an understanding about jobs are called job analysis.[6] It is through job analysis that managers decide what kind of people to hire.

Sources of job information.   Job analysis is the process of determining the tasks that make up the job and the skills, abilities, and responsibilities an employee needs to successfully accomplish the job. There are numerous methods used to collect and classify job analysis information. Interviews, surveys, self-reports, and expert-observer rating scales are some of the more popular job analysis data collection procedures. The facts about a job are found in what are called a *job description* and a *job specification.* The relationship between these is shown in Figure 9–2.

An efficient job analysis program provides information that is used by

---

[4] Gary Dessler, *Personnel Management* (Reston, Va.: Reston Publishing, 1984), p. 120.

[5] Ann Coil, "Job Matching Brings Out the Best in Employees," *Personnel Journal,* January 1984, pp. 54–61.

[6] Sidney Gael, *Job Analysis* (San Francisco: Jossey-Bass, 1983), p. 35.

FIGURE   9–2   Sources of Job Information

Job analysis provides the HRD with the criteria for evaluating applicants for a specific job in the organization.

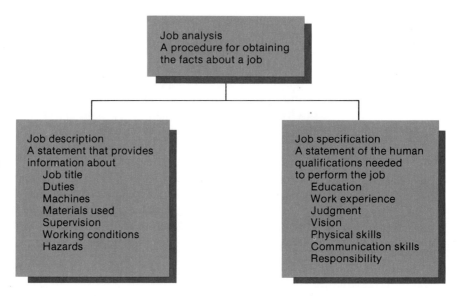

every division within the human resource management department. For example, to recruit and select effectively, it is necessary to match qualified personnel with job requirements. The full set of job information is provided by the description and specification. Another example involves the establishment of proper rates of pay. If equitable pay systems are to emerge, it is necessary to have a complete job description. An example of a job description is provided in Figure 9–3.

Two widely used, systematic job analysis approaches are functional job analysis (FJA) and the position analysis questionnaire (PAQ).[7]

Functional job analysis focuses on four dimensions of an individual job:

1. What the worker does in relation to data, people, and jobs.
2. What methods and techniques the worker uses.
3. What machines, tools, and equipment the worker uses.
4. What materials, products, subject matter, or services the worker produces.

The first three dimensions relate to job performance *activities,* and the fourth relates to job *outcomes.* Thus, FJA provides a description of jobs that can be the basis for classifying them according to any one of the four dimensions.

---

[7] Marc J. Wallace, Jr., N. Fredric Crandall, and Charles H. Fay, *Administering Human Resources* (New York: Random House, 1982), pp. 187–97.

FIGURE   9–3   Job Description

Job: New-Products Manager
 Victoreen Electronics (plant)
 Palos Park, Illinois

The new-products manager reports directly to the vice president of product planning.

The new-products manager plans, organizes, and directs the development and testing of electronic products produced for industrial customers of the organization.

Responsibility Domain

A. Plans from worksheet to final production all electronic products requested by the vice president of product planning.
B. Establishes appropriate project teams to carry out plans within time and budget constraints.
C. Provides managerial guidance and counseling to project team leaders on all phases of the project.
D. Develops adequate quality testing for all newly developed products.
E. Prepares cost-benefit analysis on each project assigned.

Supervision Domain

Project leaders (3)   Accountant/economist (1)
Operational engineers (15)   Drafter (1)
Process technicians (3)   Secretary (1)
Apprentice operational engineers (3)

Coordination Domain

• Coordinates activities with each new-products manager through preparation of prework planning document.
• Coordinates with purchasing department in arranging for the purchase of necessary materials to complete projects.
• Coordinates with personnel department in arranging for proper recruiting, selection, training and development, and compensation of employees within the supervision domain.

Job description completed   _____
                                                                    Date
Prepared by job analyst   _____
                                                               Signature
Accepted by vice president of product   _____
planning   Signature
Filed by vice president of personnel   _____
                                                               Signature

FJA can also be the basis for defining standards of performance. For example, managers can prescribe what an individual should do with what methods and machines to produce a standard level of output. FJA is the most widely used systematic job analysis method[8] and is the basis for the most extensive listing of occupational titles.[9]

The *position analysis questionnaire* focuses on the actual behavior of the individual in the performance of the job. PAQ has been the object of considerable attention by both researchers and practitioners who believe that position analysis must take into account not only job-oriented dimensions but also worker-oriented dimensions.[10] A PAQ analysis attempts to identify six dimensions:

1. Information sources critical to job performance.
2. Information processing and decision making critical to job performance.
3. Physical activity and dexterity required by the job.
4. Interpersonal relationships required by the job.
5. Physical working conditions and the reactions of individuals to those conditions.
6. Other job characteristics, such as work schedule and work responsibility.

PAQ and FJA overlap considerably. Each attempts to identify work activities and outcomes. But PAQ includes the additional consideration of the employees' psychological responses to the job demands and context. Thus, PAQ attempts to acknowledge that job performance is a combination of job dimensions and human characteristics. It enables managers to set standards and obtain information about the individual, the performance of work and the results of work (see Figure 9–4).

Performing accurate job analysis for many jobs is a complex task. For example, the job of managing is difficult to analyze. Planning, organizing, and controlling involve abstract thinking and decision making. And these activities are difficult to quantify. However, if performance appraisals are to be meaningful, fair, and comprehensive for the manager's job or any job, a systematic job analysis that results in the identification of standards is essential.

Legal aspects of recruiting.   Individuals responsible for recruiting are faced with legal requirements. For example, a certain percentage of minority group members and women must now be recruited for positions that have seldom been filled by these people. These requirements are enforced by laws administered by the Equal Employment Opportunity Commission (EEOC).

---

[8] Ibid., p. 196.

[9] U.S. Department of Labor, *Dictionary of Occupational Titles,* 4th ed., (Washington, D.C.: U.S. Government Printing Office, 1977).

[10] E. J. McCormick, P. R. Jeanneret, and R. C. Mecham, "A Study of Job Characteristics and Job Dimensions as Based on the Position Analysis Questionnaire (PAQ)." *Journal of Applied Psychology,* August 1972, pp. 347–68.

The federal government attempts to provide equal opportunities for employment without regard to race, religion, age, creed, sex, national origin, or disability through Title VII of the Civil Rights Act of 1964 and the Equal Employment Opportunity Act of 1972.[11] These laws have broad coverage and apply to any activity, business, or industry in which a labor dispute would hinder commerce. The laws also cover state and local governments, governmental agencies, and agencies of the District of Columbia.

Some of the specific provisions of the Equal Opportunity Act of 1972 are:

- It is unlawful for an employer to fail or refuse to hire or to discharge any individual, or otherwise to discriminate against any individual with respect to compensation, conditions, or privileges of employment because of race, color, religion, sex, age, or national origin. This applies to applicants for employment as well as current employees.
- Employers may not limit, segregate, or classify employees in any way that would deprive them of employment opportunities because of race, color, age, religion, sex, or national origin.
- The EEOC now has the power to file action in a federal district court if it is unable to eliminate alleged unlawful employment practices by the informal methods of conference, conciliation, and persuasion.
- Employment tests may be used if it can be proven that they are related to the job or promotion sought by the individual. Tests should be validated for each company.
- No discriminatory statements may be included in any advertisements for job opportunities.

The EEOC attempted at first to encourage employers to follow the guidelines of the law. Now the EEOC is more aggressive and asks employers to prepare *affirmative action programs;*[12] the employer must spell out how the company plans to increase the number of minority and female employees. If EEOC investigators do not like the distribution of employees, they can propose adjustments. The employer may then state why these adjustments can or cannot be made.

Even if the EEOC does not get involved with an employer, an individual who feels that discrimination is taking place may sue. The number of complaints of job discrimination has increased from 8,800 in 1966 to over 75,000 in 1985.[13] However, as of December 1985, the EEOC is bringing only approximately 300 suits per year against employers.

The hiring practices of airlines have been the subject of two important court decisions on recruitment. One held that female gender is not a bona

---

[11] Kenneth Sovereign, *Personnel Law* (Reston, Va.: Reston Publishing, 1984).

[12] Paul S. Greenlaw, "Affirmative Action or Reverse Discrimination," *Personnel Journal,* September 1985, pp. 84–86.

[13] Correspondence and discussions with EEOC, Washington, D.C., September 1985.

fide occupational qualification for the job of cabin flight attendant. Another held that an airline's policy that stewardesses must be single is unlawful. No other female employees were subject to the policy, and there was no formal policy restricting employment to single male stewards. Another court ruled it illegal to fire a female employee because she is pregnant and unmarried. A sex discrimination case against a New York law firm was settled, before a court ruling, when it agreed to recruit, hire, and promote women attorneys on the same basis as men.

The legal procedures regarding equal employment opportunities and recruitment are important to employers. Organizations have to adjust to and work with these laws. Although adjustments are sometimes difficult, they seem to be a better alternative than becoming involved in long and costly court battles. Providing equal opportunities to all qualified job applicants makes sense both legally and morally. The vast majority of managers in organizations believe that all citizens have a right to any job they can perform reasonably well after a sufficient amount of training.

An interesting legal twist was uncovered in a case involving an executive-search recruiting firm (firms hired to find candidates for employers). The Management Focus describes that case.

MANAGEMENT FOCUS
Obtaining Confidential Information May Lead to a Court Appearance

McGraw-Hill, Inc., publisher of *Business Week,* sued a San Francisco executive-search firm, F. R. Bacci & Co., charging that one of its recruiters had posed as a *Business Week* reporter in an effort to get sensitive information from several companies. Bacci was not penalized for the misrepresentation but did agree to obey a judge's order to stop the practice.

The case was unusual in that it initiated a lawsuit. However, the use of ruse calling to check on a company or a job candidate happens quite frequently. Often companies unwittingly reveal to unprincipled recruiters what many consider to be confidential information. An aggressive recruiter can ferret out information about a person's approximate salary and fringe-benefit package, home address, family, names of previous employers, and how many people work for him or her. The best sources of information seem to be switchboard operators, receptionists, and secretaries. These employees have typically never been instructed about what kind of information is confidential.

Some firms like Bacci are paid for the time and effort they use

> **MANAGEMENT FOCUS** *(continued)*
>
> to locate a job for their clients. They are paid a retainer even if the candidate is not successful. Other search firms are referred to as "contingency recruiters." They receive no compensation unless they find a candidate for a position and the person is actually hired. Contingency recruiting is highly competitive and relies heavily on information as the most important resource. By finding out personal and job information about a person, they can determine whether the job they are trying to fill would be attractive. Also, by getting a person's home address and telephone number, they can reach the potential candidate at home and talk at greater length.
>
> The *McGraw-Hill* v. *Bacci* case indicates that the courts will not sit idly by while aggressive recruiters practice the ruse technique to find talent for clients. Violations against EEO and affirmative action programs and now misrepresentation by recruiters are all causes for lawsuits and concern among managers.
>
> ---
>
> Adapted from John C. Perham, "How Recruiters Get the Lowdown," *Dun's Business Month,* May 1985, pp. 60–61.

Recruiting actions. If the needed human resources are not available from within the company, outside sources must be tapped. A well-known firm such as General Mills has a file on previous applicants. Even though such applicants were not hired, they frequently maintain an interest in working for a company with a good reputation and image. By careful screening of these files, some good applicants can be added to the pool of candidates.

Advertisement in newspapers, trade journals, and magazines is a means to secure new applications.[14] Occasionally, a company will list a post-office box number and not provide the company name. This form of advertisement is called a *blind advertisement.* Blind ads are used to eliminate the necessity of contacting every applicant, since some will be unqualified. However, a blind ad does not permit the company to use its name or logo, which is a form of promotion.

One of the most important sources for recruiting lower-level managers is the college campus. Many colleges and universities have placement centers that work with organizational recruiters. The applicants read advertisements and information provided by the companies and then are interviewed. The most promising students are invited to visit the company, where other interviews are conducted.

---

[14] Allan Halcrow, "Anatomy of a Recruitment Ad," *Personnel Journal,* August 1985, pp. 64–65.

In locating experienced employees, organizations can use private employment agencies, executive-search firms, or state employment agencies. Some are no-fee agencies, which means that employers pay the fee (if there is one) instead of the applicant. An organization is not obligated to hire any person referred by an agency, but the agency is usually informed when the right person is located.

Employee Selection and Placement

The selection and placement of personnel begins with a need for human resources and depends on legal requirements. Discriminatory practices in recruiting, testing, and offering a job are illegal, as stated in the Civil Rights Act of 1964 and the Equal Employment Opportunity Act of 1972.

The selection process is a series of steps that starts with the initial screening and ends with the orientation of newly hired employees. Figure 9–4 is a flow diagram showing each step in the process. Preliminary interviews are used to screen out unqualified applicants. This screening is often the first personal contact an applicant has with a company. The applicant who passes the preliminary screening usually completes an application blank.

Applications.   The application blank is used to obtain information that can help in reaching an employment decision. It is important that the questions on the blank be able, even in a general sense, to predict job success. The appropriate questions are usually developed after a careful job analysis is completed. The application form should be complete enough to provide necessary information and yet concise enough not to be a jumbled mass of unnecessary information.

Interviews.   Interviews are used throughout the selection process, but there are three basic interviewing steps.[15] First, interviewers must acquaint themselves with the job analysis. Second, they must analyze the information on application blanks. Third, interviewers need to ask questions that can add to what is included on the application blank. While performing these three interviewing steps, the interviewer must be courteous, create a favorable atmosphere, and provide the applicants with information and a positive image of the organization.[16]

---

[15] William L. Donoghy, *The Interview: Skills and Applications* (Glenview, Ill.: Scott, Foresman, 1984), p. 18.

[16] Richard A. Fear, *The Evaluation Interview* (New York: McGraw-Hill, 1984), p. 78.

FIGURE   9–4   Steps in the Selection Process

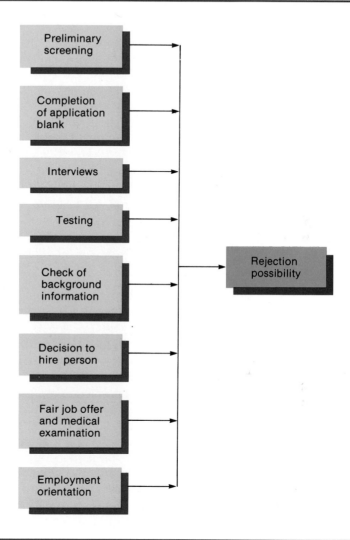

Legal requirements and human resource needs influence each step in the selection process.

Interviewing involves some science and some art. The Management Focus on provocative questions shows how a Philadelphia firm has used interviewing as a main aid in finding the right person for the job. The firm is hired by employers to develop a series of carefully phrased questions to screen job applicants.

MANAGEMENT FOCUS
Provocative Interview Questions: A Selection Tool

When you enter the interview room seeking a job, are you ready to answer some provocative questions? A skilled interviewer can ask such questions to detect the real candidates from the pretend candidates. How would you answer these questions:

"If I (the interviewer) were to call your immediate past supervisor, what would I be told about you?"

"Do you think you should be able to criticize management?"

"How do you react to rumors on the job?"

These kind of thought-provoking interview questions have been developed by a Philadelphia legal firm specializing in labor law and industrial relations. Pechner, Dorfman, Wolffe, Rownick, & Cabot has spent more than 10 years refining interview questions for job candidates.

The questions are geared to seek out positive traits such as a sense of achievement, a desire for success and recognition, goal and teamwork orientation, and pride in one's work. Employers also attempt through the use of the interview questions to spot chronic complainers, people who will do only one job at a time, nonteam workers, and those who don't believe in management authority.

Questions like Pechner's don't address candidate style or preference directly. Rather they subtly prompt replies on such indicators as abnormal nervousness and rebelliousness (on the negative side) or creativity and independence (on the positive side).

Let's take another look at the three loaded questions. For the first question, the candidate doesn't know if you will make a call or not. Asking about criticizing management looks for whether the prospect has respect for authority and has enough self-confidence to question management. The candidate that pays no attention to rumors may be displaying a lack of interest. The ideal answer to this question is, "Generally, I don't pay attention to rumors on the job. However, if I hear something that concerns me, I want to check it out with my boss."

The Pechner type of questions do not offer perfectly accurate measures of a candidate's job skills or interest. However, after 10 years of refinement and modification, they appear to be good enough for many firms to use to help them hire the best people.

Adapted from Thomas M. Rohan, "Loaded Questions . . . Help to Hire the Right People," *Industry Week,* January 21, 1985, pp. 43–44.

Testing.   For years, selection tests have been used to screen applicants.[17] Widespread use of tests started with World War II, when the Army Alpha Test was used to measure intelligence. The installation of a sound testing program is costly and time consuming, and it must be done by experts. Just because a test has been useful for selecting sales personnel in one company is no reason to believe that it will be just as useful in another company.

The advantages of a testing program include:

- *Improved accuracy in selecting employees.* Individuals differ in skills, intelligence, motivation, interests, and goals. If these differences can be measured and if they are related to job success, then performance can be predicted to some extent by test scores.
- *An objective means for judging.* Applicants answer the same questions under the same test conditions, so one applicant's score can be compared to the scores of other applicants.
- *Information for present employee needs.* When tests are given to present employees, they can provide information about training, development, or counseling needs. Thus, they can objectively uncover needs.

Despite these advantages, tests have become controversial in recent years. Important legal rulings and fair-employment codes have resulted in strict procedures for developing tests. The following criticisms have been directed at testing programs:

- *Tests are not infallible.* Test may reveal what people can do but not what they will do.
- *Tests are given too much weight.* Tests cannot measure everything about a person. They can never be a complete substitute for judgment.
- *Tests discriminate against minorities.* Ethnic minorities, such as blacks and Mexican-Americans, may score lower on certain paper-and-pencil tests than whites. Title VII, Equal Employment Opportunity, of the Civil Rights Act of 1964, prohibits employment practices that artificially discriminate against individuals on the basis of test scores.[18]

Despite the problems, controversies, and costs involved, tests are widely used. Testing is a part of the employment process, one of the tools that can help the manager make decisions. In summary, test results provide some usable information, but they do not provide a total picture of how well the person will perform.

The hiring decision.   After the preliminary screening—evaluating the application form, interviewing, and testing—the company may decide to make an offer. If so, a background check is usually made. By consulting references,

---

[17] Anne Anastasi, *Psychological Testing* (New York: Macmillan, 1982), p. 12.

[18] Dale Yoder and Paul D. Standoher, "Testing and EEO: Getting Down to Cases," *Personnel Administrator,* February 1984, pp. 67–76.

the background check verifies information, usually by letter, by telephone, or in person. One important group of references is previous employers; the company tries to gather facts about the applicant's previous record of job performance. Under the Fair Credit and Reporting Act, the prospective employer is required to secure the applicant's permission before checking references.

When the reference check yields favorable information, the line manager and an employment division representative meet to decide what the offer will be. The offer is usually made subject to successful completion of a physical examination. This examination can be conducted by a company physician or a doctor outside the organization. The objective is to screen out people whose physical deficiencies might be expensive liabilities and to place people on jobs they are physically able to handle.

TRAINING AND DEVELOPMENT

Training and development programs include numerous activities that inform employees of policies and procedures, educate them in job skills, and develop them for future advancement. The training and development program's importance to the organization cannot be overemphasized. Through recruitment and placement, good employees can be brought into the company, but they need orientation and continual education and development so that their needs and the objectives of the organization can be achieved simultaneously.[19]

Training Programs

Training is a continual process of helping employees perform at a high level from the first day a person starts to work. It may occur at the place of work or at a special training facility, but it should always be supervised by experts in the educational process.

To be effective, a training program must accomplish a number of goals. First, it must be based on organizational and individual needs. Training for training's sake is not the aim. Second, the training objectives should spell out what problems will be solved. Third, all training should be based on sound theories of learning; this is a major reason that training and management development are not tasks for amateurs. Finally, training must be evaluated to determine whether a training program is working.[20]

1. *Locating problems.*   Before a training program can be developed, prob-

[19] David F. Jones, "Developing a New Employee Orientation Program," *Personnel Journal,* March 1984, pp. 86–87.

[20] Elaine I. Berke, "Keeping Newly Trained Supervisors from Going Back to Old Ways," *Management Review,* February 1984, pp 14–16.

lem areas must be pinpointed. Organizations can use a number of techniques to identify problems, including reviewing safety records, absenteeism, data, job descriptions, and attitude surveys to see what employees think about their jobs, bosses, and the company.

2. *Setting objectives.*   Once training needs have been identified, objectives need to be stated in writing. These objectives provide a framework for the program. The objectives need to be concise, accurate, meaningful, and challenging. There are usually two major categories of objectives: skills and knowledge. Skill objectives focus on developing physical abilities; knowledge objectives are concerned with understanding, attitudes, and concepts.

3. *Conducting programs.*   A variety of methods are available for reaching the skill and knowledge objectives. Such factors as cost, available time, number of persons to be trained, background of trainees, and skill of the trainees determine the method used. Some of the more widely used are:

- *On-the-job training.*   A supervisor or other worker may show a new employee how to perform the job.
- *Vestibule training.*   This term describes training in a classroom or away from the actual work area.
- *Classroom training.*   Numerous classroom methods are used by business organizations. The lecture or formal presentation is one method. Another, a conference or small discussion group gets the student more involved than the lecture method.

Developmental Methods

Training is generally associated with operating employees; management development is associated with managerial personnel. Management development refers to the process of educating and developing selected personnel so that they have the knowledge, skills, attitudes, and understanding needed to manage in future positions. The process starts with the selection of a qualified individual and continues through that individual's career.

The objectives of management development are to ensure the long-run success of the organization, to furnish competent replacements, to create an efficient team that works well together, and to enable each manager to use his or her full potential. Management development may also be necessary because of high executive turnover, a shortage of management talent, and our society's emphasis on lifelong education and development.

There are two main ways employees can acquire the knowledge, skills, attitudes, and understanding necessary to become successful managers.[21] One is through formal development programs; the other involves on-the-job development. On-the-job programs include:

---

[21] Peter Petre, "Games That Teach You to Manage," *Fortune,* October 29, 1984, pp. 65–72.

- *Understudy programs.* A person works as a subordinate partner with a boss so that eventually he or she can assume the full responsibilities and duties of the job.
- *Job rotation.* Managers are transferred from job to job on a systematic basis. The assignment on each job generally lasts about six months.
- *Coaching.* A supervisor teaches job knowledge and skills to a subordinate. The supervisor instructs, directs, corrects, and evaluates the subordinate.

These on-the-job development plans emphasize actual job experience. They are used to increase the manager's skill, knowledge, and confidence.

Formal management development programs are often conducted by training units within organizations or by consultants in universities and specialized training facilities around the country. In the very large corporations (such as General Electric, Westinghouse, and AT&T), full-time training units conduct regular management development courses. For example, one major course offered at General Electric, the Advanced Management Course, is designed for the four highest levels of management. It is conducted over a period of 13 weeks, and its content includes business policy, economics, social issues, and management principles.

Performance Appraisal

Performance appraisal involves the formal evaluation of an individual's job performance. It includes feedback to the individual and determination of whether and how the performance can be improved. As a control technique, effective performance appraisal requires standards, information, and corrective action: The *standard* in performance evaluation is prior specification of acceptable levels of job performance. *Information* must be available to measure actual job performance in comparison to standard job performance. Finally, managers must be able to take *corrective action* to restore any imbalance between actual and standard job performance.

Because performance appraisal involves individuals judging the quality and quantity of job performance of other individuals, the process is inherently emotion laden; it brings into play ideas and perceptions of fairness, equity, and equal treatment. The human element of performance appraisal must be taken into account if it is to serve individual and organizational purposes.

As shown in Figure 9–5, a performance appraisal system has the characteristics of all feedback control methods. Through the system, managers can obtain information related to inputs (employees), activities (job performance), and outputs (outcomes). Corrective action is directed toward changing employee's abilities and skills, plus job performance actions, activities, and behaviors. The effectiveness of a performance appraisal system depends on the

---

FIGURE   9–5   Performance Appraisal

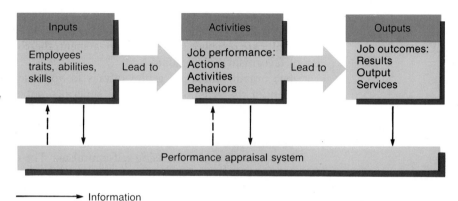

Feedback is an integral facet of effective performance appraisal.

---

quality of the three elements of all control techniques: standards, information, and corrective action.

Performance appraisal standards.   The most crucial aspect of performance appraisal is identifying the standard of effective performance. In performance evaluation systems, it is customary to refer to standards as "criteria"—ways of identifying success in an activity.[22] A criterion for a major-league pitcher is earned-run average; a criterion for a student is the grade earned in a course or the grade-point average after one year at college. An important and necessary step in developing a performance appraisal system is development of criteria that indicate successful performance.

Primary sources of individual job performance criteria are the organization's overall objectives and strategies. It is an important principle that individual performance should contribute to organizational performance. Although this principle seems self-evident, it remains difficult to implement, particularly when organizational objectives change.

Performance appraisal information.   Information enables managers to judge the performance of subordinates. Managers must decide three issues regarding performance information: (1) the source, (2) the schedule, and (3) the method.

Sources of information.   Five possible parties can provide appraisal information: (1) the supervisor or supervisors of the appraisee; (2) peers; (3) the

---

[22] Frank J. Landy and Don A. Trumbo, *Psychology of Work Behavior* (Chicago: Dorsey Press, 1980), p. 99.

appraisee; (4) subordinates of the appraisee; and (5) individuals outside the work environment. In most situations, the appraiser is the immediate supervisor of the person rated and should be most familiar with the employee's performance. In addition, many organizations regard performance appraisal as an integral part of the immediate supervisor's job. The supervisor's appraisals usually are reviewed by higher management, thereby reducing the possibility of favoritism and personal bias.

Some organizations use group ratings to appraise managerial personnel. Members of the group could include superiors, subordinates, and peers; in some companies, peer appraisal systems are used. Lack of success with peer appraisal is not unusual. Peers need mutual cooperation to do their jobs, and performance appraisal undermines the spirit of cooperation.

There is some interest in using self-appraisals. The major claims in support of this approach are that it improves the employee's understanding of job performance, increases the personal commitment of employees because of their participation in the performance appraisal process, and reduces the hostility between superiors and subordinates over ratings. Some employers fear that self-appraisals will be unusually high and not sufficiently critical of current performance.

There is some support for the use of multiple appraisers. The major advantage of using superior, peer, and self-ratings is that this provides a great deal of information about the appraisee. In making decisions about promotion, training and development, and career planning, as much information as possible is needed to suggest the best alternative courses of action for the employee.

Schedule of appraisal.   There is no specific schedule for appraising all types of employees. In general, one formal appraisal a year is provided for older or tenured employees. Recent hirees usually are appraised more frequently than other employees. The time to appraise will depend on the situation and on the intent of the appraisal. If performance appraisals either are too far apart or occur too frequently, the appraisee may not be able to use the feedback received to make improvements.

An appraisal program conducted solely for the sake of appraising employees soon will lose impact unless it becomes integrated with the main emphasis of the organization. The performance appraisal program should be considered a continual process that focuses on task accomplishment, personal development, and the organization's objectives.

Appraisal methods.   At one extreme of simplicity, the method of information gathering consists solely of the manager's periodic observations of the subordinate's work behavior. Based on these observations, the manager makes judgments of the subordinate's work performance. At the other extreme are complex systems that involve documents, procedures, and reviews. In such formal systems, the manager completes forms documenting the subordinate's performance during the period covered by the appraisal. A number of performance evaluation systems have been developed.

Graphic Rating Scales.   The oldest and most widely used performance evaluation procedure, the graphic-scaling technique, appears in many forms. Generally, the rater is supplied with a printed form, one for each subordinate to be rated. The form contains a number of job performance criteria to rate. The rating scales are distinguished by (1) how the criteria are defined, (2) the degree to which the person interpreting the ratings can tell what response was intended by the rater, and (3) how carefully the performance criteria are defined for the rater.

Some common rating-scale formats are depicted in Figure 9–6. The first distinguishing feature, the meaning of the possible response categories, usually is handled by the use of "anchor statements." Anchor statements or words are placed at points along a scale. For example, Rating Scales *a, b, c,* and *h* use anchors.

The second distinguishing feature among rating scales is the degree to which the person interpreting the ratings can tell what response is intended. The clarity of the intended response is better with Scales *(e), (f),* and *(g)* than with the other scales shown. "Quality of work" can be interpreted differently by various raters.

A performance criterion must be defined carefully. For example, Scales *a, b, e,* and *g* give the rater little help in defining the criterion. Scales *c* and *h* provide the rater with fairly good definitions.

Behaviorally Anchored Rating Scales.   Behaviorally anchored rating scales (BARS) are constructed through the use of critical incidents.[23] Once the important areas of performance are identified and defined by employees who know the job, critical-incident statements are used as criteria to discriminate among levels of performance. The form for a BARS usually covers 6 to 10 specifically defined job behaviors, each uniquely described. Each description is based on observable behaviors and is meaningful to the employees being evaluated.

An example of a BARS for engineering competence is presented in Figure 9–7. The criterion is defined for the appraiser; the descriptions defining the particular response categories are easy to interpret. The feedback provided by the BARS is specific and meaningful. For example, if the appraisee is given a 1.50 on this criterion, the individual is provided with the specific performance incident that the appraiser used to make the rating.

A number of advantages are associated with the use of BARS. Since job-knowledgeable employees participate in the actual development steps, the final rating form is assumed to be reliable, valid, and meaningful and cover all aspects of the job. A common problem of many performance appraisal techniques is that they do not evaluate all aspects of a job. The use of BARS also provides valuable insights for developing training programs. The skills to be developed are specified in terms of actual behavioral incidents rather

---

[23] P. C. Smith and L. M. Kendall, "Retranslation of Expectations: An Approach to the Construction of Unambiguous Anchors for Rating Scales," *Journal of Applied Psychology,* April 1963, pp. 149–55.

FIGURE 9–6 Samples of Rating-Scale Formats

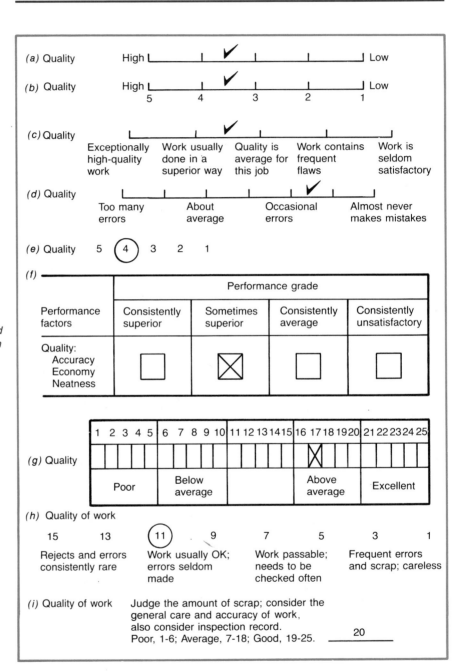

Anchor statements and response interpretation are crucial features.

FIGURE 9-7 A BARS Performance Dimension

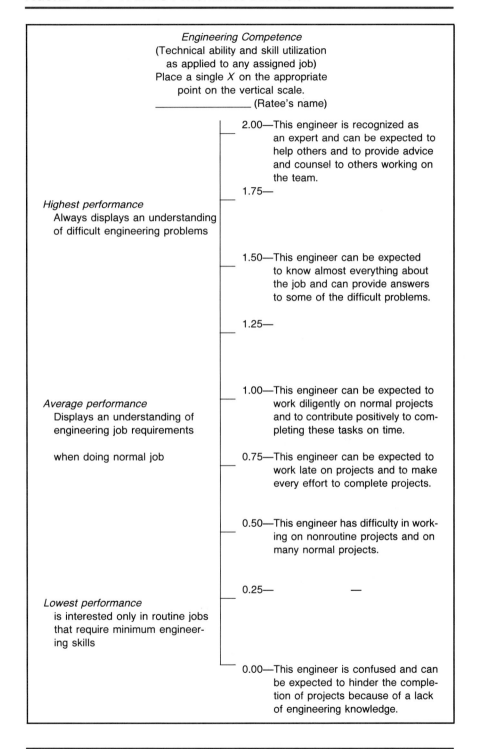

Engineering Competence
(Technical ability and skill utilization
as applied to any assigned job)
Place a single X on the appropriate
point on the vertical scale.
_____ (Ratee's name)

2.00—This engineer is recognized as an expert and can be expected to help others and to provide advice and counsel to others working on the team.

1.75—

Highest performance
Always displays an understanding of difficult engineering problems

1.50—This engineer can be expected to know almost everything about the job and can provide answers to some of the difficult problems.

1.25—

1.00—This engineer can be expected to work diligently on normal projects and to contribute positively to completing these tasks on time.

Average performance
Displays an understanding of engineering job requirements

when doing normal job

0.75—This engineer can be expected to work late on projects and to make every effort to complete projects.

0.50—This engineer has difficulty in working on nonroutine projects and on many normal projects.

0.25—   —

Lowest performance
is interested only in routine jobs that require minimum engineering skills

0.00—This engineer is confused and can be expected to hinder the completion of projects because of a lack of engineering knowledge.

than abstract or general skills. Trainees could learn expected behaviors and how job performance is evaluated.

Despite the time, cost, and procedural problems of developing and implementing BARS, this system seems to possess some advantages. Specifically, a BARS program could minimize subordinate or appraisee defensiveness toward evaluation. By being involved in the development of BARS, appraisees have input, which can be incorporated into the final BARS. The BARS development steps could include both superiors and subordinates. In a sense then, all of the parties involved can contribute to the creation of the evaluation criteria.

Another advantage of using BARS is that the appraisal program concentrates on job-specific and job-relevant behaviors. Many performance appraisal programs are abstract and not meaningful to either the appraised or the appraiser. Thus, when providing feedback to employees, the appraisers must convert the ratings to examples of actual job behavior. There are, in many cases, variances in the appraiser's ability to make these conversions from the rating scale to meaningful job behaviors. BARS already contain behaviors that the superior can use in developing the appraisal counseling interview.

WAGE AND SALARY MANAGEMENT

In modern society, money is important both economically and psychologically. Without it, a person can't buy the goods and services that make life comfortable. Money is also equated with status and recognition. Because money is so important, employees are quite sensitive about the amount of pay they receive and how it compares to what others in the company and in society are earning. It is important for employees to believe that they are being fairly compensated for the time, effort, and results they provide the employer.[24]

Employee Compensation

The most common system by which operating or nonmanagerial employees are compensated is *wages* based on time increments or number of units produced. Blue-collar workers traditionally have been paid at an hourly or daily rate, although some blue-collar employees are now being paid biweekly or monthly. Employees who are compensated on a weekly or longer schedule are paid *salaries*. Hewlett-Packard is one organization that has eliminated

---

[24] George Milkovich and Jerry M. Newman, *Compensation* (Plano, Tex.: Business Publications, 1984), pp. 269–87.

the daily rate of pay and now considers all personnel at all levels to be salaried employees.[25]

Wages.   Some organizations try to motivate employees to improve performance by paying on the basis of the number of units produced. This is called a piecework system. Piece rates are calculated by dividing the hourly wage for the job by the number of units an average employee is expected to produce in an hour. For example, if the rate of pay is $5 per hour and the average employee is expected to produce 25 units per hour, then the piece rate is 20 cents per unit. If a worker produced 40 pieces under this plan, he or she would earn $8 for the hour.

A daily rate of pay is easier than a piece rate to understand and use, because time standards and records of the employee's output are not needed. Unions generally prefer the daily rate of pay over systems that involve piecework or incentive payments. This preference is based on the belief that a piecework system tends to reduce a group orientation. By being paid on the basis of individual effort, a worker can produce at any level he or she wants to. The union prefers to encourage group solidarity and a united front.

Many factors help determine the wage rate for a nonmanagerial job. Wages for certain jobs are affected by the availability of and demand for qualified personnel, although unions and the government may hinder the effects of supply and demand. Through strike threats and contract agreements, for example, unions can prevent employers from lowering wage rates, even when qualified personnel abound.

The existing wage rates in competing companies or in the community also help determine wage scales. Organizations typically conduct wage surveys to assess hourly rates, piecework or other incentive rates, and fringe benefits offered by other organizations. If the wage rates of an organization are too low, it may not continue to attract qualified personnel.

In many organizations, the relative worth of a job and the wage adjustments for it are determined by using *job evaluation* systems. A job is compared with others within the organization or with a scale. Under the ranking method, all jobs are ranked, from highest to lowest, on the basis of skill, difficulty, working conditions, contribution to goods or services, or other characteristics. This is a simple plan but not totally objective. The personalities of the current jobholders often distort rankings. Nor are unions enthusiastic about job evaluation. With such a system, the union negotiator has almost no role to play.

Wage and salary administration, like other areas of HRM, has been the target of various laws. For instance, full-time employees must be paid at least $3.35 per hour. Since the first minimum wage law, enacted in 1938, the rate has risen over 1,000 percent, from 25 cents to $3.35 as of January

---

[25] Edward E. Lawler III, "The New Pay," *New Management,* Summer 1985, pp. 52–59.

1, 1986. In addition, the Fair Labor Standards Act (1938) forbids the employment of minors between 16 and 18 years of age in such hazardous occupations as coal mining, logging, and woodworking. And the Equal Pay Act (1963) forbids employers to pay employees differently on the basis of sex. Women performing the same work as men must receive the same wage or salary. AT&T was required to pay $6.3 million to 6,100 women employees whose pay had suffered because of their sex.[26] The act does not prohibit compensation differences based on seniority, merit, or performance.

Salaries.   Salaried employees are assumed to have more influence over the way they perform their jobs than are employees who are paid wages.[27] But in developing an equitable compensation system for executives, a similar approach is used: Comparisons are made, surveys are conducted, and both the supply and demand of candidates and the job duties and responsibilities are analyzed.

One method developed specifically for evaluating middle- and top-level management positions was initiated by Hay Associates. First, analysts evaluate each position from information provided in the job description. Three factors are analyzed: job know-how, problem solving, and accountability. Then, through a statistical procedure, the evaluation for the jobs in a particular company are converted to the Hay control standards, a special ranking system. Hay Associates publishes annual surveys showing the compensation practices of a number of companies for jobs of similar control standards. All Hay clients use the same evaluation method, so they can compare management salaries.

BENEFITS AND SERVICES

Benefits and services are forms of supplementary compensation. They represent monetary and nonmonetary payments over and above wage and salary rates. Benefits are financial in nature, whereas services are employer-supplied programs, facilities, or activities (such as parks, gymnasiums, housing, transportation) that are considered useful to employees.

If benefits and services are to yield a return to the employer and provide something positive to employees, they must be developed and used systematically. Too often, the so-called fringes are improperly installed. It is important to determine what benefits and services are preferred by employees and what resources are available to meet these preferences, and then select the best

---

[26] Michael F. Carter, "Comparable Worth: An Idea Whose Time Has Come?" *Personnel Journal,* October 1981, pp. 792–94.

[27] Paul G. Engel, "Salaried Plants: Panacea for Productivity?" *Industry Week,* January 21, 1985, pp. 39–42.

FIGURE   9–8   Weekly Employee Benefit Costs by Industry, 1980

Industry	Cost per Employee
All industries	$117.00
Manufacturing:	
Petroleum industry	203.42
Chemicals and allied industries	114.10
Primary metal industries	143.73
Transportation equipment	142.29
Machinery (excluding electrical)	127.15
Electrical machinery, equipment, and supplies	121.02
Fabricated metal products (excluding machinery and transportation equipment	119.46
Printing and publishing	114.50
Food, beverage, and tobacco	111.69
Stone, clay, and glass products	110.94
Instruments and miscellaneous products	108.50
Rubber, leather, and plastic products	106.96
Pulp, paper, lumber, and furniture	104.37
Textile products and apparel	67.96
Nonmanufacturing:	
Public utilities	158.42
Banks, finance, and trust companies	112.08
Miscellaneous nonmanufacturing industries (research, engineering, education, government agencies, construction, etc.)	109.81
Insurance companies	106.83
Wholesale and retail trade	80.96
Hospitals	74.13
Department stores	70.31

"Employee Benefits," *Nation's Business,* December 1981, p. 76.

package within the means of the company.[28] Some of the important points to consider in developing a benefit and service package for employees is its ability to:

1. *Attract and retain competent personnel.* Employees and candidates looking at opportunities evaluate the total compensation package—wage plus fringes or salary plus fringes. A company gains popularity when people in the community see it as having a competitive compensation package.
2. *Satisfy security needs.* Through a sound program of benefits and services, an organization can satisfy employees' security needs, including retirement income, disability income, death benefits, medical and dental protection,

---

[28] Robert Levering, Milton Moskowitz, and Michael Katz, *The 100 Best Companies to Work For in America* (Reading, Mass.; Addison-Wesley Publishing, 1984), p. 350.

and educational assistance. These needs may be too expensive for employees
to provide themselves.

3. *Meet government regulations.* Federal and state laws require companies
   to support such benefits as unemployment compensation and survivors'
   insurance. The states provide unemployment compensation to unemployed
   people who are seeking employment. These benefits are typically provided
   for at least 26 weeks.

The benefits and services offered to employees are significant. The average
firm pays about 33 percent of its payroll to benefits. A breakdown of this
payment appears in Figure 9–8.

Some benefits are provided because of union-management bargaining. Procter & Gamble and Nunn-Bush Shoe Company have a guaranteed annual
wage (GAW). These plans guarantee employees a certain number of weeks
of employment, but strike periods are not covered in the program. Companies
with employees in the United Auto Workers Union provide supplemental
unemployment benefits (SUB). Both GAW and SUB are negotiated by labor
and management as a part of the collective-bargaining process. For example,
the contract would require company contributions to a fund that supplements
the unemployment compensation available to employees from federal and
state sources or both.

Another type of benefit can be found in the availability of employee assistance programs (EAPs). The Management Focus on EAPs suggests that
such programs can benefit both employee and employer.

MANAGEMENT FOCUS
Employee Assistance Programs: A Helping-Hand Benefit

The main purpose of employee assistance programs (EAPs) is
to help employees. Although the original purpose of EAPs was to
help employees with alcohol and other substance abuse problems,
there is the belief among managers today that helping employees
with any kind of personal or work-related problem can be important
from both a humanitarian and an economic perspective.

At Hughes Tool, the EAP was originated in 1976 with a labor-
management task force on alcoholism. The program today helps
employees with marital problems, problems with children, stress,
and family disorders. At Chevron, the EAP initially was focused on
a visible alcoholism problem and today is like the Hughes EAP,
addressing other employee problems.

Mary Kane, manager of the EAP of the 11,000-employee Kemper
Group, Long Grove, Illinois, emphasizes the issue of privacy. Most
EAPs, like Kemper's, attempt to identify problems that are work

---

MANAGEMENT FOCUS *(continued)*

related and then refer employees to out-of-company professionals for help or treatment. This helps keep the diagnosis and treatment as private as possible. Professionals that are used as outside resources in EAPs include marriage counselors, physicians, psychiatrists, psychologists, and consumer credit counselors. Many employees prefer outside professionals to insure confidentiality.

To encourage involvement in EAPs, companies often promote the programs with posters, payroll inserts, and messages in weekly newsletters. Most firms include the immediate dependents of workers in their insurance plans, and many allow them to use EAPs as well. On-site assessment, counseling and referral are uniformly free to employees.

Some EAP directors do not keep records that can show whether the programs are a success. Keeping detailed records makes confidentiality a problem. Cost effectiveness doesn't seem to be that critical when companies are talking about employees with substance abuse problems, money management problems, or marital difficulty. Getting help for people is a benefit that more and more firms are attempting through EAPs.

Adapted from Madeleine Udeleff, "Extending a Helping Hand," *Corporate Fitness & Recreation,* October–November 1985, pp. 29–32.

As a result of the efforts of unions, employees, the government, insurance companies, and society in general, the *Occupational Safety and Health Act* (OSHA) became a law on April 28, 1970. The act directs the secretary of labor to enforce safety and health standards in over 4 million businesses and for over 57 million employees. The core of the act may be the system of standards that must be met. For example, OSHA has set a limit for industrial noise of 90 decibels where there is eight hours of exposure per day. OSHA puts special emphasis on improving safety conditions in the five industries with injury rates more than double the national average of 15.2 disabling injuries per 1 million employee-hours worked. These industries are longshoring (69.9 injuries per 1 million), meat and meat products (43.1), roofing and sheet metal (43.0), lumber and wood products (34.1), and miscellaneous transportation equipment (33.3).[30]

Enforcement of OSHA standards is accomplished through a system of inspectors, citations, and penalties. Labor Department representatives may enter any business, at a reasonable time, to inspect the health and safety

---

[30] James W. Lahey, "Safety and the Future," *National Safety News,* October 1983, p. 63.

conditions. They may also question the employer, employees, or employee representatives. Criminal penalties can go as high as $20,000 and/or one year in prison. Four categories of violations may result from an inspector's visit:

De minimus: A minor violation not directly job related.

Nonserious: A minor violation that is job related; can result in a penalty of up to $1,000.

Serious: One in which there is a chance of serious injury or death; can result in a penalty of over $1,000.

Imminent danger: One in which serious injury or death is almost certain; penalty assessed by the federal courts.

SUMMARY OF KEY POINTS

- Human resource management (HRM) is the process of accomplishing organizational objectives by acquiring, retaining, terminating, developing, and properly using the human resources in an organization.

- The human resource department in a firm (usually a medium-sized or large firm) typically includes employment, training and development, wage and salary, employee benefits and services, and labor relations divisions.

- Human resource planning is an important activity that involves estimating the size and makeup of the future work force.

- Job analysis is an important process used in HRM to determine both the tasks that make up the job and the skills, abilities, and responsibilities an employee needs to successfully accomplish the job.

- The federal government attempts to provide equal opportunities for employment without regard to race, religion, age, creed, sex, national origin, or disability through Title VII of the Civil Rights Act of 1964 and the Equal Employment Opportunity Act of 1972.

- Selection for employment is a process with a number of hurdles a candidate must pass. The steps in the process include application blanks, interviews, tests, reference checks, and a medical examination.

- Training and development programs are used to inform employees of policies and procedures, educate them in job skills, and develop them for future advancement.

- Management development refers to the process of educating and developing selected personnel so that they have the knowledge, skills, attitudes, and understanding needed to manage future positions.

- Performance appraisal requires managers to make decisions about how well individuals perform their jobs.

- Performance appraisal requires standards of acceptable job performance.

These standards are called criteria, and they measure aspects of the job that are critical to effective job performance.

■ Nonmanagerial employees are usually paid wages on the basis of time worked. Managerial employees are usually paid salaries or on the basis of a weekly or monthly rate.

■ Benefits and services are forms of supplementary compensation. Benefits are financial (insurance protection); services are programs provided by the employer (a gymnasium).

DISCUSSION AND REVIEW QUESTIONS

1. Discuss with a small-business owner the types of human resource management that owner engages in. What did you find out?
2. Why are organizations so interested in benefits and services for employees?
3. What is the difference between a job description and a job specification?
4. How active is the government in the HRM activities conducted by an organization?
5. Why is testing such a controversial part of the selection sequence?
6. Why is job analysis such a vital step in the development of any performance appraisal technique or method?
7. An engineer stated, "My job is so complex and dynamic that it is virtually impossible to find criteria for assessing job performance." What do you think about this claim? Why?
8. Why is it costly to develop a behaviorally anchored rating scale?
9. Why is forecasting such an important part of human resource planning?
10. Are equal employment opportunity and affirmative action programs the same concept or activity? Explain.

CASES

APPLICATION I

SOUTHERN BELL'S APPRAISAL PROGRAM

Recently, Southern Bell Telephone & Telegraph Company (an AT&T operating company) implemented what they call the management development and evaluation plan (MDEP). The specific purposes of MDEP are to help develop skills and job knowledge in the managerial ranks, to provide useful performance-based information for salary decisons, to evaluate a manager's potential for advancement, and to provide feedback to the appraisees. Southern Bell believes that all employees should be provided with a formal appraisal of their job performance.

One of the first steps in the Southern Bell MDEP program is the identification and description of major responsibilities. These responsibilities relate to the job itself, self-development, and affirmative action. From the responsibilities, a program of objectives is set for each appraisee.

To assist appraisers in determining the value of accomplishing these objectives, Southern Bell has identified six factors to use as measurement criteria. These factors are:

1. Difficulty of accomplishment.
2. Amount of supervisor and/or manager support required.
3. Other circumstances outside employee's control that facilitated or inhibited the achievement.
4. Effectiveness of the employee in reducing barriers to future achievements.
5. Employee's effort to facilitate the achievement of others.
6. Contribution to organizational objectives.

Bell system managers seldom use all six factors for measuring achievements. They have found that the first three factors apply more frequently than do the last three. It is also likely that a certain factor may be weighted more heavily in a certain situation by an appraiser than at another time. Management believes that the six factors stimulate the appraiser to be more aware of the context of the situation and the total worth of accomplishing the objective.

The performance appraisal process is one in which feedback provides the information necessary to improve objective-oriented performance and encourages and assists employees to develop and grow to the fullest of their potential. After the appraiser (usually the immediate supervisor) completes the MDEP ratings, a group of supervisors who work in the same department join together to perform a group review. This group can accept or modify the ratings of the original appraisal.

After completion of the appraisal and group review, the immediate supervisor and subordinate have a formal feedback and career counseling session. At this meeting, both sets of ratings are reviewed, compared, discussed, and analyzed.

Questions for Analysis

1. Does the use of the six factors as measurement criteria in Southern Bell's MDEP program eliminate the need for appraiser judgment? Why?
2. Why would a group review differ from the ratings given by an appraiser?

APPLICATION II

GOAL SETTING AT TENNECO*

Tenneco is a large, diversified company operating in eight major industries. Among the Tenneco companies are J. I. Case, manufacturer and marketer of farm and construction equipment; Newport News Shipbuilding and Dry Dock Company; Walker Manufacturing Company and Monroe Auto Equipment Company, manufacturers of automotive equipment; Packaging Corporation of America, a supplier of paperboard, folding cartons, and corregated containers; Tenneco Oil, producer, refiner, and marketer of petroleum and related products; Tennessee Gas Transmission Company, marketer of a wide range of industrial chemical products; and Tenneco West, which produces and markets agricultural products. Tenneco employs about 85,000 people, of which 15,000 are managers and professionals.

A task force with representatives from each divisional company of Tenneco recommended to the president that a performance planning and evaluation (PP&E) and goal-setting program be implemented. The president, in support of the PP&E program, stated:

> If we fail to offer maximum opportunity to any one person in our organization, we are failing in one of our basic management responsibilities. . . . Accordingly, I expect this philosophy and method of management to receive enthusiastic support at all levels within Tenneco.

Simply stated, Tenneco's top management wanted the PP&E program to create an atmosphere that encouraged self-motivation and personal satisfaction.

The PP&E program involved the diagnosis of each job by incumbents, who were then expected to broadly define the key responsibilities of their jobs. Next, specific objectives and priorities of these objectives were spelled out. Emphasis was placed on work performance and personal-development objectives. Many goal-setting programs place primary emphasis only on the work objectives, disregarding development objectives. This is not the case in the PP&E program. A balance between work performance and personal-development objectives is reached through dialogue, transaction, and agreement between the supervisor and each subordinate. The supervisor and each subordinate are expected to work out the balance in a formal meeting.

After one year, the results of the subordinate's actual performance and

---

* Source: This case is based on the experiences and research of John M. Ivancevich, J. Timothy McMahon, J. William Striedl, and Andrew D. Szilagyi, Jr.

development progress are measured against stated objectives and priorities. The performance evaluation session focuses on results, with special attention paid to specific plans and accomplishments in personal development. This special concern about personal development highlights the most unique feature of the Tenneco PP&E program, which has some other important features:

1. Active top management support displayed by participation of senior executives in all phases of PP&E.
2. The use of external evaluations to monitor the impact, if any, of PP&E on attitudes and performance of participants.
3. The use of data collected by external evaluators to make modifications. Presently, each company is able to develop its own feedback plan. Feedback in the PP&E programs means the use of the evaluator's information, collected and related to the divisional company management, to make modifications.

The Tenneco PP&E system contains areas in which subjective measures and judgments are used. However, the care exercised in planning, implementing, supporting, and evaluating the PP&E program appears to have had some impact on the attitudes of Tenneco managers about goal setting. Tenneco managers seem stimulated and interested in performance and personal-development goal setting. The secret may be that goal setting is used not only to assess performance contributions but also to develop managers for more responsible duties in the future.

Questions for Analysis

1. What advantages were there in using a task force with representatives from each divisional company to develop performance planning and evaluation (PP&E) at Tenneco?
2. Does Tenneco's president seem concerned about the development of people? How did you reach this conclusion?
3. What would be the value of Tenneco's top management supporting the PP&E program?

EXPERIENTIAL EXERCISE

A CONTROL PROCEDURE: YOUR PERSONAL PERFORMANCE APPRAISAL

Purpose

The purpose of this exercise is to apply performance appraisal guidelines to your own activities and objectives.

The Exercise in Class

1. Write a paragraph (150 words or less) describing a successful you. What would make you successful? Select school, your job, your family, or personal life as a reference point. In your paragraph, list the outcomes (results) that would mean you were successful (e.g., *school*—grade point average, 3.3, graduated with honors, receiving highest grade on final; *job*—promoted to next level in two years, receiving recognition, receiving large merit increase).
2. For the reference point (choose one), select five areas of major concern and the measure of success you would use. Determine whether the measures of success are subjective or objective? Do they have a time frame?

Major Area of Concern	How Is Success Measured?	Subjective/ Objective	Time Frame Yes/No
1.			
2.			
3.			
4.			
5.			

3. Develop the major areas of concern into specific personal objectives— one for each major area of concern. The objectives should be one *single* sentence, clearly stated, with a time period specified. Rank the objectives from the most important to the least important.

Ranked Objectives

1. _____
2. _____
3. _____
4. _____
5. _____

4. The instructor will form groups of three students to share their success stories, measures of success, and objective statements. Are there differences in what are considered success measures, objectives, and priorities?

The Learning Message

Even self-performance appraisal is a control procedure. It serves to direct individual behavior toward objectives that are meaningful, clear, comprehensive, and challenging. Explicit objectives that are well stated must be carefully worked on. Skill in developing objectives can be improved with practice. Good objectives can be helpful in planning, organizing, and controlling behavior and attitudes.

COMPREHENSIVE APPLICATION FOR PART II

MANAGING WORK AND ORGANIZATIONS

MIRACLE CORPORATION*

Introduction

Earl E. Brown, president of Miracle Corporation, a large conglomerate with 20 divisions, was surprised to hear the rumor that major problems were developing in his company. This was related to him by a personal friend who is an investment banker. Mr. Brown was dumbfounded, since the annual results just released revealed the best year ever in the history of the Miracle Corporation with regards to sales, profit, asset utilization, etc. Upon consultation with the partner in charge of the audit, it was decided that Mr. Wayne Riddlebarger of the management service division of the CPA firm should investigate the possible problems and their causes. Excerpts from Mr. Riddlebarger's findings are given below.

History of Miracle Corporation

The Miracle company was started rather modestly in the late 1920s. It experienced during World War II a tremendous expansion that has continued at an accelerated pace until now. During the 1950s, the engineers received most of top management's attention. In the early 60s, the greatest influence on policies was assumed by marketing personnel, with most attention and money spent on advertising and market research, as these topics were the "in thing." In the late 60s and early 70s, diversification and expansion received the greatest emphasis of top management. The corporation had to borrow extensively to maintain the growth rate, and the corporate debt became gigantic. During the mid-1970s, the postwar recession hit the industry, along with double-digit inflation that began in 1973.

These adverse factors increased the cost of doing business considerably, particularly the expense of interest. Some of the expansion and diversification schemes proved less than satisfactory, and profit dropped 65 percent from the high of 1971. The profit margin has fallen each year since and was 2.1

---

* Source: Prepared by Felix P. Kollaritsch, The Ohio State University. Permission to publish granted by the author.

percent in 1975, down from an average of 7.3 percent in 1960. Feeling that costs have gotten out of control, bankers and investors demanded, in a stormy meeting, better controls, higher returns, and a more favorable financial ratio position.

Vice President for Planning, Information, and Control

Mr. Brown hired Patrick Kelly, partner in charge of the audit, as vice president for planning, information, and control. This newly created position was to replace the controller of the company, who was retiring. Mr. Kelly was to be in charge of coordination of planning, operational control, appraising marketing programs, analyzing acquisition opportunities, reporting to top management, and other regular accounting matters. Kelly, who accepted this position with the provision that he be given a free hand and the support of top management for three years, was aiming at the following objectives:

1. His highest priority was to cut the costs of doing business. This goal would include evaluation of all projects and elimination if their returns were far below the expected rate.
2. New investment must provide at least a 20 percent return.
3. The profit margin must be improved.
4. Corporate debts should be reduced as rapidly as possible.

Actions by Mr. Kelly.   The first year on the job, Mr. Kelly did very little but tour all the divisions (there are 20), studying their operations and problems and promoting his ideas of planning and control to divisional and top management. Successful, he quickly moved to develop a reporting system tailor-made for this corporation. He also hired his own people for the corporate controller's staff and the divisional staff. With the consent of nearly all division managers, the divisional controller was now reporting to him. He also created a corporate internal auditing group.

The Planning Process

Mr. Kelly introduced elaborate information-gathering and planning systems and made sure that observance of each detail was strictly enforced.

Division managers were asked to prepare a five-year plan. These plans were approved by the executive committee, composed of President Brown, the executive vice president, and the corporate vice presidents for sales, production, finance, personnel, and planning. The detailed outline of the corporate command structure is shown in Exhibit 1. In February of each year, these plans were extended for one year.

EXHIBIT   1   Miracle Corporation: Organization Chart

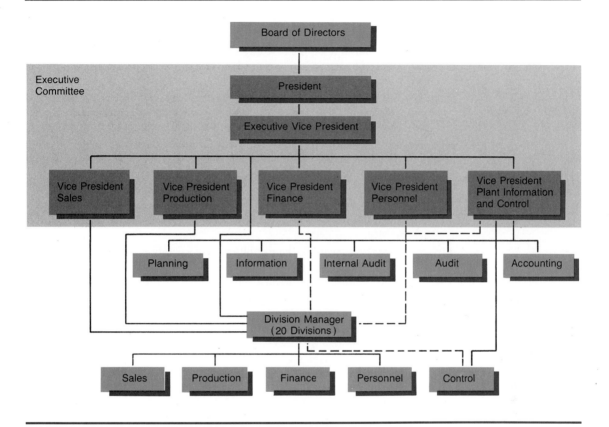

From the five-year plans, a yearly budget was prepared by division managers, including details on sales, expense figures, sales price, volume, projections by products, working-capital position, and so on. These budgets were broken down into quarterly budgets. Towards the end of the second month of any quarter, the division managers would meet to update next quarter's budget. They planned to identify factors that might alter their forecasts.

Each division controller had to submit a report at the middle of each month to the vice president of planning, stating whether or not the division can meet its goals as set out in the monthly budget, to pinpoint possible problems before they are facts. Mr. Kelly called this "anticipatory planning." This is a modification of the original procedure, which necessitated a monthly meeting of all the divisional managers for the purpose described above. However, these midmonthly division managers' meetings were resented so much that Kelly had to discontinue them and replace them with the division controllers' midmonth report.

Followup Interviews

Top management.   Here are some representative comments that Mr. Riddlebarger received from interviews with company executives:

President: "So far at least, the new way has apparently paid off." "To our business
today, financial and operating controls have become important for success and,
most of all, survival."

Executive Vice President: "What more can one ask? Our return on equity has
improved from 6.7 percent to 10.5 percent since Mr. Kelly joined us." "We
are making things happen; we don't wait for them to happen."

Vice President, Production: "The company has been successful in paring down
the inventories considerably because of tighter control." "So far the controls
have led to the shutdown of five plants with rates of return not up to our expectations."

Vice President, Finance: "Economic conditions and pressure dictate that we get
more out of our investment, and now we are." "Our working capital position
has improved considerably."

Vice President, Personnel: "The payroll of the corporation is down from 6,000 in
1973 to 5,000 right now."

Vice President, Sales: "The product mix has been upgraded. We dropped about
13 percent of our product lines." "We are finally facing up to economic facts
and problems."

Vice President, Planning. *(Mr. Kelly):*   "Today the job of good management involves
elaborate monitoring and cross-checking of all kinds of data." "I know that
some division managers are unhappy, but they must realize that planning and
controls are necessary and are here to stay."

Divisional managers.   The following are excerpts from some of the most
frequently repeated remarks of the various division managers:

1. "Political infighting? No more—we have an open war. The result has
   been that dozens of operating executives have left—and I mean the best
   of the lot." "It takes a month to get an appointment with the executive
   vice president or the president, and then you can't talk to them without
   Mr. Kelly being present."
2. "Sure he has good ideas. I'm sold on them. But whenever he applies
   controls, they turn out differently from the way they were explained to
   me. They inhibit our ability to produce and sell."
3. "I think he wants to support some universities. He hired more M.B.A.s
   for his shop than we have in the total organization. Yes, they have attractive
   credentials, but very little experience." "These whiz kids have ready access
   to top management. It takes me an eternity to get their ear."
4. "The corporate operating force has grown 30 percent; yet Mr. Kelly's
   office has grown 38 percent in the same period." "Expenses of his office
   have increased 82 percent. Those of the operating force, only 39 percent."

5. "These are short-sighted measures. Top management is seeking quick returns at the expense of long-term payoffs." "Too many opportunities have slipped by because the payoff comes too late."

6. "We are overstressing mechanistic controls and management tools. Our continued success depends on creativity, and creativity has been put into a straitjacket." "His policies raise serious questions about the future growth of this corporation."

7. "We are open to raiding and cannot attract competent managers any more. Five years ago, when my sales manager died in a car accident, I had 50 well-qualified persons apply for this opening. This year, when our sales manager left because he was fed up, I had five applications. None of them came close to the quality of those 50 of five years ago."

8. "Sure I was mad at him! When he required a large allowance for overdue accounts receivable, my profit (and with it, my bonus) went down. But we corrected the situation, and he was right. But these controls are requiring more and more of my employees' time and reduce the productivity." "Do you want to hear something? I wanted to buy a pencil sharpener; but since it had a motor, it was considered a machine, and I had to fill out a capital asset requisition form. Since I could not document a 20 percent return, there was no sense in forwarding it. If I had bought for a few hundred dollars a real antique handcranked pencil sharpener, I could have authorized that. Besides, I'm an engineer but was unable to fill out the capital requisition form. I needed my controller to do it. Needless to say, I bought it as an office furnishing."

Questions for Analysis

1. Evaluate Mr. Kelly's overall approach to solving the problems of Miracle Corporation.

2. What potential organizational problems has Mr. Kelly set in motion by having the divisional controllers report directly to him?

3. Evaluate Mr. Kelly's four objectives in terms of explicit criteria.

4. What type of organizational structure does Miracle Corporation have? Evaluate whether it "fits" the demands and opportunities of the company's environment and strategy.

5. Why did the divisional managers resent the midmonthly meetings with Mr. Kelly. Explain whether the controllers' midmonthly reports are adequate substitutes for these meetings.

6. What performance standards should be used to evaluate Mr. Kelly's performance? What performance standards should be used to evaluate divisional managers' performance?

7. Explain why top management and divisional managers have quite different opinions about the effects of Mr. Kelly's efforts.

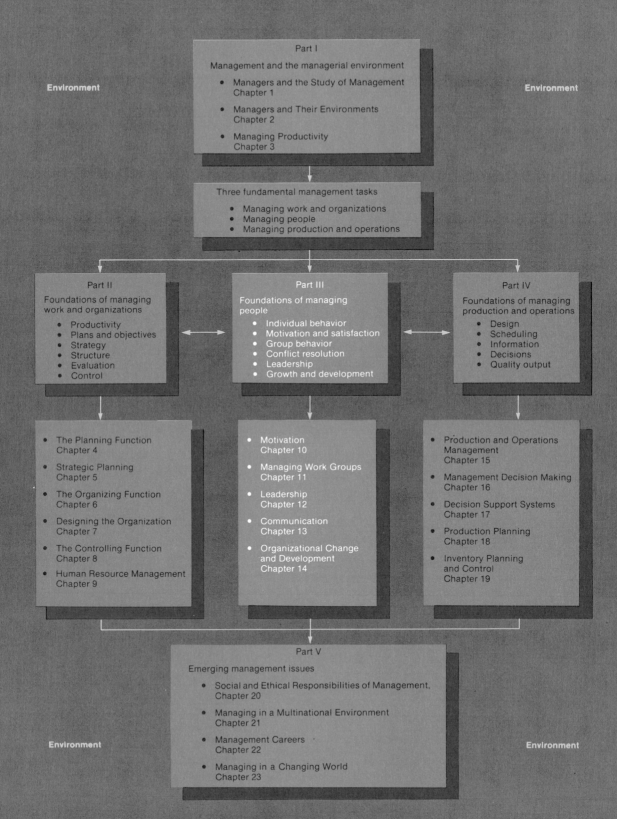

Environment

Part I

Management and the managerial environment

- Managers and the Study of Management
  Chapter 1
- Managers and Their Environments
  Chapter 2
- Managing Productivity
  Chapter 3

Environment

Three fundamental management tasks

- Managing work and organizations
- Managing people
- Managing production and operations

Part II

Foundations of managing work and organizations

- Productivity
- Plans and objectives
- Strategy
- Structure
- Evaluation
- Control

Part III

Foundations of managing people

- Individual behavior
- Motivation and satisfaction
- Group behavior
- Conflict resolution
- Leadership
- Growth and development

Part IV

Foundations of managing production and operations

- Design
- Scheduling
- Information
- Decisions
- Quality output

- The Planning Function
  Chapter 4
- Strategic Planning
  Chapter 5
- The Organizing Function
  Chapter 6
- Designing the Organization
  Chapter 7
- The Controlling Function
  Chapter 8
- Human Resource Management
  Chapter 9

- Motivation
  Chapter 10
- Managing Work Groups
  Chapter 11
- Leadership
  Chapter 12
- Communication
  Chapter 13
- Organizational Change
  and Development
  Chapter 14

- Production and Operations
  Management
  Chapter 15
- Management Decision Making
  Chapter 16
- Decision Support Systems
  Chapter 17
- Production Planning
  Chapter 18
- Inventory Planning
  and Control
  Chapter 19

Part V

Emerging management issues

- Social and Ethical Responsibilities of Management,
  Chapter 20
- Managing in a Multinational Environment
  Chapter 21
- Management Careers
  Chapter 22
- Managing in a Changing World
  Chapter 23

Environment

Environment

MANAGING PEOPLE

■ **FOUNDATIONS OF MANAGING PEOPLE**

Early approaches to management were built on the notion that if management could properly plan, organize, and control jobs and organizations, productivity could increase. The early approaches emphasized the technical aspects of work, at the expense of work's personal aspects. Therefore, it is not surprising that theories were developed that challenged some of the early fundamentals. The fundamentals of managing people evolved into two branches with heavy behavioral and humanistic orientations. One branch may be identified as *human relations;* it became popular in the 1940s and early 1950s. The second branch is *behavioral science,* which came into popular use in the early 1950s and today receives much emphasis in the literature on management. Both branches and important characteristics of each are illustrated in Figure 1.

THE HUMAN RELATIONS APPROACH

Human relations writers brought to managers' attention the important role played by individuals in determining the success or failure of an organization. Basically, the human relations approach accepted the major premises of the classical approach. However, the human relations approach showed how these premises should be modified in view of differences in individual behavior and the influence of work groups upon the individual—and vice versa. Thus, the formulators of human relations theory concentrated on the *social* environment surrounding the job, while classical writers were concerned mainly with the *physical* environment. For the student of management, the human relations movement has produced a wealth of important ideas, research findings, and values about the role of the individual in an organization.

The Hawthorne Studies

In 1924, the National Research Council (NRC) of the National Academy of Sciences decided to study how lighting in the workplace influenced individual efficiency. From 1924 to 1927, the NRC studied this relationship at the Chicago Hawthorne Plant of Western Electric. The initial experiments were so inconclusive that everyone was ready to abandon the whole project.[1] Despite the inconclusive early results, a team of Harvard University industrial psychologists became involved in the Hawthorne studies. This research team originally set out to study the

---

[1] For a complete account of these studies, see Fritz J. Roethlisberger and W. H. Dickson, *Management and the Worker* (Cambridge, Mass.: Harvard University Press, 1939). Also, see a report on a symposium held to celebrate the 50th anniversary of the original Hawthorne studies in Eugene L. Cass and Frederick G. Zimmer, *Man and Work in Society* (New York: Van Nostrand Reinhold, 1975).

FIGURE 1   Fundamentals of Managing People: Two Approaches

Human relations approach
• Stimulated by the Hawthorne studies
• Concern for individual dignity
• Concern for developing human potential
• Concern for social environment

Behavioral science approach
• Involved in the scientific search for understanding behavior
• The use of psychology, sociology, and anthropology to understand behavior
• Use of research to gain knowledge
• Acceptance of total person

relationship between productivity and physical working conditions.

The research.   The general progression of the research at Hawthorne can be grouped in four phases;[2] each successive phase developed as an attempt on the part of the researchers to answer questions raised by the previous phase. The four stages were:

1. Experiments to determine the effects that changes in illumination have on productivity.
2. Experiments to determine the effects of changes in hours and other working conditions (for example, rest periods, refreshments) on productivity (the relay assembly test room experiment).
3. Conducting a plantwide interview program to determine worker attitudes and sentiments.

---

[2] Paul R. Lawrence and John A. Seiler, *Organizational Behavior and Administration* (Homewood, Ill.: Richard D. Irwin, 1965), p. 165.

4. Determination and analysis of social organization at work (the bank wiring observation room experiment).

Experiments   in   illumination. The researchers divided the participating workers into two separate groups. One group was exposed to varying intensities of illumination. Since this group was subjected to experimental changes, it was termed the *experimental* group. Another group, called the *control* group, continued to work under constant intensities of illumination. Surprisingly the researchers found that as they increased the illumination in the experimental group, both groups increased production. When the researchers decreased the intensity, output continued to rise for both groups. Finally, the illumination in the experimental group was reduced to that of moonlight. Then, and only then, was there a significant decline in output. The researchers concluded that illumination in the workplace had little or no effect on the productivity of the two groups.

At this point, the research team from Harvard became involved.

Relay assembly test room experiment.   In the second phase of the study, several persons volunteered to work under controlled conditions isolated from the other workers. Several changes were made in the conditions of the job (for example, refreshments and workplace temperature) with little effect on productivity. In another phase, a group of women employees was placed together in an isolated part of the assembly department. The experimental group was given a special group incentive as a wage payment. In this case, output increased for each operator.

Overall, the relay assembly test room experiment was designed to determine the effects of changes in various job conditions on group productivity. The researchers concluded that these factors had little or no effect.

Employee interviews.   After the first two phases, the researchers concluded that their attempt to relate physical conditions of the job to productivity did not produce any significant results. So they postulated that the *human element* in the work environment apparently had a significantly greater impact on productivity than the technical and physical aspects of the job. The researchers summarized this impact as follows:

> In brief, the increase in the output rate of the women in the relay assembly test room could not be related to any change in their physical conditions of work, whether experimentally induced or not. It could, however, be related to what

can only be spoken of as the development of an organized social group and a peculiar and effective relation with its supervisors.[3]

On the basis of their extensive interview program, the researchers proposed the premise that the work group as a whole determined the production output of individual group members by enforcing an informal norm of what a fair day's work should be.

Bank wiring observation room experiment.   To test the premise formulated at the conclusion of the interview program, the researchers conducted a final experiment. The procedure in this part of the study was similar to that used in the relay assembly test room, except that nine males who assembled terminal banks for telephone exchanges were selected.

This experiment focused on the effect of a group piecework incentive pay plan. The assumption was that the workers would seek their own economic interests by maximizing their productivity and that faster workers would pressure the slower ones to improve their efficiency. However, the researchers found that pressure was actually a form of social behavior. In order to be accepted in the work group, the worker had to act in accord with group norms and not be a "rate buster" by overproducing or a "chiseler" by underproducing. The group defined what constituted a day's work, and as soon as they knew that they could reach this out-

[3] Ibid., p. 173.

put level, they slacked off. This process was more marked among the faster workers than the slower ones.

The researchers concluded that the work group set the fair rates for each of its members. They found no relationship between productivity and intelligence, dexterity, and other skills. They concluded that the wage incentive plan was less important in determining an individual worker's output than group acceptance and security.

Review and critique of the Hawthorne studies. The Hawthorne studies have been widely criticized by some behavioral scientists because of the lack of scientific objectivity used in arriving at conclusions. Some critics feel that there was bias and preconception on the part of the Harvard researchers. One writer developed a detailed comparison between the conclusions drawn by the researchers and the evidence they presented, and found that their conclusions were almost entirely unsupported.[4]

Although they have been criticized, the Hawthorne studies had a significant impact on management practice, teaching, and research.[5] Obviously, the assumptions of early management writers began to be questioned.[6] Subsequent studies of the behavior of workers confirmed criticism of early assumptions and led to revised assumptions about human nature.[7] Behavioral scientists began attacking the "dehumanizing" aspects of the scientific management approach and bureaucratic forms of organization; a great number of training programs were undertaken to teach managers how to better understand people and groups in the work situation. With this, the pendulum began to swing away from the supposed depersonalized view of classical management to a more personalized (some would say *over*personalized) view. Consequently the worker, rather than the job or production standards, became the focus.

The Hawthorne studies may not have been a model application of scientific methodology to problems of human behavior, but the studies do represent a pioneering effort. If nothing else, they stimulated an interest in human behavior and needs. It was a beginning in bringing new, people-oriented insights to the attention of managers. Although the assumptions and methods of human relations and behavioral science are not the same, it was the human relations foundation—with its concern for individual dignity, development of human potential, and the social environment of the employee—that provided the impetus for the present-day behavioral science emphasis in management theory.

[4] Alex Carey, "The Hawthorne Studies: A Radical Criticism," *American Sociological Review,* June 1967, pp. 403–16.

[5] Ibid., p. 403.

[6] Henry A. Landsberger, *Hawthorne Revisited* (Ithaca, N.Y.: New York State School of Industrial and Labor Relations, Cornell University, 1958).

[7] Elton Mayo, *The Social Problems of an Industrial Civilization* (Cambridge, Mass.: Harvard University Press, 1945).

THE BEHAVIORAL SCIENCE APPROACH

The behavioral science approach to management began to appear in the early 1950s, after the Foundation for Research on Human Behavior was established. The goals and objectives of this organization were to promote and support behavioral science research in business, government, and other types of organizations. The behavioral science approach to the study of management can be defined as:

> The study of observable and verifiable human behavior in organizations, using scientific procedures. It is largely inductive and problem centered, focusing on the issue of human behavior and drawing from any relevant literature, especially in psychology, sociology, and anthropology.[8]

Many things about the classical management and human relations approaches bothered advocates of the behavioral science approach. For example, they recognized that managers did indeed plan, organize, and control. But they believed that viewing management solely in this way led mainly to *descriptions* of what managers do rather than to an analysis and understanding of what they do.

Many individuals also believed that while the "economic man" model of the classical writers was an oversimplification, the "social man" model of the human relations ap-

proach likewise was oversimplified. You will see later how the emphasis of the behavioral science approach has shifted more and more to the nature of work itself and the degree to which it can fulfill the human need to use skills and abilities.

Finally, advocates of the behavioral science approach were bothered by the fact that both practitioners and scholars had accepted without scientific validation much of the management theory that preceded them. These advocates wanted to test theory against reality and see what was successful and unsuccessful. Their scientific approach has added greatly to the body of knowledge, since they provided a means of testing the earlier theories. Through their work, some aspects of the classical approach have been modified, while others have withstood the test of scientific validation. Because of the emphasis on the behavioral sciences and on science itself, let us examine each of these briefly.

The Behavioral Sciences

First, we must distinguish between the social sciences and the behavioral sciences. The term *social sciences* usually refers to six disciplines: anthropology, economics, history, political science, psychology, and sociology. When we use the term *behavioral sciences,* we refer to the disciplines of psychology, sociology, and anthropology.

Psychology is the study of human behavior. The many branches of general psychology have provided concepts and theories useful to the study

---

[8] Alan C. Filley, Robert J. House, and Steven Kerr, *Managerial Process and Organizational Behavior* (Glenview, Ill.: Scott Foresman, 1976), p. 16.

of management. For example, *social psychology* deals with behavior as it relates to other individuals. It studies how groups and individuals influence and modify each other's behavior. *Organizational psychology* is a relatively new branch dealing with behavior and attitudes within an organizational setting. It studies the effect of the organization upon the individual and the individual's effect upon the organization.

Sociology attempts to isolate, define, and describe human behavior in groups. It strives to develop laws and generalizations about human nature, social interaction, culture, and social organization.

One of sociologists' major contributions to management thought has been their focus on emergent groups, which often are treated in management literature as the informal components of organizations. Sociologists also have an interest in formal organizations, which they approach as the study of bureaucracy. They focus on bureaucratic behavior as well as the structural relationships in bureaucratic organizations. Sociologists have provided managers with knowledge regarding leader and follower roles and how patterns of power and authority are applied in organizations.

Anthropology examines the learned behaviors of people, including all of the social, technical, and family behaviors that are a part of the broad concept known as culture. Cultural anthropology, the science devoted to the study of different peoples and cultures of the world, is important to the behavioral sciences because the ways in which individuals behave, the

priority of needs they attempt to satisfy, and the means they choose to satisfy them are all functions of culture.

While psychology and sociology have had greater impact in shaping management thought, cultural anthropology has made significant contributions regarding the effect of culture on organizations. In the future, as firms expand their activities overseas, anthropology undoubtedly will provide managers with valuable insights as they attempt to perform the functions of planning, organizing, and controlling in different cultural environments.

The Scientific Approach and Human Behavior

The scientific approach has been used successfully in many fields, such as the study of human behavior and the physical sciences. In addition, it has produced information about human behavior that has become established knowledge. The greatest advantage of the scientific approach has been summarized:

The scientific approach has one characteristic that no other method of attaining knowledge has: self-correction. There are built-in checks all along the way to scientific knowledge. These checks are so conceived and used that they control and verify the scientist's activities and conclusions to the end of attaining dependable knowledge outside himself.[9]

[9] Fred N. Kerlinger, *Foundations of Behavioral Research* (New York: Holt, Rinehart & Winston, 1973), p. 6.

The one word that best describes this approach is *objectivity*. The scientific approach forces the researcher or manager to be as objective as possible. Most writers agree that there is no single scientific method (the term often used) but rather several methods that scientists can and do use. Thus, it is probably better to say that there is a *scientific approach*.

The scientific approach is a method of inquiry used by scientists to study a problem. The steps in the approach are:

1. Define the problem by *observing* the situation.
2. Through observation and problem identification, *construct* a framework (model).
3. Use the framework, or model, to *deduce* how something that is being observed will behave under various conditions. In other words, you develop *hypotheses* about the variables being studied (e.g., if illumination is improved, productivity will increase).
4. The model is *tested* by performing an experiment to see if the changes predicted in the hypotheses occur as predicted.

Methods of Inquiry Used by Behavioral Scientists

Just as other scientists have certain tools and methods for obtaining information, so does the behavioral scientist, whose tools and methods usually are referred to as *research designs*. In broad terms, there are three basic designs used by behavioral

scientists: the experiment, the sample survey, and the case study.

The experiment. To be considered an experiment, an investigation must contain two elements: manipulation of some variable by the researcher and observation or measurement of the results. The several different forms an experiment can take will not be examined here.[10]

An example of a simple experiment might be one in which management is trying to determine the effect of increases in piece rates on quantity produced. Since they probably already have measures of present levels of productivity, they would have a "before" measure with which to compare the results. Their first step would be to assign workers randomly to two groups. The *experimental* group would have its rates altered while the *control* group would continue working under the existing rates. After a period of time (for example, six months), the output of both groups would be compared with their productivity before the experiment began. This might give some idea as to the effect of a higher piece rate on this one performance indicator.

This experiment is an oversimplification used for illustrative purposes. Obviously, there would have to be provisions made to keep the results from being distorted (for example, workers being aware that they are

---

[10] The interested reader should consult Kerlinger, *Foundations,* chaps. 17–21. Also see Eugene Stone, *Research Methods in Organizational Behavior* (Santa Monica, Calif.: Goodyear Publishing, 1978).

participating in an experiment). However, this example does illustrate the two major elements of an experiment: manipulation of some variable by the researcher (piece rates), and observation or measurement of the results (productivity).

The sample survey. In the sample survey, data are collected from a limited number of subjects assumed to be representative of an entire group. For example, suppose we decide to study full-time homemakers. This is the group, or "population," we are concerned about. We then select a sample of this group and collect some measures on particular characteristics in which we are interested (for example, attitudes toward domestic roles, or spouse, or child-rearing). It should be clear that there are certain kinds of questions, such as the attitudes of homemakers toward their spouses, that can be answered only

by a sample survey. However, it is often necessary to develop provisions to study changes in attitudes over time to improve the usefulness of the findings.

The case study. Unlike the sample survey, which attempts to measure one or more characteristics in many people, usually at set points in time, the case study attempts to examine numerous characteristics of one person or group, usually over an extended time period. For example, a behavioral scientist who spends time with a group of blue-collar workers can report the results (for example, the key factors and incidents leading up to a strike) in the form of a case study.

While this method is extremely useful for exploratory purposes, the case study's major limitation is that the ability to generalize from it is uncertain. The results usually are based

---

TABLE 1 Comparison of Three Basic Research Designs Used by Behavioral Scientists

Basic Design Type	Data Collection Method	When Data Are Collected
1. Experiment		
a. In laboratory or setting away from job. *b.* In organization on the job.	Observe employees. Self-report questionnaire. Interview subjects. Use records.	Before change is introduced and after (e.g., illumination experiment in Hawthorne studies).
2. Sample survey	Self-report questionnaire. Interview. Use records.	At some specific point in time (e.g., asking managers about their roles).
3. Case study	Observation. Interview. Use records.	Over a period of time (e.g., observing workers in blast furnace area of steel mill for three months).

on a sample of one instance. Perhaps, in another firm, the same incidents would not result in a strike. A case study, therefore, usually does not prove or disprove anything.

A comparison of the three basic designs used by behavioral scientists is presented in Table 1. Each design is presented in terms of how and when information about people is collected.

Contributions of the Behavioral Approach to Management

The development of the fundamentals of managing people has gained much attention during the last three decades. An underlying rationale of the behavior-oriented approach is that since a manager must "get work done through others," and must know how to motivate, be a leader, and understand interpersonal relations and the behavior of groups (among other things), management really is applied behavioral science. Therefore, the logic is, future managers must be prepared in these behavioral areas. While we would argue that management is more than applied behavioral science, the basic assumption of the behavioral science approach appears valid: Managers *must* know how to deal with people.

One of the vital tasks performed by managers is decision making. To make decisions, they must have possible alternatives from which to choose, authority to implement the alternative, and information.

Managers need two kinds of infor-
mation: (1) facts about the particular system, the people and machines involved, and the cost; (2) theory to aid in explaining what will happen if one variable is altered, and how the different variables are related to each other.

If the behavioral approach is to be useful to managers in improving productivity, it must suggest to them what to do in problem situations, provide them with a description of their environment, or provide them with a framework on which to rely in problem-solving situations. In other words, the approach must provide managers with guides for correct problem definition, problem solving, explanation of behavior, and control of variables. In order to be useful, it must make them better practitioners.

CONCLUSION

The fundamentals of managing people should in no way be viewed separately from the fundamentals of managing work and organizations. Management writers have identified management as a process consisting of the functions of planning, organizing, and controlling and have provided insights into the nature and demands of these tasks. While reading through Part III, the question the reader should ask is: How can behavioral science theory and research help managers be regarded as contributing to the human aspects of the management process.

Chapter 10

MOTIVATION

LEARNING OBJECTIVES

After studying Chapter 10, you should be able to:

■ **Define**
the meaning of motivation.

■ **Describe**
the difference between content and process theories of motivation.

■ **Discuss**
why the integrating model of motivation must use both content and process theories of motivation.

■ **Identify**
the five core motivational dimensions of jobs.

■ **Compare**
the distinguishing characteristics of the reinforcement and expectancy theories of motivation.

☐ MANAGEMENT IN ACTION

Theory Z: Is It the Key to Motivation?*

Management Professor William G. Ouchi has explored the reasons why Japan's national productivity rate is soaring while the U.S. productivity growth rate has stalled. The secret of the Japanese success, the author believes, is the great concern Japan's managers show for the well-being and development of employees. The Japanese, according to Ouchi, recognize that motivated people do make a difference.

Ouchi states that as a nation, the United States has developed a sense of the value of technology and science but has taken people and their needs too much for granted. He proposes that neither monetary incentives nor new technologies will remedy the low-productivity problem. Instead, Ouchi believes that creating a motivational climate that encourages workers to join together and rely on each other is the key to improved performance.

In line with the philosophy that motivation is the key, Japanese managers use three particular practices: (1) lifetime employment, extending to 35 percent of the work force, and a guarantee of job security; (2) identical salary increases and promotion appointments for those in the same age group; and (3) career paths that provide each employee with experience in every phase of the organization's operations. These practices occur in organizations with internal structures that permit the simultaneous satisfaction of organizational and of individual needs. The Type Z organization approximates this form, Ouchi asserts.

Some U.S. managers believe that Theory Z is nothing more than a fad, a brand name to peddle an old ideological package. B. Bruce-Briggs, a management consultant, believes that Japanese workers do what is expected of them: work hard, work right, and not hinder productivity improvements. American workers, he notes, are told what to do but do not do it reliably. In Japan, the social organizations and ideology are based on hierarchy—the old over the young, the husband over the wife, the eldest over the youngest, the teacher over the student. Everyone knows his or her place. Under such a system, decision making by consensus is easy; no one challenges the boss.

Both Theory Z and Bruce-Briggs' critique make sense in explaining the motivation of some individuals. It will be evident in this chapter that motivation is a complex challenge that managers must deal with every day.

_____
* Source: Adapted from "Theory Z: The Sun Rises" and "Refuting Theory Z: The Sun Sets," *Management World,* December 1982, pp. 14–15.

Motivation is concerned with the "why" of human behavior. Why do people do things? Why does Harry have frequent run-ins with the boss? Why does Dianne work so much harder than Jim? These questions can be partially answered with an understanding of human motivation. In this chapter, motivation will be the main focal point because it is important to management for three reasons: First, employees on the job must be motivated to perform at an acceptable level. Second, managers themselves must be motivated to do a good job. Third, employees (managerial and nonmanagerial) must be motivated to join the organization.

WHAT IS MOTIVATION?

Motivation has been defined as "all those inner-striving conditions described as wishes, desires, drives, etc. . . . It is an inner state that activates or moves."[1] From a manager's perspective, a person who is motivated can be described as follows:

The person works hard.
The person sustains a pace of hard work.
The person's behavior is self-directed toward important goals.

Thus, motivation involves effort, persistence, and goals.[2]

THE MOTIVATION PROCESS

An unsatisfied need is the starting point in the process of motivation. A deficiency of something within the individual, it is the first link in the chain of events leading to behavior. The unsatisfied need causes tension (physical or psychological) within the individual, leading the individual to engage in some kind of behavior to satisfy the need and thereby reduce the tension. Note in Figure 10–1 that this activity is directed toward a goal. Achieving the goal satisfies the need, and the process of motivation is complete. For example, an achievement-oriented person is driven by the desire to succeed and is motivated by a desire for a promotion and/or accomplishment in order to satisfy the need.

Is everyone goal directed? A lot of people are asking this question. The Management Focus on the motivation responsibilities of management discusses the impression given by some workers that they are not goal directed but are instead lazy.

---

[1] Bernard Berelson and Gary A. Steiner, *Human Behavior: An Inventory of Scientific Findings* (New York: Harcourt Brace Jovanovich, 1964), p. 239.

[2] Herbert L. Petri, *Motivation: Theory and Research* (Belmont, Calif.: Wadsworth Publishing, 1981), p. 4.

FIGURE   10–1   The Process of Motivation

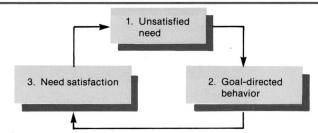

Motivation starts with an unsatisfied need.

MANAGEMENT FOCUS
Is Management Responsible for a Lack of Motivation?

Harold Geneen, the retired chairman of ITT, tells about the maintenance man who worked at Jones & Laughlin Steel for 20 years and did no work at all. The man simply picked up a pail at one plant, carried it across a bridge into another building, sat out of sight all day, carried the pail back at the end of the day, and went home. Is this what lazy means, and is this a view of how motivated American workers really are? After all, in Hungarian, the verb "amerikazik" means to slow down or goof off.

Robert Half, president of a New York recruiting firm, proposes that the example of the maintenance man is not surprising. According to Half, time theft—the deliberate and persistent abuse of paid work time—costs U.S. business $150 billion a year. His surveys indicate that employees steal 4 hours and 22 minutes a week by getting to work late, leaving early, making personal telephone calls, socializing, reading, and doing personal business on company time. He cites some examples:

- In a Denver company, an employee took daily on-the-job naps in the storage room.
- In a Boston financial services firm, a $40,000-a-year employee spent four hours a day during the football season placing and recording bets.
- In a Houston printing firm, a woman sold insurance on company time.

MANAGEMENT FOCUS (*continued*)

Not everyone, however, sees the American worker as having no goals, stealing time, and acting lazy. Sidney Harman, head of Harmon International Industries, a manufacturer and distributor of audio products, believes that the maintenance man example illustrates inept management. The worker has not exerted the effort to accomplish anything because management has ignored him and has implied that his job is not important. Harmon states that "management has only begun to create an environment in which that natural interest on the part of workers . . . for self-reliance and self-esteem on the job can be satisfied."

Adapted from Joani Nelson-Horchler, "Are U.S. Workers Lazy?" *Industry Week,* June 10, 1985, pp. 47–52.

UNDERSTANDING MOTIVATION: THE USE OF THEORIES

There are many theories of motivation that managers can use to improve their understanding of why people behave as they do. None provides a universally accepted explanation of human behavior. People are far too complex. Our purpose in presenting the most popular theories is not to identify the one best approach. Rather, it is to introduce ideas that managers can use to develop their own motivational approach.

The two most discussed groups of theories are content theories and process theories. *Content theories* are concerned with identifying what it is within an individual or the work environment that energizes and sustains behavior.[3] That is, what specific things motivate people?

On the other hand, *process theories* try to explain and describe the process of how behavior is energized, directed, sustained, and finally stopped. Process theories first attempt to define the major variables necessary for explaining choice (e.g., should I work hard), effort (e.g., how much do I need to work), and persistence (e.g., how long do I have to keep this pace).

First, two content theories—Maslow's need hierarchy and Herberg's two-factor theory—will be discussed. Second, two process theories—expectancy and reinforcement—will be introduced. After each theory is explained, we will show how it can be applied by managers.

---

[3] John P. Campbell, Marvin D. Dunnette, Edward E. Lawler III, and Karl E. Weick, Jr., *Managerial Behavior, Performance and Effectiveness* (New York: McGraw-Hill, 1970), p. 341.

CONTENT THEORIES OF MOTIVATION

Maslow's Hierarchy of Needs

Maslow's need hierarchy theory has enjoyed widespread acceptance, since it was introduced around 1943. His theory of motivation stresses two fundamental premises:

1. Man is a wanting animal whose needs depend on what he already has. Only needs not yet satisfied can influence behavior. In other words, a satisfied need is not a motivator.
2. Man's needs are arranged in a hierarchy of importance. Once one need is satisfied, another emerges and demands satisfaction.

Maslow hypothesized five levels of needs. These needs are (1) physiological, (2) safety, (3) social, (4) esteem, and (5) self-actualization.[4] He placed them in a framework referred to as the *hierarchy of needs* because of the different levels of importance. This framework is presented in Figure 10–2.

Maslow states that if all of a person's needs are unsatisfied at a particular time, satisfaction of the more predominant needs will be more pressing than the others. Those that come first must be satisfied before a higher-level need comes into play. Let us briefly examine each need level:

1. *Physiological needs.* This category consists of the human body's primary needs, such as food, water, and sex. Physiological needs will dominate when they are unsatisfied, and no other needs will serve as a basis for motivation. As Maslow states, "a person who is lacking food, safety, love, and esteem probably would hunger for food more strongly than for anything else."[5]

2. *Safety needs.* When physiological needs are adequately met, the next higher level of needs assumes importance. Safety needs include protection from physical harm, ill health, economic disaster, and the unexpected. From a managerial standpoint, safety needs show up in an employee's attempts to ensure job security and fringe benefits.

3. *Social needs.* These needs are related to the social nature of people and their need for companionship. Here, the hierarchy departs from the

---

[4] Less described, and hence not as well known, are the cognitive and aesthetic needs hypothesized by Maslow. Examples of cognitive needs are the need to know or understand and the manipulation of the environment as the result of curiosity. The aesthetic needs are satisfied by moving from ugliness toward beauty. Maslow did not include them in the formal hierarchy framework. Abraham H. Maslow, *Motivation and Personality* (New York: Harper & Row, 1954), pp. 93–98.

[5] Ibid., p. 82.

FIGURE   10–2   Maslow's Hierarchy of Needs Theory

People have and attempt to satisfy these five basic needs.

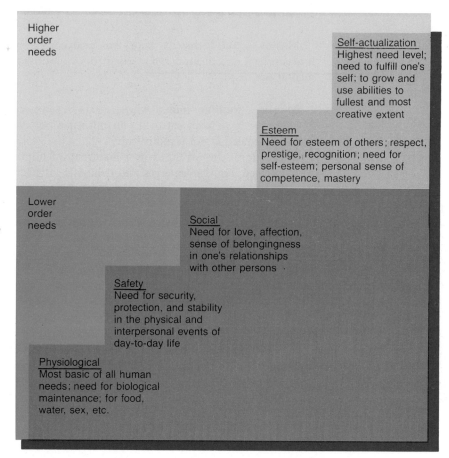

physical or quasi-physical needs of the two previous levels. Nonsatisfaction of this level of need may affect the mental health of the individual.

   4. *Esteem needs.*   The need for both awareness of importance to others (self-esteem) and actual esteem from others is included. Esteem from others must also be felt as warranted and deserved. Satisfaction of these needs leads to a feeling of self-confidence and prestige.

   5. *Self-actualization needs.*   Maslow defines these needs as the "desire to become more and more what one is, to become everything one is capable of becoming."[6] This means that the individual will realize fully the potentiali-

---

[6] Ibid., p. 92.

TABLE   10–1   Areas of Management Influence in the Five Need Hierarchy Categories

Need Category	Management Influence Areas
Self-actualization	Challenges in job. Provide advancement opportunities. Permit creativity. Encourage high achievement.
Esteem	Recognize and publicize good performance. Significant job activities. Respectful job title. Responsibility.
Social	Permit social interaction. Keep groups stable. Encourage cooperation.
Safety	Safe working conditions. Job security. Fringe benefits.
Physiological	Fair salary. Comfortable working conditions. Heat, lighting, space, air conditioning.

Managers can help employees satisfy needs.

ties of talents and capabilities. Obviously, as the role of an individual varies, so will the external aspects of self-actualization. In other words, whether the person is a college professor, corporate manager, parent, or athlete, the need is to be effective in that particular role. Maslow assumes that satisfaction of the self-actualization needs is possible only after the satisfaction of all other needs. Moreover, he proposes that the satisfaction of the self-actualization needs will tend to increase the strength of those needs. Thus, when people are able to achieve self-actualization, they tend to be motivated by increased opportunities to satisfy that need.[7]

Applying Maslow's theory in management.   The need hierarchy theory is widely accepted and referred to by practicing managers. Although it does not provide a complete understanding of human motivation or the means to motivate people, it does provide an excellent starting point for the student of management. The hierarchy is easy to comprehend, has a great deal of commonsense validity, and points out some of the factors that motivate people in business and other types of organizations. For example, most organizations in industrialized nations such as the United States, Canada, Japan, and West Germany have been extremely successful in satisfying lower-level needs.

---

[7] Abraham H. Maslow, *Motivation and Personality* (New York: Harper & Row, 1970), p. 81.

Through wages or salary, individuals are able to satisfy the physiological needs of themselves and their families. Organizations also aid in satisfying security or safety needs through both salary and fringe-benefit programs. Finally, they aid in satisfying social needs by allowing interaction and association with others on the job. Some work-related examples that managers can influence under each of the five need categories are presented in Table 10–1.

Herzberg's Two-Factor Theory

Another content explanation of motivation was advanced by Frederick Herzberg in 1959. He based his theory on a study of need satisfactions and on the reported motivational effects of these satisfactions on 200 engineers and accountants. The theory is referred to as the two-factor theory of motivation.[8]

In the study of engineers and accountants, Herzberg and his associates asked the subjects to think of times both when they felt especially good and when they felt especially bad about their jobs. Each employee was then asked to describe the conditions that led to these particular feelings. It was found that the employees named different kinds of conditions as causes of each of the feelings. For example, if recognition led to a good feeling about the job, the lack of recognition was seldom indicated as a cause of bad feelings. Based on the study, Herzberg reached two conclusions:

1. Some conditions of a job operate primarily to dissatisfy employees when they are not present. However, the presence of these conditions does not build strong motivation. Herzberg called these *maintenance factors,* since they are necessary to maintain a reasonable level of satisfaction. He also noted that many of these have often been perceived by managers as factors that can motivate subordinates but that they are, in fact, more potent as dissatisfiers when they are absent. He named 10 maintenance factors:

Company policy and administration.
Technical supervision.
Interpersonal relations with supervisor.
Interpersonal relations with peers.
Interpersonal relations with subordinates.

Salary.
Job security.
Personal life.
Work conditions.
Status.

2. Some job conditions build high levels of motivation and job satisfaction. However, if these conditions are not present, they do not prove highly dissatisfying. Herzberg described six of these *motivational factors,* or satisfiers:

---

[8] See Frederick Herzberg, B. Mausner, and B. Snyderman, *The Motivation to Work* (New York: John Wiley & Sons, 1959).

Achievement.   The work itself.
Recognition.   The possibility of personal growth.
Advancement.   Responsibility.

In summary, the maintenance factors cause much dissatisfaction when they are not present but do not provide strong motivation when they are present. On the other hand, the factors in the second group lead to strong motivation and satisfaction when they are present but do not cause much dissatisfaction when they are absent. Herzberg's study of engineers and accountants suggested to him that the opposite of satisfaction is not dissatisfaction but simply "no satisfaction." Figure 10–3 compares his view of job satisfaction to a traditional view.

The reader probably has noted that the *motivational factors* are job centered; that is, they relate directly to the job itself, the individual's performance, the job's responsibilities, and the growth and recognition obtained from it. *Maintenance factors* are peripheral to the job itself and more related to the external environment of work. Another important finding of the study is that when employees are highly motivated, they have a high tolerance for dissatisfaction arising from the maintenance factors. However, the reverse is not true.

The distinction between motivational and maintenance factors is similar to what psychologists have described as *intrinsic* and *extrinsic* motivators.

FIGURE   10–3   Contrasting Views of Satisfaction and Dissatisfaction

Herzberg's versus traditional view

Traditional versus Herzberg's view of satisfaction and dissatisfaction.

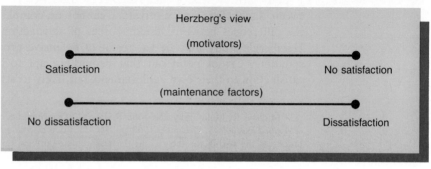

Intrinsic motivators are part of the job and occur when the employee performs the work. The opportunity to perform a job with intrinsic motivational potential is motivating because the work itself is rewarding. Extrinsic motivators are external rewards that have meaning or value after performing the work or away from the workplace. They provide little, if any, satisfaction when the work is being performed. Pay, of course, is a good example of what Herzberg classifies as a maintenance factor and what some psychologists call an extrinsic motivator.

Applying Herzberg's theory in management.   Few would argue that Herzberg still contributes substantially to our thinking on motivation at work. He certainly has extended Maslow's ideas and made them more applicable to the work situation. He has drawn attention to the critical importance, in work motivation, of job-centered factors previously given little attention by behavioral scientists. This insight has resulted in an increased interest in *job enrichment,* an effort to restructure jobs to increase worker satisfaction.

Herzberg's response to motivation problems is an important one. Traditionally, managers would respond to motivation problems with more money, increased fringe benefits, and improved working conditions. Often, the result of such actions was still no more effort to work harder. Herzberg's theory offers an explanation for this situation. If managers focus only on maintenance factors, motivation will not occur. The motivators must be built into the job to improve motivation.

Criticisms of Herzberg's theory.   One limitation of Herzberg's original study and conclusions is that the subjects consisted of engineers and accountants. That these individuals were in such positions indicates that they had the motivation to seek advanced education and expected to be rewarded. The same may not hold true for the nonprofessional worker. In fact, some testing of Herzberg's model on blue-collar workers showed that some of the factors considered as maintenance factors by Herzberg (pay and job security) are considered by blue-collar workers to be motivational factors.[9]

Some critics believe that Herzberg's inference concerning differences between dissatisfiers and motivators cannot be completely accepted and that the differences between stated sources of satisfaction and dissatisfaction in Herzberg's study may be the result of defensive processes within those responding. Critics point out that people are apt to attribute the causes of satisfaction to their own achievements but likely to attribute their dissatisfac-

---

[9] Michael R. Malinovsky and John R. Barry, "Determinants of Work Attitudes," *Journal of Applied Psychology,* December 1965, pp. 446–51. For a discussion of other alternative interpretations of the two-factor theory and the research support for the various interpretations, see N. King, "Clarification and Evaluation of the Two-Factor Theory of Job Satisfaction," *Psychological Bulletin,* July 1970, pp. 18–31; D. A. Ondrack, "Defense Mechanisms and the Herzberg Theory: An Alternate Test," *Personnel Psychology,* March 1974, pp. 79–89.

tion more to obstacles presented by company policies or superiors than to their own deficiencies.[10]

Other critics believe that the two-factor theory is an oversimplification of the true relationship between motivation and dissatisfaction as well as between the sources of job satisfaction and dissatisfaction.[11] Reviews of several studies show that one factor can cause job satisfaction for one person and job dissatisfaction for another.

Since his original study, Herzberg has cited numerous replications of the original study that support his position.[12] These subsequent studies were conducted on professional women, hospital maintenance personnel, agricultural administrators, nurses, food handlers, manufacturing supervisors, engineers, scientists, military officers, managers ready for retirement, teachers, technicians, and assemblers. And some were conducted in other cultural settings: Finland, Hungary, Russia, and Yugoslavia.

However, some researchers have used the same research methods employed by Herzberg and obtained results different from what his theory would predict,[13] while several using different methods have also obtained contradictory results.[14]

Comparing Herzberg's and Maslow's Models

There is much similarity between Herzberg's and Maslow's models. A close examination of Herzberg's ideas indicates that what he actually is saying is that some employees may have achieved a level of social and economic progress such that the higher-level needs of Maslow (esteem and self-actualization) are the primary motivators. However, they still must satisfy the lower-level needs for the maintenance of their current state. Thus, we can see that money might still be a motivator for nonmanagement workers (particularly those at a low wage level) and for some managerial employees. In

[10] See the classic Victor H. Vroom, *Work and Motivation* (New York: John Wiley & Sons, 1964), pp. 128–29.

[11] For one of the earliest criticisms, see R. J. House and L. A. Wigdor, "Herzberg's Dual-Factor Theory of Job Satisfaction and Motivation: A Review of the Evidence and a Criticism," *Personnel Psychology,* Winter 1967, pp. 369–89.

[12] Frederick Herzberg, *Work and the Nature of Man* (Cleveland: World Publishing, 1966). This is a classic work by Herzberg.

[13] An early study is Donald P. Schwab, H. William DeVitt, and Larry L. Cummings, "A Test of the Adequacy of the Two-Factor Theory as a Predictor of Self-Report Performance Effects," *Personnel Psychology,* Summer 1971, pp. 293–303.

[14] Marvin D. Dunnette, John P. Campbell, and Milton D. Hakel, "Factors Contributing to Job Satisfaction and Job Dissatisfaction in Six Occupational Groups," *Organizational Behavior and Human Performance,* May 1967, pp. 143–74; C. L. Hulin and P. A. Smith, "An Empirical Investigation of Two Implications of the Two-Factor Theory of Job Satisfaction," *Journal of Applied Psychology,* October 1967, pp. 396–402.

FIGURE   10–4   A Comparison of the Maslow and Herzberg Theories: Similarities*

Complementary ideas with different labels

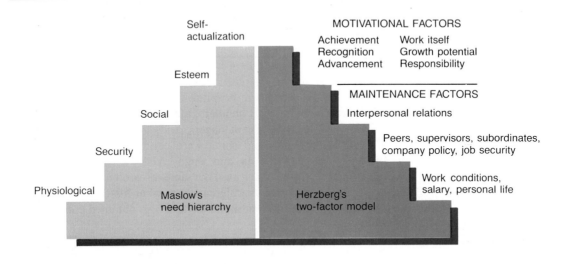

*Also see Keith Davis, *Human Behavior at Work* (New York: McGraw-Hill, 1977), p. 53.
Maslow and Herzberg: similar ideas with different labels.

addition, Herzberg's model adds to Maslow's model, because it breaks down the five need levels into two job-oriented categories: maintenance and motivational. Figure 10–4 compares the structure of the two. Table 10–2 compares areas in which they differ.

TABLE   10–2   Comparing Maslow's and Herzberg's Theories: Differences

Topic	Maslow's Need Hierarchy	Herzberg's Two-Factor Theory
1. Relevance	People in society in all types of jobs and in retirement.	Most relevant to white-collar and professional employees.
2. Impact of needs on behavior	All needs can motivate behavior.	Only some intrinsic needs serve as motivators.
3. Role of financial rewards	Financial reward can motivate.	Financial reward is not a key motivator.
4. Perspective	Applies to all people and their lives.	Is work centered.
5. Type of theory	Descriptive (what is).	Prescriptive (what should be).

Maslow and Herzberg: five points of comparison.

PROCESS THEORIES OF MOTIVATION

In contrast to the two content theories—Maslow's need hierarchy and Herzberg's two-factor theory—expectancy theory and reinforcement theory are process theories. They concentrate upon how motivation occurs.

Vroom's Expectancy Theory

The expectancy theory of motivation as initially presented in 1964 by psychologist Victor Vroom views motivation as a process governing choices.[15] The theory suggests that individuals are motivated at work to make choices among different behaviors, for example intensities of work effort. A person may choose to work at a moderate rate or an accelerated rate. The choice is made by the individual. If a person believes that his or her work effort will be adequately rewarded, there will be motivated effort: a choice will be made to work so that a preferred reward is received. The logic of expectancy motivation is that *individuals will exert work effort to achieve performance that will result in preferred rewards.*

The Management Focus about rewards as motivators gives examples in a computer manufacturer, a bank, and at Tupperware International. In some cases, reward systems create a competitive spirit that can reduce overall performance. The Focus examines how effort, reward, and competition are associated.

MANAGEMENT FOCUS
Is Increased Competition the Key to More Effort?

To encourage branch managers to work harder and perform better, a European bank encouraged them to compete against each other to produce the best results. The winner was promised a bonus. But the outcome was disappointing. The bank discovered that a jealous and greedy officer had steered a customer to a rival bank rather than help another manager win the bonus.

Sales contests, another widespread form of competition, also have produced some awkward situations for the companies that sponsor them. Data General Corporation, a Westboro, Massachusetts, computer maker, caught its salesperson for the Texas area poaching in Oklahoma, which was another salesperson's territory.

Some companies embarrass workers to motivate them. Data General used to award a statue of a horse's rear end to the region

---

[15] Vroom, *Work and Motivation.*

MANAGEMENT FOCUS (*continued*)

with the worst quarterly record of meeting its goals. But when Bill Adams, a manager, had to accept the statue in front of his 75 employees, he had to quell a minor insurrection. His four subordinate managers wanted to walk out, to quit the firm.

Issuing formal performance evaluations and rewarding those who produce are recommended to head off problems with motivational approaches that encourage cutthroat competition. For example, at Tupperware International, the sales agents who host Tupperware parties (where the firm's household containers are marketed) meet to compare results. Everyone gets some type of ribbon or prize at these meetings. Regularly reviewing performance and rewarding good performance are the motivational techniques used at Tupperware.

Three primary variables in the expectancy theory of motivation are choice, expectancy, and preference.[16] *Choice* designates the individual's freedom to select from a number of alternative behaviors. For example, a person's work may be fast or slow, hard or moderate; the employee may stay home or come to work. In some cases, working fast may lead to more pay if compensation is based on the number of units produced. *Expectancy* is the belief that a particular behavior will or will not be successful. It is a subjective probability. Expectancy would be zero if a person believed that it was impossible to produce, say, 50 units a day; it would equal one if a person felt certain of being able to produce 22 units a day. *Preferences,* also referred to by Vroom as valences, are the values a person attaches to various outcomes (rewards or punishment).

Another issue covered in the expectancy motivation model is called *instrumentality*—the probability that a person assigns to the performance-outcome link. It is the probability that a particular performance level will lead to a specific outcome.

Figure 10–5 presents a general explanation and a work-oriented example of the expectancy theory. The work-oriented example is presented to show how the theory can be applied. To predict whether a person will select Path A or B you need to examine the interrelationships of the variables in the model. The motivation to work is expressed as:[17]

$$M = E \times I \times P$$

---

[16] Ibid.

[17] Because the preference variable is also called valence, the expression may be $M = E \times I \times V$.

FIGURE   10–5   How the Expectancy Theory of Motivation Works

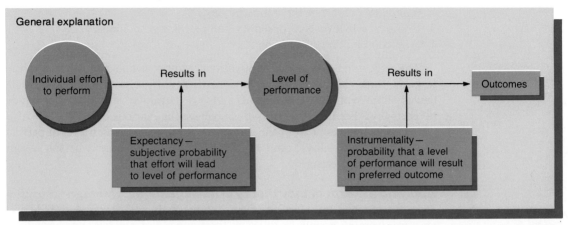

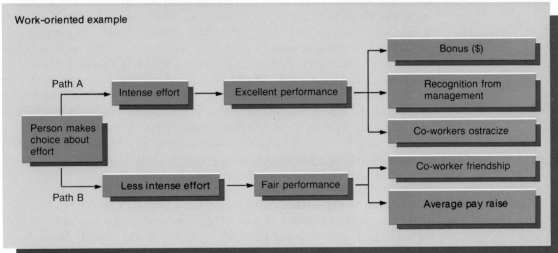

Examples of expectancy theory that show how the theory works.

That is, motivation to work (M) results from expectancy (E) times instrumentality (I) times preference (P). Because this is a multiplicative interrelationship, think about the consequences if E, I, or P approaches zero in value.

Suppose that the work example in Figure 10–5 applies to Nan Brewer and her manager Nick. Nick is not sure whether a pay bonus will motivate Nan to perform better. Using the expectancy theory, Nick would predict that Nan's motivation to work hard would be low if:

1. Expectancy is low: Nan feels that she really can't achieve the bonus level of performance.
2. Instrumentality is low: Nan is uncertain about whether excellent performance will result in the bonus money.
3. Preference is low: Nan doesn't value receiving the bonus.
4. Any combination of 1, 2, or 3.

The expectancy theory of motivation requires a manager such as Nick to know three things when applying the theory: First, what are the person's beliefs about working hard and achieving a particular level of performance (expectancy)? Second, does the person believe that various outcomes (positive or negative) will result from the achievement of the particular level of performance (instrumentality)? And third, how much value does a person assign to outcomes (preferences)?

Applying the expectancy theory in management.   Managers can influence expectancies by selecting (hiring) individuals with particular skills and abilities, training people to improve their skills and abilities, and providing individuals with the leadership support to achieve a particular level of performance. The manager also can influence instrumentalities by being supportive, realistic, and offering advice. The manager can influence preferences by listening to employee needs, guiding employees to help them accomplish desired outcomes, and providing proper resources to achieve the desired performance.

It is important for managers to understand the vital role of perception in motivation. A person's expectancies, instrumentalities, and valences depend upon a person's perceptions. The importance of perceptual differences among workers with similar skill levels is made obvious by the expectancy theory. Different levels of motivation among people with similar skills could be explained in terms of perceptual differences.

Criticisms of expectancy theory.   The expectancy theory is more complex than either Maslow's or Herzberg's theory.[18] There also are problems of measuring and studying the main variables in the model. How should preferences be determined? How should expectancy be determined? However, despite the lack of tested validity, the expectancy model still adds insight into the role that perception plays in choices, expectancy, and preferences.[19]

---

[18] See Victor H. Vroom, "Organizational Choice: A Study of Pre- and Post-Decision Processes," *Organizational Behavior and Human Performance,* August 1966, pp. 212–25; J. Galbraith and L. L. Cummings, "An Empirical Investigation of the Motivational Determinants of Task Performance: Interactive Effects between Instrumentality—Valence and Motivation—Ability," *Organizational Behavior and Human Performance,* August 1967, pp. 237–57. For a critical review of field research on expectancy and D. P. Schwab, "Expectancy Theory Predictions of Employee Performance: A Review of the Theory and Evidence," *Psychological Bulletin,* July 1972, pp. 1–9.

[19] Terence Mitchell, "Expectancy-Value Models in Organizational Psychology," in *Expectancy, Incentive, and Action,* ed. N. Feather (Hillsdale, N.J.: Erlbaum & Associates, 1980).

We might ask each reader: Do you make choices? Do you have expectancies? Do you have reward preferences?

Reinforcement Theory

Reinforcement theory is another widely discussed process theory of motivation. Reinforcement theory considers the use of positive or negative reinforcers to motivate or create an environment of motivation. This theory of motivation is not concerned with needs or why people make choices. Instead it is concerned with the environment and its consequences for the person. That is, behavior is considered to be environmentally caused. For example, suppose John Lofton, a hard-working employee, is given a $100 bonus for doing a good job. In the future, John continues to work hard, expecting another bonus payment. Why does John continue to work hard? When John first worked hard, his behavior was reinforced by a $100 bonus. This reinforcement is an environmental consequence of good performance.

The explanation of why John continued to work hard, according to reinforcement theory, centers on Thorndike's law of effect, which states that *behavior that results in a pleasing outcome will be likely to be repeated; behavior that results in an unpleasant outcome is not likely to be repeated.* [20]

Operant conditioning is a powerful tool used for changing employee behavior. The term *operant conditioning* in the management literature applies to controlling work behavior by manipulating the consequences. It is based on the research work of psychologist B. F. Skinner and is built on two principles: (1) Thorndike's law of effect and (2) properly scheduled rewards influence individual behaviors.[21] *Behavior modification* is the contemporary term used to describe techniques for applying the principles of operant conditioning to the control of individual behavior.

Applying reinforcement theory in management.
Suppose you are a manager and your employee Mary Banner is always late with required budget reports. There are four types of reinforcement that you could use. First, you could focus on reinforcing the desired behavior (which, in this example, is preparing budget reports on time). You could use positive or negative reinforcement. *Positive reinforcement* would include rewards such as praise, recognition, or a pay bonus. *Negative reinforcement* also focuses on reinforcing the desired behavior. However, instead of providing a positive reward, the "reward" is that the employee avoids some negative consequence. Thus, Mary would complete the report on time to avoid the negative consequence of being reprimanded by her manager.

[20] E. L. Thorndike, *Animal Intelligence* (New York: McGraw-Hill, 1911), p. 244.

[21] B. F. Skinner, *Science and Human Behavior* (New York: Macmillan, 1953); B. F. Skinner, *Contingencies of Reinforcement* (New York: Appleton-Century-Crofts, 1969).

Alternatively, the manager might focus on reducing the tardiness of submitting the budget report by use of two other reinforcements: extinction or punishment. Through the use of *extinction* (withholding positive reinforcement), Mary might unlearn her bad habit of submitting late reports. Another method that reduces the frequency of undesired behavior is called *punishment*. In this case, punishment could involve the public reprimand of Mary by the manager for submitting a late report. The Management Focus on Tampa Electric Company suggests that discipline without punishment is the preferred approach there.

MANAGEMENT FOCUS
Tampa Electric Decides that Nonpunitive Discipline Is Better

At Tampa Electric Company, a confrontation between a line worker and a supervisor turned into a problem. The supervisor became so upset with the worker that he grabbed him by the shirt collar and shoved him severely. This was unacceptable behavior, and the supervisor was suspended for 13 days. The supervisor temporarily changed his behavior; but five months later, another incident occurred. The punitive suspension only treated the symptoms.

Tampa Electric management decided to use a nonpunitive system, the basics of which are:

1. Manager issues an oral reminder that behavior is not acceptable. This discussion is recorded in a file.
2. If the problem continues, the manager prepares a written reminder. Also, the manager talks about the problem and attempts to develop an action plan for solving the problem.
3. If the discussions and reminder fail, then management places the individual on a paid, one-day leave. The company pays for the day.
4. On returning to the job, the employee meets with the supervisor to state that he or she has solved the problem. The statement is written up, and a copy is placed in the file. If the employee fails to live up to the statement, he or she is terminated.

The nonpunitive approach attempts to require problem employees to make a choice: to become either committed employees or former employees.

Adapted from David H. Campbell, R. L. Fleming, and Richard D. Grote, "Discipline without Punishment—At Last," *Harvard Business Review*, July–August 1985, pp. 162–164, 168, 170, 174, 176, 178.

FIGURE   10–6   Four Types of Reinforcement Available to Managers: Illustration

---

Stimulus	Employee's Work Behavior (Mary Banner)	Possible Action	Type of Reinforcement
You (as a manager) want all budget reports submitted on time.	1. Is consistently on time submitting budget reports.	1. Praise and publicly recognize Mary's behavior.	Positive reinforcement.
		2. Do not reprimand Mary.	Negative reinforcement.
	2. Is considerably late with submittal of budget reports.	3. Withhold praise and recognition that Mary values.	Extinction.
		4. Publicly reprimand Mary.	Punishment.

Four types of reinforcement that a manager can use.

Positive and negative reinforcement addresses the notion of having employees learn desired behaviors. On the other hand, unlearning undesired behaviors involves the use of extinction or punishment. Figure 10–6 summarizes the Mary Banner example.

In applying positive reinforcement to motivate desired behaviors, managers can use different schedules. A *continuous* reinforcement schedule involves administering a reward each time a desired behavior occurs. For example, every time a budget report is submitted on time, Mary would be rewarded. An *intermittent* reinforcement schedule involves rewarding desired behavior only periodically. According to research results:[22]

1. Continuous reinforcement schedules usually result in the fastest learning.
2. Intermittent reinforcement schedules result in slower learning but stronger retention of what is learned.

Criticisms of reinforcement theory.   Some critics state that the idea of rewarding or reinforcing performance is bribery and that it is used to

---

[22] H. Davis and H. M. B. Hurwitz, eds., *Operant-Pavlovian Interactions* (Hillsdale, N.J.: Erlbaum & Associates, 1977).

manipulate one person to fit a manager's concept of the ideal employee.[23] Others argue that motivating employees through behavior modification relies solely on extrinsic rewards such as pay. What about intrinsic rewards, such as feeling the challenge of doing a good job?[24] Other issues of concern include: What reinforcers should be used? For whom? How long will a reinforcer be successful? Can reinforcers be effectively used with employees who are independent, creative, and self-motivated?

It is helpful to keep these criticisms in mind when considering the managerial use of reinforcement theory. They help illustrate some of the problems associated with this approach. Also, a word of caution: Reinforcement theory (like any of the other motivation theories) is not a solution to every motivation problem.

AN INTEGRATING MODEL OF MOTIVATION

All of the motivation theories presented contain the theme that motivation is goal directed. Although the theories use different terms and appear to be quite different, they are not in conflict with each other. Basically each looks at some segment of overall motivation or looks at the same aspect of motivation from a slightly different perspective.

Porter-Lawler Model

Psychologists Lyman Porter and Edward Lawler offer a model that attempts to integrate ideas, variables, and relationships presented in other explanations of motivation such as the need hierarchy, two-factor theory, expectancy theory, and reinforcement theory.

The Porter-Lawler model is presented in Figure 10–7. It points out the relationship of performance, satisfaction, and rewards and introduces the importance of having individuals performing jobs for which they have the proper skills, abilities, and traits. There also is the issue of performance measurement. Performance must be measured accurately and systematically so that rewards can be distributed equitably. If they are not distributed fairly, expending the necessary effort to do the job will seem senseless to employees. If no meaningful difference in rewards is made between high and low performers, high performers will lose motivational intensity and probably cut back on their performance.

---

[23] H. Waird, "Why Manage Behavior? A Case for Positive Reinforcement?" *Human Resource Management,* Spring 1976, pp. 15–20.

[24] Craig Schneier, "Behavior Modification in Management: Review and Critique," *Academy of Management Journal,* September 1974, pp. 528–48.

FIGURE   10–7   An Integrative Motivational Model

Bringing together content and process theories of motivation

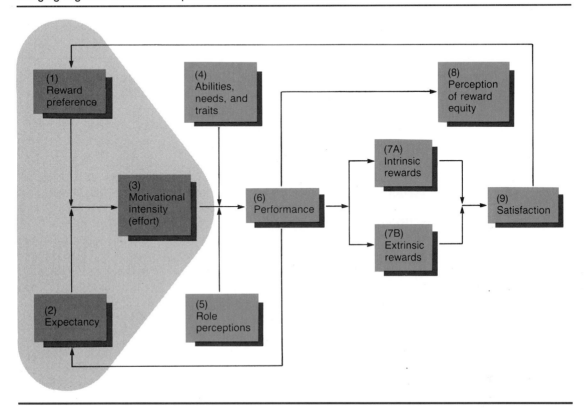

Source: Adapted from Lyman W. Porter and Edward E. Lawler III, *Managerial Attitudes and Performance* (Homewood, Ill.: Richard D. Irwin, 1968), p. 165.

Effective management must combine theories of motivation.

The model relates motivational intensity to job performance. The extent to which greater efforts yield higher performance depends on the characteristics of the person and what the individual understands the conduct of the job's duties to be. Motivational intensity also depends on the rewards received. If rewards are received and distributed fairly (7A and 7B), satisfaction (9) results.

Expectancy.   The boxes numbered 1, 2, and 3 illustrate critical expectancy theory variables. Motivational intensity (Box 3) depends on the attractiveness (Box 1) of the reward and the perception that effort will result in reward (expectancy, Box 2).

Performance.   The accomplishment of goals is successful performance (Box 6). Note that effort alone does not yield successful performance. The individual also must possess the abilities, needs, and other personal traits (Box 4) to do the job well. No matter how sincerely an employee wishes to succeed, ability is needed. Also, performance is affected by the job duties as perceived by the person performing the job (Box 5).

Performance-expectancy loop.   The feedback loop between performance (Box 6) and expectancy (Box 2) and then to effort (Box 3) and back again to performance suggests learning or a "history" effect. Employees, over time, recognize patterns according to which rewards are distributed. Reinforcement theory introduced the idea of learning desirable behaviors.

Rewards.   Rewards are preferred outcomes. *Intrinsic* rewards (Box 7A) are part of the job and occur when the employee performs the work. Recall that Herzberg discussed them in his two-factor model. *Extrinsic* rewards (Box 7B) are administered by managers or supervisors. Examples would be job security, working conditions, and fringe benefits. These are areas managers can influence to satisfy physiological and safety needs (see Table 10–1).

The notion of reward equity (Box 8) is affected by the level of rewards, type of rewards, and the person's performance. The extent of satisfaction received is related not only to the level and type of rewards but whether the rewards are considered fair.

Satisfaction-reward preference loop.   The feedback loop connecting satisfaction (Box 9) and reward preference (Box 1) recycles the motivational process. Individuals weigh what has occurred, then establish a level of effort for the future.

Using the Model

The Porter-Lawler model and the individual theories discussed in the chapter point out that motivation is a complex process. Managers should consider the types of variables shown in the integrative model. Certainly, it indicates that motivation holds some important keys for understanding performance and satisfaction. A periodic review of the motivation process can be beneficial if managers ask themselves:

1. What are the needs of this subordinate?
2. Can I play a role in helping this subordinate satisfy these needs?
3. Are the rewards that I control and administer contingent on performance? Are they sufficient to induce the type of effort needed to do the job?
4. Does the employee have the skill, traits, behaviors, and experience necessary to perform the job?

5. Am I accurately measuring performance? If not, why not?
6. For how long will the employees continue to be motivated? What must I do to sustain motivation?

MANAGEMENT STRATEGIES FOR INCREASING MOTIVATION

Behavioral scientists have called attention to a number of programs that motivate workers to improve performance. Two programs that have been beneficial to some managers are job enrichment and relating pay to job performance.

Job Enrichment

The "quality of life" at work receives much attention from practicing managers, government officials, and union leaders;[25] there is a current wave of interest in humanizing jobs. It appears that many workers are becoming increasingly dissatisfied and frustrated by routine, mechanically paced tasks and are reacting negatively with output restrictions, poor-quality work, absenteeism, high turnover, pressure for higher wages, expanded fringe benefits, and greater participation in decisions that directly affect their jobs.

Earlier we discussed the Herzberg two-factor theory. The practical contribution of Herzberg's theory is a motivational technique known as *job enrichment,* supported by many managers as a solution to the problem of the quality of life at work.[26] As Herzberg describes it, job enrichment:

> seeks to improve both task efficiency and human satisfaction by means of building into people's jobs, quite specifically, greater scope for personal achievement and recognition, more challenging and responsible work, and more opportunity for individual advancement and growth. It is concerned only incidentally with matters such as pay and working conditions, organizational structure, communications and training, important and necessary though these may be in their own right.[27]

Herzberg emphasizes the importance of differentiating between *job enrichment* and *job enlargement.* He views job enrichment as providing the employee with an opportunity to grow psychologically and mature in a job, while job enlargement merely makes a job larger by increasing the number of tasks.

---

[25] A report on a major project is found in Barry A. Macy, "A Progress Report on the Bolivar Quality of Life Project," *Personnel Journal,* August 1979, pp. 527–30, 558–59.

[26] Frederick Herzberg, "One More Time: How Do You Motivate Employees?" *Harvard Business Review,* January–February 1968, p. 53.

[27] William J. Paul, Jr., Keith B. Robertson, and Frederick Herzberg, "Job Enrichment Pays Off," *Harvard Business Review,* March–April 1969, p. 61.

Basically, what this means is that job enrichment occurs by increasing a job's scope and depth.[28] *Scope* refers to the number of activities performed on the job, while *depth* refers to the autonomy, responsibility, and discretion or control over the job. Job enrichment means that the scope and depth of a job are increased. On the other hand, job enlargement means that a job's scope, but not necessarily its depth, is increased.

The core dimensions of jobs.

Building on Herzberg's work, Hackman and others have identified five core dimensions that, if present, provide enrichment for jobs.[29] Hackman, after conducting research on many different occupations, concludes that these core dimensions are often not found in many managerial and blue-collar jobs. He also states that there are large individual differences in how employees react to core dimensions. Not all employees want or can benefit from enriched jobs.

1. *Variety.* The first core dimension is variety in the job. Variety allows employees to perform different operations using several procedures and perhaps different equipment. Jobs that are high in variety often are viewed as challenging because they require the use of the full range of an employee's skills.

2. *Task Identity.* The second core dimension, task identity, allows employees to perform a complete piece of work. Overspecialized jobs tend to create routine job duties that result in a worker performing one part of the entire job. There is a sense of loss or of nonaccomplishment in doing only a part of a job. Thus, broadening the task to provide the worker with a feeling of doing a whole job increases task identity.

3. *Task Significance.* The amount of impact that the work being performed has on other people is called task significance. This impact may be within the organization or outside in the community. The feeling of doing something worthwhile is important to many people. For example, an employee may be told by a respected supervisor that she has done an outstanding job that has contributed to the overall success of the department. The task has significance because it is recognized as important for the entire department.

4. *Autonomy.* The fourth core dimension, autonomy, refers to the idea that employees have some control over their job duties and work area. This seems to be an important dimension in stimulating a sense of responsibility. The popular practice of management by objectives is one way of establishing more autonomy, because it provides employees with an opportunity to set work and personal goals.

---

[28] James L. Gibson, John M. Ivancevich, and James H. Donnelly, *Organizations: Behavior, Structure, Processes* (Plano, Tex.: Business Publications, 1985), p. 457.

[29] J. Richard Hackman, Greg Oldham, Robert Janson, and Kenneth Purdy, "A New Strategy for Job Enrichment," *California Management Review,* Summer 1975, pp. 57–71; J. Richard Hackman and Greg Oldham, "Development of the Job Diagnostic Survey," *Journal of Applied Psychology,* April 1975, pp. 159–70.

FIGURE   10–8   Profiles of Core Dimensions for Two Jobs

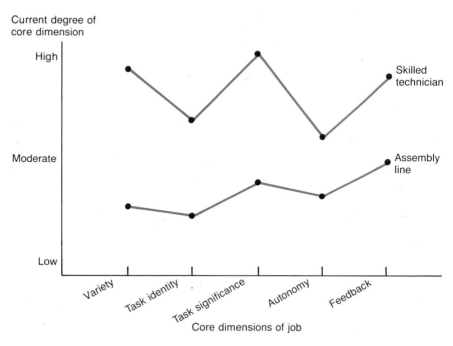

Current degree of
core dimension

High

The technician job will
be harder to enrich.
Why?

Moderate

Skilled
technician

Assembly
line

Low

Variety   Task identity   Task significance   Autonomy   Feedback

Core dimensions of job

5. *Feedback.* Feedback, the fifth core dimension, refers to information that workers receive on how well they are performing. People in general have a need to know how they are doing. They need this feedback frequently so that necessary improvements can be made.

Diagnosing jobs. These five core dimensions are what Hackman and his associates believe need to be modified to accomplish job enrichment. They suggest that organizations can study jobs to determine the quantity and quality of the core dimensions for each job. A procedure developed to study the quantity and quality of the core dimensions is called the job diagnostic survey (JDS).[30]

Profiles of two jobs are presented in Figure 10–8, one a skilled technician, the other an assembly-line position. By use of the JDS, worker opinions, and managerial opinions, a job's core dimensions can be studied in depth and the weak dimensions can be pinpointed. Managerial attention to these problem areas can result in job enrichment. Not all jobs can be enriched

_____

[30] Hackman and Oldman, "Job Diagnostic Survey."

in each core dimension. This constraint, however, should not stop managers from attempting to search further for methods to improve the total job or a specific core dimension.

Hackman's diagnostic approach to job enrichment attempts not only to profile jobs but to examine the employee's readiness for enrichment and the special problems that may hinder any job redesign. The employee who does not have a need for autonomy and feedback may not respond favorably to job enrichment. Thus, an employee's need strength is an important factor in developing the most appropriate job enrichment strategy.

One special problem of job enrichment that needs to be considered is how the program can be continued after it is started. How far will management go in each core dimension area? What is the limit of autonomy that management is willing to build into the job? If management is reluctant to continually diagnose and modify the job enrichment program, further improvement will be difficult. The management team needs to consider the following questions when reviewing job enrichment:

1. Can the employee accept more responsibility?
2. Can the employee work with more autonomy?
3. Is management able to accept changes in jobs that may result in more worker autonomy and more feedback?

Organizational applications of job enrichment.   An attempt to enrich jobs was built into a General Foods plant that opened in 1971.[31] The new plant management established work teams of 7 to 14 employees. Teams were given large amounts of autonomy and frequent feedback. There also was a high degree of variety built into each job. Most routine work was mechanized. The five core dimensions appear to have been provided, to a large extent.

Preliminary results indicate that the plant compared favorably to more traditionally operated plants: productivity was greater, and absenteeism and turnover was less. It has been suggested that the positive results may have occurred because the facility was new, since they began to weaken in the late 1970s.[32]

The Non-Linear Systems experiment offers a caution to advocates of job enrichment.[33] The firm manufactured digital electrical measuring instruments. Management replaced an assembly line with teams of 3 to 12 employees

---

[31] Richard E. Walton, "How to Counter Alienation in the Plant," *Harvard Business Review,* November–December 1972, pp. 70–81; Richard E. Walton, "The Diffusion of New Work Structures: Explaining Why Success Didn't Take," *Organizational Dynamics,* Winter 1975, pp. 3–22. Also see Lyman D. Ketchum, "How to Start and Sustain a Work Redesign Program," *National Productivity Review,* Winter 1981–1982, pp. 75–86.

[32] "Stonewalling Unit Democracy," *Business Week,* March 28, 1977, pp. 78, 81–82.

[33] Erwin L. Malone, "The Non-Linear Systems Experiment in Participative Management," *Journal of Business,* January 1975, pp. 52–64.

having minimal supervision. The teams decided how the instruments would be produced. Work could be rotated and the pace controlled by the team. Each group was also responsible for resolving conflicts and handling disciplinary problems.

The first set of findings at Non-Linear revealed increased productivity and morale. Over a period of years, however, productivity and quality began to suffer. The teams were not able to make quick decisions, because there was little structure within the units. The team members became dissatisfied. After approximately four years of experimenting, the firm reverted to its previous managerial practices.

These two experiences suggest that the implementation of job enrichment principles can be successful in some situations but not in others.[34] There also is the question of how long performance improvements can continue, an important issue in the General Foods example. Job enrichment should not be viewed as a universally desirable program. Some workers and managers cannot operate effectively under job enrichment conditions. Therefore, both worker and managerial reactions need to be considered before implementing job enrichment.

Relating Pay to Job Performance

The money that employees receive for working is actually a package made up of pay and various fringe benefits, such as health insurance, vacation pay, life insurance, and sick leave. Each of the content and process theories of motivation suggest that money can have some influence on effort and persistence.

In Maslow's need hierarchy, pay has the potential to satisfy each of the five needs. However, according to Herzberg's two-factor model, pay is a maintenance factor that should not contribute significantly to workers' motivation. The expectancy theory would indicate that since pay can satisfy a variety of needs, it has an attraction. Pay would be a good motivator if workers perceive that good performance is instrumental to obtaining it. The reinforcement theory would view pay as an environmental consequence that could be used to stimulate positive work behaviors.

A number of research studies suggest to managers that a pay plan, in order to motivate, must (1) create a belief that good performance leads to high levels of pay, (2) minimize the negative consequences of good performance, and (3) create conditions so that desired rewards other than pay

---

[34] For more thorough reviews of job enrichment, see Ricky W. Griffin, *Task Design: An Integrative Approach,* (Glenview, Ill.: Scott, Foresman, 1982; Randall Dunham, "Job Design," in *Organizational Behavior,* ed. Steven Kerr (Columbus, Ohio: Grid, 1979); Ramon J. Aldag and Arthur P. Brief, *Task Design and Employee Motivation* (Glenview, Ill.: Scott, Foresman, 1979).

FIGURE   10–9   The Consequences of Pay Dissatisfaction

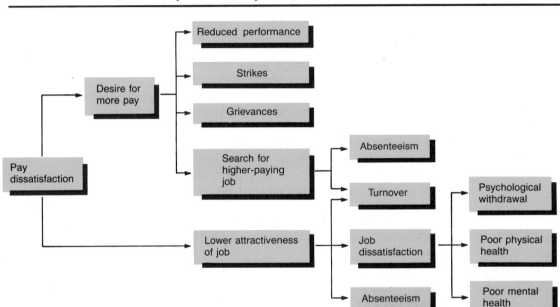

Source: From *Pay and Organizational Effectiveness: A Psychological View* by Edward E. Lawler III. Copyright © 1971 McGraw-Hill Book Company. Used with permission of McGraw-Hill Book Company.

Being dissatisfied with pay has negative consequences.

are seen to be related to good performance.[35] Research findings suggest that many organizations do not do a very good job of relating pay to performance. This conclusion applies to both managers and nonmanagers. Surprisingly, in the managerial ranks (where no unions exist), pay is not related to performance. This may mean that pay is not a very powerful motivator or that money is being wasted when offered in hopes that it will motivate better managerial performance. Managers use numerous methods in their attempt to relate pay to performance.

One survey of personnel practices reported high dissatisfaction with pay programs,[36] which can affect performance and other variables. Figure 10–9 illustrates some of the potentially negative consequences of being dissatisfied with pay. Managers must understand that pay is very important to some

[35] Good discussions of pay and performance appear in George T. Milkovich and Jerry M. Newman, *Compensation* (Plano, Tex.: Business Publications, 1984); Edward E. Lawler, III, *Pay and Organizational Effectiveness* (New York: McGraw-Hill, 1971).

[36] Campbell, et al., *Managerial Behavior,* pp. 51–59.

people and is a highly valued reward. It can serve to satisfy needs and to increase the motivation intensity of the employee. If a worker's desire for more pay is not satisfied, the consequences could be reduced performance, filing of grievances, interest in going on strike, or even seeking a job elsewhere.

In order to head off pay dissatisfaction problems, a number of organizations have used some innovative plans. A few of these innovative efforts will be briefly introduced.

Money as a motivator.   Nucor Manufacturing Corporation has a management team that believes, unlike Herzberg, that money is the best motivator. Most Nucor employees are unskilled and semiskilled when they are hired. Furthermore, Nucor employees seem to place a high value on job security, which management attempts to provide.

Nucor currently operates five steel joist fabrication plants. The entire organization has five organizational levels from the president to the operating employee. There are no assistant managers, group managers, or directors. All of Nucor's facilites are in rural areas. These organizational features and plant locations are rather unusual in the steel joist fabrication industry.

The company currently has four incentive compensation programs. The focal point of these programs is groups, not individuals. The incentive systems are for production employees, department heads, secretaries, accounting clerks, accountants, engineers, and senior officers alike. The groups range in size from 25 to 30. Approximately 2,500 Nucor employees are under the main program, called the production incentive system.[37]

To a certain extent, Nucor views each of the 25 to 30 groups of production employees as being in business for itself. What workers earn is largely dependent upon their performance. There are no bonuses paid when equipment is not operating. The rules for absenteeism at Nucor are simple. There are four grace days per year. Additional days off are approved for military service or jury duty. Anyone not there for other days loses the week's bonus. Additionally, being more than a half-hour late means losing the bonus for the day.

The production incentive program is only one part of the Nucor system. At the department-head level, the company has an incentive compensation program based on the contribution of the particular department to the company as a whole.

The third incentive plan applies to employees who are neither in a production function nor at the department-manager level: accountants, secretaries, clerks, and so on. The bonus they receive is based on either the division's return on assets or the corporation's return on assets. Every month, each division receives a report showing, on a year-to-year basis, their return on

---

[37] John Savage, "Incentive Programs at Nucor Corporation Boost Productivity," *Personnel Administrator,* August 1981, pp. 33–36, 49.

assets. This chart is posted in the employee cafeteria or break area, together with the chart showing the bonus payout.

The fourth Nucor program is for senior officers. They receive no profitsharing, no pension or retirement plans, or other similar executive perks. More than half of each officer's compensation is based directly on company earnings. If the firm is doing well, the executives do well. Their base salaries are set at 70 percent of what an individual in a comparable position with another company would receive.

Nucor does not have a retirement plan that is actuarially based; rather, it has a profit-sharing plan with a deferred trust. Under the plan, 10 percent of the firm's pretax earnings is put into profit sharing annually. Of this amount, 20 percent is set aside to be paid to employees in March of the following year as cash profit sharing. The remainder is put into a trust.

Vesting in the profit-sharing trust is much like that of a retirement plan. An employee is 20 percent vested after a year in profit sharing, with an additional 10 percent vesting each year thereafter.

Another example of incentive at Nucor is the service awards program. Instead of handing out pen and pencil sets, money clips, or gift certificates for seniority, Nucor issues company stock. After five years of service, an employee receives five shares of Nucor stock. Another five years of service and they receive another five shares, and so on.

Salaried payments.   Companies like Eaton Corporation, TRW, Dow Chemical, Dana Corporation, and Rockwell International have implemented all-salaried compensation payments for most of their employees.[38] TRW, for instance, now has 20 plants on a salary basis, compared with just 3 a decade ago. An employee relations survey by the Conference Board found that all-salaried compensation systems ranked ahead of flexitime, payment-for-knowledge plans, autonomous work teams, and productivity or gain-sharing bonuses among a list of approaches that managers of nonunion groups are encouraged to develop or sustain.

Implementing a salaried system is complex, and eventual improvement in morale and performance depends on a host of variables. Geographic location, the strength of organized labor, and the climate of management-employee relations are important variables. The ideal scenario for management, according to a consultant in New York, is "to move down South and open a new plant in a right-to-work state with weak unions. You don't have a lot of inbred attitudes."

At Dow Chemical, a gradual shift to salary plans over an 18-year period has involved both old and new facilities. However, it should be noted that the Dow shift has resulted in the creation of salaried plants in the firm,

---

[38] Paul G. Engel, "Salaried Plants: Panacea for Productivity?" *Industry Week,* January 21, 1985, pp. 39–42.

more of which are unionized. Whether unions and salaried employees are mutually exclusive entities is an issue that will take more time to analyze.

Paid personal leave plans.   A study of employee behaviors at Rapid City Regional Hospital indicated that approximately 20 percent of the employees were using more than 50 percent of the paid sick leave at the hospital.[39] The existing plan at that time provided full-time employees with:

- 10 vacation days after 1 year of employment, increasing to 15 days after 5 years and 20 days after 10 years.
- Eight fixed holidays.
- One day of sick leave accrued per month to a maximum of 45 days.

The plan, as the study indicated, was being abused by some employees and had become very expensive.

The new paid personal leave program (PPL) was combined with the existing plan; 40 hours of guaranteed sick leave was combined with vacation and holiday hours in a lump-sum account. Since Rapid City Hospital did not have any long-term disability plan, management decided to double the previous maximum accumulation of 45 days to 90 days, put into a separate account called the extended-illness accrual bank (EIAB). EIAB would be accrued on the basis of six days per year.

The PPL plan would mean that an employee with one to four years of service would accrue an annual total of 23 days of paid leave a year; employees with 10 years of service or more would accrue 33 days per year of paid leave. Each employee would have to use at least 75 percent of his or her earned PPL each year. The difference between the 75 percent taken and the total hours earned could be accrued from one year to the next until a maximum of 30 days is reached. Any excessive accrued PPL could be cashed in or transferred to a person's EIAB account if the employee so desired.

The major emphasis of the PPL is that the leave is an earned benefit that employees should use. The employees appear to like having the responsibility for scheduling their time off on the basis of the earned benefits. Surveys indicate that a majority of employees like the plan, view it as rewarding, and understand that time off is an earned benefit. Comments also indicate that morale has been improved because employees believe that they are receiving their fair share of time off.

SUMMARY OF KEY POINTS

- Motivation is an inner state that helps describe the wishes, desires, drives, and needs of individuals.

---

[39] James H. Brockman, "Give Employees the Responsibility of Scheduling Their Time Off," *Personnel Journal,* October 1985, pp. 96–102.

■ Two important content theories of motivation are Maslow's need hierarchy theory and Herzberg's two-factor theory. Maslow arranges five needs in a hierarchy based on different levels of importance. Herzberg presents two sets of job conditons: maintenance and motivational. The maintenance factors are external to the job and cause dissatisfaction when they are not present. The motivational factors are job centered and tend to motivate individuals.

■ The expectancy theory of motivation is a process theory that suggests that individuals are motivated to make choices among different behaviors or intensities of work effort. An individual will exert effort to achieve performance that will result in receiving preferred rewards.

■ The reinforcement theory of motivation relies on the use of reinforcers (positive, negative, extinction, punishment) to motivate. It is concerned with the environment and its consequences for the person.

■ Job enrichment seeks to improve both task efficiency and human satisfaction by building into jobs greater scope for personal achievement and recognition, more challenging and responsible work, and more opportunity for individual advancement and growth.

■ In order for a pay plan to motivate, it must (1) create a belief that good performance leads to high levels of pay, (2) minimize the negative consequences of good performance, and (3) create conditions so that desired rewards other than pay are seen to be related to good performance.

DISCUSSION AND REVIEW QUESTIONS

1. Why, in Table 10–2, is Maslow's need hierarchy referred to as a descriptive theory and Herzberg's two-factor theory shown as a prescriptive approach?

2. Why would a nonpunitive approach to discipline be considered more potentially motivating to employees than a punitive approach?

3. The manager of a team of engineers in a manufacturing plant was overheard to say, "I believe that money is the best of all possible motivators. You can say what you please about all that other nonsense; but when it comes right down to it, if you give a guy a raise, you'll motivate him. That's all there is to it." In light of what we have discussed in this chapter, advise this manager.

4. Why would the union be opposed to all-salaried payments for employees?

5. Some critics of job enrichment and behavior modification programs state that most of the declared successes are based on faulty measurements or short periods of time. A proper evaluation over a longer period of time would show less positive results with these programs. Comment.

6. Why would a man or woman who has attained vast wealth by, say, his or her early 40s continue for years to work very hard to achieve outstanding job performance?

7. In this chapter, it was emphasized that managers must be familiar with the

fundamental needs of people in order to motivate employees successfully. Select two individuals you know well. Do they differ, in your opinion, with respect to the strength of various needs? Discuss these differences and indicate how they could affect behavior. If you were attempting to motivate those persons, would you use different approaches for each? Why?

8. Can a student's "job" be enriched? Assume that you are to consult with your professor about applying the two-factor motivation model in your class. You are to answer these questions: Can you apply this approach to the classroom? Why? If you can, differentiate between maintenance and motivational factors and develop a list of motivational factors your professor can use to enrich the student's job.

9. Assume that you have just read Vroom's thoughts on how the *goals* of individuals influence their *effort* and how the behavior the individual selects depends upon an assessment of the probability that the behavior will successfully lead to the goal. What is your goal in this management course? Is it influencing your effort? Do you suppose another person in your class might have a different goal? Is that person's effort (behavior) different from yours? If your professor was aware of this, could it be of any value?

10. What argument could be made to support the position that some employees consider pay earned to be the most significant intrinsic reward associated with the job?

ADDITIONAL REFERENCES

Arehart-Treichel, J. *Biotypes.* New York: Times Books, 1980.

Arvey, R. D., and Ivancevich, J. M. "Punishment in Organizations: A Review, Propositions, and Research Suggestions." *Academy of Management Review,* January 1980, pp. 123–32.

Baird, L. S., and W. C. Hamner. "Individual versus System Rewards: Who's Dissatisfied, Why, and What Is Their Likely Response?" *Academy of Management Journal,* December 1979, pp. 783–92.

Brennan, E. J. "Merit Pay: Balance the Old Rich and the New Poor." *Personnel Journal,* May 1985, pp. 82–85.

Brennan, E. J. "The Myth and the Reality of Pay for Performance." *Personnel Journal,* March 1985, pp. 73–75.

Chase, M. "Intel to Cut Salaries Up to 10%, Impose 1-Year Freeze." *The Wall Street Journal,* November 18, 1982, p. 24.

Hackman, J. R. "The Design of Work in the 1980s," *Organizational Dynamics,* Summer 1978, pp. 3–17.

Henderson, R. I. "Designing a Reward System for Today's Employee." *Business,* July–September 1982, pp. 2–13.

Herzberg, F. "Herzberg on Motivation for the 1980s." *Industry Week,* 1979, pp. 58–63.

Kazdin, A. E. *Behavior Modification in Applied Settings.* Homewood, Ill.: Dorsey Press, 1980.

Lawler, E. E., III. "The New Pay." *New Management,* Summer 1985, pp. 52–59.

Lindroth, J. "Inflation, Taxes and Perks: How Compensation Is Changing." *Personnel Journal,* December 1981, pp. 934–40.

Petty, M. M.; G. W. McGee; J. W. Cavender. "A Meta-Analysis of the Relationships between Individual Job Satisfaction and Individual Performance." *Academy of Management Review,* October 1984, pp. 712–21.

Sims, H. P., Jr. "Further Thoughts on Punishment in Organizations." *Academy of Management Review,* January 1980, pp. 133–38.

Steers, R. M., and L. W. Porter, eds. *Motivation and Work Behavior.* New York: McGraw-Hill, 1982.

Stein, Jeannine. "Flexible Benefits." *Houston Post,* August 29, 1982, 1BB.

Sussman, M., and R. P. Vecchio. "A Social Influence Interpretation of Worker Motivation." *Academy of Management Review,* April 1982, pp. 177–86.

"Upsurge in ESOPs." *Dun's Business Month,* February 1983, pp. 76–79.

CASES

APPLICATION I

PHYSICAL FITNESS, RECREATION, AND MOTIVATION

Organizations have used both monetary and nonmonetary rewards to motivate employees. However, performance, absenteeism, turnover, and loyalty problems still exist and trouble managers. One new move to create an atmosphere and working climate conducive to better performance and motivation is the use of recreational programs:

1. Peoples Jewelry Company has a program that provides discount tickets for amusement parks, hotels, resorts, and cultural events. The company has found that since the program has started, absenteeism is down 23 percent.
2. Eastman Kodak has a 300,000-square-foot recreational area that includes a putting green, tennis courts, softball diamonds, a gymnasium, physical-fitness rooms, bowling lanes, squash courts, and pistol ranges.
3. Xerox has a $3.5 million recreation center with facilities for swimming, golf, handball, racquetball, soccer, squash, and basketball.
4. Integon Corporation, an insurance company with about 600 employees, hired a professional to run its recreation program, which includes tennis, racquetball, Christmas parties for adults and children, pizza nights, arts and crafts classes, and subsidized memberships at the local YMCA.

Most recreation programs include families in at least some of their activities. James H. Hoke, president of Practical Management Consultants of Southfield, Michigan, says, "A perceptive recreation director will produce several couples' activities yearly to avoid job jealousy and fantasies about unknown company people that can build resentments at home."

Recreation programs also can be helpful for employees nearing retirement. They can develop interests and hobbies to pursue in retirement, and some retired employees volunteer to help run the recreation programs.

Operating costs for recreation programs vary almost as widely as the programs themselves. While some programs have annual budgets of more than $750,000, others manage on less than $5,000. The average is about $11,000, according to a recent study.

Sources of funding for such programs usually include employee dues and special assessments for activities, employer contributions, and frequently the profits from vending machines. Some programs also receive profits from canteens, food service, and company stores. Incorporated employees' associations that operate with such funding usually are approved by the Internal Revenue Service as nonprofit organizations.

There is no question that employees benefit from recreational facilities; management finds them advantageous as well. They make recruiting easier and reduce turnover because happy employees are less likely to quit or be lured away, are absent less, and often are more productive. This makes for more-profitable companies whose managers view their recreation programs as sound investments.

Questions for Analysis

1. Would you (do you) participate if the organization you worked for had recreation activities similar to the Xerox, Eastman Kodak, Integon, and Peoples Jewelry programs?
2. How could a recreational program be used as a positive motivator of on-the-job performance?
3. Recreation programs date back to the 1800s. Why is there a renewed interest in the potential impact of recreation programs on employees?

APPLICATION II

FORD AND GENERAL MOTORS MOVE TOWARD LIFETIME EMPLOYMENT PROGRAMS

One feature of the Japanese system of management that has caught the attention of many employees in the United States is lifetime employment. In Japan, lifetime employment is not a legal contract. More like a psychological contract between the company and employees, it is used to mitigate, as much as possible, the difference in social and economic status between management and operating employees. The Japanese have found lifetime employment valuable as a factor in creating a sense of team spirit, loyalty, and organizational commitment.

In Japan, organizations attempt to cushion the effects of economic decline by maintaining steady employment while making downward adjustments of various other forms of income payments. Saving the job while cutting back on compensation and fringe benefits is the rule rather than the exception. Also, mandatory retirement age is about 57 or, at best, 60 years old for most individuals. Only those who reach the rank of corporate officer continue to work in their 60s.

Whether lifetime employment is a viable technique for motivation in the United States is, in general, untested. Today, however, there are firms considering some type of lifetime guarantee for employees. Ford Motor Co. began an experiment in lifetime employment in two plants in 1981. In November 1982, General Motors Corp. and the United Automobile Workers Union agreed to conduct a lifetime employment plan in four plants.

In these plants, "lifetime" jobs will be guaranteed to 80 percent of the workers, chosen by seniority. Decisions on just how the program is to work—to what extent, for example, workers can be shifted from one department function to another—will be made by union-management agreement at each Ford and General Motors plant. Lifetime employment has been extended in the 1985 contract agreements. It is now agreed that only a disaster, such as a flood or fire that puts a plant out of business, will interfere with job security. Whether the concept will catch on and continue to be included in future contracts will be negotiated later.

Job security has become an important concern. Layoffs, plant closings, and economic uncertainty are everyday realities. Although Maslow presents job security as a lower-level need and Herzberg considers it a maintenance factor, there are now many individuals in the work force who consider job security a top-priority need. At Ford and General Motors, management is attempting to address the job security needs of at least some of their employees.

Questions for Analysis

1. Would guaranteed lifetime employment generally be considered an extrinsic or intrinsic reward?

2. Do you feel that lifetime employment guarantees can become as popular in the United States as they are in Japan? Why?

3. Which needs could possibly be satisfied by a guarantee of lifetime employment?

EXPERIENTIAL EXERCISE

YOUR JOB PREFERENCES COMPARED TO OTHERS

Purpose

This exercise identifies what makes a job attractive or unattractive to you. Preferences of employees, if known, could be used as information by managers to develop and restructure jobs that are more attractive, rewarding, and generally more fulfilling. It is this type of information that would permit a manager to create a positive motivational atmosphere for subordinates.

The Exercise in Class

1. Think about your present job (if you have one) or the type of job you would like. Decide which of the following job factors is most important to you. Place a *1* in front of it. Then decide which is the second most important to you and place a *2* in front of it. Keep ranking the items in order of importance until the least important job factor is ranked *14*. Individuals differ in the order in which these job factors are ranked. What is your present preference?

   _____ Advancement (opportunity for promotion).
   _____ Pay (income received for working).
   _____ Fringe benefits (vacation period, insurance, recreation facilities).
   _____ Schedule (hours worked, starting time).
   _____ Location (geographic area: Midwest, South, West, East, Southwest).
   _____ Supervisor (a fair, influential boss).
   _____ Feedback (receiving prompt, meaningful, and accurate feedback on job performance).
   _____ Security (steady work, assurance of a future).
   _____ Challenge (interesting and stimulating work).
   _____ Working conditions (comfortable and clean work area).
   _____ Co-workers (colleagues who are friendly, interesting).
   _____ The organization (working for a company you are proud of).
   _____ Responsibility (having responsibility to complete important job).
   _____ Training and development opportunities (the ability to receive training and development in the organization or through external sources).

2. Now rank the job factors as you think other members of your class would rank them. Look around and think how the average person in your class would rank the job factors.

_____ Advancement
_____ Pay
_____ Fringe benefits
_____ Schedule
_____ Location
_____ Supervisor
_____ Feedback
_____ Security
_____ Challenge
_____ Working conditions
_____ Co-workers
_____ The organization
_____ Responsibility
_____ Training and development
       opportunities

3. The instructor will form four-to-six-person groups to discuss the *individual* and *other* rankings. Each group should calculate averages for both rankings. What does this show? The members of the group should discuss these average scores.
4. The average individual and average other rankings should be placed on the board or flip chart and discussed by the entire class.

The Learning Mesage

Individuals consider different factors important. Can a manager realistically respond to a wide range of different preferences among subordinates?

MANAGING WORK GROUPS

LEARNING OBJECTIVES

After studying Chapter 11, you should be able to:

■ **Define**
in a concise manner such terms as work groups, group cohesiveness, and group norms.

■ **Describe**
the conditions under which group decision making is preferred over individual decision making, and vice versa.

■ **Discuss**
the four stages of work group development.

■ **Compare**
the causes of and solutions to intragroup and intergroup conflict.

■ **Identify**
the key attributes of quality circles.

MANAGEMENT IN ACTION

PATCO versus the Government: Two Groups in Conflict*

Earlier in this decade, 11,500 air traffic controllers walked off their jobs in what was one of the most shocking labor conflicts in recent decades. The Reagan administration, pointing to the law, had insisted that there would be no negotiations if the air traffic controllers went out on strike. Both sides meant business, and the struggle between the Professional Air Traffic Controllers' Organization (PATCO) and the Federal Aviation Administration (FAA) had reached a feverish pitch that summer. Instead of open and constructive bargaining between the two groups, there were hostility, threats, and disruptive action.

A number of unusual elements and events in the PATCO and FAA conflict led up to the strike:

- A strike was illegal under federal law.
- The large majority of PATCO members were trained only in air traffic controller skills and had few other job opportunities open to them.
- PATCO issued an ultimatum that the union would strike unless its members received a $10,000 across-the-board pay increase and a 32-hour work week.
- The secretary of transportation responded that in the event of a walkout, termination notices would be prepared.

Eighty percent of the PATCO membership struck. Furthermore, given a 48-hour "window" in which they could return to their jobs, only a handful did return.

The fact that groups must work together, within and between organizations, offers unique challenges to managers. While it is unrealistic to assume that intergroup conflict can be eliminated, management must attempt to minimize any discord. This chapter will examine some of the methods used to control intergroup conflict so that it doesn't deteriorate into the kind of situation that resulted in 11,500 air traffic controllers walking off their jobs and then being fired by the President of the United States.

---

* Source: Adapted from David G. Bowers, "What Would Make 11,500 People Quit Their Jobs?" *Organizational Dynamics,* Winter 1983, pp. 5–19; FAA Task Force Report; Management and Employee Relationships within the Federal Aviation Administration, vols. I and II (Report to the Department of Transportation), March 1982.

ew managers question the existence of work groups. For over six decades,
behavioral scientists have paid special attention to the processes occurring
within groups and affecting individuals and organizations. Therefore, any
examination of the fundamentals of managing people must provide a framework for understanding the nature of work groups. This chapter will provide
(1) a classification of the different types of work groups; (2) the reasons for
formation and development of work groups; (3) the characteristics of groups;
and (4) the results of group membership.

*A work group is a collection of employees (managerial or nonmanagerial)
who share certain norms and who strive to satisfy their needs through the
attainment of the group goal(s).* Students often ask why work groups should
be studied in a management text. Many different answers can be provided:

1. The formation of work groups is inevitable. Managers create some work
   groups to perform work and tasks. Others form to satisfy employees'
   social needs. Therefore, it is in management's interest to understand what
   happens within work groups, because they are found throughout the organization.
2. Work groups strongly influence the overall behavior and performance of
   members. To understand the forces of influence exerted by the group
   requires a systematic analysis.
3. Group membership can have both positive and negative consequences
   on the organization. If managers are to avoid the negative consequences,
   it is in their interest to learn about work groups.

The common thread found in most answers is that groups exist and affect
the attitudes and behaviors of employees.

Kurt Lewin, a recognized scholar, perhaps explained it best in a classic
speech on why groups need to be understood:

> Although the scientific investigations of group work are but a few years old,
> I don't hesitate to predict that group work—that is, the handling of human
> beings not as isolated individuals, but in the social setting of groups—will
> soon be one of the most important theoretical and practical fields. . . . It is
> easier to affect the personality of 10 people if they can be melted into a group
> than to affect the personality of any 1 individual separately.[1]

CLASSIFICATION OF GROUPS

Every organization has technical requirements that arise from its objectives.
The accomplishment of these objectives requires certain tasks to be performed,
and employees are assigned to groups to perform these tasks. In addition,
other types of groups form that are not the result of deliberate design. Accord-

---

[1] Alvin Zander, "The Psychology of the Group Process," *Annual Review of Psychology,*
1979, p. 418.

ingly, we can identify two broad classes of groups in organizations: formal and informal.

Most employees belong to a group based on their positions in the organization. These *formal groups* are the departments, units, and so forth that management forms to do the work of the organization. The demands and processes of the organization lead to the formation of these groups.

On the other hand, whenever employees associate on a fairly continuous basis, there is a tendency for groups to form whose activities may be different from those required by the organization. These *informal groups* are natural groupings of people in the work situation in response to social needs. In other words, they do not arise as a result of deliberate design but rather evolve naturally. While this distinction is convenient for our discussion on specific types of groups in organizations later in the chapter, both formal and informal groups exhibit the same general characteristics. Thus, throughout the chapters, the term *work group* will include both formal and informal groups unless otherwise specified.

The influence of informal groups on employee behavior and performance was spelled out in our discussion of the Hawthorne studies in the Part III Foundation. In the bank wiring room portion of the study, a group of workers was observed for approximately three months. The group decided to produce two units a day and to finish the second unit exactly at quitting time. Any group member who tried to speed up the work was ridiculed. These behaviors existed despite the fact that the group had the capability to produce more and despite the existence of what management believed was a good pay incentive plan.

TABLE   11–1   Formal and Informal Group Characteristics: A Comparison

		Characteristics	
	Dimensions	*Formal Group*	*Informal Group*
1.	Major objectives	Profit, efficiency, service.	Member satisfaction, member security.
2.	Origin	Planned by organization.	Spontaneous.
3.	Influence on members	Position authority, monetary rewards.	Personality, expertise.
4.	Communication	Flows from top down, use of formal channels.	Grapevine, person-to-person, using all channels.
5.	Leader	Appointed by organization.	Emergence from group.
6.	Interpersonal relations	Established by job and work-flow pattern.	Developed spontaneously.
7.	Control	Reliance on threat, use of monetary rewards.	Strong social sanctions.

Formal and informal groups. The key characteristics.

The point of the Hawthorne example is not that informal groups are disruptive to managers. Rather, it illustrates the powerful influence that work groups can exert over their members. This influence can be economic, social, psychological, or even physical. Table 11–1 compares some of the main characteristics of formal and informal groups.

FORMATION OF WORK GROUPS

Chapter 10 stated that individuals have a number of needs, most of which are satisfied when interacting with others. Groups form because they sustain and satisfy these needs.

Physical Reasons

In organizations, a typical procedure is to place together workers in similar occupations. For example, in the construction of a home, bricklayers perform their jobs in close proximity to each other. The same situation exists in offices where secretaries are located elbow to elbow.[2] People in close proximity to each other tend to interact and communicate with each other. If workers are not able to do this on a fairly regular basis, there is less tendency to form a group.[3]

Economic Reasons

In some situations, work groups form because individuals believe they can derive more economic benefits from their jobs if they form into groups. For example, individuals working at different stations on an assembly line may be paid on a group incentive basis. Whatever the particular group produces determines the wages for each member. Because of the interest of the workers in their wages, they will interact and communicate with each other. By working as a group instead of as individuals, they may perceive and actually obtain higher economic benefits.

Another example of the economic motive for informal work group formation might be a nonunion organization. The workers form to bring pressure against management for more economic benefits. The group members would

---

[2] William G. Scott and Terence R. Mitchell, *Organization Theory* (Homewood, Ill.: Richard D. Irwin, 1976), p. 171.

[3] Darwin Cartwright and Ronald Lippitt, "Group Dynamics and the Individual," *International Journal of Group Psychotherapy,* January 1957, p. 88.

have a common interest—increased economic benefits—that would lead to group affiliation.

Sociopsychological Reasons

Workers in organizations also are motivated to form work groups to satisfy safety, social, esteem, and self-actualization needs.

Safety.   Work groups can protect members from outside pressures, including serving as a buffer from management demands for better quality and quantity of production, insistance that they punch the clock on time, and recommendations for change in their work area layouts. By being a member of a group, individual employees can become involved in group activities and openly discuss these management demands with fellow workers who usually support their viewpoint. Without the group to lean on when various management demands are made, employees often assume that they stand alone against management and the entire organization. This "aloneness" leads to a degree of insecurity.

Another form of safety need occurs in instances when a new employee is asked to perform a difficult job task over an extended period of time. Not wanting to contact the supervisor continually for help in correctly performing the job, the employee depends largely upon the group for help, gaining a form of security need satisfaction. Whether the supervisor believes that continual requests for help by a new employee are signs of inability to perform the job is not the main issue. The important point is how new workers perceive their situation and job security.

Social.   Employees often join work groups because of their need for affiliation. The basis of affiliation ranges from wanting to interact with and enjoy other employees to more complex desires for group support of self-image. A management atmosphere that does not permit interaction and communication suppresses the desire of employees to feel a sense of belonging.

We learned from our discussion of motivation in Chapter 10 that people have social needs. Informal and formal group affiliations permit people to satisfy these needs. Management's blocking or frustrating of these needs will probably lead to a significant degree of defensive behavior. The employee who is not able to satisfy social needs is likely to withdraw, become aggressive against management, and compensate in other areas such as absenteeism or work slowdowns.

Esteem.   Some employees are attracted to a work group because they think they gain prestige by belonging. In an organization, a particular group may be viewed by employees as being a top-notch work group. Consequently membership among the elite bestows upon the members prestige that is not enjoyed by nonmembers. This prestige is conferred on members by other employees (nonmembers), which often leads to more gratification of the esteem need. And by sharing in the activities of a high-prestige work group, the individual identifies more closely with the group.

Self-Actualization.   The desire of individuals to utilize their skills with maximum efficiency and to grow and develop psychologically on the job is interpreted as the self-actualization need. Employees often believe that rigid job requirements and rules do not enable them to satisfy this need sufficiently. One reaction is to join a work group, which is viewed as a vehicle for communicating among friends about the use of a job-related skill. The jargon utilized and the skill employed are appreciated by the knowledgeable group members, which can lead to a feeling of accomplishment. This feeling and other similar feelings related to a belief that one is creative and skillful can lead to more satisfaction of the self-actualization need.

SPECIFIC TYPES OF GROUPS IN AN ORGANIZATION

Both managers and nonmanagers belong to a number of different groups within the organization. Memberships in multiple groups often overlap.[4] In some instances, individuals are members of a group because of position in the organization. However, through group contacts, they begin to affiliate with some of its members on an informal basis.

To illustrate the point that individuals rarely belong to just one group, look at the case of Joe DiNardo, an electrical engineer who works for American Bridge and Iron in Chicago. Joe is friendly with each worker on his project team (a formal group): a senior mechanical engineer, an industrial designer, a safety specialist, and three technicians. He also regularly discusses project problems with two electrical engineers and the design specialists who work at the Barrington, Illinois, project site. Joe always eats lunch with office accountant Mickey Wright, drafting supervisor Don Spellman, and production analyst Mike Jackson. And every Wednesday he bowls with Mickey, as well as ironworker Mel Perkowski and district manager Mitch Kelso. Each of the groups to which Joe belongs has a different membership. Some of the groups are formal, and some are informal.

Another, more specific way to classify groups is to refer to them as command, task, interest, and friendship groups.[5] Command and task groups are *formal* groups because they are defined by the organization structure; interest

[4] Rensis Likert, *New Patterns of Management* (New York: McGraw-Hill, 1961), chap. 8.

[5] This is the widely used and insightful framework offered by Leonard R. Sayles, "Research in Industrial Human Relations," *Industrial Relations Research Association* (New York: Harper & Row, 1957), pp. 131–45.

and friendship groups are not defined by the organization structure and are *informal* groups.

Command Groups

The command group is represented in the organization chart as the subordinates who report directly to a given supervisor. The relationship between the department manager and the three supervisors in a machine shop is spelled out in the organization chart. As the span of control of the department manager increases, the command group grows in size.

Task Groups

Employees that work together to complete a project or job are considered a task group. Assume that three office clerks are required for (1) securing a file of an automobile accident claim; (2) checking the accuracy of the claim by contacting persons involved; and (3) typing the claim, securing the required signatures of those involved, and refiling the claim.

These activities create a situation in which three clerks must communicate and coordinate with each other if the file is to be handled properly. Their activities and interactions facilitate the formation of the task group. Joe Di-Nardo's project team, mentioned previously, can be referred to as a task group. Another form of task group is portrayed in the Management Focus on Wang Laboratories.

MANAGEMENT FOCUS
Wang Laboratories' Use of Group Concepts to Improve Productivity

Wang Laboratories in Tewksbury, Massachusetts, has recently eliminated the traditional form of assembly-line work. Wang management has initiated what they call the "production module" concept.

Under the production module approach, specific groups of employees are organized into work teams that manufacture designated products from beginning to end in work cells. A work team is able to build a single unit in a few hours, while an assembly line takes much longer. The work teams are able to work quickly, efficiently, and produce high-quality products that are identified as being made by the teams. They are more flexible than an assembly line, since they involve only one product and a small cohesive group of individuals.

MANAGEMENT FOCUS (*continued*)

Since the work teams develop norms, structure, and an informal network, they become cohesive. They also develop a pride in what the team is producing, since everyone is committed to do a better job. A sense of competition emerges, with each team attempting to establish a reputation for high-quality workmanship.

Since Wang introduced the work team concept, there has been a major increase in quality and quantity of output as well as in the morale of members. Instead of management attempting to create a positive motivational atmosphere, the group itself exerts influence on the membership. Wang has been satisfied with the work teams and the use of group concepts for productivity improvement as well as the development of a high degree of pride in quality of work.

Source: Adapted from "Work Cells: A Unique Alternative," *Management Review*, May 1985, p. 9.

Interest Groups

Another type of group formation occurs when workers organize to present a united front on a particular issue. This type of group is called an interest group, since the members have joined together to achieve some common objective, such as an equitable pension plan. Its members may or may not be members of the same command or task group.

When the desired objective has been achieved or is thought to be within reach, the interest group might disband. Thus, it typically exists for a shorter period of time than other types of groups.

Friendship Groups

Because of some common characteristic such as age, ethnic background, political sentiment, interest in sports, or desire to drink coffee in the lounge at 10:30 A.M., employees may form a friendship group. These groups often extend their interaction and communication to off-the-job activities. For example, they get to know each other in the workplace and then bowl together or take their families on picnics. Mickey Wright and Joe DiNardo ate lunch together and bowled together, thus forming a friendship group.

The membership patterns of interest and friendship groups are not tightly controlled by the organization. However, managerial actions such as laying out a work area, allowing workers to take coffee breaks at a specified time, and demanding a certain level of productivity can influence the interaction and communication patterns of employees, causing certain individuals to affiliate with each other so that interest and friendship groups emerge.

Committees: Special Kinds of Groups

Many unkind things have been said about committees: "A camel is a horse designed by a committee"; "A committee is a body that keeps minutes and wastes hours"; and "A committee is a group that works hard at making common sense seem difficult."[6] Despite this, the use of committees in organizations is very common[7] for such purposes as resolving conflict, recommending action, generating ideas, and making decisions.

Behavioral scientists recommend that a committee be kept relatively small, since size affects the quality of a group's decision[8] and the ability of its members to communicate. As size increases, a growing number of members seem to feel threatened and less willing to participate actively, which can increase stress and conflict.

The committee chairperson.   In most committees, a chairperson is expected to provide direction. Successful committees often have chairpersons who understand group processes and keep the committee moving toward its objectives without becoming constrained by endless debates, conflict, and personality clashes.

A committee chairperson must walk a fine line: A passive one may lose the members' respect. On the other hand, an overly dominating one will not usually acquire the group's acceptance. Without group respect, the chairperson is a leader without a group.

A few managerial guidelines that can aid committee chairpersons are:

1. Listen carefully and with an open mind.
2. Allow each member to voice opinions and do not place your opinions above others.
3. Get everyone involved in the committee's activities.
4. Display an active interest in the purpose of the committee and the ideas of the membership.
5. Help the committee focus on the task at hand and the progress being made.[9]

---

[6] Ralph L. Woods, *The Modern Handbook of Humor* (New York: McGraw-Hill, 1967), p. 8.

[7] Rensis Likert and Jane Gibson Likert, *New Ways of Managing Conflict* (New York: McGraw-Hill, 1976), pp. 213–15.

[8] Alan C. Filley, "Committee Management Guidelines from Social Science Research," *California Management Review,* Fall 1970, pp. 13–21.

[9] G. M. Prince, "How to Be a Better Chairman," *Harvard Business Review,* January–February 1969, pp. 98–108.

Committee members.   The image of a committee is that of a group cooperating to reach an objective. But what is found in some committees is negative
competition and a general lack of cooperation. Behavioral studies indicate
that in cooperative groups, as distinguished from competitive groups, one
finds stronger motivation to accomplish the task, more effective communication, more ideas generated, more membership satisfaction, and more group
productivity.

These findings suggest that when cooperation prevails, there are generally
positive results. Thus, the importance of the chairperson should not be underestimated.

Quality Circles: An Action-Oriented Group Approach

Quality circles have taken American and Canadian industry by storm.
A 1982 study by the New York Stock Exchange showed that 44 percent of
all companies with more than 500 employees had quality-circle programs.[10]
A *quality circle* is a task group. It usually consists of a small number of
employees and their supervisor from the same work area who voluntarily
meet on a regular basis to study quality control and productivity improvement
techniques and to identify and solve work-related problems. Some specific
features of quality circles are:

1. Small groups ranging in size from 4 to 15 members. Eight or nine seems
   to be the most popular size.
2. Members located in the same work area.
3. A work area supervisor who is usually, though not always, the leader of
   the circle.
4. Voluntary participation.
5. Meetings once every week on company time for one-half to one hour,
   with pay.
6. Training in the techniques of problem solving (for example, brainstorming,
   cause-and-effect analysis, flow charts).
7. Choice of the problems and projects that members will work on.
8. Circles exist as long as the members wish to meet.

The quality circle as a managerial technique was first used in Japan. Today,
600,000 quality circles involving about 6 million workers—about 1 in every
8 employees—are established within Japanese companies.[11]

Structure and process.   The term *quality circle* refers to both a structure
and a process. Its structure is basically the composition of the group, defined

---

[10] Edward E. Lawler III and Susan A. Mohrman, "Quality Circles after the Fad," *Harvard
Business Review,* January–February 1985, p. 65.

[11] David Bain, *The Productivity Prescription* (New York: McGraw-Hill, 1982), p. 202.

FIGURE   11–1   The Quality-Circle Process

How a quality circle achieves results.

by the positions of its members in the wider organization. For example, a group of mechanics, technicians, and assembly-line operators and the first-line supervisor would constitute the quality circle. The circle members are represented on an organization chart as a task or command group. Quality circles typically follow a four-step process to solve problems.

1. Identification of problems and development of solutions.
2. Managerial review of the proposed solution and a decision on whether or not to implement it.
3. Organizational implementation of the solution.
4. Evaluation of the success of the solution by the quality circle and the organization.

These subprocesses in the quality-circle process are presented in Figure 11–1.

Quality circles at Toyota.   Toyota Auto Body Company has over 800 quality circles. The firm produces bodies for passenger cars, trucks, and commercial vans, then sells them to Toyota Motor Company. Of the 6,000 employees in the company (three fourths of them blue-collar workers), about 72 percent are participating in quality circles.[12]

Originally, supervisors led the quality circles at Toyota Auto Body, but today senior workers lead many of the groups. Some leaders are elected or serve on a rotation basis. The circles meet after regular hours, and members receive overtime pay at half their regular pay.

---

[12] Philip C. Thompson, *Quality Circles* (New York: AMACOM, 1982), pp. 19–26.

To provide technical assistance to quality circles, Toyota Auto Body formed an industrial engineering project team. The team has 45 members, half of whom are engineers and half of whom are shop employees who have received special training.

The company promotes two major incentives for participation in quality circles: competition and money. Circles compete regularly for the best solution to the problem and the best presentation at the department level. Each month, the best of these compete against those of other departments for companywide honors. The winner enters regional and national competitions.

As financial incentives, the company pays for quality-circle participation. In addition, it pays more for suggestions submitted by quality circles, $272, than it pays for suggestions from individuals, only $227. On the average, 75 percent of all suggestions submitted come from quality circles.

To promote, train, and coordinate quality-circle activities, Toyota Auto Body has set up a quality-circle general office that coordinates the quality-circle activities and is responsible for quality-circle training and results. This office, which reports directly to the plant manager, also conducts monthly meetings of quality-circle leaders in which information is exchanged, problem-solving topics discussed, and mutual respect and support encouraged.

The total commitment to quality circles by upper management is an important key to the success of the groups at Toyota Auto Body. For 18 years, the quality circles have existed and been involved in changing the organization. The organization views the quality circles as their most important technique for successful management.

The bottom-line score card.   Advocates of quality circles feel their greatest advantage is that they tap brainpower at all levels of the organization. Participating employees also are able to improve communication and gain a new sense of respect for each other as they work together. The result is that the traditional adversarial "we-they" relationship between the workers and their supervisor is replaced by an attitude of "all of us working together."[13]

A few examples of quality-circle results are:

- A quality circle of line operators at Texas Instruments increased output of an assembly-line operator from 10,000 to 18,500 units per day. As a result, the company saved $1.2 million annually.[14]
- A circle of clerical employees in a corporate mailroom reduced misdirected mail by 50 percent and saved the company $62,000 per year.[15]
- A quality circle at Hughes Aircraft in one meeting listed 22 problems

---

[13] Michael Le Boeuf, *The Productivity Challenge* (New York: McGraw-Hill, 1982), p. 143.

[14] Ibid., p. 142.

[15] Ibid., p. 143.

and in the next few weeks was able to save the company over $100,000 by solving some of the problems.[16]

Despite these success stories about quality circles, there does need to be some caution. Robert C. Cole, director of the Center for Japan Studies at the University of Michigan, raises the issue of how much the Japanese culture contributes to quality-circle success in that country. He states: "The task of evaluating the applicability of Japanese management practices in the United States and judging what are to be the needed adaptations is a Herculean task."[17] He cautions U.S. managers to look closely at and evaluate results over an extended time period—four, five, six years.

Also, what is referred to as "group decline" may emerge over time. That is, the quality circle meets less often, it becomes less productive, and fewer resources are committed to the program; the quality circle limps along because of social satisfaction rather than the group's problem-solving effectiveness. As a result, the commitment to quality circle shrinks, and opponents become more aggressive in resisting the quality-circle approach.[18]

Although there are some glowing success reports pointing to positive impact, some managers are learning that quality circles are not able to solve structural deficiencies, poorly designed reward systems, managerial conflict, union-management strife, and other difficulties. Organizations considering the use of quality circles need to examine employee receptivity, costs, expectations, goals, and employee preparedness before leaping into this form of group participation.[19]

DEVELOPMENT OF WORK GROUPS

Task groups, committees, or quality circles go through various stages of development. Initially a group flounders while searching for an identity and a direction. Later the group begins to focus on helping each other and supporting the group's goals. Finally the group is able to utilize fully the skills and abilities of members. These changes occur gradually and are often difficult to recognize.

Groups primarily develop along two main dimensions: member relationships and task and problem-solving activities. The development of work groups

---

[16] Vernon M. Buehler and Y. Krishna Shetty, eds., *Productivity Improvement* (New York: McGraw-Hill, 1981), p. 95.

[17] Ron Zemke, "What's Good for Japan May Not Be Best for You or Your Training Department," *Training/HRD,* October 1981, p. 63.

[18] Lawler and Mohrman, "Quality Circles," p. 69.

[19] Gordon W. Meyer and Randall G. Stott, "Quality Circles: Panacea or Pandora's Box?" *Organizational Dynamics,* Spring 1985, pp. 34–50.

FIGURE   11–2   Four Phases of Group Development

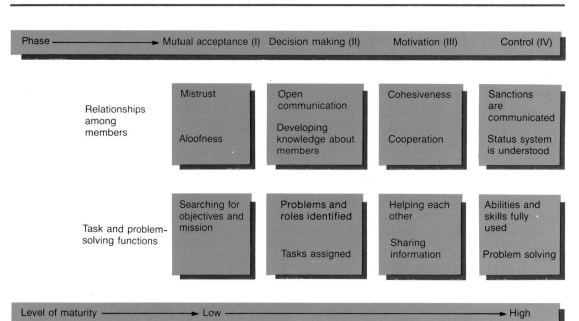

Source: Leonard R. Sayles and George Strauss, *Human Behavior in Organizations,* © 1966. Reprinted by permission of Prentice-Hall, Inc., Englewood Cliffs, N.J.

A group matures from a state of infancy to adulthood. The four phases.

is distinctly related to learning—learning to work together, to accept each other, and to trust each other. These phases are referred to as the maturation of a group.[20] Bernard Bass has identified a four-phase process that clearly points out some characteristics and attitudes inherent in group development.[21]

I. Mutual acceptance: Members of a group are often hampered by their mistrust of each other, the organization, and their superiors. They are fearful that they do not have the necessary training or skill to perform the job or to compete with others. These feelings of insecurity motivate employees to seek out others in the same predicament and to express their feelings openly.

___

[20] Warren G. Bennis and Herbert A. Shepard, "A Theory of Group Development," *Human Relations,* Summer 1963, pp. 415–57.

[21] The discussion of the development of groups is based largely upon Bernard Bass, *Organizational Psychology* (Boston: Allyn & Bacon, 1965), pp. 197–98. A number of alterations were made by the authors. Also see J. Stephen Heiner and Eugene Jacobson, "A Model of Task Group Development in Complex Organizations and a Strategy of Implementation," *Academy of Management Review,* October 1976, pp. 98–111.

After an initial period of uneasiness and learning about the feelings of others, individuals begin to accept each other.

II. Decision making: During this phase, open communication concerning the job is the rule. Problem solving and decision making are undertaken. The workers trust each other's viewpoints and beliefs; they develop strategies to make the job easier and to help each other perform more effectively.

III. Motivation: The group is reaching maturity and the problems of its members are known. Members have accepted that it is better to cooperate than to compete. Thus, the emphasis is on group solidarity.

IV. Control: A group reaching this phase has successfully organized itself, and members are contributing according to their abilities and interests. The group exercises sanctions when control is needed to bring members into line with the group's norms.

As employees develop from a "bunch" to a mature group, they display and acquire personal trust, interactions, and friendships. Figure 11–2 illustrates the four phases of development.[22] Management needs to determine which phase of development a group is in at any particular point. This is, of course, difficult but important, since it can provide answers about a group's capability. A mature group is able to be a positive force in completing projects and setting a good example for other employees.

CHARACTERISTICS OF WORK GROUPS

The creation of a formal organization structure results in characteristics such as specified relationships between subordinates, superiors, and peers; leaders assigned to positions; communication networks; standards of performance; and a status rank order according to the position an individual is filling. Logically, if an organization is to accomplish its objectives, retain its personnel, and project a favorable image to the public, it must have structure and a favorable work atmosphere (that is, the employees must enjoy going to work to some extent). Work groups have characteristics similar to those of formal organizations and include standards of conduct, communication systems, and reward and sanction mechanisms.[23] These and other characteristics of groups are discussed here.

Group Structure

As a group progresses through each developmental phase, structures emerge. Members begin to take on roles or a set of activities and behavior

---

[22] Fremont E. Kast and James E. Rosenzweig, *Organization and Management* (New York: McGraw-Hill, 1979), p. 290.

[23] Leonard R. Sayles and George Strauss, *Human Behavior in Organizations* (Englewood Cliffs, N.J.: Prentice-Hall, 1966), pp. 90–100.

expected by others. The ability to carry out expected roles provides the group with an arrangement or a pattern for its members. If roles are not carried out according to the expectations of members, it is difficult to maintain a group structure.

How the failure to maintain a group structure can have disastrous effects on satisfaction, group morale, and overall effectiveness has been vividly described by researchers who studied Chinese prisoner-of-war camps established during the Korean War.[24] The Chinese separated officers from noncommissioned officers so that a formal hierarchy couldn't be established. Squad leaders were appointed by the Chinese. Often the lowest-ranking enlisted prisoners were selected. All organized activity was prohibited. No emergent leaders were permitted to stay in the group. The Chinese used spies, gossip, and rumor to disrupt group structure and activities. They passed misinformation into the groups, creating an atmosphere of mistrust among squad members. The disruption, instability, and normlessness conditions resulted in little group structure. The prisoners had no view of what roles they were to perform. The lack of a group structure resulted in poor morale, reduced resistance, and a dampening of the will to attempt escape.

Group Goals

Work groups generally have two sets of goals. The organization's managers set goals for work groups. These *manager-assigned* goals reflect the reason for the group's formation. A second set of goals is the *group goals*.[25]

Within the groups, there are *achievement goals* that serve to provide the group with direction and an end-result target. *Maintenance goals* sustain the group and maintain its existence. Of course, not all members always agree with either the achievement or maintenance goals. On occasion, conflict with group goals is why members drop out and form new groups or join other groups.

As a group develops, the goals become clearer and more meaningful to members. Research indicates that a number of factors increase a person's commitment to the achievement and the maintenance of group goals. Some of these factors are participating in group activities, tying incentives to goal achievement, providing feedback on goal accomplishment, and training group members in the goal-setting process.[26]

---

[24] E. P. Schein, J. Schneier, and G. H. Barker, *Coercive Persuasion: A Socio-Psychological Analysis of the Brainwashing of American Prisoners by the Chinese Communists* (New York: W. W. Norton, 1961).

[25] Jerry C. Wofford, *Organizational Behavior* (Boston: Kent Publishing, 1982), p. 311.

[26] John M. Ivancevich, "Different Goal Setting Treatments and Their Effects on Performance and Job Satisfaction," *Academy of Management Journal,* September 1977, pp. 406–19.

Leadership

As a group attempts to accomplish an objective such as producing a product without a single defect and as individual members get acquainted, one or more of the many group roles become filled. One of the most important is that of the group leader, who emerges from within and is accepted by the informal group. In the formal organization, however, the leader is appointed.

The leaders in formal organizations are followed and obeyed because employees perceive them as possessing power and influence to reward or punish them for not complying with requests. The formal leaders possess the power to regulate the formal rewards of the members of a work group. On the other hand, informal group leaders do not possess this power.

The informal leader typically serves a number of facilitating functions. First, any group of individuals that does not have a plan or some coordination becomes an ineffective unit. The individuals are not directed toward the accomplishment of objectives, and this leads to a breakdown in group effectiveness. The leader serves to initiate action and provide direction. If there are differences of opinion on a group-related matter, the leader attempts to settle the differences and move the group toward accomplishing its objectives. Second, some individual must communicate to nonmembers the group's beliefs about policies, the job, the organization, the supervision, and other related matters. In effect, the group leader communicates the values of the group.

A number of research studies have been made on the personal characteristics of group leaders, which can be summarized as follows:

1. The leadership role is filled by an individual who possesses attributes the members perceive as being critical for satisfying their needs.
2. The leader embodies the values of the group and is able to perceive these values, organize them into an intelligible philosophy, and verbalize them to nonmembers.[27]
3. The leader is able to receive and decipher communications relevant to the group and effectively communicate important information to group members.[28]

Status within the Group

Managers in an organization are accorded status because of position in the hierarchy; that is, the top management group of the firm has more prestige or status than middle managers in the organization, while middle managers

---

[27] Scott and Mitchell, *Organization Theory,* pp. 175–82.
[28] Ibid.

have more prestige or status than lower-level managers. The basic cornerstone of status in the formal organization is a comparative process. The top-level positions embody more authority, responsibility, power, and influence and are accorded more status. In effect, a status hierarchy emerges with the top-level positions listed first and the lower-level positions listed last.

In an informal group, a similar type of status system develops for many different reasons. The individuals performing in leadership roles possess prestige because of the role; consequently, they are ranked by group members as being at a particular level of status in the group hierarchy. The seniority of a member is a factor many groups consider to be important. A worker having more seniority is often thought of as "organizationally intelligent," which means knowing how to adapt to the demands of supervisors, subordinates, or peers. This ability to adjust is an important status factor with group members.

The skills of an individual in performing a job is another factor related to status. An individual who is an expert in the technical aspects of the job, managerial or nonmanagerial, is given a high status ranking in some groups. This type of status does not mean that the individual actually utilizes the skill to perform more efficiently but that the group members perceive this skill in the individual.

Thus, the status system in a work group is formed around such factors as leadership, seniority, and skill. These and other factors are weighted differently by each type of work group; the varying amount of importance placed on them affects the status system.

Norms and Control

Once a group addresses specific task goals, a pattern of behavior begins to emerge. The pattern becomes a regular feature of the group dynamics and is called a *norm,* which is an agreement among the group membership as to how members should regularly behave.[29] The more an individual complies with norms, the more that person accepts the group's standards of behavior. Work groups utilize norms to bring about job performance acceptable to the group. In the workplace, a number of different production-related norms can exist. For example: (1) don't agree with management in its campaign to change the wage structure; (2) present a united front to the supervisor concerning the displeasure of the group about the firing of Mr. Jones; (3) resist the suggestions of the new college graduate assigned to the group's work area; (4) do not produce above the group leader's level of production; (5) help members of the group to achieve an acceptable production level if

---

[29] Joseph A. Litterer, *The Analysis of Organizations* (New York: John Wiley & Sons, 1973), p. 96.

they are having difficulty and if you have time; and (6) don't allow the union steward to convince you to vote for his favorite union presidential candidate.

Three specific social processes bring about compliance with group norms: group pressure, group review and enforcement, and the personalization of norms.

Group pressure.   In groups, pressure can be applied to members to conform to group norms. Pressure is excessive when it interferes with the group's goal accomplishment. On the other hand, pressure is inadequate when lack of conformity to group norms is detrimental to a member, the group, or the organization. Conformity is optimal when it results in cooperation, efficiency, and the accomplishment of group goals.[30]

A number of factors influence the level of conformity in a group. *Task characteristics* such as the nature of a particular job affect conformity. An employee faced with a difficult, unfamiliar, and ambiguous task is more inclined to conform to a group norm.

The *personality* makeup of an individual influences that person's conformity behavior. A person who is deficient in self-esteem is more likely to conform than one who has the opposite personality traits.[31] Also, the more intelligent the individual, the less likely he or she is to conform to group norms.

Group characteristics affect conformity. For example, as size increases, pressures to conform increase. Also, when the majority of a group strongly supports a position, a member is more inclined to conform than when he or she has one or more partners who disagree with the majority view.[32] There is a tendency to conform when the consequence for deviance is social isolation by the group.

Although many individuals prefer to be independent in thoughts and behaviors, there usually is some degree of conformity in dress, work habits, language, attitudes, or effort to perform. Conformity is simply a fact of group membership. Without it, there would be chaos and disruption.

Group review and enforcement.   When individuals become members of a group, they quickly become aware of group norms. The group position on such matters as production, absenteeism, and quality of output is communicated. The group members then observe the actions and language of new members to determine whether the group norms are being followed.

---

[30] L. A. Rosenberg, "Conformity as a Function of Confidence in Self and Confidence in Partner," *Human Behavior,* Spring 1963, pp. 131–39.

[31] Ibid.

[32] Solomon E. Asch, "Opinions and Social Pressures," *Scientific American,* November 1955, pp. 31–35.

If individual members, both old-timers and newcomers, are not complying with generally accepted norms, a number of different approaches may be employed. A "soft" approach would be a discussion between respected leaders and those persons deviating from the norm. If this does not prove effective, more rigid corrective action is used, such as the membership scolding the individual or individuals both privately and publicly. The ultimate type of enforcement would be to ostracize the nonconforming members, which might take the form of not communicating with them.

These are only a few of the numerous strategies to bring deviants into line. Other, more severe techniques, such as sabotaging the nonconformer's performance, have also been utilized. Review and enforcement occur at managerial levels in a form similar to that in nonmanagerial ranks.

Personalization of norms.   The behavioral patterns of people are influenced significantly by their value systems.[33] Their values in turn are influenced by the events occurring around them; values are learned and become personalized. For example, the norm of a work group may encourage group members to treat college graduates and noncollege individuals equally and courteously. This norm may be accepted by the person as morally and ethically correct. Prior to group affiliation, the member may have displayed little interest in a "fair treatment of all" philosophy. However, based on a latent feeling of fairness, the member personalizes this group-learned norm. It becomes a standard of conduct correct from a group and social vantage point.

In some but definitely not in all instances, group pressures, group review and enforcement, and personalization of norms may conflict with organizational objectives such as higher production, improved quality of output, lower absenteeism, and loyalty to the firm. The emphasis here is on the word *some*. It is incorrect to assume that all groups are established to resist the achievement of organizational goals. In fact, some groups are very loyal and committed to the success of their organization.

Cohesiveness

Cohesiveness is another important group characteristic. Group cohesiveness is defined as the attraction of members to the group and the strength of forces on the individual member to remain active in the group and resist leaving it.[34]

---

[33] Litterer, *Analysis,* p. 96.

[34] This definition is based upon the group cohesiveness concept presented by Stanley E. Seashore, *Group Cohesiveness in the Industrial Work Group* (Ann Arbor: University of Michigan, Institute for Social Research, 1954).

FIGURE   11–3   Some Factors Contributing to Group Cohesiveness

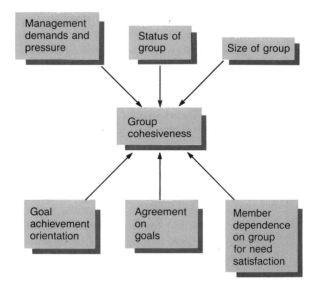

The forces that produce a cohesive group.

All of these characteristics of groups are influenced to some degree by the cohesiveness within the group.[35] For example, the greater the attraction within the group, the more likely it is that the membership will adhere closely to a group norm.

Factors contributing to cohesiveness.   Research findings have allowed those interested in work group cohesiveness to isolate some of the more important factors that affect it. The factors identified in Figure 11–3 are examples of some of the variables uncovered in research studies, but they are representative of the types of conditions that can enhance or reduce cohesiveness of work groups.

Size.   One important and necessary condition for the existence of a group is that members interact and communicate with each other. If the group is so large that members do not get to know each other, there is little likelihood that the group will be high in cohesiveness. Research studies indicate that

[35] Sayles and Strauss, *Human Behavior,* p. 101.

an inverse relationship exists between size of group and group cohesiveness.[36]

In addition to affecting cohesiveness, a group's size can influence how much effort members apply to a task. A phenomenon called "social loafing" has been identified.[37] This involves the tendency of individuals in a group not to work hard, because there are others around to carry the workload. In cohesive groups, social loafing would not be tolerated once it was identified. Also, there are more opportunities for social loafing in large groups. A person not doing the share of work is often hard to identify. If a group leader is able to point out each member's contribution, it would reduce the tendency to loaf. Social loafing is found not only in the workplace but also within family units, student groups, and volunteer groups.[38]

Dependence of members upon the work group.   A group that is able to satisfy a significant portion of an individual's needs will appear attractive to that individual. Group processes such as communication and overall friendship make the group a key factor in the individual's life. Thus, what the group stands for, its norms, and its membership are bonds that relate the individual to the group. The greater the individual's dependency upon the group, the stronger will be these bonds of attraction.

Goal agreement.   Membership agreement on the goals of the group provides the basis for cohesiveness. Inability to agree results in internal conflict, disharmony, and dissatisfaction, which contributes to a lack of focus and direction. Consequently the accomplishment of achievement and maintenance goals suffers when group cohesiveness declines.[39]

Achievement of goals.   The attainment of a set of group-established goals (for example, better production than another group) has an influence on members. For example, a work group that attains a highly desired rating for completing a task enhances the value of being a group member; individuals feel a pride in being members of a work group that has performed in such a manner that they are recognized as being superior.

Work groups that successfully have attained preestablished goals are likely to be highly cohesive units, the members tending to be more attracted toward each other because they have worked together in the past and because their efforts have resulted in achieving a desired goal. Thus, success and cohesiveness are interrelated: Success in goal achievement encourages cohesiveness, and cohesive work groups are more likely to attain preestablished goals. It

---

[36] Seashore, *Group Cohesiveness,* pp. 90–95. Also see Robert C. Cummins and Donald C. King, "The Interaction of Group Size and Task Structure in an Industrial Organization," *Personnel Psychology,* Spring 1973, pp. 87–94.

[37] S. Latane, S. Harkins, and K. Williams, "Many Hands Make Light the Work: Causes and Consequences of Social Loafing," *Journal of Personality and Social Psychology,* 1979, pp. 822–32.

[38] Robert Albanese and David D. Van Fleet, "Rational Behavior in Groups: The Free-Riding Tendency," *Academy of Management Journal,* April 1985, pp. 244–55.

[39] G. H. Graham, "Interpersonal Attraction as a Basis of Informal Organization," *Academy of Management Journal,* December 1971, pp. 483–95.

is important to consider that although group cohesiveness can lead to successful achievement of goals, it can prove detrimental when group and organization goals are not congruent.

Status of group.   In an organizational setting, work groups typically are ranked in a status hierarchy. An intergroup status hierarchy may develop for many different reasons, including the following:

1. One group is rated higher than another in overall performance; this is a measure of success in the organization.
2. To become a member of the group, individuals must display a high level of skill.
3. The work being done by the group is dangerous or financially more rewarding or more challenging than other work.
4. The group is less closely supervised in comparison to other groups.
5. In the past, members of the group have been considered for promotion more often than members of other groups.

These are only some of the criteria that affect the status hierarchy of groups.[40] Generally, the higher a group ranks in the intergroup status hierarchy, the greater its cohesiveness. However, the higher-status groups appear attractive only to some nonmembers. Individuals on the outside of the group may not want to become members of a high-status group, because membership then entails close adherence to group norms.

Management demands and pressure.   It is certainly true in many organizations that management has a significant impact on group cohesiveness. The members of work groups tend to stick together when they are pressured by superiors to conform to some organizational norm (for example, punching in at 8:00 and not 8:05 A.M., or producing at least five more units of output per day).

The group cohesiveness attributed to managerial demands may be a short-run or long-run phenomenon. A group may be loosely knit (low in cohesiveness), and a company policy statement interpreted as a threat to the job security of group members causes the members of the group to become a more cohesive and unified whole in order to withstand the perceived management threat. In some cases, after the danger is past (that is, the policy statement is rescinded), the group gradually drifts back toward low cohesiveness. In other cases, the cohesiveness may be a longer-lasting phenomenon.

Consequences of cohesiveness.   The cohesiveness of a group affects a number of important factors, such as satisfaction and performance. Members of cohesive units usually are more satisfied with their group affiliation than are members of noncohesive groups. This is not to say that cohesive group members are more satisfied with their jobs, their bosses, or the organization.

---

[40] For a listing of other status criteria, see Sayles and Strauss, *Human Behavior,* p. 102.

FIGURE   11–4   Relationship between Cohesiveness and Productivity

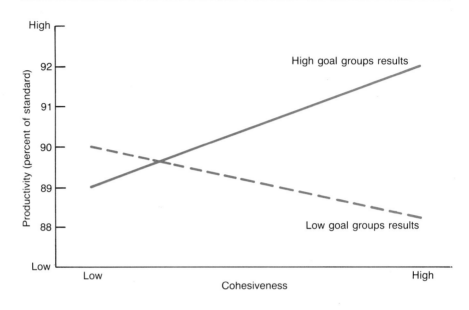

The group goal is a factor in whether cohesiveness is good for management.

Source: Adapted from Stanley E. Seashore, *Group Cohesiveness in the Industrial Work Group.* Ann Arbor: University of Michigan, Institute for Social Research.

Cohesive groups are more highly motivated to attain group goals. However, recall from our discussion of goal achievement and cohesiveness that group and organizational goal congruence is an important consideration. Cohesive groups that have high productivity goals and good relationships with management generally will have high productivity. Cohesive groups having poor relationships with management often have low productivity. The preferred condition is a highly cohesive group whose goals align with management expectations and goals.

Figure 11–4 points out the cohesiveness-productivity relationship. Note that groups with low productivity goals (contrary to management's goals) are increasingly lower in productivity with increasing cohesiveness. This is shown as a decreasing dashed line in the figure. On the other hand, the groups with high productivity goals (solid line) increase production as cohesiveness increases.

Group ownership.   An attempt to increase production and also profitability involves the concept of group ownership. The Management Focus on group ownership cites three slightly different examples of that concept used to promote motivation and cohesiveness.

MANAGEMENT FOCUS
Group Ownership: A Motivation Technique

On January 10, 1984, Wierton Steel's 7,700 employees purchased the 80-year-old company. The employees pooled their money, talent, and energy to become group owners of a problem-ridden firm. While most steel companies lost money in 1984, Wierton Steel racked up $48 million in profits in the first nine months of group ownership. What the employee purchase has accomplished is to create a large, cohesive team of owners.

Phoenix-based America West Airlines requires every new employee to become a shareholder in the company through the purchase of an amount of stock equal to 20 percent of his or her first year's pay. The policy, says president and cofounder Mike Conway, "is predicated on the simple idea that if we're successful, there's enough for everyone. And if we're not successful and don't have profits, the whole thing comes apart like a cheap watch."

The theory being used at America West Airlines involves motivation that is created through group ownership. Motivation theories usually focus on the individual; however, group motivation uses the notion of equity participation to create cohesiveness within the firm.

Joseph Nederlander, chairman of Ticket World Inc., based in New York, also subscribes to the concept of equity participation to build group cohesion; he shares in profits with six key associates. Nederlander saw Arthur Miller's play *Death of a Salesman* and was struck by the importance of loyalty and commitment among employees. In the play, Willy Loman gets fired by the son of the man for whom he has been working all those years. ("There were promises made across the desk," Willy says. "You can't eat the orange and throw the peel away—a man is not a piece of fruit!") Nederlander says thank you for your loyalty, hard work, and commitment by sharing the earnings with his key associates.

These three examples show that two consequences of cohesiveness resulting from group ownership may be more effort and more loyalty. An issue that has not been sufficiently studied at this point is whether equity participation can be sustained over time. Do employees who own the business become complacent, or do they maintain false expectations of what they can do monetarily or in the form of job security? There are some risks involved, and these need to be openly explored before group ownership is considered to be the answer to an organization's problems.

Source: Adapted from Steven Greenhouse, "Employees Make a Go of Weirton," *New York Times,* January 6, 1985, p. 16; Bruce G. Posner, "In Search of Equity," *Inc.,* April 1985, pp. 51–60.

Intragroup Conflict

Conflict is an everyday occurrence in life. *Conflict results when there are incompatible goals, cognitions, or emotions within or between individuals or groups, that lead to opposition or antagonistic interaction.* [41]

Conflict among members of a group can arise in a variety of ways. In the mutual acceptance and decision-making phases of group development, there are likely to be disagreements over member roles, plans, schedules, and standards. These disagreements can cause the group to be ineffective and fragmented. Coalitions and power centers emerge and create anxiety for the membership. Management needs to be alert for these types of conflicts, especially in the relatively immature group.

Interpersonal conflict among members always is present to some extent. Differences in opinions, attitudes, values, and beliefs create tension. We tend to like people with values, beliefs, and opinions similar to our own. The "personality clash" not only happens between superiors and subordinates but among members of groups. Individuals who are in a state of conflict with other members are also likely to be dissatisfied with the interpersonal features of the group. In addition, the member who is having interpersonal conflicts is likely to withdraw from engaging in most group activities.

Of course, if group performance is affected by intragroup conflict, management has a stake in determining the reasons for the problems. However, before managerial prescriptions are implemented, it is necessary to fully understand the reasons. This requires careful diagnostic work: observation, discussions, and reviews of performance records. Management's intent is not to eliminate intragroup conflict but to minimize it so that individual and organizational goals can be achieved.

Intergroup Conflict

Management prefers that groups cooperate and work toward the accomplishment of organizational and individual goals. However, conflicts often develop between groups. If the groups are working on tasks that are interdependent (i.e., Department A's output flows to Department B, and B's output flows to Department C), the coordination and effectiveness of working together are crucial managerial issues. The relationships can become antagonistic and so disruptive that the entire flow of production is slowed or even stopped.

Cooperation is not always the most desirable result of group interaction. For example, two groups can cooperate because they both oppose the introduction of new equipment. The equipment is being introduced to improve cost

---

[41] Don Hellriegel, John W. Slocum, Jr., and Richard Woodman, *Organizational Behavior* (St. Paul, Minn.: West Publishing, 1983), p. 459.

control, but the groups working together can make the period of testing the new equipment a bad experience for management.

Determinants of intergroup conflict.   Conflict develops between groups for many reasons.[42] Some of the more important ones relate to limited resources, communication problems, differences in interests and goals, different perceptions and attitudes, and lack of clarity about responsibilities.

1. *Limited resources.*   Groups that possess an abundance of materials, money, and time usually are effective. However, when a number of groups are competing for limited resources, there is a good chance that conflict will result. The competition for the limited equipment dollars, merit-increase money or new positions can become fierce.

2. *Communication problems.*   Groups often become very involved with their own areas of responsibility. Each tends to develop its own vocabulary. Paying attention to an area of responsibility is a worthy endeavor, but it can result in communication problems. The receiver of information must be considered when a group communicates an idea, proposal, or decision. This often is not the case, and there are misinformed receivers who become irritated and hostile.

3. *Different interests and goals.*   A group of young workers may want management to do something about the inadequate promotion system. However, management is being accused by older workers of ignoring improvements in the company pension plan. Management recognizes the two different goals but believes that the pension issue is the most pressing and addresses it. The groups may want management to solve both problems, but this is not currently possible. Thus, one group becomes hostile because it is ignored.

4. *Different perceptions and attitudes.*   Individuals perceive differently. The groups to which they belong also can have different perceptions. Groups tend to evaluate in terms of their backgrounds, norms, and experiences. Since each of these can differ, there is likely to be conflict between groups. Most groups tend to overvalue their own worth and position and undervalue the worth and position of other groups.

5. *Lack of clarity.*   Job clarity involves knowing what others expect in terms of task accomplishment. In many cases, it is difficult to specify who is responsible for a certain task. This difficulty exists in most organizations. Who is responsible for losing a talented management trainee—the personnel department or the training department? Who is responsible for the increased interest in the product line—marketing, advertising, or research and development? The inability to pinpoint positive and negative contributions causes groups to compete for control over those activities that are recognized.

The causes of conflict just cited are common. Each needs to be managed. The management of intergroup conflict involves determining strategies to minimize such problems.

---

[42] Likert and Likert, *New Ways of Managing Conflict.*

Management strategies.   Management reaction to disruptive intergroup conflict can take many different forms.[43] There is a typical sequence of events. Management first will try to minimize the conflict indirectly; if this fails, it will become directly involved.

Indirect approaches.   Initially, managers often avoid direct approaches to solving conflict between groups. *Avoidance* is easy in the short run, since the causes of conflict are unknown and giving attention to conflict admits that it exists. Unfortunately, avoidance does not always minimize the problem. Matters get worse because nothing seemingly is being done about the problem and the groups become more antagonistic and hostile.

Another indirect strategy is to encourage the groups to meet and discuss their differences and work out a solution without management involvement. This strategy can take the form of *bargaining, persuasion,* or *working on a problem together.*

Bargaining involves the groups agreeing about what each will get and give to the other. For example, a group may agree to give another group quick turnaround time on the repairs of needed equipment if the other group agrees to bring complaints about the quality of repairs to them before going to management. Bargaining can be successful if both groups are better off (or at least no worse off) after an agreement is reached.

Persuasion involves the groups finding common areas of interest. They attempt to find points of agreement and show how these are important to each in attaining organizational goals. Persuasion is possible if clashes between group leaders do not exist.

A problem can be an obstacle to a goal. In order for groups to minimize their conflicts through *problem solving,* they must generally agree on the goal. Then the groups can propose alternative solutions that satisfy the parties involved. For example, one group may want the company to relocate the plant in a suburban area, and the other group may want better working conditions. If both agree that a common goal is to maintain their jobs, then building a new facility in an area that does not have a high tax rate may be a good solution.

Direct approaches.   Management may use *domination* to minimize conflict. It may exercise authority and require that the problem be solved by a specific date. If management uses authority, the groups may join together and resist the domination. Management becomes a common enemy, and they forget their differences in order to deal with their opponent.

Another direct approach is to *remove the key figures* in the conflict. If two individuals are in conflict because of personality differences, this may be a possible alternative. Three problems exist with this approach: First, the figures who are to be removed may be respected leaders of the groups.

---

[43] Alan C. Filley, *Interpersonal Conflict Resolution* (Glenview, Ill.: Scott, Foresman, 1975); Louis Pondy, "Organizational Conflict: Concepts and Models," *Administrative Science Quarterly,* September 1972, pp. 296–320.

This could lead to the groups becoming more antagonistic and to greater conflict. Second, it is difficult to pinpoint accurately whether the individuals in conflict are at odds because of personal animosities or because they represent their groups. Third, removal is not always good, because there is a danger that "martyrs" will be created. The causes of the removed leaders will be remembered and fought for even though the persons themselves are gone.

A final, direct strategy to minimize conflict is that of finding *superordinate goals*. These goals are desired by two or more groups but only can be accomplished through cooperation of the groups. Studies have shown that when conflicting groups are faced with the necessity of cooperating in order to accomplish a goal, conflict can be minimized and cooperation increased.[44] For example, a companywide profit-sharing plan may be used to encourage groups to work together. At the end of the year, a percentage of company profits will be distributed equally to each employee. Conflict between groups can reduce the amount of profits each person receives. Thus, the superordinate goal, generating optimal profits, takes precedence.

END RESULTS: MEMBER SATISFACTION AND EFFECTIVE DECISIONS

Two potential end results, or consequences, of group membership are the satisfaction of members and the reaching of effective group decisions. Behavioralists and managers have, in recent years, increased their efforts to understand the causes of member satisfaction and decision making within groups.

Member Satisfaction

Perhaps the most provocative integrative analysis of work group member satisfaction is presented by Richard Heslin and Dexter Dunphy.[45] They report on a survey of 37 studies that show specific relationships between work group member satisfaction and (1) perceived freedom to participate, (2) perceived goal attainment, and (3) status consensus:

Perceived freedom to participate.   A member's perception of freedom to participate influences need satisfaction. Individuals who perceived themselves as active participators reported themselves more satisfied, while those who perceived their freedom to participate to be insignificant typically were the least-satisfied members in a work group.

---

[44] M. Sherif and C. W. Sherif, *Groups in Harmony and Tension* (New York: Harper & Row, 1953).

[45] Richard Heslin and Dexter Dunphy, "Three Dimensions of Member Satisfaction in Small Groups," *Human Relations,* May 1964, pp. 99–112.

The freedom-to-participate phenomenon is related to the entire spectrum of economic and sociopsychological needs. For example, the perceived ability to participate may lead individuals to believe that they are valued members of the group. This assumption can lead to the satisfaction of social, esteem, and self-actualization needs.

Perceived goal attainment. A number of studies indicate that a group member's perception of progress toward the attainment of desired goals is an important factor in satisfaction.[46] Groups that progressed toward the attainment of goals indicated higher levels of member satisfaction, while members of groups not adequately progressing showed a lower satisfaction level.

Status consensus. This concept is defined as agreement about the relative status of all group members. Several studies indicate that when the degree of status consensus is high, member satisfaction tends to be high; where status consensus within the group is low, member satisfaction tends to be low. It also is concluded that status consensus is more readily achieved in groups where:

1. The group task specialist is perceived by the membership to be competent.
2. A leader emerges who plays a role that is considered an important group task.
3. A leadership role emerges and is filled by an individual who concentrates on coordinating and maintaining the activities of the group.

The insightful review of Heslin and Dunphy suggests that the perceptions of the membership concerning freedom to participate, movement toward goal attainment, and status consensus significantly influence the level of need satisfaction attained by group members. Their review also clearly indicates that when an individual member's goals and needs are in conflict with the goals and needs of the overall group, lower levels of membership satisfaction result.

The degree of satisfaction among employees in health and welfare agencies toward their place of work was the focus of a study by Bagley, Hage, and Aiken.[47] These researchers measured the flow of communication among staff members in formally scheduled meetings as well as informal contacts. The total communication among colleagues was not associated with satisfaction. But the direction of the flow, whether it was up or down the hierarchy or among peers at the same level, was correlated with satisfaction. That is, when most of the informal talk was from subordinates to supervisors, more unfavorable views of the workplace existed. And when most of the informal

---

[46] Clovis R. Shepherd, *Small Groups: Some Sociological Perspectives* (San Francisco: Chandler Publishing, 1964), p. 101.

[47] C. B. Bagley, J. Hage, and M. Aiken, "Communication and Satisfaction in Organizations," *Human Relations,* 1975, pp. 611–26.

messages were directed from superiors to subordinates, favorable workplace attitudes were the rule.

Group Decision-Making Effectiveness

A number of research studies have raised the question of whether group decision making is superior, inferior, or equal to individual decision making. Maier, instead of developing an exact answer to the question, discusses assets and liabilities of group decision making.[48]

Group assets.   In a group, there is a greater total of knowledge and information. Thus, decisions that require knowledge should give groups an advantage over individuals. This additional information is helpful in reaching the best decision possible.

Many problems require making decisions that depend on the support of other group members. More members accept a decision when a group solves the problem than when one person solves it. A person reaching a decision must persuade others in the group who may resist being told what the best solution is for the problem. Individuals, by working on the problem, believe that they are more responsible for the solution. This feeling of shared responsibility is satisfying to some people.

A decision made by an individual, which is to be carried out by others, needs to be communicated to those who must execute it. Thus, the individual decision maker must communicate effectively before positive action is taken. The chances for communication breakdowns are reduced when the individuals who must execute the decision have participated in making it. They were involved in reaching the decision and are aware of how it was reached, which improves understanding.

Group liabilities.   Making a decision in a group exerts pressure on each member. The desire to be an accepted and cooperative group member tends to silence individual disagreement and favors agreement. If the majority is forceful enough, its decision usually will be accepted regardless of whether the quality is adequate.

In some groups, a dominating individual takes over. This person, because of a strong personality, organizational position, reputation, or status can dominate the group. None of these traits or characteristics is necessarily related to decision-making skill. And they can inhibit group discussion, reduce creativity among other members, and stop members from making positive contributions.

---

[48] Norman R. F. Maier, "Assets and Liabilities in Group Problem Solving," *Psychological Review,* July 1967, pp. 239–49.

"Stand taking" may hinder a group in reaching a good solution. Most problems have more than one possible solution, and individual group members may have personal preferences. Sometimes a member may take a stand on his or her preference and will feel that a defeat means loss of face. Thus, the member becomes more concerned with winning than with finding the best group decision.

Group versus individual decision making.   The logic of using a group instead of an individual to solve a problem or make a decision is based on the premise that "two heads are better than one." This premise rests on the notion of synergy. *Synergy* exists when the whole is greater than the sum of its parts.[49] In some cases, synergy may not be a positive result. The Management Focus discussing the Edsel failure gives a classic example of a group making a poor set of decisions.

MANAGEMENT FOCUS
The Edsel: A Group Decision That Failed

Are two heads really better than one? In 1957, Ford Motor Co. proudly announced its development of the Edsel. It was Ford's entry into the medium-priced field. Ernest Breech, board chairman of Ford, set the 1958 goal for the Edsel Division at 3.3 to 3.5 percent of the total auto market. In a 6 million-car year, this would be about 200,000 cars. Ford invested about $250 million in the Edsel.

The Edsel was planned, designed, and promoted by a specially created group of Ford executives and specialists. The group worked for more than 10 years on its new entry. As it turned out, the Edsel is now known as one of the ugliest cars to appear in an automotive era dominated by ornate chrome decorations and high-sweeping tail fins. Within two years after its entry, Ford had lost over $350 million on the Edsel. For all of 1958, only 34,481 Edsels were sold. Between 1957 and 1960, the end of Edsel era, about 109,000 Edsels were sold.

The Edsel decision illustrates that even careful, thorough, and expert analysis by a group of decision makers is not always successful. Many things contributed to the failure. Among them was poor judgment by a group confident in its preplanning, personal tastes, and marketing research. They failed to seriously consider the economy and other conditions outside their control.

---

[49] Robert Albanese and David D. Van Fleet, *Organizational Behavior* (Hinsdale, Ill.: Dryden Press, 1983), p. 273.

MANAGEMENT FOCUS (continued)

In the case of the Edsel, two heads, or a group decision, were not better than an individual decision. Perhaps one executive would have reached the decision that the world simply was not ready for the Edsel. If this brave executive had made this kind of decision, Ford would have saved $350 million.

Source: Adapted from Al Ries and Jack Trout, Positioning the Battle for Your Mind (New York: McGraw-Hill, 1981), p. 74; Robert F. Hartley, Marketing Mistakes (Columbus, Ohio: Grid, 1976), pp. 59–70.

Work groups generally are superior to individuals in reaching decisions when it is desirable to have a wealth of information that no one person possesses; however, if an expert is present, it would not always be advantageous to use a group. Groups also are superior to individuals in most cases when accuracy is important: By taking a number of judgments together and averaging them, random error is reduced. Also, there is the opportunity in a group to critically evaluate judgments so that accuracy improves.

But group decision making produces some drawbacks. If a group is dominated by one member or a small coalition, the contributions of other members are sacrificed. Also, members who do not contribute to problem solving and decision making are less inclined to accept the group solution. In fact, the noncontributing members may harm the group's attempts to implement a solution. And there is the issue of time. Group decision making generally requires more time than individual decision making.

Instead of stating that either group or individual decision making is superior, it is better to consider the issues and tasks involved. Complex and large-scale tasks, such as building an airplane, could benefit from group effort because of the magnitude of the job and the physical and mental effort required.[50] On the other hand, assembly of an electric generator may be more efficiently completed by an individual, since there are fewer tasks.

It also is important for managers to weigh a few group disadvantages such as (1) group decision making is more time consuming; (2) intragroup conflicts are likely to occur and must be resolved; (3) there is a possibility of social loafing in groups;[51] and (4) "groupthink."[52] Groupthink occurs when group pressures lead to reduced mental efficiency, poor testing of reality,

---

[50] J. R. Campbell, "Individual versus Group Problem Solving in an Industrial Sample," Journal of Applied Psychology, April 1968, pp. 205–10.

[51] B. Latane, K. Williams, and S. Harkins, "Social Loafing," Psychology Today, October 1979, p. 104; M. N. Dobosh, "Peril of Work within Groups: Social Loafing," The Wall Street Journal, March 19, 1981, pp. 1, 27.

[52] I. L. Janis, Groupthink (Boston: Houghton Mifflin, 1983).

and lax moral judgment. Highly cohesive groups that stress unanimous acceptance of group decisions encourage the onset of groupthink. Political examples of groupthink include the Watergate fiasco and the planning done by the Kennedy administration for the April 1961 invasion of the Bay of Pigs by 1,400 Cuban exiles. Of course, not all cohesive groups exhibit groupthink.

SUMMARY OF KEY POINTS

- Work groups are formed formally and informally in organizations. Groups are extremely important because they influence individual and organizational goals and performance.
- Groups are formed because of physical proximity and to satisfy needs.
- There are numerous and overlapping groups in organizations. Employees are members of multiple groups at the same time. Formal groups include command and task groups. Informal groups include interest and friendship groups.
- Committees are special kinds of task groups. Committees exist to accomplish such purposes as resolving conflict, recommending action, generating ideas, and making decisions.
- Quality circles are the new management craze in the United States and Canada. This type of group has been exported from Japan. A quality circle is a small group of employees and their supervisor, who voluntarily meet on a regular basis to study quality-control and productivity improvement techniques and to identify and solve work-related problems.
- Groups move through various phases of development or maturity. This development occurs along two dimensions: (1) relationships among members and (2) task and problem solving. The four phases of development are called mutual acceptance, decision making, motivation, and control.
- Group characteristics have a potential impact on how groups function. A summary of some main points about characteristics appears in Exhibit 1.
- Groups perform better than individuals in some situations and equal to or worse than individuals in others. Groups usually outperform individuals when complex and large-scale tasks must be completed.

EXHIBIT   1   Summary of Key Group Characteristics

Characteristics	Major Point(s)
Group goals	Groups typically have two sets of goals: managerial assigned goals and group goals.
Leadership	In informal groups, leaders emerge from within. In the formal organization, the leader is appointed.
Status	Status systems develop over time. Seniority, skill, and expertise influence a person's status within the group.
Norms	Work groups utilize norms to affect dress, language used, and job performance.
Cohesiveness	High group cohesiveness aligned with high performance goals is associated with high group performance.
Intragroup conflict	There is likely to be disagreement among different members because of plans, schedules, and standards.
Intergroup conflict	A few of the crucial reasons for intergroup conflict are limited resources, different perceptions, different interests, and lack of clear communication channels.

What makes groups tick: another reminder.

DISCUSSION AND REVIEW QUESTIONS

1. What did Lewin mean when he stated that "it's easier to affect the personality of 10 people if they can be melted into a group than to affect the personality of any 1 individual separately"?
2. How would social loafing be handled within a highly cohesive group?
3. Informal groups exist in organizations and are very important to their members. If an organization has a number of informal groups, is this an indication that the company is being poorly managed?
4. Should management encourage and aid in the development of cohesive work groups? Why?
5. How is the concept of group norms and control used by weight-watcher clinics and stop-smoking clinics?
6. If quality circles are so successful, why doesn't every organization use them?
7. How would a group's structure influence the members' behavior and attitudes?
8. When would a group's norms not be acceptable to an organization?
9. It is generally agreed that a group influences individual behavior. Can an individual significantly influence a group's behavior? Why?
10. How can one individual dominate the discussion or activities of a group attempting to reach decisions?

ADDITIONAL REFERENCES

Biddle, B. J. *Role Theory: Expectations, Identities, and Behaviors.* New York: Academic Press, 1979.

Hackman, J. R. "The Design of Self-Managing Work Groups." In *Managerial Control and Organizational Democracy.* Edited by B. King, S. Streufert, and F. E. Fiedler. Washington, D.C.: Winston and Sons, 1978.

Herzberg, F. "Group Dynamics at the Roundtable." *Industry Week,.* November 16, 1981, pp. 39–40.

Klein, S. M. *Workers under Stress: The Impact of Work Pressure on Group Cohesion.* Lexington: University of Kentucky Press, 1971.

Martins, L., and Jacobs, M. "Structured Feedback Delivered in Small Groups." *Small Group Behavior,* February 1980, pp. 88–107.

Ohmae, K. "Quality Control Circles: They Work and Don't Work." *The Wall Street Journal,* March 29, 1982, p. 19.

Roark, A. E., and Wilkinson, L. "Approaches to Conflict Management." *Group and Organization Studies,* December 1979, pp. 440–52.

Shaw, M. E. *Group Dynamics: The Psychology of Small Group Behavior.* New York: McGraw-Hill, 1981.

Shaw, M. E. "An Overview of Small Group Behavior." In *Introduction to Organizational Behavior.* Edited by L. L. Cummings and R. B. Dunham. Homewood, Ill.: Richard D. Irwin, 1981, pp. 280–82.

Shea, G. P. "Work Design Committees: The Wave of the Future." *Journal of Applied Management,* March–April 1979, pp. 6–11.

Tervell, R. "How to Keep Quality Circles in Motion." *Business,* January–March 1982, pp. 47–50.

Zander, A. *Motives and Goals in Groups.* New York: Academic Press, 1971.

CASES

APPLICATION I

MARATHON STEEL USES A COMMITTEE EFFECTIVELY*

At Marathon Steel in Phoenix, Arizona, absenteeism was rampant and productivity was low. Administrators in the firm were on the East Coast, and the plant was operating in Phoenix. A plan was developed by Donald Bartlett, Marathon's employee relations manager. He believed that getting

---

* Source: Adapted from John Aberth, "LMRC: A New Solution for Old Problems," *Management Review,* November 1985, p. 16.

the managers and labor to sit and talk was a needed first step in reducing the hostility and conflict between the groups. Therefore, he started the Labor-Management Relations Committee (LMRC).

Before the LMRC, Marathon Steel was overrun with grievances. Everyone seemed to have a complaint. In addition, absenteeism kept increasing every year. Once the LMRC began to function, absenteeism decreased and general grievances dropped from an annual average of 318 to 117. The primary advantage of the LMRC was to have representatives from each side talk to each other. Three representatives from each group (administrative and labor) would discuss job-related issues.

The Marathon LMRC became involved in generating ways to improve work, recommending changes in the workplace, and communicating how each group viewed the other. Open communication of perceptions improved the overall respect each had for the other. It also appeared to improve morale, confidence, and creativity. (New ideas leading to innovative changes were rarely generated prior to the use of the LMRC.) Another spin-off benefit of the LMRC is the pervading spirit of cooperation throughout the company. Instead of conflict and argument, there is respect, problem solving, and attempts to make Marathon a better company.

The LMRC attempts to be fair when hearing complaints and working to correct problems. Instead of always supporting a particular position (management versus labor), each problem is analyzed in open discussion. Pinpointing the cause is the objective of the analysis.

The LMRC spirit of cooperation has trickled down into the workplace and has influenced the perceptions and behavior of employees. Whether some other approach would have been as effective as the LMRC is not known. However, it is reasonable to assume that both management and labor wanted to resolve their conflicts in such a way as to improve Marathon's overall performance.

Questions for Analysis

1. Would the LMRC be as successful in a unionized situation? Why?
2. Is it safe to assume that the LMRC contributed to the reduction in absenteeism? Why?
3. What factors would contribute to the development of cohesiveness in a group like the LMRC?

APPLICATION II

LAKELAND POLICE DEPARTMENT

The mission of the Lakeland Police Department is to protect the life and property of the citizens and visitors to the city of Lakeland. Recently Bob Lukash, chief of police, has been faced with two major problems. First, there is a serious lack of understanding between residents of low-income areas and the police. This problem has generated a number of suggested solutions from politicians, community leaders, and police officers. Second, some embarrassing conflicts are occurring between the Personnel Department and the Training Division. They have become so disruptive that newspaper articles about it are appearing in the *Lakeland Times*. Chief Lukash wants to resolve the problem between the units as soon as possible.

The first problem has led to charges of police brutality and discrimination. The chief is now considering two suggestions for improving understanding between residents and the police:

- To train officers who work in the low-income area in human relations. The rationale is that through training, the officers will become more understanding.
- To form a neighborhood committee, comprised of local leaders and a few police officers trained in social problems. The committee would discuss the problems and attempt to find reasonable solutions.

The chief currently is thinking through these two alternatives and will make a decision in a few days.

The second problem involves two divisions in the department. The Training Division is responsible for police training and the investigation of applicants seeking to join the department. The division's training school offers a six-week course for new recruits twice a year. Between 10 and 12 people attend each session. The Personnel Division recruits through interviews, advertisements, and word of mouth. In the past year, the Personnel Division has been accused by the Training Division of not doing a good job in attracting qualified candidates. The Training Division's commanding officer Nick Tandy has met with Chief Lukash twice to voice this complaint. He asked the chief to lean on personnel director Martin Rossano to make him more aggressive in recruiting quality candidates.

Martin Rossano informed the chief that the Training Division has suddenly raised its requirements without notifying the Personnel Division. He believes that this is why good candidates are lacking. The failure to communicate these changes in requirements has resulted in bad feeling between Tandy and Rossano for the past year.

The chief has told both commanding officers that he will not tolerate this type of conflict. The newspapers have had a field day with it, and the chief wants it stopped. He has scheduled a meeting for Monday morning and ordered both officers to attend. Tandy and Rossano also have been told to bring with them a suggested solution to the problem.

Questions for Analysis

1. Which solution do you consider to be the best for improving community-police relations?
2. Why has the conflict between Tandy and Rossano become disruptive?
3. What are some feasible solutions to the conflict between Personnel and Training?

EXPERIENTIAL EXERCISE

GROUPS AND CONFLICT RESOLUTION

Purpose

The purpose of this exercise is to compare individual versus group problem solving and to examine conflict.

The Exercise in Class

1. Each individual has 15 minutes to read the story and respond to the 11 statements about the story. Individuals may not refer to the story when answering the questions and may not confer with anyone else. Each person should circle T if the answer is clearly true; F if the answer is clearly false; or ? if it isn't clear from the story whether the answer is true or false.
2. Next, form small groups of four to five and make the same decisions, using group consensus. (No one should change any answers on the individual questions.) The ground rules for group decisions are:

   a. Group decisions should be made by consensus, without reference to the story. It is illegal to vote, trade, average, flip a coin, and so forth.
   b. No individual group member should give in only to reach agreement.
   c. Every group member should be aware that disagreements may be resolved by facts. Conflict can lead to understanding and creativity if it does not make group members feel threatened or defensive.

3. After 20 minutes of group work, the instructor should announce the correct answers. Scoring is based on the number of correct answers out of a possible total of 11. Individuals are to score their own individual answers, and someone should score the group's answers. The exercise leader should then call for:

   a. The group-decision score in each group.
   b. The average individual score in each group.
   c. The highest individual score in each group.

4. Responses should be posted on the tally sheet. Note those groups in which the group score was (1) higher than the average individual score and (2) higher than the best individual score. Groups should discuss the way in which individual members resolved disagreements and the effect of the ground rules on such behavior. They may consider the obstacles experienced in arriving at consensus and the possible reasons for the difference between individual and group decisions.

The story.   A businessman had just turned off the lights in the store when a man appeared and demanded money. The owner opened a cash register. The contents of the cash register were scooped up, and the man sped away. A member of the police force was notified promptly.

Statements about the story.

1. A man appeared after the owner had turned off his store lights.   T   F   ?
2. The robber was a man.   T   F   ?
3. A man did not demand money.   T   F   ?
4. The man who opened the cash register was the owner.   T   F   ?
5. The store owner scooped up the contents of the cash register and ran away.   T   F   ?
6. Someone opened a cash register.   T   F   ?
7. After the man who demanded the money scooped up the contents of the cash register, he ran away.   T   F   ?
8. While the cash register contained money, the story does *not* state *how much*.   T   F   ?
9. The robber demanded money of the owner.   T   F   ?
10. The story concerns a series of events in which only three persons are referred to: the owner of the store, a man who demanded money, and a member of the police force.   T   F   ?
11. The following events in the story are true: Someone demanded money, a cash register was opened, its contents were scooped up, and a man dashed out of the store.   T   F   ?

Tally Sheet

Group Number	Group Score	Avg. Individual Score	Best Individual Score	Group Score Better than Avg. Indiv?	Group Score Better than Best Indiv?

The Learning Message

The influence of a group on individual performance will be displayed in this exercise.

12

Chapter

LEADERSHIP

LEARNING OBJECTIVES

After completing Chapter 12, you should be able to:

■ **Define**
what is meant by the preferred leader/manager mix.

■ **Describe**
the difference between the terms leadership and management.

■ **Discuss**
the power bases that leaders can use to influence the work behavior of followers.

■ **Compare**
the similarities and differences in the University of Michigan, Ohio State, and Managerial Grid personal-behavioral explanations of leadership.

■ **Identify**
the unique features of the Fiedler, House, and Vroom-Yetton situational approaches to leadership.

◻ MANAGEMENT IN ACTION

Leaders Replacing Managers: Is It a New Trend?*

The A. E. Staley Company operates an automated plant in Lafayette, Indiana, virtually without managers. The plant's 265 employees work in small teams with leaders of their own choosing; they make their own work assignments and do their own hiring and firing. The Diamond Fiber Products plant in Palmer, Massachusetts, recently changed owners. Some managers were let go, but the employee "100 Club" to recognize good work was kept. Bankers who financed the purchase said the club was essential to the plant's future. Don Hewitt, producer of the top-rated CBS television show "60 Minutes" is so committed to a conversational, face-to-face leadership style that he never sends anyone a memo and refuses to attend meetings. These three operations are vastly different. But all recognize the importance of leadership.

There is a movement in the United States away from hierarchical and authoritarian management structures to some form of participative leadership. For years, some managers were trained to be autocrats—to supervise closely, to control, and to monitor. Today, however, the autocratic model is not well received by workers, who are different than their predecessors. Today's worker is better educated, more self directed, and wants some say in designing working conditions.

It was three years before the leadership approach at A. E. Staley began to pay off. Since then, productivity has skyrocketed. Operating costs are below those of other plants; absenteeism and turnover are under 1 percent; downtime in a 24-hour workday is less than 1 percent; and production runs at 115 percent of engineering specifications. Leaders are the key to the company's success. Instead of relying on managers, the firm has decided to place the future in the hands of a nonhierarchy team leader arrangement.

This approach may work at Staley's Lafayette plant but not in another plant site. The leadership style needs to match the situation context and the people involved. The importance of matching will be highlighted in this chapter.

---

* Source: Adapted from Harry Bacas, "Who's in Charge Here?" *Nation's Business,* May 1985, pp. 57–64.

nterest in the subject of leading others has existed throughout the history of studying human behavior. However, behavioral scientists in the past 40 years have scientifically analyzed leadership in organizational settings, finding that leadership is a complex process that can be explained by various theories and models. And many of the available theories and models are contradictory or overlap.[1]

WHAT IS LEADERSHIP

Some writers have given the impression that leadership is a synonym for management. This assumption is not correct. Leaders are found not only in the managerial hierarchy but also in informal work groups. The difference between leadership and management is stated as follows:

> Leadership is a part of management but not all of it. . . . Leadership is the ability to persuade others to seek defined objectives enthusiastically. It is the human factor which binds a group together and motivates it toward goals. Management activities such as planning, organizing, and decision making are dormant cocoons until the leader triggers the power of motivation in people and guides them toward goals.[2]

Figure 12–1 emphasizes graphically that managers are not always effective leaders. Of course, organizations of all sizes prefer to have and attempt to develop managers who also are leaders.

An important feature of the above definition of leadership is that leadership is a process whereby one individual exerts influence over others. Several attempts have been made to clarify and depict the basis upon which a superior might influence a subordinate or a group of subordinates. One of the most concise and insightful approaches is offered by John French and Bertram Raven.[3] They define influence in terms of *power*—the control a person possesses and can exercise on others—and propose five different bases for such power:

1. *Coercive power.*   This is power based upon fear. A subordinate perceives that failure to comply with the wishes of a superior would lead to punishment (for example, an undesirable work assignment, a reprimand). Coercive power is based upon the expectations of individuals that punishment is the consequence for not agreeing with the actions, attitudes, or directives of a superior.

2. *Reward power.*   This is the opposite of coercive power. A subordinate

---

[1] Gary Yukl, "Toward a Behavioral Theory of Leadership," *Organizational Behavior and Human Performance,* July 1971, p. 414.

[2] Keith Davis, *Human Relations at Work* (New York: McGraw-Hill, 1967), pp. 96–97.

[3] John R. P. French and Bertram Raven, "The Bases of Social Power," in *Group Dynamics,* 2nd ed., ed. Dorwin Cartwright and Alvin F. Zander (Evanston, Ill.: Row, Peterson, 1960), pp. 607–23.

FIGURE   12–1   The Preferred Leader/Manager Mix

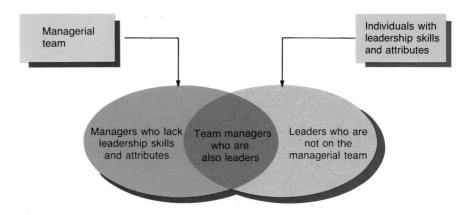

Leaders = Managers only in some cases.

perceives that compliance with the wishes of a superior will lead to positive rewards. These rewards could be monetary (increases in pay) or nonmonetary (a compliment for a job well done).

3. *Legitimate power.*   This type of power comes from the position of a superior in the organizational hierarchy. For example, the president of a corporation possesses more legitimate power than the vice president, and the department manager has more legitimate power than the first-line supervisor.

4. *Expert power.*   An individual with this type of power is one with an expertise, special skill, or knowledge. The possession of one or more of these attributes gains the respect and compliance of peers or subordinates.

5. *Referent power.*   This power is based on a follower's identification with a leader. The leader is admired because of one or more personal traits, and the follower can be influenced because of this admiration.

Coercive, reward, and legitimate power are specified primarily by the individual's position in the organization. The first-line supervisor in an organization is at a lower managerial level than the department manager and consequently has significantly less coercive, reward, and legitimate power than does the department manager. The head operating-room nurse has more freedom to make job-related decisions than a floor nurse. Position also affects the use of power in regard to the discipline process. A first-line supervisor can reprimand subordinates (coercive power), while the department manager can reprimand the first-line supervisor.

The degree and scope of a manager's referent and expert power are dictated primarily by individual characteristics. Some managers possess specific qualities (for example, skills or attributes) that make them attractive to subordinates. Managers could be considered attractive because of an ability to express themselves clearly or because they appear completely confident in performing the job. Thus, the individual leader controls the referent and expert power bases, while the organization controls the coercive, reward, and legitimate power bases.

THE LEADERSHIP JOB: A MUTUAL–SHARING VIEW

Unquestionably, the manager has the legitimate power to run a plant, establish new accounting procedures, or discard the present performance appraisal system. These rights to influence and make decisions are granted by the organization. However, influence should be viewed as a mutual exercise. In order to influence, one must be influenced to some degree. That is, the leader must be influenced by followers.

A leader who attempts to influence through coercion or fear will eventually face problems. This is not to say that the leader should be stripped of the right to discipline followers in an equitable manner. It does suggest, however, that the leader should be viewed as approachable, equitable, and considerate. The leader can exert more influence if viewed as being open to influence in some situations.

This mutual-sharing view of leadership has an important message: Influence can be divided or shared and both parties can gain. A leader, by sharing influence with followers, can benefit from establishing better interaction and more respect. The followers can benefit by learning more about the leader. It has been shown that managers and employees in effective organizations perceive themselves as having greater influence. The greater the total influence leaders and followers have in the organization, the better seems to be the performance of the total system.[4]

An example of the mutual-sharing view is what is happening at Photocircuits, a division of Kollmorgen Corporation in Glen Cove and Riverhead, New York. Managers have their performance assessed by—and get feedback from—their subordinates.[5] So far, participation has been voluntary. This reverse performance review has become a matter of company policy.

The objective of the reverse performance review is to build a mutual relationship between managers and subordinates. It is designed to encourage them to talk to each other as equals. And some of its original skeptics seem to be changing their tune. Frank Fuggine, vice president of human resources, stated: "I was skeptical when the reverse review was proposed. But it's been a real eye-opener. I learned more about myself. . . . I found people in general

---

[4] See D. C. Pelz, "Influence: A Key to Effective Leadership in the First-Line Supervisor," *Personnel,* 1952, pp. 201–21; M. Rosner et al., "Worker Participation and Influence in Five Countries," *Industrial Relations,* 1973, pp. 200–212, for two classic studies.

[5] "Another Perspective of Managers' Performance—from Subordinates," *Management Review,* August 1982, pp. 29, 32, 33.

were very candid and in most cases welcomed the opportunity. That really surprised me."

LEADER ATTITUDES: IMPORTANT ASSUMPTIONS

Douglas McGregor introduced the idea that the attitudes that managers hold about the nature of people will greatly influence their behavior. If managers view their subordinates as being lazy, uncooperative, and possessing poor work habits, they will treat them accordingly.[6] Likewise, if managers see their employees as hardworking, cooperative, and possessing positive work habits, they will treat them in this manner. McGregor referred to this attitude-behavior link as the "self-fulfilling prophecy."

McGregor's views about manager attitudes were presented in terms of assumptions. McGregor distinguished between what he called Theory X and Theory Y managers. Theory X managers behaved according to these assumptions:

- The average employee inherently dislikes work and will avoid it when possible.
- Most employees must be coerced, directed, and closely supervised to get them to put forth the effort to achieve organizational objectives.
- Most employees have little ambition and prefer job security above all other outcomes.
- Most employees avoid taking on responsibilities.

The Theory X manager making these assumptions would use an authoritarian and directive style of leadership.

On the other hand, Theory Y managerial behaviors would be based on the following assumptions and would reflect a less authoritarian leadership style.

- The expenditure of physical and mental effort in work is as natural as play or rest.
- Most people prefer to exercise self-direction and self-control.
- People learn, when encouraged, to accept and seek responsibilities.
- People are interested in displaying imagination, ingenuity, and creativity to solve organizational problems.

Under a Theory X manager, the employee who is having difficulty meeting standard output levels is seen as lazy, one that needs to be closely supervised. However, the Theory Y manager would view this employee as perhaps needing training, more support, or more autonomy to do the job.

---

[6] Douglas McGregor, *The Human Side of Enterprise* (New York: McGraw-Hill, 1960). This is McGregor's original work.

The self-fulfilling prophecy of managing and leading others is aptly stated as follows:

> What a manager expects of his subordinates and the way he treats them largely determines their performance and career progress. A unique characteristic of superior managers is their ability to create high performance expectations that subordinates fulfill.[7]

SELECTED LEADERSHIP THEORIES

Attempts to explain and understand leadership have shown a trend toward integrating various theories of leadership. Instead of creating more theories of leadership behavior, the focus here is upon systematically organizing and categorizing what is already available. There appear to be three broad categories of leadership theories. They are: trait theories, personal-behavioral theories, and situational theories. Some of the situational theories have borrowed from the trait theories and from various personal-behavioral theories. Therefore, it is best to consider the three theories as having many similarities and some differences.

TRAIT THEORIES

The identification of various personal traits of leaders as criteria for describing or predicting success has been used for some time. Some executives engaged in recruitment and selection of managers believe that the trait approach is as valid as any other method. However, the comparison of leaders by various physical, personality, and intelligence traits has resulted in little agreement among researchers.

Physical Traits

Some advocates of the trait theory contend that the physical stature of a person affects ability to influence followers. For example, in an early extensive review of 12 leadership investigations, Ralph Stogdill determined that 9 of the studies found leaders to be taller than followers, two found them to be shorter, while one concluded that height was not the most important factor.[8] Other physical traits that have been studied with no conclusive results include weight, physique, and personal appearance.

[7] J. Sterling Livingston, "Pygmalion in Management," *Harvard Business Review,* July–August 1969, p. 82.

[8] Ralph Stogdill, "Personal Factors Associated with Leadership," *Journal of Applied Psychology,* January 1948, pp. 35–71.

Personality

A research study by Edwin Ghiselli reports on several personality factors that are related, in most though not all cases, to effective leadership.[9] He found that leaders who have the drive to act independently and are self-assured (for example, have confidence in their leadership skills) are successful in achieving organizational objectives.

The work of Fred Fiedler suggests that successful leaders may be more perceptive than unsuccessful leaders.[10] He found that effective leaders are more proficient in differentiating between their best and poorest followers than are the less effective leaders. The leaders of the more effective groups maintain greater psychological distance between themselves and their followers than do leaders of less effective groups.

A test attempting to identify personality traits of successful leaders has been developed. The Management Focus discusses the test and some research.

MANAGEMENT FOCUS
A Test of Personality Traits: Some Unfinished Business

What makes an effective leader? Ask 20 experts this question and you will receive 20 different views. Tracing the development of personality-oriented trait theories, it seems reasonable to consider the role that family behaviors (especially of the parents) play in each person's development. Thus, if we are to understand the personality makeup of the leader, it will be necessary to trace or assess a person's ego development.

Jane Loevinger, a psychologist from Washington University, proposed that all human traits evolve along four distinct dimensions: physical, intellectual, psychosexual, and ego development. Loevinger and associates have spent considerable time developing a test that reveals these four dimensions in terms of each respondent's state of development. The test includes sentence-completion questions asking people how they feel about themselves, about others, and about reality; what they are concerned with; and how they manage their impulses. For example, 1 of the 36 test questions is, "What gets me into trouble is . . ."

A person's responses are processed in terms of a number of

---

[9] See the classic, Edwin E. Ghiselli, "Managerial Talent," *American Psychologist,* October 1963, pp. 631–41.

[10] Fred Fiedler, "The Leader's Psychological Distance and Group Effectiveness," in *Group Dynamics,* ed. Cartwright and Zander, pp. 586–605.

MANAGEMENT FOCUS (*continued*)

development stages—impulsive, self-protection, conformist, conscientious, autonomous, and integrated. The integrated stage is attained by those rare individuals who not only cope with internal conflicts but also transcend them. Ideally organizations would nurture and encourage the development of their leaders to an integrated state.

In a recent study on the relationship between ego development and decision-making style, more than 70 leaders, men and women, took the test. They included corporate managers from a number of organizations. Despite the many demographic differences among these managers, 95 percent of them were within a range of two stages of ego development. Almost all of the managers were in the conformist ego stage or were in the transition stage between the conformist and conscientious stages; very few managers were in the integrated stage. The conformist believes that rules, structure, and controls are necessary to ensure worker performance. These necessary requirements need to be strictly followed.

Loevinger's test needs to be examined in terms of the stages of ego development of highly successful, moderately successful, and unsuccessful leaders before more managers pay closer attention to using the test as a screening tool.

Source: Adapted from Alan Gratch, "Testing for Traits that Make a Manager," *New York Times,* February 3, 1985, p. 17.

Intelligence

After surveying the literature, Stogdill concluded that leadership ability is associated with the judgment and verbal facilities of the leader.[11] Ghiselli also concluded that an individual's intelligence is an accurate predictor of managerial success within a certain range. Above and below this range, the chances of successful prediction significantly decrease.[12] It should be noted, however, that the leader's intelligence should be close to the followers. The leader who is too smart or not smart enough may lose the followers' respect.

Ghiselli has studied eight personality traits and five motivational traits.[13]

---

[11] Stogdill, "Personal Factors."

[12] Ghiselli, "Managerial Talent."

[13] Edwin E. Ghiselli, *Explorations in Management Talent* (Santa Monica, Calif.: Goodyear Publishing, 1971).

Personality traits
    Intelligence: of a verbal and symbolic nature.
    Initiative: the willingness to strike off in new directions.
    Supervisory ability: the ability to direct others.
    Self-assurance: favorable self-evaluation.
    Affinity for the working class.
    Decisiveness.
    Masculinity/femininity.
    Maturity.

Motivational traits
    Need for job security.
    Need for financial reward.
    Need for power over others.
    Need for self-actualization.
    Need for occupational achievement.

His research on these traits is well respected because of the scientific quality of the work. Table 12–1 summarizes the results of Ghiselli's studies, which suggest the relative importance of the traits. They must be tempered, however, because the traits are not totally independent from each other. There are some interesting pieces of information: First, intelligence and self-actualization are important for success. Second, the concept of power over others is not very important. (This tends to support McGregor's Theory Y orientation.) Third, the supervisory-ability trait basically refers to the ability to use planning, organizing, and controlling to direct subordinates. This is an extremely

---

TABLE   12–1   The Importance of Personal Traits to Management Success

Some personal traits predict leadership success and some have little predictive power.

Importance	Personal Trait
Great	Supervisory ability.
	Occupational achievement.
	Intelligence.
	Self-actualization.
	Self-assurance.
	Decisiveness.
Moderate	Lack of need for security.
	Affinity for working-class.
	Initiative.
	Lack of need for high financial reward.
	Maturity.
Little	Masculinity-femininity.

Source: Adapted from Edwin E. Ghiselli, *Explorations in Management Talent* (Santa Monica, Calif.: Goodyear Publishing, 1971).

important trait in the classical explanation of management. Finally, masculinity/femininity seems to have little to do with managerial success.

Shortcomings in Trait Theory

There are some shortcomings in using a trait approach and assuming that a manager who is confident, independent, and intelligent has a higher probability of succeeding. First, the trait theory of leadership ignores the subordinates. The followers have a significant effect on the accomplishments of the leader. Second, except for Ghiselli, trait theorists do not specify the relative importance of various traits. Should an organization attempt to find leaders who are confident or those who act independently—which should be weighted more? Third, the research evidence is inconsistent. For every study that supports the idea that a particular trait is positively related to improved effectiveness, there seems to be one that shows a negative relationship or no relationship at all. Finally, though large numbers of traits already have been uncovered, the list grows annually, suggesting that still others will be found in the future. The cumbersome listings lead to confusion and disputes and provide little insight into leadership.[14]

The assumption that a certain set of traits can be used to predict leader effectiveness is still appealing to some executives. However, it has not yielded strong evidence that specific traits can predict leader success.

PERSONAL-BEHAVIORAL THEORIES

Personal-behavioral (P–B) theories contend that leaders may best be classified by personal qualities or behavioral patterns (styles). P–B theories of leadership focus on what the leader does in carrying out the managerial job. Of these, there is no specific style that is universally accepted.

A Continuum of Leadership

Robert Tannenbaum and Warren Schmidt propose that managers often have difficulty deciding what type of action is most appropriate for handling a particular problem.[15] They are not sure whether to make the decision or to delegate the decision-making authority to subordinates.

To provide insight into the meaning of leadership behavior with regard

---

[14] See Rodman L. Drake, "Leadership: It's a Rare Blend of Traits," *Management Review,* August 1984, pp. 24–26. For another listing that is based on research findings, see Bernard M. Bass, *Stogdill's Handbook of Leadership* (New York: Free Press, 1982), pp. 75–76.

[15] Robert Tannenbaum and Warren H. Schmidt, "How to Choose a Leadership Pattern," *Harvard Business Review,* May–June 1973, pp. 162–80.

FIGURE   12–2   Continuum of Leadership Behavior

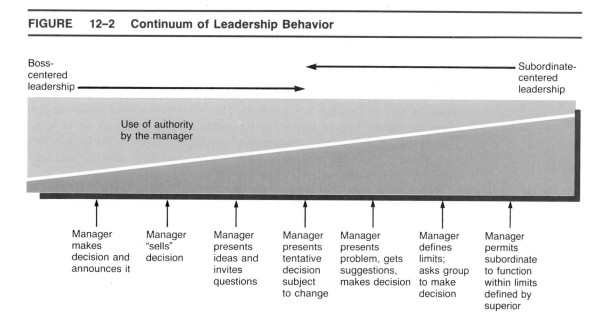

Boss-
centered
leadership

Subordinate-
centered
leadership

Use of authority
by the manager

| Manager makes decision and announces it | Manager "sells" decision | Manager presents ideas and invites questions | Manager presents tentative decision subject to change | Manager presents problem, gets suggestions, makes decision | Manager defines limits; asks group to make decision | Manager permits subordinate to function within limits defined by superior |

Autocratic to democratic: A number of behavioral differences to consider.

to decision making, Tannenbaum and Schmidt suggest a continuum, presented in Figure 12–2. Leadership actions are related to the degree of authority used by managers and to the amount of freedom available to the subordinates in reaching decisions. The managerial actions depicted on the left characterize managers who maintain a high degree of control, while those on the right are those of managers who delegate decision-making authority. Along the continuum, there are a number of leadership styles. According to this theory, effective leaders would be those who are adaptable—that is, who can delegate authority effectively because they consider their capabilities, subordinates' capabilities, and objectives to be accomplished. Thus, Tannenbaum and Schmidt imply that leaders should not choose either a strict "autocratic" or "democratic" style but should be flexible enough to cope with different situations.

Job-Centered/Employee-Centered Leaders

Since 1947, Rensis Likert and a group of social researchers at the University of Michigan have conducted studies of leadership.[16] They have studied leaders

---

[16] Rensis Likert, *New Patterns of Management* (New York: McGraw-Hill, 1961). For a discussion of the history of Likert's work, see Rensis Likert, "From Production- and Employee-Centeredness to Systems 1–4," *Journal of Management,* Fall 1979, pp. 147–56.

in industry, hospitals, and government, obtaining data from thousands of employees.

After extensive analyses, the leaders studied were classified as job centered or employee centered. The *job-centered leader* structures the jobs of subordinates, closely supervises to see that designated tasks are performed, uses incentives to spur production, and determines standard rates of production, based on procedures such as time study. The *employee-centered leader* focuses attention on the human aspects of subordinates' problems and on building effective work groups with high performance goals. Such a leader specifies objectives, communicates them to subordinates, and gives subordinates considerable freedom to accomplish their jobs.

The University of Michigan research showed that the majority of high-producing groups were led by supervisors who displayed an employee-centered style. In a study of clerical workers, the employee-centered manager was described as a general supervisor and the job-centered manager as a close supervisor. Once again, productivity data clearly indicated that the general type of supervision (employee centered) was more effective than the close supervision style (job centered).

Based on his extensive research, Likert suggested that the type of leadership style significantly influences various performance criteria. Such criteria as productivity, absenteeism, attitudes, turnover, and defective units were found to be more favorable from an organizational standpoint when employee-centered, or general, supervision was utilized. Likert implied that the choice is of the either-or variety—that is, management can be categorized and practiced as employee centered or job centered. His recommendation was to develop employee-centered managers whenever possible.

Two-Dimensional Theory

In 1945, a group of researchers at Ohio State University began extensive investigations of leadership, focusing on the study of leader behavior. Their effort uncovered many provocative insights and changed the conceptual foundation of leadership research from a trait-based approach to a behavior base.

Perhaps the most publicized aspect of the studies was the isolation of two dimensions of leadership behavior, identified as "consideration" and "initiating structure."[17] These two dimensions were used to describe leadership

---

[17] See any of the following for excellent presentations of the two-dimensional theory: E. A. Fleishman, "The Measurement of Leadership Attitudes in Industry," *Journal of Applied Psychology*, June 1953, pp. 153–58; E. A. Fleishman and D. A. Peters, "Interpersonal Values, Leadership Attitudes and Managerial Success," *Personnel Psychology*, Summer 1962, pp. 127–43; Abraham K. Korman, "Consideration, Initiating Structure, and Organizational Criteria—a Review," *Personnel Psychology*, Winter 1966, pp. 349–61; Chester A. Schreisheim and Barbara J. Bird, "Contributions of the Ohio State Studies to the Field of Leadership," *Journal of Management*, Fall 1979, pp. 135–45.

behavior in organizational settings. The researchers assessed how supervisors think they should behave in leadership roles. They also attempted to ascertain subordinates perceptions of supervisory behavior. The findings allowed the Ohio State researchers to classify leaders on consideration and initiating-structure dimensions.

Leaders who scored high on the consideration dimension reflected a work atmosphere of mutual trust, respect for subordinates' ideas, and consideration of subordinates' feelings. Such leaders encouraged good superior-subordinate rapport and two-way communication. A low consideration score indicated that leaders were more impersonal in their dealings with subordinates.

A high initiating-structure score indicated that leaders structured their roles and those of subordinates toward the attainment of goals. They were actively involved in planning work activities, communicating pertinent information, and scheduling work.

One early research study attempted to compare supervisors having different consideration and initiating-structure scores with various performance measures.[18] The first measure was obtained from proficiency ratings made by plant management. Other measures were unexcused absenteeism, accidents, formally filed grievances, and employee turnover. Indexes for each of these measures were computed for each foreman's work group for an 11-month period.

Supervisors who worked in production divisions were compared to supervisors in nonproduction divisions on consideration scores, initiating-structure scores, and proficiency ratings. In the production divisions, the supervisors who were rated by their superiors as most proficient scored high on structure and low on consideration. In the nonproduction divisions, the relationships were reversed.

After comparing the leadership scores and proficiency ratings, the researchers compared leadership scores to the other performance measures: unexcused absenteeism, accidents, formally filed grievances, and employee turnover. In general, it was determined that high structure and low consideration were related to more absenteeism, accidents, grievances, and turnover.

A number of studies have supported the general findings cited above, while other research findings present contradictory evidence.[19] Despite these differences, it certainly is true that the Ohio State researchers have stimulated the interest of practitioners and researchers in systematically studying leadership.

---

[18] E. A. Fleishman, E. F. Harris, and H. E. Burtt, *Leadership and Supervision in Industry* (Columbus: Bureau of Educational Research, Ohio State University, 1955).

[19] For a number of studies that dispute some of the findings of the Ohio State researchers, see Korman, "Consideration." For more supportive studies see S. Kerr and Chester A. Schriesheim, "Consideration, Initiating Structure, and Organizational Criteria: An Update of Korman's 1966 Review," *Personnel Psychology,* Winter 1974, pp. 558–68.

Managerial Grid Theory

Another P–B theory is the Managerial Grid®. Robert Blake and Jane Mouton propose that leadership style can be plotted on a two-dimensional grid.[20] Individuals are asked questions about their leadership style and, based on the responses, are placed at the appropriate point on the grid. Blake and Mouton use the Managerial Grid as a framework to help managers learn what their leadership style is and to track their movement toward the ideal (9,9) team management style. This grid is presented in Figure 12–3.

Five specific leadership styles are used to highlight different approaches to leading others. Of course, these are only five of the many possible styles of leadership that can be and are utilized.

1,1 *Impoverished:* A minimum effort to accomplish the work is exerted by the leader.

9,1 *Task:* The leader concentrates on task efficiency but shows little regard for the development and morale of subordinates.

1,9 *Country club:* The leader focuses on being supportive and considerate of employees. However, task efficiency is not a primary concern of this easygoing style.

5,5 *Middle of the road:* Adequate task efficiency and satisfactory morale are the goals of this style.

9,9 *Team:* The leader facilitates production and morale by coordinating and integrating work-related activities.

Blake and Mouton assume that the leader who is a 9,9 individual would be using the most effective style; however, defining a 9,9 leader for every type of job is very difficult. Blake and Mouton imply that a managerial development program can move leaders *toward* a 9,9 style. They recommend a number of management development phases to aid the manager in acquiring concern for fellow employees and expertise to accomplish objectives such as productivity and quality. The six phases are:

1. *Laboratory-seminar groups.* Typically, one-week conferences are used to introduce the leaders to the grid approach and philosophy. Leadership training is conducted by line managers of the firm who already are familiar with the ideas of Blake and Mouton. A key part of the phase is to analyze and assess one's own leadership style.

2. *Teamwork.* This is an extension of Phase 1, which included leaders from different departments in the conference groups. In the second phase, managers from the same department are brought together, and each department works out and specifies its own 9,9 description. The intent of Phases

---

[20] Robert R. Blake and Jane S. Mouton, *The Managerial Grid* (Houston: Gulf Publishing, 1964).

FIGURE   12–3   Blake and Mouton's Managerial Grid

Leadership style is plotted on a grid, 9,9 being the ideal.

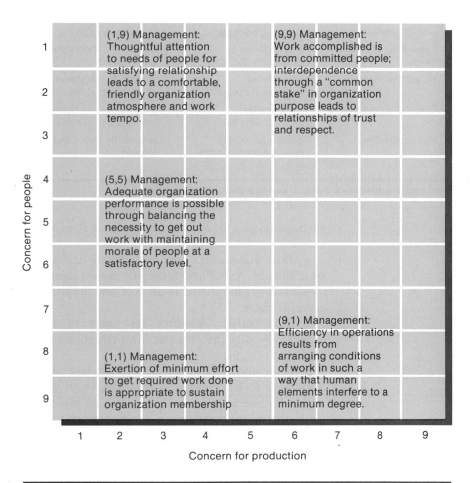

Source: Robert R. Blake and Jane S. Mouton, *The Managerial Grid* (Houston: Gulf Publishing, 1964).

---

1 and 2 is to enable leaders to learn the grid philosophy, to improve their ability to assess their own leadership style, and to develop cohesiveness among the participants.

3. *Intergroup interaction.*   This phase involves intergroup discussion and analysis of 9,9 specifications. Tensions and conflicts that exist between groups are analyzed by group members.

4. *Organizational goal setting.*   Goal setting on the part of the leaders in the program is discussed and analyzed. Such problems as profits, cost control, and safety are placed in a goal-setting context (for example, one

TABLE   12–2   Personal-Behavioral Theories of Leadership

Theories	Two Concepts	Derivation	Theory Development
1. Leadership continuum theory	Boss centered Subordinate centered	Opinions of Tannenbaum and Schmidt	By authors' description
2. Supportive theory	Job centered Employee centered	Research at the University of Michigan—Likert	By field research studies
3. Two-dimensional theory	"Consideration" "Initiating structure"	Research at Ohio State University—Fleishman	By field research studies
4. Managerial Grid	Concern for people Concern for production	Research by Blake and Mouton	By description and limited research

Four personal-behavioral theories and how they were developed.

participant vows to reduce direct expenses 20 percent over the next six-month period).

5. *Goal attainment.*   The participants attempt to accomplish the goals set in Phase 4. As in Phase 1, the participants meet, but this time the discussion focuses on organizational issues and how to accomplish the goals set in the previous phase.

6. *Stabilization.*   Attempts are made to stabilize the improvements brought about in the program. An evaluation of the entire program is conducted at this point.

The Managerial Grid approach relates task effectiveness and human satisfaction to a formal managerial development program. This program is unique in that (1) line managers, not academicians or consultants, run the program; (2) a conceptual framework of management (the grid) is utilized; and (3) the entire managerial hierarchy undergoes development, not just one level (for example, first-line supervisors).[21]

Synopsis of the Personal-Behavioral Approach

Examination of the various P–B theories presented in this section indicates that similar concepts are discussed but different labels are utilized. For example, the continuum, Likert, the Ohio State researchers, and the Managerial Grid approach each utilize two broadly defined concepts, summarized in Table 12–2.

Each approach in Table 12–2 focuses on two concepts; however, some differences should be emphasized: (1) The continuum theory is based primarily

---

[21] Robert R. Blake and Jane S. Mouton, "Using the Managerial Grid to Ensure MBO," *Organizational Dynamics,* Spring 1974, pp. 50–62.

upon personal opinions. Although the opinions of the originators are respected, they should be supported with research evidence before much faith
can be placed in this particular theory. (2) Likert's supportive theory implies
that the most successful leadership style is employee centered. He suggests
that we need look no further. However, the critical question is whether the
employee-centered style works in all situations. Some studies dispute Likert's
claim. (3) The Ohio State researchers found that from a production standpoint,
the leader with a high initiating-structure score was preferred by the executives
of the company. Thus, Likert's claim, or any other claim, that one best
leadership approach has been discovered, is subject to debate. (4) Blake and
Mouton's Managerial Grid is an intuitively sound proposal. However, only
limited research has been reported to test the grid. Also, it is not safe to
assume that a 9,9 leader will always be successful. The need is obvious for
research testing 9,9 in different settings, with various types of leader-follower
situations, and with diverse sets of constraints (e.g., time, monetary resources,
technology).

SITUATIONAL THEORIES OF LEADERSHIP

An increasing number of managers are questioning the premise that a
particular leadership style is effective in all situations. They believe that a
manager behaving as a considerate leader, for example, cannot be assured
of effective results in every situation. As noted earlier in this chapter, the
Ohio State researchers found that supervisors who scored high on initiating
structure were relatively more proficient when managing production rather
than nonproduction workers. Thus, evidence exists, even in the literature
on personal-behavioral theories, to support the view that effective leadership
depends upon the interaction of the situation and the leader's behavior.

The identification of key situational factors and the determination of their
relative importance are difficult undertakings. Behavioral scientists who have
devoted considerable time and energy to such undertakings are Fiedler (contingency theory), Robert House (path-goal theory), and Victor Vroom and
Philip Yetton (leadership-style theory).

Fiedler's Contingency Theory

With a considerable body of research evidence behind him, Fiedler has
developed a dynamic situational, or contingency, theory of leadership.[22] Three

---

[22] Fred E. Fiedler, *A Theory of Leadership Effectiveness* (New York: McGraw-Hill, 1967);
Fred E. Fiedler and Martin M. Chemers, *Leadership and Effective Management* (Glenview,
Ill.: Scott, Foresman, 1975).

important situational dimensions are assumed to influence the leader's effectiveness:

1. *Leader-member relations:*   The degree of confidence the subordinates have in the leader. It also includes the loyalty shown the leader and the leader's attractiveness.
2. *Task structure:*   The degree to which the followers' jobs are routine as contrasted with nonroutine.
3. *Position power:*   The power inherent in the leadership position. It includes the rewards and punishments typically associated with the position, the leader's formal authority (based on ranking in managerial hierarchy), and the support that the leader receives from superiors and the overall organization.

FIGURE   12–4   Summary of Research Findings on Leadership Styles According to Situational Conditions

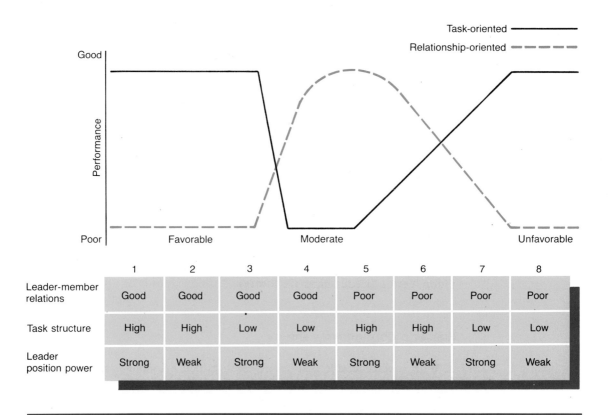

	1	2	3	4	5	6	7	8
Leader-member relations	Good	Good	Good	Good	Poor	Poor	Poor	Poor
Task structure	High	High	Low	Low	High	High	Low	Low
Leader position power	Strong	Weak	Strong	Weak	Strong	Weak	Strong	Weak

Source: Reprinted, by permission of the publisher, from "The Leadership Game: Matching the Man to the Situation," Fred E. Fiedler, *Organizational Dynamics,* Winter 1976. © 1976 by Amacom, a division of American Management Associations, p. 11.

Where task-oriented and relationship-oriented leaders work best: The situational mix.

Fiedler measures leadership style by evaluating leader responses to what is called a least preferred co-worker (LPC) questionnaire. The leaders who rate their least preferred co-worker in more positive terms (high LPC) are assumed to be people oriented and supportive. Those leaders who give low LPC ratings are more task oriented.

In developing his theory, Fiedler uses the term *situational favorableness,* defined as the degree to which a situation enables a leader to exert influence over the group. In other words, leader-member relations can be either good or poor; task structure can be high or low; and position power can be either strong or weak. The various combinations of these three dimensions can be favorable, moderate, or unfavorable. Figure 12–4 shows that task-oriented leaders performed most effectively in the more favorable situations (1, 2, and 3), as well as in one relatively unfavorable situation (8). On the other hand, research indicates that relationship-oriented leaders are better performers in moderately favorable situations (4 and 5). In effect, the Fiedler model suggests that leaders who are directive and leaders who are permissive can function best in certain types of situations. Instead of stating that a leader must adopt this or that style, Fiedler identifies the type of leader who functions best in a given situation.

According to Fiedler, we should not talk simply about good leaders or poor leaders. A leader who achieves effectiveness in one situation may or may not be effective in another. The implication of this logic is that managers should think about the situation in which a particular leader performs well or badly. Fiedler assumes that managers can enhance leader effectiveness if they carefully choose situations that are favorable to the leaders' style.

The situational-leadership logic is extended in Table 12–3. The examples represent the various combinations of the three dimensions. Furthermore, suggestions on what leadership action to take in the eight situations are indicated.

As Table 12–3 suggests, there may be a need to engineer the situation to fit the leader's style, as suggested by Fiedler in his contingency theory. Fiedler suggests some pragmatic procedures for improving a leader's relations, task structure, and position power:

1. *Leader-member relations* could be improved by restructuring the leader's group of subordinates, so the group is more compatible in terms of background, education level, technical expertise, or ethnic origin. It should be noted that this would be extremely difficult in a unionized group, since they may assume that this restructuring is a management plan to weaken the union.

2. The *task structure* can be modified in the structured or the nonstructured direction. The task can be made more structured by spelling out the jobs in greater detail. A task can be made less structured by providing only general directions for the work that is to be accomplished. Some workers like minimum task structure, while others want detailed and specific task structure.

3. *Position power* can be modified in a number of ways. A leader can be

TABLE   12–3   Situational Leadership Applied to Eight Situations

Situation	Leader-Member Relations	Task Structure	Position Power	Most Effective Leadership	Reason(s) for Effectiveness
1. First-line supervisor at Ford Motor Co.	Good	High	Strong	Task oriented	Employees respect task expertise, recognize power, and permit supervisor to lead.
2. Chairperson of college department	Good	High	Weak	Task oriented	Faculty member elected because he/she possesses group values. Understands what the group needs to do and pushes for task completion.
3. Sales manager at Procter & Gamble	Good	Low	Strong	Task oriented	Manager has formal authority and power, but salespeople work all over territory. They must have some autonomy because of unstructured nature of job.
4. Committee chairperson	Good	Low	Weak	About equally task and relationship oriented	Chair has little power and must rely on both types of leadership to accomplish job.
5. Middle-level manager at IBM	Poor	High	Strong	Relationship oriented	Manager is not well liked but has power to motivate. Can accomplish more if relationship approach is used.
6. Supervisor at General Mills	Poor	High	Weak	Relationship oriented	Employees know what they're supposed to accomplish. Supervisor is unpopular and has little say-so. More effective to use relationship style instead of creating more hostility.
7. Operating-room nurse supervisor	Poor	Low	Strong	Almost equally task and relationship oriented	Difficult to control unstructured activities through use of power. Because person is unpopular, it is best to use relationship orientation when appropriate and task orientation if necessary.
8. Detective in charge of other detectives working on a case	Poor	Low	Weak	Task oriented	Detective has little power, is not well-liked, and case is unstructured. Concentrate on solving the case.

Eight situations and the best leadership style to use.

given a higher rank in the organization or more authority to do the job. A memo can be issued indicating the rank change or the authority a leader now possesses. In addition, a leader's reward power can be increased if the organization delegates authority to evaluate the performance of subordinates.

Fiedler's suggestions may not be feasible in every organizational setting. Such factors as unions, technology, time, and costs of changes must be considered. For example, a unionized company that has a highly routine technology and currently is faced with intense competition in new-product development may not have the patience, time, and energy to modify the three situational dimensions so that its leaders become more effective.

Interestingly, Fiedler's suggestions do not include leadership training.[23] In fact, he believes that training is not an effective approach, reporting that his own research has shown disappointing results from training. On the average, people with much training perform about as well as people with little or no training.

Critics question Fiedler's methodology for measuring LPC, the subjects he uses in some of his research (for example, basketball teams, the Belgian Navy, and students), and the fact that only high and low LPC scores are considered.[24] Despite critics and some glaring shortcomings, Fiedler provided a starting point for leadership research in the 1970s and 1980s.

The Path-Goal Theory

A leadership approach that draws heavily on the expectancy theory of motivation is called the path-goal theory.[25] It proposes that the leader is a key individual in bringing about improved subordinate motivation, satisfaction, and performance. The theory suggests that four leadership styles can be and are used:

1. *Directive.* The leader directs, and there is no subordinate participation in decision making.
2. *Supportive.* The leader is friendly and is interested in subordinates as people.
3. *Participative.* The leader asks for, receives, and uses suggestions from subordinates to make decisions.

---

[23] Fred E. Fiedler, "The Leadership Game: Matching the Man to the Situation," *Organizational Dynamics,* Winter 1976, pp. 6–16.

[24] An early review article that is critical of the situational, or contingency, model of leadership is George Graen, Kenneth Alvaris, James B. Orris, and Joseph A. Martella, "Contingency Model of Leadership Effectiveness: Antecedent and Evidential Results," *Psychological Bulletin,* October 1970, pp. 285–96.

[25] See Martin G. Evans, "The Effect of Supervisory Behavior on the Path-Goal Relationship," *Organizational Behavior and Human Performance,* May 1970, pp. 277–98 and Robert J. House, "A Path-Goal Theory of Leader Effectiveness," *Administrative Science Quarterly,* September 1971, pp. 321–38 for two early works.

4. *Achievement oriented.*   The leader sets challenging goals for subordinates and shows confidence that they can achieve the goals.

The path-goal theory, unlike Fiedler's theory, suggests that these four styles are used by the *same* leader in different situations.[26]

The important key in this theory is the way the leader affects the "paths" between subordinate behavior and goals. In a sense, the leader is the coach who charts out realistic paths for the team. The leader can affect the paths by:

1. Recognizing and stimulating subordinates' needs for rewards over which the leader has some control.
2. Rewarding goal achievement.
3. Supporting subordinates' efforts to achieve the goals.
4. Helping reduce frustrating barriers to achieving goals.
5. Increasing the opportunities for personal satisfaction for subordinates.

Basically, the leader attempts to help the subordinate find the best path, to set challenging goals, and to remove stressful barriers along the way.

Since the path-goal theory was proposed, there have been a limited number of studies testing its assumptions. One study of 10 different samples of employees found that supportive leadership has its most positive effect on satisfaction for subordinates who work on stressful and frustrating jobs. Another study determined that in three separate organizations, subordinates doing nonroutine job tasks working for achievement-oriented leaders were more confident that their efforts would result in better performance.[27]

The Vroom-Yetton Theory

Another situational-leadership theory is offered by Vroom and Yetton.[28] Their theory attempts to identify the appropriate leadership style for a given set of circumstances, or situations. Five leadership styles are suggested by the Vroom-Yetton theory:

A–I: The leader solves the problem or reaches a decision using available information.

A–II: The leader obtains the information from followers, then decides on the solution to the problem. The leader may or may not inform

---

[26] Robert J. House and Terence R. Mitchell, "Path-Goal Theory of Leadership," *Journal of Contemporary Business,* Autumn 1974, pp. 81–97.

[27] See Alan C. Filley, Robert J. House, and Steven Kerr, *Managerial Process and Organizational Behavior* (Glenview, Ill.: Scott, Foresman, 1976), pp. 256–60.

[28] Victor Vroom and Philip Yetton, *Leadership and Decision Making* (Pittsburgh: University of Pittsburgh Press, 1973). It should be recognized that much of the validation of this model and some of the refinements have been initiated by Arthur Jago of the University of Houston.

followers what the problem is in acquiring information from them. The role of followers is to supply information.

C–I: The leader shares the problem with subordinates individually, getting their ideas and suggestions without bringing them together as a group. The leader makes the decision, which may or may not reflect followers'· influence.

C–II: The leader shares problems with subordinates as a group, obtaining their ideas and suggestions. The leader then makes a decision that may or may not reflect follower's influence.

G–II: The leader shares a problem with followers as a group. Together the group generates and evaluates alternatives and attempts to reach consensus on a solution. The leader acts as a chairperson. The solution that has the support of the entire group is accepted and implemented.

The letters in the code identify the leadership practice: A stands for autocratic; C stands for consultative; and G stands for group. The appropriate style of leadership (A–I, A–II, C–I, C–II, G–II) depends on seven attributes of the

---

TABLE   12–4   Problem Attributes and Diagnostic Questions Developed by Vroom and Yetton

Problem Attributes	*Diagnostic Questions*
A. The importance of the quality of the decision.	Is there a quality requirement such that one solution is likely to be more rational than another?
B. The extent to which the leader possesses sufficient information/expertise to make a high-quality decision.	Do I have sufficient information to make a high-quality decision?
C. The extent to which the problem is structured.	Is the problem structured?
D. The extent to which acceptance of commitment on the part of subordinates is critical to the effective implementation of the decision.	Is acceptance of decision by subordinates critical to effective implementation?
E. The probability that the leader's autocratic decision will receive acceptance by subordinates.	If I were to make the decision by myself, is it reasonably certain that it would be accepted by my subordinates?
F. The extent to which the subordinates are motivated to attain the organizational goals are represented in the objectives explicit in the statement of the problem.	Do subordinates share the organizational goals to be obtained in solving the problem?
G. The extent to which subordinates are likely to be in conflict over preferred solutions.	Is conflict among subordinates likely in preferred solutions?

Seven situational factors in the Vroom-Yetton theory.

problem situation. The attributes, along with diagnostic questions, are shown in Table 12–4. The leader, if interested in, say, the importance of the quality of a decision (the first problem attribute), could ask himself or herself the diagnostic question: "Is there a quality requirement such that one solution is more likely to be rational than another?"

Vroom and Yetton use a decision tree for determining the best leadership

FIGURE 12–5 The Vroom-Yetton Decision Tree

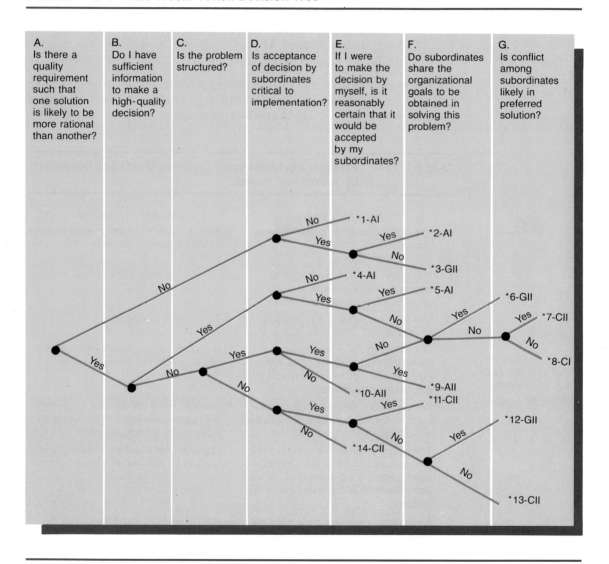

Using the seven situational factors and a decision tree to select a leadership style.

TABLE   12-5   Comparison of Three Popular Situational Theories of Leadership

Points of Comparison	Contingency Theory (Fiedler)	Path-Goal Theory (House)	Vroom-Yetton Theory *
1. Theme	No best style. Leader success determined by the interaction of environment and leader personality variables.	Most successful leaders are those who increase subordinate motivation by charting out and clarifying paths to effective performance.	Successful leadership style varies with the situation. Leader can learn how to recognize the requirements of the situation and how to fit style to meet these requirements.
2. Leadership styles (range of choices)	Autocratic or democratic.	Instrumental to achievement.	Autocratic to participative.
3. Research base (number of supportive studies)	Large, in many settings: military, educational, industrial. Some contradictory results.	Moderate to low, generally supportive.	Low but increasing, generally supportive.
4. Application value for managers	Moderate to low: leaders can't generally be trained.	Moderate.	High: Leaders can be trained.

* The contributions of Arthur Jago to the refinement and testing of this model have led some to refer to this approach as the Vroom-Yetton-Jago theory.
Comparing the characteristics of the three major situational theories of leadership.

style for a problem situation. Figure 12-5 illustrates how the diagnostic questions are asked from A to G, and where a yes or no answer takes a person along the tree. The person using the decision tree works across it as the questions are answered. In this way, a leader can identify the appropriate situation and leadership style.

The Vroom-Yetton theory is being tested and validated in various settings. One study by Jago has found that managers higher in the management hierarchy tend to use more participative styles than managers lower in the hierarchy.[29] Another study indicated that managers of retail franchises who more closely conformed to the style identified by the Vroom-Yetton decision tree were more successful and had employees who reported higher amounts of job satisfaction.[30]

---

[29] Arthur G. Jago, "Hierarchical Level Determinants of Participative Leader Behavior," (Ph.D. dissertation, Yale University), *Dissertation Abstracts International* 30 (1977), p. 2921B; Arthur G. Jago and Victor H. Vroom, "An Evaluation of Two Alternatives to the Vroom/Yetton Normative Model," *Academy of Management Journal,* June 1980, pp. 347–55.

[30] C. Margerison and R. Glube, "Leadership Decision-Making: An Empirical Test of the Vroom and Yetton Model," *Journal of Management Studies,* February 1979, pp. 45–55.

Comparison

There certainly are a growing number of situational theories of leadership. However, each approach adds insight into a manager's understanding of leadership. Table 12–5 contains a brief explanation of the three popular leadership theories that stress the importance of situational variables. Although the Fiedler theory has the largest research base and has been around for years, the Vroom-Yetton theory appears to offer the most promise for managerial training. At present, there is not enough evidence available to say how effective training is in applying the Vroom-Yetton theory to managerial problem solving and decision situations.

SELECTED FACTORS INFLUENCING
LEADERSHIP EFFECTIVENSS

We have defined leadership as the ability to persuade others to seek defined objectives enthusiastically. We also have identified three approaches to the study of leadership: trait, personal-behavioral, and situational. The trait and personal-behavioral approaches indicate that effective leadership depends on a number of variables such as intelligence, decisiveness, and style. No one trait or style is best for all situations.

Since the magic trait or style was never discovered, researchers and practitioners have turned to the situational approach. The leader's effectiveness in today's work organization is considered to be influenced significantly by various situational factors.

An interesting trait analysis was conducted at the Center for Creative Leadership in Greensboro, North Carolina. The Management Focus highlights some of that study's findings. If one important trait was showing through in the research, it was that successful managers have a better understanding of people than nonsuccessful managers do.

MANAGEMENT FOCUS
Successful and Unsuccessful Managers

The Center for Creative Leadership, a nonprofit research and educational institution in Greensboro, North Carolina, was formed to improve the practice of management. Two of the center's experts on leadership are behavioral scientists Morgan McCall, Jr., and Michael Lombardo. They are interested in understanding the differences between successful and unsuccessful managers.

MANAGEMENT FOCUS (*continued*)

McCall and Lombardo studied 21 *derailed managers*—successful people who were expected to go higher in the organization but who reached a plateau late in their careers, were fired, or were forced to retire early. They also studied 20 *arrivers*—those who made it all the way to the top. To McCall and Lombardo's surprise, the two groups had somewhat similar characteristics. Every one of the 41 managers possessed strengths, and every one had one or more weaknesses. More often than any other flaw, insensitivity to others was cited as a reason for derailment. But it was never the only reason. Most often, a combination of personal qualities and external circumstances put an end to a manager's rise.

The 10 most frequently found traits of unsuccessful managers were:

1. Insensitive to others; abrasive, intimidating, bullying style.
2. Cold, aloof, arrogant.
3. Betrayal of trust.
4. Overly ambitious; thinking of next job, playing politics.
5. Specific performance problems with the business.
6. Overmanaging; unable to delegate or build a team.
7. Unable to staff effectively.
8. Unable to think strategically.
9. Unable to adapt to boss with different style.
10. Overdependent on mentor.

When the researchers compared the arrivers and the derailed, a few identifiable differences showed up. Derailed managers often were described by peers as moody or volatile under pressure. Also, although neither group made many mistakes, all the arrivers handled theirs with poise and grace. Moreover, derailed managers tended to react to failure by going on the defensive, trying to keep it under wraps while they fixed it or, once the problem was visible, blaming it on someone else. Finally, the arrivers had the ability to get along with all types of people. They were direct but diplomatic. Arrivers also were outspoken but did not offend people when they revealed this characteristic.

The researchers concluded that managers are like the rest of us: a patchwork of strengths and weaknesses. There is no one best way to be successful.

Source: Adapted from Morgan W. McCall, Jr., and Michael W. Lombardo, "What Makes a Top Executive?" *Psychology Today,* February 1983, pp. 26–31.

Perceptual Accuracy

McGregor indicated how perception plays a role in leadership. Managers who misperceive employees may miss the opportunity to achieve optimal results. If you feel someone is lazy, you tend to treat him/her as a lazy person. Thus, managerial perceptual accuracy is extremely important. It is important in each of the three situational models.[31]

Background, Experience, and Personality

The leader.   The leader's background and experience will affect the choice of style. A person who has had success in being relationship oriented probably will continue the use of this style. Likewise, a leader who doesn't trust followers and who has structured the task for years will use a close supervision or autocratic style.

Despite Fiedler's opinion, the majority of leadership researchers believe that what has been used can be altered. That is, a leader who perceives that his or her preferred style is not working well can change it accordingly. Of course, some individuals are so rigid in their preferences and personality makeup that alteration is extremely difficult.

The follower.   Followers are an important factor in the leader's choice of style. As stated earlier, the leadership job is a mutual-sharing process. For example, a leader with technically proficient followers is best advised to be more participative and less autocratic. On the other hand, inexperienced, recent hirees with a minimum of work knowledge may prefer a leader who structures the task and is firm. Then an autocratic or job-centered leader works best.

The astute leader attempts to determine the background and experience of followers, which may signal the style that is most appropriate. In any event, the followers must be given serious consideration in making a judgment about which leadership style can achieve the desired results. (Recall the Management in Action at the beginning of the chapter.)

Superior's Expectations and Style

Superiors are comfortable with and prefer a particular leadership style. A superior who prefers a job-centered, autocratic approach encourages followers to adopt a similar approach. Imitation of the superior's example is a powerful force in shaping leadership styles.

---

[31] Douglas McGregor "On Visionary Leadership," *New Management,* Winter 1985, pp. 46–52.

Since superiors possess various power bases, their expectations are important. For example, many firms seek to improve the relationship skills of first-line supervisors and send these managers to an off-the-job training program. Research indicates that during and immediately after these programs, supervisors' relationship skills are improved. However, soon after returning to the job, the learned skills often disappear. Why? A reasonable explanation is that the supervisors' superiors prefer more task-oriented behaviors instead of relationship-oriented behaviors.

Task Understanding

The task of a group or an individual refers to what is to be done on a job. Tasks are imposed by management or self-generated by the employee. A task has physical properties and behavioral features. The physical properties are the stimuli surrounding the job; these stimuli may be a set of instructions from management or the way the employee interprets the job. The behavioral properties are the requirements or kinds of responses expected of a person doing the task.

The task may be very structured, such as the job duties of a worker on an assembly line. The worker is instructed by management what to do with the products being processed. The goal or requirement of this type of job is to produce as many units as possible of good quality.

Other tasks, such as those of a research and development engineer or planning expert, may be unstructured. In these jobs, the goals are not easily defined. Thus, the leader may have to work hard to display "paths" and goals for the employees.

Leaders must be able to assess correctly the tasks their followers are performing. In an unstructured task situation, directive or autocratic leadership may be very inappropriate; the employees need guidelines, freedom to act, and the necessary resources to accomplish the task. Leaders must properly diagnose the tasks of followers so that proper leadership style choices are made. Because of this requirement, a leader must have some technical knowledge of the job and its requirements.

Peer Expectations

Leaders form relationships with other leaders. These peer relationships are used to exchange ideas, opinions, experiences, and suggestions. A leader's peers can provide support and encouragement for various leadership behaviors, thus influencing the leader in the future. Often, for example, when peers inform a leader that he was too easy on an uncooperative follower, the leader may respond by becoming very harsh and restrictive. Peers are

FIGURE   12–6   Selected Factors that Influence Leadership Effectiveness

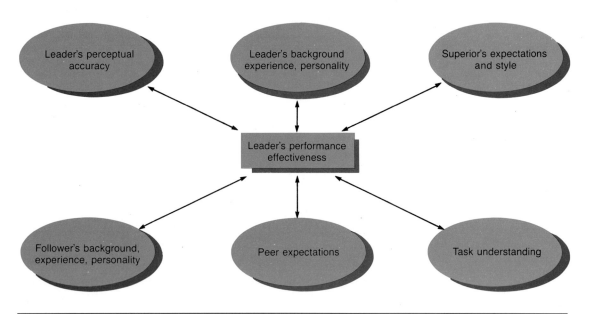

Leaders must diagnose themselves and the total leadership environment in order to effect good leadership.

an important source of comparison and information in making leadership style choices and modifications.

Integrating Influence Factors

Figure 12–6 integrates these six important factors influencing leadership effectiveness. Leadership also influences these factors. Although many other factors that are not presented also influence leadership effectiveness, these six seem to be as important as any and serve to illustrate concisely the reciprocal nature of leadership.

The emphasis in Figure 12–6 is on leaders' ability to diagnose themselves and their total leadership environment. Perhaps if leadership training programs are used, they should stress diagnostic skills. It should not be concluded that individuals can be trained easily to accurately diagnose work situations and to develop appropriate leadership abilities. This type of training difficulty was summed up by Fiedler:

> Industrial psychologists and personnel men typically view the executive's position as fixed and immutable and the individual as highly plastic and trainable. When we think of improving leadership performance, we generally think first of training the leader. Yet, we know all too well from our experience with psychotherapy, our attempts to rehabilitate prison inmates, drug addicts or juvenile delinquents—not to mention our difficulties with rearing our own progeny—that our ability to change personality has its limitations.[32]

If leaders are to become skilled at diagnoses and flexible enough to adapt leadership style to the circumstances at hand, patience is essential. The organization must be willing to plan and to fund development programs that are time-consuming. The approach we are suggesting is not applicable in those instances where changing the situation is less costly than changing the leader. Lessons on patience and training in leadership can be found in comparisons between Japanese and American leadership practices.

AMERICAN AND JAPANESE LEADERSHIP: WHAT ARE THE DIFFERENCES

In 1945, Japan's industrial capacity was totally destroyed; and in the 1950s, "Made in Japan" was a catchphrase for shoddy, second-rate merchandise. Things have changed in the 1970s and 1980s.[33] There appear to be several reasons for such a change. Leadership is one of them. And some distinct differences exist between Japanese and American management styles:[34]

1. *Cultural Differences.* There are significant cultural differences. In Japan, there is a strong sense of national purpose. The role of each Japanese man and woman is to help achieve the ultimate goal of a more prosperous Japan. Each worker works for the company, which in turn works for the industry, which in turn works for Japan. This national purpose has helped create a spirit of teamwork among government, banking, and industry interests. Management, labor, and government have pulled together. This type of cooperation simply doesn't exist in the United States. Japanese subsidiaries in the United States are hiring more American managers, who have some problems with corporate culture differences. These differences are pointed out in the Management Focus on that topic.

---

[32] Fiedler, *Theory of Leadership,* p. 247.

[33] M. LeBoeuf, *The Productivity Challenge* (New York: McGraw-Hill, 1982), p. 53.

[34] Michael Lombardo, "How Do Leaders Get to Lead?" *Issues and Operations,* February 1982, pp. 1–4.

MANAGEMENT FOCUS
Corporate Culture Differences

As increasing numbers of Japanese companies either set up or expand operations in the United States, more American executives are getting telephone calls that open something like this: "I'm an executive recruiter, and I have a job that might interest you. It's with a Japanese company."

For many who accept the offer, working for a Japanese company will be the high point of their careers. Frequently they will be given more authority, power, and responsibility than they could expect at an American company. But for some, the job could be a disaster. There are major style and corporate culture differences in Japanese firms. American managers have become accustomed to a hierarchy, preferred treatment, and frequent feedback on performance. In Japanese firms, there is a vague environment, little hierarchy, and not much feedback. The Japanese want their managers to be leaders who are self-motivated and able to define their jobs.

There are some disincentives to taking a job with a Japanese company. One involves compensation. While salaries will be competitive with those in American companies, other kinds of compensation (especially bonus and stock options) are rarely offered. There is also the issue of promotion. Even if the American executive becomes an effective leader, how likely is a non-Japanese to be promoted? The evidence suggests that moving to the top is very difficult for any non-Japanese.

Americans who need large offices, status symbols, frequent feedback, and many assistants are going to have a difficult time succeeding in Japanese subsidiaries in the United States. Japanese executives and leaders think of the company as a big family, and their job is to help the family do well. American managers tend to compare themselves to other managers. In Japanese subsidiaries, comparisons are fine only if they occur after the family is in excellent shape.

Adapted from Douglas R. Sease, "Working for a Japanese Subsidiary: A Life's Thrill—Or a Career Disaster," *The Wall Street Journal,* August 29, 1985, p. 21.

2. *Individual versus group goals.* At the organizational level, Japanese managers—to a far greater extent than their American counterparts—place group goals ahead of individual goals.[35] In the United States, a manager is

[35] K. Tobioka, "Japan's Matrix of Nature, Culture, and Technology," *Management Review,* May 1985, pp. 42–47.

in charge (and hopefully also is a leader). In Japan, on the other hand, there is not a clear concept of who is in charge. Everyone is in charge, instead of one person being in charge. Since everyone is in charge, there is a need for teamwork and group goals. In American firms, policies are set at the top and are communicated downward. The group orientation in Japan encourages consultation among team members. Thus, even lower-level employees help formulate policy. The Japanese approach tends to reduce resistance to policies, rules, and procedures. There is little need to exercise power and authority, since the team established the policies, rules, and procedures.

3. *Competition.*   Although teamwork is part of the Japanese cultural fabric, fierce competition is the rule throughout life in Japan. Competition for entrance into top schools and colleges is strong; and competition between firms and industries is harsh. Competition also exists in the United States but not in this degree. What happens to the losers in Japan? The strong survive, and the weak suffer the consequences of failure. Whether this results in more benefits than costs to Japan is debatable. The costs of failure in Japan are extremely high in terms of people and their attitudes, emotions, and mental well-being.

4. *Paternalism.*   The Japanese leader is a paternalistic figurehead. Paternalism is not well received in the United States. About 35 percent of Japan's labor force enjoys the security of guaranteed employment until age 55.[36] When business is poor, everyone receives lower salaries or bonuses instead of being fired or furloughed. The Japanese approach tends to encourage company loyalty.

5. *Training.*   Japanese managers are trained to lead. Lengthy training programs emphasize learning each phase of a firm's operations. In-class and on-the-job training are required. It is not uncommon to see trainees and even company executives working in overalls along with other operating employees on an assembly line. Managerial trainees become personally familiar with jobs of operating employees. They listen to, observe, and work with the employees they will be leading in the near future. Most Japanese firms require management trainees to keep a diary of their experiences. At the end of the training, participants are asked to submit a report of their experiences and impressions. This type of training intensity is generally not found in American firms. The American manager learns by going directly to the job and by attending off-the-job training programs.

6. *Patience.*   Japanese leaders practice patience. Unlike American leaders, they tend to stress the long run, the future. Japanese leaders think in terms of 5-year and 10-year plans. The relationship between the government, labor, and management encourages a more long-run perspective than that found in the United States.

---

[36] N. Hatvany and V. Pucik, "Japanese Management in America: What Does and Doesn't Work," *National Productivity Review,* Winter 1981–82, pp. 61–74.

A Closing Word of Caution

These six distinct differences are not intended to imply that Japanese leadership is superior. They do indicate some of the advantages that the Japanese seem to have in accomplishing leadership effectiveness. There are, however, a number of characteristics that American organizations do not and will not support. For example, the selection of managers (leaders) in Japan is limited to men who are chosen before they are hired; there is little or no opportunity for workers to move up through the ranks. And Japanese corporations have virtually no female executives. Such managerial practices are incompatible with the American ethic of equal and unlimited opportunity.

Disregarding Japanese and American leadership differences is not recommended. But in considering Japanese practices that might be applicable in the United States, a number of points must be kept in mind: (1) Japan is a homogeneous, group-oriented culture, and America is a heterogeneous culture that places a high premium on individualism. (2) It is probably more difficult to lead and manage a group of strong-willed individuals than a team-oriented and culturally supported group.

SUMMARY OF KEY POINTS

- Leadership and management are not synonymous terms. Leadership is the ability to persuade others to seek defined objectives enthusiastically.

- Leaders possess five potential power bases to influence followers: coercive, reward, legitimate, expert, and referent.

- McGregor believed that a manager's attitudes and assumptions explain his/her behavior toward followers. These attitudes were referred to as Theory X and Theory Y. The attitude-behavior relationship generates a self-fulfilling prophecy. If a manager assumes a person is a winner, then the manager will treat the person as a winner.

- Numerous attempts to study and understand leadership have been made. Three major approaches are trait, personal-behavioral, and situational.

- Trait theories attempt to discover various traits that describe or predict leadership success. Some of the more important traits are intelligence, self-assurance, and decisiveness. A new and not fully tested trait was presented in the Management in Action: a strong sensitivity toward people.

- Personal-behavioral theories contend that leaders may be classified by personal qualities or behavioral patterns. Continuums of leadership, two-dimensional models, and managerial grids are used to explain leadership in personal-behavioral terms.

- The situational factors that influence leadership are given prominence in Fiedler's contingency theory, the House path-goal theory and the Vroom-Yetton theory.

- Leadership effectiveness is affected by numerous factors. Some of the prominent factors are: the leader's perceptual accuracy, the background, experience, and personality of both follower and leader, superior's expectations and style, peer expectations, and task understanding.
- Japanese and American leadership styles differ because of cultural differences, individual versus group goals, competition, paternalism, training, and patience.

DISCUSSION AND REVIEW QUESTIONS

1. When and under what conditions should a person consider using participative leadership?
2. Does the Vroom-Yetton approach to leadership suggest that leaders can or cannot be trained to improve their effectiveness?
3. What role is the leader expected to play in the path-goal leadership theory?
4. Why is the diagnostic skill of the leader so vital to the situational approach to leadership?
5. Why should leaders be aware of their impact on followers?
6. Explain how the three situational dimensions discussed by Fiedler can be modified in an organization.
7. Which of your personal traits probably influence or will influence the style of leadership you usually use?
8. What other factors not included in Figure 12–6 are important in achievement of leadership effectiveness?
9. What advice would you give to American executives who are considering the possibility of going to work for Japanese subsidiaries in the United States?
10. Why should Japanese leadership techniques not be accepted carte blanche in the United States or Canada?

ADDITIONAL REFERENCES

Bass, B. M. "Leadership: Good, Better, Best." *Organizational Dynamics,* Winter 1985, pp. 26–40.

Bennis, W., and B. Nanus. *Leaders' Strategies for Taking Charge.* New York: Harper & Row, 1985.

Boyatzis, R. E. *The Competent Manager: A Model for Effective Performance.* New York: John Wiley & Sons, 1982.

Hatakeyama, Y. "The Unsung Hero of Japanese Management: The Middle Manager." *Management Review,* July 1982, p. 33.

Jago, A. G., and V. H. Vroom. "Sex Differences in the Incidence and Evaluation of Participative Leader Behavior." *Journal of Applied Psychology,* December 1982, pp. 776–83.

Maccoby, M. *The Leader.* New York: Simon & Schuster, 1981.

McClelland, D. C., and R. E. Boyatzis. "Leadership Motive Pattern and Long-Term Success in Management." *Journal of Applied Psychology,* December 1982, pp. 737–43.

Miller, S. S. "Make Your Plant Manager's Job Manageable." *Harvard Business Review,* January–February 1983, pp. 69–74.

Rehder, R. R.; R. W. Hendry; and M. M. Smith. "Nummi: The Best of Both Worlds?" *Management Review,* December 1985, pp. 36–41.

Thompson, P. H.; K. L. Kirkham; and J. Dixon. "Warning: The Fast Track May Be Hazardous to Organizational Health." *Organizational Dynamics,* Spring 1985, pp. 21–33.

Yukl, G. M. *Leadership in Organizations.* Englewood Cliffs, N.J.: Prentice-Hall, 1981.

CASES

APPLICATION I

A LEADERSHIP TEAM AT MENNEN COMPANY: WILL IT WORK?

Mennen Company is a privately held toiletries manufacturer attempting to make the transition from management by family owners to management by outsiders—professionals. Mennen, for the first time in its 103-year history, now is being led by a chairman and chief executive officer, L. Donald Horne, and a president, Harold Danenberg, who have no blood ties to the Mennen family.

The company has been plagued in the past by conflict between the family and top-level professional managers. Three chief operating officers quit or were fired during a recent eight-year period. Pointing up the sensitivity of what is happening at Mennen, Horne and Danenberg have embarked on an aggressive, growth-oriented strategy that appears to clash with the cautious, take-few-risks management style established under three generations of Mennen chief executive officers. There is another complication to the Horne and Danenberg aggressive-team approach in the presence of G. Jeff Mennen, 41, who has held the job of vice chairman since his father retired.

Based in Morristown, New Jersey, the company was one of the nation's pioneer marketers of consumer packaged goods. It helped break down American male inhibitions about using sweet-smelling aftershave lotions and colognes, and it was the first to sell shaving cream in a tube and talcum in sifter cans. But despite these feats, it was never in the league of Procter & Gamble, Johnson & Johnson, or Colgate-Palmolive. Mennen's profit margins consistently have lagged behind its competitors'. Mennen was satisfied with making a comfortable living and not dominating any market. Family-run companies often have this kind of philosophy of management and success.

In addition to a shortage of new products and a sluggish growth record, Mennen consistently has had sour relations with retailers. Operating inefficiencies, poor promotional efforts, and little shelf display creativity or enthusiasm by Mennen have helped create this situation.

The Horne and Danenberg team has moved in with new products (Hawk and Millionaire men's fragrances), increased the advertising budget by $20 million annually and introduced jazzier store displays. They also have weeded out some marginal products such as Balm Barr, a women's cocoa-based skin product.

The Horne and Danenberg style of leading Mennen can be described as aggressive, risk taking, and fast moving. These characteristics are much different than the conservative, slow, limited-growth orientation previously used by Mennen's.

Questions for Analysis

1. The Horne and Danenberg leadership style is described as being loved by some and totally hated by others at Mennen—there is no middle ground. In your opinion, why is this the case?
2. Using the Ohio State leadership terminology, how would you describe the Mennen leadership approach prior to the arrival of Horne and Danenberg?

APPLICATION II

THE TROUBLED HOSPITAL SUPERINTENDENT

Tyler Medical Center consisted of four buildings, had 475 patient beds, and employed 1,850 people. It was known in Illinois as a quality medical institution and a good place for medical researchers and interns to work. The Board of Trustees of the hospital relied heavily on the judgment of the superintendent of the hospital, Don Gloversmen, regarding hospital administration.

Tyler was organized around six functionally defined areas. Each area had a head who reported to Don. The areas were:

1. Medical Services.
2. Nursing Services.
3. Accounting Services.
4. Dietary Services.
5. Plant and Housekeeping Services.
6. Pharmaceutical Services.

Don, as superintendent, was the only person in the hospital who had legitimate power to make decisions concerning administrative matters. He had to handle complaints and requests from administrators in each of the areas. Two that were extremely difficult to work with were Medical Services and Nursing Services.

Don analyzed each of the personnel components of these units:

Medical Services: Medical doctors and laboratory technicians. Included are such individuals as physician in charge of neurology, physician in charge of pediatrics, director of surgery, director of clinical laboratories, and director of anesthesiology. The medical doctors are largely male, while the technicians are split about evenly between male and female.

Nursing Services: Primarily females in charge of providing nursing care at bedside and staffing operating rooms, delivery rooms, and nurseries. The nursing group and staff include approximately 975 employees.

Don communicated in most instances with the administrators in these two service areas. He found that his leadership style of being frank, open, and direct worked better with the Medical Services heads than with the Nursing Service heads. He wanted to be the best superintendent the hospital ever had but found that his approach of being the same kind of leader for all the people he worked with was not effective.

Don reached the conclusion that he was not effective in his relationship with the nursing administrators. They seemed to be hostile toward him and the other functional areas, especially the Medical Service area. In addition, a number of patients had complained about rudeness by the nurses. The strain in his relationship with Nursing Services always seemed to peak at the monthly meeting of nursing administrators.

Each month, the 42 nursing supervisors met with Don. In these sessions, he attempted to ascertain how the nursing area was performing. The nursing administrators complained that no standards for assessing performance were used to determine effectiveness. They also complained that they were being watched closely, while Medical Services never had discussions with the superintendent about performance.

After last month's disruptive and volatile meeting, Don decided to look at the problem. He assumed that there might be a serious flaw in his leadership ability. He also thought about what he had read about the situational approach to leadership.

Questions for Analysis

1. What are some of the causes of Don's problem with the nursing administrators?

2. As a superintendent in Tyler Medical Center, would it be necessary to consider situational leadership theories? Why?

3. What kind of modification in the three situational dimensions—leader-member relations, task structure, and position power—could aid Don in improving his relationship with Nursing Services?

EXPERIENTIAL EXERCISE

LEADERSHIP SKILLS: SETTING THE TONE FOR PROBLEM SOLVING

Purpose

The purpose of this exercise is to demonstrate an effective approach to problem solving and to indicate the attitudes and skills required of a leader.

The Exercise in Class

An assembly-line scenario will be acted out by students. The assembly job is an arrangement in which a crew of seven, working in a circle, assembles an electronic generator in a manufacturing plant. Each person does a particular job and sends the unit to the next person, and so forth. There are eight such assembly circles, each one with a supervisor. The average production per day of the circles is as follows:

1.	83	5.	80
2.	78	6.	76
3.	64	7.	60
4.	78	8.	70

The total department production is dependent on the output of the eight assembly circles. The desired total output for the eight circles is 675 units.

The assembly line is simple and requires little formal training. The crew members must be alert, have good finger dexterity and eyesight, and be in good physical condition to keep up with the pace. The materials for each crew member are located in bins right next to the workstation. The stations (1–7) are of equal difficulty, and pay for all crew members is based on hourly rates.

Exhibit 1 illustrates the assembly work area. The assembly-line members work for the leader and report directly to him or her. There seems to be a bottleneck at Station 3 of Circle 3. The crew member there is 59 years old

EXHIBIT   1   Assembly Work Area: Circle 3

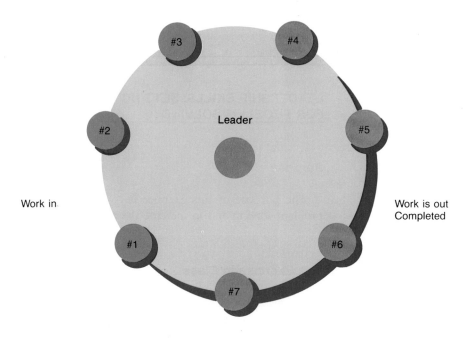

with 33 years of service. The emphasis on improvement of output has pointed out his/her deficiencies.

1. Eight students are needed to play the roles: one supervisor and seven crew members. Role players can be male or female in any combination. Students not participating as role players will serve as observers. Teams of three to four observers should be established as consulting teams. The assembly line should be recreated as closely as possible to the circular arrangement in Exhibit 1.
2. The class should individually read the instructions.
3. The role players should be given their role-play instructions (instructor will have them) and individually read them carefully. Only their roles should be given to them.
4. Observers should read the instructions for observers. The observer-consultants will be asked to come up with a feasible solution.
5. The *crew members,* after reading and learning the role sheets, discuss in front of the class and with the supervisor a solution to the production problem.
6. Observers should watch and listen to the role-play, which should cover

about 20 to 25 minutes. The instructor will stop the role-play at a natural stopping point.

7. After the role-play, the observers/consultants and crew and supervisor discuss solutions.

8. The observers should answer questions on the instruction sheets that were issued to them.

The Learning Message

Notice how the supervisor's style and interactions in the first few minutes will determine the quality of the solution. The leader will set the tone and direction for the exercise.

COMMUNICATION

LEARNING OBJECTIVES

After completing Chapter 13, you should be able to:

■ **Define**
each element in the process of communication.

■ **Describe**
communication in organizations.

■ **Discuss**
interpersonal communications and interpersonal communication styles.

■ **Compare**
the situations in which an informal and a formal channel of communication would be utilized.

■ **Identify**
the major reasons why communications break down.

☐ MANAGEMENT IN ACTION

Communication Clarity: A Managerial Challenge*

An important key to success in the tasks of a project team, quality circle, executive committee, or department in an organization is informed participation. If individuals are to pull together, they must understand their mutual goals and have a solid sense of how their efforts toward achievement relate to those of others. Thus, the responsibility of keeping oneself and others informed is a basic part of any manager's job.

The difficulty of fulfilling this responsibility cannot be underestimated. Even in a conversation between two people, misunderstandings arise if either fails to listen clearly or makes too poor an effort to understand the other person's point of view.

Ensuring that communications are understood, especially in a sizable organization, can be a challenge. It is important for managers and leaders to find a way. A possibly apocryphal story about General Robert E. Lee concerns a Colonel Smith who served on the Confederate Army head-quarters staff. By all accounts, Smith was not distinguished by his bril-liance, and some wondered why General Lee tolerated him. One day, a new brigadier asked the general how Colonel Smith managed to keep his position. General Lee replied that despite Smith's limitations, he per-formed a vital service. If Smith could understand an order, he reasoned, then everyone down to the lowest private could understand it too.

In most companies, it is not too difficult to communicate the top execu-tive's view throughout the system. However, it is quite another thing to get reliable and honest feedback from the bottom to the top. Numerous techniques—attitude surveys, grapevines, and suggestion systems—exist to help improve upward communication. Yet formal programs, while valu-able, cannot substitute for person-to-person communication.

An important aspect of effective person-to-person communication is trust. If employees feel that everyone's opinion is valued, they will commu-nicate upward often, reliably, and with conviction.

Good organizational communication doesn't simply happen; knowl-edgeable managers work at making it happen. This chapter will discuss some of the obstacles to open upward, downward, lateral, and diagonal communication. Understanding such obstacles is a first step in overcom-ing and minimizing many communication problems.

---

* Source: Adapted from Thomas R. Horton, "Unblocking the Channels of Communication," *Management Review,* December 1985, p. 3.

Managing people effectively requires an understanding of several behavioral factors. Understanding of communication is surely one of them. Managers rarely work with "things" but rather with "information about things"; so communication pervades the management functions of planning, organizing, and controlling.

But what is communication? How can we communicate with each other? And how do we know when we have? "Telling isn't teaching, and listening isn't learning." This old adage known to instructors expresses in a few words the essence of poor and ineffective communication. In the context of our discussion, it can be restated as: "Writing isn't communicating, and reading isn't understanding." Why not? There are many reasons for ineffective communication. The one cited most often is that we tend to think in too-simple terms about this very complicated process. To communicate something to someone involves the emotional, psychological, and mental characteristics of both persons, as well as the technical characteristics of the medium used to communicate. The understanding that the teller intended to impart may be far different from what was actually imparted to the listener. Effective communication is so important for the effective management of people that we hope that our discussion of what it is and how it is achieved "communicates" its complexity fully.

THE IMPORTANCE OF COMMUNICATION

The following statements, or ones very similar, are heard on a regular basis in most organizations: "The purchase order has not been sent because you never said it was a rush request." "I really never thought she was serious about resigning." "When the president says as soon as possible, he means now." In these and similar situations, we often hear, "What we have here is a failure to communicate." That statement communicates clearly to everyone, because all of us have faced situations in which the problem was poor communication. Whether it be on a person-to-person basis, nation to nation, in large organizations, or in small groups, breakdowns in communication seem to be pervasive.

It is difficult to find an aspect of a manager's job that does not depend on communication. Problems arise when directives are misunderstood, rumors spread, informal remarks by an executive are misinterpreted or distorted, or when casual kidding in a work group leads to anger. Thus, the real issue is not whether managers communicate but whether they do it effectively or ineffectively. Everything a manager does or (in many cases) doesn't do communicates something to some person or group. The only question is, "With what effect?"

FIGURE   13–1   Critical Elements in the Process of Communication

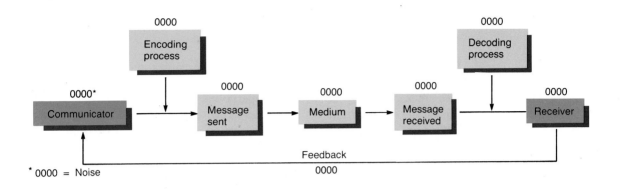

* 0000 = Noise

The communication process can be summarized as who (communicator) says what (message) in what way (medium) to whom (receiver) with what effect (feedback).

UNDERSTANDING THE PROCESS OF COMMUNICATION

Communication is *the transmission of common understanding through the use of symbols.* The term *communication* is derived from the Latin *communis,* meaning "common." In other words, unless a common understanding results from the transmission of symbols (verbal or nonverbal), there is no communication.

Figure 13–1 presents our definition and the key elements of communication.[1] It identifies the basic elements of communication as *communicator, encoding, message, medium, decoding, receiver, feedback,* and *noise.* In simple terms, an individual or group (the communicator) has an idea, message, or understanding to transmit to another individual or group (the receiver). To transmit the idea, the communicator must translate the idea into a meaningful form (encoding) and send the message by verbal, nonverbal, or written means (the medium). The message is received through the senses of the receiver and translated into a form meaningful to the receiver (decoded).

---

[1] The most widely used contemporary model of the process of communication has evolved mainly from the work of Shannon and Weaver, and Schramm. See Claude Shannon and Warren Weaver, *The Mathematical Theory of Communication* (Urbana: University of Illinois Press, 1948); Wilbur Schramm, "How Communication Works," in *The Process and Effects of Mass Communication,* ed. Wilbur Schramm (Urbana: University of Illinois Press, 1953), pp. 3–76.

With a nod of the head, a facial expression, or some action, the receiver acknowledges whether understanding has been achieved (feedback). The intended message can be distorted by the presence of distractions in each element (noise).

Let us examine each element more closely in an organizational setting.

The communicator.   Communicators in an organization can be managers, nonmanagers, departments, or the organization itself. Managers communicate with other managers, subordinates, supervisors, clients, customers, and parties outside the organization. Nonmanagers likewise communicate with managers and nonmanagers, clients, customers, and external parties. People in sales departments communicate with people in production departments, and engineering personnel communicate with product design teams. Communications within the organization are important means for coordinating the work of separate departments. And more and more organizations communicate with employees, unions, the public, and government. Each of these communicators has a message, an idea, or information to transmit to someone or some group.

Encoding process.   With the communicator, an encoding process must take place that translates the communicator's ideas into a systematic set of symbols expressing the communicator's purpose. The major form of encoding is language. For example, accounting information, sales reports, and computer data are translated into a message. The function of encoding then is to provide a form in which ideas and purposes can be expressed as a message.

The message.   The result of the encoding process is the message—either verbal or nonverbal. Managers have numerous purposes for communicating, such as to have others understand their ideas, to understand the ideas of others, to gain acceptance of themselves or their ideas, and to produce action. The message, then, is what the individual hopes to communicate, and the exact form that the message takes depends to a great extent on the medium used to carry it. Decisions relating to the two are inseparable.[2]

The medium.   The medium is the carrier of the message. Organizations provide information to their members by a variety of means, including face-to-face communication, telephone, group meetings, computers, memos, policy statements, reward systems, production schedules, and sales forecasts. Video-

---

[2] D. A. Level, "Communication Effectiveness: Method and Situation," *Journal of Business Communication,* Fall 1972, pp. 19–25; T. R. Mitchell, *People in Organizations: Understanding Their Behavior* (New York: McGraw-Hill, 1978), p. 214.

tapes are a message carrier being used more frequently, as the Management Focus indicates.

MANAGEMENT FOCUS
Smile, You're on Videotape

General Motors Acceptance Corporation (GMAC) has implemented a new way for managers and subordinates to communicate with each other: the GMAC Video Network. This is a program that combines television techniques with audio messages. The first videotape, a message from GMAC president Bob Murphy describing the results of a recent survey of GM dealers' opinions of GMAC, was presented to company employees via video tape recordings and monitors.

Developing the videotapes is expensive (the cost of producing audiovisual programming exceeds the expense of distributing comparable printed material), but GMAC believes that the method can provide many benefits. Studies have shown that audiovisual presentations are more effective than print in conveying information. This was confirmed in a recent survey by the management consulting firm of Towers, Perrin, Forster, and Crosby, which showed that both management and labor found audiovisual presentations to be more enjoyable, dramatic, and interesting.

The major challenge with videotape technology is keeping the message timely. If a videotape is not timely, the message is viewed as not being credible. Thus, a manager using videotapes to explain a job change, a new compensation system, or how to conduct a performance appraisal feedback interview must be up-to-date in order to be viewed as credible.

The early results indicate that GMAC employees believe that they are more informed and in closer touch with management. Such enthusiastic employee response to the program will result in additional videotapes. The plan is to produce tapes on a regular basis—several a month. Cost-benefit comparisons point to developing more and more videotapes.

Source: Adapted from "Video Communiques," *Management Review,* May 1985, p. 9.

Less obvious, however, are *unintended* messages that can be sent by silence or inaction on a particular issue, as well as decisions about which goals and objectives are *not* to be pursued and which methods are *not* to be utilized.

Finally, such nonverbal media as facial expressions, tone of voice, and body movements also communicate.[3]

Decoding process.   For the process of communication to be completed, the message must be decoded in terms relevant to the receiver. Decoding is a technical term for the thought processes of the receiver. Thus, it involves interpretation. Receivers interpret (decode) the message in light of their own previous experience and frames of reference. The closer the decoded message is to the intent desired by the communicator, the more effective is the communication. In a business organization, if the message that the chief executive receives from the marketing research department includes technical terms that are known only to marketing researchers, no communication exists. In fact, an often-cited complaint in organizations that employ staff specialists is that they frequently cannot communicate. Each staff group (for example, accountants, personnel and marketing research) has a unique language and symbols that persons outside the group cannot decode.

The receiver.   Whether there is sound when a tree falls in a deserted forest is a philosophic problem. But whether communication occurs without a receiver is not a philosophic problem. By definition, communication requires a communicator and a receiver. The foregoing discussion of decoding difficulties underlines the importance of taking the receiver into account when a communicator attempts to transmit information. "Telling isn't teaching" if the teacher uses language that the student cannot understand (cannot decode). Engineers cannot expect to communicate to nonengineers if the symbols they use are beyond the receivers' training and ability to comprehend. Effective communication requires the communicator to anticipate the receiver's decoding ability, to know where the receiver "comes from." Effective communication is receiver oriented, not media oriented.

Feedback.   *One-way* communication processes do not allow receiver-to-communicator feedback. *Two-way* communication processes provide for such feedback.[4] It is desirable to make provision for feedback in the communication process.[5] It decreases the potential for distortion between the intended message and the received message. A feedback loop provides a channel for receiver response, enabling the communicator to determine whether the message has

---

[3] A. Mehrabian, *Nonverbal Communication* (Hawthorne, N.Y.: Aldine Publishing, 1972).

[4] The classic experiment comparing one-way and two-way communication is described in Harold J. Leavitt and R. A. H. Mueller, "Some Effects of Feedback on Communications," *Human Relations,* 1951, pp. 401–10. Also see Harold J. Leavitt, *Managerial Psychology* (Chicago: University of Chicago Press, 1978).

[5] See P. H. Lewis, Organizational Communications: The Essence of Effective Management (Columbus, Ohio: Grid, 1975), p. 95; D. M. Herold and M. M. Greller, "Feedback: The Definition of a Construct," *Academy of Management Journal,* March 1977, pp. 142–47.

been received and has produced the intended response. For the manager, communication feedback may come in many ways. In face-to-face situations, *direct* feedback is possible through verbal exchanges as well as through such subtle means as facial expressions that indicate discontent or misunderstanding. In addition, communication breakdowns may be indicated by *indirect* means, such as declines in productivity, poor quality of production, increased absenteeism or turnover, and conflict or a lack of coordination between units.

Noise.   In the framework of communications, noise is a factor that, if present, can distort the intended message. Noise can be present in any element (as noted in Figure 13–1). Later in this chapter, a number of sources of noise are identified, including differing frames of reference, stereotyping, and semantics.

COMMUNICATION IN ORGANIZATIONS

The design of an organization should provide for communication in four distinct directions: downward, upward, horizontal, and diagonal.[6] These four directions establish the framework within which communication takes place in an organization. Examining each of them will enable the manager to better appreciate the barriers to effective organizational communication and the means for overcoming those barriers.

Downward Communication

Downward communication flows from individuals at higher levels of the hierarchy to those at lower levels. The most common mediums for such communications are job instructions, official memos, policy statements, procedures, manuals, and company publications. Researchers have identified the five most common types of downward organizational communication as job instructions, job rationale, organization policy, procedures and practices, employee performance feedback, and indoctrination of company goals.[7]

In many organizations, downward communication often is both inadequate and inaccurate, as reflected in the often-heard statement among organization members that "we have absolutely no idea what's happening." Such complaints are indicative of inadequate downward communication—and the need individuals have for information relevant to their jobs. The absence of job-

---

[6] Also see S. B. Bacharach and M. Aiken, "Communication in Administrative Bureaucracies," *Academy of Management Journal,* March 1977, pp. 365–77.

[7] F. M. Jablin, "Superior-Subordinate Communication: The State of the Art," *Psychological Bulletin,* November 1979, pp. 1201–22.

related information can create unnecessary stress among organization members.[8]

Philips Industries, a British firm, communicates downward with members of its seven unions for reasons other than negotiating a contract. In the late 1970s, Philips initiated annual conferences of management and labor. The principal purpose of the conferences is to allow the firm to give a "state of the company" report to the union leadership, focusing on the broad economic problems facing Philips. The communication of ideas and views between the management and union officials is carried on without reference to salaries and contracts. The proceedings of the conference are videotaped and made available to all personnel in the 25 Philips plants in the United Kingdom.

In large organizations, communicating with employees is typically undertaken by a trained staff of communication experts. The usual function of the staff is to produce a publication aimed at these three purposes: (1) to explain the organization's plans and programs as they are implemented; (2) to answer complaints and criticisms; and (3) to defend the status quo and those who are responsible for it. The medium often selected to accomplish these purposes is a periodic publication, the "house organ." The publication's intended messages are those that present the organization's side of issues. Large organizations are viewed more and more with distrust and suspicion. Although they may not always be successful in convincing the general public that their actions are public minded, it has become increasingly necessary for them to win the support of their employees.

Upward Communication

A high-performing organization needs effective upward communication as much as it needs effective downward communication. Effective upward communication is difficult to achieve, especially in larger organizations. However, it often is necessary for sound decision making. Widely used upward communication devices include suggestion boxes, group meetings, reports to supervisors, and appeal or grievance procedures. In the absence of these flows, employees find ways to adapt to nonexistent or inadequate upward communication channels. Consider the emergence of "underground" employee publications in many large organizations.

The practices of ESCO Corporation of Portland, Oregon, reveal the company's commitment to upward communications. Employees in this company who wish to communicate directly with top management—whether to express complaints, suggestions, questions, compliments, or comments—simply dial

---

[8] John M. Ivancevich and James H. Donnelly, Jr., "A Study of Role Clarity and Need for Clarity in Three Occupational Groups," *Academy of Management Journal,* March 1974, pp. 28–36.

a listed telephone number and state their views. The calls are recorded, transcribed, and reviewed by ESCO's vice president of industrial relations in charge of personnel. The vice president forwards the transcriptions to the appropriate department managers for reply and action. If callers give their names, they receive a written answer; if they choose to be anonymous, the answers are posted on the bulletin board. No call is unanswered, and each call is answered within 48 hours.

Effective upward communications are important because they provide employees with opportunities to have a say. They are equally important because top management depends on subordinates for vital information. An example is the dependence of generals on lieutenants and sergeants for tactical information. The outcomes of battles and maneuvers are reported upward. History is replete with instances in which upward communications became distorted and the consequences of such distortions.

Horizontal Communication

Often overlooked in the design of most organizations is provision for the horizontal flow of communication. When the supervisor of the accounting department communicates with the director of marketing concerning advertising budget expenditures, the flow of communication is horizontal. Although vertical (upward and downward) communication flows are the primary considerations in organizational design, effective organizations also need horizontal communication. Horizontal communication—for example, between production and sales in a business organization and between different departments within a hospital—is necessary for the coordination of diverse organizational functions.

Diagonal Communication

Although diagonal communication probably is the least used channel of communication in organizations, it is important in situations in which members cannot communicate effectively through other channels. For example, the comptroller of a large organization may wish to conduct a distribution-cost analysis, and one part of the analysis may involve having the sales force send a special report directly to the comptroller rather than through the traditional channels in the marketing department. Thus, the flow of communication would be diagonal rather than upward and then horizontal. In this case, the use of a diagonal channel would minimize the time and effort expended by the organization.

Figure 13–2 illustrates the four directions in which organizational communication flows. While these are the major communication flows, many others can and do exist.

FIGURE   13–2   Communication in Organizations

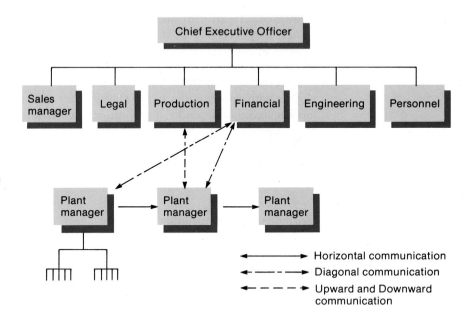

Communication in organizations flows in four distinct directions and must be provided for in the design of the organization.

INTERPERSONAL COMMUNICATIONS

Communication flows from individual to individual in face-to-face and group settings. Such flows, called "interpersonal communications," vary in form from direct orders to casual expressions. The primary manner in which managers relate to and learn from people in their environment is through interpersonal communication—information the managers receive and transmit. And the way in which managers receive and transmit information depends in part on how they relate to two very important *senders* of information, themselves and others.

Regions of Information

Information is held by oneself and by others, but each of us does not fully have or know that information. The different combinations of knowing and not knowing relevant information are shown in Figure 13–3. The figure

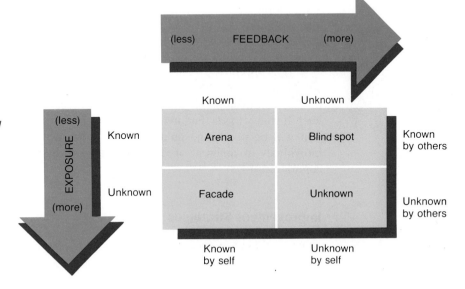

FIGURE   13–3   Regions of Information Influencing Communication

The four regions of information known and not known by the self and others.

identifies four combinations, or regions, of information known and unknown by the self and others.[9]

1. *The arena.*   The region most conducive for effective interpersonal relationships and communication is termed the *arena*. In this setting, all the information necessary to carry on effective communication is known to both the communicator (self) and the receivers (others). For a communication attempt to be in the arena region, the parties involved must share identical feelings, data, assumptions, and skills. The arena is the area of common understanding.

2. *The blind spot.*   When relevant information is known to others but not to the self, a *blind spot* area results. In this context, one is at a disadvantage when communicating with others, because one cannot know their feelings, sentiments, and perceptions. Consequently interpersonal relationships and communications suffer. The blind spot presents an interpersonal handicap for the self, since one hardly can understand the behaviors, decisions, or potentials of others without having data on which these are based. Others

---

[9] The discussion in this section is based on J. Hall, "Communication Revisited," *California Management Review,* Fall 1973, pp. 56–67.

have the advantage of knowing their own feelings, while the self is unaware of these.

3. *The facade.*   When information is known to the self but unknown to others, a person (self) may resort to superficial communications; that is, present a "false front," or *facade.* This situation is particularly damaging when a subordinate "knows" and an immediate supervisor "does not know." The facade, like the blind spot, diminishes the arena and reduces the possibility of effective communication.

4. *The unknown.*   This region, the *unknown,* constitutes that portion where the relevant information is not known by the self or by other parties to the relationship: "I don't understand them, and they don't understand me." It is easy to see that under such circumstances, interpersonal communication will be poor. The unknown area often occurs in organizations when individuals in different specialties must coordinate what they do through communications.

Improvement Strategies

Figure 13–3 indicates that an individual can improve interpersonal communications by utilizing two strategies, exposure and feedback:

1. *Exposure.*   Increasing the arena area by reducing the facade area requires that the individual be open and honest in sharing information with others. The process that the self uses to increase the information known to others is termed *exposure,* because it leaves the self in a sometimes vulnerable position. Exposing one's true feelings over "telling it like it is," often will involve risks.

2. *Feedback.*   When the self does not know or understand, more effective communications can be developed through feedback from those who do know. Thus, the blind spot can be reduced with a corresponding increase in the arena. Of course, whether the use of feedback is possible depends on the individual's willingness to "hear" it, and on the willingness of others to give it. Thus, the individual is less able to control the provision of feedback than the provision of exposure. Obtaining feedback is dependent on the active cooperation of others, while exposure requires the active behavior of the individual and listening of others.

Management Styles

Interpersonal style refers to *the way in which an individual prefers to relate to others.* The fact that much of the relationships among people involve communication indicates the importance of interpersonal style.

The day-to-day activities of managers place a high value on effective interpersonal communications. Managers provide *information* (which must be *understood*); they give *commands* and *instructions* (which must be *obeyed* and *learned*); and they make *efforts to influence* and *persuade* (which must be *accepted* and *acted upon*). Thus, the way in which managers communicate, both as senders and receivers, is crucial for obtaining effective performance.

Theoretically managers who desire to communicate effectively can use both exposure and feedback to enlarge the area of common understanding, the arena. As a practical matter, such is not the case. Managers differ in their ability and willingness to use exposure and feedback. At least four different managerial styles can be identified:

Type A: Managers who use neither exposure nor feedback are said to have a Type A style. The unknown region predominates in this style because the manager is unwilling to enlarge the area of his or her own knowledge or the knowledge of others. Such managers exhibit anxiety and hostility and give the appearance of aloofness and coldness toward others. If an organization has a large number of Type A managers in key positions, then we would expect to find poor and ineffective interpersonal communications and a loss of individual creativity. Type A managers often display the characteristics of autocratic leaders.

Type B: Some managers desire a degree of satisfying relationships with their subordinates; but because of their personalities and attitudes, these managers are unable to open up and express their feelings and sentiments. Consequently they cannot use exposure and they must rely on feedback. The facade is the predominant feature of interpersonal relationships when managers overuse feedback to the exclusion of exposure. The subordinates likely will distrust such managers, because they realize that these managers are holding back their own ideas and opinions. Type B behavior often is displayed by managers who desire to practice some form of permissive leadership.

Type C: Managers who value their own ideas and opinions but not the ideas and opinions of others will use exposure at the expense of feedback. The consequence of this style is the perpetuation and enlargement of the blind spot. Subordinates soon will realize that such managers are not particularly interested in communicating, only in telling. Consequently Type C managers usually have subordinates who are hostile, insecure, and resentful. Subordinates soon learn that such managers are mainly interested in maintaining their own sense of importance and prestige.

Type D: The most effective interpersonal communication style is one which uses a balance of exposure and feedback. Managers who are secure in their positions will feel free to expose their own feelings and to obtain feedback from others. To the extent that the manager practices Type D behavior successfully, the arena becomes larger, and communication becomes more effective.

To summarize our discussion, we should emphasize the importance of interpersonal styles in determining the effectiveness of interpersonal communication. The primary force in determining the effectiveness of interpersonal communication is the attitude of managers toward exposure and feedback.

The most effective approach is that of the Type D manager. Type A, B, and C managers resort to behaviors detrimental to the effectiveness of communication and to organizational performance.

WHY COMMUNICATIONS BREAK DOWN

Why do communications break down? On the surface, the answer is relatively easy. We have identified the elements of communication as the communicator, encoding, the message, the medium, decoding, the receiver, and feedback. If noise exists in these elements *in any way,* clarity of meaning and understanding will be impaired. A manager has no greater responsibility than to develop effective communications. In this section, we shall discuss some barriers to effective communication: differing frames of reference, selective perception, value judgments, source credibility, semantic problems, filtering, time pressures, and overload. These sources of noise can exist in both organizational and interpersonal communications.

Differing Frames of Reference

Individuals can interpret the same communication differently, depending on their previous experience. The result is variations between the *encoding* and *decoding* processes. When the processes are alike, communication is most effective. When they are different, communication tends to break down. In terms of interpersonal communication, the arena is relatively small when compared to blind spots, facades, and unknown areas. To the extent that individuals have distinctly different frames of reference, effective communication among those individuals will be difficult to achieve.[10]

One result of different frames of reference is that communications become distorted. For example, teenagers have different experiences than do their parents (the oft-cited generation gap?); district sales managers have different perceptions than do salespersons. In an organization, the *jobs* that people perform will create barriers and distortions in communications. For example, a pricing problem will be viewed differently by the marketing manager and by the plant manager. An efficiency problem in a hospital will be viewed by the nursing staff from its frame of reference and its experiences; this may result in interpretations that differ from those of the staff physicians.

Different *levels* in the organization also will have different frames of reference. First-line supervisors have frames of reference that differ in many respects from those of vice presidents, because they are in different positions

---

[10] For a related study, see J. D. Hatfield and R. C. Huseman, "Perceptual Congruence about Communication as Related to Satisfaction: Moderating Effects of Individual Characteristics," *Academy of Management Journal,* June 1982, pp. 349–58.

in the organization's structure. As a result, the needs, values, attitudes, and expectations of these two groups will differ, and this often will produce unintentional distortions of the communications between them. Neither group is wrong or right.

In any situation, individuals will choose that part of their own past experiences that relates to their current experiences and is helpful in forming conclusions and judgments. Unfortunately such incongruities in encoding and decoding result in barriers to effective communication.

Selective Perception

Each of us "catalogs" the world in our own way. *Selective perception* occurs when people block out new information, especially if it conflicts with what they believe. Thus, when people receive information, they are apt to hear only those parts that conform to or reaffirm their beliefs. Information that conflicts with preconceived notions either is not processed or is distorted to confirm our preconceptions.

For example, a notice may be sent to all operating departments that costs must be reduced if the organization is to earn a profit. Such a communication may not achieve its desired effect, because it conflicts with the "reality" of the receivers. Operating employees may ignore or be amused by the notice in light of the large salaries, travel allowances, and expense accounts of some managers. Whether these expenditures are justified is irrelevant; what is important is that such preconceptions result in breakdowns in communication.

Finally, selective perception results in *stereotyping.* When an individual has preconceived ideas about other people and refuses to discriminate between individual behaviors, that person is applying selective perception to his relationships with other people. Stereotyping is a barrier to communication, because those who stereotype others use selective perception in their communications and tend to hear only those things that confirm their stereotyped images. For example, some managers stereotype union stewards, some men stereotype successful females, and some women stereotype aggressive men.

Poor Listening Skills

Listening should consume about half of the time that a superior and subordinate spend together; it doesn't, because one or both persons fail to listen.[11] For example, a meeting between a boss and employee might go something like this: "Boss, I really have a problem finishing the report." "Is that so, Bob? Well, sit down a minute and let me hear about it." However, before

---

[11] William C. Hemstreet and Wayne M. Baty, *Business Communications* (Boston: Kent Publishing, 1984), p. 308.

Bob can even start his story, the boss begins to cite his current problem. "I've got to do something about the production unit. It is producing at 15 percent below standard rate. I am really on the carpet with the chief." As the boss finishes, he says: "Sorry Bob, I've got a meeting to attend, so come on back tomorrow and we can get to your problem." Bob leaves completely frustrated, his problem still on his mind and no one to talk to about a solution.

The boss simply failed to listen. He heard what Bob said, but he really wasn't listening. Failing to listen may result from a host of personal habits. We speak at rates of 100 to 200 words a minute, read at two or three times our speaking rate, and think several times faster than we read. As a result, a listener can move through a discussion much faster than can a speaker. Because of the speed involved, we typically develop poor listening habits. Bad listening habits are of particular interest in work settings. For example, if either a manager or a subordinate fails to listen to the other, the objectives of the discussion, feedback session, or job instruction will not be accomplished.

Value Judgments

In every communication situation, receivers make value judgments by assigning an overall worth to a message prior to receiving the entire communication. Such value judgments may be based on the receiver's evaluation of the communicator, the receiver's previous experiences with the communicator, or the message's anticipated meaning. Thus, a hospital administrator may pay little attention to a memorandum from a nursing-team leader because "she's always complaining about something." An employee may consider a merit-evaluation meeting with the supervisor as "going through the motions," because the employee perceives the supervisor as being concerned about administrative matters to the exclusion of performance.

Source Credibility

Source credibility refers to the trust, confidence, and faith that the receiver has in the words and actions of the communicator. The level of credibility that the receiver assigns to the communicator directly affects how the receiver views and reacts to the words, ideas, and actions of the communicator.

Thus, how subordinates view a communication from their manager is affected by their evaluations of the manager. The degree of credibility they attach to the communication is heavily influenced by their previous experiences with the manager. A group of hospital medical staff who view the hospital administrator as less than honest, manipulative, and not to be trusted are apt to assign nonexistent motives to any communication from the administrator. Union leaders who view managers as exploiters, and managers who view union leaders as inherent enemies are likely to engage in little real communication.

Semantic Problems

Communication is the transmission of information and understanding through the use of common symbols. Actually, we cannot transmit understanding. We can only transmit information in the form of words, which are the common symbols. Unfortunately the same words may mean entirely different things to different people. The understanding is in the receiver, not in the words.

When a plant manager announces that a "budget increase" is necessary for the growth of the plant, the manager may have in mind the necessity for new equipment, an expanded parts inventory, and more personnel. To the existing personnel, however, growth may be perceived as excess funds that can be used for wage and salary increases.

Again, because different groups use words differently, communication often can be impeded. This is especially true with abstract or technical terms and phrases. A "cost-benefit study" would have meaning to persons involved in the administration of the hospital but probably would mean very little to the staff physicians; in fact, it might even carry a negative meaning to the latter. Such concepts as trusts, profits, and Treasury bills may have concrete meaning to bank executives but little or no meaning to bank tellers. Because words mean different things to different people, it is possible for a communicator to speak the same language as a receiver but still not transmit understanding.

Occupational, professional, and social groups often develop words and phrases that have meaning only to group members. Such special language can serve many useful purposes. It can provide group members with feelings of belonging, cohesiveness, and (in many cases) self-esteem. It also can facilitate effective communication *within* the group. The use of in-group language can, however, result in severe semantic problems and communication breakdowns when outsiders or other groups are involved. Technical and staff groups often use such language in an organization, not for the purpose of transmitting information and understanding but rather in order to communicate a "mystique" about the group or its function.

Filtering

Filtering is a common occurrence in upward communication in organizations. It amounts to "manipulating" information so that the information is perceived as positive by the receiver. Subordinates "cover up" unfavorable information in messages to their superiors. The reason for such filtering should be clear. Upward communication carries control information to management. Management makes merit evaluations, grants salary increases, and promotes individuals based on what it receives by way of the upward channel. The temptation to filter is likely to be strong at every level in the organization.

The shape of the organization determines the extent to which information can be filtered. An organizational design with many levels of management (a "tall" organization) will experience more information filtration than will one with fewer levels (a "flat" organization). The reason is fairly simple: the more levels through which upward communications must flow, the greater is the opportunity for each successive layer of management to take out what it does not want the next level to know. An advantage of flat organizational designs is that they minimize the problem of filtration.

Time Pressures

The pressure of time is an important barrier to communication. An obvious problem is that managers do not have the time to communicate frequently with every subordinate. However, time pressures can often lead to serious problems. *Short-circuiting* is a failure of the formally prescribed communications system that often results from time pressures. What it means simply is that someone who normally would be included has been left out of the formal channel of communication.

For example, suppose that a salesperson who needs a rush order for a very important customer goes directly to the production manager with the request, since the production manager owes the salesperson a favor. Other members of the sales force get word of this and become upset over this preferential treatment and report it to the sales manager. Obviously, the sales manager would know nothing of the deal, since the sales manager has been short-circuited.

In some cases, going through formal channels is extremely costly or impossible from a practical standpoint. Consider the impact on a hospital patient if a nurse had to report a malfunction in some critical life-support equipment in an intensive care unit to the nursing-team leader, who in turn had to report it to the hospital engineer, who then would instruct a staff engineer to make the repair.

Communication Overload

One of the vital tasks performed by a manager is decision making. One of the necessary ingredients for effective decisions is *information*. The last decade has been described as the Information Era, or the Age of Information.

Because of the advances in communication technology, difficulties may arise, not from the absence of information but from excessive information. Managers often are deluged by information and data. As a result, they cannot absorb or adequately respond to all of the messages directed to them. They "screen out" the majority of messages, which in effect means that these messages are never decoded. Thus, the area of organizational communication is one in which more is not always better.[12]

The barriers to communication discussed here, though common, are by no means the only ones that exist. Examining these barriers indicates that they are either *within individuals* (e.g., frame of reference, value judgments) or *within organizations* (e.g., in-group language filtering). This point is important because *attempts to improve communications must focus on changing people and/or changing the organization structure.*[13]

IMPROVING COMMUNICATION IN ORGANIZATIONS

Managers striving to become better communicators have two separate tasks. First, they must improve their messages—the information they wish to transmit. Second, they must improve their own understanding of what other people are trying to communicate to them. They must become better encoders and decoders; *they must strive not only to be understood but also to understand.* Techniques for improving communication are following up, regulating information flow, utilizing feedback, empathy, simplifying language, effective listening, and utilizing the grapevine.

Following Up

Following up involves assuming that you may have been misunderstood and, whenever possible, attempting to determine whether your intended meaning was actually received. As we have seen, meaning often is in the mind of the receiver. An accounting unit leader in a government office forwards notices of openings in other agencies to the accounting staff members. Although this may be understood among longtime employees as a friendly gesture, a new employee might interpret it as a negative evaluation of performance and a suggestion to leave.

---

[12] Charles A. O'Reilly III, "Individuals and Information Overload in Organizations: Is More Necessarily Better?" *Academy of Management Journal,* December 1980, pp. 684–96.

[13] See P. M. Muchinsky, "Organizational Communication: Relationships to Organizational Climate and Job Satisfaction," *Academy of Management Journal,* December 1977, pp. 592–607, for a recent study.

Regulating Information Flow

Regulating the flow of communications ensures an optimum flow of information to managers, thereby eliminating the barrier of "communication overload." Both the quality and quantity of communications are controlled. The idea is based on the *exception principle* of management, which states that only significant deviations from policies and procedures should be brought to the attention of managers. In terms of formal communication, then, managers should be communicated with only on matters of exceptions and not for the sake of communication.

Certain types of organizational designs are more amenable to this principle than are other types. Certainly, in neoclassical organization, with its emphasis on free-flowing communication, the principle would not apply. However, classical organizations would find the principle useful.

Utilizing Feedback

Feedback is an important element in effective two-way communication. It provides a channel for receiver response, enabling the communicator to determine whether the message has been received and has produced the intended response.

In face-to-face communication, direct feedback is possible. In downward communication, however, inaccuracies often occur because of insufficient opportunity for feedback from receivers. Thus, a memorandum addressing an important policy statement may be distributed to all employees, but this does not guarantee that communication has occurred. One might expect that

---

TABLE   13–1   Characteristics of Effective and Ineffective Feedback in Human Resource Management

Effective Feedback	Ineffective Feedback
1. Intended to help the employee	1. Intended to belittle the employee
2. Specific	2. General
3. Descriptive	3. Judgmental
4. Useful	4. Inappropriate
5. Timely	5. Untimely
6. Employee readiness for feedback	6. Makes the employee defensive
7. Clear	7. Not understandable
8. Valid	8. Inaccurate

Source: Fred Luthans and Mark J. Martinko, *The Practice of Supervision and Management* (New York: McGraw-Hill, 1979), p. 183.

feedback in the form of upward communication would be encouraged more in neoclassical organizations, but the mechanisms discussed earlier that can be utilized to encourage upward communication are found in many different organizational designs. A healthy organization needs effective upward communication if its downward communication is to have any chance of being effective. Table 13–1 presents some of the major characteristics of effective and ineffective feedback for employee performance.

Empathy

Empathy is the ability to put oneself in the other person's role and to assume the viewpoints and emotions of that person. This involves being receiver oriented rather than communicator oriented. The form of a communication should depend largely on what is known about the receivers. Empathy requires communicators to place themselves in the receivers' positions for the purpose of anticipating how the message is likely to be decoded.

It is vital that a manager understand and appreciate the process of decoding. Decoding involves perceptions, and the message will be filtered through the perceptions of the receiver. For vice presidents to communicate effectively with supervisors, for faculty to communicate effectively with students, and for government administrators to communicate effectively with minority groups, empathy is often an important ingredient. Empathy can reduce many of the barriers to effective communication that have been discussed above. The greater the gap between the experiences and background of the communicator and the receiver, the greater is the effort that must be made to find a common ground of understanding—ground on which there are overlapping fields of experience.

Simplifying Language

Complex language has been identified as a major barrier to effective communication. Students often suffer when their instructors use technical jargon that transforms simple concepts into complex puzzles.

Colleges and universities are not the only places, however, where complex language is used. Government agencies also are known for their often incomprehensible communications. We already have noted instances in which professional people attempt to use their in-group language in communicating with individuals outside their group. Managers must remember that effective communication involves transmitting understanding as well as information. If the receiver does not understand, then there has been no communication. In fact, many of the techniques discussed in this section have as their sole purpose the promotion of understanding.

Effective Listening

Just listening is not enough; one must listen with understanding. Can managers develop listening skills? Numerous pointers for effective listening have been found to be useful in organizational settings. For example, one writer cites "Ten Commandments for Good Listening": stop talking; put the speaker at ease; show the speaker you want to listen; remove distractions; empathize with the speaker; be patient; hold your temper; go easy on argument and criticism; ask questions; and stop talking. Note that "stop talking" is both the first and last commandment.[14]

Such lists of guidelines can be useful for managers. However, more important than these lists is the *decision to listen.* The above guidelines are useless unless the manager makes the conscious decision to listen. The realization that effective communication involves being understood as well as understanding probably is far more important than lists of guidelines. Then and only then can such guidelines become useful.

Utilizing the Grapevine: Informal Communication System

The grapevine is an important informal communication channel that exists in all organizations. It basically serves as a bypassing mechanism and in most cases is faster than the formal system it bypasses. In most cases, managers can count on the fact that the grapevine is fast, efficient, accurate, and fulfills people's need to communicate. Because it is flexible and because it usually involves face-to-face communication, the grapevine is capable of transmitting information rapidly. Through the grapevine, the resignation of an executive may become common knowledge long before it has been officially announced.

The grapevine can be used to spread rumors. It is important for managers to understand the rumor characteristics identified in the Management Focus.

MANAGEMENT FOCUS
Tracking Rumors Is Elusive

How do rumors start and where do they come from? We simply don't know. They don't really begin the way a bridge is constructed or a new product is developed in a laboratory. A rumor evolves through group interaction, putting together observations and bits of information until a message is formed of sufficient relevance to be worth passing on.

There is a strong tendency to attribute individual responsibility

---

[14] K. Davis, *Human Behavior at Work* (New York: McGraw-Hill, 1985), p. 387.

MANAGEMENT FOCUS (continued)

for rumors. Some companies have actually hired detective agencies to try to trace back through the sources to a person in the office or on the shop floor who is spreading rumors. This is generally a hopeless search.

Of more concern is why rumors emerge and why they circulate. Nothing happens without a reason—people listen to and pass on a rumor because it satisfies some need. Different people have different needs:

- Some people are receptive to rumors because of boredom; other individuals like some stories because they are entertaining. Rumors circulate because they are interesting or a source of diversion.
- Rumors, in the words of sociologist Tamotsu Shibutani, provide "closure in that they can pull together events and fill in gaps to make sense and provide explanations for what is going on." He refers to rumors as improvised news.
- Rumors can validate and support a point of view.
- Rumors reconcile one's psychological state with what one sees as actually going on. If one has anxieties or unfocused apprehensions, a message that contains forecasts of major or minor calamities supports and legitimizes anxieties. Studies have shown that people who are high in anxiety are more frequent participants in the rumor process, and groups in stressful situations have more rumor activity.
- Rumors are a means of getting attention. An important and often neglected feature of rumors is that they bring momentary prestige to the bearer.

In organizations, it is important to understand that a rumor is an actively transmitted, unverified message. Nothing in this definition implies truth or falsehood. Once the message has been established and accepted, however, it is no longer a rumor but is news or history or a false story.

Source: Adapted from Frederick Koenig, "Rumors that Follow the Sun," *Across the Board,* February 1985, pp. 25–30.

For management, the grapevine frequently may be an effective means of communication. It is likely to have a stronger impact on receivers because it is face-to-face and allows for feedback. Because it satisfies many psychological needs, the grapevine will always exist. No manager can do away with it. Research indicates that over 75 percent of the information in the grapevine is accurate.[15] Of course, the 25 percent that is distorted can be devastating.

If the grapevine is inevitable, managers should seek to utilize it or at least attempt to assure its accuracy. One way to minimize the undesirable aspects of the grapevine is to improve other forms of communication. If information exists on issues relevant to subordinates, then damaging rumors are less likely to develop.

SUMMARY OF KEY POINTS

- The quality of managerial decisions depends in large part on the quality of information available. Communication is the process of achieving common understanding; for managerial purposes, it is undertaken to achieve an effect.

- If the intended effect is not achieved, communication has not taken place.

- The elements of communication are the communicator, encoding, the message, the medium, decoding, the receiver, and feedback. All of these elements must be in harmony if communication is to achieve understanding and effect.

- A crucial factor in determining the effectiveness of communication in organizations is the way in which the organizations are structured. Upward, downward, diagonal, and horizontal communication flows are more likely to occur in neoclassical than in classical organization structures.

- The extent to which individuals share understanding depends on their use of feedback and exposure. People differ in this regard, with some preferring feedback and others preferring exposure. A balanced use of both is the most effective approach.

- Numerous barriers exist that contribute to communication breakdowns. Managers must be aware of barriers relevant to their situations. Major barriers are differing frames of reference, selective perception, poor listening skills, value judgments, source credibility, semantic problems, filtering, time pressures, and communication overload.

- Improving communications in organizations involves following up, regulating information flow, utilizing feedback, empathy, simplifying language, effective listening, and utilizing the informal communication system.

DISCUSSION AND REVIEW QUESTIONS

1. During disagreements, we often hear someone say: "What you heard is not what I said." Discuss what this statement means in terms of the elements of communication presented in the chapter.

---

[15] Ibid., p. 267.

2. What steps can a manager take in preparing for a feedback session with a subordinate?

3. Based on your own experience, which element of communication has most often been the cause of your failures to communicate? What do you believe you can do to improve your communication effectiveness?

4. Are you a Type A, B, C, or D person when you engage in interpersonal communications? Are you satisfied to be what you think you are? Why? If not, how could you change?

5. Think of your management course in terms of the basic elements of communication. For example, who is the communicator; what is the message; who is the receiver? Is effective communication occurring? Why? Identify where, if at all, breakdowns are occurring and why.

6. In your experience, what kinds of people—in terms of personality, needs, and motivation—are most likely to use one-way communication?

7. How can a manager improve his or her credibility as a communicator with subordinates?

8. Describe a situation in which you have been the receiver in a one-way communication process. Can you think of some reasons why some people might prefer it?

ADDITIONAL REFERENCES

Centron, M.; A. Pagano; and O. Port. "The Telecommunications Boom." *Management Review,* November 1985, pp. 57–59.

Larson, J. R., Jr. "The Supervisory Feedback Process: A Preliminary Model." *Organizational Behavior and Human Performance,* 1984, pp. 42–76.

Liden, R. C., and T. R. Mitchell. "Reactions to Feedback: The Role of Attributions." *Academy of Management Journal,* June 1985, pp. 291–308.

Penley, L. E., and B. Hawkins. "Studying Interpersonal Communication in Organizations: A Leadership Application." *Academy of Management Journal,* June 1985, pp. 309–26.

Poole, M. S. "An Information-Task Approach to Organizational Communication." *Academy of Management Journal,* July 1978, pp. 493–504.

Roberts, K. H., and C. A. O'Reilly III. "Failures in Upward Communication in Organizations: Three Possible Culprits." *Academy of Management Journal,* June 1974, pp. 205–15.

———. "Some Correlates of Communication Roles in Organizations." *Academy of Management Journal,* March 1979, pp. 42–57.

Rockey, E. H. *Communicating in Organizations.* Cambridge, Mass.: Winthrop Publishers, 1977.

Saunders, C. S. "Management Information Systems, Communications and Departmental Power: An Integrative Model." *Academy of Management Review,* July 1981, pp. 431–42.

Tubbs, S. L., and S. Moss. *Human Communication.* New York: Random House, 1977.

Tushman, M. L. "Impacts of Perceived Environmental Variability on Patterns of Work Related Communications." *Academy of Management Journal,* September 1979, pp. 482–500.

Watson, K. "An Analysis of Communication Patterns: A Method for Discriminating Leader and Subordinate Roles." *Academy of Management Journal,* March 1982, pp. 107–20.

Weiner, N. *The Human Use of Human Beings.* New York: Doubleday Publishing, 1954.

CASES

APPLICATION I

THE POWER OF THE GRAPEVINE*

Chicago—In the communications department of one of Chicago's largest banks, a staff member and supervisor have successfully avoided speaking to each other for 18 months. Any necessary correspondence is done by memo. They keep unofficial tabs on each other through the office grapevine.

A Loyola University professor often tests the waters with superiors for a plan in the offing by first leaking part of it through the grapevine.

At First Federal Savings and Loan Association of Chicago, the grapevine nearly had a senior executive resigned and out the door before it buzzed across a correction. It was the same first name, wrong last one and a much lower position on the management ladder.

Every company, every organization, every industry has a grapevine.

It's the unofficial source of information for everyone from the lowliest clerk to the chief executive officer and the chief executive's spouse. It hums loudest at a company that is autocratically managed or in a state of turmoil.

While it nearly always carries negative connotations, the office grapevine can be put to good use. In fact, in some instances, it is absolutely essential to the survival of an organization.

"Despite the stigma of the company grapevine, it can be used to supplement formal communications," wrote Vanessa Dean Arnold in a recent issue of *Management World,* a trade publication. She is an assistant professor of business communications at the University of Mississippi.

She added, "In a healthy organization, there will be both formal and informal channels of communications. Managers should listen to and study

---

* Source: Article by Sally Saville Hodge, *Chicago Tribune,* 28 August 1983, B6. Reprinted by permission.

the grapevine to learn who its leaders are, how it operates, and what information it carries."

By being plugged in that way, management can frequently defuse potentially explosive situations by "feeding" the grapevine accurate or positive information, Arnold wrote. Failure to do so means the fear and insecurity that frequently set the grapevine humming will result in decreased productivity.

Despite the best efforts, however, defusing bad situations is difficult when an organization is in turmoil.

For example, International Harvester Co., always a formal company where lines of communication were rigidly defined, had the busiest grapevine in Chicago even before it began skirting Chapter 11 bankruptcy in 1981.

An executive with another Chicago institution that has an uncertain future sighs over the problems of keeping one step ahead of what he considers the frequently inaccurate company and industry grapevines.

"I try to keep one ear to the ground, so I can act with official communications (in response to the rumors)," he said.

He recalls being in a company elevator recently, carrying a file bearing the name of a firm that, with much publicity, had earlier considered buying his. Inside the file was a marketing backgrounder that he thought might be of use to a new employee.

On the elevator was a passenger, however, who couldn't have known that. "The guy practically bent over backwards trying to read what was on the cover of the file," the executive said with a laugh. "I told him what it was, and he got off the elevator kind of embarrassed, but I can imagine what the grapevine would have made of that if I hadn't told him."

More executives than one might think depend on the grapevine's tidbits. Frank Corrado, head of Communications for Management in Chicago who also works with Hay Associates, a well-known management consulting firm, said, "A senior manager who is not assigned a secretary who is always wired in is at a tremendous disadvantage."

Gloria Lewis, head of the Department of Counseling Psychology and Higher Education at Loyola University, said she frequently plugged into the grapevine to test ideas on superiors.

"It's a way of gradually exposing part of a master plan ahead of time, so that by the time something happens, no one is surprised," she said. "But I only use it going up; that's not the way I would deal with colleagues, or students, or my support section."

Despite the fact that studies indicate many executives make as much use of the grapevine as Lewis does, Corrado insisted, "I'd much rather see (my clients) open up their formal lines of communication.

"Research on employee communications shows that the grapevine is the least desirable way of communicating with employees, but in some instances it is a survival mechanism that has to be used."

A classic case is the Environmental Protection Agency, until recently operating in a near-state of siege when top-level officials were accused of conflicts of interest.

Corrado said, "The lower-level managers kept the agency running, and it was the grapevine that kept everything glued together, because they weren't being told anything from the top.

"They got their information from car pools, from old friends networks, from field offices. The grapevine was absolutely critical to (the agency's) survival." Now, under new Director William Ruckelshaus, who has retained Corrado to revitalize official lines of communication, the grapevine is less necessary and not quite as active, Corrado said.

"He is trying to better establish the vertical lines of communication over the lateral lines, and a big turnaround in morale is built into it," Corrado added.

Educator Arnold points to a couple of other aspects of the maligned grapevine:

- Some studies have indicated the grapevine to be 80 to 85 percent accurate, with inaccuracies in the form of incompleteness rather than wrong information. Arnold writes that many researchers, in fact, believe much of the grapevine's information may be more accurate than information relayed by formal channels, particularly where managers are less frank and honest than they should be.
- Despite the generally held idea that women participate more actively in grapevine activity than men, other studies indicate men and women are equally active.

The grapevine does not necessarily follow the organizational hierarchy. It can go from secretary to president or from vice president to clerk. Arnold writes that in one firm, an executive bypassed in the formal channels learned grapevine information from supervisors who were given news by their superior.

"The vice president of a large firm was surprised at both the speed and range of the grapevine when learning that his wife knew of a proposed relocation that had only been finalized that day," Arnold wrote. "It seems she heard it from their maid, whose husband was a custodian at the plant."

Questions for Analysis

1. Is the grapevine an effective communication channel in an organization?
2. What characteristics should a manager be familiar with before using a grapevine to initiate a message?
3. In what type of company is the grapevine most likely to be active? Why?

APPLICATION II

DO YOU KNOW WHAT I LIKE ABOUT YOU?

Jim McCabe, only 33, is a successful bloodstock agent in the highly volatile and competitive thoroughbred horse industry. He locates thoroughbred buyers and sellers for his clients, as well as breeding rights for stallions and mares. It is a complicated and risky business. His knowledge of thoroughbred horses and their bloodlines, along with much hard work, has enabled him to achieve success. Educated in the physical sciences (master's degree), he chose the thoroughbred industry because of his love of horses. His firm, which he began alone five years ago, now employs five other agents, three researchers whose task it is to research thoroughbred bloodlines, three secretaries, an office manager, and myself. My title when I was hired four months ago was assistant office manager, but no one ever told me what I was supposed to do. For a part-time job while in college, the pay is good, and I'm learning a great deal about a business I knew nothing about previously. In addition, there is always some kind of excitement around the office.

I stood by the door of McCabe's office. He was on the phone, and before I could knock, he motioned for me to come in and sit down. Every inch of his desk was covered by reports, memos, horse-sale catalogs, telephone messages, and racing results. Other reminders on bits of paper were taped to the wall, and a "to do" list with at least 10 entries on it was taped to the base of the telephone. Evidently these were things that he had "to do" immediately. While talking on the phone, he added another item to this list.

As he continued the phone conversation, he was shaking his head and signing letters at the same time. Finally, he put his hand over the phone and said to me, "This is Robinson in Florida on that two-year-old filly deal. All the tests on her leg are not in yet, but he insists on giving me every detail on the entire test procedure. The guy is going to drive me nuts."

Turning his attention back to the phone he removed his hand and resumed talking. "Right, Robbie, OK . . . Great . . . OK . . . Sure . . . Call me back on that . . . Terrific . . . 'Bye."

He hung up the phone with a sigh of relief and looked at me. "Do you know what I like about you, Tinsley?" I didn't have time to answer, nor did he, because the phone rang again. "Yea . . . Fine . . . Terrific . . . Count me in . . . 'Bye." At this point, his secretary looked in and said, "John Towne of Winthrop Farms is on hold. It sounds urgent."

McCabe shook his head again and went back to the telephone. After a few minutes of conversation, he put his hand over the receiver and called to his secretary. "Get Johnson and Burke in here, fast." Johnson was the office manager, and Burke was an agent. They arrived as he hung up the phone.

"Burke," he said, "you know that deal you put together for the syndication of that three-year-old, Ol' Blue? Well, they don't like it. Put this information into it and tell me what effect the changes will have on us. When you get it finished, bring it to me so I can call Towne back." Burke left.

"Johnson, I want all of the training fees, jockey expenses, and all other expenses on that horse. Don't give them to me by the month like you did last time. I need totals in *all* categories; and for crying out loud, this time break out the 'other' category a little better. I looked real good last week when Towne asked me what the $6,300 in 'other expenses' was for. I want all the information at my fingertips in case we've got to go to war with these people." Johnson left.

"Now, Tinsley, what did you need me for?"

"Just sign this bill of sale," I said. "No reason to spend a lot of time on it. It's for the sale of that yearling you asked me to take care of."

"That's what I like about you, Tinsley," he said as he leaned back in his chair and signed the bill of sale. "When I give you a job, you listen. Then you do it right the first time and tell me when it's done. You don't tell me how you did it, the problems you're having doing it, who you met while doing it, and every other Mickey Mouse detail. If the rest of the people around here had that ability, I might be able to get some work done. I think I got more work done five years ago when I had nobody working for me."

As I left his office, I didn't have time to thank him, because the phone began ringing.

Questions for Analysis

1. What is your impression of McCabe?
2. What is your opinion of his communications to the other employees of the firm?
3. What might be the reasons for his demands on employees?
4. Could this influence the effectiveness of the organization? In what ways?

Chapter 14

ORGANIZATIONAL CHANGE AND DEVELOPMENT

LEARNING OBJECTIVES

After completing Chapter 14, you should be able to:

■ **Define**
the term *organization development*.

■ **Describe**
a five-step model or framework that displays the organization change process.

■ **Discuss**
four major reasons why people resist change.

■ **Compare**
specific techniques that are used to bring about structural, people, and technological changes.

■ **Identify**
some of the productivity and human resource advantages and disadvantages associated with robotics in work settings.

MANAGEMENT IN ACTION

Honeywell: A Strategy to Manage Change Effectively*

In 1971, a Honeywell Corporation human resource planning study estimated that the Minneapolis-based multinational manufacturer of computers and controls would grow from 75,000 to 150,000 in less than six years. The problem would be how to increase the managerial population from 5,000 to 10,000.

No one in Honeywell had the slightest idea how to achieve this mammoth increase in managerial talent. A research effort was initiated by a small band of creative individuals.

The team used interviews, self-report analysis, discussions in conferences, and analysis to reach a number of conclusions.

- The assumption was incorrect that managers learn to manage in an 80–10–10 percent ratio from job experiences, relationships, and formal training and development. The more appropriate ratio was 50–30–20. In other words, relationships with others (bosses, colleagues) and training and development are more important than previously thought.
- The finding that 20 percent of a manager's know-how comes from formal training and development is remarkable, since the average manager spends less than 1 percent of his or her time in such a setting.
- To develop subordinates, managers need to be supportive and provide autonomy.
- The key barriers to the development of managers are a lack of time devoted to personal development, the lack of opportunity for advancement, and a boss who places heavy emphasis on short-term results.

The results of the team's analysis indicated that senior executives at Honeywell would need to make changes and to (1) establish a philosophy of development, (2) incorporate training for managers, (3) make more cross-functional, cross-divisional, and cross-country assignments for developmental purposes, and (4) set specific goals and reward managers for developing subordinates.

The Honeywell example of problem solving used an approach similar to that presented in Figure 14–1 (a model for managing change). The company recognized a need, diagnosed the problem with a team, examined various solutions, selected a solution, and implemented a program that has resulted in developing the managers needed.

* Source: Adapted from Ron Zemke, "The Honeywell Studies: How Managers Learn to Manage," *Training,* August 1985, pp. 46–51.

Organizational change is a pressing problem for modern managers; and in recent years, a great deal of literature has appeared focusing on the need for *planning* for change.[1] Some companies have instituted staff units whose mission is organizational planning.[2] The planning units are specific responses to the need for systematic, formalized procedures to anticipate and implement changes in the structure, technology, and personnel of the organization.

In this chapter, the processes of organizational change and development are discussed. Before beginning, however, we must explain the manner in which we are using the terms *change* and *development*. As even the casual reader of management literature soon must realize, the term *organization development* (OD) involves a variety of meanings and management strategies. In its most restrictive sense, it refers specifically to some form of sensitivity training; in a larger and more encompassing sense, it refers to any systematically planned, programmatic effort to improve the effectiveness of an organization through the application of behavioral science concepts, theories, and approaches. The change effort may focus on the way in which the organization is structured, the behavior of employees, or the technology that is used in getting the work done. Therefore, *OD is a method for facilitating change and development in structures and processes (e.g., relationships, roles), people (e.g., styles, skills), and technology (e.g., more routineness, more challenge).*[3]

The growing realization that organizations can be changed and made more effective through managerial applications of behavioral science knowledge has created a wealth of literature.[4] This chapter presents some of the established ideas from this literature, in the context of practical management. In order to provide a theme, we present the material in terms of a model describing the important factors of the change and development process. For simplicity, we will use the phrase "the management of change" to include the concept of organization development in its broadest sense.

RESISTANCE TO CHANGE

Most organizational change efforts eventually run into some form of employee resistance. Change triggers rational and irrational emotional reaction

---

[1] Organizational change is broadly interpreted for purposes of this discussion. Some management students restrict the term to changes in the formal structure, but we will include changes in employee behavior and technology.

[2] Donald L. Kirkpatrick, *How to Manage Change Effectively* (San Francisco: Jossey-Bass, 1985).

[3] Frank Friedlander and L. Dave Brown, "Organization Development," *Review of Psychology,* 1974.

[4] Michael Beer, *Organization Change and Development* (Santa Monica, Calif.: Goodyear Publishing, 1980); Wendell L. French and Cecil H. Bell, Jr., *Organization Development* (Englewood Cliffs, N.J.: Prentice-Hall, 1978); Edgar Huse, *Organization Development* (St. Paul, Minn.: West Publishing, 1980).

because of the uncertainty involved. Instead of assuming that employees will resist change or act in a particular manner, it is better to consider in a general way the reasons why people resist change. There are four common reasons why people resist change.[5] As you read about each of them, think about your own reasons for resisting change. Do any of the discussed reasons fit you?

Parochial self-interest.   One reason some people resist organizational change is the fear of losing something they value. Individuals fear the loss of power, resources, freedom to make decisions, friendships, and prestige. In cases of fearing loss, individuals think of themselves and what they may have to give up. The fearful individual only has his or her parochial self-interest in mind when resisting change. The organization and the interests of co-workers are not given much priority.

Misunderstanding and lack of trust.   When individuals do not fully understand why the change is occurring and what its implications are, they will resist change. Misunderstanding about the intent and consequences of organizational change is more likely to occur when trust is lacking between the individual and the person initiating the change. In organizations characterized by high levels of mistrust, it is likely that misunderstandings will be associated with any organizational change.

Different assessments.   Since individuals view change—its intent, potential consequences, and personal impact—differently, there are often different assessments of the situation. Those initiating changes see more positive results because of the change, while those being affected and not initiating the changes see more costs involved with the change. Take, for example, the introduction of robots. Management might view the change to robots as a benefit, while subordinates may consider the robot introduction as a signal that they will lose their jobs.

The initiators of change often make two overly broad assumptions: (1) They have all the relevant data and information available to diagnose the situation. (2) Those to be affected by the change also have the same facts. Whatever the circumstances, the initiators and the affected employees often have different data and information. This leads to resistance to change. However, in some cases, the resistance is healthy for the firm, especially in the situation where the affected employees possess more valid data and information.

---

[5] Four reasons are discussed in John P. Kotter and Leonard A. Schlesinger, "Choosing Strategies for Change," *Harvard Business Review,* March–April 1979, pp. 106–14. The discussion of resistance to change is based on this article.

Low tolerance for change.   People resist change because they fear they will not be able to develop the new skills necessary to perform well. Individuals may understand clearly that change is necessary, but they are emotionally unable to make the transition. For example, this type of resistance is found in offices that are introducing computerized word processing systems. Some secretaries and even their bosses are resisting these changes that are clearly needed if office productivity is to be improved.

A low tolerance for change also is found in individuals who resist change to save face. Making the necessary adjustments and changes would be, they assume, an open admission that some of their previous behavior, decisions, and attitudes were wrong.

TABLE   14–1   Methods for Reducing Resistance to Change

Approach	Situational Use	Advantages	Drawbacks
Education + Communication	Where there is a lack of information or inaccurate information and analysis.	Once persuaded, people often will help with the implementation of the change.	Can be very time consuming if many people are involved.
Participation + Involvement	Where the initiators do not have all the information they need to design the change, and where others have considerable power to resist.	People who participate will be committed to implementing change, and any relevant information they have will be integrated into the change plan.	Can be very time consuming if participators design an inappropriate change.
Facilitation + Support	Where people are resisting because of adjustment problems.	No other approach works as well with adjustment problems.	Can be time consuming, expensive, and still fail.
Negotiation + Agreement	Where someone or some group will clearly lose out in a change, and where that group has considerable power to resist.	Sometimes it is a relatively easy way to avoid major resistance.	Can be too expensive in many cases if it alerts others to negotiate for compliance.
Manipulation + Co-optation	Where other tactics will not work or are too expensive.	It can be a relatively quick and inexpensive solution to resistance problems.	Can lead to future problems if people feel manipulated.
Explicit + Implicit Coercion	Where speed is essential, and the change initiators possess considerable power.	It is speedy, and can overcome any kind of resistance.	Can be risky if it leaves people angry at the initiators.

Source: Reprinted by permission of the *Harvard Business Review*. An exhibit from "Choosing Strategies for Change" by John P. Kotter and Leonard A. Schlesinger, March/April 1979. Copyright © 1979 by the President and Fellows of Harvard College; all rights reserved.

MINIMIZING RESISTANCE TO CHANGE

Resisting change is a human response, and management needs to take steps to minimize such resistance. Minimizing resistance can reduce the time it takes for a change to be accepted or tolerated. Also, the performance of employees can rebound more quickly if resistance is kept at a minimal level.

A number of methods have been useful in minimizing resistance to change. Table 14–1 summaries six action steps:

1. *Education and communication.* One of the most common ways to reduce resistance is to communicate and educate before the change occurs. This helps people prepare for the change. Paving the way, showing the logic, and keeping everyone informed helps cut down resistance.

2. *Participation and involvement.* Having those to be affected help design and implement the change helps increase their commitment to the change. If individuals feel their ideas and attitudes are being included in the change effort, they tend to become less resistant and more receptive. Involvement and participation by workers at the Rochester Products plant in Tuscaloosa, Alabama, is discussed in the Management Focus. In this plant, management, the union, employees, and students and faculty from a nearby university all cooperated in introducing needed changes.

MANAGEMENT FOCUS
Participating to Save a Plant

In the early 1970s, when employee participation programs began to catch on, most activities focused on creating better jobs and more meaningful work. Today the programs are often pointed toward saving jobs, plants, and even communities. The Rochester Products plant in Tuscaloosa, Alabama, was faced with a declining market for carburetors. Management decided that unless a way was found to save $2 million annually, the plant would be permanently closed. Employees attempted, through an aggressive suggestion system, to save $1.5 million. This was short of the $2 million goal, and the company began the closedown process.

The union (Local 1097 of the United Auto Workers) and the Tuscaloosa community arranged a special agreement with the company. The firm agreed to lease floor space to the University of Alabama in exchange for finding ways to reduce costs and introduce changes in production methods.

Within a short time, students and faculty consultants from the university, along with employees, engineers, and managers found ways to reduce the operating budget by $645,000 per year. Through

MANAGEMENT FOCUS (*continued*)

a cooperative and participative effort, the goal of $2 million savings was met. The company decided to keep the plant open and save the 225 jobs.

The changes in work flow, production methods, work scheduling, and cost control systems have meant higher morale and more productivity. There has also been an increase in new work being brought into the Tuscaloosa plant because of its efficiency. In this case, the participative change efforts saved jobs, a plant, and helped the economy of a community.

Source: Adapted from Peter Lazes, "Employee Involvement Activities: Saving Jobs and Money Too," *New Management,* Winter 1986,, pp. 58–61.

3. *Facilitation and support.*   Being supportive is an important management characteristic when change is implemented. It is especially important for managers to be supportive (for example, showing concern for subordinates, being a good listener, going to bat for subordinates on an issue that is important) and help facilitate the change when fear and anxiety are at the heart of resistance.

4. *Negotiation and agreement.*   Reducing resistance can be brought about through negotiation. Discussion and analysis can help managers identify points of negotiation and agreement. Negotiated agreement involves giving something to another party to reduce resistance. For example, getting a person to move to a less desirable work location may require paying him a bonus or increasing his monthly salary. Once this negotiation agreement is reached, others may expect the manager to grant them the same concessions in the future.

5. *Manipulation and co-optation.*   Manipulation involves the use of devious tactics to convince others that a change is in their best interests. Holding back information, playing one person against another, and providing slanted information are examples of manipulation. Co-opting an individual involves giving him or her a major role in the design or implementation of the change. The ethical problems associated with manipulation and co-optation are obvious and should preclude the widespread use of these techniques.

6. *Explicit and implicit coercion.*   In using explicit and/or implicit coercion, the manager engages in threatening behavior. He or she threatens the employees with job loss, reduced promotion opportunities, poor job assignments, and loss of privileges. The coercion is intended to reduce a person's resistance to the management-initiated change. Coercive behavior can be risky because of the bad feelings and hostility generated.

Each of these six approaches has advantages and drawbacks that need

FIGURE   14–1   The Process of Managing Organizational Change

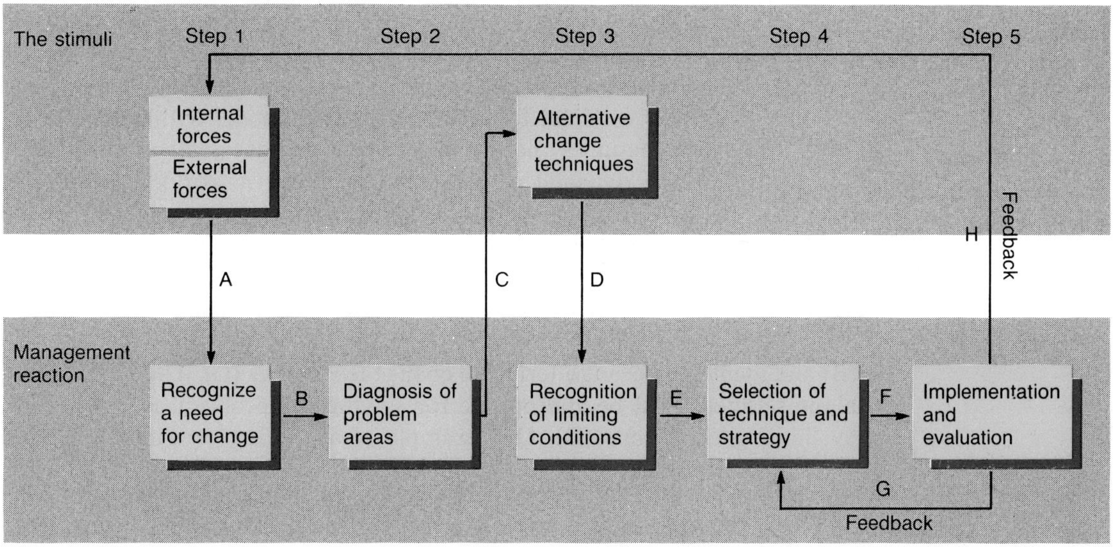

Stimuli and reactions of managers in organizational change decision making.

to be carefully considered. Managers can use them in different situations and in various combinations. Use of any of the six approaches depends on a systematic analysis of the particular situation. Often this involves the use of a model, or framework, to help provide guidelines and an overview of the situation.

A MODEL FOR MANAGING CHANGE

The management of change can be broken down into subprocesses or steps. A model describing this process is illustrated in Figure 14–1 and consists of five steps linked in a logical sequence. The prospects for initiating successful change and minimizing resistance are enhanced when the manager explicitly and formally goes through each successive step. For this reason, each step and process is discussed in a separate section of this chapter.

The knowledgeable manager is one who recognizes the multiplicity of alternatives and is not predisposed toward one particular approach to the exclusion of all others.[6] At the same time, the effective manager avoids the

---

[6] See the range of change strategies in Wendell L. French, Cecil H. Bell, Jr., and Robert A. Zawacki, *Organization Development* (Plano, Tex.: Business Publications, 1983).

pitfalls of stagnation. The sign of decay, as Larry Greiner has observed, is "managerial behavior that *(a)* is oriented more to the past than to the future, *(b)* recognizes the obligations of ritual more than the challenges of current problems, and *(c)* owes allegiance more to department goals than to overall company objectives."[7] Thus, the management of change implies a flexible, forward-looking stance for the manager.[8]

This attribute is essential for using the change model outlined in Figure 14–1. The model assumes that forces for change continually act upon the firm, reflecting the dynamic character of the modern world. At the same time, it is the manager's responsibility to sort out the information received from the firm's control system and other sources that reflect the magnitude of change forces (A). This information is the basis for recognizing the need for change; it is equally desirable to recognize when change is *not* needed. But once the problem is recognized, the manager must diagnose the problem (B) and identify relevant alternative change techniques (C). The change technique selected must be appropriate for solving the problem, as constrained by limiting conditions (D). One example of a limiting condition discussed in an earlier chapter is the prevailing character of group norms. A work group may support some of the change techniques but may sabotage others.

The fact that a change program can be thwarted underscores the fact that the choice of change *strategy* is as important as the change technique itself (E). Finally, managers must implement the change and monitor the change process and change results (F). The model includes feedback to the selection-of-strategy phase and to the forces-for-change phase. These feedback loops (G and H) suggest that the change process itself must be monitored and evaluated. The implementation strategy may be faulty and lead to poor results, but prompt action could correct the situation. Moreover, the feedback loop to the initial step recognizes that *no* change is final. A new situation is created within which other problems and issues will emerge; a new setting is created that will itself become subject to change. The model suggests no final solution. Rather, it emphasizes that managers operate in a dynamic setting where the only certainty is change itself.

STEP 1: STIMULI—FORCES FOR CHANGE

The forces for change (stimuli) can be classified into two groups: external and internal forces. *External forces* include changes in the marketplace, technology, and environment; they usually are beyond the control of the manager.

---

[7] Larry E. Greiner, "Patterns of Organization Change," *Harvard Business Review,* May–June 1967, p. 119.

[8] See Paul Hersey and Kenneth H. Blanchard, "The Management of Change," *Training and Development Journal,* January 1972, pp. 6–11, for the first of a three-part discussion of the management of change (parallels the model developed in this chapter).

Internal forces operate inside the firm and are generally within the control of management.

External Forces

Managers of business firms historically have been concerned with reacting to changes in the *marketplace.* Competitors introduce new products (Diet Pepsi versus Tab), increase advertising (General Motors versus Toyota), reduce prices (Delta Airlines versus United), or improve customer service (Apple versus IBM). In each case, a response is required unless the manager is content to permit the erosion of profit and market share. At the same time, changes occur in customer tastes and incomes. The firm's products may no longer have customer appeal; customers may be able to purchase less expensive, higher-quality forms of the same product.

Another source of market forces is that of the supply of resources to the firm. A change in the quality and quantity of human resources can dictate changes in the firm. For example, the adoption of automated processes can be stimulated by a decline in the supply of labor. The techniques of coal mining and tobacco farming have changed greatly during recent years because of labor shortages. We also can understand how changes in the supply of materials and energy can cause the firm to attempt to substitute one material for another. Rayon stockings and synthetic rubber tires are direct outgrowths of World War II–induced shortages of raw materials. We need not catalog the whole range of possible changes in the resource markets that can stimulate organizational change. The potential is great, however, and must be recognized.

The second source of external change forces is *technology.* The knowledge explosion since World War II has introduced new technology for nearly every management function. Computers have made high-speed data processing and the solution to complex production problems possible. New machines, new processes, and robots have revolutionized the way in which many products are manufactured and distributed. High rates of obsolescence have encouraged many firms to adopt payback criteria as low as two years, so that they will not be caught with obsolete equipment. Computer technology and automation have affected not only the technical conditions of work but the social conditions as well. New occupations have been created, and others have been eliminated. Slowness in adopting new technology that reduces costs and improves quality will show itself in the financial statements sooner or later. Technological advance is a permanent fixture in contemporary society and, as a force for change, will continue to demand attention as managers attempt to master the dynamics of change.[9]

---

[9] Leon Martel, *Mastering Change* (New York: Simon & Schuster, 1986).

Finally, the third external force consists of *environmental changes*. Managers must be "tuned in" to great movements over which they have no control but that, in time, affect the firm's fate. For example, since the 1960s and 1970s, there has been a distinct increase in social awareness; the drive for social equality poses for managers new issues not previously confronted. Sophisticated mass communication and international markets create enormous potential but also pose a great threat to those managers unable to understand what is going on. Finally, to add to the problem, the relationship between government and business has become much more involved as new regulations are imposed or taken away. These pressures for change reflect the increasing complexity and interdependence of modern living. The traditional function of business is being questioned and new objectives are being advanced. No doubt the events of the future will intensify environmental forces for change.

Internal Forces

The forces for change occurring within the organization can be traced to *processes* and *people*. Process forces include decision making, communications, and interpersonal relations. Breakdowns or problems in any of these processes can create forces for change. Decisions either are not being made, are made too late, or are of poor quality. Communications are short-circuited, redundant, or simply inadequate. Tasks are not undertaken or not completed because the person responsible did not "get the word." Because of inadequate and nonexistent communications, a customer order is not filled, a grievance is not processed, an invoice is not filed , or a supplier is not paid. Interpersonal and interdepartmental conflicts reflect breakdown in the interaction between people.

Low levels of morale and high levels of absenteeism and turnover are symptoms of people problems that must be followed up. A wildcat strike or a walkout may be the most tangible sign of a problem; such tactics usually are employed because they arouse the management to action. There is in most organizations a certain level of employee discontent; a great danger is to ignore the complaints and suggestions. But the process of change includes the *recognition* phase, and it is at this point that management must decide to act or not to act.

STEP 1: REACTION—RECOGNITION OF THE NEED FOR CHANGE

Information helps managers comprehend the magnitude of the change forces. Some of the important sources of information were discussed above. Certainly the most important information comes from the firm's preliminary, concurrent, and feedback control data. Indeed, the process of change can be viewed as a part of the control function, specifically the corrective-action requirement. Financial statements, quality-control data, budget and standard cost information are important mediums through which both external and internal forces are revealed. Declining profit margins and market shares are tangible signs that the firm's competitive position is deteriorating and that change may be required. Spiraling hospital costs may be a sign of inefficient hospital management. These sources of feedback control information are highly developed in most organizations because of their crucial importance.

Two examples in the automobile industry highlight the recognition reaction by managers. In 1974, General Motors had the worst gasoline mileage average among U.S. automakers—about 12 miles per gallon. This was during an oil crisis, and GM's market share declined to about 45 percent, the lowest since 1952. GM management recognized their situation and decided to "downsize" most of their cars. They recognized a problem and changed the style of their product. The cost of recognizing and changing was enormous: about $1 billion annually. But this change in technology had to be faced if GM was to hold on to its market share. By 1977, the average mileage of GM cars was around 18 miles per gallon—the best among the U.S. automakers—and its market share was about 55 percent.[10]

Chrysler Corporation for years was the third largest automaker in the United States. It held about a 15 percent market share in 1976, which declined to about 9 percent by 1979.[11] The company reported a loss of more than $1 billion on revenues of $12 billion in 1979, and it had to rely on a loan guarantee of $1.5 billion from the government plus loans of $2 billion from other sources just to stay in business. Why? Chrysler didn't recognize the need to downsize the product line in time. The company's small cars, Omni and Horizon, were selling well, but they were introduced too late to produce enough cars to meet the demand.

STEP 2: REACTION—DIAGNOSIS OF THE PROBLEM

Before appropriate action can be taken, the symptoms of the problem must be analyzed to discover the problem itself. Experience and judgment are critical to this phase unless the problem is readily apparent to all observers. However, managers often disagree as to the nature of the problem. There is no magic formula. The objectives of this phase can be described by three questions:

1. What is the problem, as distinct from the symptoms of the problem?
2. What must be changed to resolve the problem?
3. What outcomes (objectives) are expected from the change, and how will such objectives be measured?

---

[10] C. G. Burck, "How GM Turned Itself Around," *Fortune,* January 16, 1978, pp. 89–100.

[11] "Driving for a Rescue Deal," *Time,* September 24, 1979, p. 70.

FIGURE   14–2   Employee Attitude Survey (Sample)*

INSTRUCTIONS

This is a survey of the ideas and opinions of Baker Company salaried employees. WHAT YOU SAY IN THIS QUESTIONNAIRE IS COMPLETELY CONFIDENTIAL. We do not want to know who you are. We do want to know, however, how employees with different interests and experience and doing different kinds of work feel about their jobs and Baker.

This is not a test. There are no right or wrong answers. Whether the results of this survey give a true picture of the Baker Company depends on whether you answer each of the questions in the way you really feel. The usefulness of this survey in making Baker a better place to work depends on the honesty and care with which you answer the questions.

Your answers will be compiled with many others and summarized to prepare a *report* for Baker. Your identity will always be protected. We do not need your name, only your impressions. Your written comments will be put in typewritten form so that your handwriting will not even be seen by anyone at Baker.

Please complete each part of the survey so that all of your impressions can be recorded. Remember, your honest impressions are all that we are asking for.

PART I: THE JOB AND CONDITIONS

The statements below are related to certain aspects of your job at Baker. Please circle the response number that best describes how you feel about each statement.

1—strongly disagree   2—disagree   3—undecided   4—agree   5—strongly agree

Pay	Strongly Disagree	Disagree	Undecided	Agree	Strongly Agree
My pay is all right for the kind of work I do.	1	2	3	4	5
I make as much money as most of my friends.	1	2	3	4	5
My pay allows me to keep up with the cost of living.	1	2	3	4	5
I am satisfied with the pay I receive for my job.	1	2	3	4	5
Most employees at Baker get paid at least what they deserve.	1	2	3	4	5
I understand how my salary is determined.	1	2	3	4	5
What changes, if any, should be made with the Baker pay system?					

Fringe Benefits	Strongly Disagree	Disagree	Undecided	Agree	Strongly Agree
Our major fringe-benefit plan provides excellent coverage.	1	2	3	4	5
I understand what our fringe benefits at Baker are.	1	2	3	4	5
I am satisfied with our fringe-benefit plan.	1	2	3	4	5
What, if anything, should be done with the Baker fringe-benefit plans?					

* This is only a portion of an attitude survey used by John M. Ivancevich and Michael T. Matteson in a study conducted for an organization.

The answers to these questions can come from information ordinarily found in organizations, such as financial statements, department reports, or attitude surveys. Or it may be necessary to generate ad hoc information through the creation of committees or task forces. Meetings between managers and employees provide a variety of points of view that can be sifted through by a smaller group. Technical operational problems may be diagnosed easily, but more subtle human relations problems usually entail extensive analysis. One approach to diagnosing the problem is the attitude survey.

Attitude questionnaires such as shown in Figure 14–2 can be administered to the entire work force or to a sample of it. Such surveys permit the respondents to evaluate and rate (1) management, (2) pay and pay-related items, (3) working conditions, (4) equipment, and (5) other job-related items. The appropriate use of such surveys requires that the data be collected (usually by questionnaires) from members of an organization, analyzed in detail, and fed back to various organization members. The objective of the survey is to pinpoint the problem or problems as perceived by the members of the organization. Subsequent feedback discussions on the survey results at all levels of the organization can add additional insights into the nature of the problem.[12]

The approach management uses to diagnose the problem is a crucial part of the total strategy for a change. As will be seen in a later section, the manner in which the problem is diagnosed has clear implications for the final success of the proposed change.

Finally, the diagnostic step must specify *objectives* for change. Given the diagnosis of the problem, it is necessary to define objectives in order to guide as well as to evaluate the outcome of the change. The objectives can be stated in terms of financial and production data, such as profits, market shares, sales volume, productivity, scrappage, or the like. Or they can be stated as attitude and morale objectives derived from attitude survey information. They also can be stated as personal-development objectives that are meaningful to the members of an organization. For example, they can focus on the personal growth or reeducation of one employee or a group. Whatever the objectives, they must be explicit, understandable, challenging, and meaningful.

STEP 3: STIMULI—ALTERNATIVE CHANGE TECHNIQUES

The choice of the particular change technique depends on the nature of the problem management has diagnosed. Management must determine which alternative is most likely to produce the desired outcome. As we have noted

---

[12] Randall B. Dunham and Frank J. Smith, *Organizational Surveys* (Glenview, Ill.: Scott, Foresman, 1979).

above, diagnosis of the problem includes specification of the outcomes management desires from the change. In this section, we will describe a number of change techniques. They will be classified according to the major focus of the technique: structure, people, or technology.[13] This classification of organizational change techniques in no way implies a distinct division among the three types. On the contrary, the interrelationships of structure, people, and technology must be acknowledged and anticipated. The majority of literature on organizational change indicates the relative weakness of efforts to change only structure (e.g., job design), only people (e.g., sensitivity training), or only technology (e.g., introducing new equipment or a new computer).[14]

The interest of behavioral scientists in managing people is concerned with the impact of structure on attitudes and behavior. Overspecialization and narrow spans of control can lead to low levels of morale and low productivity.[15] At the same time, the technology of production, distribution, and information processing affects the structural characteristics of the firm[16] as well as attitudes and sentiments.[17] The fact that the interrelationships among structure, people, and technology are so pronounced might suggest a weakness in the classification scheme; but the techniques described below can be distinguished on the basis of their *major* thrust or focus: structure, people, or technology.

Structural Change

Changes in the structure of the organization ordinarily follow changes in strategy.[18] Logically, the organizing function follows the planning function since the structure is a means for achieving the goals established through planning.

Structural change in the context of organizational change refers to managerial action that attempts to improve performance by altering the formal structure of task and authority relationships. At the same time, we must recognize that the structure creates human and social relationships that gradually can

---

[13] See Harold J. Leavitt, "Applied Organizational Change in Industry: Structural, Technological and Humanistic Approaches," in *Handbook of Organizations,* ed. James G. March (Skokie, Ill.: Rand McNally, 1965), pp. 1144–68.

[14] Clayton P. Alderfer, "Change Processes in Organzation," in *Handbook of Industrial and Organizational Psychology,* ed. Marvin D. Dunnette (Skokie, Ill.: Rand McNally, 1976).

[15] Rensis Likert, *The Human Organization* (New York: McGraw-Hill, 1967).

[16] Joan Woodward, *Industrial Organization* (New York: Oxford University Press, 1967); Frank J. Jasinski, "Adapting Organization to New Technology," *Harvard Business Review,* January–February 1959, pp. 79–86.

[17] Harriet O. Ronken and Paul R. Lawrence, *Administering Changes: A Case Study of Human Relations in a Factory* (Boston: Division of Research, Harvard Business School, 1952).

[18] Alfred Chandler, *Strategy and Structure* (Cambridge, Mass.: MIT Press, 1962).

become ends for the members of the organization. These relationships, when they have been defined and made legitimate by management, introduce an element of stability.[19] Members of the organization may resist efforts to disrupt these relationships.

Structural changes alter some aspect of the formal task and authority definitions. As we have seen, the design of an organization involves the definition and specification of job depth and scope, the grouping of jobs in departments, determination of the size of groups reporting to a single manager, and the provision of staff assistance. Within this framework, the communication, decision-making, and human interaction processes occur.

Changes in the nature of jobs. Changes in the nature of jobs originate with the implementation of new methods and new machines. Job enrichment, work simplification, and job enlargement are examples of methods changes. Scientific management introduced significant changes in the way work is done, through the use of motion and time studies. These methods tend to create highly specialized jobs. Job enrichment (see Chapter 10 for a discussion of motivation and job enrichment), however, moves in the opposite direction, toward despecialization.

An interesting example of attempted job enrichment took place in the stock-transfer department of a large metropolitan bank.[20] The department was responsible for transferring the ownership of securities from one owner to another and recording the transfer. In order to remain competitive with other banks in the area, the entire stock transfer had to be completed within 48 hours. At the time of the study, 300 employees worked in the department.

Each employee reported to a "work coordinator," who was responsible for 8 to 12 employees performing the same function. A job enrichment plan was developed in which the work of the department was divided into 13 modules. The modules focused on total responsibility for a group of corporations whose stock was handled by the bank. Under the old arrangement, employees arbitrarily handled whatever work was assigned.

It was hoped that the assignment of a specific set of corporations to each group working on a module would increase the employees' identification with and commitment to the work. These feelings were to be strengthened by allowing the workers in the module to leave work together when the security transactions from their assigned companies had been completed.

Modules were scheduled to be introduced one at a time. The researchers collected data after each module was installed. Data on the nature of the jobs themselves, employee performance, and the change process were collected by use of questionnaires, interviews, company records, and actual observations.

---

[19] R. K. Ready, *The Administrator's Job* (New York: McGraw-Hill, 1967), pp. 24–30.

[20] Linda L. Frank and J. Richard Hackman, "A Failure of Job Enrichment: The Case of the Change that Wasn't," *Journal of Applied Behavioral Science,* October 1975, pp. 413–36.

Employees reported almost no impact from the changes in the characteristic of the jobs. The researchers concluded that the type of changes in structure that, if performed, should have increased performance and effectiveness were not initiated as planned. For example, it was planned that employees would experience more autonomy in the modules, because each module would be making its own decisions. In fact, however, no structural changes were made to encourage the module members to take more responsibility. Moreover, managers continued to give orders and to supervise rather closely. In effect, management did not delegate as had been planned. And employees had the same feeling as before the modules were started—namely, that they had little autonomy.

This example illustrates the value of research even on unsuccessful job changes. In a "pure" sense, this change in the job did not occur. However, it provided a valuable lesson about the interrelationships between people and structure. It also indicated that job enrichment is not always a simple solution to managerial work-related problems.

Enlargement.   Job enlargement involves making a job "larger" by increasing the number of tasks to perform. A traditional assembly line can be converted to a line with enlarged jobs. The assembly line is created by breaking down the total product (a television set, an automobile, a clothes dryer) into specialized stations. Each station has tools and workers that do a specific job. Stations are connected to each other by a workflow plan. At a General Motors assembly plant in Lordstown, Ohio, the average time cycle that a worker performs on a job at a station is 36 seconds. Thus, a worker faced a new automobile part over 700 times in each eight-hour shift.

Saab Company in Sweden decided to build a new automobile engine assembly plant and considered alternative ways of setting up jobs on the assembly

FIGURE   14–3   Saab Engine Assembly Line before Enlarging Jobs

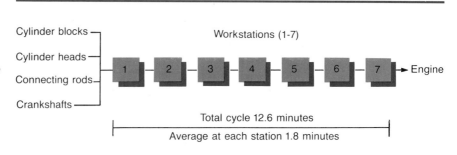

A typical assembly line with seven work stations at Saab.

Cylinder blocks
Cylinder heads
Connecting rods
Crankshafts

Workstations (1-7)

1 — 2 — 3 — 4 — 5 — 6 — 7 → Engine

Total cycle 12.6 minutes
Average at each station 1.8 minutes

FIGURE   14–4   Saab Engine Assembly after Enlarging Jobs

A new work flow at Saab: each worker has a total job.

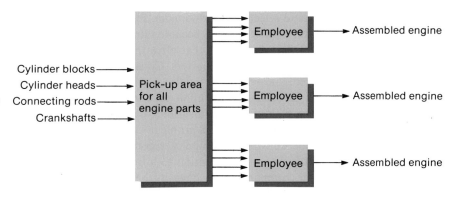

---

line.[21] The engineering team working on the problem decided that the typical system of assembly with a cycle of 12.6 minutes to put an engine together (1.8 minutes per station) at seven workstations could be improved. The traditional assembly system is presented in Figure 14–3.

Instead of using a GM-type system, Saab wanted to use a system that improved the quality of work life on the assembly line. Management decided to use job enlargement. Rather than have seven specialists (one at each workstation on the line), they elected to have one person follow an engine from start to finish. The new arrangement is presented in Figure 14–4. The average time a worker spent on the assembly of an engine was about 30 minutes, as opposed to the 1.8 minute spent at the old workstation (Figure 14–3). By assembling an entire engine, a worker might find the work more interesting and challenging. Of course, whether the work becomes more interesting and challenging depends on the person and the enlargement. Adding on tasks that are meaningless may be enlargement, but it may have negative effects on performance and morale.

Changes in line-staff relationships.   The usual approach in changing line-staff relationships is to create staff assistance as either an ad hoc or permanent solution. An illustrative case is a company that had grown quite rapidly since its entry into the fast-food industry. Its basic sources of field

---

[21] W. F. Dowling, "Job Design in the Assembly-Line: Farewell to the Blue Collar Blues?" *Organizational Dynamics,* Spring 1973, pp. 51–67; P. G. Gyllenhammer, *People at Work* (Reading, Mass.: Addison-Wesley Publishing, 1977).

control were area directors who supervised the operations of sales outlets of particular regions. During the growth period, the area directors had considerable autonomy in making the advertising decisions for their regions. They could select their own media, formats, and budgets within general guidelines. But as their markets became saturated and as competitors appeared, corporate officials decided to centralize the advertising function in a staff unit located at corporate headquarters. Consequently the area directors' freedom was limited, and an essential job aspect was eliminated.[22]

A second illustration of changes in line-staff relationships is based on the case of a large insurance company that hired a management consulting firm to analyze the problem created by a deteriorating market position.[23] The consulting company recommended a program of decentralization by changing a staff position to a line manager. The consultants' belief was that the company must have its best personnel and resources available at the branch office level to increase premium income. Accordingly, the consultants recommended that assistant managers be converted to first-level supervisors reporting to branch managers. The transformation required a significant change in the work of both assistant managers and managers throughout the organization.

These examples only suggest the range of alternatives managers must consider. In exploring such changes, both students and managers must recognize the interrelationships of structural parts. A change in job content does not take place in a vacuum; on the contrary, the change affects all other directly related jobs, supervisory and nonsupervisory alike. *The management of structural change must be guided by the point of view that all things are connected.*

Changes in sociotechnical systems.

The term *sociotechnical systems* is identified with research orginally done by the Tavistock Institute in Great Britain. Change efforts have attempted to develop a better fit between the technology, the structure, and the social-interaction patterns of a unit, department, or office.[24]

While jobs, rewards, physical equipment, work schedules, and other factors may be altered in sociotechnical change, none of these is the central focus of the change activities. Instead employees, union members, nonunion members, and managers examine all aspects of the work operation. Potential

---

[22] See Herbert A. Simon et al., *Centralization versus Decentralization in Organizing the Controller's Department* (New York: Controllership Foundation, 1954), for a classic discussion of the key issues to be resolved in deciding where to locate staff units—in this case, an accounting unit.

[23] Jeremiah J. O'Connell, *Managing Organizational Innovation* (Homewood, Ill.: Richard D. Irwin, 1968).

[24] Marvin R. Weisbord, "Participative Work Design: A Personal Odyssey," *Organization Dynamics,* Spring 1985, pp. 5–20; J. Richard Hackman and Greg R. Oldman, *Work Redesign* (Reading, Mass.: Addison-Wesley Publishing, 1980), p. 62.

changes emerge from the collaboration and discussion of employees. A distinct feature of sociotechnical systems change is that groups of employees share the responsibility for initiating changes.

One of the earliest studies of sociotechnical change was in British coal mining. A team approach was used to develop enlarged jobs and team pay incentive plans. This study indicated improved productivity, safety, and morale after the team initiated changes.[25] Using the British results, a study was conducted at the Rushton Coal Mine in Phillipsburg, Pennsylvania. A steering committee comprised of management and local union officials met to consider methods for improving mine safety. It was decided to train crew members in all jobs in a section, to train members in state and federal mine laws, to train members in group problem solving, and to make crew members responsible for the production of coal and any initial handling of grievances.[26]

The results after one year indicated fewer violations of federal laws by the crews in the study, lower absenteeism, increased job satisfaction and cooperation, and generally better performance. The crews involved in recommending and initiating the sociotechnical changes were overall better performers and reported higher morale than counterparts not collaborating in changing the system.

Despite some reported successes with changes in sociotechnical systems, there are problems with the approach. Sociotechnical system change approaches have, in many cases, ignored individual differences in how people react to various changes. There are some people who do not want the sociotechnical aspects of their jobs or work environment altered. There also are union representatives who claim that collaborative efforts between management and operating employees to initiate sociotechnical system changes will undermine the union's influence on rank and file members. Likewise, some managers claim that collaborative efforts will permanently undermine management's right to manage. These types of problems will be addressed by managers and behavioral scientists who are learning more about the strengths, weaknesses, and future uses of changes in sociotechnical systems.

People Change

People-change techniques refer to efforts to redirect and improve employee attitudes, skills, and knowledge bases. The major objective is to enhance the capacity of individuals to perform assigned tasks in coordination with others.

The early efforts to engage in people change date back to scientific management work improvement and employee training methods. These attempts

---

[25] E. L. Trist et al., *Organization Choice* (London: Tavistock Publications, 1965).

[26] T. Mills, "Altering the Social Structure in Coal Mining: A Case Study," *Monthly Labor Review,* October 1976, pp. 3–10.

were directed primarily at improving employee skills and knowledge bases. The employee counseling programs that grew out of the Hawthorne studies were (and remain) primarily directed at improving employee attitudes. Rosabeth Kanter, in the following Management Focus, outlines some important pointers for increasing the commitment of people to changes in the workplace. These pointers are guidelines that managers can use in introducing any form of change—structural, people, or technological.

MANAGEMENT FOCUS
How Managers Can Improve Commitment to Change

1. Allow room for participation in the planning of the change.
2. Leave choices within the overall decision to change.
3. Provide a clear picture of the change, a "vision" with details about the new state.
4. Share information about change plans to the fullest extent possible.
5. Divide a big change into more manageable and familiar steps; let people take a small step first.
6. Minimize surprises; give people advance warning about new requirements.
7. Allow for digestion of change requests—a chance to become accustomed to the idea of change before making a commitment.
8. Repeatedly demonstrate your own commitment to the change.
9. Make standards and requirements clear; tell exactly what is expected of people in the change.
10. Offer positive reinforcement for competence; let people know they can do it.
11. Look for and reward pioneers, innovators, and early successes to serve as models.
12. Help people find or feel compensated for the extra time and energy change requires.
13. Avoid creating obvious "losers" from the change (but if there are some, be honest with them—early on).
14. Allow expressions of nostalgia and grief for the past; then create excitement about the future.

Source: Adapted from Rosabeth Moss Kanter, "Managing the Human Side of Change," *Management Review,* April 1985, pp. 52–56.

Training and development programs for managers typically have emphasized supervisory relationships. These programs attempt to provide supervisors with basic technical and human relations skills. Since supervisors are primarily concerned with overseeing the work of others, the content of these traditional programs emphasizes techniques for dealing with people problems: how to handle the malcontent, the loafer, the troublemaker, the complainer. The programs also include conceptual material dealing with communications, leadership styles, and organizational relationships. The vehicles for training include role playing, discussion groups, lectures, and organized courses offered by universities.[27] A number of programs include materials about the Managerial Grid, participative leadership, and other ideas derived from the behavioral approach or from individuals who are interested particularly in improving the management of people.

Training continues to be an important technique for introducing people changes. Training has taken on quite a different form in some applications from that which developed in classical management theory.[28] Among some managers, a popular behavioral change approach is sensitivity training.

Sensitivity training.   This change technique attempts to make the participants more aware of themselves and of their impact on others. "Sensitivity" in this context means sensitivity to self and to relationships with others. An assumption of sensitivity training is that the causes of poor task performance are the emotional problems of people who collectively must achieve a goal. If these problems can be removed, a major impediment to task performance is consequently eliminated. Sensitivity training stresses the *process* rather than the *content* of training and . . . *emotional* rather than *conceptual* training.[29] We can see that this form of training is quite different from traditional forms stressing the acquisition of a predetermined body of concepts with immediate application to the workplace.

The process of sensitivity training includes a group of managers (training group or T group) that, in most cases, comes together at some location other than their place of work. Under the direction of a trainer, the group usually engages in a dialogue with no agenda and no focus. The objective is to provide an environment that produces its own learning experiences.[30] The unstructured dialogue encourages one to learn about self in dealing with others. One's motives and feelings are revealed through behavior toward

---

[27] Ernest Dale and L. C. Michelon, *Modern Management Methods* (New York: World Publishing, 1966), pp. 15–16.

[28] A survey of alternative training methodologies is presented in Edward C. Ryterband and Bernard M. Bass, "Management Development," in *Contemporary Management,* ed. Joseph W. McGuire. (Englewood Cliffs, N.J.: Prentice-Hall, 1974), pp. 579–609.

[29] L. This and G. L. Lippit, "Managerial Guidelines to Sensitivity Training," *Training and Development Journal,* June 1981, pp. 144–50; Henry C. Smith, *Sensitivity to People* (New York: McGraw-Hill, 1966), p. 197.

[30] L. P. Bradford, J. R. Gibb, and K. D. Benne, *T-Group Theory and Laboratory Method* (New York: John Wiley & Sons, 1964).

others in the group and through the behavior of others. The T group typically is unstructured. As Alfred Marrow points out in a report of his own sensitivity training, "It [sensitivity training] says, 'Open your eyes. Look at yourself. See how you look to others. Then decide what changes, if any, you want to make and in which direction you want to go.' "[31]

The role of the trainer in the T group is to facilitate the learning process. According to Kelly, the trainer's mission is "to observe, record, interpret, sometimes to lead, and always to learn."[32] The artistry and style of the trainer are critical variables in determining the direction of the T group's sessions. The trainer must walk the uneasy path of unobtrusive leadership, able to interpret the roles of participants and encourage them to analyze their contributions without being perceived as a threat. Unlike the group therapist, the T-group trainer is dealing with people who are not having emotional problems but who have come together to learn. The ordinarily prescribed role of the trainer is that of "permissive, nonauthoritarian, sometimes almost nonparticipative" leadership.[33]

The critical test of sensitivity training is whether the experience itself is a factor leading to improvement in task performance. It is apparent that even if the training induces positive changes in the participant's sensitivity to self and others, such behavior may be either not possible or not permissible back in the workplace. The participant must deal with the same environment and the same people as before the training. The open, supportive, and permissive environment of the training sessions is not likely to be found on the job. Even so, proponents of sensitivity training would reply that it makes the participant better able to deal with the environment. We also should recognize that sensitivity training may well induce negative changes in the participant's ability to perform organizational tasks. The training sessions can be occasions of extreme stress and anxiety. The capacity to deal effectively with stress varies among individuals, and the outcome may be dysfunctional for some participants.

The research evidence to date suggests mixed results on the effectiveness of sensitivity training as a change technique.[34] A detailed review of 100 research studies found that sensitivity training was most effective at the personal level.[35] The studies compared the influence of 20 or more hours of training on the participants' attitudes or behaviors. The review concluded that sensitivity training:

---

[31] Alfred J. Marrow, *Behind the Executive Mask* (New York: AMACOM, 1964), p. 51.

[32] Joe Kelly, *Organizational Behavior,* 3rd ed. (Homewood, Ill.: Richard D. Irwin, 1980), p. 569.

[33] Leavitt, "Applied Organizational Change," p. 1154.

[34] Robert Golembiewski and A. Blumberg, eds., *Sensitivity Training and the Laboratory Approach: Readings about Concepts and Applications* (Itasca, Ill.: F. E. Peacock Publishers, 1977).

[35] P. B. Smith, "Controlled Studies of the Outcome of Sensitivity Training," *Psychological Bulletin,* July 1975, pp. 597–622.

- Stimulated short-term improvement in communication skills.
- Encouraged trainees to believe that they controlled their behavior more than others.
- Was likely to increase the participative orientation of trainees in leadership positions.
- Improved the perceptions of others toward the trainee.

Managers should critically examine this technique in terms of the kinds of changes desired and those that are possible. Our model suggests the existence of conditions that limit the range of possible changes. In this light, managers must determine whether the changes induced by sensitivity training are instrumental for organizational purposes and whether the prospective participant is able to tolerate the potential anxiety of the training.

A major limitation of sensitivity training is the assumption that when people are aware of themselves, positive changes will be made. This assumption evolves from principles of psychotherapy, where individuals are encouraged to confront their emotions, values, and experiences. Of course, each person has a different capacity to confront values, emotions, and experiences, and some simply refuse.

Team building.   Team building is a change technique that involves an entire group (e.g., a unit, a department) that works on a problem facing the members.[36] Figure 14–5 presents the events that typically occur in team buildings. First the problem is identified. Then the full group participates to diagnose the problem. The main contributing reasons to the problem are identified. After the problem and reasons are clarified, alternative solutions and their positive and negative features are discussed. A solution is selected and then implemented.

An important potential benefit of team building as an organizational change approach is that through interaction in solving problems, the group members become more familiar with each other and the solution. This results in an increased commitment to the solution and its implementation.

A number of barriers to effective team building have been concisely outlined for managers to consider before they adopt it as a change strategy. In order for team building to have a chance at being a successful change approach, it must meet four conditions:[37]

1. The group must have a natural reason (e.g., task completion) for existing.
2. Group members must be mutually dependent on one another in terms of task experience and abilities. If dependence is not present, there is less commitment.

---

[36] S. Jay Liebowitz and Kenneth P. DeMeuse, "The Application of Team Building," *Human Relations,* January 1982, pp. 1–18.

[37] P. Palleschi and P. Heim, "The Hidden Barriers to Team Building," *Training and Development Journal,* July 1980, pp. 14–18.

3. Group members must have similar status.
4. Group communications must be open and trusting.

In recent years, there has been an increase in the use of team building to bring about problem-solving changes that focus on task performance. There is, however, a lack of empirical evidence that team building over a period of time enhances group members' trust, openness, commitment, and performance. Until more studies are available, the growth of team building will continue but not at a rapid pace.

Life and career planning. Company-sponsored programs for life and career planning are growing in popularity. These programs use formal classroom or counseling settings. Participants are asked to focus on their past,

FIGURE   14–5   Team Building: Sequence of Events

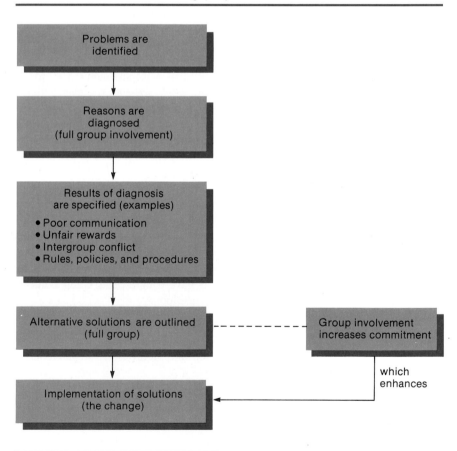

present, and future[38] and to work out their life and career plans. Typically plans are developed after some self-assessment and self-study,[39] These plans may be discussed with colleagues, a human resource development specialist, or a manager. The objective is to have people look at their lives and career plans in a systematic and thorough manner.

The sequence of steps in many life and career planning programs is:

1. Assess life and career paths up to now, noting highlights.
2. Formulate objectives for both desired lifestyle and career path, and forecast the future.
3. Develop a plan of action for achieving the goals and schedule target dates.

Generally life planning and career planning are done concurrently because career planning is but one subset of life planning.

Herbert Shepard is an originator of a life-goals exercise that is often used in life and career planning programs. The exercise is as follows:

I. First phase.
   A. Draw a straight horizontal line from left to right to represent your life span.
   B. Indicate where you are now.
   C. Prepare a life inventory of important "personal events." Note the following:
      1. Peak experiences you have had.
      2. Things you do well.
      3. Things you do poorly.
      4. Things you want to stop doing.
      5. Things you would like to learn.
      6. Peak experiences you would like to have.
      7. Goals you want to achieve.
      8. Things you want to start doing now.
   D. Discuss the inventory with others in small groups.
II. Second phase.
   A. Write your obituary.
   B. Form pairs. Take 20 to 30 minutes to write a eulogy for your partner.
   C. Discuss in pairs.

The life-goals exercise is designed to get people thinking about their life and career plans and to provide data to be shared and discussed with others.[40]

---

[38] Margaret Butteress and Karl Albrecht, *New Management Tools* (Englewood Cliffs, N.J.: Prentice-Hall, 1979), pp. 57–62.

[39] William F. Rothenback, "Career Development: Ask Your Employees for Their Opinions," *Personnel Administrator,* November 1982, pp. 43–51.

[40] Wendell L. French and Cecil Bell, Jr., *Organizational Development* (Englewood Cliffs, N.J.: Prentice-Hall, 1978), pp. 146–48.

Whether life and career planning has any impact on individual attitudes and behaviors has not been scientifically determined at this time. Most of the support for this type of program is found in the form of testimonials of those who have participated in life and career planning. Those who complete such exercises enthusiastically claim that they understand themselves, their careers, and their lifestyles better. They also report less anxiety about the future.

Technological Change

This category of change includes any application of new ways to transform resources into the product or service. In the usual sense of the word, technology means new machines—robots, lathes, presses, computers, and the like. But we expand the concept to include new techniques, with or without new machines. From this perspective, the work improvement methods of scientific management can be considered as technological breakthroughs.

Robots.   The word conjures visions of complex machines that both look and perform like human beings. R2D2 in the popular *Star Wars* movies helps create these viewpoints. Yet in organization reality, robots are quite different; they scarcely resemble people and perform a limited range of job tasks.[41] However, robots are a technological force that is creating resistance and fears among many people—namely workers in the automobile and electrical-component industries.

The Robotics Institute of America defines a robot as a "reprogrammable multifunctional manipulator designed to move material, parts, tools, or specialized devices through programmed motions for the performance of a variety of classes."[42] The more sophisticated robots are called intelligent, while their less sophisticated counterparts are labeled as dumb, slaves, grasshoppers (an automobile industry term), and CAM (computer-aided manufacturing).

Robot use is expected to continue to grow throughout the remainder of this century because of wage inflation and the development of the microprocessor, a computer small enough to use as the brains of a robot.[43] In the 1960s, a typical assembly-line robot cost $4.20 an hour (averaged over its lifetime), which was slightly higher than the average factory worker's wages and fringe benefits. Today the robot still can be operated for less than $5 an hour, while the employee now makes between $15 and $20 an hour.

One of the earliest countries to realize the economic benefits of robots

---

[41] Jeffrey G. Miller and Thomas E. Vallmann, "The Hidden Factory," *Harvard Business Review,* September–October 1985, pp. 142–50.

[42] George L. Whaley, "The Impact of Robotics Technology upon Human Resource Management," *Personnel Administrator,* September 1982, p. 61.

[43] Robert A. Pierson, "Automation," *Management Review,* July 1985, pp. 33–35.

was Japan. Although most of the original research and development on robotic technology occurred in the United States, Japan had about 30,000 of the world's 45,000 robots in 1984. The United States had about 7,000.[44]

General Motors has about 2,000 robots in place or on order; GM will have 6,000 robots on the job by the end of 1986 and an estimated 20,000 by 1990. Chrysler Corporation used 100 robotic welders in their assembly plants where K-cars were made.

The changes in organizational efficiency brought about by a new machine or robot are calculable in economic and engineering terms. Whether the robot or machine is a good investment is a matter of estimating its future profitability in relation to its present cost. These calculations are an important part of the managerial control function. Here, however, we are interested in the impact of the machine or robot on the structure of the organization and on the behavior of the people in the organization.

As some scholars have observed, technology is a key determinant of structure.[45] They tentatively conclude that firms with simple and stable technology should adopt a structure that tends toward classical organization, whereas firms with complex and dynamic technology ought to move toward the more open and flexible neoclassical structure.[46] Thus, it would appear that the adoption of new technology involves a concurrent decision to adapt the organzational structure to that technology. Whether an inexorable and deterministic relationship between technology and structure exists, the fact remains that the introduction of technological innovation has far-reaching effects on the organization.

The most recognizable impact of the robot technology is likely to be upon the behavior of groups and individuals. In the short run, robots have displaced some employees. This displacement creates feelings of insecurity, uncertainty, and fear, which lead to resistance on the part of workers.[47] Some organizations have attempted to minimize this type of resistance by having workers participate in planning the introduction of robots.

In order to catalog the impact of technological change on structure and behavior, Floyd C. Mann analyzed a number of actual cases and concluded that the adoption of new machines in the factory involves:[48]

---

[44] Fred K. Foulkes and Jeffrey L. Hirsch, "People Make Robots Work," *Harvard Business Review,* January–February 1984, pp. 94–102.

[45] Woodward, *Industrial Organization;* Jasinski, *"Adapting Organization,"* among others.

[46] Tom Burns and G. M. Stalker make this point in their analysis of the ways Scottish electronics firms responded to technological change. They use the terms *mechanistic* to refer to relatively tight, highly structured organizations and *organic* to refer to relatively loose, flexibly structured organization. Tom Burns and G. M. Stalker, *The Management of Innovation* (London: Tavistock Publications, 1961).

[47] Vandra L. Huber and Geri Gay, "Channeling New Technology to Improve Training," *Personnel Administrator,* February 1985, pp. 49–57.

[48] Floyd C. Mann, "Psychological and Organizational Impacts," in *Automation and Technological Change,* ed. John T. Dunlop (Englewood Cliffs, N.J.: Prentice-Hall, 1962), pp. 50–55.

1. Major changes in the division of labor and the content of jobs.
2. Changes in social relations among workers.
3. Improving working conditions.
4. The need for different supervisory skills.
5. Changes in career patterns, promotion procedures, and job security.
6. Generally higher wages.
7. Generally higher prestige for those who work.
8. Around-the-clock operations.

The degree and extent of these observed changes in structure and behavior depend upon the magnitude of the technological change. Obviously, the introduction of a new offset printing press will not cause the great dislocations and changes that Mann observes, but the introduction of robots on a previously human-paced manufacturing process would include many, if not all, of them.

FIGURE   14–6   Selected Programs, Techniques, and Outcomes of Organizational Change

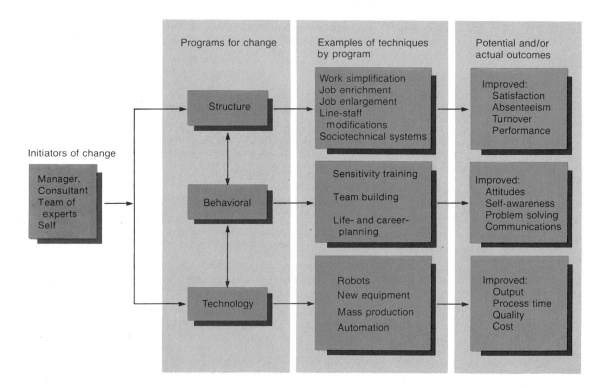

Structural, behavioral, technological change techniques and what they are supposed to accomplish.

Comparison of Three Major Change Approaches

The three major approaches to organizational change we have presented are structure, people, and technology. Each of these, and any combination of them, is designed to improve the effectiveness, well-being, and attitudes of employees (managers and nonmanagers). The use of these change approaches is based on the assumption that modifying structure, people, and technology can result in individual, group, and organizational improvements. Figure 14–6 portrays the three approaches, the types of programs in each approach, and the anticipated outcomes. The potential and actual accomplishment of such outcomes is why managers search out, test, and evaluate various change techniques.

STEP 3: REACTION—RECOGNITION OF LIMITING CONDITIONS

The selection of the change technique is based on diagnosis of the problem. But the choice is tempered by certain conditions that exist at the time. Three sources of influence on the outcome of management development programs have been identified. They can be generalized to cover the entire range of organizational change efforts, whether structural, behavioral, or technological. They are leadership climate, formal organization, and organizational culture.

Leadership climate refers to the nature of the work environment resulting from the leadership style and administrative practices of superiors. Any change program that does not have the support and commitment of management has slim chance of success; managers must be at least neutral toward the change. The style of leadership itself may be the subject of change. For example, sensitivity training is a direct attempt to move managers toward a certain style—open, supportive, and group centered. But the participants may be unable to adopt styles that are not compatible with their own superiors' styles.

The *formal organization* must be compatible with the proposed change. This includes the effects on the environment that result from the philosophy and policies of top management, as well as legal precedent, organizational structure, and the system of control. Of course, each of these sources of impact may be the focus of the change effort; the important point is that a change in one must be compatible with all others. For example, a change in technology that eliminates jobs contradicts a policy of guaranteed employment.

The *organizational culture* refers to the impact on the environment resulting from "group norms, values, philosophy, and informal activities."[49] The impact of traditional behavior, sanctioned by group norms but not formally

---

[49] Edgar H. Schein, *Organizational Culture and Leadership* (San Francisco: Jossey-Bass, 1985).

acknowledged, was first documented in the Hawthorne studies. A proposed
change in work methods or the installation of an automated device can run
counter to the expectations and attitudes of work groups. The concept of
culture is rooted in theories of group dynamics and group growth. Such
being the case, the change strategist must anticipate the resulting resistance
that can evolve from the group.[50] An assessment procedure for examining
culture is presented in the Management Focus on culture gaps.

MANAGEMENT FOCUS
Organizational Culture Gaps: A Limiting Condition

The contrast between desired and actual norms in any company
or department can be significant. Ralph Kilman and Mary Jane Sex-
ton have developed an interesting measurement tool for detecting
what they call cultural gaps (what it is and what it should be). The
Kilman-Sexton Culture Gap Survey was developed by first collecting
over 400 task, personal, and job performance norms from managers
and employees in more than 25 different organizations.

A final set of 28 norm pairs are on the survey form. An example
of a norm pair is: (A) Share information only when it benefits your
own work group versus (B) Share information to help the organization make better decisions. Each respondent chooses the A or B
for each norm pair in two ways: first, according to the pressures
the work group puts on its members (actual norms); and second,
according to which norms should be operating in order to promote
high performance and morale.

The differences between the actual norms and the desired norms
represent the culture gaps. There are four types of culture gaps
made up of seven norm pairs each:

1. *Task support:* Norms having to do with information sharing, helping other groups, and concern with efficiency.
2. *Task innovation:* Norms for being creative, being rewarded for
   creativity, and doing new things.
3. *Social relationships:* Norms for socializing with one's work group
   and mixing friendships with business.
4. *Personal freedom:* Norms for self-expression, exercising discretion, and pleasing oneself.

---

[50] Lawrence A. Benningson, "Managing Corporate Cultures," *Management Review,* February
1985, pp. 31–32; Ralph H. Kilman, *Beyond the Quick Fix* (San Francisco: Jossey-Bass, 1984),
pp. 21–124.

> **MANAGEMENT FOCUS** (*continued*)
>
> The survey can be used to develop, for each unit or department, a profile that can reveal where gaps exist in the organization and which employees see culture gaps. Correcting culture gaps can prove to be valuable in creating a common mission and strategy in an organization. The Kilman-Sexton work on organizations suggests that cultures can be fixed and improved.
>
> ─────────
>
> Source: Adapted from Ralph H. Kilman, *Beyond the Quick Fix* (San Francisco: Jossey-Bass, 1984, pp. 105–21.

In a real sense, when managers evaluate the strength of limiting conditions, they simultaneously are considering the problem of setting objectives. Many managers have been disappointed when change efforts fall short of their expectations. Particularly frustrated are those who cannot understand why the simple issuance of a directive does not produce the intended response. Thoughtful managers will recognize that even as they operate as forces for change, other conditions are operating as forces for stability. The realities of limiting conditions are such that managers often must be content with modest change or no change at all.[51]

STEP 4: REACTION—THE STRATEGY FOR CHANGE

Selection of a strategy for implementing the change technique has consequences in the final outcome. Greiner analyzes a number of organization changes to determine the relationship of various change strategies to the relative success of the change itself.[52] He identifies three approaches, located along a continuum, with unilateral authority at one extreme and delegated authority at the other extreme. In the middle of the continuum are approaches he calls shared authority.

Unilateral approaches can take the form of an edict from top management describing the change and the responsibilities of subordinates in implementing it.[53] *Shared approaches* involve lower-level groups in the process of either

─────────

[51] Herbert Kaufman, "The Direction of Organization Evolution," *Public Administration Review,* July–August 1974, pp. 300–307, has made a strong plea for reality-centered objectives in organizational change programs.

[52] Greiner, "Patterns."

[53] Greiner identifies replacement of key personnel and structural changes as two other forms of unilateral change. For our purposes, personnel and structural changes are change techniques, not strategies for implementing change. Techniques specify *what* is to be done, strategies specify *how* it is to be done.

(1) defining the problem and alternative solutions or (2) defining solutions only after higher-level management has defined the problem. In either case, the process engages the talents and insights of all members at all levels. Finally, *delegated approaches* relinquish complete authority to subordinate groups. Through freewheeling discussions, the group ultimately is responsible for the analysis of the problem and proposed solutions. According to Greiner, the relatively more successful instances of organizational change are those that tend toward the shared position of the continuum.

Why would this be the case? As has been observed, most instances of organizational change are accompanied by resistance from those involved in the change. The actual form of resistance may range in extreme from passive resignation to deliberate sabotage. The objective of shared approaches is at least to minimize resistance and at most to maximize cooperation and support. The manner in which the change is managed from beginning to end is a key determinant of how employees and lower-echelon managers react.

The shared approach for implementing change is fairly popular and involves the participation of superiors and subordinates in the entire process. But there is no guarantee that the strategy will work in all cases. Indeed, before employees can meaningfully participate in the change process, four very basic preconditions must exist:[54]

1. An intuitively obvious factor: employees must want to become involved. For any number of reasons, they may reject the invitation. They may have other, more pressing needs, such as getting on with their own work. Or they may view the invitation to participate as a subtle (but not too subtle) attempt by managers to manipulate them toward a solution already predetermined. Perhaps they do not want to become associated with a program that is uncertain and may fail. If the leadership climate or organizational culture has created an atmosphere of mistrust and insincerity, most attempts to involve workers will be viewed by them in cynical terms.

2. The employees must be willing and able to voice their ideas. Even if they are willing, they must have expertise in some aspect of the analysis. The technical problems associated with computer installation or automated processes may be beyond the training of assembly-line workers, yet they may have valuable insights into the impact of the machinery on their and co-workers' jobs. And even if they have the knowledge, they must be able to articulate their ideas.

3. The managers must be secure in their own positions. Insecure managers

---

[54] Based upon Arnold S. Judson, *A Manager's Guide to Making Changes* (New York: John Wiley & Sons, 1966), pp.109–13. Much popular and scientific literature treats employee participation in decision making. For an example of each type, see W. L. Mandry, "Participative Management: The CIL Experience," *Business Quarterly,* Winter 1971, pp. 80–87; Joseph A. Alutto and James A. Belasco, "A Typology for Participation in Organizational Decision-Making," *Administrative Science Quarterly,* March 1972, pp. 117–25.

would perceive any participation by employees as a threat to their authority. They might view employee participation as a sign of weakness or as undermining their status. They must be able to give credit for good ideas and to give explanations for ideas of questionable merit. As is evident, the managers' personalities and leadership styles must be compatible with the shared-authority approach if it is to be a successful strategy.

4. The managers must be open minded to employees' suggestions. If they have predetermined the solution, the participation of employees soon will be recognized for what it is. Certainly managers have final responsibility for the outcome and can control the situation by specifying beforehand what latitude will be given the employees: They may define objectives, establish constraints, or whatever, so long as the employees know the rules prior to their participation.

If any of the conditions that limit effective participation are present, the use of shared- or delegated-authority approaches must be viewed with caution. As we have seen, the same factors limiting the range of viable alternative change techniques also limit the range of alternative change strategies. Leadership style, formal organization, organizational culture, and characteristics of the employees are key variables constraining the entire change process. Also, the nature of the problem itself affects the choice of strategy. If, for example, the problem is one requiring immediate action, a unilateral approach may be the only means, since alternative approaches consume time. We can summarize by observing that the appropriate change strategy depends upon three factors: the problem, the participants, and various organizational dimensions.

STEP 5: REACTION—IMPLEMENTATION AND EVALUATION

The implementation of the proposed change has two dimensions: timing and scope. *Timing* is the selection of the appropriate time to initiate the change. *Scope* is the selection of the appropriate scale of the change. The matter of timing is strategic and depends upon a number of factors, particularly the company's operating cycle and the groundwork preceding the change. Certainly, if a change is of considerable magnitude, it is desirable that it not compete with ordinary business operations. Thus, it might well be implemented during a slack period. On the other hand, if the problem is critical to the survival of the organization, immediate implementation is in order. The scope of the change depends on the strategy. The change may be implemented throughout the organization and become an established fact in a short period of time. Or it may be phased into the organization, level by level, department by department. The strategy of successful changes, according to Greiner, makes use of a phased approach, which limits the scope but provides feedback for each subsequent implementation.

Evaluation is an important and often overlooked step in organizational change programs. Essentially, evaluation should be made by comparing the results (the benefits) with the objectives of the organizational change program. It is difficult to evaluate the effectiveness of most change efforts. But it is crucial to know what has resulted in terms of attitudes, productivity, and behavior.

There are three types of criteria for evaluating organizational change programs: internal, external, and participant reaction. *Internal criteria* are directly associated with the basis of the program. For example, did the sociotechnical change result in increased frequency of employee exchange of job information, or did the employees in the job enrichment seminar learn the core dimensions of the job? *External criteria* are related to the effectiveness of employees before and after the change is implemented. Possible external criteria include increased number of units produced per work-hour, increased sales volume, and better quality of workmanship. *Participant reaction criteria*

FIGURE   14–7   An Evaluation Matrix: Issues to Consider

Relevant Issues to Cover and Evaluate	Examples of What to Measure	Who or What to Examine for Answers	How to Collect Data to Answer Issue Questions
1. Are the employees learning, changing attitudes, and/or improving skills?	Employees' attitudes and/or skills before and after (even during) training or development sessions.	Comments. Method of participation. Co-workers. Superiors.	Interviews. Questionnaires. Records. Observation.
2. Are organizational change materials used on the job?	Employees' on-the-job performance, behavior, and style.	Subordinate performance, attitudes, and style.	Records. Interviews. Questionnaires. Critical Incidents. Observation.
3. What are the costs of organizational change programs and techniques?	The fixed and variable costs of conducting the change programs.	Cost of consultants. Participant time. Travel expenses. Training aids. Rent. Utilities.	Budget records.
4. How long does the organizational change program have an effect on employees?	Employees' on-the-job performance, behavior, and style over an extended period of time.	Subordinate performance, attitudes, and style.	Records. Interview. Questionnaires. Critical incidents. Observation (repeated).

attempt to determine how the individuals affected by the change feel about it.

One useful device encourages the use of multiple and systematic assessment. Figure 14–7 presents a guideline (in the form of a matrix) for managers to use. The costs and benefits of any organizational change effort can be determined only if evaluation programs are used. Simply asking individuals if they like the sensitivity training program or the job enlargement changes is not very thorough. It would be more systematic and thorough to monitor changes in structure, people, and technology over long periods of time.

SUMMARY OF KEY POINTS

- Organization development (OD) is a method for facilitating change and development in structures and processes (e.g., relationships, roles), people (e.g., styles, skills), and technology (e.g., more routineness, more challenge).

- There are numerous reasons for resisting change. Some of the most commonly cited are parochial self-interest, misunderstanding and lack of trust, different assessments, and a low tolerance for change.

- Managers can take some steps to minimize resistance: education and communication, participation and involvement, facilitation and support, negotiation and agreement, manipulation and co-optation, and explicit and implicit coercion.

- A five-part model presented in Figure 14–1 provides some order and a framework for the study of organizational change and development. Step 1 includes stimuli such as internal and external forces that trigger a reaction or recognition of the need for change. Step 2 involves the diagnosis for problem areas. Step 3 involves stimuli in the form of alternative change techniques that can be selected and a reaction by managers in that limiting conditions are recognized. In Step 4, a decision is made on the strategy and the technique to use. Step 5 involves the implementation and evaluation of the change.

- The choice of a particular change technique depends upon the nature of the problem management has diagnosed. We classify them according to the major focus of the change technique: structure, people, or technology. Techniques to change structure include changes in the nature of jobs, job enlargement, changes in line-staff relationships, and changes in sociotechnical systems. Techniques to change people include sensitivity training, team building, and life and career planning. Techniques to change technology include any application of new ways to transform resources into the product or service, such as new technology (e.g., robots).

■ Strategies for introducing change are *unilateral* (an edict for change from top management), *delegated* (control for the change is relinquished to those being affected by the change), and *shared* (participation between the initiators and recipients of change in deciding on the problem or solution).

■ In many cases, not enough time and effort are spent on the evaluation of change. Evaluation of behavior, results, and attitudes is needed to examine the costs and benefits of any structural, people, or technological change effort.

DISCUSSION AND REVIEW QUESTIONS

1. How could team building enhance commitment to a structural change in an organization?

2. How could culture gaps such as those identified with the Kilman-Sexton survey hinder the effectiveness of organizational change?

3. The notion of planned change is assumed to be more effective than a nonplanned approach. In fact, some state that the federal government could benefit from a planned approach in efforts to bring about changes in various agencies. Do you believe this is true? Why?

4. Can you present an example that you are familiar with in which a job can be enlarged? Use the Saab example to help you think through the necessary features for job enlargement.

5. It has been claimed that as the tasks performed by humans become more complex, the probability of robots replacing human labor increases. Do you agree?

6. Would employees' resistance to change be more or less intense during times of high unemployment? Why?

7. A manager stated: "It took me 30 years to develop a set of defense mechanisms that enable me to live and function in this crazy world. I refuse to participate in any training program whose objective is to tear them down." Comment.

8. Behavioral change is difficult to measure accurately. Some changes in employee behavior occur subtly, over time. Why would it be difficult to measure subtle changes in behavior that may be occurring during a sensitivity training program? Should these changes, if they are occurring, be measured at all?

9. A model can serve as a guideline for someone actually managing employees. The model used can alert managers to various constraints or issues that may appear. Would there be any value for a manager in understanding the parts of the model represented in Figure 14–1? Explain.

10. Are participative management systems an example of people, structural, or technological change? Explain.

ADDITIONAL REFERENCES

Calvert, R., Jr. "Training America: The Numbers Add Up." *Training and Development Journal,* Novemeber 1985, pp. 35–37.

Eden, D. "Team Development: A True Field Experiment at Three Levels of Rigor." *Journal of Applied Psychology,* February 1985, pp. 94–100.

Gordon, J. "Games Managers Play." *Training/HRD* July 1985, pp. 30–47.

Hatcher, L. L., and T. L. Ross. "Organization Development through Productivity Gainsharing." *Personnel,* October 1985, pp. 42–50.

Kimberly, J. R., and R. E. Quinn. *Managing Organizational Transitions.* Homewood, Ill.: Richard D. Irwin, 1984.

Maxey, C., and T. Cummings. "Organization Development and Labor Law: Implications for Practice/Malpractice." Center for Effective Organizations Working Paper, University of Southern California, 1985.

Naisbitt, J., and P. Aburdene. *Re-Inventing the Corporation.* New York: Warner Books, 1985.

Sayles, L. R., and V. L. Wright. "The Use of Culture in Strategic Management." *Issues and Observations,* November 1985, pp. 1–9.

Seashore, S. E.; E. E. Lawler; P. H. Mirvis; and C. Cammann. *Assessing Organizational Change.* New York: John Wiley & Sons, 1983.

Sullivan, S. M. "Management a la Francais." *Management Review,* June 1985, pp. 11–14.

Vicars, W.M., and D. D. Hartke. "Evaluating OD Evaluations: A Status Report." *Groups and Organization Studies,* 1984, pp. 177–88.

Woodman, R. W., and S. J. Wayne. "An Investigation of Positive-Finding Bias in Evaluation of Organization Development Intervention." *Academy of Management Journal,* December 1985, pp. 889–913.

CASES

APPLICATION I

MOTOROLA MAKES SOME BOLD CHANGES*

Motorola, Inc.'s Chief Executive Officer Robert Galvin believes that the firm's openness to change is a major reason it has fared better than Philco, Zenith, and Admiral. Motorola has been able to move from relatively low

---

* Source: Adapted from James O'Toole, "How Motorola Got to Be Number One," *New Management,* Fall 1985, pp. 4–13.

technology to leadership in the most sophisticated high-tech fields: microprocessors, semiconductors, and cellular mobile phones.

What happened at Motorola is interesting in that there was no crisis to
change. The company and the industry appeared to be in good shape. Galvin
did something highly unusual for an American executive: He anticipated
the need for future change even though the company was not in any imminent
trouble.

Galvin saw that his plan could only be realized through the active support
of *all* of Motorola's employees. In fact, Galvin saw in the 1960s that to
get the support he needed, he would have to involve as many of his people
as possible in *creating* that plan. As the Motorola plan developed, it became
clear to top management that a centralized, highly directive corporate structure would not produce the kind of commitment, effort, and innovation needed
to succeed. To more fully engage Motorola's managers in his "mission impossible," Galvin radically decentralized the company, creating many new "presidents" in the process, each with a small entrepreneurial business to run as
he saw fit (as long as the actions of each complemented and abetted the
thrust of the overall corporate plan). Galvin created an incentive system
for these managers that made them feel they were the "owners" of their
businesses (including a general bonus pool that rewarded innovation, risk
taking, and superior performance).

But that wasn't enough—certainly not enough to remain competitive with
the Japanese, who coveted the same markets Motorola planned to enter.
By the 1970s, Galvin and his managers realized that to compete with the
Japanese, Motorola would need high productivity and high-quality goods.
They also realized that they, Motorola's managers, could not achieve those
objectives by themselves. What was required was employee dedication at
all levels to high standards of quality, productivity, cost control, inventory
control, customer service, and delivery. They realized that they needed a
system that would turn out well-designed products—products with low cost,
high yield, and high reliability. Their goal was nothing less than perfection—
zero defects.

To beat the Japanese competitors at their own game, would Galvin and
his managers have to mimic them? Not on your life! Instead Galvin went
to his roots, to the management principles established by Motorola's founder,
his father Paul Galvin. Under Paul Galvin, Motorola had pioneered some
fairly "radical" employee practices: In 1947, Motorola started a profit sharing
fund into which the company placed 20 percent of pretax earnings. In the
1950s, Motorola jettisoned their last time clock, putting all workers on an
honor system. At about the same time, Motorola created an employee advisory
commitee that reported directly to the board of directors and separate employee task forces to review such subjects as benefits (to ensure that workers
got what they needed and not just what managers wanted to give them).
Motorola workers were also among the first in a large U.S. corporation to

gain a measure of job security: A decision by the CEO was (and still is) needed to fire any worker with 10 years or more service in the company. Significantly, the burden of appeal is on the manager who wishes to do the firing, *not* on the worker. All of this seems to have set well with Motorola employees. In five decades, only one union election has ever been contested in a Motorola plant, and that was in a bargaining unit with only 20 workers (the union lost 17–3).

Motorola's PMP

Throughout the 1970s, the engine of change at Motorola was what they called their participative management program (PMP). It is misnamed. For it is not a "program" at all; rather, it has become synonymous with the way they manage at Motorola. Building on the highly participative style of founder Paul Galvin, Motorola's managers have created a system in which employees now have a greater stake in Motorola than Japanese workers have in the best-run corporations in Japan. Even if the latter point is found to be overstated, it is no doubt the case that working conditions at Motorola are better suited to American workers than would be any Japanese alternative. As one Motorola employee explained to me, "Like the Japanese, we play softball and volleyball on the excellent facilities the corporation provides for us. But, unlike the Japanese, we play when we want to, not on cue!"

The Motorola system of worker participation is much simpler to describe than it was to create, for it was not easy to devise a system in which employees could all legitimately feel they have a say in management. At the start, it was recognized that it would be impossible for all Motorola's 60,000 domestic employees to function effectively if they each acted as individuals. For purposes of coordination, then, Motorola employees have been grouped into teams of some 50 to 250 workers. This system is similar to the Scanlon plan that has been successful for three decades at Herman Miller (the furniture manufacturer).

The genius of the Motorola system is that it has been made to work in a very large corporation. A key element in this successful translation of a small-company idea into big-company practice is Motorola's intricate process of communications. Each working team has one of its members on a steering committee at the next higher level in the company (which, in turn, has a member on another committee at the subsequent higher level). The steering committees perform several critical functions:

1. *Coordination.* A steering committee will act on ideas that come from a working group and require cooperation with one or more other working groups.

2. *Lateral communication.* A steering committee will disseminate the ideas or practices of one working group to other groups, thus facilitating organizational learning.

3. *Downward communication.* A steering committee will ensure that each work group has all the managerial information it requires to do its job.

4. *Upward communication.* Since each steering committee is linked to the next-level steering committee (which, in turn, reports to top management), shop-floor issues reach Motorola executives after going through only four levels in the hierarchical chain (this is an extremely flat organizational structure for a company with 95,000 workers worldwide).

5. *Control.* A steering committee negotiates output standards and measures of performance with the work teams that report it. This is a continuing process in which trust is built by clearly establishing the performance criteria by which work teams will be measured in advance of the evaluation process.

6. *Evaluation.* Based on the negotiated measures of performance, a steering committee evaluates the record of the work teams that report to it and allocates rewards based on a prenegotiated formula.

This system is clearly designed for manufacturing and production workers. Recently Motorola has augmented it with a parallel plan for professional, clerical, marketing, research, and other staff people. These employees also are organized into teams and partake in a bonus program based on performance measures appropriate to their tasks.

Questions for Analysis

1. What are the risks involved in changing a system when it is not in trouble or faltering?

2. Why would some employees resist the participative management program (PMP) at Motorola?

3. How could the success, if any, of the Motorola PMP be evaluated?

APPLICATION II

GENERAL MOTORS' QUALITY–OF–WORK–LIFE SURVEY

General Motors has decided to use a survey questionnaire called "The Quality of Your Work Life in General Motors" to learn about employee

---

EXHIBIT   1   Dimensions of GM's Quality-of-Work-Life Survey Questionnaire*

Employee commitment: Feelings of loyalty to GM; a commitment to and concern for the future of the organization.

Absence of developing apathy: A measure of employees' concern and ambition regarding their work.

On-the-job development and utilization: Opportunity for the employees to learn and apply skills and abilities in a meaningful and challenging way.

Employee involvement and influence: The extent to which employees feel involved in decision making.

Advancement based on merit: The extent to which management is interested in the progress of individuals and rewards people on the basis of ability, performance, and experience.

Career goal progress: Making progress in the achievement of career objectives and the belief that there are opportunities for further progress.

Relations with supervisor: The working relationship with one's supervisor as reflected in fairness, honesty, and mutual respect.

Work group relations: The way employees in a work group provide mutual support and encouragement.

Respect for the individual: The feeling of being treated as an adult, with respect and dignity.

Confidence in management: Belief that management is aware of and concerned about employee problems and interests.

Physical working environment: Conditions affecting employees' health, comfort, and convenience.

Economic well-being: Receiving adequate financial rewards and having income protection.

Employee state of mind: Whether the employees feel upset or depressed while at work.

Absence of undue job stress: The relative absence of excessive work demands and pressures that might interfere with doing the job well.

Impact on personal life: The spillover effect of the job on employees' personal lives.

Union-management relations: The extent to which the union and management recognize mutual goals and are working together.

---

* The survey form has 90 items and uses a five-point scale to record employee responses. Additionally, there are 11 items for recording such information as sex, length of service, educational level, salary level, and kind of work performed. Space has also been provided so that local units can include up to 20 additional items.

---

attitudes and to locate potential trouble spots. The survey is a part of the company's organizational development efforts. The dimensions of GM's quality-of-work-life survey questionnaire are presented in Exhibit 1, and the instructions and some sample questions are presented in Exhibit 2.

This type of survey can provide management with important information from employees. However, sole reliance on survey data is questioned by some who believe that honest responses are rarely provided by individuals because of an innate sense of insecurity. On the other hand, one of the most efficient ways to gather a general picture of what employees think in different units and locations is to ask them in a survey.

EXHIBIT   2   "The Quality of Your Work Life in General Motors"

Instructions and sample questions from GM's questionnaire

Instructions

This survey is aimed at getting your ideas about what it is like to work here. We are trying to learn more about the quality of work life where you work. The purpose of this survey is to measure the attitudes, opinions, and work climate of GM organizations from the employee's point of view.

You should answer each question as honestly as you can so your answers, along with those of other employees, will provide a good measure of the quality of work life at this location.

The best answer is *always* just what you think.

Your answers are completely confidential. Except for the survey administrator, no one in your organization will see your filled-out survey. The survey administrator will see to it that your survey, together with all others taken today, is sent to an independent company. The filled-out surveys will be processed by computers for groups of people, and your survey copy will be destroyed. To be sure that your answers will not be identified, please do *not* write your name on the form.

Sample Questions*

1. What happens to GM is really important to me.   ① ② ③ ④ ⑤

2. I feel very little loyalty to this GM organization.   ① ② ③ ④ ⑤

3. I could care less what happens to GM as long as I get my paycheck.   ① ② ③ ④ ⑤

4. I often think of quitting.   ① ② ③ ④ ⑤

5. I really care about the future of this GM organization.   ① ② ③ ④ ⑤

6. I used to care about my work more than I do now.   ① ② ③ ④ ⑤

7. I used to be more ambitious about my work than I am now.   ① ② ③ ④ ⑤

8. Around here, I am asked for my ideas.   ① ② ③ ④ ⑤

9. GM rewards those who do their jobs well.   ① ② ③ ④ ⑤

10. People who get ahead in this part of GM deserve it.   ① ② ③ ④ ⑤

11. In this part of GM, getting ahead is based on ability.   ① ② ③ ④ ⑤

12. Job experience is financially rewarded in GM.   ① ② ③ ④ ⑤

13. GM management is really interested in my getting ahead.   ① ② ③ ④ ⑤

14. I think more job opportunities should be given to women and minorities around here.   ① ② ③ ④ ⑤

---

* Meaning of ratings are: 1—strongly disagree; 2—disagree; 3—neither agree nor disagree; 4—agree; and 5—strongly agree.

Questions for Analysis

1. What is your opinion about the dimensions covered in the GM survey? It is comprehensive?

2. Is the use of a survey worthwhile for diagnosing the attitudes in a large organization such as General Motors?

3. Why would some employees feel insecure in answering an attitude survey?

COMPREHENSIVE APPLICATION FOR PART III

MANAGING PEOPLE*

NOTE: Do not read this case until directed to do so by your instructor. It has been set up as a Prediction Case so that you can test your analysis by answering questions before reading the entire case.

Part I

During the summer of my freshman year in college, I worked for a small private landscaping company planting shrubs, seeding new lawns, cutting grass, and tending flower gardens. The company was located in my hometown of Seaview, New Jersey, which is a rural community on the coast about 80 miles from Philadelphia. The company was owned and run by Joe Brewster, a 45-year-old man who had lived in Seaview all his life. He had started the company some years ago and not only handled the paperwork (payroll, bills, estimates, and so on) but also worked along with the crew six days a week.

The crew consisted of five guys ranging in age from 17 to 20 years. We all lived in towns around Seaview and had gone to the regional high school, which was physically located in Seaview. Only two of us were attending college, but all had been hired personally by Joe following a short, informal interview. I can't be completely certain about the others, but I think all of us and several others sought the job because we needed work, enjoyed the outdoors, and had heard that Joe paid well and was an OK guy to work for. Working hours were from 8 A.M. to 4:30 P.M. with an hour off for lunch, Monday through Saturday. Once in a while we'd work overtime to help out some customer who had an urgent need. Each worker began at the same wage with the understanding that hard workers would be rehired the next summer at a higher wage. Several of the crew I was part of had been rehired under this policy.

Most of the customers we serviced lived in Seaview, knew Joe personally, and seemed to respect him.

Joe owned one truck, which he used to transport all of us and necessary supplies and equipment from job to job. Each morning he would read off a list of houses that had to be completed that day. He would then leave it

* *Source:* A. R. Cohen, S. L. Fink, H. Gadon, and R. D. Willits, *Effective Behavior in Organizations,* 3rd ed. (Homewood, Ill.: Richard D. Irwin, 1984), pp. 454–58.

up to us to decide among ourselves who would do what task while at a particular house. We also were the ones who determined by our work pace how long we would spend at each house.

In doing the work itself, we were able to use our own ideas and methods. If we did a good job, Joe would always compliment us. If we lacked the necessary know-how or did a poor job, Joe was right there willing to help us.

At each house, Joe worked along with us doing basically the same work we did. He dressed the same as we did and was always very open and friendly towards us. He seldom "showed his authority," and treated us as equals. Although our workday was scheduled to begin at 8, Joe never became upset nor penalized us if we were 10 to 15 minutes late. Our lunch hour was usually an hour long starting anytime between 11:30 and 12:30 depending on what time we, the crew, felt like eating. Each member brought his own lunch to work and anytime during the day could take time off to go to the truck for a snack.

The crew itself became very well acquainted, and we were always free to talk and joke with each other at any time and did so. We enjoyed each other's company, although we did not socialize after hours.

We also became very friendly with the customers. They were always eager to talk to us as we worked, and Joe never objected. All in all, the job had a very relaxed, easygoing atmosphere. I for one felt little pressure to hurry and, like the others, respected and liked Joe very much.

Prediction Question

1. What will be the productivity in terms of quantity and quality of the work crew? Why?

Part II

The attitude we had toward the job was very high. We sometimes talked among ourselves about how we felt a sense of responsibility toward the job. While we talked and joked a lot while working, little horseplay occurred; and the talking and joking did not interfere with the work. We were always working steadily, and efficiently, seeking to keep ahead of schedule. The days seemed to go fairly quickly, and a lot seemed to get done. I know Joe said that our output was 15 percent above that which other landscaping companies experienced with summer crews.

We also took a lot of pride in our work. Feeling responsible for the job we did, we were constantly checking and rechecking every job to be sure it was perfect. We were always willing to work overtime for Joe when he needed us to do so.

Case Question

1.   What elements in the situation contributed to these positive results?
     Can you think of things that, if present, might have led to very different
     results? Explain how.

Part III

I returned the following summer to work for Joe because of the strong
satisfaction I had with the job the summer before. So did the others. However,
we were in for a surprise. Many things had changed. Joe had increased the
number of workers to 10, bought another truck, and hired two young college
graduates from Philadelphia as crew supervisors. His plan was to concentrate
on the paperwork and on lining up new customers, leaving the direct guidance
of the two work crews to the new supervisors.

Joe had hired the two supervisors during the early spring after interviewing
a number of applicants. Both were young (23 and 24), from the city, and
had degrees in agricultural management from Penn State but had not known
each other previously.

We "old-timers" were assigned to one crew, and five new workers were
hired for the other crew. These new workers had little experience in landscaping. Except for the working hours, which were the same as during the previous
summer, the two supervisors were told that they could run their crew in
any manner they wished as long as they kept to the schedule prepared by
Joe.

No one on the crew had known the supervisors before. Joe had found
them through ads in the paper. The supervisors didn't dress quite as informally
as Joe did, perhaps because they didn't do as much actual physical work,
but they did dress casually in dungarees and shirts, the same as the crew.
Though we called the supervisors by their first names, they did some nit-
picky things. For example, Joe never cared who drove the truck or who
did what job; sometimes a crew member would drive, and Joe would talk
with the rest of us. But the supervisors always drove the truck and decided
when we would eat. Nor did the supervisors help us unload the tools as
Joe had done. They stood around and watched us.

Both supervisors refused to tolerate tardiness in the morning and immediately set up a scheduled lunch hour that would remain the same throughout
the summer. We were no longer allowed to go to the truck for a snack
during the day and were constantly being watched over by our supervisor.
The supervisors assigned us to specific tasks to be done at each job and
told us how "they" wanted them to be completed. They also told us how
much time we were to spend doing each job. They refused to let us talk to
each other or to the customers (except about business) saying that it "only

wasted time and interfered with our work." It was a more structured, more formal atmosphere than the summer before.

Prediction Questions

1. What kind of issues or problems are likely to develop during the second summer? Why?
2. How will productivity compare with that of the previous summer in terms of quantity and quality? Why?
3. What would have been your advice to the two supervisors about how they could best approach their new role?

Part IV

I was disappointed at the new setup and a little bit surprised that Joe hadn't hired one of the more experienced members of the old crew as supervisor. But I figured it was necessary because of the increased volume of business so I tried to make the best of it. However, very soon my attitude and that of the rest of the old crew changed significantly. We began to hate the new supervisors and soon developed a great disinterest in the work itself. While I'm a person who usually is very conscientious and responsible, I have to admit that before long I along with the others began to put little care or concern into my work. The supervisors soon found it very difficult to get anyone to work overtime.

The new employees didn't react as strongly as we did, but I could tell that they weren't working with much enthusiasm either.

I thought about talking to the supervisors but didn't because I'd only worked there the one year and figured that it was not my place to. The others were older than I and had worked there longer, so I figured that they should, but no one did. Instead, we talked among ourselves and individually griped to Joe.

Joe didn't seem to know how to deal with our complaints. He passed them off by saying "Oh . . . I'll talk to the supervisors and straighten it out with them." But nothing changed, and in fact they seemed to clamp down more and push even harder. This only made us madder. Our work rate continued to fall.

Incidentally, throughout this period we had little social interaction with the supervisors, but I noticed that they became more and more friendly with each other.

Meanwhile the new crew's difficulties increased. Being new and inexperienced, they couldn't do the work as easily as we could. Also, the supervisors didn't, or couldn't, give them any adequate training. Their productivity went lower and lower. The supervisors were very upset and yelled at them, pushing them to get out their quota. We felt sorry for them and tried to help them; but we concentrated on reluctantly meeting our own quota.

I don't think Joe realized that the supervisors were not teaching the new crewmen. He was very busy and not around much, and I think he assumed that they were training the new men. I think he began to put pressure on the supervisors as the work rate fell, because things continued to get worse. We couldn't even accept drinks. Production lagged greatly as compared to the previous summer, and the two supervisors struggled to meet the schedule and deal with customer complaints about quality. By July 15th, the overall productivity of the company was 5 percent below "normal" and way below the previous summer.

As Joe became aware of this huge decrease in production, he became very concerned and wondered what to do about it.

Case Questions

1.   What caused the poor production condition during the second summer?
2.   How might this situation have been avoided from the beginning?
3.   What should Joe do now?
4.   Do you think the supervisors could have effectively adopted Joe's style of leadership? What kind of problems might they have had if they did? How should they have conducted themselves?

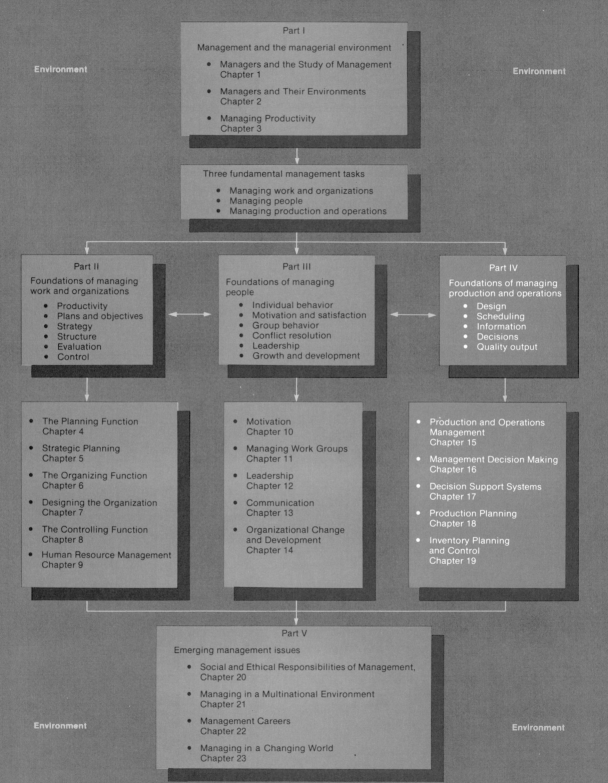

Environment

Part I

Management and the managerial environment

- Managers and the Study of Management
  Chapter 1
- Managers and Their Environments
  Chapter 2
- Managing Productivity
  Chapter 3

Three fundamental management tasks

- Managing work and organizations
- Managing people
- Managing production and operations

Part II

Foundations of managing work and organizations

- Productivity
- Plans and objectives
- Strategy
- Structure
- Evaluation
- Control

Part III

Foundations of managing people

- Individual behavior
- Motivation and satisfaction
- Group behavior
- Conflict resolution
- Leadership
- Growth and development

Part IV

Foundations of managing production and operations

- Design
- Scheduling
- Information
- Decisions
- Quality output

- The Planning Function
  Chapter 4
- Strategic Planning
  Chapter 5
- The Organizing Function
  Chapter 6
- Designing the Organization
  Chapter 7
- The Controlling Function
  Chapter 8
- Human Resource Management
  Chapter 9

- Motivation
  Chapter 10
- Managing Work Groups
  Chapter 11
- Leadership
  Chapter 12
- Communication
  Chapter 13
- Organizational Change
  and Development
  Chapter 14

- Production and Operations
  Management
  Chapter 15
- Management Decision Making
  Chapter 16
- Decision Support Systems
  Chapter 17
- Production Planning
  Chapter 18
- Inventory Planning
  and Control
  Chapter 19

Part V

Emerging management issues

- Social and Ethical Responsibilities of Management,
  Chapter 20
- Managing in a Multinational Environment
  Chapter 21
- Management Careers
  Chapter 22
- Managing in a Changing World
  Chapter 23

Environment

MANAGING PRODUCTION AND OPERATIONS

Foundations

▦ FOUNDATIONS OF MANAGING PRODUCTION AND OPERATIONS

Part IV explores the third major contribution to modern management theory and practice: the *management science approach.* The central theme of management science is *to provide managers with quantitative bases for decisions regarding the operations under their control.*[1] A more complete definition of the field is that it "is the science devoted to describing, understanding, and predicting the behavior of complicated systems of men and machines operating in natural environments."[2] The ideas and concepts of management science are, in fact, extensions of scientific management, which was a major part of the classical approach, even as the behavioral approach is an extension of earlier developments arising out of the Hawthorne studies and human relations. Thus, we can see the thread of continuity that runs through each of the three contributions to contemporary management.

DEVELOPMENT OF MANAGEMENT SCIENCE

The field of management science has formally existed only for approxi-

---

[1] This definition is based on an early and influential book in management science, Philip M. Morse and George E. Kimball, *Methods of Operations Research* (New York: John Wiley & Sons, 1951), p. 1.

[2] John C. Anderson and Thomas R. Hoffman, "A Perspective on the Implementation of Management Science," *Academy of Management Review,* July 1978, p. 564.

mately 40 years. During this period, individuals associated with the field began to have a noticeable impact on the solution of complex military and business problems through the use of engineering and mathematical skills. Also during this period, a new profession emerged: the management scientist.

The terms *management science* (MS) and *operations research* (OR) are synonymous. In recent years, the field is generally designated MS/OR. The use of different terms for essentially the same set of ideas is a characteristic of emerging bodies of knowledge; management science is no exception. But the reader should keep in mind that an aim of management science is *to provide managers with quantitative bases for decisions.*

By the end of World War II, enthusiasm for management science spread throughout business and industrial organizations around the world. It was predicted that this scientific interdisciplinary approach to problem solving would drastically change the practice of management. However, somewhere between the management scientists' "theories, tools, and techniques" and the managers' application of what the scientists were recommending, something happened. The rift between management scientists and managers was stated this way by one expert:

> Management science got its start working on problems that were too big for any one individual to ap-

TABLE 1 Survey Results

Implementation Problem	Percentage of Respondents
1. Selling management science methods to managers.	35%
2. Neither top nor middle managers have the educational background to appreciate management science methods.	34
3. Lack of good clean data.	32
4. There is never enough time to analyze a real problem using a sophisticated approach.	23
5. Lack of understanding by those who need to use the results.	22
6. Hard to define problems for applications.	19
7. The payoff from using unsophisticated methods is sufficient.	16
8. Shortage of personnel.	12
9. Poor reputation of management scientists as problem solvers.	11
10. Individuals feel threatened by management scientists and their methods.	10

The 10 most cited reasons for problems in implementing management science methods.

Source: Reprinted by permission of Hugh J. Watson and Patricia Gill Marett, "A Survey of Management Science Implementation Problems," *Interfaces* 9 (August 1979), p. 125. Copyright 1979 The Institute of Management Sciences.

proach. It was seen that a team effort to synthesize different perspectives was needed to tackle large problems. Many managers disliked this new field because it threatened to take away their jobs and thus somehow the whole discipline was shunted off towards science, with mathematics, rather than problems, being the rationale for existence. . . . A group of people called "managers" would look at operations, make decisions, and manage the company. Another group called "scientists" would do research on theoretical problems and develop algorithms: they were relegated to the back room with the computer experts and accountants.[3]

Concerned with the fact that many management science solutions to organizational problems were not being implemented, people started to ask why. In a survey, 112 management scientists were asked to rank the difficulties they had in implementing their solutions.[4] Table 1 presents a summary of the findings. Interestingly, management scientists suggest that implementation is a problem caused by others (except for Reason 9). They do not indicate that their techniques, style, or knowledge of management could be the major problem.

[3] Rick Hesse, "Management Science or Management/Science?" *Interfaces,* February 1980, p. 104.

[4] Hugh J. Watson and Patricia Gill Marett, "A Survey of Management Science Implementation Problems," *Interfaces,* August 1979, pp. 124–28.

CONTRIBUTIONS OF THE APPROACH

The activities of management scientists have emphasized the mathematical modeling of systems. Applications of these models by operations research specialists, mostly confined to the production segment of business firms, began after World War II. During the war, operations researchers had successfully solved a number of military problems ranging from those of a logistical nature (equipment and troop movements) to developing strategy for submarine warfare. As a result, management science caught on in some of the larger firms in the United States after the war. Such companies as E. I. du Pont de Nemours and H. J. Heinz pioneered the use of early operations research applications. However, not until these bolder firms had tried it with success did civilian operations research make any major headway in the United States.

While it is difficult to place clear boundary lines around the management science process, it is possible to distinguish certain characteristics of its approach. It is generally agreed that most management science tools and techniques possess the following characteristics.[5]

1. *A primary focus on decision making.* The principal end result of the analysis must have direct implications for management action. Deci-

sion making is still the central activity for production and operations managers today, as will be illustrated in Chapter 16.

2. *An appraisal resting on economic effectiveness criteria.* A comparison of feasible actions must be based on measurable values that reflect the future well-being of the organization. Examples of such measured variables include costs, revenues, and rates of return on investment.

3. *Reliance on formal mathematical models.* These models, stated in mathematical form, are actually possible solutions to problems. The procedures for manipulating the data must be so explicit that another analyst can derive the same results from the same data. This *replicability* requirement is not new to the reader, who saw in the previous section that this was also a major requirement of the behavioral science approach to management. In fact, replication is the keynote of scientific analysis.

4. *Dependence on an electronic computer.* This requirement is necessitated by either the complexity of the mathematical model, the volume of data to be manipulated, or the magnitude of computations needed to implement the model.

Managers were faced with the problem of *planning, organizing, and controlling* their organizations' operations long before the advent of the electronic computer and management science models; they are still performing these functions. In other words, it must be recognized that management science *is not* a substitute for management. Mathematical models can be especially useful as an *aid* to

---

[5] Efraim Turban and Jack R. Meredith, *Fundamentals of Management Science* (Plano, Tex.: Business Publications, 1981), pp. 15–23.

FIGURE   1   Managing Production and Operations

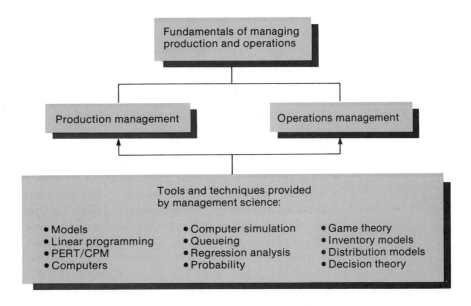

P/OM stresses the application of management science techniques.

the manager performing the functions of *planning* and *controlling production and operations,* as shown in Figure 1. In order to justify its existence to the practicing manager, however, management science models must provide for more efficient and effective planning and controlling.

While management scientists were constructing sophisticated quantitative models and theories, managers in organizations were struggling to manage their day-to-day production and operations more efficiently. What has emerged from this partnership of managers and scientists is a distinct area of inquiry, analysis, and application that focuses on the management of production and operations in manufacturing and service industries.

This area is known as production and operations management (P/OM).[6]

MANAGEMENT SCIENCE: PRODUCTION AND OPERATIONS MANAGEMENT

Probably the most widespread application of management science tools and techniques in modern organizations has been in the area of production and operations management.

The term *production* focuses on manufacturing technology and the flow of materials in a manufacturing

———
[6] Charles G. Andrew and George A. Johnson, "The Crucial Importance of Production and Operations Management," *Academy of Management Review,* January 1982, pp. 143–47.

plant. The production function in a business organization is specifically concerned with the activity of producing goods—that is, the design, implementation, operation, and control of people, materials, equipment, money, and information to achieve specific production objectives. The term *operations* is broader in scope and refers to the goods- or service-producing activity in any organization—public, private, profit, or nonprofit. Thus, a bank and a hospital have operations functions although they have nothing to do with manufacturing technology, production assembly lines, and assembled products. Operations management, therefore, is similar to production management except that it focuses on a wider class of problems and includes organizations whose technologies may be quite different from those of a manufacturing organization. However, there are important similarities between the flow of materials in a manufacturing plant, customers waiting in line at a bank or supermarket, the processing of claims in an insurance company, student registration in a college or university, and the provision of health care in a hospital.

Production and operations management has management science as its foundation. To understand the P/OM approach, it is essential to understand the relationship between the two areas, graphically portrayed in Figure 1.

THE ROLE OF MATHEMATICAL MODELS

Mathematical models play a significant role in production and opera-

tions management. Before defining mathematical models, however, let us examine two points. First, in the previous section of the book, we saw that experimentation is an important part of the scientific approach. However, rarely if ever can a manager perform what would be considered a bona fide scientific experiment to test the feasibility of taking a particular action. The practicalities of the real world preclude any manager from doing this. In other words, a manager cannot usually experiment with inventory to determine which level minimizes carrying costs and ordering costs. However, an accurately constructed mathematical model enables the decision maker to experiment with possible solutions without interrupting the ongoing system. If the model accurately represents the ongoing system, it will provide the decision maker with the results of proposed solutions. In other words, it will react as the real system would react, enabling the decision maker to simulate the behavior of the real system. It is this experimental role of mathematical models that makes them useful to managers.

Second, while there are several different types of models used, the emphasis in P/OM is on mathematical models. Thus, the models examined in this section of the book are quantitative, or mathematical, in nature.

What do we mean by mathematical model? *A mathematical model is a simplified representation of the relevant aspects of an actual system or process.* The value of any model depends on how well it represents the system, or process, under consideration. A highly simplified model that accurately describes a system or process still provides a more clearly understood starting point than a vague conception that a manager mentally creates. Such a model forces the manager to consider systematically the variables in the problem and the relationships among the variables. And forcing the manager to formalize thinking reduces the possibility of overlooking important factors or giving too much weight to minor factors.

You are probably more familiar with models for decision making than you think. The accounting equation $A = L + C$ is a mathematical model. It is a mathematical model showing a simplified relationship between assets, liabilities, and capital. It does not resemble the actual system physically, but it does *behave as the real system behaves*. It is an abstraction of the financial condition of a particular enterprise at a given moment of time.

TYPES OF MATHEMATICAL MODELS

Before managers can understand, evaluate, and utilize mathematical models, they must be aware of the major types of these models. Mathematical models may be classified by the *purpose* (descriptive or normative) of the model and/or by the *types of variables* (deterministic or probabilistic) included in the model.

Purpose of the Model: Descriptive or Normative

A *descriptive model* describes how a system works. That is, *it describes*

things as they are and makes no value judgments about the particular phenomenon being studied. A model constructed solely to describe a real-world phenomenon can be used to display the situation more clearly or to indicate how it can be changed. Descriptive models reveal alternative choices and, in some cases, help the decision maker determine the consequences or outcomes of each alternative. However, a descriptive model *does not* select the best alternative.

A *normative* (or *prescriptive*) *model* selects the best alternative based on some previously determined criteria that are included in the model. *It tells how the system should be* in order to achieve a particular objective. These models are also referred to as optimizing models and decision models, since they seek the optimum from among all the possible solutions. An example of a normative model is the Vroom-Yetton model of leadership that was covered in Chapter 12. It is normative in the sense of specifying the manner in which managers should make decisions.

Types of Variables in the Model: Deterministic or Probabilistic

A model is *deterministic* when the law of chance plays no role. In other words, the model contains no probabilistic considerations. For example, the model Profit = Revenue − Costs is a deterministic mathematical model. All of the factors taken into account are exact (deterministic) quantities, and the solution is determined by this set of exact relationships. In other words, in a determinis-

---

Figure   2   Types of Mathematical Models

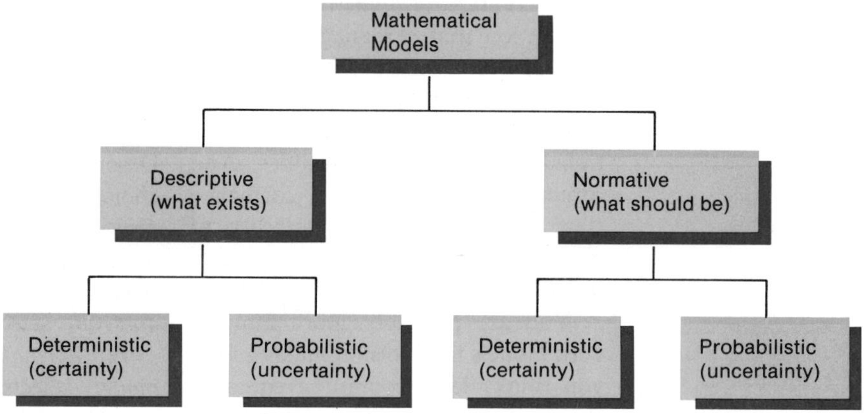

Mathematical models are classified as descriptive or normative and as deterministic or probabilistic.

---

tic model, we assume conditions of certainty.

Once chance or random variables are introduced, conditions of uncertainty exist, and the model is said to be *probabilistic*. Probabilistic models are based on the mathematics of statistics. Conditions of uncertainty introduced in the model are often based on observations of real-world events. For example, insurance companies make heavy use of actuarial tables that give the probability of death as a function of age. These tables can be considered probabilistic models.

Figure 2 summarizes our discussion to this point. Now let us briefly examine some of the models used to aid managers in solving production and operations problems.[7]

---

[7] John M. Wilson, "Classification of Models in Operations Research," *Journal of the Operations Research Society,* March 1985, pp. 253–56.

SOME POPULAR P/OM MODELS

Allocation models. Allocation models are used in a variety of situations in which numerous activities are all competing for limited resources. These models enable the decision maker to allocate scarce resources to maximize some given objective. In certain departments, the resources may include labor time that the production manager must allocate to several different products to maximize the objective of profit. One of the most widely used allocation models is the linear programming (LP) model. Linear programming, as discussed in Chapter 18, expresses the objective to be achieved in the form of a mathematical function, the value of which is to be maximized (for example, profits) or minimized (for example, costs).

Network models. Network models are extremely useful in planning and controlling both simple and complex projects. Actually, network models are as old as scientific management. The Gantt chart was Henry Gantt's contribution to the managerial task of managing work and organizations. While network models are more sophisticated than the Gantt chart, both are based on the same philosophy. The basic type of network model is PERT (Program Evaluation and Review Technique). PERT (to be discussed further in Chapter 18) is a method of planning and controlling nonrepetitive projects—projects that have not been done before and will not be done again in the same exact manner (for example, the space shuttle).

Inventory models. Inventory models provide answers to two questions: how much, and when. Just as the business organization is concerned with obtaining goods to be sold at the most favorable price, it must also be concerned with the time at which orders are placed for repeat goods and the quantity of each order. On the one hand, enough inventory must be available at all times to ensure that there are no lost sales or loss of customer goodwill due to stockouts; on the other hand, frequent orders result in increased costs, such as the storage costs from carrying an excessive inventory. The costs of ordering and carrying an inventory are inversely related: one increases while the other decreases. Inventory models enable the manager to compute the economic order quantity

(EOQ) and the optimum reorder point. Because these models can be applied wherever inventories are kept, they have also found wide use in nonbusiness organizations. Chapter 19 will discuss inventory models.

LIMITATIONS OF THE MANAGEMENT SCIENCE APPROACH

The reader should not construe our discussions in this section of the book as implying that mathematical models can provide the entire basis for *all* management decisions. This is inconceivable. We saw in the prior section that there are many kinds of management decisions that cannot rest solely on the manipulation of quantitative data. Many behavioral models are utilized in which all variables are not quantified. Also, successful implementation of a mathematical model must apply behavioral as well as mathematical science, because the resultant solution must be implemented by human beings.

The next five chapters give an introductory view of managing production and operations. Covering the entire production and operations field is beyond the scope of this book. Thus, we have selected an overview of production and operations management; decision making, decision support systems, production planning, and inventory planning and control as representative areas to highlight the fundamentals of managing production and operations.

15

Chapter

PRODUCTION AND OPERATIONS MANAGEMENT

LEARNING OBJECTIVES

After completing Chapter 15, you should be able to:

■ **Define**
the term *product (service) quality.*

■ **Discuss**
why the production process at Burger King is a worker-paced system.

■ **Describe**
the area of influence of production and operations management.

■ **Identify**
some of the main factors that affect quality.

■ **Compare**
the four specific functions of design, scheduling, operation, and transformation control.

☐ MANAGEMENT IN ACTION

Effective Production Management Equals Productivity and Quality*

What is the difference between good plants and poor plants? What distinguishes factories that manufacture high-quality goods and services year-in and year-out without sacrificing productivity, from factories that do not do as well? These questions and their answers are of great importance to the American economic system and to the managers of firms that make up the system. Remaining competitive in an increasingly international marketplace requires American managers to evaluate every avenue of potential productivity and quality gains.

To obtain some answers to these questions, FORTUNE magazine examined the 10 best factories in America to determine what they have in common. Included were factories bearing logos of well-known firms: AT&T, GE, IBM, and Hewlett-Packard. The 10 plants were selected because of their record of high productivity, high product quality, or both. According to the author of the study, these 10 plants do many things the same way: they all make use of the most current production management methods for planning and controlling the process. But in addition to those technically oriented practices, these plants have other practices in common.

They all begin by reducing the barriers between product design and manufacturing. In the typical plant, there exists considerable friction and even hostility between the group that designs the product and the group that manufactures the product. The most successful plants manage to design the product and the required manufacturing process concurrently rather than sequentially. This means merging the two groups into a single unit for the entire process, from the initial idea to the final production layout.

Another characteristic of the 10 excellently managed factories is the ability to create working conditions that allow employees to make quality products. They include enabling employees to stop the production line to correct defects and to hold the line until the source of the product defect is discovered. In effect, these factories have turned every employee into a quality inspector. To obtain employee commitment to quality, competitors' products are displayed prominently on the factory floor so as to demonstrate what is at stake.

---

* Source: Gene Bylinsky, "America's Best-Managed Factories," *Fortune,* May 28, 1984, pp. 16–24.

The terms *manufacturing management, production management,* and *operations management* are used interchangeably to refer to the functional field of production and operations management (P/OM). Traditionally, the word *production* brings to mind smokestacks, assembly lines, and machine shops. However, P/OM refers to the broader idea of the producing activities of all kinds of organizations—manufacturing or service, public or private, large or small, profit or nonprofit.[1]

P/OM as a field of study and practice uses concepts and principles from scientific management and management science. It also uses ideas from the behavioral sciences. As a part of management, P/OM is quite eclectic and application oriented.[2] As the opening Management in Action indicated, the achievement of high levels of productivity and quality depends on good management of people as well as machines. In this chapter, the nature and area of influence of P/OM will be surveyed. We will emphasize the analytical side of P/OM while acknowledging the importance of people-related issues.

THE NATURE OF PRODUCTION AND OPERATIONS MANAGEMENT

P/OM goes well beyond manufacturing operations involving the assembly of products. It also covers the operation of banks, transportation companies, hospitals and clinics, school systems, insurance companies, and high-technology firms. Any system that generates tangible products (e.g., a Ford automobile, a Sunbeam shaver) or intangible services (e.g., a flight on American Airlines, advice on computer programming) is part of the domain of P/OM.

A Systems View

P/OM practitioners view organizations in terms of systems. A *system* is a collection of objects united by some form of regular interaction and interdependence. We noted in Chapter 2 that organizations themselves are systems made up of interacting subsystems. One of the significant subsystems of many organizations is the production and operations management department. Figure 15–1 illustrates the organization as a system that takes in and transforms

---

[1] K. Jarvis and K. Flint, "Productivity Programs," *Credit,* October 1984, pp., 23–25; Christopher W. Hart and Gregory D. Casserly, "Quality: A Brand-New, Time-Tested Strategy," *Cornell Hotel and Restaurant Administration Quarterly,* November 1985, pp. 52–63; H. D. Sherman, "Improving the Productivity of Service Businesses," *Sloan Management Review,* Spring 1984, pp. 11–23.

[2] Numerous texts survey the field of P/OM. See Richard B. Chase and Nicholas J. Aquilano, *Production and Operations Management: A Life Cycle Approach,* 4th ed. (Homewood, Ill.: Richard D. Irwin, 1985); Elwood S. Buffa, *Production/Operations Management* (New York: John Wiley & Sons, 1983); Donald Del Mar, *Operations and Industrial Management: Designing and Managing for Productivity* (New York: McGraw-Hill, 1985).

FIGURE   15–1   Scope of Production and Operations Management

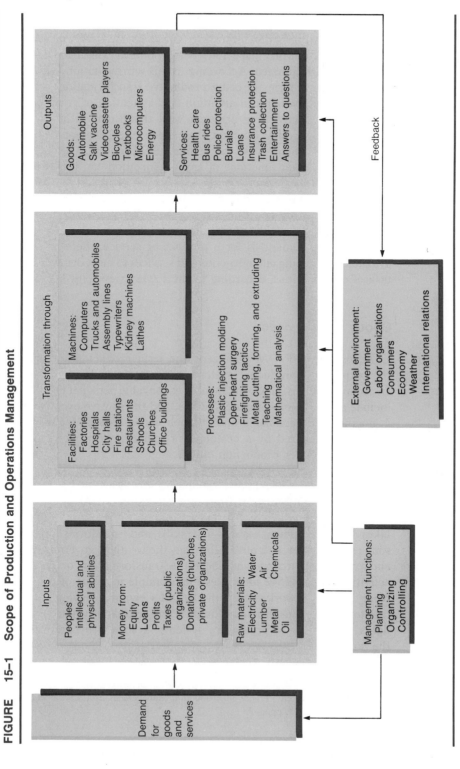

Source: Adapted form Franklin G. Moore and Thomas E. Hendrick, *Production/Operations Management*, 9th ed. (Homewood, Ill: Richard D. Irwin, 1985), p. 11. *P/OM is an Input → Transformation → Output system.*

inputs and then provides outputs that are consumed or demanded. The transformation portion of Figure 15–1 is the point at which P/OM activities, or processes, are conducted. According to this representation, organizations can be thought of in terms of being productive transformation systems. The P/OM executive gives special attention to the creation of goods and services—that is, the productive transformation work that occurs within an organization.

P/OM is a specific function that affects the behavior and performance of other major functions like marketing and accounting. The interrelationships of these three main functions of any organization can be better understood by thinking of an organization as a system. The marketing subsystem deals primarily with the demand side of business; the accounting subsystem addresses the control side of business; the P/OM subsystem centers around converting inputs into outputs, or the supply side of business. No matter how great the demand is for a product or service, there must be a supply available. Producing enough goods and services to meet demand is the primary task of organizations, according to the P/OM viewpoint.[3]

Goods and Services

According to P/OM managers, the term *product* is a generic label for the output of a productive system. A product can be a good or a service. In economic terms, *goods* are defined as movable personal property; examples include autos, home computers, desks, and microwave ovens. A *capital good* is nonmovable personal property, such as a house or factory. A *service*— an activity required by a customer or a client, or work done for another person—is another production output.

Economists refer to the transformation of inputs into goods and services as the "production function." Managers are aware of the fact that simply moving goods and services from input to transformation to output is often affected by unpredictable or random events. For example, a farm manager takes land, equipment, labor, and skills and transforms them into goods such as grain, beef, and milk. However, the weather, government regulations, and equipment breakdowns affect the transformation or productive work activities. Figure 15–2 illustrates this example in terms of a systems framework. The framework reflects the P/OM viewpoint, paying particular attention to inputs, transformation, outputs and feedback cycles. Table 15–1 highlights the variety of productive systems in society by examining a few of the various input transformations, random events, and outputs of some typical organizations.

---

[3] Vincent G. Reuter, "Trends in Production Management Education," *Industrial Management,* May–June 1983, pp. 1–3.

FIGURE   15–2   Transformation Process for a Farm Manager

Farm management can be viewed as a P/OM system.

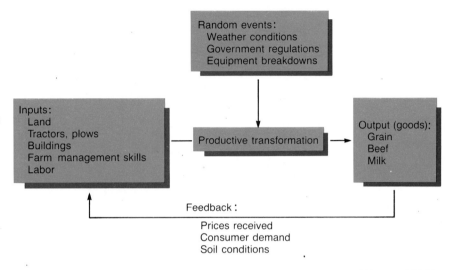

MANAGING THE TRANSFORMATION PROCESS

When managing the transformation process, P/OM managers pay particular attention to four specific functions: design, scheduling, operation, and transformation control.[4] Table 15–2 categorizes the major responsibilities of managers from a P/OM perspective.

1. *Design.* Designing the transformation process involves making decisions on equipment selection, type of production process, and work flow patterns.[5] Transformation processes are usually either continuous, intermittent, or "one-shot" projects. Continuous processes are generally very specialized, producing one type of product (for example, Oldsmobiles) or service (for example, H & R Block tax services). Intermittent processes are more general and utilize a variety of equipment; for example, an intermittent process is used in a job shop (e.g., a shop that produces a product to meet a customer's specifications). The one-shot project is found in building, bridge, and highway

---

[4] R. Wild,"Survey Report—The Responsibilities and Activities of UK Production Managers," *International Journal of Operations and Production Management* 4, no. 1 (1984), pp. 69–74.

[5] R. P. Sadowski and N. J. Tracey, "Concepts to Increase Productivity Are Used in the Design of a Manufacturing Facility," *Industrial Engineering,* September 1982, pp. 61–65.

TABLE 15–1 Productive Systems and Their Characteristics

System	Main Inputs	Transformation Activities	Random Events	Main Outputs
Chrysler Motors	Steel, glass.	Assembly of autos.	New government regulation, new car of competitor.	Automobiles
Methodist Hospital, Houston, Texas	Patients.	Diagnosis, surgery, rehabilitation.	Reduction in medicare payments.	Well patients.
Apple Computer	Electrical circuits, computer languages.	Assembly of personal computers and development of software.	Competitive product from IBM.	Computers and software.
Tadich's Grill, San Francisco, California	Lobsters, hungry patrons, waiters.	Preparation of food.	Price increase for lobsters, strike by waiters.	Satisfied patrons who want to come back.
College or University	High school graduates.	Classroom instruction, lecture enrichment, discussions with alumni who are brought back to the campus, use of library.	Missing books in library, cancellation of course with outstanding instructor.	Educated and employable graduates.

Every organization can be considered a productive system.

TABLE   15–2   P/OM Responsibilities of Managers

The Design,
Scheduling, Operation,
and Control Functions:
Some specific activities
for P/OM practitioners.

	Design	**Scheduling**
	1. Product design	1. Aggregate planning
	2. Job and process design	2. Scheduling manpower levels
	3. Capital equipment selection	3. Project management
	4. Setting labor standards	4. Timing inventory replenishments
	5. Developing labor skills	5. Routing and sequencing
	6. Plant location and layout	6. Job shop scheduling
	Operation	**Control**
	1. Purchasing	1. Quality control
	2. Forecasting requirements	2. Inventory control policies
	3. Process redesign	3. Monitoring production processes
	4. Operating transformation process	4. Cost control
	5. Maintenance	5. Resource allocation

Source: Adapted from Thomas M. Cook and Robert A. Russell, *Contemporary Operations Management: Text and Cases* (Englewood Cliffs, N.J.: Prentice-Hall), © 1980, p. 10. Reprinted by permission of Prentice-Hall, Inc.

construction. The decision on which process to utilize is based on economic considerations, volume required, and labor resources and skills available.

2. *Scheduling.*   Once the optimal process is designed, it must be scheduled to produce the desired product or service at the right time. Scheduling in P/OM terms covers both long and short runs. In long-range scheduling, forecasts and estimates of product or service demand are developed so that manpower, capacity, raw materials, and other input needs can be met. Scheduling also can involve the management of projects over time. Short-range scheduling involves employees' daily or weekly work activities: the sequencing of work flow, raw materials, patients, or other similar inputs.[6]

3. *Operation.*   Operating the transformation process involves the actual implementation of P/OM procedures. The planning, organizing, and controlling of operations directly affect the output of a productive system. The operating function also involves such activities as purchasing, redesigning the process if necessary, and forecasting requirements.

4. *Control.*   The transformation control function requires some method of measuring the product or service before it is sold or used. For example, computers are used to monitor sales in Kroger and Safeway stores. By using the computer, the store manager can monitor inventory levels so that stock reorders can be placed and outages minimized. Another means of control is by inspection. For example, inspectors monitor the waterproof protection of upholstery in Ford automobiles in the Chicago assembly plant.

Effective management of the transformation process achieves high levels

---

[6] Richard Schonberger, *Operations Management* (Plano, Tex.: Business Publications, 1981), pp. 200–241.

of productivity and quality. Systems designed to transform outputs into inputs are dynamic. They change from day to day as employees change. Raw materials and machines change and become obsolete, and customer expectations change. The management of transformation processes involves constant awareness of the need to consider alternatives. Many organizations have ongoing efforts or programs to improve production systems. An example of an ongoing program at Beatrice Companies is described in the Management Focus.

MANAGEMENT FOCUS
Beatrice Companies' Productivity Improvement Program

The concern of managers for productivity improvements remains unabated in the last few years of the 1980s. The effects of the rampant inflation and high interest rates that ushered in the decade have eased, but managers now face the problem of passing on cost increases to the consumer. Periods of low inflation have their own problems, which are eased when productivity gains can be obtained.

The efforts of many companies to achieve productivity gains are reported daily by the press and in business literature. One such effort is that of the Beatrice Companies.

This conglomerate began its efforts to improve productivity in the late 1970s, and they continue today. The company's productivity program, which includes every one of its 440 profit centers, consists of eight steps. Modified substantially during the past 10 years to suit the situations encountered at Beatrice, these eight steps are:

1. Getting started by asking questions whose answers give direction to the program.
2. Assessment of the current state of the department or unit that is the focus of the program.
3. Analysis of opportunities for reducing the amount of effort required to perform routine tasks.
4. Establishing objectives for the program in terms of increases in productivity.
5. Preparing action plans that enable the objectives to be met.
6. Developing measures of progress toward achieving the established objectives.
7. Identifying and providing rewards to those who contribute to the achievement of objectives.
8. Evaluating progress toward the objectives.

> **MANAGEMENT FOCUS** (*continued*)
>
> Although the Beatrice program has accomplished some notable productivity increases, the company believes that even greater success could have been realized if it had appointed a full-time top-level executive to coordinate the program.
>
> ---
>
> Source: Michael S. Bremer, "Productivity Improvement at Beatrice Companies, Inc.," *National Productivity Review,* Spring 1985, pp. 111–20.

P/OM practitioners, by addressing the supply side of business, become involved in many different areas of an organization. Table 15–3 presents the kinds of questions asked by P/OM practitioners.

THE QUALITY CONCERN OF P/OM

The last set of questions presented in Table 15–3 addresses quality control—an extremely important responsibility of managers. The P/OM manager works very hard at improving quality control, but other managers may emphasize quantity. Why? While outputs such as assembled autos, manufactured pipes, or tons of grain processed can be easily quantified by counting or weighing, it is generally more difficult to evaluate their quality. And often quality is judged on subjective opinions rather than on objectively based data. But emphasizing quantity may lead to a lack of concern for quality.

Quality is important. Fine-quality products lead to customer goodwill and satisfaction that manifest themselves in the form of repeat sales, loyal customers and clients, and testimonials to prospective customers or clients. One of the Big Three automakers has a case on record where the irate owner of a luxury car cost the company no fewer than 100 lost sales in a single year.[7] However, to achieve total customer satisfaction not only would be cost prohibitive but also would lead to unrealistic expectations.[8] Even though total customer satisfaction is not attainable, a reasonable record of quality must be established.

Webster defines quality as the degree of excellence a thing possesses. The problem with this definition centers on the word *excellence.* Excellence is in the eye of the beholder; it is subjective rather than objective. Instead of discussing quality in broad terms such as excellence, it seems more realistic to consider quality in terms of *accuracy* and *timeliness.* A firm like IBM or General Motors must provide the customer with products that accurately

---

[7] Edward M. Stiles, *Handbook for Total Quality Assurance* (Englewood Cliffs, N.J.: Prentice-Hall, 1977), p. 3.

[8] Madhav Sinha and Walter O. Willborn, *The Management of Quality Assurance* (New York: John Wiley & Sons, 1985).

TABLE   15-3   Questions Asked by P/OM Executives

Subject	Questions
Capital investment analysis	When should new machinery be bought to replace old machines? When should investments be made in machines in order to economize on labor? What methods of analysis need to be used when making such decisions?
Design of products and services	Are our products safe for consumers to use? How long a life should our products have before they wear out or become obsolete? Are they energy efficient?
Facilities location and design	Where should facilities be located? What building and equipment design will allow work to be done in the most economical manner? What are the best ways to make products or to deliver services. What machines, labor skills, and processes are required?
Maintenance	How shall the organization's facilities be maintained and kept in repair? Should repairs be done on a preventive basis or confined to taking care of breakdowns? Which work should be done by inside crews, and which should be contracted to outsiders?
Energy management	Are we using energy efficiently in our processes? Can alternate energy sources be used?
Work measurement and standards	How much output can reasonably be expected from workers? How much is being turned out, and how can discrepancies between expected and actual be corrected?
Safety	Are our facilities and machines safe for people to operate? Do the processes produce harmful fumes? Are machines too noisy? Are injuries more than rare? How and at what cost can we meet federal and state regulations in these areas?
Production scheduling and control	How should work priorities be determined? How should work be assigned to machines and labor so that the capacity is used effectively while, at the same time, customers get good service?
Inventory management	How much inventory of finished products should we carry in order to give good customer service? What raw material and work-in-process inventories should be carried? Should we make or buy component parts? How much should be ordered or produced at a time, and when should it be ordered so that materials are available as needed?
Purchasing	From whom should we buy our raw materials and component parts? How can we tell if their quality and delivery reliability will meet our needs?
Quality standards and control	How can the organization produce goods and services of the quality required by the marketing department? How can internal operations be controlled so that unacceptable deviations in quality can be detected, and how can they be remedied?

Production and operations managers' questions address key issues of design, scheduling, operation, and control functions.

Source: Adapted from Franklin G. Moore and Thomas E. Hendrick, *Production/Operations Management,* 9th ed. (Homewood, Ill.: Richard D. Irwin, 1985), p. 12.

match specifications and expectations.[9] That is, a personal computer should be able to provide relevant information; an automobile should be fuel efficient, safe, and ride comfortably. A firm must also provide products when they are needed. Providing a good or service after the need has dissipated reduces a customer's or client's satisfaction. Both accuracy and timeliness are extremely important quality issues faced by managers.

Factors Affecting Quality

Quality depends upon a number of factors: policy, engineering/design, equipment, and field support.

Policy. Management establishes policies concerning product quality. The market for the product is one important consideration. There is generally a relationship between quality level and the price of a product.[10] In most cases, if quality increases, so will the price. Because Mercedes and Honda are aimed at different markets, the price customers are willing to pay determines to some extent, the effort, attention, and money spent for quality concerns at Mercedes and Honda. Figure 15–3 shows the price = quality relationship.

In addition to considering the market and the price customers are willing to pay, management must consider the organization's image. A firm might damage its long-term interests by coming out with a product whose quality is not consistent with the firm's image. For example, producing a very low-priced Mercedes or Gucci handbag or a new and low-priced Baskin-Robbins ice cream flavor may create a backlash from regular customers. Customer images of these firms may be tarnished if they associate a lower-priced product or service with lower quality.

Engineering/design. Once management has formulated a policy concerning quality, it is the engineer/designer who must translate the policy into an actual product or service. Designing a product that will appeal to customers, can be produced at a reasonable cost, and will fare well against competition involves making decisions that affect both the quality and the cost of a product.

Equipment. The ability of equipment, tools, and machinery accurately and reliably to produce desired outputs has an important impact, especially in manufacturing industries. If the equipment can meet acceptable tolerances at reasonable costs and quality, then an organization will have an opportunity to compete in the marketplace.

---

[9] David Bain, *The Productivity Prescription: The Manager's Guide to Improving Productivity and Profits* (New York: McGraw-Hill, 1982), p. 114.

[10] Everett E. Adams, Jr., James C. Hershauer, and William A. Ruch, *Productivity and Quality* (Englewood Cliffs, N.J.: Prentice-Hall, 1981).

FIGURE   15–3   The Price = Quality Relationship

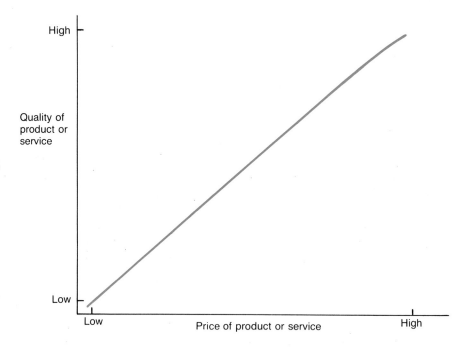

The higher the quality, the higher the price.

Field support.   Often the field support provided by the supplier will determine a product's quality image. IBM, General Electric, and Sears, Roebuck have reputations of providing field support for their products. This is not to say that the products of these firms are necessarily the best in their industries. Remember, quality is in the eye of the beholder. Many customers select IBM computers, GE refrigerators, and Sears dishwashers because the field support of these firms is considered excellent.

Quality-Control Programs: Five Steps

Managers can systematically design and implement quality-control programs. Most have five steps.[11]

Step 1: Defining quality characteristics.   The first step is to define the quality characteristics desired by the customer or client. Examining customer preferences, technical specifications, marketing suggestions, and compe-

---

[11] Bain, *Productivity Prescription,* pp. 119–27.

titive products provides necessary information. Customer preferences are extremely significant, since repeat sales are unlikely unless a reasonable degree of customer satisfaction is achieved. A Rolex customer wants accuracy, a long service life, and a stylish watch. But a Timex watch customer has other quality standards and preferences. The Timex keeps reasonably accurate time and sells at a much lower price than the Rolex. The exact quality characteristics for the Rolex and Timex watches meet different customer preferences.

Step 2: Establishing quality standards.
Once the quality characteristics have been defined (e.g., a Rolex or Timex), the next step is to determine the desired quality levels. The cost of achieving and sustaining a specific level of quality must be estimated and compared to the cost of potential rejections.

Figure 15–4 represents what is often referred to as the quality *funnel principle*. The nearer to the start of the production process, the lower the cost of rejection. As the product or service progresses through the process, more resources are invested. The greater the amount of resources invested, the higher the cost of rejection. The greatest cost is incurred when the customer or the client is the source of rejection. In this case, the cost of processing the complaint and the cost of lost goodwill are added to the cost of resources. For example, complaints about the Ford Pinto automobile were costly in

FIGURE   15–4   The Funnel Principle: Quality Costs as a Function of Time

The cost of rejects increases with time.

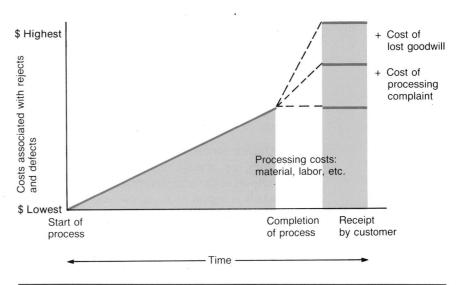

Source: Adapted from David Bain, *The Productivity Prescription: The Manager's Guide to Improving Productivity and Profits* (New York: McGraw-Hill, 1982), p. 120

the form of lost repeat sales, customer lawsuits, and recalls to repair defective parts.

Quality standards serve as the reference point to compare what is "ideal" to what actually "is." In organizations, standards for factors such as size, color, weight, texture, accuracy, reliability, and time of delivery and support are set by management.

Step 3: Developing the quality-review program.

The methods for quality review, where and by whom reviews will be conducted, when they will occur, how the review will be reported and analyzed by managers, and other review procedures must be formalized.

One important management decision involves how many products will be checked for quality. Will all products be inspected for quality, or will there be a representative sampling? The greater the number of products inspected, the greater the inspection costs associated with quality review. Representative sampling is less costly than inspecting all products manufactured. But inspecting only a sample and not every product for quality creates (1) the risk that a greater number of low-quality products will get into the hands of customers; (2) more likelihood that customer goodwill can be tarnished; and (3) the need to make a decision on what constitutes an acceptable number of defects or poor-quality products.

The sampling used in manufacturing firms can take one of many forms. A random spot check, in which a number of products (e.g., cars, generators, computers) are inspected for quality, is used by some organizations. When a formal random spot check is used, the results can be meaningful and can provide adequate control. Other forms of sampling plans using statistical analysis are also available.[12] In each case, the decision about which plan to use involves making inferences about the entire production, based on samples. Representative sampling means that defective products will occasionally slip through the quality-check network.

Step 4: Building quality commitment.

Generating a spirit and a commitment to quality among the work force within an organization requires three ingredients:

- *Quality commitment.* There must be a sincere belief by employees, from top management to operating employees, that quality of all outputs is the accepted practice. Satisfying customer or client quality needs is a goal of all employees.
- *Quality intelligence.* Employees must be aware of the acceptable quality standards and how the standards can be met.
- *Quality skills.* Employees must have the skills and abilities to achieve the quality standards set by management.

---

[12] Sherie Posesorski, "Here's How to Put Statistical Process Control to Work for You," *Canadian Business,* December 1985, p. 163.

The commitment of employees to producing high-quality output is imperative.[13] It can be obtained through the application of motivational programs; any number of approaches are available, as was noted in the presentation on managing people. Job enrichment, goal setting, positive reinforcement, and team development are but a few of the available approaches. An approach that has many adherents is participative management, involving employees in important management decisions. The Management Focus on Ringer Hut describes the use of quality circles to enlist employees' support to improve the quality of the firm's service.

MANAGEMENT FOCUS
Quality Control at Ringer Hut

The experience of Ringer Hut, a Japanese restaurant chain, provides some valuable insights into how to implement a quality-management program. Quality assurance is becoming increasingly important due to the keen sensitivity of consumers to product and service quality. Consumerism, continued technical progress, and the ability of businesses to produce quality products have spurred consumers' demands for quality. The chief lesson to be learned from Ringer Hut's experience is that quality assurance cannot be imposed by top management but must be accepted by all employees and come from the bottom up.

The company devised a quality-assurance program when it began to experience problems in key areas. These included lack of product uniformity, unclean restaurants, and deterioration of service quality. All these problems could be traced to the chain's rapid growth and the subsequent loss of central control. More and more, top management had to depend on the field managers to implement control.

The technique that Ringer Hut used to enlist employee commitment to quality was that of quality circles. The use of quality circles is a unique contribution of Japanese management and was the central feature of Ringer Hut's efforts to restore quality to its products and services. Quality circles are sure ways to involve employees in quality-assurance efforts.

Source: Christopher W. Hart and Gregory D. Casserly, "Quality: A Brand-New, Time-Tested Strategy," *Cornell Hotel and Restaurant Administration Quarterly*, November 1985, pp. 52–63.

---

[13] Allen E. Puckett, "People Are the Key to Productivity," *Industrial Management,* September–October 1985, pp. 12–15; Philip E. Atkinson and Brian W. Murray, "Managing Total Quality," *Management Services,* October 1985, pp. 18–21.

Step 5: The design and use of quality measurements, and the reporting system.   To control and improve product or service quality, management requires feedback in the form of quality measurements and progress reports:

- Measures of inputs entering the transformation process are important indicators of how good, questionable, or poor inputs are. These input measures prepare management for possible transformation and output problems.
- Measures of quality at the point of transformation are also valuable. Such in-process information indicates the need to alter, regulate, or shut the process down. These changes and decisions can prevent faulty outputs from reaching customers or clients.
- The final outputs must be checked and the results reported. Measures prior to shipment can result in last-minute corrections. Measures and reports from customers or clients also provide crucial data.

Without a measurement and reporting system, critical quality problems can be overlooked. The consequence of such faulty control can mean the loss of customers or clients.

When customers or clients perceive quality as being good—up to expectations—the image of the product or service is enhanced. It is these perceptions that the five-step quality program is ultimately attempting to influence.

P/OM: A VISIT TO BURGER KING

To clearly portray P/OM management, nothing serves better than to see it in a real-world setting. Burger King, an organization that most readers know about and probably have visited, provides an example of managing a production and operation system in the real world. As you read, relate the concepts and techniques of P/OM discussed above to the management of Burger King.

On the Assembly Line[14]

Burger King Corporation is a wholly owned subsidiary of the Pillsbury Company. Today over 4,000 Burger King fast-food restaurants are producing a wide selection of hamburger, ham and cheese, and fish sandwiches, french

---

[14] The discussion is based on Roger W. Schmenner, *Production/Operations Management: Concepts and Situations* (Chicago: Science Research Associates, 1981), pp. 97–109.

fries, onion rings, soft drinks, shakes, apple pie, and a frozen dessert. In general, the Burger King restaurant is square in design, stands on about one acre of land, and is constructed largely of brick and glass. The restaurant seats about 100 customers.

Making sandwiches and filling orders at Burger King is viewed as an assembly-line operation. All burgers follow a straight path from the back of the kitchen to the front (order) counter; along this assembly line are a series of workstations. At Burger King, a "board" is used as one workstation. The board is where buns and meat (inputs) are transformed into Whoppers and other sandwiches and products. The board is a long table on which pickles, onions, cheese slices, plastic squeeze bottles of ketchup and mustard, sliced tomatoes, shredded lettuce, mayonnaise, and tartar sauce are kept.

Each Burger King workstation is staffed differently, depending on the pace of demand at the restaurant. At any time, the preferred ratio of front-counter hostesses to back-room production workers (cooks, preparers) is about 1 to 1.5. During a peak period, the crew in a Burger King often increases to 12 to 15 workers.

The typical Burger King employee works part time and is a high school student. Wages are paid for hours worked. The days and hours to be worked are scheduled in advance. The use of high school labor permits day-to-day and peak-to-slow time adjustments.

The Management System

Most Burger King restaurants have a manager and two assistant managers. Since the week contains 14 shifts and each manager works about 5 shifts a week, one of the three is always present in the restaurant.

Management's primary responsibility is to ensure that a quality product is promptly served in a clean environment. Quality is stressed in every part of the production process. While management's abilities to control costs are valued, meeting the Burger King Corporation service goals always comes first. Achieving service goals requires management to motivate and develop the work force. Thus, managers at Burger King have line responsibilities, and this means that they need to effectively *manage work,* the *organization, people,* and the *production process.*

Other specific responsibilities of Burger King management include ordering materials, receiving and checking deliveries, checking on standards of performance (e.g., how much time it takes to service a customer at the order counter and at the drive-in window), supervising the clean-up and maintenance work, and scheduling the work assignments. One of the most difficult managerial tasks is scheduling work assignments, because labor is the chief controllable cost. More labor is scheduled when there are higher sales, longer hours of operation, and more service provided, such as a drive-in window.

FIGURE   15–5   A Production Process Flow Diagram for a Burger King Restaurant

Nonpeak period

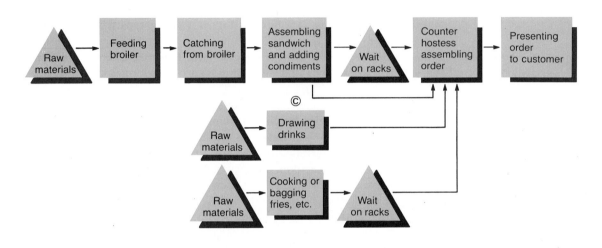

Source: From *Production/Operations Management: Concepts and Situations* by Roger W. Schmenner, p. 106. © 1980. Science Research Associates, Inc. Reprinted by permission of the publisher.

Making a Whopper, bagging fries, and drawing drinks is a production process that is organized well at Burger King.

The Production Process

In most service industries, the time delay between service requests (placing an order) and service consumption (receiving the order) must be short. In other words, service is rarely put in an inventory.[15] A doctor's recommendation, tips for making investments, or a hot, tasty Whopper cannot be inventoried. It is one of Burger King's service objectives to customize its services to fit customer needs—to make the sandwich the way the customer wants it.

Figure 15–5 is a production process flow diagram for assembling a Burger King order. Responsibilities are clearly specified, and yet the famous Burger King customizing can be done by the workers at the main assembly point—at the board, (shown as C on the diagram). The information flow at a Burger King is displayed in Figure 15–6. The free-flowing information permits rapid changes in the work being performed.

The customizing feature of Burger King requires flexibility from the work

---

[15] Peter K. Mills and Dennis J. Moberg, Perspectives on the Technology of Service Operations," *Academy of Management Review,* July 1982, pp. 467–78.

FIGURE   15–6   An Information Flow Diagram at a Burger King Restaurant

Nonpeak period

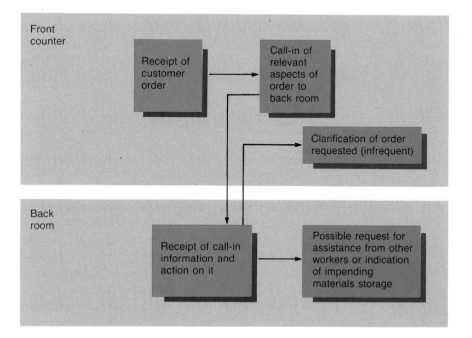

Customer satisfaction requires clear communication between Burger King employees.

Source: From *Production/Operations Management: Concepts and Situations* by Roger W. Schmenner, p. 107. © 1980, Science Research Associates, Inc. Reprinted by permission of the publisher.

force. The job content and production pace vary throughout any worker's shift during the day. What management encourages on a worker-paced assembly line (as opposed to a machine-paced assembly line) is a team atmosphere and effort. Each worker depends on the other workers.

The manager at Burger King plans, organizes, and controls the work. He or she is also expected to perform the four specific P/OM functions: design, scheduling, operation, and transformation control. Burger King's status as a service operation heightens the importance of quality, and this goal always requires special management attention.

LOOKING AHEAD

The remaining four chapters in this part of the book will examine some of the specific tools and techniques used by P/OM managers. Tools and techniques such as decision making (Chapter 16), decision support systems

(Chapter 17), linear programming and PERT (Chapter 18), and inventory control and material requirements planning (Chapter 19) are the basis for making P/OM decisions and for performing the functions of management. It will become clear that whether we discuss Burger King, Methodist Hospital, the Tennessee Valley Authority, or New York University there is a need to study and understand the production process of organizations. It is P/OM that brings into clear focus the importance of design, scheduling, operation, transformation control, and quality. Very few organizations can survive very long without these factors being properly managed.

SUMMARY OF KEY POINTS

- Any productive system that generates tangible products or intangible services is within the sphere of influence of production and operations management.

- P/OM views organizations in terms of systems, or a collection of objects united by some form of regular interaction and interdependence. Thus, according to this view, organizations are a productive transformation system.

- Managing a productive transformation system involves the planning, organizing, and controlling functions. However, some specific P/OM functions must also be performed: design, scheduling, operation, and transformation control.

- A primary responsibility of P/OM is assuring quality. Customer/client satisfaction and goodwill are affected by quality. In managerial terms, quality is measured in terms of accuracy and timeliness.

- Specific factors that affect quality include policy, engineering/design, equipment, and field support.

- Management can, through the development of a quality-control program, improve quality. A five-step program to achieve quality improvement includes (1) defining quality characteristics; (2) establishing quality standards; (3) developing the quality-review program; (4) building quality commitment; and (5) the design and use of quality measurements and a reporting system.

DISCUSSION AND REVIEW QUESTIONS

1. How important is worker cohesiveness in a worker-paced service operation such as a Burger King restaurant?
2. How could international politics affect the inputs required for a production process? Provide some recent examples of this in American organizations.
3. What production activities are involved in a Kroger or Safeway supermarket?

4. Does a city like Lincoln, Nebraska, have a production system? What is produced?

5. Pick a specific organization (other than a fast-food restaurant) and identify its inputs, transformation processes, and outputs.

6. There are some quality specialists who believe that quality control starts right on the drawing board. What do they mean?

7. If maintaining quality is so important to the success of an organization, why isn't a 100 percent inspection always used?

8. Folklore says that you should not buy a car assembled on a Monday, Friday, or during hunting season. Why?

9. How does the design of services differ from the design of products?

10. How does P/OM generally fit in with other functional areas of business, such as marketing and accounting?

ADDITIONAL REFERENCES

Achabal, D. D.; J. M. Heineke; and S. H. McIntyre. "Issues and Perspectives on Retail Productivity." *Journal of Retailing,* Fall 1984, pp. 107–27.

Adams, F. P., and J. F. Cox. "Manufacturing Resource Planning: An Information System Model." *Long Range Planning,* April 1985, pp. 86–92.

Andrew, C. G., and G. A. Johnson. "The Crucial Importance of Production and Operations Management." *Academy of Management Review,* January 1982, pp. 143–47.

Bhada, Y. K. "A Framework for Productivity Measurement." *Business,* January–February–March 1984, pp. 27–33.

Brown, R. M., and K. F. Murrmann. "Productivity Measurement in Manufacturing Firms." *Cost and Management,* January–February 1984, pp. 25–29.

Gaither, N. *Production and Operations Management.* Hinsdale, Ill.: Dryden Press, 1984.

Gold, B. "Foundations of Strategic Planning for Productivity Improvement." *Interfaces,* May–June 1985, pp. 15–20.

Greenwood, F., and J. Gupta. "Improving Small Business Productivity." *American Journal of Small Business,* Spring 1983, pp. 15–18.

Hendrick, T. D., and F. G. Moore. *Production/Operations Management.* Homewood, Ill.: Richard D. Irwin, 1985.

Kearns, D. T. "Xerox's Productivity Plan Is Worth Copying." *Planning Review,* May 1985, pp. 14–17.

Ross, J. E., and Y. K. Shetty. "Making Quality a Fundamental Part of Strategy." *Long Range Planning,* February 1985, pp. 53–58.

Schuster, M., and D. DeSalvia. "Productivity Improvement Programs for Smaller Firms." *Journal of Small Business Management,* January 1983, pp. 14–20.

Shetty, Y. K. "Corporate Responses to the Productivity Challenge." *National Productivity Review,* Winter 1984–85, pp. 7–14.

Steck, R. N. "Strategies for Boosting Productivity." *D & B Reports,* January–February 1985, pp. 44–46.

Weeks, J. K. "Stochastic Dominance: A Methodological Approach to Enhancing the Conceptual Foundations of Operations Management Theory." *Academy of Management Review,* January 1985, pp. 31–38.

Williams, J. L. "Microcomputing: Production Planning's Liaison," *Production and Inventory Management Review,* April 1984, pp. 54–56.

Young, J. A. "The Quality Focus at Hewlett-Packard." *Journal of Business Strategy,* Winter 1985, pp. 6–14.

CASES

APPLICATION I

FORD USES A DR. QUINCY TYPE OF AUTOPSY*

Engineering/design work is an extremely important function in P/OM. Robert Camron does engineering/design work with a small staff at Ford Motor Co.'s research center in Dearborn, Michigan.

In a sense, Mr. Camron is Ford's chief "pathologist." As the "Dr. Quincy" of Ford Motor Co., he dismantles or dissects automobiles to find out what the competition is up to. As soon as rival competitors introduce a car, Mr. Camron and his team go to work, systematically disassembling, cataloging, and examining each of its 30,000 or so parts. In the process, they look for production, safety, or any other ideas that might be applied to Ford's own cars.

The job of Mr. Camron and his team is extremely important, according to Ford. Scrambling to improve quality and cut costs, Ford is hungry for innovations that can help its products work better and can save money. The philosophy of engineering/design is that when someone has a better idea, use it.

To keep posted on models that are nearing public introduction, Mr. Camron constantly reads trade magazines, travels to auto shows, and evaluates companies that supply the industry. When a car is introduced, he buys it through a local dealer. His current inventory that is ready for disassembly includes two J-cars built by General Motors, a Nissan Stanza, a Toyota Supra, and the engine from a Chevrolet Chevette.

Before he recommends a competitor's idea to management, Mr. Camron often puts it through a series of torture tests, using machines that spray parts with salt, roll windows up and down, and turn electrical equipment

* Source: Adapted from Kevin Totlis, "Auto Makers Look for Ideas in Rivals' Cars," *The Wall Street Journal,* July 20, 1982, p. 1.

on and off. One machine pounds the heel of a women's shoe into the carpet to test durability.

Because both GM and Chrysler Corporation have operations similar to Mr. Camron's at Ford, the companies sometimes wind up reimproving one another's innovations. This practice raises the issue of patent infringements, which must be carefully handled to avoid legal suits.

Of course, not everything Mr. Camron uncovers is usable in Ford products. He also finds competitor mistakes and helps Ford avoid such problems. He found that a plastic strip window regulator in the door of a Chevrolet didn't stand up well to wear and tear. Ford decided to use metal rods to avoid the problems with plastic rods.

When Mr. Camron finishes one of his autopsies, he mounts all of the parts on long white boards for display for Ford executives. They visit, look over the display, and experiment with their own approaches to products and parts.

Questions for Analysis

1. What is your opinion of the engineering/design work done by Mr. Camron at Ford? Do you consider it ethical to conduct such work?

2. If Ford relies solely on Mr. Camron to improve engineering/design work, would this effort be sufficient to compete with firms like Toyota, Nissan, and Honda? Why?

3. Some might claim that Mr. Camron's work affects all phases of the production process—inputs, transformation, and outputs—as well as quality. Do you agree? Why?

APPLICATION II

PRATT & WHITNEY'S PRODUCTION SYSTEM THREATENED BY A COBALT SHORTAGE*

Any P/OM system must have sufficient inputs (raw materials) to be transformed into outputs. Today many American firms face crucial shortages of strategic raw materials. If substitutes for materials like columbium, strontium, manganese, cobalt, and platinum metals could be found readily, American manufacturers wouldn't be paying $475 an ounce for some of them.

---

* Source: Adapted from Lad Kuzela, "Are We Ready to Deal with Strategic Material Shortages?" *Industry Week,* September 6, 1982, pp. 45–47.

The United States depends on foreign sources for 93 critical materials. These materials are stockpiled by the U.S. government for use in time of war or other national emergencies. Stockpiling is, however, not without its problems. It is expensive to initiate and maintain. There is also debate over how much of each material is needed. And manufacturers are not guaranteed that their needs for critical raw materials will be met from the stockpile.

Substitution efforts are under way for almost every critically important material. For industry, the most important question is who will foot the bill for their development. Producers wonder if there will be a market at the end of the development road. The government policy in strategic materials was announced in April 1982: technological assistance will be given only where market forces are incapable of achieving clearly defined national objectives.

The cutoff of a critical raw material can shut down the production process in many organizations. Not too long ago, United Technologies Corporation's Pratt & Whitney Aircraft group faced just such a major threat to its production system.

Pratt & Whitney produces jet engines for military and commercial aircraft. The jets' power plants use a substantial amount of cobalt, a critical imported raw material. In 1978, political upheaval in Zaire closed down cobalt mines in that country and reduced the supply of cobalt to firms like Pratt & Whitney. Zaire has the richest mines in the world, supplying about 59 percent of the world's cobalt. From a low of $6 per pound, cobalt shot to $50 to $60 per pound within weeks.

Production work at Pratt & Whitney was threatened. However, since the Zaire upheaval was not a national U.S. emergency, Pratt & Whitney could not ask for release of cobalt from the U.S. stockpile. The production team at Pratt & Whitney began to work on reducing the requirements of cobalt. They developed a cobalt-free turbine vane. In several other engine parts, they reduced the use of cobalt by substituting more nickel and nickel-based iron in combination with cobalt. Overall consumption of cobalt was reduced by about 20 percent.

The real problems with developing substitutes for strategic materials like cobalt are the costs of research and development, new equipment and new production processes, and redesigning parts. Luckily Pratt & Whitney was able to come out of the situation with a substitute, but they might not be so lucky when the next crisis occurs.

Questions for Analysis

1. What type of studies should management at firms like Pratt & Whitney conduct to determine whether they will have the inputs (raw materials) necessary to furnish products to customers?

2. An organization is a system. This means that the environment can influence the production system. What recent environmental events similar to the Zaire cobalt situation have threatened the slowing or shutting down of production in American companies.

3. Should the research and development work to find substitutes for critical materials like that conducted at Pratt & Whitney be considered a part of the input phase in a production system? Why?

MANAGEMENT DECISION MAKING

LEARNING OBJECTIVES

After completing Chapter 16, you should be able to:

■ **Define**
programmed and nonprogrammed decisions.

■ **Describe**
how the types of decisions managers make are related to their level in the organization.

■ **Discuss**
the process of decision making.

■ **Compare**
decision making under conditions of certainty, risk, and uncertainty.

■ **Identify**
the major sources for locating problems that require management decisions.

Chapter 16

■ MANAGEMENT IN ACTION

Hallmark Uses Payoff Matrix*

Hallmark Cards, Inc. and the local newsstand have at least one management problem in common: No one wants to buy leftover inventory. On December 26, there is likely to be scant demand for either Christmas cards or December 25 newspapers. Managers at Hallmark Cards and newsstands must somehow produce and order just enough product to satisfy demand without running either short or over. To run short means lost sales; to run over means excessive inventory costs.

Hallmark's production managers face many such decisions each year. The company produces numerous special theme cards and promotional materials that have never before been made. Consequently they have little basis for deciding how many to produce. Prior to 1982, production managers decided how many first-time and specialty cards to produce by applying the "similar experience" approach, a method by which one looks for the most similar past experience and projects that experience to the new one. Thus, the production run for a specialty card featuring a Walt Disney character could be determined by consulting the sales experience of a previously issued Disney character card. These past experiences enabled production managers to obtain "best estimates" as the basis for their production decisions.

Beginning in 1982, Hallmark began to apply somewhat more sophisticated decision-making techniques to their production problems. The new techniques enable production managers to use their judgment to make probabilistic estimates (e.g., the chance that something will happen) of the effects of different production runs. For each level of production, an associated revenue and cost can be combined to obtain a "payoff." When the managers apply probabilistic estimates to each level of production, they can calculate expected payoffs. Such estimates of expected sales and costs enable the managers to take into account all their collective, pertinent information about an uncertain future event—expected sales—to make a production decision.

---

* Source: Based on F. Hutton Barron, "Payoff Matrices Pay Off at Hallmark," *Interfaces,* July–August 1985, pp. 20–25.

Managers at all levels in an organization make decisions. The ultimate influence of these decisions may extend to the survival of the organization or only the starting salary of a new college trainee. All decisions, however, have some influence—large or small—on performance. Thus, it is important for managers to develop decision-making skills. The quality of the decisions that they reach is the yardstick of their effectiveness and of their value to the organization. Like it or not, managers are evaluated and rewarded on the basis of the importance, number, and results of their decisions.

TYPES OF MANAGERIAL DECISIONS

Although managers in large business organizations, government offices, hospitals, and schools may be separated by background, lifestyle, and distance, they must all make decisions involving several alternatives and outcomes. In this section, we will discuss various types of decisions.

Programmed and Nonprogrammed Decisions

If a particular problem occurs often, managers will develop a routine procedure for solving it. Thus, a decision is programmed if it has a repetitive and routine solution. The managers of most organizations face great numbers of programmed decisions in their daily operations. Such decisions should be made without expending unnecessary time and effort on them. When a problem has not previously arisen in exactly the same manner or it is complex or extremely important, it will require a nonprogrammed decision. Decisions are nonprogrammed when they are for novel and unstructured problems. The two classifications are broad, yet they point out the importance of differentiating between programmed and nonprogrammed decisions.[1] Figure 16–1 presents examples of programmed and nonprogrammed decisions in different types of organizations.

What is important, however, is that the need for nonprogrammed decisions be properly identified. On the basis of this type of decision making, billions of dollars in resources are allocated in our nation every year. Government organizations make decisions that influence the lives of every citizen; business organizations make decisions to manufacture new products; hospitals and schools make decisions that influence patients and students years later. Unfortunately, very little is known about the nonprogrammed type of human decision making.

Managers can usually handle programmed decisions through rules, standard operating procedures, and the development of specific policies. In this

---

[1] Herbert Simon, *The New Science of Management Decision* (New York: Harper & Row, 1960), pp. 5–6.

FIGURE   16–1   Types of Managerial Decisions

Type of Decision	Type of Problem	Procedures	Examples
Programmed	Repetitive, routine	Rules Standard operating procedures Policies	Business: Processing payroll vouchers College: Processing admission applications Hospital: Preparing patient for surgery Government: Using state-owned motor vehicle
Nonprogrammed	Complex, novel	Creative problem solving	Business: Introducing a new product College: Constructing new classroom facilities Hospital: Reacting to regional disease epidemic Government: Solving spiraling inflation problem

Programmed and nonprogrammed decisions apply to different types of problems and, therefore, require different procedures.

---

section of our book we shall see that through the development of mathematical models, the management science approach has made a great contribution to handling these types of decisions.

Nonprogrammed decisions have traditionally been handled by general problem-solving processes, judgment, intuition, and creativity.[2] The Management Focus on Napco illustrates a nonprogrammed decision that relied on intuition.

MANAGEMENT FOCUS
A High-Risk Decision at Napco Industries Pays Off

Few companies gamble with the stakes that Napco Industries Inc. put up when it completely rebuilt its corporate strategy. Five years ago, executives of the slow-growing, Minneapolis-based manufacturer huddled together at a suburban hotel for several days to find a way to improve Napco's prospects. They settled on a risky path: selling the businesses that produced two thirds of sales (the manufacturers of axles and electronic products) to enter into a new service business.

---

[2] Paul C. Nutt, "Types of Organizational Decision Processes," *Administrative Science Quarterly,* September 1984, pp. 414–50.

> ### MANAGEMENT FOCUS (*continued*)
>
> Using the $32 million proceeds from the sale, Napco began to acquire small service companies that specialized in the distribution of nonfood products to supermarkets as well as pricing and keeping inventory tabs on them. It established a successful network in the South and the Central Plains. Its timing proved impeccable; Napco got out of a capital-intensive business before interest rates soared. Now Napco has begun to expand westward, aiming to become the first national service merchandiser.

Some managers, however, are uncomfortable with basing decisions on intuition. Unfortunately, modern management techniques have not made the same advances in improving managerial performance in nonprogrammed decision making as they have in programmed decision making.

Types of Decisions and Level of Management

Problems that arise infrequently and have a great deal of uncertainty surrounding them are often of a strategic nature and should be the concern of top management. Problems that arise frequently and have fairly certain outcomes should be the concern of lower levels of management.

Middle managers in most organizations concentrate mostly on programmed decisions. As Figure 16–2 indicates, the nature of the problem,

FIGURE   16–2   Types of Problems, Types of Decisions, and Management Level in the Organization

Programmed decisions should be made by lower management; nonprogrammed decisions should be made by top management.

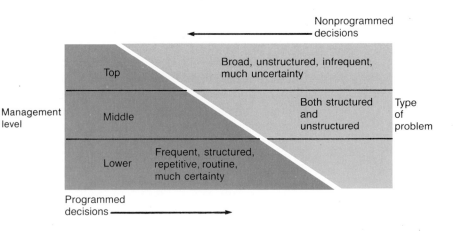

how frequently it arises, and the degree of certainty surrounding it should dictate at what level of management the decision should be made.

THE PROCESS OF DECISION MAKING

There are numerous approaches to decision making. Which approach is best will depend on the nature of the problem, the time available, the costs of individual strategies, and the mental skills of the decision maker.

Decisions should be thought of as *means* rather than ends. They are mechanisms by which a manager seeks to achieve some desired state. They are the manager's (and hence the organization's) responses to problems. Every decision is the outcome of a dynamic process influenced by a multitude of forces. Thus, decision making is the process of thought and deliberation that results in a decision; the process influences how good the decision is likely to be.

Decision making is not a fixed procedure, but it is a sequential process.[3] In most decision situations, managers go through a number of stages that help them think through the problem and develop alternative strategies. The stages need not be rigidly applied; their value lies in their ability to force the decision maker to structure the problem in a meaningful way. Figure 16–3 enables us to examine each stage in the normal progression that leads to a decision. You may find it helpful to develop your own list of stages for the decision-making process.

The process represented in Figure 16–3 is more applicable to nonprogrammed decisions than to programmed decisions. Problems that occur infrequently with a great deal of uncertainty surrounding the outcome require the manager to utilize the entire process.[4] In contrast, problems that occur frequently are often handled by policies or rules, so it is not necessary to develop and evaluate alternatives each time these problems arise.[5]

An Example of the Process

Suppose the operations officer of a local bank has established a specific error rate (number of errors per 1,000 transactions) for all of the bank's tellers. At the end of the year, the error rate has consistently been above

---

[3] James E. Hopper and Kenneth J. Euske, "Facilitating the Identification and Evaluation of Decision Objectives," *Cost and Management,* July–August 1985, pp. 36–40.

[4] Jane M. Booker and Maurice C. Bryson, "Decision Analysis in Project Management: An Overview," *IEEE Transactions on Engineering Management,* February 1985, pp. 3–9.

[5] J. W. Boudreau, "Decision Theory Contributions to HRM Research and Practice," *Industrial Relations,* Spring 1984, pp. 198–217.

FIGURE   16–3   The Process of Decision Making

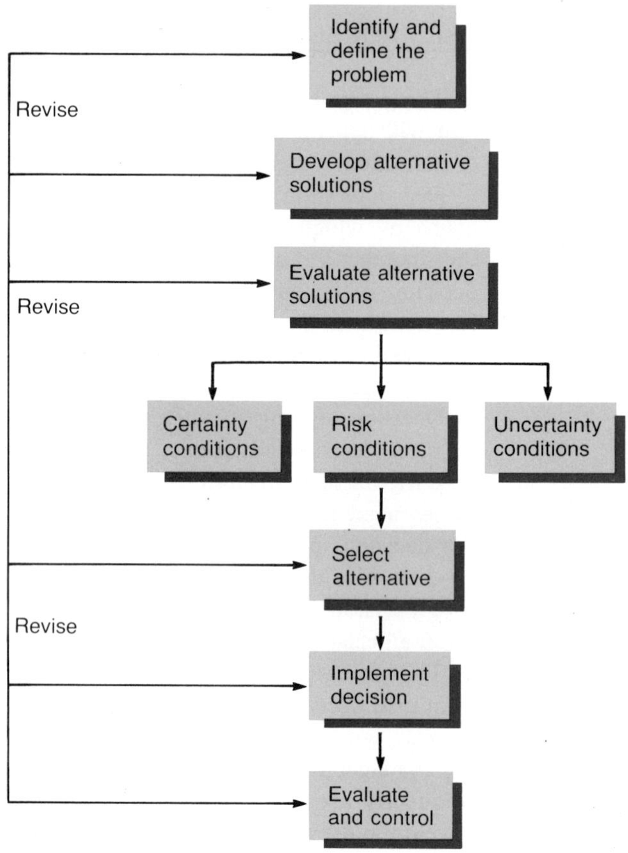

A systematic approach to decision making is most useful for handling nonprogrammed decisions.

the desired rate. The operations officer must then *identify and define the problem* and make some kind of decision to solve the problem.

Identifying problems is not as easy as it may seem. If the problem is incorrectly identified or defined, any decisions made will be directed toward solving the wrong problem. There are several criteria managers use to locate problems:

1. *Deviation from past performance.*   A sudden change in some established pattern of performance often indicates that a problem has developed. When employee turnover increases, sales decline, student enrollments decline, selling expenses increase, or more defective units are produced, a problem usually exists. Thus, if the error rate among tellers had always been below the standard

until this year, this departure from the historical pattern could signal a problem.

2. *Deviation from the plan.*   When results do not meet planned objectives, a problem is likely. For example, a new product fails to meet its market share objective, profit levels are lower than planned, or the production department is exceeding its budget. In our example above, the teller error rate exceeded the performance objective. These occurrences signal that some plan is off course.

3. *Outside criticism.*   Outsiders may identify problems: Customers may be dissatisfied with a new product or with their delivery schedules; a labor union may present grievances; investment firms may not recommend the organization as a good investment opportunity; alumni may withdraw their support from an athletic program.

In the above example, once the bank operations officer has clearly defined the problem, it will be necessary to *develop* a number of *alternative solutions*—potential strategies or solutions to the problem. Next the operations officer would have to *evaluate* each of the *alternative solutions.* Evaluation involves measuring and comparing the potential payoffs and possible consequences of each alternative solution. For example, suppose the bank operations officer decides that two possible solutions are (1) to invest in the latest electronic technology for recording teller transactions or (2) to invest in an intensive teller training program. He would carefully consider the potential payoffs and consequences of each solution and *select one alternative.*

Once selected, the decision must be implemented. A decision is only an abstraction if it is not implemented. It is possible that a "good" decision can be damaged by poor implementation. It is also possible that a "poor" decision can be helped by good implementation. Thus, implementation may be just as important as the actual activity of selecting an alternative.

Finally, the solution must be *evaluated* and *controlled.* The bank operations officer would have to continue periodic measurement of the teller error rate, compare the results with the established standard, and if problems still exist, face new decisions.

Terms Used in Decision Making

The term *state of nature* is used to describe an *event beyond a manager's control that could actually happen.* For example, a manufacturer of children's toys knows that the accuracy of production forecasts will depend in large measure upon the state of the overall economy—an event that is beyond the firm's control. The executive of a tobacco company must make decisions on how much and what type of each of the firm's cigarettes to produce, given the government campaign against certain tobacco products. In each of these examples, the decision maker must make a decision while facing an uncontrollable state of nature.

The term *strategies* is used to describe the alternative solutions available to the decision maker. As noted, decision making involves selecting one of several alternative solutions (*strategies*), which in combination with a future *state of nature* yields some desired result. The desired result may be to maximize profit, revenue, or market share or to minimize some objective such as costs, absenteeism, defective output, or teller error rates.[6]

Now that you are familiar with the process of decision making, we shall devote the remainder of the chapter to a detailed analysis of a decision problem in production and operations, using the management science approach to decision making.

DECISION MAKING IN PRODUCTION AND OPERATIONS

To illustrate the use of decision making in production and operations, we will develop an example with many of the same characteristics as the Management in Action presented at the beginning of the chapter. Publishers of specialty books face a production problem similar to Hallmark's. If the publisher knows exactly how many books will be demanded, then the number of books to produce is obvious. However, this is frequently not the case. Often a book will commemorate a special event such as the nation's bicentennial celebration. Since the book is unique, the publisher may have only sketchy information about its potential sales.

Let us assume that the publisher has established the price of the book at $1.75 and that the incremental cost of each book is $1.00. Thus, each book that is sold will contribute $.75 to overhead and profit. Assume also that there is no secondary market for the book. If it is not sold by the end of the bicentennial celebration period, there will be no market for it. As we noted in the opening Management in Action, such production and operations decisions are characteristic of situations having perishable products. With that in mind, we can understand that if the publisher prints one book and one book is demanded, then the contribution is $.75; if two books are printed and two are demanded, the contribution is $1.50. But if two books are printed and three are demanded, the contribution remains $1.50, and the publisher has no more books to sell. By the same reasoning, if the publisher prints three books and two are demanded, the contribution is $.50: The revenue is $3.50 (2 × $1.75), the incremental cost is $3.00 (3 × $1.00), and $3.50 − $3.00 = $.50. The contribution for any combination of production and demand can be calculated in this manner.

Say that the publisher decides it is only necessary to investigate four levels of possible demand, in 5,000-unit intervals (that is, rather than dealing with the infinite range of production and demand combinations, we will illustrate

[6] D. V. Lindley, *Making Decisions* (New York: John Wiley & Sons, 1985).

TABLE   16–1   Conditional-Value Payoff Table for Production Decision

---

Strategies: Books Printed	States of Nature: Number of Books Demanded			
	5,000	*10,000*	*15,000*	*20,000*
5,000	$ 3,750	$3,750	$ 3,750	$ 3,750
10,000	−1,250	7,500	7,500	7,500
15,000	−6,250	2,500	11,250	11,250
20,000	−11,250	−2,500	6,250	15,000

---

only four): 5,000, 10,000, 15,000, and 20,000 books. With this information, we can determine the contribution for each of the four levels of sales and each of the four production levels. In the terminology of decision theory, each level of sales is called a state of nature, and each production level is a strategy. The contribution associated with each state of nature and strategy is a conditional value. The conditional values, or payoffs, for each of the 16 possible combinations of production and demand are presented in Table 16–1.

In the present example, the payoffs associated with each possible strategy and state of nature are based on the previously presented price ($1.75) and cost ($1.00). Thus the payoff associated with producing 5,000 books and selling 5,000 books (Revenue − Cost = Payoff) is:

Revenue (5,000 × $1.75)	$8,750
Cost (5,000 × $1.00)	$5,000
Payoff	$3,750

If, however, the publisher prints 15,000 books and only 10,000 are demanded, the payoff is:

Revenue (10,000 × $1.75)	$17,500
Cost (15,000 × $1.00)	$15,000
Payoff	$2,500

Each payoff in Table 16–1 is calculated in the above manner. The fact that some of the values are negative simply reflects the cost of overproducing.

The payoff table is useful, but it does not make the decision; it simply organizes the important information on which to base the decision. But how can the publisher make such a decision? Let's examine three different conditions the publisher might face: certainty, risk, and uncertainty.

Decision Making: Certainty Conditions

If a manager knew exactly which state of nature would occur (e.g., knowing that on April 15 income taxes are due), the decision could be made with certainty. A certainty situation means that a perfectly accurate decision will be made time after time. Of course, decision making under certainty is rare.

For illustrative purposes, however, assume that the publisher knows with certainty that 10,000 books will be demanded. The maximum payoff associated with this state of nature is to produce 10,000 units: The payoff of $7,500 associated with the joint occurrence of 10,000 books produced and demanded is greater than any other payoff associated with that state of nature.

The publisher in this situation is fortunate to have perfect information about future states of nature. In most situations, of course, the publisher will not know with certainty which state of nature will occur. When facing a decision where the state of nature is uncertain, a manager is forced to use probabilities.

Decision Making: Risk Conditions

Probabilities fall into two categories. *Objective* probability is based on historical evidence. For example, the probability of obtaining either heads or tails on the toss of a fair coin is .50 (50 percent); the coin is equally likely to come up a head or a tail. In many cases, historical evidence is not available, so a manager must rely on a personal estimate, or *subjective* probability, of the situation outcome.

Even a manager who is able to estimate the likelihood that the various states of nature will occur faces risk conditions. A risk situation requires the use of probability estimates. The ability to estimate may be due to experience, incomplete but reliable information, or intelligence.

Decision making under risk conditions also necessitates the use of expected values. (Recall that the payoffs listed in Table 16–1 are conditional values because they will occur only if a specific state of nature occurs and a specific strategy is chosen.) The expected value of an alternative is the long-run average return; in other words, you would obtain the same results, on average, if you made the same decision in the same situation over and over again. In decision making, the average return or *expected value,* is found by taking the value of an outcome if it should occur (the conditional value) and multiply-

---

TABLE   16–2   Expected-Value Table for Production Decision

	States of Nature: Number of Books Demanded				
Strategies: Books Printed	5,000 (.20)*	10,000 (.40)*	15,000 (.30)*	20,000 (.10)*	Expected Value
5,000	$ 750 +	$1,500 +	$1,125 +	$ 375 =	$3,750
10,000	−250 +	3,000 +	2,250 +	750 =	5,750
15,000	−1250 +	1,000 +	3,375 +	1,125 =	4,250
20,000	−2,250 +	−1,000 +	1,875 +	1,500 =	125

---

* Estimated probability.

ing that value by the probability that the outcome will occur. This is a standard and acceptable procedure. Remember that:

$$\text{Expected Value} = \text{Conditional Value} \times \text{Probability}$$

If the book publisher is able to estimate subjectively the probabilities associated with each of the four levels of demand (states of nature), these estimates can be used to construct a table of expected values. Suppose, for example, that the publisher estimates the following probabilities:[7]

Demand	Probabilities
5,000 books	.20
10,000	.40
15,000	.30
20,000	.10

Table 16–2 presents the expected values for each of the four strategies. For example, the expected value for the strategy of printing 10,000 books (refer to Row 2 in Table 16–1) is computed as follows:

$$(.2 \times -\$1250) + (.4 \times \$7500) + (.3 \times \$7500) + (1. \times \$7500) = \$5750$$

The proper decision for the book publisher is to print 10,000 books. The expected value of that strategy exceeds the expected value of any alternative strategy. When given the probabilities of different states of nature, decision theory can aid managers make decisions that maximize the value of some

---

[7] The calculation of such probabilities involves mathematical computations beyond the scope of this book. Interested readers may wish to consult a basic text on statistics or economics.

outcome. Decision theory has many applications, including decisions that require the minimization of costs. The following Management Focus describes just such an application.

MANAGEMENT FOCUS
The Use of Decision Theory in Forest Management

To most of us, the forestry industry's use of fire as a management tool would seem unusual. After all, fire destroys, and a major aim of forestry management is to preserve. So how can deliberately set (prescribed) fires be useful?

The fact of the matter is that prescribed fires can be used to reduce fire hazards, to enhance wildlife, and to control disease and insects. Prescribed fires burn off forest residue, the tinder of naturally set fires. The costs of naturally set fires is calculable in terms of the value of houses, buildings, and other physical structures that the fires destroy. Thus, the value of removing the causes of naturally set fires through the use of prescribed fires equals the value of those things that would have otherwise been destroyed. Whether to use the prescribed-fire method in a particular forest is a matter of comparing the expected value saved to the cost of setting the prescribed fire.

One application of this analysis involved the decision to set fire to parts of the Prescott National Forest lands in central Arizona. The decision depended on probabilities pertaining to the two key variables in the problem: (1) the number and value of the structures that could be expected to be destroyed by natural fires and (2) the number and value of structures that could be expected to be destroyed by prescribed fires that get out of control. In the area subject to the analysis, there were some 2,000 homes and other structures with an average value of $50,000. The decision makers used historical data to estimate the probability distributions of the two key variables and then compared the expected loss from natural fires to the expected loss from prescribed fires (including the known costs of setting and managing a prescribed fire). The analysis indicated that expected loss due to prescribed fires was half the expected loss due to natural fires.

Based on David Cohan, Stephen M. Haas, David L. Radloff, and Richard F. Yancik, "Using Fire in Forest Management: Decision Making under Uncertainty," *Interfaces*, September–October 1984, pp. 8–19.

What if the decision maker has absolutely no basis for estimating probabilities of future states of nature? As we have seen, probabilities are necessary if one is to calculate expected values. But in many instances, decision makers confront problems that do not lend themselves to the application of expected-value methods. The next section presents some ways that decision theory can assist decision makers with such problems.

Decision Making: Conditions of Uncertainty

When no historical data exist concerning the probabilities for the occurrence of the states of nature, the manager faces conditions of uncertainty. The management science approach focuses on improving the decision-making process under such conditions. A number of different decision criteria have been proposed as possible bases for decisions under uncertainty, including:

1. Maximax criterion (optimistic): maximizing the maximum possible payoff.
2. Maximin criterion (pessimistic): maximizing the minimum possible payoff.
3. Minimax criterion (regret): minimizing the maximum possible regret to the decision maker.
4. Insufficient-reason criterion: assuming equally likely probabilities for the occurrence of each possible state of nature.

As with conditions of certainty and risk, the first step in making decisions under conditions of uncertainty is to construct a conditional-value payoff table. The next step is to select and apply one of the above decision criteria. Using the conditional-value payoffs in Table 16–1, we will illustrate the four criteria for decision making under conditions of uncertainty.

Maximax criterion. Some decision makers think optimistically about the occurrence of events influencing a decision. A manager with this attitude will examine the conditional-value table and select the strategy allowing the most favorable payoff. But this criterion is dangerous to employ, because it ignores possible losses and the chances of making or not making a profit.

Using a maximax criterion, the publisher would assume that no matter what strategy is selected, the best possible state of nature will occur. Therefore, the publisher should print 20,000 books because that strategy is associated with the maximum payoff of $15,000 (see Table 16–1).

Maximin criterion. Some managers act on the belief that only the worst possible outcome can occur. This pessimism results in the selection of the strategy that maximizes the least favorable payoff. Using this criterion, the publisher would locate the worst possible outcome associated with each alternative. Table 16–1 indicates that the worst possible payoffs associated with each strategy and state of nature to be as follows:

Strategy	Worst Outcome
Print 5,000 books	$ 3,750
Print 10,000 books	−1,250
Print 15,000 books	−6,250
Print 20,000 books	−11,250

The publisher will minimize the worst possible outcome by selecting the strategy of printing 5,000 books. Of the four worst possible outcomes, that one is the least—the maximum of the minimums.

Minimax criterion.   If a manager selects a strategy and if a state of nature occurs that does not result in the most favorable payoff, regret occurs. The manager is regretful that the strategy selected did not lead to the best payoff.

A manager who does not know and does not want to guess which state of nature will occur selects a regret strategy. Managerial regret is the payoff for each strategy under every state of nature, subtracted from the most favorable payoff that is possible with the occurrence of the particular event. For example, if the publisher prints 5,000 books and the demand is for 10,000, the publisher will experience regret of $3,750 (the difference between the realized payoff for that strategy and the potential payoff associated with printing 10,000 books). The regret for any particular strategy is the difference between the best possible outcome and the actual outcome.

Applying the minimax criterion requires the development of regret tables. These tables indicate the amount of regret associated with each strategy and state of nature. Table 16–3 presents the amounts of regret associated with the book publisher's production decisions.

Next the regret values for each strategy are identified:

Strategy	Regret
Print 5,000 books	$11,250
Print 10,000 books	7,500
Print 15,000 books	10,000
Print 20,000 books	15,000

The minimax criterion indicates that the publisher should print 10,000 books because that strategy produces the minimum regret.

Insufficient-reason criterion.   The three preceding decision criteria assume that without any previous experience, it is not worthwhile to assign probabilities to the states of nature. The insufficient-reason criterion, however,

---

TABLE 16–3 Regret Table for Production Decisions

Strategies: Books Printed	States of Nature: Number of Books Demanded			
	5,000	10,000	15,000	20,000
5,000	0	$ 3,750	$7,500	$11,250
10,000	$ 5,000	0	3,750	7,500
15,000	10,000	5,000	0	3,750
20,000	15,000	10,000	5,000	0

---

states that if managers do not know the probabilities of occurrence for the various states of nature, they should assume that all are equally likely to occur. In other words, managers should assign equal probabilities to each state of nature.

Using the insufficient-reason criterion, the publisher would assign a one-in-four ($\frac{1}{4}$) probability to each of the four states of nature (see Table 16–4).

Based on those probabilities, the publisher should print 10,000 books.

Reviewing the choices.   The application of the four criteria to the decision faced by the book publisher results in different choices, depending on the orientation of the decision maker:

1. The optimist would print 20,000 books.
2. The pessimist would print 5,000 books.
3. The regretter would print 10,000 books.
4. The insufficient-reasoner would print 10,000 books.

Different criteria result in different decisions. Each decision problem has unique data that lead to unique situations.

One point should be clear. The greater the amount of reliable information, the more likely it is that the manager will make a good decision. Making sure the right information is available at the right time to the right decision

---

TABLE 16–4 Expected Values, Using Insufficient-Reason Criterion

Strategies: Books Printed		Calculation	Expected Value
5,000	¼	($ 3,750 + $3,750 + $ 3,750 + $ 3,750) =	$3,750.00
10,000	¼	(−1,250 + 7,500 + 7,500 + 7,500) =	5,312.50
15,000	¼	(−6,250 + 2,500 + 11,250 + 11,250) =	4,687.50
20,000	¼	(−11,250 − 2,500 + 6,250 + 15,000) =	1,875.00

maker is the function of a decision support system. The relationship of decision support systems to the decision-making process is the subject of the next chapter.

SUMMARY OF KEY POINTS

- Managers make both programmed and nonprogrammed decisions. Programmed decisions are responses to repetitive and routine problems. Nonprogrammed decisions are responses to novel and unstructured problems.

- The focus of top management should be on nonprogrammed decisions, while first-level management should be concerned with programmed decisions. Middle managers in most organizations concentrate mostly on programmed decisions.

- Decisions should be thought of as means rather than ends. They are mechanisms through which a manager seeks to achieve some desired state. They are the manager's (and hence the organization's) responses to problems.

- Problems must exist in order for decisions to be necessary. Managers use the following criteria to locate problems: (1) deviation from past performance, (2) deviation from the plan, and (3) outside criticism.

- The approach to decision making suggested in this chapter encourages the manager to discover and enumerate potential strategies and possible states of nature. In addition, it (1) encourages logical definition of objectives and assumptions, (2) encourages precise definition of problems, (3) facilitates systematic consideration of a large number of factors, (4) facilitates the identification of alternative strategies, and (5) facilitates the prediction of outcomes.

- While a manager may not actually construct payoff tables, the disciplined process of specifying possible states of nature enables the manager to add some clarity to a situation where none existed previously.

DISCUSSION AND REVIEW QUESTIONS

1. Interview managers in one or more organizations where you work or otherwise have some connection. Attempt through your questioning to identify the programmed and nonprogrammed decisions of the organization(s). List them and compare the ways in which each organization goes about deciding among alternatives for both types of decisions.

2. Review your understanding of the differences between classical and neoclassical organization designs as we described them in Chapter 7. Explain how the distinction between programmed and nonprogrammed decision making helps you to understand how managers make decisions in these two types of organizations.

3. Use the process of decision making as depicted in Figure 16–3 to describe how a personnel manager would decide whom to hire, how a production manager would decide how many units to produce, how a marketing manager would decide which salesperson to assign to which territories, and how a financial manager would decide between debt and equity as sources of additional funds.

4. The Ace Music Company is considering two strategies for promoting the records of a new recording artist: (1) concentrate entirely on television advertising and (2) concentrate entirely on newspaper advertising. In the past, the company's profits have been influenced by general economic conditions. The profit payoffs for each strategy depend on future economic conditions, as noted:

	States of Nature: Economy		
Strategies	Downturn	Stable	Upturn
1. Television advertising	$ 4,000	$40,000	$60,000
2. Newspaper advertising	10,000	20,000	30,000

    a. What would the maximax choice be?
    b. What would the minimax choice be?
    c. What would the maximim choice be?
    d. What would the insufficient-reason choice be?

5. A dairy store manager observes the daily sales of skim milk for a 100-day period and develops this table of sales:

Quantities Purchased	Number of Days
40	20
50	15
70	15
100	30
120	20

The milk sells for $.30 a quart, and the cost to the store manager of securing the milk from the dairy is $.20.

    a. If 70 units are stocked every day, what will be the firm's expected profit per day over the long run?
    b. Using the data presented in the table, what quantity (40, 50, 70, 100, or 120) should be purchased every day to maximize long-run profits?

6. Distinguish between decisions under conditions of risk and those under uncertainty. Under what circumstances can a manager convert an uncertain decision to a risky decision.

7. Explain in ordinary language the meaning of the term *expected value*. With this meaning in mind, how useful is the term for reaching solutions to nonprogrammed decisions?

8. An analysis and forecast of next year's sales results in the following probability distribution:

Total Demand	Probability
1,000 units	.20
1,200	.20
1,400	.40
1,600	.20

The price per unit is $58. The cost of the product is $38. If the product is not sold during the year, it is worthless.

a. Prepare a table of conditional values.
b. Prepare a table of expected values and indicate the optimum choice if management is attempting to optimize profits.

9. What kinds of managers would most likely use the maximax criterion as the basis for deciding among alternatives? Would these managers be likely to have a record of good decisions?

10. Explain why decisions under uncertainty depend so much on factors unrelated to the nature of the decision itself. For example, why is the decision maker's personality such a key factor in these decisions?

ADDITIONAL REFERENCES

Archer, E. R. "How to Make a Business Decision: An Analysis of Theory and Practice." *Management Review,* February 1980, pp. 54–61.

Bass, B. M. *Organizational Decision Making.* Homewood, Ill.: Richard D. Irwin, 1983.

Bell, D. E. "Disappointment in Decision Making under Uncertainty." *Operations Research,* January–February 1985, pp. 1–27.

Booker, J. M., and M. C. Bryson. "Decision Analysis in Project Management: An Overview." *IEEE Transactions on Engineering Management,* February 1985, pp. 3–9.

Chao, H. P.; B. R. Judd; P. A. Morris; and S. C. Peck. "Analyzing Complex Decisions for Electric Companies." *Long Range Planning,* April 1985, pp. 46–55.

Churchman, C. W. *Challenge to Reason.* New York: McGraw-Hill, 1968.

Clough, D. B. *Decisions in Public and Private Sectors.* Englewood Cliffs, N.J.: Prentice-Hall, 1984.

Davis, D., and R. M. Cosenza. *Business Research for Decision Making.* Boston: Kent Publishing, 1985.

Dixon, D. N. *Using Logical Techniques for Making Better Decisions.* New York: John Wiley & Sons, 1983.

Donaldson, G., and J. W. Lorsch. *Decision Making at the Top: The Shaping of Strategic Direction.* New York: Basic Books, 1983.

Dung, N. "An Analysis of Optimal Advertising under Uncertainty." *Management Science,* May 1985, pp. 622–33.

Eppen, G. D., and F. J. Gould. *Introduction to Management Science.* Englewood Cliffs, N.J.: Prentice-Hall, 1984.

Fallon, R. *Subjective Assessment of Uncertainty.* Santa Monica, Calif.: Rand Corporation, 1976.

Harrison, F. L. "Decision Making in Conditions of Extreme Uncertainty." *Journal of Management Studies,* May 1977, pp. 169–78.

Hertz, D. B., and H. Thomas. *Risk Analysis and Its Applications.* New York: John Wiley & Sons, 1983.

Hunsaker, P. L., and J. S. Hunsaker. "Decision Styles in Theory and in Practice." *Organizational Dynamics,* Autumn 1981, pp. 23–36.

Menzefricke, U. "Using Decision Theory for Planning Audit Sample Size with Dollar Unit Sampling." *Journal of Accounting Research,* Autumn 1984, pp. 570–87.

McCall, M. W., and R. E. Kaplan. *Whatever It Takes: Decision Makers at Work.* Englewood Cliffs, N.J.: Prentice-Hall, 1985.

Moody, P. *Decision Making: Proven Methods for Better Decisions.* New York: McGraw-Hill, 1983.

Nigro, L. G., ed. *Decision Making in the Public Sector.* New York: Marcel Dekker, 1984.

Pennings, J. M. ed. *Decision Making: An Organizational Behavior Approach.* Bridgeport, Conn.: Wiener, 1983.

CASES

APPLICATION I

GENERAL INSTRUMENT CORPORATION: LUCKY OR SMART*

General Instrument Corporation (GI) was at one time a rather lackluster and heavily in debt maker of $375 million worth of electronic and electromechanical products annually. Then something very nice happened. The company caught a fast ride on two rising stars. The first was the video games market, to which it supplies specialized semiconductor chips, including those

---

* Source; Adapted from "Mixing Luck and Knowhow," *Business Week,* October 18, 1982, pp. 118, 120–21.

that run Mattel, Inc.'s Intellivision and Atari, Inc.'s Pac Man. The second is cable TV, for which General Instrument builds distribution gear and converter boxes, products that generate 43 percent of the company's revenues and 70 percent of its operating profits.

Entering the mid-1980's, the company experienced six consecutive years of growth despite a recession and reached $1 billion in annual sales. But some observers agree with one of the firm's competitors, who says: "GI didn't create the demand for game chips. And they didn't create the cable business. They just got lucky."

Executives at GI agree with that observation but only up to a point. They believe, like many others, that the company also got smart. For example, chief executive officer Frank G. Hickey cut GI's long-term debt from nearly 36 percent of equity to less than 8 percent. He also mapped out a growth plan to put the company in other selected communications markets and invested in outside companies to acquire the remaining technology GI needs to compete in those markets. Mr. Hickey believes that the company can parlay its position in targeted markets into 25 percent annual growth. He states: "We're beginning another era. We've got a vision of the portfolio of our businesses again. We're going to become a $3 billion communications company in five years."

In an even more aggressive decision, GI moved into the risky but highly visible business of direct satellite-to-home television broadcasting. Through its part ownership of—and exclusive supply contract with—United Satellite Television Corp., GI expects to sell at least $1.5 billion worth of direct broadcast satellite (DBS) gear to some of the 30 million homes in rural and other areas that will not be supplied by cable systems.

Such decisions have given GI a new popularity as a high-technology stock on Wall Street. The company is on the "buy lists" of most brokerages. One broker says, "Hickey has done an absolutely incredible job. GI has a shot at becoming the hottest technology stock on the Big Board over the next three years. It's a combination of being lucky and being good."

Mr. Hickey observes that the DBS decision has resulted in "the single largest growth opportunity ever available to our company." This decision apparently underscores the company's strategy. As Hickey says, "The strength of our business mix is such that we don't have to rely only on the semiconductor industry or only on telecommunications or anything else."

To a large number of observers GI's plan is more than just luck. One comments, "They did get lucky, but they have exploited their position to the hilt."

Questions for Analysis

1. Do you believe GI was lucky? Why?
2. What does this case indicate to you about decision making? Be specific.

APPLICATION II

THE "OLD MAN"

Ted Gray smiled as he carried some of his belongings into the huge, oak-paneled office that would be his on Monday. At the relatively young age of 46, he had been appointed president of Newtown Developers (the nation's largest developer of planned model cities) three months ago when Don Stevens announced his retirement.

Stevens, or the "Old Man" as he was affectionately known in the organization, had been the only other president Newtown ever had. Most agreed he was responsible for the tremendous growth and success the company had achieved in the last two decades. Ted had worked closely with the Old Man for the past seven years and was his choice to succeed him.

Ted had learned all he could from Stevens. The two were very close and had spent much time together discussing management philosophies, decision making, and human relations. While they sometimes differed in opinion, the discussions were always helpful to Ted.

When he opened the top drawer in his new desk, Ted was surprised to find two old and worn pieces of paper that Don had apparently left behind. Both contained statements from Clarence Randall, head of the Inland Steel Company during the 1950s. The first read as follows:

> Decision making is a lonely business, and the greater the degree of responsibility, the more intense the loneliness. It is human to wish to share the risk of error and to feel the comforting strength of outside support, like the flying buttresses along the wall of a medieval cathedral. But the strong man, the one who gives free enterprise its vitality, is the man who weighs thoughtfully the entire range of available opinion and then determines policy by relying solely on his own judgment.

The second piece of paper contained Randall's response to the question "What, then, are the outward attributes displayed by a man who comes to be regarded by his associates as one who may be highly trusted with the authority to say yes or no?" It read as follows:

> The instinct for recognizing when a problem exists.
> The ability to articulate the problem with clarity.
> The ability to saturate himself with pertinent data.
> The ability to maintain an open mind until the evidence is in.
> A sense of urgency that forces him to work as rapidly as possible.
> The courage not to look back after a decision is made.

Ted put the pieces of paper in his briefcase to give to Stevens the next time he saw him. Then he thought, "I'm still learning from that old goat. I bet he left them here for me."

As Ted left the building on his way home, he thought, "On Monday, I'll be the Old Man." He wasn't sure now if he was glad or scared.

Questions for Analysis

1. Given today's technology, rapidly changing environment, and the increased complexities facing managers, what should Ted Gray do with the two pieces of paper? In other words, would they be of any use to him as he begins his term as president? Discuss in detail.
2. In the statements about decision making, is there anything that has changed in the past 30 years?

EXPERIENTIAL EXERCISE

LOST-AT-SEA DECISION MAKING

Purpose

The purpose of this exercise is to offer you the opportunity to compare individual versus group decision making.

The Exercise in Class

You are adrift on a private yacht in the South Pacific. As a consequence of a fire of unknown origin, much of the yacht and its contents have been destroyed. The yacht is now slowly sinking. Your location is unclear because of the destruction of critical navigational equipment and because you and the crew were distracted trying to bring the fire under control. Your best estimate is that you are approximately 1,000 miles south-southwest of the nearest land.

Exhibit 1 contains a list of 15 items that are intact and undamaged after the fire. In addition to these articles, you have a serviceable rubber life raft with oars, large enough to carry yourself, the crew, and all the items listed here. The total contents of all survivors' pockets are a package of cigarettes, several books of matches, and five $1 bills.

1. Working independently and without discussing the problem or the merits of any of the items, your task is to rank the 15 items in terms of their importance to your survival. Under Column 1, place the number 1 by the most important item, the number 2 by the second most important,

---

EXHIBIT   1   Worksheet

Items	(1) Individual Ranking	(2) Group Ranking	(3) Ranking Key
Sextant	——	——	——
Shaving mirror	——	——	——
Five-gallon can of water	——	——	
Mosquito netting	——	——	——
One case of U.S. Army C rations	——	——	——
Maps of the Pacific Ocean	——	——	
Seat cushion (flotation device approved by the Coast Guard)	——	——	——
Two-gallon can of oil-gas mixture	——	——	——
Small transistor radio	——	——	——
Shark repellent	——	——	——
Twenty square feet of opaque plastic	——	——	——
One quart of 160-proof Puerto Rican rum	——	——	——
Fifteen feet of nylon rope	——	——	——
Two boxes of chocolate bars	——	——	——
Fishing kit	——	——	——

Individual accuracy index	————————
Group accuracy index	————————
Average of group's individual accuracy indexes	————————
Lowest individual accuracy index (correct ranking)	————————

---

and so on through number 15, the least important. When you are through, *do not discuss* the problem or rankings of items with anyone.

2. Your instructor will establish teams of four to six students. The task for your team is to rank the 15 items, according to the group's consensus, in the order of importance to your survival. Do not vote or average team members' rankings; try to reach agreement on each item. Base your decision on knowledge, logic, or the experiences of group members. Try to avoid basing the decision on personal preference. Enter the group's ranking in Column 2. This process should take between 20 and 30 minutes, or as the instructor designates.

3. When everyone is through, your instructor will read the correct ranking, provided by officers of the U.S. Merchant Marine. Enter the correct rankings in Column 3.

4. Compute the accuracy of your individual ranking. For each item, use the absolute value (ignore plus and minus signs) of the difference between

Column 1 and Column 3. Add up these absolute values to get your *individual accuracy index.* Enter it here on the worksheet.

5. Perform the same operation as in Step 4, but use Columns 2 and 3 for your group ranking. Adding up the absolute values yields your *group accuracy index.* Enter it on the worksheet.

6. Compute the *average* of your group's individual accuracy indexes. Do this by adding up each member's individual accuracy index and dividing the result by the number of group members. Enter it.

7. Identify the *lowest* individual accuracy index in your group. This is the most correct ranking in your group. Enter it on the worksheet.

The Learning Message

This exercise is designed to let you experience group decision making. Think about how discussion, reflection, and the exchange of opinions influenced your final decision.

DECISION SUPPORT SYSTEMS

LEARNING OBJECTIVES

After completing Chapter 17, you should be able to:

■ **Define**
decision support systems and their increasing importance.

■ **Describe**
how the types of decisions a manager makes relate to the types of information the manager needs.

■ **Discuss**
the organization of decision support systems.

■ **Compare**
decision support systems and management information systems.

■ **Identify**
the major functions performed by a decision support system.

☐ MANAGEMENT IN ACTION

Decision Support Systems at IBM*

International Business Machines Corp. (IBM) operates a manufacturing facility in Poughkeepsie, New York. The plant develops and manufactures processors for the highly competitive international market.

The plant's 150-person Purchasing Department is responsible for procurement of all production and nonproduction parts from outside vendors. These parts range from inexpensive screws to relatively expensive frames. Because the cost of purchased parts comprises a large percentage of total product cost, the procurement manager constantly seeks ways to attain cost savings.

The purchasing decision at IBM involves selecting specific vendors to supply specific parts in specific quantities to arrive at specified times. The decision is extremely complex, involving a great number of considerations. For example several different vendors can each supply several different parts. The prices each vendor charges for the parts will depend on the quantity ordered. Seldom will a single vendor specialize in supplying IBM with only one kind or type of part. Thus, the decision involves selecting a particular combination of vendors, parts, quantities, and times that minimizes the sum of purchasing, transportation, and inventory costs over multiple time periods.

IBM began its effort to achieve minimum costs by realizing that the solution required a *model* that simulates the relationships among the vendors, parts, quantities, and time, *data* that specify the relationships, and *information* that portrays the relationships according to the model. After an investment of considerable time and money, the Poughkeepsie Purchasing Department developed a system that enabled it to make the optimal decision. The system is termed a vendor selection system (VSS) because it enables the decision maker to specify the decision variables and constraints and select the optimal combination of vendors. The system is no more complicated to use than an electronic spreadsheet routine such as VisiCalc® or Lotus.® It is an excellent example of how management science analysis can be combined with computer capability to produce an information system dedicated to the production of decision-relevant information: a decision support system.

---

* Source: Based on Paul S. Bender, Richard W. Brown, Michael H. Isaac, and Jeremy F. Shapiro, "Improving Purchasing Productivity at IBM with a Normative Decision Support System," *Interfaces,* May–June 1985, pp. 106–15.

As organizations grow in complexity, managers depend more heavily upon various internal and external sources of information. Growing complexity also increases the number of points at which decisions must be made, ranging from individual decision makers at the lowest operating levels to strategic decision makers at the top. Management information systems, designed to provide information to these decision makers, are certainly not new. Many firms have accounting information systems, marketing information systems, customer information files, warehouse information systems, and others. But one very important idea moves beyond the management information system: the decision support system.

THE NEED FOR DECISION SUPPORT SYSTEMS

You know from the last chapter that the quality of a decision depends greatly on understanding the circumstances surrounding an issue and knowing the available alternatives and states of nature. The better the information, the better the resulting decision, because there is less risk and uncertainty. If new, advanced information technology is to support management decision making, organizations must plan now. The need for comprehensive decision support systems has resulted from three factors: (1) the importance of information in decision making,[1] (2) mismanagement of current information,[2] and (3) the increased use of personal computers by individual decision makers.[3]

The Importance of Information in Decision Making

Information is really a fuel that drives organizations. A major purpose of a manager is to convert information into action through the process of decision making. Therefore, a manager and an organization act as an *information-decision system.*

> Information-decision systems should be considered in conjunction with the fundamental managerial functions: planning, organizing, and controlling. If organization is to implement planning and control, if organization is tied to communication, and if communication is represented by an information-decision system, then the key to success in planning and controlling any operation lies in the information-decision system.[4]

---

[1] Cornelius H. Sullivan, Jr., "Systems Planning in the Information Age," *Sloan Management Review,* Winter 1985, pp. 3–12.

[2] C. Wood, "Countering Unauthorized Systems Accesses," *Journal of Systems Management,* April 1984, pp. 26–28.

[3] E. W. Robak, "Toward a Microcomputer-Based DSS for Planning Forest Operations," *Interfaces,* September–October 1984, pp. 105–11; W. L. Fuerst and M. P. Martin, "Effective Design and Use of Computer Decision Models," *MIS Quarterly,* March 1984, pp. 17–26.

[4] Richard A. Johnson, Fremont E. Kast, and James E. Rosenzweig, *The Theory and Management of Systems* (New York: McGraw-Hill, 1978), p. 108.

Viewing an organization as an information-decision system points out the importance of only generating information that is necessary for effective decisions. If management converts information into action, then how effective the action is depends on how complete, relevant, and reliable the information is. The effectiveness of an organization is more often than not at the mercy of the information available to its managers.[5]

Mismanagement of Current Information

The ability of organizations to generate information is really not a problem, since most are capable of producing massive amounts of information and data. In fact, the last decade has often been described as the Age of Information. Why then do so many managers complain that they have insufficient or irrelevant information on which to base their everyday decisions? Specifically, most managers' complaints fall into the following categories:

1. There is too much of the wrong kind of information and not enough of the right kind.
2. Information is so scattered throughout the organization that it is difficult to locate answers to simple questions.
3. Vital information is sometimes suppressed by subordinates or by managers in other functional areas.
4. Vital information often arrives long after it is needed.

Historically managers did not have to deal with an overabundance of information. Instead they gathered a bare minimum of information and hoped that their decisions would be reasonably good. In fact, in some business organizations, marketing research came to be recognized as an extremely valuable staff function during the 1930s and 1940s because it provided information for marketing decisions where previously there had been little or none.

Today, by contrast, managers often feel buried by the deluge of information and data that comes across their desks. This deluge of information, much of which is not useful, has led to the mismanagement of current information. More is not always better.

The Increased Use of Personal Computers

Many experts believe that before this decade is over, most managers will be sharing their desk space with a personal computer. Personal computers

---

[5] D. Lynch, "MIS: Conceptual Framework, Criticism, and Major Requirements for Success," *Journal of Business Communication,* Winter 1984, pp. 19–31; Michael Davis and Joseph L. Sardinas, Jr., "Creating the Right Decision Support System—Pitfalls," *Management Accounting,* June 1985, pp. 12, 69.

have the capability of increasing both the productivity of managers and the quality of their decisions. First, the capacity of computers to extract, process, and analyze data swiftly and accurately is awesome. Second, computers have gotten smaller, faster, and smarter in a shorter period of time than any other technological innovation in history. A common desktop personal computer can solve ordinary arithmetic problems 18 times faster than the world's first large-scale computer (weighing 30 tons) built only 38 years ago. Present-day computers have become extremely inexpensive compared to earlier models. Just 30 years ago, a medium-sized computer cost a quarter of a million dollars. A firm can now buy a desktop computer with three times the memory capacity for less than $2,000. Consequently many firms are now making personal computers widely available to their employees as described in the Management Focus on J. C. Penney.

MANAGEMENT FOCUS
Personal Computers at J. C. Penney

J. C. Penney Company recently created a new corporate entity, the Personal Computer Information Center. The mission of this new department is to provide assistance to employees throughout the corporation who plan to use PCs. The company began encouraging employees to determine ways to increase their productivity through the use of personal computers in 1983. Since that time, employees in all the major departments have used personal computers to do the routine number-crunching tasks as well as to do more sophisticated analyses.

The company purchases a machine for any employee who can outline and justify the need for it. The justification can be in terms of the employee's own job or of other, related employees' jobs. The idea of the program is now spreading to include nonmanagerial jobs as well as managerial jobs.

The inclusion of nonmanagers in the program is consistent with J. C. Penney's overall personnel policy of treating all employees as "associates." Accordingly, any benefits of computerization that might make managers' jobs easier and more fulfilling should also be made available to nonmanagers. The advent of the inexpensive personal computer has opened up avenues for information use and information sharing that were closed only a few years ago.

Based on Nancy Madlin, "Personal Computing at J. C. Penney," *Management Review,* August 1985, pp. 59–60.

The means necessary to produce information are available. Still, managers complain of information losses, delays, and distortions. Apparently many managers have been so concerned about advancing technology and the ready availability of computers that they have overlooked the planning necessary for their effective use. To enable managers to make swift and effective decisions, however, present management information systems must be developed into more effective decision support systems.

MANAGEMENT INFORMATION SYSTEMS (MIS) AND DECISION SUPPORT SYSTEMS (DSS)

Decision support systems have one primary purpose: *to provide the manager with the necessary information for making intelligent decisions.*

The critical point here is that not just any information will do. A system is needed that converts raw data into information that management can actually use. Such systems are known as *decision support systems* (DSS's). They can be described as

> a wide variety of systems which have the direct objective of supporting managerial decision making. Thus, a *management information system* (MIS) is a DSS if, and only if, it is designed with the primary objective of managerial decision support. A computerized data processing system is *not* a DSS—despite that it may, as a byproduct, produce aggregated operating data that are useful to management in making decisions. Only those systems that have the direct and primary objective of supporting managerial decision making are considered DSS's.[6]

Thus, a DSS is a specialized MIS designed to support a manager's skills at all stages of decision making—identifying the problem, choosing the relevant data, picking the approach to be used in making the decision, and evaluating the alternative courses of action. A DSS must produce information in a form managers understand and at a time when such information is needed, and place the information under the managers' direct control. Thus, a DSS is an MIS, but an MIS is not always a DSS; their purposes are different, as shown in the Management Focus comparing several systems.

---

[6] William R. King, "Developing Useful Management Decision Support Systems," *Management Decision,* Fall 1978, pp. 262–73; R. W. Blanning, "What Is Happening in DSS?" *Interfaces,* October 1983, pp. 71–80.

An MIS at United Services Automobile Association

The United Services Automobile Association, the nation's eighth-largest insurer of passenger cars, purchased a $4 million information system that now contains virtually all of the company's written records. When a customer reports an accident, an adjustor can call up the customer's file, check the coverage, and keep track of all the paperwork through the final settlement of the claim. The company figures that it used to take five people a day and a half to perform tasks that one person now handles in 20 minutes.

An MIS at Savin Corporation

Savin Corporation has installed a computer terminal in each of its warehouses to keep track of every item in its inventory. The system identifies the quantity on hand, the location and movement of stock, and the status of all orders. The major purposes of this system are to plan shipments, locate single items in inventory, and locate customer records.

A DSS at Crocker National Bank

Crocker National Bank in San Francisco has purchased desktop terminals for most of its top-level executives. Each terminal is tapped into the huge computers that record all bank transactions. The executives are able to make comparisons, analyze problems, and prepare charts and tables in response to simple commands. For example, they can analyze emerging trends in deposits and loans and monitor the influence of various interest rates and loan maturities on the bank.

A DSS at Gould, Inc.

Gould, Inc. has developed a decision support system to help managers retrieve, manipulate, and display information needed for making decisions. The system combines a large visual display and video terminals with a computerized information system. The system is designed solely to help managers make comparisons and analyze problems for decision-making purposes. The DSS instantly prepares tables and color charts in response to simple commands.

In short, an MIS provides information, but a DSS shapes that information to management's needs. Thus, a DSS discussed in the previous chapter provides support for the types of decisions—programmable and nonprogrammable—as well for decision making under certainty, risk, and uncertainty conditions.

PROVIDING THE RIGHT INFORMATION FOR THE RIGHT DECISIONS

The preceding chapter discussed how the types of problems faced and the procedures used for dealing with them vary according to a manager's level in the organization. The same factors—level in the organization and the type of decision being made—also affect managerial information requirements. To ensure that the types of information match the types of decisions being made, appropriate information must be directed to the proper decision points.

Types of Decisions and Types of Information

The types of information needed are classified by the types of decisions being made: planning decisions, control decisions, and operations decisions. Decision support systems must generate the right types of information for particular types of decisions.[7] Planning, control, and operations decisions require planning, control, and operations information.

■ *Planning decisions* are made by top management. These decisions involve formulating objectives for the organization, the amounts and kinds of resources necessary to attain these objectives, and the policies that govern the use of the resources. Much of this *planning information* comes from external sources and relates to such factors as the present and predicted state of the economy, availability of resources (nonhuman as well as human), and the political and regulatory environment. Planning information forms the input for nonprogrammed types of decisions made at this top level in the organization.[8]

■ *Control decisions* are made by middle management to ensure that the organization's performance is consistent with its objectives. *Control information* comes mainly from internal sources (often interdepartmental) and involves such problems as developing budgets and measuring performance of

---

[7] L. Mann, "User Profiles for Systems Planning and Development," *Journal of Systems Management,* April 1984, pp. 38–40.

[8] Robert Fildes, "Quantitative Forecasting—the State of the Arts," *Journal of the Operations Research Society,* July 1985, pp. 549–80; Kelvin Cross, "Manufacturing Planning with Computers at Honeywell," *Long Range Planning,* December 1984, pp. 64–75.

first-line supervisors. The nature of problems faced may be either programmable or nonprogrammable.[9]

■ *Operations decisions* focus on the day-to-day activities of the organization and how efficiently its resources are being used. *Operations information* comes from routine and necessary sources, such as financial accounting, inventory control, and production scheduling. This information is generated internally; and since it usually relates to specific tasks, it often comes from one designated department. First-line supervisors are the primary users. Since decision making at this level in the organization usually involves programmed types of problems, many problems at the operations level are stated as mathematical models.[10] Some examples of such models and the information they require are presented in the next two chapters.

DESIGNING A DECISION SUPPORT SYSTEM

The first step in designing a DSS is to develop a clear understanding of the various information flows that must be dealt with.

Understanding Information Flows

An organization must deal with two broad types of information flows (see Figure 17–1):

External information flows.   These proceed from the organization to its environment and/or from the environment to the organization. The inward flow is referred to as intelligence information and the outward flow as organizational communications.

Intelligence information includes data on the various elements of the organization's operating environment—such as clients, patients, customers, competitors, suppliers, creditors, and the government—for use in evaluating short-run trends in the immediate external environment. It also includes long-run, strategic planning information on the economic environment—such as consumer income trends and spending patterns for a business organization—as well as tracing developments in the social and cultural environment in which the organization operates. This type of information has long-run significance to the organization and aids in long-range strategic planning.

---

[9] John Murdoch, "Forecasting and Inventory Control on Micros," *Journal of the Operations Research Society,* July 1985, pp. 607–8.

[10] John Bowers, "Network Analysis on a Micro," *Journal of the Operations Research Society,* July 1985, pp. 609–12; A. C. McKay, "Linear Programming Applications on Microcomputers," *Journal of the Operations Research Society,* July 1985, pp. 633–36.

FIGURE   17–1   Information Flows and Types of Information

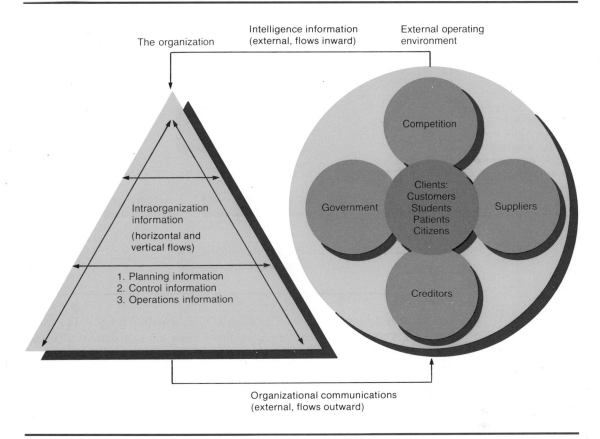

Information flows both to and from an organization. Once inside the organization, it flows both vertically and horizontally.

Organizational communications flow outward from the organization to the various components of its external operating environment. Advertising and other promotional efforts are considered organizational communications. Whatever the type of organization, the content of this information flow is controlled by the organization. Although an important information flow, it nevertheless is an *outward* flow, with which we will not be concerned in this book.

Intraorganization flows.   This term means exactly what the name says: information flowing within an organization. To be useful, intelligence information must, along with internally generated information, reach the right manager at the right time. Within every organization, there are *vertical* (both

FIGURE   17–2   The Functions of a Decision Support System

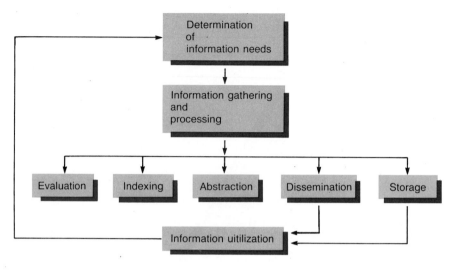

Because it is a system, the outputs from information utilization are channeled back into the DSS as inputs for determining information needs.

upward and downward) as well as *horizontal* information flows.[11] The rationale of a DSS is that all information flows must become part of a master plan and not be allowed to function without a formal scheme and direction. The objective of the master plan is to circulate information to the proper person at the right time.

The Functions of a Decision Support System

An effective DSS should provide managers with four major services: determination of information needs, information gathering, information processing, and utilization (see Figure 17–2).

Determination of information needs.   At the start, the manager must attempt to answer such questions as: How much information is needed? How, when, and by whom will it be used? In what form is it needed? In other words, the manager begins with an examination of the output requirements. Questions helpful for identifying a manager's information needs are presented in Table 17–1.

As discussed earlier in this book, research and practical experience have demonstrated the need to involve people in changes that affect them. No

---

[11] Lawrence W. Foster and David M. Flynn, "Management Information Technology: Its Effects on Organizational Form and Function," *MIS Quarterly,* December 1984, pp. 229–36.

TABLE   17–1   Checklist for Manager's Information Needs*

Determining information needs is the initial task for a manager using a DSS.

1. What types of decisions do you make regularly?
2. What types of information do you need to make these decisions?
3. What types of information do you regularly get?
4. What types of information would you like to get that you are not now getting?
5. What information would you want daily? Weekly? Monthly? Yearly?
6. What types of data analysis programs would you like to see made available?

---

* Source: Adapted from Philip Kotler, *Principles of Marketing,* 3rd ed. (Englewood Cliffs, N.J.: Prentice-Hall, 1986).

less is true if a decision support system is being installed: Managers expected to use it should be involved in implementing it.[12] Thus, output requirements are based on answers to such questions as: What information is necessary for planning and controlling operations at different organizational levels? What information is needed to allocate resources? What information is needed to evaluate performance? These types of questions recognize that a different kind of information is needed for formulating organizational objectives than for scheduling production. They also recognize that too much information may actually hinder a manager's performance. The manager must distinguish between "need to know" types of information and "nice to know" types of information. Remember the point we made at the beginning of this chapter: More information does not always mean better decisions.

Determining what information a manager needs for decision making is a useless exercise unless that information can be obtained. For example, any production manager would like to know exactly how many employees are going to show up each day. With that information, the production manager could always schedule the use of part-time and temporary employees. But such information is seldom available. Other information that a manager might need is likely to be found in the mind of experts who have done a particular task for many years but are unable to articulate what it is that they do. For example, Campbell Soup Company recently faced the problem of replacing an employee who was retiring after 44 years with the company. This particular employee knew more about operating the company's huge soup kettles than anyone in the organization. To replace him was next to impossible.[13]

---

[12] William J. Doll, "Avenues for Top Management Involvement in Successful MIS Development," *MIS Quarterly,* March 1985, pp. 17–36; Robert I. Mann and Hugh J. Watson, "A Contingency Model for User Involvement in DSS Development," *MIS Quarterly,* March 1984, pp. 27–36.

[13] Emily T. Smith, "Turning an Expert's Skill into Computer Software," *Business Week,* October 7, 1985, pp. 104, 108.

In response to the problem of obtaining information about the kettle operation, Campbell developed an *expert-decision system*. [14] The system incorporates the latest in decision system technology and includes computer software that simulates the thought processes that the retired employee had used when running the kettles. Other companies are engaged in the development of these systems, and the field of knowledge engineering, as it is called, is just now beginning to develop. It promises to be an exciting extension of decision support systems.

Information gathering and processing.   The purpose of this service is to improve the overall quality of the information. It includes five component services: *Evaluation* involves determining how much confidence can be placed in a particular piece of information. Such factors as the credibility of the source and reliability of the data must be determined. *Abstraction* involves editing and reducing incoming information in order to provide the managers with only information relevant to their particular task. Once information has been gathered, the service of *indexing* provides classification for storage and retrieval purposes. *Dissemination* entails getting the right information to the right manager at the right time; indeed, this is the overriding purpose of a DSS. The final information-processing service is that of *storage*. As noted earlier, an organization has no natural memory, so every DSS must provide for storage of information so that it can be used again if needed. Modern electronic information storage equipment has greatly improved the "memory" capabilities of organizations.

Information utilization.   How information is used depends greatly on its quality (accuracy), presentation (form), and timeliness. Effective utilization is only possible if the right questions to determine information needs are asked in the beginning and if the system is planned carefully. *The major goal of a DSS is to provide the right information to the right decision maker at the right time.* To this end, timeliness may take precedence over accuracy.[15] If information is not available when it is needed, then its accuracy is not important. In most cases, however, both accuracy and timeliness are critical.

Timeliness is not the same for every manager; it is determined by the nature of the decisions that must be made. For example, a sales manager may find accurate weekly reports of sales for each company product to be adequate, while an investment manager may need accurate information every few minutes.

---

[14] Richard Vedder and Chadwick H. Nestman, "Understanding Expert Systems: A Companion to DSS and MSS," *Industrial Management,* March–April 1985, pp. 1–8.

[15] Kenneth M. Drange, "Information Systems: Does Efficiency Mean Better Performance?" *Journal of Systems Management,* April 1985, pp. 22–29.

ORGANIZING A DECISION SUPPORT SYSTEM

In most organizations, many different independent information systems exist for different organizational functions. Along with the development of accounting information systems, other line and staff groups in businesses have developed management information systems uniquely suited to their own needs. While management information systems are critical for effective performance within functional areas, what happens when a decision maker requires information from other functional areas? Organizing a DSS means developing a central data bank and an information center, plus viewing information as an important organizational resource.

The Central Data Bank

A central data bank is the core of a decision support system. Information in one area of an organization is made readily available for decision making in other areas through use of a central data bank. Recent developments in computer and communications technology have made such decision support systems both possible and affordable. And the idea is simple: Centralizing information means that sales data would not have to be stored in accounting, marketing, and production but would be available in one central data bank. Since its data can be accessed at will by any decision maker needing it, the central data bank increases both the quality and timeliness of decisions. Figure 17–3 presents the central data bank concept, illustrating two subsystems in more detail.

The Information Center

The information requirements of most managers have greatly changed in the past decade, while the information arrangements within most organizations have remained essentially the same. Because both users and suppliers of information are scattered throughout an organization, some unit is needed to oversee the operation of the central data bank. In fact, a basic weakness in most organizations has been the absence of a central entity—known as the information center—for the gathering and processing of information.

To develop an information center, three tasks are necessary:

1. Dispersed information activities must be identified throughout the organization.
2. These activities must be viewed as parts of a whole.
3. These activities must be brought under the management of a separate, centralized information center.

A central data bank ensures that information in one area of the organization is readily available for decision makers in other areas.

The information center is a consultant, coordinator, and controller for the functions of a DSS—determination of information needs, information gathering and processing, and information utilization. In order to justify its existence, it must facilitate improved managerial performance through more as well as better information availability and use.

Many "information-oriented" organizations have developed a separate, centralized, companywide information office. The use of such an office is probably more widespread in highly competitive, volatile consumer-goods industries. However, the need is becoming greater in both private industry and the public sector.[16] This organizational arrangement offers several advantages (such as increased efficiency and more effective use of information) because all computer facilities, knowledge, and storage and retrieval facilities become available to all other functions in the organization. As the Management Focus on Travelers Insurance illustrates, the information center becomes the organizing unit for decision support systems.

MANAGEMENT FOCUS
The Information Center at Travelers Insurance

Since International Business Machines Corp. began promoting the concept in the late 1970s, about 50 percent of the users of its largest computers have installed information centers. Judging from users' early experiences, the concept is likely to spread. For example, Travelers Insurance Co., opened a center in December 1981 with 10 consultants answering 200 calls for assistance a month; within a year, Travelers had twice as many consultants fielding 4,000 calls a month from managers.

The kind of quick response made possible by the information center encourages executives to pursue the sudden unanticipated question. That speed also gives them the flexibility to test various options. For example, the vice president of management information systems at Travelers now uses the information center to compare quarterly sales of 10 types of insurance against policies from 20 competitors. Previously the computer department did make comparisons, but it could not quickly switch the factors to be compared. The vice president commented, "Being able to change directions in the middle of the problem is very important."

---

[16] John C. Henderson and David A. Schilling, "Design and Implementation of Decision Support Systems in the Public Sector," *MIS Quarterly,* June 1985, pp. 157–70.

Information as an Organizational Resource

Developing a central data bank and an information center does not guarantee that information will be used wisely. A frequent problem in many organizations is that a great deal of information is generated for no real purpose and should be eliminated. The tendency to generate large quantities of information is based on the assumption that a direct relationship exists between the amount of information and the quality of decisions. But as we have seen, the quality rather than the quantity of information is more important for decision making.[17] To promote effective utilization of a DSS is to see information as a basic resource of the organization, just as we do money, materials, personnel, and plant and equipment. Thus, as a basic resource, information:

1. Is vital to the survival of the organization.
2. Can only be used at a cost.
3. Must be at the right place at the right time.
4. Must be used efficiently for an optimal return on its cost to the organization.

Each user of information should consider the cost of the information relative to its utility for decision making. For example, the cost of compiling complete information for a decision must be weighed against the expected value of a decision made with incomplete information.

While the concept of a DSS is relatively new, we have seen in this chapter that it is a reality in small[18] and large[19] organizations. Certainly, one of the major reasons for the increased interest in and the development of DSS has been the growth in information technology. However, the development of DSS is more than technology; its purpose is more effective management decision making.

SUMMARY OF KEY POINTS

- More comprehensive decision support systems are necessary because of the importance of information in decision making, mismanagement of current information, and the increased use of personal computers by decision makers.

- A management information system is a decision support system if, and

---

[17] T. Hirouchi and T. Kosaka, "An Effective Database Foundation for Decision Support Systems," *Information and Management,* August 1984, pp. 183–95.

[18] Stewart C. Malone, "Computerizing Small Business Information Systems," *Journal of Small Business Management,* April 1985, pp. 10–16.

[19] G. Nigel Gilbert, "Decision Support in Large Organizations," *Data Processing,* May 1985, pp. 28–30.

only if, it is designed with the primary objectives of managerial decision support. Thus, a DSS is an MIS, but an MIS is not necessarily a DSS.

- A DSS must be designed to support a manager's skills at all stages of the decision-making process—from identifying and defining problems to evaluating alternative courses of action.

- The types as well as sources of information required for management decisions will vary by level in the organization. We identify three types of information—planning, control, and operations—based on the types of decisions made.

- Designing a DSS involves understanding information flows as well as the functions of such a system. The functions of a DSS are determination of information needs, information gathering and processing, and information utilization.

- Organizing a DSS involves developing a central data bank and an information center, plus viewing information as an important organizational resource.

DISCUSSION AND REVIEW QUESTIONS

1. What reasons account for the growing importance of information in management decision making? Can a manager make a decision without information? Explain.

2. Do you believe that it is easy to mismanage information in contemporary organizations? Why? What personal experiences have you had with organizations that mismanaged information.

3. What are the key differences between management information systems and decision support systems?

4. What kinds of information would a manager need to make the following decisions?
   a. Hiring a new employee.
   b. Promoting an employee.
   c. Purchasing a computer system.
   d. Assigning salespersons to regions.
   e. Assigning shelf space to a product.

5. Provide examples of decisions other than the ones listed in Question 4 to illustrate the differences between planning, control, and operations decisions.

6. What are the different external and internal information flows that the college or university you attend must deal with? If possible, interview campus administrators and determine which of these flows they consider most critical for the effectiveness of their decisions.

7. What are the different functions of a decision support system? How do these functions differ in manufacturing as compared to service organizations?

8. Explain how a manager could make sure that the centralized information center does not become overly powerful in the organization by virtue of its position as monopolist of information?

9. If information is a resource, as suggested by the chapter discussion, should it be valued in the balance sheet like other assets? Why or why not?

10. In the modern age of information, is the study of information little more than the study of computer technology, including hardware and software? Explain your answer.

ADDITIONAL REFERENCES

Ayers, A. F. "Decision Support System—New Tool for Manufacturing." *Computerworld,* June 1985, pp. 35–38.

Bahl, H. C., and R. G. Hunt. "Problem-Solving Strategies for DSS Design." *Information and Management,* February 1985, pp. 81–88.

Brown, D. C. "The Anatomy of a Decision Support System: How Abbott Labs Puts DSS to Work for 2,000 Products." *Business Marketing,* June 1985, pp. 80–86.

Chan, K. H. "Decision Support Systems for Human Resource Management." *Journal of Systems Management,* April 1984, pp. 17–25.

Ford, F. N. "Decision Support Systems and Expert Systems: A Comparison." *Information and Management,* January 1985, pp. 21–26.

Gilbert, G. N. "Decision Support in Large Organization." *Data Processing,* May 1985, pp. 28–30.

Horn, S. "Managers Analyze Data with DSS, Make Future Planning Decisions." *Bank Systems and Equipment,* April 1984, pp. 66–69.

Keen, P. G. W., and M. S. Morton. *Decision Support Systems: An Organization Perspective.* Reading, Mass.: Addison-Wesley Publishing, 1978.

Kroeber, D. W. *Management Information Systems.* New York: Free Press, 1982.

McCosh, A. M., and M. S. Morton. *Management Decision Support Systems.* New York: John Wiley & Sons, 1977.

Meador, C. L.; P. G. Keen; and M. J. Guyote. "Setting Priorities for DSS Development." *MIS Quarterly,* June 1984, pp. 117–29.

Schoderbek, P. P.; C. G. Schoderbek; and A. G. Kefalas. *Management Systems: Conceptual Considerations.* Rev. ed. Plano, Tex.: Business Publications, 1980.

Taylor, T. C. "Honeywell's Computer Makes Managers out of Salespeople." *Sales and Marketing Management,* May 14, 1984, pp. 59–61.

Vedder, R., and C. H. Nestman. "Understanding Expert Systems: Companion to DSS and MSS." *Industrial Management,* March–April 1985, pp. 1–8.

Wedley, W. C., and R. H. G. Field. "A Predecision Support System." *Academy of Management Review,* October 1984, pp. 696–703.

CASES

APPLICATION I

STEALING ELECTRONIC INFORMATION AT THE L.A. COUNTY SHERIFF'S DEPARTMENT*

A deputy sheriff resigned from the Los Angeles County Sheriff's Department to become a private investigator, but he continued to use the department's files. The sheriff's department discovered that the man made 286 unauthorized phone calls in one year for his own investigations to check criminal histories, automobile registrations, and outstanding warrants. He was, in effect, stealing information.

This example is only one of a growing number of information crimes. This kind of crime is increasing for a variety of reasons. First, storing information electronically in a centralized place makes it more available than when it was printed and stored on paper. It is faster and easier to steal important information stored in a computer rather than in individual departments. Second, electronic equipment facilitates crime. For example, two securities salesmen who were about to resign their jobs with one firm did not have to spend any time and effort copying customer names and addresses; they simply ordered a computer printout, which they took with them to their jobs at a competitor. Third, information stored on magnetic disks or tapes is far less bulky than the same amount of information printed on paper, making the information easier to steal. Finally, information can be changed in a computer without leaving any trace.

The problem is complicated by the difficulty in prosecuting information crime. Larceny is defined as depriving someone of their possessions permanently. But when someone steals information, it is still left in the computer.

In response to the growing crime rate, more and more corporations are increasing their information security. Most companies have always carefully guarded their market data, product designs, and other secrets. However, few of them have bothered to update their security practices for the new electronic equipment.

For the growing problem of information crime, however, experience is still the best teacher. One expert notes: "The places doing the best jobs of protecting their information are those that have had previous problems."

* Source: Adapted from "Locking the Electronic File Cabinet," *Business Week,* October 18, 1982, pp. 123–24.

Questions for Analysis

1. As a student and a customer, you are probably part of numerous information systems. Can information crime have any impact on you? Discuss.
2. With the rapid growth in technology, are there any ethical concerns associated with information systems? How would you deal with these concerns?

APPLICATION II

HOW DO WE EVER MAKE A DECISION?

Return on investment for Lobo Enterprises had not been over 7 percent for the last five years. Late last year, when it became apparent that it would not reach 5 percent for the year, top management finally decided that something needed to be done. One of the nation's largest management consulting firms was contracted to examine the company's operations from top to bottom.

Seven weeks later, the consultants submitted their report with numerous suggestions and recommendations. One of the strongest recommendations read as follows:

Decision makers at the present time are relying on an inefficient, ineffective information system. In fact, Lobo Enterprises does not have anything that resembles an information system. We strongly recommend the design of an information system to include all levels of the organization. Its major goal should be to provide decision makers with relevant, accurate, and timely information for use in making decisions in their specific areas of responsibility.

The top management agreed with the recommendation and ordered the EDP (electronic data processing) Department to work with the consultants in designing a DSS. As part of the initial phase of the project, all decision makers in the organization were asked to think carefully about the information needed and used in making decisions related to their area of responsibility. Each manager was asked to submit a report within three weeks, relating information needs and the specific types and sources of information utilized on a regular basis.

Two weeks later, Ralph Reeves, the chief purchasing agent for Lobo, had just completed a rough draft of his report. He called in one of his purchasing agents, Scott Reed, and asked him to take the report home for the weekend, read it, and be prepared to comment on it and make recommendations for changes on Monday. Here is Reeves' report:

Information Needs and Sources of
Information for Purchasing Function

In order to make effective purchasing decisions, an industrial buyer needs a certain amount and quality of information. Primarily, our information needs are related to the following:

1. Price of the items.
2. Quantities to be purchased.
3. Number of sources of supply.
4. Urgency of the buy.
5. Complexity of the items.
6. Current market situation relative to the items.
7. Authority over details of the purchase decision.

The specific informational needs will for the most part be of two types: technical or quantitative. The technical needs relate to such things as dimensional prints, engineering specifications, and quality requirements. The quantitative requirements are things such as lot size, estimated prices, and terms of shipment.

A careful analysis of the purchasing task reveals numerous and diverse sources of information. Some of our most important and widely used sources are the following:

1. Engineering Department
2. Research and Development Department.
3. Production Control.
4. Supplier literature.
5. Trade papers and magazines.
6. Supplier salespersons.
7. Accounting Department.
8. Receiving Department.
9. Competitors.
10. Other buyers in the department.
11. Production Department.
12. Legal Department.

Exhibit 1 illustrates more completely the sources of information used by a buyer prior to most procurement decisions. We in the Purchasing Department believe it clearly illustrates the need for some type of formal systemization of information.

On Monday, Scott Reed brought the report in to Ralph Reeves. "What do you think?" asked Reeves.

"Ralph, it's excellent. I believe you have accurately detailed the information needs and sources for most purchasing decisions. I have no suggestions or recommendations for changes. One thing did cross my mind as I saw all of our information needs and numerous sources all laid out before my eyes."

"What's that?" asked Reeves.

There was a slight pause before Reed said, "How do we ever make a decision?"

EXHIBIT   1   Sources of Information Used by an Industrial Buyer at Lobo Enterprises

---

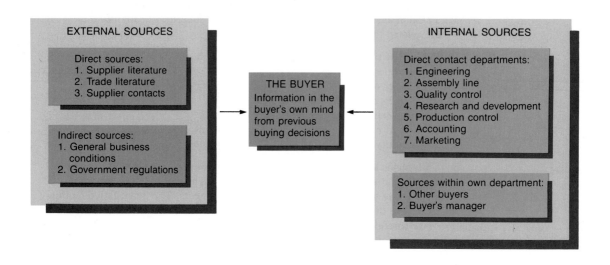

Questions for Analysis

1. What would be your answer to Scott Reed's question?
2. Could Figure 17–2 be of use to Lobo Enterprises? How?
3. Could the concept of a central data bank be of use to Lobo Enterprises? Why? Illustrate, using specific examples.

18

PRODUCTION PLANNING

LEARNING OBJECTIVES

After completing Chapter 18, you should be able to:

■ **Define**
the concept of production planning in terms of competing products and activities.

■ **Describe**
the differences between types of production planning settings for which linear programming (LP) and program evaluation review techniques (PERT) are applicable.

■ **Discuss**
the concepts and assumptions that are the bases for linear programming and program evaluation review techniques.

■ **Compare**
the informational requirements of linear programming and program evaluation review techniques.

■ **Identify**
the optimal production plan for a two-product, three-process firm, given the required information.

☐ **MANAGEMENT IN ACTION**

Bank Financial Planning with and without Linear Programming*

Linear programming is a mathematical technique for finding the best uses of a firm's limited resources. The adjective *linear* is used to describe a relationship between two or more variables.

Central Carolina Bank and Trust Company (CCB) used a linear programming model for financial planning from 1975 to 1980. The model in effect determined the optimal bank "inventory" of assets (sources of bank earnings) and liabilities and equities (sources of bank costs). The development and refinement of the model took many hours of executive time. Eventually it was fully accepted as an important method in bank operations.

The linear programming model generated target balance sheets and rank orderings of the relative profitability of the bank's services. With these outputs, bank executives could make decisions that would maximize the difference between total yields on all assets and total costs of all liabilities. Bank assets include cash, treasury securities, consumer loans, commercial loans, and others. Bank liabilities include demand deposit accounts, savings accounts, certificates of deposit, and others. Each of these liabilities has as associated cost. A bank's earnings depend, then, on its inventory of assets and its inventory of liabilities.

In order to maximize the difference between yields and costs, it is necessary to specify the constraints that must be observed. Banking is subject to many operational, legal, and policy guidelines, and linear programming handled them satisfactorily. But in the late 1970s, the banking industry began to experience changes that created constraints the linear programming model could not handle. Prior to 1978, the industry was heavily regulated by federal and state banking authorities. But with deregulation came intense competition that resulted in dramatic and unpredictable changes in interest rates for both assets and liabilities. Planning horizons changed from an annual to a weekly and sometimes daily basis. The linear programming model, as a deterministic model (one that contains no elements of chance), was less and less satisfactory as an adjunct to profit planning.

---

* Source: Based on Sheldon D. Balbirer and David Shaw, "An Application of Linear Programming to Bank Financial Planning," *Interfaces,* October 1981, pp. 77–83; Sheldon D. Balbirer and David Shaw, "The Evolution of Financial Planning Models at a Commercial Bank," *Interfaces,* November–December 1984, pp. 67–69.

Production planning is a key recurring decision in production and operations management. In this chapter, production planning will be presented in the context of two situations. The first is that of a manufacturer with multiple products. These products are demanded by large numbers of consumers who are willing to buy them at particular prices. Manufacturers of autos, home products, appliances, and textiles are representative of this first situation. The production planning decision requires managers to determine the specific number of each product to produce given the resource constraints of the firm and the relative profitability of each product.

The second situation deals with the firm that takes on few, but large-scale, construction or product development projects. These projects are typically one of a kind. The firm may never again produce an identical or even similar product. Builders of roads, buildings, ships, missiles, spacecraft, and dams are but a few examples of this type of firm. In this second situation, the production planning decision requires managers to determine the combination and sequence of activities to complete the project given the cost and time constraints of each activity.

These two situations depict a range of typical production planning possibilities. The management science approach offers numerous techniques applicable to each. In this chapter, we will describe two of the more widely used techniques: linear programming and program evaluation review technique.

PLANNING REPETITIVE PRODUCTION: LINEAR PROGRAMMING

Determining which specific combination of products to manufacture during a time period becomes more complex as the number of products increases. To assist management in making this decision, a class of techniques called "programming methods" is available. The simplest of these methods is linear programming (LP). Since World War II, linear programming models increasingly have been used to solve management problems. With the growth of the electronic computer, complex linear programming models are now being utilized on a wide scale.[1]

The model is called linear because the mathematical equations employed to describe the particular system under study and the objective to be achieved are in the form of linear relations between the variables. A linear relationship between two or more variables is directly and precisely proportional.

A linear programming model enables managers to maximize an objective (such as profits) or minimize an objective (such as costs) by determining

---

[1] H. O. Guenther, "Comparison of Two Classes of Aggregate Production Planning Models under Stochastic Demand," *Engineering Cost and Production Economics,* April 1982, pp. 89–97.

the future value of certain variables affecting the outcome. These variables are ones that the manager can control.

Specific Applications of Linear Programming

Linear programming has been applied to a number of specific management problems:

1. *Production planning.*   In production planning (the specific interest of this chapter), a manager must determine the levels of a number of production activities for the planning period. For example, if a firm manufactures two products, both of which must go through the same three production processes, the manager faces a problem of this nature. The two products compete for time in the three production processes, and the task of the linear programming model in this case would be to allocate the limited resources (available time in the three processes) in such a way as to produce the number of each product that will maximize the firm's profit.

Applications of linear programming are widespread and have few geographical boundaries. Textile mills in India, for example, use linear programming to plan the allocation of loom time (the scarce resource) to alternative fabric types (the competing products).[2]

2. *Feed mix.*   Large farming organizations purchase and mix together several types of grains for different purposes. For one situation, the production manager must mix the different grains to produce feed for livestock. Each grain contains different amounts of several nutritional elements. The mixture must meet minimal nutritional requirements at the lowest cost. Linear programming is used to allocate the various grains so that the resulting mixture meets both nutritional and dietary specifications at the minimum cost. A number of different problems in agriculture lend themselves to application of linear programming.[3]

3. *Fluid blending.*   This variation of the feed-mix problem requires the manager to blend fluids such as molten metals, chemicals, and crude oil into a finished product. Steel, chemical, and oil companies make wide use of linear programming models for problems of this type. Computing the right mixture of octane requirements in the blending of different gasolines is an example of such a problem in the oil industry.[4]

4. *Transportation.*   The managers at many manufacturers and large retail chains must select transportation routes that minimize total shipping costs,

---

[2] S. C. Bhatnagar, "Implementing Linear Programming in a Textile Unit: Some Problems and a Solution," *Interfaces,* April 1981, pp. 87–93.

[3] Keith Butterworth, "Practical Applications of Linear Programming in U.S. and Canadian Agriculture," *Journal of the Operations Research Society,* January 1985, pp. 99–108.

[4] Thomas E. Baker and Leon S. Lasdon, "Successive Linear Programming at Exxon," *Management Science,* March 1985, pp. 264–74.

given a number of supply sources (for example, warehouses) and destinations (for example, customers) and the cost of shipping a product from the source to each destination. This problem becomes even more complex if the firm has many warehouses and thousands of customers in different parts of the country. Other interesting transportation-related applications of linear programming include scheduling ports of call for oceangoing tankers[5] and scheduling optimal routes for school buses.[6]

5. *Advertising media mix.* In most organizations, a manager must sooner or later face a media-mix problem. Given an advertising budget, how can the funds be allocated over the various advertising media to achieve maximum exposure of the product or service? Linear programming enables the manager to make these decisions regarding a number of media (for example, five magazines) all competing for limited resources (the advertising budget). In fact, many advertising agencies use linear programming for problems of this type.

While these problems are probably the most popular areas of application, there are many other practical problems for which linear programming has proved its worth. For example, it has aided allocation of tax dollars to public projects,[7] space and time to tree development,[8] credit to customers,[9] dollars to investments,[10] and hospital resources to patients.[11]

Production Planning with LP

To illustrate the application of LP to production planning, assume that Apex Corporation manufactures two products, both of which must go through the same three production processes. The firm's manager, using linear programming, must decide on the optimal allocation of limited resources to produce the number of each product that will maximize profits. This production and operations decision recurs frequently in repetitive manufacturing settings such as textile manufacturing.

[5] Raymond F. Boykin and Reuven R. Levary, "An Interactive Decision Support System for Analyzing Ship Voyage Alternatives," *Interfaces,* March–April 1985, pp. 81–84.

[6] A. J. Swersey and W. Ballard, "Scheduling School Buses," *Management Science,* July 1984, pp. 844–53.

[7] Colin O. Benjamin, "A Linear Goal Programming Model for Public-Sector Project Selection," *Journal of the Operations Research Society,* January 1985, pp. 13–24.

[8] T. H. Mattheiss and S. B. Land, "A Tree Breeding Strategy Based on Multiple Objective Linear Programming," *Interfaces,* September–October 1984, pp. 96–104.

[9] John D. Stowe, "An Integer Programming Solution for the Optimal Credit Investigation/ Credit Granting Sequence," *Financial Management,* Summer 1985, pp. 66–76.

[10] Gordon J. Alexander and Bruce G. Resnick, "Using Linear and Goal Programming to Immunize Bond Portfolios," *Journal of Banking and Finance,* March 1985, pp. 35–54.

[11] William L. Hughes and S. Y. Soliman, "Short-Term Case Mix Management with Linear Programming," *Hospital and Health Services Administration,* January–February 1985, pp. 52–60.

The manager of the Apex Corporation has the choice of producing two different products, A and B. Furthermore, both products must go through three departments—X, Y, and Z—to be completed. Assume that Department X is production, Department Y is assembling, and Department Z is packaging. Both products require the same amount of time in Department X. Because of special features, however, Product B requires twice as much time in Department Y as Product A does but less time in Department Z. Product A contributes $10 per unit to profits, and Product B contributes $12 per unit. Given these facts, the manager must determine a production program for the two products.

Key elements of LP.   In this particular problem, Products A and B are the competing users; the available time in the three processes (production, assembling, and packaging) represents the limited resource. The capacity of this resource is limited because there is only so much time per day available in each of the three departments. If we assume that no expansion plans are called for, then this limitation is expressed as a set of constraints on the values that can be assigned to the competing products.

Apex Corporation's desired outcome is maximum profit. In linear programming, the desired outcome is formulated as a mathematical expression termed an *objective function.* The value of the objective function depends on the values of all other variables.

To review, then, it should be clear that the linear programming model is *normative* in purpose, since it selects the best alternative to optimize some objective (profit in this case), and contains *deterministic* variables, since all variables are assumed to be known with certainty. Also, note that in order to utilize the linear programming model, it is necessary to *assume certainty* (all factors are exact or deterministic quantities) and to *simplify relationships* (assume linear relationships among variables) in the problem. These simplifying assumptions limit the application of LP to relatively certain environments, as we saw in this chapter's Management in Action. The variables in the Apex Corporation example are given numerical values in Table 18–1.

TABLE   18–1   Apex Corporation's Resources Requirements and Constraints

Linear programming depends upon accurate assessment of the organization's available resources, product requirements for those resources, and capacity for each resource.

Department	*Minutes Required per Unit*		*Capacity per Day in Minutes*
	Product A	*Product B*	
X (production)	6	6	300
Y (assembling)	4	8	320
Z (packaging)	5	3	310
Profit contribution per unit	$10	$12	

The LP Solution.   To begin solving this problem by means of linear programming, we must restate it in mathematical form. Since the goal is to maximize profit (P), the objective function can be stated:

$$\text{Objective function} = P = \$10A + \$12B$$

This equation is read: Profit equals $10 multiplied by the number of Product A produced plus $12 multiplied by the number of Product B produced. Assuming we produced and sold 20 of each, profit would equal $10 (20) plus $12 (20), or $440.

The next step is to express the constraints in mathematical form. The time used in the three departments cannot exceed the total time available per day in each of the departments. For example, the time needed to produce one Product A times the number produced *plus* the time needed to produce one Product B times the number produced must be equal to or less than the 300 minutes available each day in the production department (Department X). Using the values from Table 18–1, the constraints for all three departments can be expressed as follows:

$$6A + 6B \leq 300 \text{ minutes in Department X (production)}$$
$$4A + 8B \leq 320 \text{ minutes in Department Y (assembling)}$$
$$5A + 3B \leq 310 \text{ minutes in Department Z (packaging)}$$

Finally, every linear programming problem has a set of *nonnegativity* constraints. These are imposed to ensure that any derived values for A and B are positive since we cannot produce a minus quantity of a product. Thus, the optimal solution must have nonnegative values for A and B; expressed mathematically, $A \geq 0$ and $B \geq 0$.

Summarizing the problem in mathematical form yields:

$$\text{Maximum profit } (P) = \$10A + \$12B$$

subject to the following constraints:

$$6A + 6B \leq 300$$
$$4A + 8B \leq 320$$
$$5A + 3B \leq 310$$

and

$$A \geq 0$$
$$B \geq 0$$

After stating the problem mathematically, the next step is to construct a two-dimensional graph. With Product A on the horizontal axis and Product B on the vertical axis, plot each of the three constraint equations.

Figure 18–1 illustrates the inequalities (constraints) for each department on a separate graph and all together on a composite graph. The arrow associated with each line shows the direction indicated by the inequality signs

FIGURE   18–1   Constraint Equations

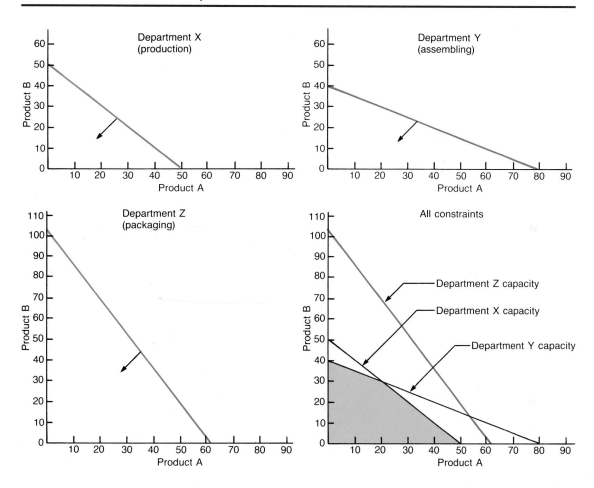

Once the production planning problem is expressed in mathematical terms, plotting the equations on a graph is one method used to reach a solution.

(less than or equal to) in the constraint equations. Any combination of Products A and B that lies in that area can be produced, assembled, or packaged without exceeding the available time in the particular department. Note that the nonnegativity constraints $A \geq 0$, $B \geq 0$ restrict us to zero or more units of Products A and B.

All values for Product A and B satisfying all three constraints are shown in the shaded region in Figure 18–1. In this particular problem, any pair of values for Products A and B that satisfies the constraints in Department X and Y also satisfies Department Z. To complete one unit of Product A or B, work must be done in all three departments. Therefore, the best combination of Products A and B falls within the shaded area in Figure 18–1. Any combination in this *feasibility space* will not exceed the maximum time in either Department X, Y, or Z.

The construction of Figure 18–1 is the first step in solving the problem by the graphical method. The goal is to locate at least one point from the shaded area in the figure that will maximize the objective function.

Finding the optimal solution.   The problem can be solved by selecting any arbitrary profit figure and determining how many units of Product A alone or Product B alone would be needed to earn such a profit. Any profit figure will suffice, but common sense tells us to select a point within the feasibility space in Figure 18–1. Let us assume a profit figure of $300. Since Product A contributes $10, we would need 30 units in order to earn a profit of $300. If we manufacture only Product B, we would need 25 units in order to earn a $300 profit, since Product B contributes a profit of $12. If we locate these two points in the feasibility space and join them, we obtain

FIGURE   18–2   Equal-Profit Lines

Equal-profit lines reflect the total profit (as defined by the objective function) for each feasible combination of the two products.

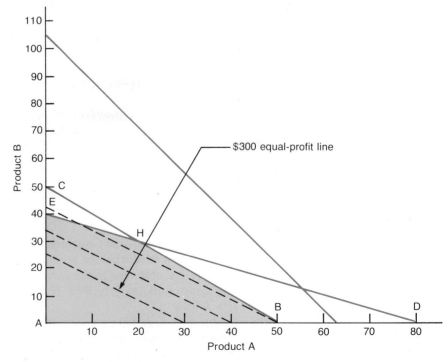

what is known as a $300 equal-profit line, which is nothing more than the locus of all points (all combinations of Products A and B) that will yield a profit of $300. This is illustrated in Figure 18–2 as the dotted line between 30 on the A axis and 25 on the B axis.

We can continue to construct these lines for higher and higher profit figures, illustrated in Figure 18–2 by dotted lines, as long as we remain within the feasibility space. We are forced to stop when we reach a boundary line or corner point of the feasibility space. The highest combination still having a point in the feasibility space provides the optimal value of the objective function.

The equal-profit line farthest from the origin and still within the feasibility space occurs at the intersection of the Department X and Department Y constraints—at Point H in Figure 18–2. Although there are an infinite number of solutions within the feasibility space, Point H provides the optimal solution.

The coordinates of Point H can be read directly from the graph if it is constructed perfectly, but they are usually found by solving simultaneously the equations of the two lines that intersect to form Point H, which is the only point common to both equations. The equations to be solved are:

$$\text{Line } BC: \quad 6A + 6B = 300$$
$$\text{Line } DE: \quad 4A + 8B = 320$$

To solve these equations simultaneously,

a. Multiply the first equation by 4.
b. Multiply the second equation by -3.
c. Add the results.

$$
\begin{array}{rrrr}
4(6A + 6B = 300) = & 24A + & 24B & = & 1200 \\
-3(4A + 8B = 320) = & -12A + & (-24B) & = & -960 \\
\hline
 & 12A & & = & 240 \\
 & A & & = & 20 \\
\end{array}
$$

d. Substitute 20 for A in the second equation:

$$4A + 8B = 320 = 4(20) + 8B = 320$$
$$80 + 8B = 320$$
$$8B = 240$$
$$B = 30$$

e. Point H is, therefore, $(20, 30)$.

We can test the four points that delineate the feasibility space in order to determine the highest dollar profit.

$$
\begin{array}{lll}
\text{Point } A \ (0,0) & = 10(0) + 12(0) & = \$0 \\
\text{Point } B \ (50,0) & = 10(50) + 12(0) & = \$500 \\
\text{Point } E \ (0,40) & = 10(0) + 12(40) & = \$480 \\
\text{Point } H \ (20,30) & = 10(20) + 12(30) & = \$560 \\
\end{array}
$$

The point that provides the most profit is Point *H,* where we manufacture 20 units of Product *A* and 30 units of Product *B* for a profit of $560.

The production planning decision is crucial in manufacturing. The outcome of the decision determines how the scarce resources are to be allocated to the alternative products. The LP method is a very flexible method that has general applicability. As we saw in the opening section, management can apply LP to numerous problems. The Management Focus illustrates the use of linear programming in textile mills.

MANAGEMENT FOCUS
Production Planning in a Textile Mill

The production planning problem of textile mills is similar to that of many manufacturing firms. It involves determination of the optimal mix of fabric styles and types. The optimal mix depends on the profitability of each fabric style and type *and* the available loom time. One approach to obtaining an optimal production plan is to use the linear programming technique.

Indian production managers have attained significant improvements through the use of LP. For example, production managers in one firm used linear programming to identify fabric styles that were unprofitable. Subsequently these styles were dropped from the production plan. More important, the profitability of each loom increased because each was used to produce an optimal quantity of the most profitable fabrics. These positive results are very encouraging because they demonstrate the superiority of linear programming over the more traditional manual planning systems that dominated the Indian textile industry.

The social and economic consequences of increasing productivity in developing countries cannot be overestimated. Improved production planning can contribute to productivity gains, as reflected in this one experience.

The Value of Linear Programming

Properly constructed linear programming models provide managers with three specific benefits:

1. *Improved planning.* Linear programming can, with the aid of an electronic computer, quickly solve a problem containing over 500 equations and 1,000 variables. This incredible capability means that linear programming

can expand the analytic ability, and therefore the planning ability, of a manager. It permits an exhaustive search of numerous alternative solutions and systematically searches for the optimum one. Previously time constraints might have permitted examination of only a few possible alternative solutions when numerous potential solutions actually existed.

2. *Improved decisions.* Linear programming models can also improve management decisions by quickly finding the optimal solution for a problem under a variety of conditions. For example, after a solution has been selected using an LP model, the manager may alter or add a constraint or change the objective. The computer can quickly provide a new solution under the revised set of conditions. Only a manager, however, can determine which of the two solutions is best.

3. *Improved understanding of problems.* Since linear programming models are highly efficient ways of analyzing very complex problems, they also improve a manager's comprehension and an appreciation of these complex problems. By structuring a problem, LP models enable the manager to comprehend more easily the effects of alternative assumptions. They not only provide a solution but also enable the manager to understand the problem.

PLANNING NONREPETITIVE PRODUCTION: PERT

Techniques used to combine resources or to control activities so that plans are carried out as stated are called *network models.* Such models are especially suited for projects that are not of a routine or repetitive nature. Coordination is needed for these projects, to ensure that prerequisite tasks are completed before subsequent tasks are started. For nonrepetitive projects, some method is needed to avoid unnecessary conflicts and delays by keeping track of all events and activities—and their interrelationships. Network models provide the means to achieve these purposes. As such, they are valuable aids in managerial *planning* and *controlling.*

Program evaluation and review technique (PERT) is a type of network model that minimizes conflicts, delays, and interruptions in a project by coordinating the various parts of the overall job. PERT's goal is to complete the job on schedule. It does not solve a manager's problems, but it does help identify what the problems are and what solutions are realistic, as well as aid in anticipating problems.

PERT is especially useful to management for nonrepetitive projects—ones that the manager has not previously encountered and is not likely to encounter again. Nonrepetitive projects pose a special problem: How can the manager learn to manage work that is done only once? Such programs have two major characteristics. First, they are extremely complex in that hundreds or thousands of interdependent tasks must be accomplished; second, most of the tasks are single-occurrence tasks that are not likely to be repeated. In contrast to repetitive processes (such as the mass production of a product or the periodic reorders of inventory for which management has past experience, standards, and costs), historical data is not available for nonrepetitive projects. However, each task in a one-of-a-kind program must be performed on time and be of the necessary quality, just as with routine work. In other words, management must still *plan* and *control* nonroutine operations. PERT is extremely helpful in such situations because it enables a manager to think through a project in its entirety. As such, it usually results in a more optimum utilization of resources.

Specific Applications of PERT

PERT (and variations of it) is probably one of the most widely used production planning models. It was developed through the cooperation of the U.S. Navy and the management consulting firm of Booz Allen & Hamilton Inc. Introduced by the Special Projects Office of the U.S. Navy in 1958 on the Polaris missile project, PERT was widely credited with helping to reduce by two years the time originally estimated for the completion of the engineering and development programs for the missile. By identifying the longest paths through all of the tasks necessary to complete the project, it enabled the program managers to concentrate efforts on those tasks that vitally affected the total project time. PERT has spread rapidly throughout the defense and space industries. Today almost every major government military agency involved in the space program utilizes PERT. In fact, many government agencies require contractors to use PERT and other network models in planning and controlling their work on government contracts.

While the aerospace business faces peculiar problems, one-of-a-kind development work is also an important element in many other kinds of organizations and industries. In addition to developing space vehicles and putting a man on the moon, PERT has also been utilized successfully in:

1. Constructing new plants, buildings, and hospitals.
2. Designing new automobiles.
3. Coordinating the numerous activities (production, marketing, and so forth) involved in managing a new product or project.[12]
4. Planning and scheduling space probes.[13]
5. Managing accounts receivable.[14]

---

[12] Gary L. Wolf and Warren C. Hauck, "PERT/CPM: A Tool for Managing Projects," *Industrial Management,* January–February 1985, pp. 22–25; James A. G. Krupp, "Project Plan Charting: An Effective Alternative," *Production and Inventory Management Review,* First Quarter 1984, pp. 31–47.

[13] James E. Zerega, "Down and Up with PERT at Goddard," *Astronautics and Aeronautics,* February 1976, p. 65.

[14] Ann Wiles and Ronald M. Horowitz, "PERT Charts Pinpoint Problems in Accounts Receivable Management," *Healthcare Financial Management,* September 1984, pp. 38–40, 42, 44, 46.

6. Coordinating the installation of large-scale computer systems.
7. Coordinating ship construction and aircraft repairs.

In addition to engineering-oriented applications, PERT has been used for coordinating the numerous activities necessary to complete mergers between large organizations as well as economic planning in underdeveloped countries. Even for smaller specific applications, such as coordinating and planning all the tasks necessary for large-scale conventions and meetings, PERT has been successful.

Production Planning with PERT

There are two fundamental steps involved in using PERT and other network models: (1) constructing the network and (2) estimating activity time requirements.

Constructing the network.   PERT networks are developed around two key concepts: activities and events. An *activity* is the work necessary to complete a particular event. An *event* is an accomplishment at a particular point in time and consumes no time. In PERT diagrams, an event is designated with a circle and an activity as an arrow connecting the two circles. These two concepts are shown in Figure 18–3.

Before the PERT network can be constructed, the activities and events that will be represented on the diagram must be identified. Table 18–2 describes the activities and events required to manufacture a prototype aircraft engine.

The information from Table 18–2 is represented by the network model shown in Figure 18–4. Examination indicates that Event 1 is the network beginning event since there are no activities leading to it, and Event 8 is the network ending event since there are no activities leading away from it. Note also that Event 2 is the beginning event for two activities and Event 6 is the ending event for two activities as well as the beginning event for one activity.

FIGURE   18–3   Two Events and One Activity

The basic building blocks of PERT are events (Circles 1 and 2) and activities (arrow →).

TABLE   18–2   PERT Network for Manufacture of Prototype Aircraft

Description of activities and events in Figure 18–4

	Activity			Event	
Arrow	**Description**	**Prerequisite**	**Circle**	**Description**	
1–2	Develop engineering specifications.		2	Specifications completed.	
2–3	Obtain test models.	1–2	3	Test models obtained.	
2–4	Locate suppliers of component parts.	1–2	4	Suppliers located.	
3–5	Develop production plans.	2–3	5	Plans completed.	
5–6	Begin Subassembly 1.	3–5	6	Subassembly 1 completed.	
4–6	Place orders for component parts and await receipt.	2–4	6	Component parts received.	
6–7	Begin Subassembly 2.	5–6 and 4–6	7	Subassembly 2 completed.	
7–8	Begin final assembly.	6–7	8	Engine completed.	

PERT's effectiveness depends on accurate assessment of all activities and events.

FIGURE   18–4   PERT Network for Information in Table 18–2

A PERT network helps the manager think through a project by representing complex steps in simple graphic form.

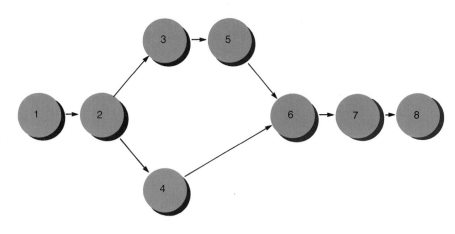

PERT emphasizes identifying events and activities with enough precision so that it is possible to monitor accomplishment as the project proceeds. There are four basic phases in constructing a PERT network.

1. Define each necessary activity.
2. Estimate how long each activity will take.
3. Construct the network.
4. Find the critical path—that is, the longest path, in time, from the beginning event to the ending event.

All events and activities must be sequenced in the network under a strict set of logical rules (for example, no event can be considered complete until all predecessor events have been completed) that allows for the determination of the critical path.[15]

The paramount variable in a PERT network is time.[16] Estimating how long each activity will take is extremely difficult, since the manager has no experience to rely on in most cases.

Estimating activity time requirements.   Since PERT projects are usually unique, they are subject to a great deal of uncertainty. PERT is designed to deal specifically with the problem of determining time estimates.

For example, assume you are trying to estimate how long it will take to complete a term project for your management class. You know that one activity will be to collect certain information. If all goes well, you believe that you could complete this one activity in eight weeks. However, if you encounter numerous obstacles (dates, parties, illness, material not available in the library), this one activity will take much longer to complete. Estimating the time needed to complete your term project becomes a complex process when you try to account for the delays that might occur.

For PERT projects, *three time estimates are required for each activity.* The individual or group chosen to make each time estimate should be that individual or group most closely connected with and responsible for the particular activity under consideration. The three time estimates needed are:

Optimistic time (a): The time in which the activity can be completed if everything goes exceptionally well and no obstacles or problems are encountered.

---

[15] For complex projects, networking is a difficult task better left to trained individuals. The reader interested in networking principles should consult Louis R. Shaffer, J. B. Ritter, and W. L. Meyer, *Critical Path Method* (New York: McGraw-Hill, 1965); Jerome D. Wiest and Ferdinand K. Levy, *Management Guide to PERT/CPM* (Englewood Cliffs, N.J.: Prentice-Hall, 1977).

[16] D. Sculli, "The Completion Time of PERT Networks," *Journal of the Operations Research Society,* February 1983, p. 155.

Most likely time (m): The most realistic estimate of how long an activity might take. If the activity were repeated, most likely time would equal the average completion time.

Pessimistic time (b): The time that would be required if everything goes wrong and numerous obstacles and problems are encountered.

It is extremely difficult to deal simultaneously with the optimistic time, the most likely time, and the pessimistic time. Fortunately a way has been developed to arrive at one time estimate. An *expected time* (t_e) can be estimated satisfactorily for each activity by using the following formula:

$$t_e = \frac{a + 4m + b}{6}$$

Note that in the formula for computing the expected time (t_e), the weight that is given to the most likely time (m) is much greater than the weight given to the optimistic and pessimistic times, since each of them has only a small chance of occurring. Also note that optimistic and pessimistic time each receive the same weight.

To illustrate the use of this formula, recall the prototype-engine project described in Table 18–2. Suppose you estimate that 3 weeks is the most likely completion time (m) for the activity of developing engineering specifications. However, you feel that there is a small chance that the activity might be completed in 1 week. Therefore, the optimistic time (a) is 1. You also feel there is a slight chance things could go wrong and it would take 8 weeks to develop specifications. Therefore, the pessimistic time (b) is 8.

In order to compute the expected time from the three time estimates, we must determine at what time there is a 50–50 chance of completing the activity. The expected time formula provides that figure. The time estimates are as follows:

Optimistic time *(a)* = 1 week
Most likely time *(m)* = 3 weeks
Pessimistic time *(b)* = 8 weeks

Substituting these time estimates into the formula yields:

$$\text{Expected time} = t_e = \frac{1 + 4(3) + 8}{6} = 3.5$$

Thus, there is a 50–50 chance that the information will be collected in 3.5 weeks.

The expected time may be either longer or shorter than the most likely time, depending on the three time estimates. To illustrate an expected time shorter than the most likely time, assume the following three time estimates for developing engineering specifications:

$$\text{Optimistic time } (a) = 2 \text{ weeks}$$
$$\text{Most likely time } (m) = 4 \text{ weeks}$$
$$\text{Pessimistic time } (b) = 5 \text{ weeks}$$

Substituting these values into the formula yields:

$$\text{Expected time} = t_e = \frac{2 + 4(4) + 5}{6} = 3.83$$

In this case, the expected time of 3.83 weeks is shorter than the most likely time of 4 weeks.

When there is a great uncertainty in a project, this three-way time estimate is an important advantage of PERT. While it does introduce a complicating feature, it recognizes realities that can cause problems in planning for the future. The three-way time estimate usually results in a greater degree of honesty and accuracy in forecasting time. If nothing else, it provides the manager with the opportunity to be aware of and to evaluate the degree of uncertainty involved, especially along the critical path.

The completed PERT networks for the aircraft-engine-prototype project are shown in Figures 18–5 and 18–6. Figure 18–5 shows the three time estimates for each of the eight activities. Figure 18–6A shows the expected time for each activity. Obviously, expected times are only estimations. But if carefully constructed, they form a solid base for subsequent management decisions.

FIGURE   18–5   PERT Network

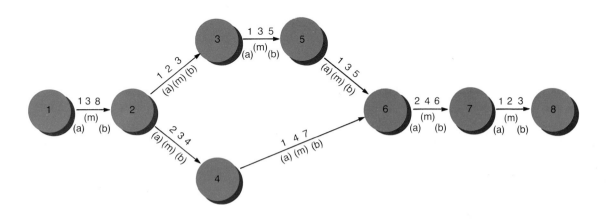

PERT networks become more complicated when time estimates are included.

FIGURE   18–6   Expected Time (t_e) for Each Activity

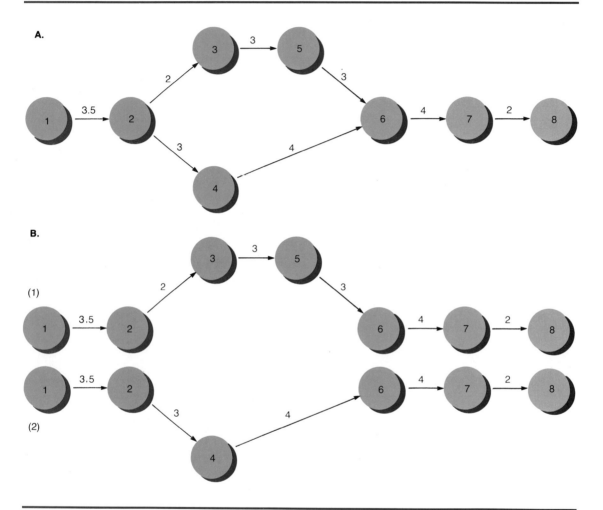

PERT networks that indicate expected time have considerable importance for scheduling nonroutine production.

Critical path.   The critical path is the most time-consuming sequence of activities from the beginning event to the ending event.[17] Therefore, the most crucial calculation in a PERT network is for the critical path.[18] Using two

---

[17] Bajis M. Dodin and Salah E. Elmaghraby, "Approximating the Criticality Indices in the Activities in PERT Networks," *Management Science*, February 1985, pp. 207–23.

[18] Richard J. Schonberger, "Why Projects Are 'Always' Late: A Rationale Based on Manual Simulation of a PERT/CPM Network," *Interfaces*, October 1981, pp. 66–70, notes the problems associated with the assumption that time estimates for each activity are assumed to be *independent* of all other activities.

steps, we can calculate the critical path for the network shown in Figure 18–6A. First we must identify each discrete path from beginning to end. In Figure 18–6B two paths are shown. Second, we must sum the expected times for each discrete path. Path 1 is expected to be completed in 17.5 weeks (3.5 + 2 + 3 + 3 + 4 + 2); Path 2 is expected to be completed in 16.5 weeks (3.5 + 3 + 4 + 4 + 2). Path 1, which takes 17.5 weeks, is the critical path.

Path 1 is "critical" because any delay in the completion of its activities will delay the total project. Yet a delay of up to one week can occur on Path 2 and the project will still be completed in 17.5 weeks. Path 1 is critical for yet another reason. If the project must be completed sooner than the expected 17.5 weeks, management can see that additional resources must be allocated to it rather than to Path 2.

In this example, the project network is rather simple; it has only two paths, and the critical path is readily identifiable. Real-world problems are seldom so simple.[19] As projects become more complex, the development of PERT networks also becomes more complex. In fact, were it not for developments in computer programming, the use of PERT would be seriously hampered.

The Value of PERT

Properly constructed, PERT and other network models provide direct aid to managers in two important areas.

Improved planning.   Network models help managers handle the uncertainties involved in projects where no standard cost and time data are available. Because it shows the manager the interconnections of tasks and provides estimated times, PERT increases the manager's ability to plan an optimum schedule before starting work. In other words, while a project is still in the planning stage, management can take a number of steps to reduce the total time needed to complete the project. Time reductions can be brought about in a number of ways:

1. By reducing the expected time on the longest path through the network (the critical path) by transferring resources or additional funds from those activities that can afford it since they do not take as long to complete.
2. By eliminating some part of the project that previously might have been considered desirable but not necessary.
3. By adding more resources—men or machines.
4. By purchasing a component if the time required to produce the component is too long.

[19] Bajis M. Dodin, "Determining the K Most Critical Paths in PERT Networks," *Operations Research,* July–August 1984, pp. 859–77.

5. By changing some work to parallel activities that had previously been planned in a series.

Better control—a major advantage of PERT.   The planning necessary to construct the network contributes significantly to the definition and ultimate *concurrent control* of the project. In the case of PERT, the construction of the network is a very demanding task that forces the planner to visualize the number, different kinds, and sequence of all the necessary activities. This kind of thinking cannot help but be a benefit in and of itself in most cases.

Used effectively, PERT can be valuable as both an internal and external control device. For internal control, it provides time schedules for each activity. Networks can therefore be revised if unforeseen difficulties arise. Resources can be shifted and activities can be rescheduled with minimal delay in the outcome of the project.[20] PERT analysis is applicable to a broad range of management control problems, including some outside the general run of production issues. For example, financial controllers in a variety of organizational settings have found PERT to be a valuable aid. The Management Focus describes an interesting application of PERT in hospital management.

For external control, in projects where subcontractors are used, the necessity for meeting scheduled dates can be stressed by showing them the negative effects a delay will have on the entire project. When subcontractors are involved, it is vital that these firms meet their scheduled delivery dates. For example, the Polaris project involved some 250 prime contractors and almost 10,000 subcontractors. The failure of any one of these subcontractors to deliver a piece of hardware on schedule could have stalled the entire project.

MANAGEMENT FOCUS
PERT Is Applicable to Hospital Financial Management

The rising cost of health care encourages health care managers to search for ways and means to manage resources more efficiently. The more efficiently they manage resources, the more competitive they are in obtaining clients for their hospitals and clinics. One opportunity to conserve resources is in the collection of patients' accounts receivable. The sooner an account is collected the sooner the cash is available for other uses. Hospital managers have discovered that PERT enables them to identify the events and activities related to accounts receivable collection cycles for different types of patients. The PERT network for the cycle begins when the patient is physician referred or self-referred and ends when the receivable for services

---

[20] D. M. Doughert and D. B. Stephens, "The Lasting Qualities of PERT," *R&D Management,* January 1984, pp. 47–56.

MANAGEMENT FOCUS (*continued*)

rendered is collected. Between the beginning and ending events are other events and activities for which critical times can be estimated.

Most hospitals require three distinct networks for each of three distinct patient types—inpatients, outpatients, and emergency room patients—because each utilizes different hospital services. But the analysis involved in each network is the same: Managers identify the critical path and then search for ways to reduce the times along the critical path. Any reduction in time in the critical path from referral to collection represents a cost saving in that the hospital has cash rather than a promise to pay cash.

Source: Ann Wiles and Ronald M. Horowitz, "PERT Charts Pinpoint Problems in Accounts Receivable Management," *Healthcare Financial Management,* September 1984, pp. 38–40, 42, 44, 46.

SUMMARY OF KEY POINTS

- Production planning involves determining the quantity of each product to manufacture, given the relative *profitability* of each product and the availability of scarce resources. It is a recurring decision that managers make with the aid of information, knowledge, and methods such as linear programming and program evaluation review technique.

- Linear programming (LP) is widely used to determine optimal production schedules when management must allocate scarce resources to alternative products. Each product competes, in a sense, with other products for the productive resources of the firm.

- Linear programming has applications for a variety of settings in which resources must be allocated. Production planning is the focus of this chapter, but LP can be applied to decisions involving optimal feed mixes, fuel blendings, transportation routes, and an advertising media mix.

- Management can determine an optimal production schedule if the decision support system provides (1) the profit contribution of each product, (2) the resource requirements of each product, and (3) the availability of resources to be allocated to the products. In addition, the LP method is most applicable if the relationships among the different variables are linear and if the required data are fairly certain.

- The value of linear programming is to improve managerial decisions, plans, and understanding of the problem. The process of setting up LP solutions requires the manager to thoroughly analyze the elements of the problem under study.

■ A great number of firms produce a single, nonrepetitive product or project. Unlike the multiproduct firm, the single, nonrepetitive product firm must find the optimal allocation of resources to activities that are necessary to complete the product or project.

■ A class of management science techniques termed network models is applicable to nonrepetitive production planning. Of this class of models, program evaluation review technique (PERT) has enjoyed the greatest popularity among production planners.

■ PERT has been a useful aid in planning new plants, building dams, and other large-scale construction projects. It is also useful for planning new-product developments, sales campaigns, computer installations, and other projects that involve sequences of activities.

■ To implement a PERT solution, the decision support system must provide data that enable managers to define the network of activities and the time required to complete those activities. Management can then determine the critical path—the longest path, in terms in time, through the network. Resources can be allocated to the critical path to expedite completion of the project.

■ The value of PERT is that it assists management in planning and controlling large-scale projects. A completed network of activities enables management to know better how resources should be allocated among the activities. The network also provides standards for gauging progress toward project completion.

DISCUSSION AND REVIEW QUESTIONS

1.   Explain the two general types of production systems and give examples of each one.

2.   Why is it useful to think of production planning as a problem that involves the allocation of scarce resources to alternative products or services?

3.   The text discusses a number of different production planning problems for which linear programming solutions are available. Describe what these problems have in common that makes them amenable to linear programming.

4.   Illustrate the practical value of linear programming by relating the benefits to the planning and controlling functions of management.

5.   Helene Manufacturers, Inc. produces two different models of professional hair dryers. Dryer A contributes $20 profit and Dryer B contributes $10. In order to be completed, each dryer must go through three manufacturing processes as shown in Exhibit 1. Using the graphic method, find the optimum combination of the products that would maximize total profit. Suppose the company could concentrate all its efforts on one model. Would this change the solution?

EXHIBIT   1   Hair Dryers' Manufacturing Processes: Time Requirements

	Time Required		
Department	Dryer A	Dryer B	Available Time
Department X	4	9	180
Department Y	5	6	150
Department Z	5	14	175

---

6. What are the specific characteristics of production problems for which PERT is an applicable technique?

7. Cite some nonrepetitive problems, other than those discussed in the chapter, for which PERT would be useful as a planning and control tool. Use your personal experiences if necessary. Which of these problems would cause you the greatest difficulty in determining expected times of completion?

8. Assume that you have been assigned a term project in one of your management courses. It is your task to collect data for the report from both library sources and personal interviews with local business people. You have a total of 10 weeks in which to complete the assignment. List the activities and their optimistic, most likely, and pessimistic times and construct a PERT network for the project.

9. Place the following activities in the form of a PERT network:

    a. Remove carburetor.   e. Clean and replace air filter.
    b. Rotate tires.   f. Test drive car.
    c. Put on snow tires.   g. Remove air filter.
    d. Tune motor.   h. Complete tune-up.

10. Assume that you have just received word to begin production on a special device that your company will make for the government. You have developed the PERT network for the project and the time estimates for each activity (Exhibit 2). Determine the critical path.

EXHIBIT   2   PERT Network for Government Project

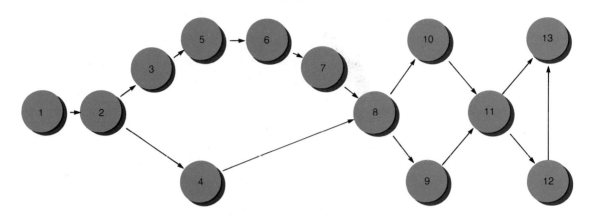

	Time Estimates (Weeks)		
Activity	Optimistic	Most Likely	Pessimistic
1–2	1	2	3
2–3	2	4	6
2–4	2	4	6
3–5	1	3	5
4–8	2	4	6
5–6	4	7	10
6–7	1	2	3
7–8	1	2	3
8–9	1	2	3
8–10	1	2	3
9–11	2	3	4
10–11	3	4	5
11–12	1	2	3
11–13	4	6	8
12–13	1	1	1

ADDITIONAL REFERENCES

Aronofsky, J. S.; J. M. Dutton; and M. T. Tayyabkhan. *Managerial Planning with Linear Programming.* New York: John Wiley & Sons, 1978.

Arranovich, D., T. M. Cook, G. D. Langston, and F. Sutherland. "A Decision Support System for Fleet Management." *Interfaces,* June 1982, pp. 1–6.

Bazaraa, M. S., and J. J. Jarvis. *Linear Programming and Network Analysis.* New York: John Wiley & Sons, 1977.

Beale, E. M. L. "The Evolution of Mathematical Programming Systems." *Journal of the Operational Research Society,* May 1985, pp. 357–66.

Boesch, F. T., ed. *Large-Scale Networks: Theory and Design.* New York: IEEE Press, 1976.

Clough, R. H. *Construction Project Management.* New York: John Wiley & Sons, 1972.

Elmaghraby, S. E. *Activity Analysis: Project Planning and Control by Network Models.* New York: John Wiley & Sons, 1977.

Hilal, S. S., and W. Erikson. "Matching Supplies to Save Lives: Linear Programming the Production of Heart Valves." *Interfaces,* December 1981, pp. 48–55.

Hoare, H. R. *Project Management Using Network Analysis.* New York: McGraw-Hill, 1973.

Kao, E. P. C., and M. Queyranne. "Budgeting Costs of Nursing in a Hospital." *Management Science,* May 1985, pp. 608–21.

Levin, R. I., and C. A. Kirkpatrick. *Planning and Control with PERT/CPM.* New York: McGraw-Hill, 1966.

Lockyer, K. G. *An Introduction to Critical Path Analysis.* Marshfield, Mass.: Pitman Publishing, 1964.

Luh, J. Y. S., and C. S. Lin. "Scheduling Parallel Operations in Automation for Minimum Execution Time Based on PERT." *Computers and Industrial Engineering* 9, no. 2. (1985), pp. 149–64.

Martino, R. L. *Finding the Critical Path.* New York: AMACOM 1964.

Park, K. S., and D. K. Yun. "Optimal Scheduling of Periodic Activities." *Operations Research,* May–June 1985, pp. 690–95.

Pritsker, A. A. B. *Modeling and Analysis Using Q-GERT.* New York: Halstead Press, 1977.

Randolph, P. H., and H. D. Meeks. *Applied Linear Optimization.* Columbus, Ohio: Grid, 1978.

Rothenberg, R. I. *Linear Programming.* New York: Elsevier North-Holland Publishing, 1980.

Spivey, W. A., and R. M. Thrall. *Linear Optimization.* New York: Holt, Rinehart & Winston, 1970.

Wendell, R. E. "The Tolerance Approach to Sensitivity Analysis in Linear Programming." *Management Science,* May 1985, pp. 564–78.

Whitehouse, G. E. *Systems Analysis and Design Using Network Techniques.* Englewood Cliffs, N.J.: Prentice-Hall, 1973.

Wiest, J. D., and F. K. Levy. *A Management Guide to PERT/CPM.* Englewood Cliffs, N.J.: Prentice-Hall, 1977.

CASES

APPLICATION I

LINEAR PROGRAMMING IN FURNITURE PRODUCTION

A furniture manufacturer had recently developed and marketed a line of self-assembly furniture. Each item (chair, table, sofa) in the line consisted of a set of rectangular, laminated plywood panels, along with the required metal fittings and hardware. The customer purchased the furniture unassembled and unfinished, but no special carpentry skills were required to assemble and finish the items.

The relatively low price, low margin, and initially low sales volume dictated high concern for cost savings at the manufacturer's sites. A major expense factor, in relation to other costs, was found to be in the panel-cutting operation. Specifically, production management believed that there was excessive waste associated with cutting the plywood panels required for each item in the line.

The complete line required 20 different panel sizes, each cut from a larger sheet of plywood. The lamination process was such that only one size of the larger plywood sheet could be used. Thus, the production problem was to determine the most efficient cutting patterns for producing the 20 different panel sizes from the laminated plywood sheets. The most efficient patterns would be ones in which there were no leftover, unusable pieces of plywood.

Of course, production management recognized that these patterns were unattainable, nevertheless they believed that the present cutting patterns produced excessive scrap. The basis for that belief was rather subjective. Management had had little experience in the production of such furniture under these conditions. Obviously the cutting of panels, spindels, legs, arms, and other parts of furniture from stock lumber was as old as the craft of carpentry itself. Yet the production of furniture in a manner roughly equivalent to an assembly-line process was new to the company's experience. Its managers recognized that a vast number of cutting patterns existed, but they were skeptical that the ones devised by a veteran employee in the cutting room were optimal.

The company contacted a group of production management professors at a nearby university and requested a review of the cutting patterns. The group arrived on the scene and immediately recognized that the problem could be set up in a linear programming format, with the objective function stated in terms of minimizing the quantity of scrap material.

The group constructed a linear programming model and then compared the results obtained from it to those obtained by the veteran employee. The comparison indicated that waste could be reduced by some 2 percent at a net cost saving of $6,000 per year through use of the linear programming solutions. These figures were not impressive, as the total annual production costs of this company were in the millions of dollars. The production manager expressed the view that the cutting patterns the company had been using were quite satisfactory, given the cost of the more sophisticated ones generated by the professors.

Questions for Analysis

1. What general principles, if any, regarding the application of linear programming models are suggested by this case?
2. How would you, as production manager, explain to the veteran employee your decision to engage the college professors? How would you avoid giving the impression that your decision expressed lack of confidence in the employee's work?
3. In addition to the problem of defining efficient cutting patterns, what are some of the other problems to which linear programming can be applied in furniture manufacturing?

APPLICATION II

PERT AT WESTINGHOUSE ELECTRIC

When Westinghouse Electric picked Harry Butler to head up purchasing for its plant being erected in South Boston, Virginia, he recognized immediately the enormity of his new assignment. The new plant was expected to cost $20 million when fully built and equipped to produce power transformers. Butler's responsibilities included arranging for capital-equipment purchases, scheduling machinery deliveries, contracting for interior designers, and buying furniture. These responsibilities were to be coordinated with the construction of the plant itself, so that the project would be completed without undue delay.

The interrelationships among purchasing and installing capital equipment and constructing the building are illustrated by Butler's experience with a punch press that cost over $250,000. To get the machine into the plant, the completion of one wall of the building had to be delayed. Because the machine was being shipped by rail, it was necessary to have the rail siding laid prior to its arrival. Moreover, the concrete footing for the press had to be poured in time; the electrical crew had to be available to install the machine; and power had to be available. Installing the punch press, however, was only one of the instances in which Butler was required to sort out interrelationships.

Butler and his associates decided that the nature of their job necessitated a procedure to schedule and control the various sequence of events and activities involved in equipping the plant. They selected PERT as the primary method to assist them in scheduling the logical sequence and in identifying the critical paths. With the network drawn, Butler was able to anticipate problems and bottlenecks and to deal with them before they became major obstacles. The PERT network enabled the Westinghouse management team to contact suppliers to expedite delivery dates. The team also found it useful to hold review sessions with major suppliers to go over the PERT network from the perspective of their commitments for timely delivery of equipment. One result of the use of the PERT method was to minimize "crash program" expediting.

As Butler stated, "A PERT diagram is extremely helpful because it indicates the way all the activities can best be coordinated. If something along the critical path fails, the network shows which other events must be either speeded up or delayed."

Questions for Analysis

1. What were the characteristics of the Westinghouse project that made PERT a useful method for scheduling and controlling it?

2. In addition to those activities for which Butler was responsible, what other activities associated with constructing and opening a new manufacturing facility might be aided by PERT?

3. What would be the effects of unexpected bad weather, labor disputes, and other unforeseen circumstances on the PERT diagram?

INVENTORY PLANNING AND CONTROLLING

LEARNING OBJECTIVES

After completing Chapter 19, you should be able to:

■ **Define**
the concept of inventory control in the context of strategic and production planning

■ **Describe**
the types and purposes of inventory found in manufacturing firms.

■ **Discuss**
the importance of inventory control.

■ **Compare**
the components and behavior of ordering and carrying costs.

■ **Identify**
the characteristics of inventories for which economic order quantity and material requirements planning are applicable.

MANAGEMENT IN ACTION

Inventory Control at Black and Decker*

Black & Decker (BD) is an international corporation with annual sales in excess of $1 billion. The world's largest manufacturer of power tools, BD's product line includes drills, saws, sanders, grinders, hedge trimmers, and lawn mowers. If it is powered by an electric motor, chances are that BD makes it.

The largest BD plant, located in Hampstead, Maryland, assembles some 120 major product groups requiring 20,000 inventory items. Because of the large required investment and costs associated with such a large inventory, managers at the Hampstead plant are especially alert for ways to control inventory. Over time, BD management has developed an effective inventory control system that has attracted much industry attention. The system, which combines the latest computer technology and control technique, has four essential features:

1. A sound materials plan that controls quantities ordered, order dates, and reorder dates in coordination with changes in specifications due to product or production changes. This materials plan is the foundation of the entire system, and the other three elements build on it.
2. A commitment to executing the plan, which in turn requires adherence to the specified order dates and lead times. Through adherence to the discipline of the plan, BD seeks to avoid unnecessary inventory costs associated with administrative mistakes.
3. Constant evaluation of ways to reduce inventory levels commits BD managers to continuous review of the inventory system. Commitment to continuous review instills the attitude that acting on potential problems is preferable to reaction to actual problems.
4. Insistence on maintaining accurate records of inventory levels and characteristics reflects BD's understanding that a major problem in any inventory control system is keeping accurate records.

These four elements come together in a unified system that Black & Decker managers believe to be an effective inventory control system. The acronym that describes the system is PACE—planned action and constant evaluation. It aptly expresses the philosophy of inventory management at this important international corporation.

---

* Source: Based on John J. Kanet, "Inventory Planning at Black & Decker," *Production and Inventory Management,* Third Quarter 1984, pp. 9–21.

Rising energy costs, increasing foreign competition, and a period of relatively low inflation are but a few of the factors that have caused managers to focus on controlling costs of production and operations activities. The development of sophisticated managerial techniques in inventory and production planning and scheduling, along with the availability of advanced computerized systems, enables production managers to become more adept at cost control. These new developments include automated and computerized methods to handle orders, manage materials, control production inventories, manage shop-floor operations, and measure product and order costs.

The pace of competition and international commercial rivalry demand that manufacturing operations be turned into a *strategic* weapon.[1] As such, production and operations must be integrated into the overall strategic plan of the organization, thus achieving a coordinated effort with marketing and financial strategies. As highlighted in this chapter's Management in Action, Black & Decker's efforts to integrate inventory management into all planning phases reflect that firm's view of the strategic importance of inventories. But not only big businesses need to be concerned about inventory control. Small businesses also have a stake in controlling the costs of inventory.[2]

An important, and indeed crucial, aspect of production and operations management (P/OM) is the utilization of appropriate methods such as linear programming, simulation, inventory models, network models, material requirements planning, and the like. But without consideration of the broader, strategic implications of production and operations, management can still fail to achieve the most efficient and effective use of the firm's resources.

A key factor in P/OM is inventory control. In its broadest sense, *inventory control implies securing and maintaining the optimal quantities and types of physical resources required by the organization's strategic plan.* The importance of inventory is underscored when we visualize a manufacturing process as a flow of materials through a process that changes the form of those materials into finished goods. Thus, inventory control is at the heart of production control; some experts do not even distinguish between the two.[3] In this chapter, two widely used inventory control methods will be discussed: economic order quantity (EOQ) and material requirements planning (MRP). But first, we must describe the various *types* of inventories and the *purposes* they serve.

---

[1] Steven A. Melnyk and Richard F. Gonzalez, "MRP II: The Early Returns Are In," *Production and Inventory Management,* First Quarter 1985, pp. 124–36.

[2] John H. Blackstone and James F. Cox, "Inventory Management Techniques," *Journal of Small Business Management,* April 1985, pp. 27–33; "Material Requirement Planning—Overcoming the Biggest Obstacle to Productivity," *Small Business Reports,* June 1985, pp. 37–40.

[3] Thomas E. Hendrick and Franklin G. Moore, *Production/Operations Management: Fundamental Concepts and Methods* (Homewood, Ill.: Richard D. Irwin, 1981), p. 63.

TYPES OF INVENTORIES

Although we usually think of inventory in the context of manufacturing and distribution firms, other types of businesses have inventory. Banks, for example, must maintain an inventory of cash to meet customer demand. Nonbusiness organizations have inventories, too: Hospitals have inventories of medicine, surgical supplies, and all kinds of housekeeping items; schools have instructional supplies; and government agencies have inventories of office supplies (and red tape, some would say).

The particular inventories that must be managed depend upon the nature of the business. But the following inventory types are generally found in all businesses.[4]

Raw Materials

Raw materials are the ingredients that go into the final product. Raw materials are the adhesive, gauze, and paper required to make surgical bandages; the grains, sweeteners, preservatives, paper, and adhesive required to make breakfast cereals; the paper, ink, and binding required to make books. The exact form of the raw material depends upon the manufacturing process.

Some manufacturers take nature's own resources and convert them into a product. Steel-making firms must have iron ore and coal to produce steel. The steel is then sold to auto manufacturers, and for them it becomes a raw material. Other manufacturers assemble component parts into a final product. Their raw-materials inventory consists of many different components supplied by other manufacturers. Corning Glass Works makes more than 60,000 different products, but its largest facility doesn't manufacture a thing. The company's Greencastle, Pennsylvania, facility packages, warehouses, and distributes some 1,250 finished-goods items from eight different manufacturing plants.[5] Despite the fact that the Greencastle plant doesn't manufacture a product, it has a considerable inventory of raw materials.

Supplies

Every business requires materials that do not become part of the final product. These materials, termed MRO items (maintenance, repair, and operating supplies), are usually small in number and expense compared to other

---

[4] For the discussion of inventory types on which this presentation is based, see Ibid., pp. 68–69.

[5] Bruce Horovitz, "Why Corning Is Sticking with MRP," *Industry Week,* January 25, 1982, p. 46.

inventories. Nevertheless, they are essential to the operation of the plant. Examples of MRO items include stationery and other office-related materials, repair tools and parts, lubricants, and cleaning supplies.

Work in Process

Raw materials moving through the stages of production are called work in process. Depending on the length and complexity of the production process, work-in-process inventory can be relatively large or small. Westinghouse Electric estimates that work in process accounts for 80 percent of its inventory investment.[6] Controlling work-in-process inventory is an important element of *scheduling:* Goods must procede through the various stages of production as rapidly as possible but also in order of priority. Multiproduct manufacturers must determine not only how many of each product to make but also when to produce each product.

Finished Goods

Finished-goods inventory consists of unsold final products. Finished goods are stored at the manufacturing facility itself or at some point in the distribution channel—at warehouses or retailers, for example. Job-order manufacturers carry little, if any, finished-goods inventory, since their products are custom made and are therefore not produced until a customer places an order. In contrast, process and assembly manufacturers typically carry a large finished-goods inventory. For example, automobile manufacturers must produce large quantities of finished goods in anticipation *of* rather than in response *to* customer demand.

When we recognize the extent of inventories, the importance of inventory control is apparent. In 1981, for the economy as a whole, the cost of carrying all the various inventories was $110 billion, almost 15 percent of the total value of the inventory itself.[7] The Management Focus on Blue Bell reflects the importance of inventory control as a source of cost savings.

---

[6] Hendrick and Moore, *Production/Operations Management,* p. 68.

[7] Lewis Berman, "A Big Payoff from Inventory Controls," *Fortune,* July 27, 1981, p. 77.

MANAGEMENT FOCUS
Blue Bell Manages Its Inventory

Blue Bell, Inc. manufactures apparel including Wrangler jeans, Red Kap work clothing and uniforms, and Jantzen sportswear. From 1979 to 1982, the company experienced hard times, as the cost of carrying inventory soared from $1.1 million to $21.9 million. Management recognized that extreme measures were called for to bring this cost down. The focus of the control measures would have to be materials and finished-goods inventories. These two inventories together made up more than 50 percent of the company's asset base, and in 1982, they were running an average of $371 million!

Controlling inventory cost would require concerted effort, including production planning that would take into account the complexities of a vast product line, more demanding customers, and sophisticated computer technology. A task force undertook the job of cutting inventories through the application of inventory control models. A key part of the overall plan was a model that forecasts sales on monthly and annual bases. These forecasts are the foundation for determining production volumes and safety stocks. The completely revised inventory control system took some 21 months to develop and install, but the results appeared to justify the effort: By mid-1984, inventory had dropped to an average of $256 million for a savings in interest expense of $16 million.

Based on Jerry R. Edwards, Harvey M. Wagner, and William P. Wood, "Blue Bell Trims Its Inventory," *Interfaces,* January–February 1985, pp. 34–52.

PURPOSES OF INVENTORIES

Inventory is costly. The organization must store it, move it from place to place, and safeguard it. The organization also incurs the cost of having funds tied up in inventory and therefore unavailable for other, profit-making investments. We will have more to say about inventory costs later. The point is that inventory is costly, and organizations would prefer to do other things with their funds. Inventory, then, must exist for a purpose. Here are the most important.[8]

---

[8] The following discussion is based on Gordon K. C. Chen and Robert E. McGarrah, *Productivity Management* (Hinsdale, Ill.: Dryden Press, 1982), pp. 74–76.

To Promote Customer Service

Inventory on hand means the product is available when customers are ready to buy it. Obviously, if it is not on hand, customers are not served, and the firm loses that sale as well as future ones. If the firm knew with *certainty* when customers would be ready to buy, it could have just enough inventory on hand to meet the demand. But such is not the case.

Manufacturers, wholesalers, and retailers all face the problem of deciding how many of what kinds of products to have available. This decision involves balancing the costs of having too little inventory versus having too much. Even those firms that manufacture goods to customer specification must maintain an inventory of materials. For example, job-order printing firms must decide how much inventory of paper, ink, and supplies to keep on hand for uncertain customer demand.

Having inventory is vital to keeping customers. Customers usually must be convinced that a product has three attributes before they buy it: the "right" price, quality appropriate to the price, and delivery service. Inventory contributes to customer service by providing delivery service: The product is available upon demand.

To Promote Manufacturing Flexibility

Most manufacturing firms produce more than one product, using the same machines in the same facility. The flexibility of being able to shift back and forth from one product to another is possible only because of inventory. Inventory promotes the use of multiproduct manufacturing in two ways. First, the inventory of raw materials enables the manufacturer to produce the specific product on schedule. Also, unless there are raw materials and components on hand, the changeover to another product is impossible. Second, a finished-goods inventory makes it possible to satisfy the demand for a product not presently being produced.[9] Gains in productivity are achieved when managers can use manufacturing equipment in flexible ways.

To Promote Certainty in Production and Operations

Decision making in nearly every aspect of business takes place in conditions of *uncertainty*. The demand for the final product is typically uncertain; the supply of materials needed to make the product is uncertain. The amount of uncertainty varies from business to business. A provider of electricity for residential consumption operates under more certain demand than the

---

[9] P. P. Kleutghen and J. C. McGee, "Development and Implementation of an Integrated Inventory Management Program at Pfizer Pharmaceutical," *Interfaces,* January–February 1985, pp. 69–87.

manufacturer of electronic games. But uncertainty, to a degree, exists in both instances.

Inventories serve as a hedge to counteract the effects of uncertainty. The greater the uncertainty, the greater the need for hedging against its effects. Consequently firms keep a reserve of raw materials, components, and other inventories on hand as "safety stocks." They are called safety stocks because they safeguard the firm against lost production or sales due to unforeseen shortages and forecasting errors.

To Promote Production Smoothing

Manufacturing firms prefer smooth—that is, relatively consistent—rates of production over time. Smooth production enables the firm to retain a stable, trained work force. It also avoids the cost of sustained downtime or, its opposite, the cost of extra-capacity production. Production smoothing involves leveling manufacturing during seasonal fluctuations. Thus, the purpose of inventory is to meet demand during periods of peak sales without having to increase the rate of production.

To Promote Profits through Price Speculation

A final, secondary purpose of inventory is that, during periods of inflation, a firm can profit by buying inventory at a lower price, holding it until prices increase, and selling it at a profit. Inventory speculation is not the primary concern of manufacturing concerns. But other organizations, such as those that trade and process farm products, could well argue that speculation in commodities is part of their business. Inventory, in such firms, can become a major source of profit.

In most instances, however, firms consider inventory a major source of cost. Managers in these firms seek approaches for controlling inventory cost. One of the most widely used approaches is the economic order quantity model.[10]

THE EOQ MODEL

The economic order quantity (EOQ) model enables managers to determine a number of key inventory decisions. Managers who order goods from a supplier can use the EOQ model to decide *how many* units to order and

---

[10] Richard R. Jesse, Jr., Amitava Mitra, and James F. Cox, "EOQ Formula: Is It Valid under Inflationary Conditions?" *Decision Sciences,* July 1983, pp. 370–74; James A. G. Krupp, "Deterministic EOQ in a Production Environment," *Journal of Purchasing and Materials Management,* Summer 1984, pp. 24–30.

how often to order them. Manufacturers use a similar method, called the economic lot size (ELS) model, to determine the size of batches to produce and when. The principles are the same whether the goods are ordered or produced; but in this chapter, we will discuss only the EOQ variation. The EOQ model is used to balance the costs of having either too much or too little inventory.

Cost Factors in Inventory Control

To effectively control inventory, the manager must initially identify cost factors. First, there are the *ordering costs* of getting a particular item into the actual inventory. These costs are incurred each time an order is placed. They are the clerical and administrative costs per order, which also include the cost of receiving the goods and placing them into inventory.

Second, there are the *carrying costs.* These include the interest on money invested in inventory; the cost of storage space, rent, obsolescence, taxes;

FIGURE   19–1   Ordering and Carrying Cost Relationship

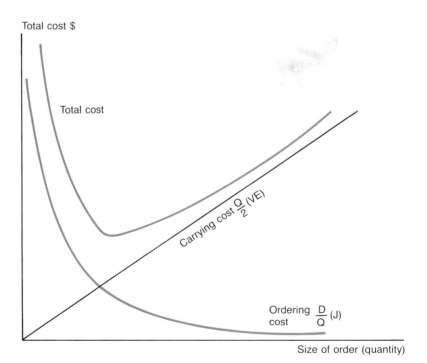

As ordering costs decrease, carrying costs increase.

and the cost of insurance on losses due to theft, fire, and deterioration. Carrying costs are usually expressed as an annual figure and as a percentage of the average inventory.

To reduce inventory costs, a manager must minimize both ordering and carrying costs. Unfortunately these two costs are related to each other in opposing directions, as shown in Figure 19–1. As the size of each order increases, the number and cost of orders decrease; but since larger quantities are being ordered and placed in inventory, the cost of carrying the inventory increases.

Computing ordering costs is relatively simple. The number of orders for a given period of time is equal to demand (D) for the period divided by the size of each order quantity (Q). The total ordering cost per period (week, month, or year) is equal to the cost of placing each order (J) multiplied by the number of orders per period. Thus, the formula for computing ordering costs reads $D/Q\ (J)$. As the order size increases, fewer orders are required to meet the demand for a period; consequently ordering costs decrease, illustrated by the downward sloping order-cost curve in Figure 19–1.

Carrying costs for one item in inventory are calculated by multiplying the value of the item (V) by a percentage figure (E), which is management's estimate of taxes, insurance, and so forth, per period as a percentage of the value of inventory. Total carrying costs are equal to the cost of carrying one item (VE) multiplied by the average inventory $Q/2$. Thus, the formula for calculating total costs is $Q/2(VE)$. For the sake of simplicity, carrying cost is shown as a straight line in Figure 19–1.

An example will illustrate why average inventory equals $Q/2$. Assume that an organization orders 500 items and uses 100 of them each week; at the midpoint of the first week it has 450 on hand. Table 19–1 lists the number in inventory at the midpoint of each week over a period of five weeks. The average inventory is found by dividing total inventory (1,250) by the number of weeks (5), yielding an average of 250. The average can also be found by utilizing the $Q/2$ formula; that is, $500 \div 2 = 250$.

TABLE   19–1   Average-Inventory Analysis

Average inventory can be easily calculated if inventory is used at a constant rate over time.

Week	Inventory at Midpoint of Week
1	450
2	350
3	250
4	150
5	50
	1,250

FIGURE   19–2   Constant Inventory Usage

When inventory is used at a constant rate, the relationship between average inventory and time can be easily illustrated.

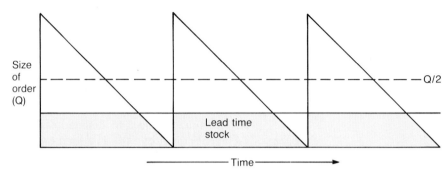

Trial-and-Error Methodology

After ordering and carrying costs have been calculated, a manager can use trial and error to determine what size of order to place. However, in attempting to select the optimal size of inventory from a cost standpoint, a number of assumptions are usually made:

1. We assume the demand for the item over the period is known with certainty. Thus, we are developing the economic order quantity model (EOQ) under conditions of certainty.
2. We assume the rate at which the inventory of the item is depleted is constant. Figure 19–2 illustrates depletion at a constant rate. The average inventory is found under conditions of constant usage (for example, selling the same amount monthly for the year).
3. We assume the lead time—the time between the placement of an order and the actual delivery of that order—is exactly known.

These assumptions are not completely realistic, but they allow us to study the development of the EOQ model in an uncomplicated manner. Further sophistication of the basic model can occur only if the simplified form is clearly understood.[11]

Assume that a production manager is attempting to solve a lot size problem involving a component part that is purchased from a supplier. The yearly demand for the part, which is constant, is estimated to be 1,000. The administrative and clerical cost of placing an order is $40. The manager estimates

---

[11] Edward F. Mykytka and John S. Ramberg, "On the Sensitivity of the EOQ to Errors in the Forecast of Demand," *IIE Transactions,* June 1984, pp. 144–51.

TABLE   19–2   Trial-and-Error Method

In the trial-and-error
method, the manager
uses a table
summarizing cost data
for various order sizes
to decide which will
yield the lowest total
cost.

Number of Orders	Size of Order Q	Order Cost D/Q (J)	+	Carrying Cost Q/2 (VE)	=	Total Cost
1	1,000	$ 40	+	$1,000	=	$1,040
2	500	80	+	500	=	580
4	250	160	+	250	=	410
10	100	400	+	100	=	500
20	50	800	+	50	=	850

insurance and taxes to be 10 percent per year. The value of a single part is $20. Thus, the variables involved are:

Demand (D)   = 1,000 units
Ordering costs (J)   = $40
Insurance and taxes (E) = 10 percent
Value of the item (V)   = $20

The manager could use this data to calculate total inventory costs by randomly choosing the size of the order to place. By compiling a table that summarizes the size of inventory order and cost relationships as shown in Table 19–2, the manager could decide at a glance how many orders to place to minimize total inventory costs.

A review of the total-cost data in Table 19–2 indicates that placing four orders of 250 each yields the lowest cost ($410). However, note that the trial-and-error method could be tedious, so management scientists have developed a formula for the economic order quantity model.

The EOQ Formula

Looking back to Figure 19–1, we see that the minimum total inventory cost is at the point directly above the intersection of carrying cost and ordering cost. Thus, the EOQ formula may be derived by utilizing this relationship. It should be noted that, for simplicity, the relationship shown is linear. The first step in algebraic derivation is to set carrying and ordering costs equal to each other.

$$\frac{Q}{2}(VE) = \frac{D}{Q}(J)$$

Solving for Q yields:

$$Q(VE) = \frac{2DJ}{Q}$$

$$Q^2(VE) = 2DJ$$

$$Q^2 = \frac{2DJ}{(VE)}$$

$$Q = \sqrt{\frac{2DJ}{(VE)}}$$

The final equation is commonly referred to as the *economic order quantity formula* and can be used to solve the inventory problem we have outlined. Using the data in our problem ($D = 1,000$, $J = \$40$, $E = 10$ percent, and $V = \$20$), we can determine the economic order size:

$$Q = \sqrt{\frac{2(1,000)(\$40)}{(\$20)(.10)}}$$

$$Q = \sqrt{\frac{\$80,000}{\$2.00}}$$

$$Q = \sqrt{40,000}$$
$$Q = 200$$

For this problem, the trial-and-error method indicates that the least costly alternative is to place four orders to satisfy the overall demand of 1,000. However, utilization of the more exact EOQ formula suggests that placing five orders of 200 each will be least costly. Since the five-order alternative was not considered in the trial-and-error solution, the manager was not able to really minimize inventory costs.

The EOQ model can also be used to consider changes in demand for a product. Assume that demand is 1,000 for the first 10 months of the year and 2,000 for the last 2 months of the year. For the January–October period, the EOQ calculations would be as follows: $D = 1,000$; $J = \$40$; $E = 10$ percent; and $V = \$20$ for 10 out of 12 months. Thus,

$$EOQ = \sqrt{\frac{2(1,000)(\$40)}{(\$20)(.10)(10/12)}}$$

$$EOQ \cong \sqrt{48,000}$$
$$EOQ \cong 219 \text{ units}$$

The November–December inventory strategy would be determined as follows: $D = 2,000$; $J = \$40$; $E = 10$ percent; and $V = \$20$ for 2 months out of 12. Thus,

$$EOQ = \sqrt{\frac{2(2,000)(\$40)}{(\$20)(.10)(2/12)}}$$

$$EOQ = \sqrt{484{,}848}$$
$$EOQ \cong 696$$

The EOQ decision for January–December is relatively clear-cut in that the demand of 1,000 can be satisfied with five orders of 200 each. Because the EOQ during the November–December peak period is approximately 696, however, the manager must decide whether two or three orders are appropriate. The human element is essential, since $2 \times 696 = 1{,}392$ and $3 \times 696 = 2{,}088$, and the exact demand is 2,000. The above example shows that, despite the use of mathematical formulas, human judgment is still an important factor in many inventory control decisions.

Limitations of the EOQ Model

The most obvious limitation of the EOQ model is that conditions of certainty rarely exist in the real world. In our problem, we have assumed that the correct time to order is known. But many times, transportation problems, order requisition difficulties, and other related problems make the lead time a highly unpredictable phenomenon.[12]

The estimation of demand is another problem. Throughout our discussion, demand is known with certainty. But the demand for any item in the real world can at best be only roughly estimated. Many variables—competitors' prices, economic conditions, social conditions, and substitutable items—can influence demand.

A final limitation of the EOQ model is that it is most applicable to control inventory that has *independent* demand. That is, the demand is unrelated to the sale or usage of other items. Finished goods and supplies are examples of inventories that have independent demand. Inventory errors for these items are isolated and have no cumulative effects. Therefore, the EOQ model can be applied to these inventories, given its inherent limitations.

MATERIAL REQUIREMENTS PLANNING

Raw-material, component, subassembly, and work-in-process inventories have *dependent* demand. The demand for these inventories depends upon the demand for the finished goods. The EOQ model is much less applicable to these inventories because errors, such as shortage, compound forward. In recent years, an inventory control method termed material requirements planning (MRP) has been developed to control inventories with dependent demand. MRP uses sophisticated computer software to plan and control

---

[12] Alvin C. Adkins, Jr., "EOQ in the Real World," *Production and Inventory Management,* Fourth Quarter 1984, pp. 50–54.

inventory costs. This method enables management to combine decision making for a vast number of interlocking areas related to ordering, scheduling, handling, and using inventories of parts and supplies that are components of the final product.

The firms that have been quickest to adopt MRP are in the transportation equipment, instruments, and electrical machinery industries. Such firms must carry a complex and expensive array of materials and components. In contrast, firms in continuous-process industries (such as paper, petroleum, lumber and wood) have not rushed to adopt MRP. Generally MRP is more useful in firms that manufacture goods to order and whose manufacturing process includes both assembly and fabrication. But what is MRP, and how does it work?

The Basics of MRP

Material requirements planning involves breaking down a product into its components and subassemblies. Management is then able to coordinate the ordering and delivery of components and the production start date of all subassemblies.[13] MRP has been applied successfully to a wide range of problems related to producing an end product with numerous components. For example, MRP has been successfully applied to the management of NASA's space operations.[14]

The basic tools of MRP are the master production schedule, the bill of materials, and inventory records. Although most manufacturing firms have some form of these schedules and records, MRP requires greater detail and sophistication than is usually present in a manual system.

The master production schedule.
The master production schedule details the *planned* quantities of finished goods to be produced during a particular time period. The schedule is based on (1) the company's strategic plan and (2) the production plan.[15] The strategic plan identifies the product-market strategies that will propel the firm toward its long-run objectives. The production plan specifies the production volume of each product or class of products. Before planning production, however, the manager must determine an optimum product mix that reflects product demand, resources, and overall profit-

[13] Charles J. Anton and Charles J. Malmborg, "The Integration of Inventory Modeling and MRP Processing: A Case Study," *Production and Inventory Management,* Second Quarter 1985, pp. 79–90.

[14] Earl Steinberg, William B. Lee, and Basheer M. Khumawala, "MRP Applications in the Space Program," *Production and Inventory Management,* Second Quarter 1982, pp. 65–77.

[15] Gerald R. Gallagher, "How to Develop a Realistic Master Schedule," *Management Review,* April 1980, pp. 19–25.

ability. Linear programming or more complex programming models can assist managers with this decision. If only one product is produced, the ELS model is most useful. In any case, the master schedule depends upon prior determination of a production plan.

The master schedule takes the information from the production schedule and adds the *timing* element; it details *what* will be produced and *when* it will be produced. Thus, the master schedule provides the bases for controlling the amount and type of work-in-process inventory during a period of time.

The bill of materials.   The bill of materials defines the required components—those items of inventory that have dependent demand—for each subassembly and finished good. The required quantity, quality, and timing of components depend upon the production schedule for the final products. In **MRP** terms, the bill of materials is the result of "exploding" each final product into its subassembly and components.

Figure 19–3 shows the relationship between the master production schedule and bills of materials.

As shown, the requirement for wheels depends upon the production schedule for baby carriages. The information could be expanded to include the

FIGURE   19–3   The Relationship between Master Schedule and Bills of Materials

Master production schedule for week of November 12, 1986:

Product:	Bicycles	Baby Carriages	Playpens
Quantity:	100	50	25

Bill of materials: Baby carriage:

Part Number	Description	Amount
1	Body assembly	1 each
2	Wheel assembly	2 each
3	Handle and frame assembly	1 each

Bill of materials: Wheel assembly:

Part Number	Description	Amount
2/A	Wheels	2 each
2/B	Axle	1 each

Inventory requirement for wheel, Part 2/A, for week of November 12, 1986, is 50 (carriages) × 2 (wheel assemblies) × 2 (wheels) = 200 wheels.

By relating the bills of materials to the master schedule, managers can clearly see the types and amounts of materials necessary for a certain production period.

bills of materials for the subassemblies and components of bicycles and play-pens.

It should be obvious that the master schedule and supporting bills of materials become considerably more complex as the number of products increases. To control the scheduling by manual and intuitive means becomes unwieldy and unproductive.

Inventory records.   The current status of each component subassembly and finished-good item must be available. This information requirement necessitates developing and maintaining records that are updated to reflect current usage and replenishment. Thus, perpetual rather than periodic inventory records are parts of an MRP system.

The MRP System

The MRP system, in practice, involves complex calculations and administrative routines. The intent of MRP is to coordinate all the activities required to produce the final product or service that sustains the organization. We can sense the complexity by outlining the basic decisions that managers must make to operate MRP.[16]

Determination of gross requirements.   Managers must determine the gross requirements for all dependent demand items, based on a production plan that specifies how many end products are to be produced. Gross requirements must be determined in terms of both quantity required *and* delivery dates. The key to successful MRP is to have just the right *amount* of inventory available at just the right *time*.

Determination of net requirements.   The calculation for *net* requirements is the remainder of inventory on hand plus quantity on order, minus the safety stock. The difference must be ordered from suppliers, or produced if the firm makes rather than buys the item. The purpose of net-requirement calculations is to set in motion the replenishment process.

Determination of safety stock and lead times.   Safety stocks enable managers to meet unexpected demand for a product. They are a hedge against the costs of being out of stock: a lost sale and a disappointed customer. MRP requires safety stocks to be decided for finished goods *only* and to be included in the production schedule. The gross-requirement calculation will automatically take into account safety stocks for dependent demand items.

---

[16] Gabriel R. Bitran, David M. Marieni, Hirofumi Matsuo, and James W. Noonan, "Multi-plant MRP," *Journal of Operations Management,* February 1985, pp. 183–203.

Another way to reduce costs, lead-time calculations enable a manager to obtain components at the time they are needed. By coordinating calculations for *time required* and *lead time,* a manager can keep the size of component inventory at a low level and thereby reduce carrying costs.

Determination of order quantities.   After net requirements have been determined, the manager must decide how many components should be ordered each time—the order quantity. Ordinarily orders are planned in exact amounts, and timing is determined in the net calculation. The EOQ method can be used to determine order size if the sources and lead times for all components can be coordinated. Otherwise there would be as many different order quantities as there are components, and the opportunity for stockouts and overages would increase.

Determination of order release.   Order release time, when the order is placed with the supplier, is calculated by subtracting lead time from the date the item is required for production. Order release calculations become as complex as PERT networks when a finished good has a lengthy bill of materials involving many assemblies and subassemblies. General Motors, Ford, and Chrysler face bills of materials of staggering complexity. In other instances, order release calculations can be quite simple.

Determination of aggregate requirements.   Planned orders and release dates for all components are aggregated in a master schedule. The complexity of the schedule is directly related to the number of different products made and the required components for those products. The aggregate-requirements data are the basic outputs of a MRP system. Their accuracy depends upon the quality of information and management decision making that went into them.

The Complete MRP System

A complete MRP system is diagrammed in Figure 19–4. The simplicity of the diagram should not disguise the complexity of the system. To fully implement MRP requires managerial commitment, adequate decision support systems, and computer facilities.[17]

One apparently successful MRP system, described in the Management Focus, is operating at the Norton Company. MRP systems at Norton and other companies contribute to productivity increases, because MRP is adaptable to unexpected changes. For example, bills of materials (the equivalent

---

[17] James F. Cox, Robert W. Zmud, and Steven J. Clark, "Auditing an MRP System," *Academy of Management Journal,* June 1981, pp. 386–402.

FIGURE 19–4 Elements of an MRP System

The master production schedule integrates information from all areas of an MRP system and is therefore the key element.

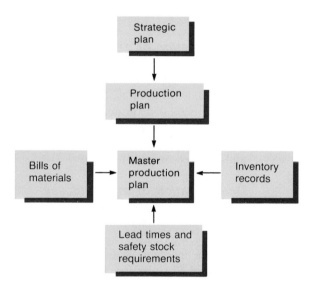

of a list of recipe ingredients) change as a consequence of engineering and technical improvements. The development of a welding technique can make obsolete a bill of materials that includes bolts and nuts that previously attached the components. Lead times and safety stock determinations can be altered by changing supplier capabilities. A key supplier may suffer a work stoppage that upsets the entire ordering schedule. The ability to adapt to these changes depends on accessing and entering the required data quickly. It is easy to see why computer capability is important for a MRP system.

MANAGEMENT FOCUS
Achieving Inventory Control at Norton Company

Inventory control at Norton Company's Construction Products Division in Gainesville, Georgia, has been a case study in the successful application of a MRP system. The division's managers implemented a broad-based effort using MRP principles to reverse the upward trend of costs due to late deliveries, downtime, excessive inventory, and record keeping. Implementation of the effort involved the application of computers, education of employees, and commit-

MANAGEMENT FOCUS (*continued*)

ment of top management—the usual three ingredients of successful efforts to implement new systems of inventory control.

The results were impressive. Some of the more tangible ones are:

1. The plant no longer must shut down to take inventory.
2. On-time delivery of stocked items to customers increased from 40 percent of the time to 99 percent.
3. Inventory levels decreased by 57 percent.
4. Record-keeping accuracy increased from 64 percent to 99 percent.

The impact of these improvements has resulted in increased profits and customer satisfaction. In addition, Norton managers are now enthusiastic searchers for other ways to increase productivity and cost savings.

Based on Richard L. Thompson, "How to Achieve and Maintain Inventory Accuracy," *Production and Inventory Management,* First Quarter 1985, pp. 38–44.

MRP, when fully operational, is more than a method for managing inventory. Because of its integrative nature, a newer term—*resource requirements planning (RRP)*—has been adopted to describe more accurately the breadth of its application. RRP expands the bill-of-materials concept to include *all* resources required of a product. A bill of resources specifies required materials *and* labor, machines, capacity, managerial and technical skills, energy, capital, and cash. Thus, planning and controlling inventory is, in the final analysis, planning and controlling the organization itself.

Just-in-Time Inventory Control

An advanced version of MRP is termed *just-in-time* (JIT). As its name implies, JIT attempts to provide the raw material or component part on the very last day, or even hour, before it is needed.[18] JIT attempts to eliminate the need for inventory by altering some of the basic conditions of manufacturing. The JIT approach originated in Japan and is one of the keys to that country's manufacturing success. The Japanese believed that if the underlying *reason* for inventory could be eliminated, inventory could be eliminated.

[18] Richard J. Schonberger, "The Transfer of Japanese Manufacturing Management Approaches to U.S. Industry," *Academy of Management Review,* July 1982, p. 480; Richard J. Schonberger, "Just-in-Time Systems Focus on Simplicity," *Industrial Engineering,* October 1984, pp. 52–63.

The underlying reason for inventory is the existence of uncertainty in the production system. Rather than being a smooth-flowing, integrated process, production systems are loosely coupled subsystems that produce component parts at different rates. The component parts do not arrive at assembly points at reliable, predictable times. Thus, it is necessary for faster-moving subsystems to have inventories of slower-moving subsystems' outputs so that production proceeds without interruption. The mismatch in the production rates of interdependent production units combines with other factors to create uncertainty that management usually copes with by investing in inventory.

The other important factors contributing to production uncertainty include unreliable deliveries of acceptable materials from vendors. If a vendor's shipment contains unacceptable units or if it is not on time, production will come to a halt unless there is an inventory on hand, a safety stock. Equipment breakdowns and insufficiently skilled or trained employees can also contribute to production uncertainty and the need for inventory. The flow of components is interrupted by unacceptable quality or quantity of components, whether internally produced or externally supplied. But even the most reliable vendors, maintained equipment, and skilled employees cannot overcome poorly designed production layouts or incompetently drawn production plans. Management also can contribute to the necessity to maintain inventory.

The Japanese and American manufacturers who have successfully implemented JIT have done so by eliminating both the human and technical reasons for inventory. The Japanese are notable for their success in developing cooperation among interdependent groups. Japanese managers, as discussed in previous chapters, use participative management and quality circles to encourage communication among groups that are connected in the work flow. They also invest heavily in employee training and development, including management. On the technical side, JIT requires effective quality control, preventive maintenance, and vendor relations programs. A full-scale and encompassing evaluation of the production system must precede the installation of JIT inventory control.

American firms such as General Electric, Goodyear, Ford, Chrysler, and General Motors have had some success with JIT.[19] It is no coincidence that these same firms face the stiffest competition from the Japanese.

EOQ AND MRP: A COMPARISON

EOQ and MRP systems are typically mutually exclusive but can be combined in some instances.[20] The EOQ model is intended for use in process

---

[19] Richard J. Schonberger and Marc J. Schniederjans, "Reinventing Inventory Control," *Interfaces,* May–June 1984, pp. 76–83; Mehran Sepehri, "Kanban and JIT: American Style," *Manufacturing Systems,* June 1985, pp. 49–50.

[20] Normal Gaither, "An Improved Lot-Sizing Model of MRP Systems," *Production and Inventory Management,* Third Quarter 1983, pp. 10–20.

manufacturing settings. In these instances, the usage of inventory is likely to be continuous and constant, a key requirement for effective use of EOQ. If demand and usage are not constant over time and not known with some certainty, then inventory shortages and overages will disrupt production schedules. Total inventory costs will be far from minimized.

MRP is ideally suited for firms that manufacture in job-lot or batch-processing technology. In such firms, production is discontinuous, varied, and dependent upon relatively uncertain customer demand. MRP systems pay special attention to each component and subassembly item, using the master production schedule, bills of materials, and inventory records. Successful applications of MRP result in synchronized orders of all inventories based upon safety stocks and lead times.

The two methods can be used simultaneously in firms that have both types of products and production. Items with constant and relatively certain demand can be controlled by EOQ; items with discontinuous, batch-type, and relatively uncertain demand can be controlled by MRP.

Finally, it must be understood that MRP can be a fully integrated production and operations system. In its most complete form, MRP (or RRP) is used for capacity planning and for establishing production priorities. Top management uses it to "run the business." But this level of sophistication is rarely attained, because the complexity of the very process being controlled defies even the most rigorous management science methods.

SUMMARY OF KEY POINTS

- A key to obtaining productivity increases in the management of production and operations is inventory control. The methods of inventory control attempt to reduce costs of inventory by maintaining a balance between the costs of having too much and too little inventory.

- The management science approach has long recognized the importance of inventory control. That recognition has resulted in a rather impressive array of ideas, theories, and methods of inventory management. Economic order quantity (EOQ) models and material requirements planning (MRP) systems are most widely used.

- A typical manufacturing firm must manage several different inventories for raw materials, supplies, work in process, and finished goods. In recent years, the annual cost of carrying these inventories has exceeded $100 billion for the economy as a whole. Such staggering inventory costs indicate the importance of improving inventory management.

- Effective management of inventory requires a distinction between items with independent and dependent demand. Independent demand inventory is unrelated to the demand or usage of other items. Finished goods (end products) have independent demand. Dependent demand inventory is related to the demand or usage of other items. Raw materials and work in process (components and subassemblies) are subject to dependent demand.

■ The economic order quantity (EOQ) model is appropriate for controlling inventories whose demand is independent, relatively constant over time, and known with certainty. The EOQ controls inventory cost by determining the order size that minimizes the total inventory cost. The economic lot size (ELS) model is related to EOQ, but it determines the lot size that minimizes inventory costs for a manufacturer.

■ EOQ is based upon the idea that the optimal order quantity is one that equates carrying cost and ordering cost. The logic is that as order size increases, carrying costs increase (because the average inventory increases) but ordering costs decrease (because the number of orders decreases). But at some point, the increase in carrying cost equals the decrease in ordering costs, and no further cost reductions can be obtained by increasing the size of the order.

■ Material requirements planning (MRP) is used if the demand or usage of independently demanded inventory is discontinuous, such as in job-lot or batch manufacturing. MRP stresses the control of the dependent inventory through computer-based ordering and scheduling.

■ The key elements of MRP are the master production schedule, the bill of materials, and inventory records. In most instances, MRP also requires computer capability. Through successive steps, the gross requirements are "exploded" into constituent items and summarized in an aggregate-requirements schedule of what items are needed by when.

■ In its most fully developed state, MRP evolves into a general production and operations management technique known as resource requirements planning (RRP). At this point, MRP is a way of "managing the business."

DISCUSSION AND REVIEW QUESTIONS

1. Why is it necessary for firms to carry inventories of finished goods? What purposes are served by such inventories?

2. Discuss how a firm could go about developing and implementing a strategic inventory control system.

3. Explain the relationship between the various inventories and the systems theory explanation of a firm's activities.

4. Why do production managers prefer relatively smooth production rates? How do inventories help them achieve this kind of production?

5. Explain why the total inventory costs of ordering and carrying move in opposite directions as the size of the inventory increases.

6. The Slag Valley Construction Corporation uses 5,000 pressure valves annually.

The cost accountants ascertain that the ordering cost for securing the valves from suppliers is $60. Each valve costs $10. The carrying charge for the valves is estimated to be 20 percent per year of the average inventory.

   a.   Utilize the trial-and-error method to derive the economic order quantity for the number of valves to order, using the following possibilities: 500, 1,000, 2,500, 5,000.

   b.   Utilize the EOQ formula to determine the economic order size.

7.   How would you redefine the variables in the EOQ formula to make it applicable to determining the lot size in the case of making rather than buying the part? What costs would have to be taken into account if you were attempting to determine the optimal number of items to produce?

8.   Under what circumstances is MRP preferable to EOQ as an inventory control method? Are EOQ and MRP mutually exclusive? That is, must a firm use one or the other for all inventory items? Explain.

9.   Define the basic tools and decisions that comprise an MRP system. Which decisions are pivotal for determining the relative effectiveness of an MRP system?

10.   Explain why MRP usually requires computer utilization. Does the computer requirement place limits on the kinds of firms for which MRP is applicable? Explain.

11.   Describe and illustrate the application of MRP in managing the university cafeterias. Assume that the menu plan for the semester is the master production schedule. What then are the bills of materials? The inventory records? How would order points and lead times be determined? How would aggregate requirements be determined?

ADDITIONAL REFERENCES

Adkins, J., and R. Tieken. "MRP Keeps Production on Schedule." *Production Engineering,* July 1985, pp. 22–23.

Aggarwal, S. C. "Purchase-Inventory Decision Models for Inflationary Conditions." *Interfaces,* August 1981, pp. 18–23.

Austin, L. M. "Project EOQ: A Success Story in Implementing Academic Research." *Interfaces,* August 1977, pp. 1–12.

Baumol, W. J. *Economic Theory and Operations Analysis.* Englewood Cliffs, N.J.: Prentice-Hall, 1965.

Buffa, E. S. *Elements of Production/Operations Management.* New York: John Wiley & Sons, 1981.

Cook, T. M., and R. A. Russell. *Production/Operations Management.* Englewood Cliffs, N.J.: Prentice-Hall, 1980.

Davis, D. J. "Transportation and Inventory Management." *Distribution,* June 1985, pp. 10–16.

Duckworth, W. E.; A. E. Gear; and A. G. Lockett. *A Guide to Operations Research.* New York: John Wiley & Sons, 1977.

Gaither, N. *Production and Operations Management.* Hinsdale, Ill.: Dryden Press, 1980.

Goyal, S. K. "Economic Order Quantity under Conditions of Permissible Delay in Payments." *Journal of the Operational Research Society,* April 1985, pp. 335–38.

Kelly, D. A. "The Principle of Complex Demand." *Production and Inventory Management,* Second Quarter 1985, pp. 115–20.

Lawler, W. "EOQ, MRP, JIT: Inventory's Alphabet Soup," *Massachusetts CPA Review,* Summer 1984, pp. 10–15.

Meredith, J. R., and T. E. Gibbs. *The Management of Operations.* New York: John Wiley & Sons, 1980.

Moore, F. G., and T. Hendrick. *Production/Operations Management.* 8th ed. Homewood, Ill.: Richard D. Irwin, 1980.

Orlicky, J. *Materials Requirements Planning—a New Way of Life in Production and Inventory Management.* New York: McGraw-Hill, 1978.

St. John, R. "The Cost of Inflated Lead Times in MRP Systems." *Journal of Operations Management,* February 1985, pp. 119–28.

Schonberger, R. J. *Operations Management: Planning and Control of Operations and Operating Resources.* Plano, Tex.: Business Publications, 1981.

Schroeder, R. G.; J. C. Anderson; S. E. Tupy; and E. M. White. "A Study of MRP Benefits and Costs." *Journal of Operations Management,* October 1981, pp. 1–9.

Sheely, L. S. "MRP and the Bottom Line." *Production and Inventory Management,* Third Quarter 1979, pp. 59–67.

Taylor, S. G., and C. E. Bradley. "Optimal Ordering Strategies for Announced Price Increases." *Operations Research,* March–April 1985, pp. 312–25.

Tersine, R. J. *Production/Operations Management.* New York: Elsevier North-Holland Publishing, 1980.

Wehrman, J. C. "Evaluating the Total Cost of a Purchase Decision." *Production and Inventory Management,* Fourth Quarter 1984, pp. 86–91.

CASES

APPLICATION I

INVENTORY CONTROL AT CORNING GLASS WORKS*

Corning Glass Works is a major U.S. corporation operating in a multinational market. The company makes 60,000 products, employs some 29,000 people in 63 plants located throughout the world, and does business in more than 90 countries. Its record of product success and reliability accounts in

---

* Sources: Based on Bruce Horovitz, "Why Corning Is Sticking with MRP," *Industry Week,* January 25, 1982, pp. 44–48; Myron Magnet, "Corning Glass Shapes Up," *Fortune,* December 13, 1982, pp. 90–96, 102, 104, 108–9.

large measure for its $1.6 billion in sales in 1981. But Corning has inventory control problems that it has just begun to deal with.

During the mid-1970s, Corning executives were disturbed to find that the company's reputation for prompt and reliable shipment of orders was being threatened. Plants were unable to complete products on time because required inventory was not on hand. For example, they could not coordinate the availability of bowls made in a Pennsylvania plant with lids for those bowls made in a West Virginia plant. When the manufacture of these two parts is not synchronized, Corning Ware cannot be shipped. Executives correctly identified the problem as inventory control and, more broadly, as production management. But they had to find a solution that could apply to this broad area.

The magnitude and complexity of Corning are suggested by the fact that it manufactures 60,000 items of great variety. Everyone is familiar with its baking dishes and coffeepots. But nearly two thirds of its business is in technical, scientific, medical, and industrial products. It makes components for computers, lenses for eyewear, glass products for autos and TVs, and even supplies for the space industry. Corning's major competitors include many of the most progressive and productive Japanese and European firms. Efficiency in production can reap big dividends. Therefore, production management at Corning takes in a lot of ground.

So, where to begin? The executives decided that to solve the inventory problems by improving production management would require a company-wide effort. Every functional area from marketing to finance to purchasing would have to be involved in the solution. The technique that appealed most to the managers was material requirements planning, and they began to implement it. Since MRP implementation would affect all parts of the company, they had to design the implementation process as carefully as they designed the technique itself.

Management selected three plants that had already made considerable progress toward managing inventories to begin the changeover to MRP. Management believed that these plants would be sure to develop and adopt MRP and become examples for the rest of the company. The plants selected are located in Greencastle, Pennsylvania, Harrodsburg, Kentucky, and Martinsburg, West Virginia. In short order, each plant implemented MRP, and plant managers were able to document productivity gains that resulted.

Dick Sphon, plant manager of the Harrodsburg facility, is an enthusiastic supporter of MRP. The system went on line in 1979, and by 1981 the plant was saving $500,000 per year. These savings resulted from elimination of the need to take physical inventory, inventory accuracy of 90 percent and balanced production. "The system and its computer do the busywork," says production supervisor Al Webber, "and we manage the plant instead of fire fighting."

Success stories are told at the other two sites as well, and these stories have spread throughout the organization. The plant managers are featured speakers at the semiannual get-togethers of Corning's plant managers. As a result of these success stories, more and more plants have begun the conversion.

According to some executives, MRP can create ego problems. Its computerized scheduling enables headquarters officials to make decisions that plant managers once made. Many managers view the system as a threat to their authority and prerogatives as plant managers. In contrast, proponents of MRP respond by noting how MRP eliminates minor problems and permits the manager to spend time on important decisions.

Corning executives believe that by 1990 all plants will be using MRP, but that considerable resistance must be overcome at the plant level to accomplish that goal.

Prior to 1982, MRP had been fully installed in the three pilot plants and partially installed in other plants. The company states that it can identify a savings of $2 million from these limited applications of MRP and that its inventory investment is down some $17 million. Consequently, in 1982, 12 of Corning's 39 U.S. plants planned to implement MRP.

MRP is but one of several approaches to productivity improvements at Corning. In recent years, the company has also implemented new manufacturing technology and quality circles to involve employees. According to industry analysts, these efforts had resulted by 1982 in the reduction of Corning's breakeven point from 63 percent to 55 percent of capacity.

Questions for Analysis

1. Evaluate the manner in which Corning implemented the MRP system.
2. Explain fully why plant managers would resist the installation of MRP at their locations.
3. Explain the productivity implications of reducing inventory levels and lowering breakdown points.

APPLICATION II

JUST–IN–TIME INVENTORY CONTROL AT THE TOYOTA TRUCK PLANT*

Long Beach, California, is the site of a truck bed manufacturing facility owned and operated by Toyota Motor Company. The plant has attracted

---

* Source: Mehran Sepehri, "How Kanban System Is Used in an American Toyota Motor Facility," *Industrial Engineering,* February 1985, pp. 50–56.

considerable attention because of its successful application of Japanese-style inventory control procedures. The Long Beach plant fabricates, assembles, and paints four models of truck beds for Toyota light trucks. It has a capacity of 150,000 units per year and an annual payroll of $10 million. The plant is a significant economic factor in the Long Beach community, as well as an enlightened user of modern inventory control methods.

The Long Beach plant's mission is to supply truck beds of appropriate style, size, and color to each of the eight ports of entry receiving truck cabs from Toyota plants in Japan. The cabs are shipped from Japan without beds, which are added upon arrival. Close coordination is required to assure that cabs and beds match at the eight ports. The system puts a high premium on production scheduling, inventory management, and shipping. At the heart of the Long Beach system is a practice and philosophy termed just-in-time (JIT) inventory control.

JIT involves a complete commitment to the idea that whatever is now done, there exists a better way to do it. Consequently there is never a sense of acceptance of the status quo. As soon as a practice or procedure is implemented in response to a problem, it itself becomes the focus of scrutiny. This critical attitude is necessary in order to attain the ideal inventory situation: lot sizes of one unit and zero work in process. At that point, the cost of raw materials and work-in-process inventories is at its absolute minimum.

The JIT system takes its name from the idea that a required inventory part or unit should arrive at the point where it is needed at the split second before it is needed. Thus, a brace for a truck bed would arrive on the assembly line at the precise moment when the worker is ready to weld it in place. As we move on down the line, we can see that the truck bed is completed at the precise instant when it is to be painted; it comes off the line at the precise moment when it is to be loaded and shipped to one of the eight ports of entry; it arrives at the port of entry precisely on time to coincide with the arrival of the cabs from Japan.

The ultimate purpose of JIT is to eliminate the need for inventory. But to eliminate the need for inventory requires the elimination of defects, late arrivals of component parts from outside vendors, assembly-line breakdowns, and work stoppages in general. The focus of JIT, then, is more than inventory; the focus is the entire manufacturing process from beginning to end.

The managers of the Long Beach plant had the advantage of knowing what to expect when they decided to adopt JIT. Other Toyota plants in Japan had adopted the method. The difference at Long Beach was that American, not Japanese, workers and managers would be responsible for planning, implementing, and operating the system. Could the Americans do the job as well as the Japanese? Could the Americans be retrained to expect perfect quality rather than acceptable quality? Could they be motivated to accept the idea that nothing is perfect, that anything can be improved? Could they be expected to develop and implement procedures that would mean the elimination of their jobs even if the company did promise to relocate them to other jobs? Could they work effectively in problem-solving groups, called quality circles, rather than working as individuals to solve knotty problems?

Apparently they not only could, they did. Some of the early performance improvements included a reduction by 45 percent of the work-in-process inventory and a reduction of 24 percent in raw-materials inventory in the first year. The warehousing costs of material were reduced by 30 percent. In the production area, the labor cost savings were 20 percent and productivity increased by 40 percent, absenteeism and turnover are reduced, and interdepartmental conflicts are down.

These gains have stirred considerable pride of accomplishment among the employees of the plant. Their successes have been publicized throughout the Toyota organization and the community. The company believes that JIT is no longer a Japanese management tool. JIT is as American as management by objectives and could be adopted by any American manufacturing plant that seeks productivity improvements in manufacturing.

Questions for Analysis

1. Do you believe that JIT can be applied in plants that do not have a "Japanese connection?" What, if anything, is there about JIT that is peculiarly Japanese?
2. Why is it necessary to consider the entire manufacturing process in order to make improvements in inventory control?
3. What features of the JIT approach have applicability in organizations that do not have inventories, such as banks, professional firms, and the like?

COMPREHENSIVE APPLICATION FOR PART IV

MANAGING PRODUCTION AND OPERATIONS

McCALL DIESEL MOTOR WORKS*

McCall Diesel Motor Works has been a pioneer in the manufacture of diesel internal-combustion engines. The plant is located on tidewater in the state of New Jersey. This site was dictated originally by the fact that the company built engines for the marine field, chiefly fishing boats and pleasure craft. Subsequently its production was extended to include stationary types of engines. They are used essentially for the production of power in small communities, in manufacturing plants, or on farms.

During the earlier years of the company's operation, its engines were largely special-order jobs. Even at the present time, about 60 percent of the output is made to order. In recent years, however, there has been a trend toward standardization, particularly in component parts but also in lines of engines. The Engineering Department has followed the principle of simplification and standardization in the case of minor parts such as studs, bolts, and springs, giving a degree of interchangeability to these components among the various sizes and types of engines. Sizes of marine engines have also been standardized to some extent, although customer requirements still necessitate special designs. In the small engines for agricultural use, there has been a genuine effort to concentrate sales on a standard line of engines of three sizes—20 HP, 40 HP, and 60 HP.

The company has always been advanced in its engineering development and design. The production phase, on the other hand, has not been progressive. The heritage of job-shop operation persists. Despite the definite trend toward standardization, production continues largely on a made-to-order basis. But the increasing popularity of diesel engines has brought many new companies into the field, with a consequent tightening of the competitive situation.

High manufacturing costs and poor service have been reflected in the loss of orders. Customer complaints, together with pressure from the Sales Department, prompted the management to call in a consulting engineer to make a survey of the Manufacturing Department and recommend what action should be taken. The engineer submitted the following findings:

1. *Manufacturing methods,* while still largely of the job-shop character, are in the main good, and no wholesale change should be made. As production

---

* Source: Prepared by Frank K. Shallenberger, Stanford University. Used with permission.

is still 60 percent special, a complete shift to line manufacture or departmentalization by product is not feasible.

2. *Machinery and equipment* is for the most part general-purpose, in line with manufacturing requirements. Some machine tools are approaching obsolescence; and for certain operations, high-production, single-purpose machines would be advisable. Extensive replacement of machine tools is not a pressing need, but an increased use of jigs and fixtures should be undertaken immediately. There are many bottlenecks existing in the plant, but contrary to your belief, as well as that of your foreman and other shop executives, there is no serious lack of productive equipment. The trouble lies in the improper utilization of the machine time available.

3. *Production control* is the major element of operating weakness, and improvement is imperative. The lack of proper control over production is evidenced by the following:

a. In-process inventory is too high, as indicated by piles of partially completed parts over the entire manufacturing floor area.

b. There are not any records concerning the whereabouts of orders in process from their initiation to delivery at assembly.

c. The number of rush orders is inordinately high, particularly in assembly but also in parts manufacture.

d. Too many parts chasers must be used to force orders through the shops by pressure methods.

e. Piece-meal manufacture—a lot of 20 parts usually is broken up into four or five lots before it is finished. Not infrequently the last sublot remains on the shop floor for months and, in a number of instances, is lost so far as records are concerned because subsequent orders for the same part are issued and new lots pass through to completion while the remains of the old lot lie in a partially fabricated condition.

f. Setup costs are excessive, resulting from the piecemeal methods mentioned in *e* as well as the failure to use proper lot sizes, even when lots are not broken up during manufacture.

g. All the necessary component parts fail to reach assembly at approximately the same time. The floor of the assembly department is cluttered with piles of parts awaiting receipt of one or more components before engines can be assembled.

h. The department lacks a definite sequence of manufacturing operations for a given part. Reliance as to the exact way by which a part is to be made rests entirely on the various departmental foremen. These men are able machinists, but they are burdened with detail and their memories cannot be relied upon to ensure that parts will always be manufactured in the best, or even the same, sequence of operations. Moreover, they have undue responsibility for determining the department to which a lot of parts should be sent when it has been completed in their department.

i. In the case of certain small standard parts, shop orders have been issued as many as six or eight times in a single month.

j. Information is lacking from which to estimate, with any degree of close approximation, the overall manufacturing time for an engine. The result is failure to meet delivery promises or high production cost due to rush or overtime work.

k. Parts in process or in stores and destined for imminent assembly are frequently taken by the Service Department to supply an emergency repair order. The question here is not the academic determination of priority between the customer whose boat may be lying idle due to a broken part and the customer who has not yet received his engine. The question is why there should be any habitual difficulty in rendering adequate repair service and at the same time meeting delivery promises.

l. Virtually all basic manufacturing data reside in the heads of the superintendent, departmental foremen, assistant foremen, and setup men.

m. Delivery dates are set by the Sales Department and generally are dates which customers arbitrarily stipulate.

n. The general superintendent shows little enthusiasm for the idea of a system of production control. In fact, he is opposed to such an installation. He is of the opinion that reasonably satisfactory results are now being obtained by placing responsibility in the foremen and maintaining contact between them and the parts chasers, who in turn are held responsible for meeting delivery promises. He believes that no system can be substituted for the foremen's knowledge of the workers' ability. He feels that operation of a production control system requires time studies of all jobs; this, he points out, is difficult because of the many operations involved, the high degree of special work, the probable resistance of the workers, and the cost which would be incurred. He states further that emergencies and rush orders would upset any rigid scheduling of work through the plant. Finally, he is convinced that any system of production control involves an excessive amount of clerical detail to which the foremen, who are practical shop men, object. The state of affairs found by the consultant was, he realized, due to two main causes:

(1) The strong influence of the original job-shop character of manufacture and the very slow evolution to large-scale operations.

(2) The fact that top management of the company was essentially sales-minded.

His [the engineer's] recommendations, therefore, had to be made with the idea of presenting a simple, straightforward program to provide adequate control over production and to enable this control to be instituted gradually and logically.

Questions for Analysis

1. Outline the essential features of a production control system for this company, giving sufficient detail to make clear how the system will function.

2. Indicate what part of your procedure should be centralized and what part decentralized. That is, what functions should be handled by a central production control office, and what functions should be carried out in the various production and assembly departments?

3. What data must be compiled before your system can become fully effective?

4. Enumerate the benefits that the company will derive when your production control system is in operation.

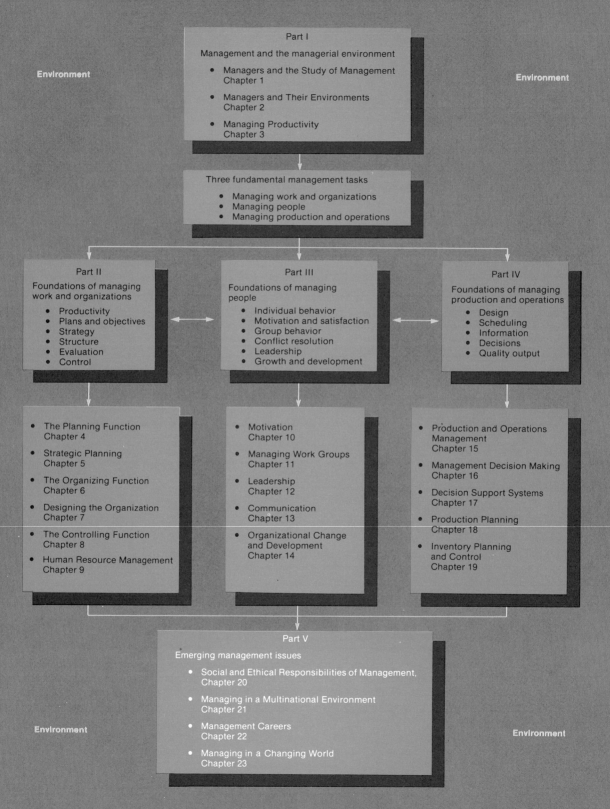

Environment

Environment

Part I

Management and the managerial environment

- Managers and the Study of Management
  Chapter 1

- Managers and Their Environments
  Chapter 2

- Managing Productivity
  Chapter 3

Three fundamental management tasks

- Managing work and organizations
- Managing people
- Managing production and operations

Part II

Foundations of managing work and organizations

- Productivity
- Plans and objectives
- Strategy
- Structure
- Evaluation
- Control

Part III

Foundations of managing people

- Individual behavior
- Motivation and satisfaction
- Group behavior
- Conflict resolution
- Leadership
- Growth and development

Part IV

Foundations of managing production and operations

- Design
- Scheduling
- Information
- Decisions
- Quality output

- The Planning Function
  Chapter 4

- Strategic Planning
  Chapter 5

- The Organizing Function
  Chapter 6

- Designing the Organization
  Chapter 7

- The Controlling Function
  Chapter 8

- Human Resource Management
  Chapter 9

- Motivation
  Chapter 10

- Managing Work Groups
  Chapter 11

- Leadership
  Chapter 12

- Communication
  Chapter 13

- Organizational Change
  and Development
  Chapter 14

- Production and Operations
  Management
  Chapter 15

- Management Decision Making
  Chapter 16

- Decision Support Systems
  Chapter 17

- Production Planning
  Chapter 18

- Inventory Planning
  and Control
  Chapter 19

Part V

Emerging management issues

- Social and Ethical Responsibilities of Management,
  Chapter 20

- Managing in a Multinational Environment
  Chapter 21

- Management Careers
  Chapter 22

- Managing in a Changing World
  Chapter 23

Environment

Environment

EMERGING MANAGEMENT ISSUES

PART V

20

SOCIAL AND ETHICAL RESPONSIBILITIES OF MANAGEMENT

Chapter

LEARNING OBJECTIVES

After completing Chapter 20, you should be able to:

■ **Define**
social responsibility in terms that reflect your view of the role of corporations in society.

■ **Describe**
the manner in which managers' ethics affect their decisions regarding social responsibility.

■ **Discuss**
why the term *social responsibility* has so many different and conflicting meanings.

■ **Compare**
arguments for and against a specific corporate action, based on your own ethical standards.

■ **Identify**
the various beneficiaries of corporate actions and the responsibilities of corporations to those beneficiaries.

■ MANAGEMENT IN ACTION

Corporate Social Responsibility*

The periodical *Business and Society Review* (published quarterly) includes in each issue the section "Company Performance Roundup." In this section, the periodical's senior editor Milton R. Moskowitz reports "notable company achievements and failures in areas of public concern." Recently Moskowitz reported the following:

- Atlantic Richfield awarded a $500,000 grant to the National Chicano Foundation to fund doctoral dissertations for Hispanics in the fields of mathematics, science, and engineering.
- In 1984, Hasbro acquired Milton Bradley Toy Company located in Chicago. Hasbro, maker of the G.I. Joe doll and other toys, became a leader in the toy industry after the acquisition, trailing only Mattel. Soon thereafter, Hasbro announced that it was moving production of the Milton Bradley toys to its plant in Massachusetts; 700 Chicagoans would lose their jobs. After considerable negotiation and legal maneuvering, the company agreed to assist the displaced workers in finding other employment.
- 3M settled six sex discrimination suits, agreeing to pay $2.3 million to 2,350 women employees. Some $525,000 of the settlement is earmarked for 1,000 or so women forced by a company rule, since scrapped, to take maternity leave four months prior to their due date.
- San Francisco requires companies to support some social program in exchange for obtaining approval of private projects. For example, Hilton, Holiday Inns, and Ramada agreed to pay 50 cents a night per room over the next 20 years to finance the construction or renovation of low-cost housing for low-income citizens.
- Employees of Union Carbide formed a relief fund for the victims of the Bhopal, India, poison gas leak. By 1986, present and retired employees had contributed over $100,000.

In this chapter, the issues associated with socially and ethically acceptable actions will be presented.

---

* Based on Milton R. Moskowitz, "Company Performance Roundup," *Business and Society Review,* Summer 1982, pp. 65–70; Milton R. Moskowitz, "Company Performance Roundup," *Business and Society Review,* Spring 1985, pp. 74–79.

The terms *social responsibility, business ethics,* and *management ethics* appear frequently in popular and technical literature. Every day, newspapers report incidents involving businesses that some people would call socially irresponsible and unethical. Yet, other individuals and groups might consider the actions to be quite proper, from both a social and ethical standpoint. For example, the Management In Action reports two recent court decisions. Each found a company guilty of sexual discrimination in personnel practices. Clearly these two incidents reflect social irresponsibility and unethical conduct: each incident was *illegal.* But other incidents may not be so clearcut. The important point is that such incidents are reported and held up for public discussion.

One of the purposes of this chapter is to provide bases for understanding the meanings and implications of social responsibility and ethics. To accomplish this purpose, we will review (1) society's expectations for corporate and managerial behavior and (2) changing business ethics. The social context in which corporate and managerial decisions and actions occur is dynamic and complex. Thus, to understand the meanings of social responsibility and business ethics is to recognize that they change with time and circumstance.[1]

Another purpose of this chapter is to provide guidelines by which managers can determine socially and ethically responsible behavior. Managers must be cognizant of their own responsibilities for instilling acceptable ethical standards throughout their organizations.[2] They must also be cognizant of the necessity to create organizational procedures and policies that encourage disclosure of unethical behavior.[3] The standard of business and managerial behavior for what is minimally responsible and ethical is that which is legal. Legality must be the recognized threshold of all managerial and organizational action.

---

[1] Ronald L. Crawford and Harold A. Gram, "Social Responsibility as Interorganizational Transaction," *Academy of Management Review*, October 1978, p. 880.

[2] George Strother, "The Moral Codes of Executives: A Watergate-Inspired Look at Barnard's Theory of Executive Responsibility," *Academy of Management Review*, April 1976, pp. 13–22; Len Peach, "Managing Corporate Citizenship," *Personnel Management*, July 1985, pp. 32–35.

[3] L. D. Alexander and W. F. Matthews, "The Ten Commandments of Corporate Social Responsibility," *Business and Society Review*, Summer 1984, pp. 62–66; Robert Boulanger and Donald Wayland, "Ethical Management: A Growing Corporate Responsibility," *CA Magazine*, March 1985, pp. 54–59.

THE MEANINGS OF SOCIAL RESPONSIBILITY

A recent review of the literature identifies no less than nine meanings for social responsibility.[4] These nine meanings can be classified in three general categories: social obligation, social reaction, and social responsiveness.[5]

Social Responsibility as Social Obligation

According to this view, a corporation engages in socially responsible behavior when it pursues a profit within the constraints of law as imposed by society. Because society supports business by allowing it to exist, business is *obligated* to repay society for that right by making profits. Thus, legal behavior in pursuit of profit is socially responsible behavior, and *any behavior not legal or not in pursuit of profit is socially irresponsible.*

This view is associated with economist Milton Friedman and others who believe that society creates business firms to pursue special and specialized purposes—producing goods and services—and that to engage in other pursuits exaggerates the legitimate place of business in society.[6] As Friedman stated: "There is one and only one social responsibility of business—to use its resources and engage in activities designed to increase its profits so long as it stays within the rules of the game, which is to say, engages in open and free competition without deception or fraud."[7] But in some instances, charitable contributions can in fact be profitmaking, as described in the Management Focus on American Express.

MANAGEMENT FOCUS
American Express Makes Profitable Donations

American Express Company (AmEx) makes cash donations to the Atlanta Arts Alliance each time one of its customers uses the American Express charge card or travel service in the greater Atlanta

---

[4] Archie B. Carroll, "A Three-Dimensional Conceptual Model of Corporate Performance," *Academy of Management Review*, October 1979, pp. 497–505.

[5] Suggested by S. Prakash Sethi, "A Conceptual Framework for Environmental Analysis of Social Issues and Evaluation of Business Response Patterns," *Academy of Management Review*, January 1979, pp. 63–74.

[6] Milton Friedman, *Capitalism and Freedom* (Chicago: University of Chicago Press, 1962).

[7] Milton Friedman, "The Social Responsibility of Business Is to Increase Its Profits," *New York Times Magazine*, September 1970, pp. 33, 122–26.

MANAGEMENT FOCUS (*continued*)

area. The amount of the donation depends upon the value of the actual use. The donation varies from $.05 each time the card is used to $5.00 each time travel arrangements are made through one of AmEx's travel offices. The program enables AmEx to obtain tangible benefits from its philanthropic contributions.

According to William M. McCormick, president of AmEx's consumer financial services group, the Atlanta program is profitable as well as philanthropic; card usage in the Atlanta area is up significantly (by how much has not been disclosed). But it is apparent that the program is a very effective marketing tactic. The company benefits from publicity associated with the donations and from television, newspaper, and point-of-purchase advertising to promote the program.

The idea that corporations can make money by giving away money is not lost on the arts community. Spokespersons for the arts see the AmEx program as an effective technique for creating an alliance with business. As one spokesperson stated, "Arts groups must . . . adopt creative, cooperative approaches with business if they hope to survive."

The idea that business should limit itself to profit-making activities within the law reflects a particular view of the rightful place for business in society. According to this view, activities other than profit seeking may work to the disadvantage of society. For example, some activities may be illegal, as when managers use company funds to support charitable causes. As a result of these contributions, the price of the company's goods and services increases, and customers pay the bill when they receive no benefit. The action would be "illegal" in the sense that managers have acted contrary to the interests of customers and, ultimately, stockholders. The proponents of this position note that nonprofit-seeking activity may be unwise and unworkable because managers are not trained to make noneconomic decisions; thus, society really doesn't benefit from the action. Perhaps the most persuasive point of this position is that to encourage managers to do more than pursue profit gives them power without accountability. Managers are not accountable to society as are publicly elected officials. Managers are accountable to stockholders or to whoever owns the resources invested in the business. To the extent that managers deviate from actions intended to make as much money as possible for their stockholders, pluralism—the very foundation of a free society—is undermined.[8]

---

[8] Friedman, "Social Responsibility of Business."

Although many people disagree with this definition, *social responsibility* can refer to behavior that is directed exclusively (but legally) toward the pursuit of profit. A manager can, with some justification, state that his or her *obligation* has been discharged to society by creating goods and services in exchange for profit within the limits defined by law. Accordingly such a manager would not knowingly engage in behavior that violated pertinent laws and regulations.

Social Responsibility as Social Reaction

A second meaning of social responsibility is behavior that is in reaction to "currently prevailing social norms, values, and performance expectations."[9] This pervasive view emphasizes that society has expectations for business and corporate behavior that go beyond the provision of goods and services. At minimum, business must be accountable for the ecological, environmental, and social costs incurred by its actions; at maximum, business must react and contribute to solving society's problems (even those that cannot be directly attributed to business). Thus, by this meaning, the actions of Atlantic Richfield would be socially responsible.

A somewhat restrictive interpretation of social responsibility as social reaction is that it involves only voluntary actions. This interpretation seeks to separate corporate actions that are *required* by economic or legal imperative and those that are initiated by voluntary, altruistic motives.[10] Thus, this more narrow view would imply that a corporation that pursues only socially obligated behavior is not socially responsible, because such behavior is required, not voluntary.

A leading spokesman for the view that social responsibility goes beyond the law, Keith Davis, states: "A firm is not being socially responsible if it merely complies with the minimum requirements of the law. . . . Social responsibility goes one step further. It [social responsibility] is a firm's acceptance of social obligation beyond the requirements of the law."[11] A firm that accepts social obligation in reaction to pressure groups, consumer boycotts, or adverse publicity would not be socially responsible. For example, the contributions of the three national hotel chains to low-cost housing construction, as noted in the Management in Action, would not be socially responsible because they are not voluntary actions.

---

[9] Sethi, "A Conceptual Framework," p. 66.

[10] H. Manne and H. C. Wallich, *The Modern Corporation and Social Responsibility* (Washington, D.C.: American Enterprise Institute for Public Policy Research, 1972), as noted in Carroll, "A Three-Dimensional Conceptual Model," p. 498.

[11] Keith Davis, "The Case for and against Business Assumption of Social Responsibilities," *Academy of Management Journal*, June 1973, p. 313.

Whether the firm's actions are voluntary or involuntary, a broader interpretation of the social reaction view identifies as socially responsible those actions that go beyond the law. Typically these actions are reactions to the expectations of specific groups—unions, stockholders, social activists, consumerists, and the like.[12] Because the expectations of these groups go beyond legal minimums, firms can decide not to react in such circumstances. Favorable reaction, however, is considered socially responsible behavior in this view.

The essence of this view of social responsibility is that firms are reactive. Demands are made of them by certain groups, and the firms are socially responsible when they react, whether voluntarily or involuntarily, to satisfy these demands. This meaning is unsatisfactory for those who believe social responsibility should refer to proactive behavior.

Social Responsibility as Social Responsiveness

According to this view, socially responsible behaviors are anticipatory and preventive rather than reactive and restorative.[13] The term *social responsiveness* has become widely used in recent years to refer to actions that go beyond social obligation and social reaction.[14] The characteristics of socially responsive behavior include taking stands on public issues, accounting willingly for actions to any group, anticipating future needs of society and moving toward satisfying them, and communicating with the government regarding existing and anticipated socially desirable legislation. According to this view, the management of R. J. Reynolds is socially responsive, as depicted in the Management Focus.

MANAGEMENT FOCUS
R. J. Reynolds Supports Minority Business

R. J. Reynolds, based in Winston-Salem, North Carolina, has a long history of supporting minority business. A recent action, announced by Vice Chairman of the Board Joseph F. Abely, Jr., commits R. J. Reynolds to a $10 million line of credit with 53 minority banks. The company's other actions include purchases amounting to more than $60 million from minority suppliers.

According to Abely, the company's actions are morally right and

---

[12] Crawford and Gram, "Social Responsibility."

[13] Sethi, "A Conceptual Framework," p. 66.

[14] Peter Arlow and Martin J. Gannon, "Social Responsiveness, Corporate Structure, and Economic Performance," *Academy of Management Review*, April 1982, p. 235.

MANAGEMENT FOCUS (*continued*)

economically sound. Minority entrepreneurs are vital parts of a healthy overall economy, but the aspirations of these entrepreneurs must be given assistance. Abely believes that business should take a leadership role in society. Supporting the development of minority business is but one expression of R. J. Reynolds' leadership effort.

In addition to its support of minority business, the company makes other contributions. For example, the company has contributed $1 million to the United Negro College Fund and has set up a $1 million scholarship program at Winston-Salem State University. It also supports local community improvement organizations, such as the National Urban League.

A socially responsive corporation actively seeks ways to solve social problems. Progressive managers, according to this view, apply corporate skills and resources to every problem—from rundown housing to youth employment, from local schools to small-business job creation. Such behavior reflects the "true" meaning of social responsibility for social-responsiveness advocates; and when corporate executives commit their organizations to such endeavors, they are likely to receive substantial public approval.[15]

The social-responsiveness view is the broadest meaning of social responsibility. It places managers and their organizations in a position of responsibility far removed from the traditional one of being concerned solely with economic means and ends. This broader view rests on two premises: (1) corporations *should* be involved in preventing as well as solving social problems and (2) corporations "are perhaps the most effective problem-solving organizations in a capitalist society."[16]

A Continuum of Social Responsibility

The three general meanings of social responsibility can be depicted as a continuum. As shown in Figure 20–1, at one extreme is social obligation—business behavior that reflects the firm's economic and legal responsibilities. Occupying the middle position is social reaction—behavior that is demanded by groups having a direct stake in the organization's actions. The farthest extreme, social responsiveness, is behavior that reflects anticipatory, proactive, and preventive expectations.

---

[15] See Neal R. Pierce, "Corporations Are Becoming Social Institutions," *Sunday Herald-Leader*, Lexington, Kentucky, October 10, 1982.

[16] H. Gordon Fitch, "Achieving Corporate Social Responsibility," *Academy of Management Review*, January 1976, p. 45.

The three classes of socially responsible behavior actually form a continuum, ranging from an emphasis on profit making to an emphasis on social and economic concerns.

FIGURE 20–1 A Continuum of Social Responsibility

Type of behavior:	Socially obligated	Socially reactive	Socially responsive
	←		→
Primary emphasis:	The organization's economic and legal responsibilities	The organization's economic, legal and social responsibilities	The organization's economic, legal, social, and citizenship responsibilities

In practice, a corporation can choose to be anywhere along the continuum. To be socially reactive implies the firm's acceptance of social obligation as well. Similarly, to be socially responsive requires both social-obligation and social-reaction behavior. In a sense, the three meanings refer to different degrees of departure from the usual economic expectations and performance of business firms.

SPECIFIC SOCIALLY RESPONSIBLE ACTIVITIES

So far, the discussion has centered on rather *abstract* meanings of socially responsible behavior. In this section, the emphasis is on *concrete* expressions of social responsibility—that is, the actual actions of a corporation.

Socially responsible activities can be classified in several different ways. One such classification includes the following categories:

1. Product line.
2. Marketing practices.
3. Employee education and training.
4. Corporate philanthropy.
5. Environmental control.
6. External relations:
   a. Community development.
   b. Government relations.
   c. Disclosure of information.
   d. International relations.
7. Employee relations, benefits, and satisfaction with work.
8. Employment and advancement for minorities and women.
9. Employee safety and health.

Each of these broad categories can be broken down into specific activities and issues. For example, product line includes issues such as quality, safety, product life, and packaging. Within each of the nine categories are necessities and opportunities for the organization to practice social responsibility ranging from producing a safe, quality product to making contributions to the arts.

A more specific classification of "areas of social concern" was devised by Sandra Holmes, who sought to identify the extent of corporate involvement in the following activities:[17]

1. Assistance to charities, welfare, health funds.
2. Assistance to public or private education.
3. Recruitment and managerial development of racial or ethnic minorities.
4. Participation in community affairs.
5. Pollution abatement.
6. Recruitment and managerial development of women.
7. Improvement of the quality of working life for employees.
8. Conservation of resources, including energy.
9. Hiring and training of hard-core unemployed.
10. Assistance to minority enterprise.
11. Urban renewal and development.
12. Assistance to the arts.
13. Consumer protection.
14. Promotion of viable political and governmental systems within the United States.

These 14 activities represent a wide range of actions that corporations can confront when they move into social-reaction and social-responsiveness behaviors. While the organization is bound by law and regulation to reach certain levels of compliance in some areas (for example, affirmative action compliance obligates the corporation to recruit and develop racial and ethnic minorities), the corporation often has considerable latitude in determining how rapidly it will comply. Thus, within a particular area of concern, a corporation's response may be deemed *social obligation*—hire and develop the minimum legal number of racial and ethnic minorities; *social reaction*—go beyond the minimum in response to concerted group pressure; or *social responsiveness*—actively pursue means to identify and recruit racial and ethnic minorities so as to *prevent* future discrimination.

Another way to classify socially responsible actions is to identify the *beneficiaries* of each action. As the discussion above indicates, in some instances, the organization's *customers* benefit; in other instances, the *employees* benefit. Beyond employees and customers are definable interest groups, such as racial and ethnic groups, women's groups, and governmental agencies. In a sense, these groups are other organizations that transact business with the corporation. The focus of these transactions is not exchange of economic goods

---

[17] Sandra L. Holmes, "Corporate Social Performance: Past and Performance Areas of Commitment," *Academy of Management Journal,* September 1977, pp. 433–38. These 14 areas are, in turn, based on the Committee for Economic Development, Research and Policy Committee, *Social Responsibilities of Business Corporations* (New York: Committee for Economic Development, 1971).

and services but exchange of concessions based upon relative power. In addition to customers, employees, and interest groups, there are ill-defined beneficiaries such as future generations, society at large, and the common good. Activities such as assistance to the arts are directed to these beneficiaries. For simplicity, two general classes of beneficiaries can be identified: internal and external.

Internal Beneficiaries

Three groups of internal beneficiaries are apparent: *customers, employees* and *stockholders* (owners). Each of these groups has an immediate and often conflicting stake in the organization. Corporate activities in response to each group can be classified as obligatory, reactive, or responsive.

Responsibilities to customers. [18]   Much of what is said about the responsibility of business toward its customers is critical. One target of criticism has been the business organization's responsibilities regarding the product and marketing.

One social obligation of business relates to product characteristics: quality, safety, packaging, and performance. The relative importance of these characteristics varies among products over time. Even within one industry, the relative importance shifts. For example, the publication of Ralph Nader's *Unsafe at any Speed* in 1965 raised the issue of automobile safety. The safety issue reached its highest point publicly in 1979 when a California jury awarded $125 million for punitive and general damages to a young boy who was riding in a Pinto when the gasoline tank exploded. Today the safety issue for automobiles is not as important as quality and fuel efficiency. But the safety of other consumer goods—children's toys, over-the-counter drugs, electrical products and appliances, and food—is high on the list of public concern.

Laws and regulations establish the bases for judging product safety, but market and competitive forces often set quality standards. A case in point involves the American automobile industry. In the early 1980s, this industry faced declining demand for its products due partly to the deepening recession and high interest rates but also to competition from Japanese auto manufacturers. The success of Japanese automobiles rests largely on their superior quality. American consumers believe that Japanese cars are of better quality than American cars, and they express this judgment in their decision to buy Japanese rather than American cars.

The response of American auto manufacturers has been to implement quality-control programs and to publicize those programs in advertisements.

---

[18] The following discussion is based on Frederick D. Sturdivant, *Business and Society: A Managerial Approach,* 3rd ed. (Homewood, Ill.: Richard D. Irwin, 1985), pp. 288–303.

Ford Motor Co., for example, indicates in its television commercials that it has achieved a 48 percent increase in quality. Its commercials state that "Quality is Job 1." Thus, the emphasis in American auto manufacturing has shifted away from safety to quality. But quality is a difficult characteristic to assess, because there are few legal guidelines that define acceptable levels of product quality. Instead, quality is often judged by vague expectations about the appropriate relationships between price and reliability, service life, and maintenance.

The social-responsibility issue toward customers is relatively fixed at one extreme (as in those instances where specific legal directives define product safety) and quite fluid at the other extreme (as in those instances where there are general expectations regarding price-quality relationships). Many firms choose to meet their responsibilities to customers by responding promptly to complaints, by providing complete and accurate product information, and by implementing advertising programs that are truthful in all respects regarding product performance.

Responsibilities to employees.   Management's responsibilities to employees can be minimally discharged by meeting the legal requirements that relate to employee-employer relationships. Such laws address issues associated with the physical conditions of work (particularly the safety and health issues), wage and hour provisions, unions and unionization, and the like. The thrust of these laws is to encourage management to create safe and productive workplaces within which employees' basic civil rights are not compromised. In addition to these responsibilities, the modern corporate practice of providing fringe benefits—retirement funds, health and hospitalization insurance, and accident insurance—has extended the range of socially obligated activity. In some instances, these practices are in response to concerted employee pressure, typically through union activity.

Other responsibilities a firm may take on include training, career development, counseling and therapy for drug and alcohol abuse, maternity leave, and day-care centers. While these issues affect only particular employees, the organizational response to them has broad implications. For example, the provision of maternity leaves and day-care centers may be socially reactive in nature if it results from action by highly organized women's groups. Yet the organization has the choice of not reacting to the pressure—but not reacting will cause some employees to consider the firm socially irresponsible. Practices neither required by law nor pushed by well-articulated groups in society clearly fall in the socially responsive category.

Business firms engage in numerous activities intended to meet the needs of their employees. Some firms restrict their activities to providing safe working conditions and competitive pay. Other firms provide a whole range of employee-related services. The Management Focus describes some of the things that Apple Computer does for its employees.

MANAGEMENT FOCUS
Apple Computer's Employee-Centered Practices

Apple Computer attempts to integrate its social values into day-to-day operations. Some observers consider the company to be a leading advocate of the "new age" corporation whose mission includes making the world a better place to live in as well as making computers at a profit. The company provides every new employee with a statement of the philosophy and values that underlie everything Apple does. The company carries out its values in such routine ways as providing all employees with a free computer after a year's service and granting stock options to every employee. It also does some nonroutine things, such as giving every employee an extra week of paid vacation when it achieved its first $100 million sales quarter.

Based on Milton Moskowitz, "The Corporate Responsibility Champs and Chumps," *Business and Society Review,* Winter 1985, pp. 4–5.

Responsibility to stockholders.   Management has a responsibility to disclose fully and accurately its use of corporate resources and the results of those uses to stockholders. The law guarantees stockholders the right to financial information and establishes minimums of public disclosure. The fundamental right of a stockholder is not to be guaranteed a profit but to be guaranteed information on which a prudent investment decision can be based. The ultimate action that a stockholder can take is to sell the stock and cease to have an ownership interest.[19]

Many individuals would argue that managers' preeminent responsibility is to the stockholder. In fact, those persons would argue that any managerial action that goes beyond socially obligated behavior to the benefit of any group other than stockholders is a violation of management's (and therefore social) responsibility. At the same time, there is evidence that firms that aggressively pursue socially responsive behavior are more profitable than those that do not. The evidence to support this position is controversial because there is little agreement on how social responsibility can be measured and how it should be related to performance measures such as profit and stock prices, the interests of stockholders. Two recent reviews of the relevant research literature suggest that if there is a relationship between socially respon-

[19] Howard R. Bloch and Thomas J. Lareau, "Should We Invest in 'Socially Irresponsible' Firms?" *Journal of Portfolio Management,* Summer 1985, pp. 27–31.

sible behavior and corporate performance, it is one that must be taken on faith.[20]

The internal beneficiaries of corporate actions are the focus of much of management's socially obligated behavior. In their relations with customers, employees, and stockholders, managers are most likely to be judged socially responsible. The relationships between the corporation and its internal beneficiaries are so circumscribed by law, regulation, and custom that the corporation is bound to act out of legal obligation. To do so involves no particular accomplishment for the corporation. But to fail to act legally, whether intentionally or not, can lead to all sorts of legal and social condemnation of the corporation and its management. Therefore, corporations have greater opportunities to be socially reactive and responsive in matters involving external beneficiaries.

External Beneficiaries

The external beneficiaries of corporate behavior are of two types, *specific* and *general*. Both types benefit from the organization's actions, even though they may have no direct or apparent stake in it.

Specific external beneficiaries.   Modern societies consist of diverse interest groups working to further the well-being of their members. These groups represent rather well-defined populations of individuals seeking to redress historical grievances: minorities and ethnics, women, the handicapped, and the aged. They pursue their interests by bringing political and popular opinion to bear on corporate actions. Some groups are able to have laws implemented that force corporations to support their efforts. For example, equal employment opportunity and affirmative action legislation creates corporation obligations to recruit, hire, and develop women and members of minority and ethnic groups. The fundamental contention of these groups is that they have been discriminated against in the past and that corporations have been an important cause of that discrimination. Thus, a larger burden of responsibility must be borne by corporations to erase the vestiges of historical discrimination and to create a new environment of equal access to employment opportunities and economic advancement.

Corporate actions involving specific external beneficiaries can be obligatory,

[20] Kenneth E. Aupperle, Archie B. Carroll, and John D. Hatfield, "An Empirical Examination of the Relationship between Corporate Social Responsibility and Profitability," *Academy of Management Journal,* June 1985, pp. 446–63; Arieh A. Ullman, "Data in Search of Theory: A Critical Examination of the Relationships among Social Performance, Social Disclosure, and Economic Performance of U.S. Firms," *Academy of Management Review,* July 1985, pp. 540–57.

reactive, or responsive. Obligatory actions are in response to antidiscrimination laws and regulations. The corporation can be judged both socially and legally irresponsible if it violates these laws. But beyond minimal compliance, a corporation has considerable latitude in the rigor with which it pursues affirmative action programs. How rapidly it fills its managerial ranks with minorities and women is largely a matter of discretion, so long as good faith can be demonstrated. A corporation can be deemed socially reactive if it goes beyond the letter of the law in implementing affirmative action. Socially responsive behavior not only seeks solutions to the immediate problems but attempts to go to the very heart of the causes. Such behavior could include doing business with minority-owned businesses, creating programs to train the hard-core unemployed, and initiating career development programs for women. When such efforts are not prompted by law or pressure, they are clearly socially responsive in nature.

The most important characteristic of these actions—whether they be obligatory, reactive, or responsive—is that the economic, social, and political well-being of a specific group of individuals is enhanced through the corporation's efforts.

General external beneficiaries.   This category of beneficiary is often considered synonymous with social responsibility because it elicits corporate efforts to solve or prevent general social problems. Examples include corporate efforts and programs (1) to solve or prevent environmental and ecological problems such as water, air, and noise pollution and waste and radiation disposal; (2) to upgrade education, the arts, and community health through outright gifts and donations of executive time; (3) to improve the quality of governmental management through leaves of absence for executives to take government positions; (4) to contribute to philanthropic causes such as United Way so as to upgrade the quality of community life. Corporations have considerable freedom in this area of social responsibility. They can choose which specific problems to become involved with—or not to become involved at all.

But why do corporations engage in behavior that cannot, except remotely, be related to their primary economic and legal responsibilities? It is a matter of fact that they do, and they do so in an atmosphere of controversy. The next section reviews the explanations for corporate social responsibility.

CHANGING EXPECTATIONS FOR CORPORATE PERFORMANCE

No thoughtful person can question the responsibility of a corporation to act within the law. Society expects no less of an individual citizen. But people disagree over other corporate responsibilities, described in the previous section as socially reactive and socially responsive behavior. Does a corporation have any responsibility to support the arts, rebuild inner-city housing, or make charitable contributions? Some people argue that corporations have been legally required to bear a disproportionate share of the cost of redressing historical discrimination in employment and degradation of the environment. Yet the prevailing mood is that large organizations, particularly corporations, are not only *capable* of contributing to social progress beyond that of producing safe and reliable goods and services but are *responsible* for doing so. This attitude did not suddenly appear. It is simply a contemporary expression of the dynamic and evolutionary relationship between society and its institutions.

The Historical Evolution of Contemporary Expectations

One scholar has observed that the relationship between organizations and society has changed in the aftermath of three business crises.[21]

The crisis of 1870.   The industrialization of America and the incorporation of its business occurred during the pre- and post–Civil War eras; the great impetus for the development of corporate power was the mobilization required by the Civil War. During the 1860s, the "captains of industry"— John D. Rockefeller, J. Pierpont Morgan, Jay Gould, and Andrew Carnegie— were creating the great railroad, steel, coal, sugar, tobacco, and oil corporations. In comparison to smaller, more traditional proprietorships and partnerships, these corporations had tremendous power—for good and for evil. The abuse of this power, in the form of kickbacks, discriminatory pricing, lockouts, and the manipulation of commodity prices, led to a public outcry for legal redress. Consequently Congress enacted various laws related to rate regulation, fair-trade practices, and labor. The landmark legislation was the Sherman Act of 1890.

The crisis of 1930.   The passage of the Sherman Act did not reverse the trend toward larger and larger business organizations; the underlying impetus and irreversible. Business organizations tended then, as today, to equate growth with profitability—the bigger, the better. As one scholar notes, three merger movements occurred between 1870 and 1930 (1870, 1890, and 1920).[22] The effect of these mergers was to create even larger yet legal corporate entities, which enabled the country to mobilize and successfully fight a world war. By 1914, the production of goods and services in the United States was *more than a third of the world's total industrial output.*[23] The

---

[21] Stahrl W. Edmunds, "Unifying Concepts in Social Responsibility," *Academy of Management Review,* January 1977, pp. 38–45.

[22] Ibid., p. 40.

[23] Sturdivant, *Business and Society,* p. 102.

Roaring Twenties was aptly named. More and more people were sharing the fruits of America's industrial development. Thus, the beneficiaries of corporate action widened beyond a small circle of owners. Many Americans owned shares of stock. Even more Americans worked for big business. And even more Americans were daily affected by the actions of corporations.

The Great Depression brought an abrupt halt to the euphoric attitude that unchecked business could bring prosperity to all. To the contrary, the blame for the Great Depression was placed squarely on business. In a sense, the country felt that business had betrayed the country's faith. As a result, the power of government to regulate and monitor business practice increased sharply through the efforts of President Roosevelt and supporters of his New Deal reforms. Government action cemented a relationship between corporations and society that placed responsibility on business for fair treatment of customers, employees, stockholders, suppliers, and other groups in society having a *direct stake* in the corporation's actions. Much of contemporary corporate legal responsibility (obligatory responsibility) can be traced to the crisis of 1930.

The post-1930-crisis era also marked the beginning of society's expectations for socially reactive behavior. After World War II, which was a watershed historical event, business regained the country's confidence as a provider of industrial goods. Employment soared, savings accounts swelled, and when the war ended, corporations converted to production of consumer goods. The country put behind it the experience, if not the memory, of the Depression. Thus, society turned again to the corporation as a singular source of "the good life," but the definition of the good life was beginning to change.

The crisis of 1970.   The closer one gets to contemporary history, the more unreliable hindsight becomes. Whether this crisis began in 1970 or 1960,[24] the fact remains that society now expects more of its corporations than it did in 1930 and much more than in 1870. But how much more? And specifically for what? The answers to these questions are now being hammered out in political debates, shaped by public relations efforts, and argued in public forums.

The background of the 1970 crisis was an uninterrupted 20-year period during which two economies came into being. One economy, the *public economy,* is run by the government. It regularly intervenes in business practice, redistributes income through taxation and entitlement programs, and regulates labeling, packaging, advertising, and many other business factors. According to some estimates, the public economy makes up one fourth of the national social system.[25] The second economy, the *private economy,* makes up the

---

[24] Thomas J. Zenisek, "Corporate Social Responsibility: A Conceptualization Based on Organizational Literature," *Academy of Management Review,* July 1979, pp. 359–68, suggests that 1960 marks the beginning of contemporary dialogue regarding the role of corporations in society.

[25] Edmunds, "Unifying Concepts," p. 40.

remaining three fourths. Of this portion, the 500 largest firms account for two thirds of all manufacturing. These two economies confront and accommodate each other. Each has power over the other, and each represents different yet compatible interests.

But in the 1960s and 1970s the business/government-as-usual relationship was challenged. New ideas—such as consumerism, feminism, environmentalism, and ecology—grew out of the social unrest fed by the unpopular Vietnam War and fanned by the Watergate scandal. As a result, new demands were made on business that went far beyond social obligations as defined by law.

The Contemporary Expectation for Corporate Social Responsiveness

The crisis of 1970 reinforced the attitude that corporations must react to problems created by their own actions. But more importantly, the crisis initiated the idea that corporations should be proactive, that they should be responsive to a wide range of social problems because they have the expertise and power to do so. The current debate on the social responsibility of business is not concerned with obligatory behavior: business must be law abiding. The debate is seldom couched in terms of reactive behavior; business should be responsible for its actions. Rather the debate has to do with socially responsive behavior.

MANAGERIAL ETHICS

The word *ethics,* as commonly understood, refers to principles of behavior that distinguish between good, bad, right, and wrong.[26] The purpose of ethics, or a code of ethics, is to enable individuals to make choices among alternative behaviors. The importance of ethics increases in proportion to the *consequences* of the outcome of a behavior. As an individual's actions become more consequential for others, the ethics of that individual become more important.

Managers, by virtue of their positions, face many consequential decisions. They have access to resources that they can use for good, bad, right, or wrong purposes. But ethics involve not only purposes (ends) but also means. Ethical ends can be achieved by unethical means. Bribing an official to obtain a government defense contract would be considered unethical by most Americans. At the same time, some individuals would judge the contract itself as unethical even if it were obtained by ethical means. For example, if the

---

[26] Verne E. Henderson, "The Ethical Side of Enterprise," *Sloan Management Review,* Summer 1982, p. 38.

contract involved producing materials for use as biological warfare weapons, many individuals would consider the contract to be wrong and bad, even if acquired ethically.

There is a whole range of behaviors that would be discredited by a code of ethics. For example, most people would agree that managers should not divulge confidential information, falsify records, pad expense accounts, use company resources for personal benefit, accept or give gifts in exchange for preferential treatment, and do personal business on company time. For that matter, these actions would be unacceptable for any employee, nonmanagerial or managerial. But important as they may be in their own right, these actions do not concern us here. Our interest is in those actions that require managers to make choices involving the organization's relationship to its internal and external beneficiaries.

Managers who aspire to social responsibility in their actions face considerably more ambiguity than those who aspire to do only that which is legal.[27] What is legal is not always clear; what is ethical is seldom clear. A manager who decides it is "right" to become involved in a community's effort to restore its inner city must make many choices among relatively right and good means and ends. The decision to become involved is itself filled with ethical content because it requires a choice between stockholders' and community interests. The manager who determines that the corporation has no *legal* obligation to become involved and acts on that basis avoids the more difficult choice of whether it has an *ethical* obligation.

Ethical Standards

Managers must reconcile competing values in making decisions. They make decisions that have consequences for (1) themselves, (2) the organization that employs them, and (3) the society in which they and the organization exist. For example, managers can be called upon to make decisions that can be good for them but bad for the organization and society.

Philosophers, logicians, and theologians have studied ethical issues. Their ideas provide guidelines, but only guidelines, for making value-laden decisions. Figure 20–2 depicts a simplified model of ethical behavior with three different bases for developing ethical guidelines.[28]

Maximum personal benefits (egoism), depicted on the vertical axis, can be the sole basis for decision making. A completely selfish individual would always do that which is personally beneficial. An extreme view of this ethical approach is that individuals should always seek that which is pleasurable;

[27] John Roberts, "The Moral Character of Management Practice," *Journal of Management Studies,* July 1984, pp. 286–302.

[28] The discussion that follows is based on Grover Starling, *The Changing Environment of Business* (Boston: Kent Publishing, 1980), pp. 252–58.

FIGURE   20–2   An Ethical Framework

Ethical behavior involves balancing what is good for the individual—egoism— and what is good for society—altruism.

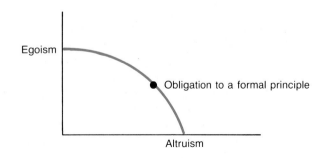

Source: Based on Grover Starling, *The Changing Environment of Business* (Boston: Kent Publishing, 1980), p. 255.

and conversely one should avoid pain. Manager's driven by egoism would evaluate alternative actions in terms of personal benefit—salary, prestige, power, or whatever they consider valuable. If the action also proves beneficial to the organization and society, all is well and good. But these other benefits are incidental and not the primary intent of the manager.

Maximum social benefits (altruism), depicted on the horizontal axis, can also be the sole consideration in decision making. An altruistic individual will select courses of action that provide maximum social benefit. A manager who follows this ethical guideline would measure right and wrong as the "greatest happiness to the greatest number." As a practical matter, decisions based on only altruistic concerns are particularly difficult to make. For example, altruism provides no means for judging the relative benefits of individuals, unless one is willing to assume that each has the same interest in and benefit from a decision.

Obligation to a formal principle is shown between the extremes of egoism and altruism. Egoism states that an act is good if the individual benefits from it. Altruism states that an act is good if society benefits from it. The criteria for both ethical guidelines are consequences. In contrast to them, the ethic of adhering to a formal principle is based on the idea that *the rightness or wrongness of an act depends upon principle, not consequences.*

Those who adhere to principle in judging their actions could, for example, follow the Golden Rule: "Do unto others what you would have others do unto you." Or they may decide that each action should be judged by the Categorical Imperative: "Act as if the maxim of your action were to become a general law binding on everyone."

But the idea that actions can be judged by one particular principle is unacceptable to many individuals. Some prefer a *pluralistic* approach that would contain several principles arranged in a hierarchy of importance. For example, one writer proposes that managers can be guided in decision making by adhering to the following principles: (1) Place the interests of society before the interests of the organization. (2) Place the interests of the organization before managers' private interests. (3) Reveal the truth in all instances of organizational and personal involvement.[29] These three principles provide guidelines but not answers. The manager must determine the relative benefits to society, company, and self. The determination of benefits and beneficiaries is seldom simple accounting. But the advantage of a pluralistic approach to ethical decision making is that the decision maker, *with intentions to do right,* has the basis for evaluating decisions.

Codes of ethical conduct do not guarantee that a manager's every decision will square with everyone's personal values. Value differences will always exist, even among like-minded persons. To give some direction to the decisions of managers, many organizations have adopted codes like the one described in the Management Focus on J. C. Penney.

MANAGEMENT FOCUS
J. C. Penney's Code of Ethics

J. C. Penney, the nation's third-largest merchandising chain, has attempted to adhere to the homespun philosophy of the Golden Rule since its founding in 1902. Throughout its history, the company has put the philosophy into practice through its dealings with customers, employees, stockholders, and the general public. The company's code of ethics is circulated widely, and it stands as a model for other companies to follow. Three of its planks are:

- To expect for the service we render a fair remuneration and not all the profit the traffic will bear.
- To reward the men and women in our organization through participation in what the business produces.
- To test our every policy, method and act in this wise manner: "Does it square with what is right and just?"

The company first proposed these principles in 1913, and its employees and customers have benefited from them ever since.

Based on Milton Moskowitz, "The Corporate Responsibility Champs and Chumps," *Business and Society Review,* Winter 1985, p. 6.

---

[29] Robert W. Austin, "Code of Conduct for Executives," *Harvard Business Review,* September–October 1961, p. 53, as cited in Sturdivant, *Business and Society,* p. 147.

FIGURE   20–3   The Corporation's Social Responsibility and Managerial Ethics

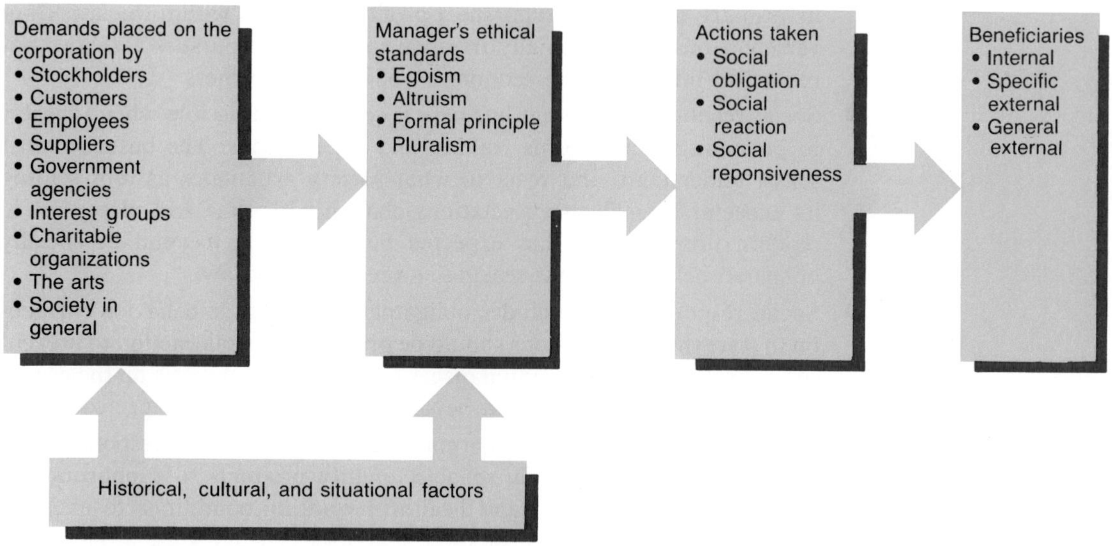

Demands placed on the corporation by
- Stockholders
- Customers
- Employees
- Suppliers
- Government agencies
- Interest groups
- Charitable organizations
- The arts
- Society in general

Manager's ethical standards
- Egoism
- Altruism
- Formal principle
- Pluralism

Actions taken
- Social obligation
- Social reaction
- Social reponsiveness

Beneficiaries
- Internal
- Specific external
- General external

Historical, cultural, and situational factors

In the final analysis, managerial ethics determine a corporation's socially responsive actions.

Ethics and Social Responsiveness

The relationship between a manager's ethical standards and social responsiveness should be apparent. Ethics serve as bases for assessing the "rightness" of potential actions. In a sense, ethical standards are filters that screen actions according to relative rightness. The ideas that have been developed in our discussion of social responsibility, expectations for corporate behavior, and ethics can be integrated as shown in Figure 20–3. Here, the corporation is seen as a *means* for achieving the *ends* of various claimants. Social responsibility involves deciding *what* means and *whose* ends are right and good. Ultimately it is the task of corporate managers to decide the relative rightness of each demand; and ethical standards are the bases for their decisions.

SUMMARY OF KEY POINTS

■ The term *social responsibility* is popularly used to prescribe and proscribe corporate activity, yet the meaning of social responsibility has many variations. Because of the numerous meanings, it is imperative to define the term when discussing the issue. The various meanings can be sorted into three categories: social obligation, social reaction, and social responsiveness.

■ Social obligation means that business is socially responsible when it meets its primary obligation: to pursue a profit for owners within the law. Conversely a business is socially irresponsible when it pursues activities not related to improving the economic well-being of owners.

■ Social reaction means that business is socially responsible when it reacts to prevailing social norms, values, and expectations. The business must sense, understand, and react to what society articulates as representing its expectations. These expectations change with time and place; but in modern times, society has expected business to go beyond its socially obligated behavior: profit seeking as prescribed by law.

■ Social responsiveness includes obligatory and reactive behavior but goes on to state that corporations should be proactive and take action to prevent social problems. This meaning places considerable emphasis on the corporation's obligations above and beyond what is legal and expected.

■ The activities through which corporations meet their social responsibilities range from producing safe, reliable, quality products to supporting the arts; from providing safe and healthful working conditions to assisting minority enterprises. Each of these activities benefits some group, often to the disadvantage of some other group. Managers must make choices among various interests both inside and outside the corporation.

■ The beneficiaries of corporate actions are either internal or external. Internal beneficiaries include customers, owners, and employees. External beneficiaries include groups representing minorities, women, the handicapped, and the aged. These groups make demands on the corporation to gain assistance in satisfying the interests of their members. More general external beneficiaries are those who benefit from the corporation's efforts to solve ecological, environmental, and social problems.

■ The contemporary demands placed on corporations are the result of an evolutionary process. In earlier times, when corporations were relatively insignificant, society expected them to meet their social obligations. As corporations became larger and more pervasive, society's expectations shifted toward social reaction and responsive corporate behavior.

■ The referees of competing demands on corporate resources are managers. It is their ethical standards—criteria of rightness and goodness—that filter these demands and determine which will be satisfied.

■ Ethical standards differ from person to person. Each individual is entitled to a unique sense of right and wrong, except that society sets certain expectations for socially acceptable behavior. Similarly corporate managers follow their own ethical standards in deciding the organization's approach to its social responsibilities.

DISCUSSION AND REVIEW QUESTIONS

1. Explain why corporations have "social responsibilities." How does society express its expectations for corporate behavior?

2. Is it possible for a corporate executive to be both personally unethical and professionally ethical? Which are more demanding: the ethics of personal life or the ethics of professional life?

3. Which of the three meanings of social responsibility reflects your opinion? Explain.

4. Identify organizations in recent events whose actions you believe to be notable expressions of social responsibility.

5. What are the basic arguments for and against each of the three meanings of social responsibility?

6. To which beneficiaries of corporate behavior is management primarily responsible? Explain your answer. Does your answer reflect *your* ethical standards?

7. Explain how a manager's ethics affect decisions regarding social responsibility.

8. Are society's expectations for corporate social responsibility likely to change in the 1980s? Explain.

9. Do you believe that the decline in American business productivity in recent years has been caused by society's demand for socially responsive corporate behavior? Explain.

10. Can American business solve pollution problems and remain competitive in international markets? Explain.

ADDITIONAL REFERENCES

Ackerman, R. W. *The Social Challenge to Business.* Cambridge, Mass.: Harvard University Press, 1975.

Berle, A. A., and G. C. Means. *The Modern Corporation and Private Property.* New York: Harcourt Brace Jovanovich, 1968.

Brown, L. "Virtue as Its Own Reward: New Evidence that Nice Guys Don't Always Finish Last." *Canadian Business,* July 1985, pp. 15–18.

Chrisman, J. J., and R. W. Archer. "Small Business Social Responsibility: Some Perceptions and Insights." *American Journal of Small Business,* Fall 1984, pp. 46–58.

Committee for Economic Development, Research and Policy Committee. *Social Responsibilities of Business Corporations.* New York: Committee For Economic Development, 1971.

Davis, K.; W. C. Frederick; and R. L. Blomstrom. *Business and Society: Concepts and Policy Issues.* New York: McGraw-Hill, 1980.

Filios, V. P. "Corporate Social Responsibilities and Public Accountability." *Journal of Business Ethics,* November 1984, pp. 305–14.

Fry, L. W.; G. D. Keim; and R. E. Meiners. "Corporate Contributions: Altruistic or For-Profit?" *Academy of Management Journal,* March 1982, pp. 94–106.

Grant, C. T. "Blacks Hit Racial Roadblocks Climbing up the Corporate Ladder." *Business and Society Review,* Winter 1985, pp. 56–59.

Grunigs, J. E. "A New Measure of Public Opinions on Corporate Social Responsibility." *Academy of Management Journal,* December 1979, pp. 738–64.

Jones, T. M., and L. D. Goldberg. "Governing the Large Corporation: More Arguments for Public Directors." *Academy of Management Review,* October 1982, pp. 603–11.

Logan, J. E.; S. P. Logan; and J. M. E. Mille. "Corporate Social Responsibility." *Business and Economic Review,* January 1985, pp. 25–27.

Mahapatra, S. "Investor Reaction to a Corporate Social Accounting." *Journal of Business Finance and Accounting,* Spring 1984, pp. 29–40.

Maitland, I. "The Limits of Business Self-Regulation." *California Management Review,* Spring 1985, pp. 132–47.

McAdams, T. "Speaking Out in the Corporate Community." *Academy of Management Review,* April 1977, pp. 196–205.

McGowan, W. "The Whistleblowers Hall of Fame." *Business and Society Review,* Winter 1985, pp. 31–36.

McQuaid, K. "Big Business and Public Policy in Contemporary United States." *Quarterly Review of Economics and Business,* Summer 1980, pp. 57–68.

Parmerlee, M. A.; J. P. Near; and T. C. Jensen. "Correlates of Whistleblowers' Perceptions of Organizational Retaliation." *Administrative Science Quarterly,* March 1982, pp. 17–34.

Preston, L. E., ed. *Research in Corporate Social Performance and Policy.* Greenwich, Conn.: JAI Press, 1981.

Saul, G. K. "Business Ethics: Where Are We Going?" *Academy of Management Review,* April 1981, pp. 269–76.

Sethi, S. P. "The Inhuman Error: Lessons from Bhopal." *New Management,* Summer 1985, pp. 40–44.

Starling, G. *The Changing Environment of Business.* Boston: Kent Publishing, 1980.

Strand, R. A. "A Systems Paradigm of Organizational Adaptations to the Social Environment." *Academy of Management Review,* January 1983, pp. 90–96.

Sweezy, P. M.; J. K. Galbraith; S. J. Tolchin; and R. S. Browne. "Can Socially Responsible Societies Compete Economically?" *Business and Society Review,* Winter 1985, pp. 11–14.

Upah, G. D., and R. E. Wokutch. "Assessing Social Impacts of New Products: An Attempt to Operationalize the Macromarketing Concept." *Journal of Public Policy and Marketing* 4 (1985), pp. 166–78.

CASES

APPLICATION I

GOVERNMENT RELATIONS AT SCOTT PAPER COMPANY*

In the early 1980s, Scott Paper Company expanded its government relations department. Its plans were based on the attitude expressed by Jeffrey P. Eves, director of government relations: "The largest competitor influencing our bottom line is not necessarily Proctor & Gamble, Kimberly Clark, Mead, or Champion. The largest competitor has become the government. It is in our interest, as a company, and our stockholders' interests, to look after that factor." Eves points out that the company spends considerable time and money complying with and implementing government laws and regulations. These resources might well be used in other ways: to improve products and deliver service to the customer, or to improve productivity.

Other groups with interests in government policy effectively lobby for passage of laws that benefit them. Scott management believes that corporations must make their positions known by the same legitimate means that other groups use. Efforts to influence government policy would involve active communications with those government individuals and groups who enunciate public policy and enact laws that carry out that policy. As Eves states: "There's a great deal at stake—in terms of both dollars and productivity."

To carry out its government relations mission, Scott identified four objectives:

1. To increase political sensitivity throughout the company.
2. To build stronger relationships with elected officials.
3. To monitor and evaluate government actions.
4. To expand the company's advocacy role.

These four objectives will be the responsibility of a larger and more visible Government Relations Department in Scott's Public Affairs Division. The primary strategy for achieving these objectives will be lobbying, although the department will devote only 20 percent of its time to that activity.

In addition to enlarging the Government Relations Department, Scott has made other organizational changes. It recently named a staff of regional managers who have responsibility for government relations in each area of company operations. Although these regional managers report to Eves, they are in advisory capacities to managers at Scott facilities around the country.

---

* Source: Based on "How Scott Is Strengthening Its Government Relations," *Management Review,* August 1981, pp. 29–30.

The same issues that are debated in Washington are also on the agenda of state officials. In fact, the company believes that state government is the most rapidly growing government sector because of the Reagan administration's push to decentralize government. The company has also established a political action committee, SCOTTPAC, which supports candidates for public office. The Government Relations Department will provide seminars on government relations for corporate management and will publish newsletters expressing company positions on pending government actions.

Questions for Analysis

1. Evaluate the attitude that government in Scott's major competitor. What are the implications of this attitude if it is widely held in industry?
2. How would you characterize Scott's attitude toward its social responsibility?
3. Who will be the primary beneficiaries of Scott's efforts to influence government action?

APPLICATION II

ANHEUSER–BUSCH AND PUSH*

Jesse Jackson, director of *P*eople *U*nited to *S*ave *H*umanity (PUSH), has had great success negotiating "trade agreements" with companies that sell to black customers. Corporations such as Heublein, Seven-Up, and Coca-Cola have signed agreements with PUSH that commit them to employing more blacks; recruiting more black franchises, wholesalers, and vendors; and using more black-owned banks, ad agencies, insurance companies, and legal services. Other organizations, such as the *S*outhern *C*hristian *L*eadership *C*onference (SCLC) and the National Association for the Advancement of Colored People (NAACP), have reached similar agreements with Food Giant, Inc., Winn-Dixie, and Walt Disney Studios.

Jackson has attracted publicity because of his flamboyant personal style and rhetoric. He is also known for driving hard bargains. He doesn't object to using the ultimate weapon—boycott. When his discussions with Coca-Cola dragged on without agreement, he announced at the PUSH convention his "withdrawal of enthusiasm" for Coke's drinks. The slogan of the day

* Source: Based on Irwin Ross, "PUSH Collides with Busch," *Fortune,* November 15, 1982, pp. 90–92, 96, 100.

became "Don't choke on a Coke." Two weeks after the announcement, Coca-Cola agreed to Jackson's terms.

Anheuser-Busch, however, has resisted Jackson's pressure. Despite the fact that black customers account for 10 percent of total sales, the company's chief executive August A. Busch III stated that he saw no reason "to fit into Jesse's format." The company has its own program, according to Busch.

The St. Louis brewery has 14,000 employees, of which 18 percent are blacks and Hispanics. Ten percent of these blacks and Hispanics are managers, 8 percent are professionals, and 17 percent are technicians. In addition to its employment practices, Anheuser has $10 million in deposits and lines of credit with minority banks, buys $18 million of goods and services annually from minority suppliers, and places $7 million of advertising annually in minority media. These numbers compare favorably with the goals of companies that have signed agreements with PUSH.

Jackson points out, however, that despite those numbers and the fact that Anheuser's board membership includes two blacks, the company has failed to open up distributorships to blacks. Of the nearly 950 distributors of Anheuser-Busch products, only one is black and only three are Hispanics. Jackson claims the company has done little to improve on that record. In response, the company says it plans to spend $5 million for loans and loan guaranties to help black entrepreneurs buy distributorships.

When a series of meetings in the summer of 1982 produced little agreement and considerable personal animosity, Jackson called for a nationwide boycott of Anheuser-Busch products. "Bud is a dud," he stated, and the slogan stuck.

Anheuser-Busch claims that the boycott has not had an adverse effect on sales. But Jackson says that time is on the side of PUSH. Moreover, Jackson's verbal assaults pose a long-term threat to the company. If more and more people believe Anheuser-Busch is unresponsive to the economic needs of blacks, the company's image could be tarnished. Those close to the controversy believe that it has become a test of wills between two proud men—Jesse Jackson and August Busch III. Jackson believes that Busch is trying to discredit him. Busch, on the other hand, takes pride in his company's efforts in minority relations and resents being a target of PUSH.

Questions for Analysis

1. Should Anheuser-Busch sign an agreement with PUSH? Why?
2. Do you believe that boycotts should be used as a tactic to achieve concessions?
3. Is Anheuser-Busch a socially responsive organization?

21

Chapter

MANAGING IN A MULTINATIONAL ENVIRONMENT

LEARNING OBJECTIVES

After completing Chapter 21, you should be able to:

■ **Define**
culture and its importance to a manager in a multinational company.

■ **Describe**
the major reasons for a company to decide to become a multinational company.

■ **Discuss**
the evolution of a company into a multinational company.

■ **Compare**
the functions of management in a domestic company and in a multinational company.

■ **Identify**
the key cultural influences in a multinational company.

■ MANAGEMENT IN ACTION

Should You Take that Overseas Job Assignment*

What would you do if you were offered an overseas job assignment? The location is great, and your family thinks the idea is terrific. Are you ready to go? The experts warn, "Not so fast." When it comes to your career, taking a foreign assignment has some risks. One job placement expert says, "The stars are going to make it, no matter what route they take to the top." But for many of the rest of us, an overseas assignment is riskier than staying with your employer in the United States.

Many experts believe that in the early stages of a career, taking an overseas assignment can be the quickest way for ambitious young executives to show their stuff. "The experience they get normally is superior—they find themselves being a big fish in a small sea," says one consultant. The lifestyle and financial rewards of an overseas job can also be very enticing.

However, far too often, executives who have been assigned abroad return to corporate headquarters after a few years only to find themselves in a kind of limbo, with no one knowing quite what to do with them. One management consultant commented, "It's not uncommon for you to have completed an assignment overseas, come back home, and find there's no position for you."

To get the career benefits of a foreign assignment while at the same time avoiding the traps, experts advise answering two key questions about one's employer before accepting an overseas assignment:

1. Do your company's senior-level executives view the firm's international operations as a critical part of their business?
2. Within top management of the firm, how many executives have a foreign assignment in their background, and do they feel it is important for their executives to have experience overseas?

Many readers of this book may face the decision described here. This chapter examines the challenge of managing in a global environment, where many firms view the world as their market.

---

* Source: "Weigh the Risks First on that Job Abroad," *U.S. News and World Report,* December 2, 1985, p. 82.

William Wordsworth complained in a 19th-century poem, "The world is too much with us. Getting and spending, we lay waste our powers." What would he make of the current era of instant communications and global business? These days, the world is "much" with almost everyone. Goods, products, services, currencies, and changing cultural values move restlessly around the planet, from country to country, city to village, and group to individual.

What once was considered "foreign" by many Americans now is considered "ours." We have adopted Oriental, Mexican, and Italian foods. We wear shoes made in Italy, shirts made in Taiwan, and jeans and slacks made in China. Many of our automobiles, electronics products, and entertainment items are made in Japan.

And international business is not a one-way street. American technology, products, and management skills are utilized worldwide. In fact, many American organizations consider themselves worldwide in perspective and scope.

THE MULTINATIONAL COMPANY

A multinational company (MNC) is an organization doing business in two or more countries. Typically, however, these firms have sales offices and, in many cases, manufacturing facilities in many countries. They usually define their scope of operation as global. For example, American firms such as Pfizer, Hoover, Otis Elevator, Mobil Oil, and Gulf Oil sell the majority of their output outside the United States. Some U.S. firms, such as Coca-Cola, Xerox, Dow Chemical, Chrysler, and IBM earn more than half their profits outside the United States.

Multinational companies are large, and they are growing.[1] Today American-based MNCs employ most of the Americans working outside the United States and are responsible for much of America's imports and exports. In addition, the present growth rate of the world's 200 largest MNCs (most of which are American) is two or three times the growth rate of individual advanced nations. Figure 21–1 shows the multinational character of a number of business organizations.

The MNC Decision

Most American managers prefer doing business domestically. Domestic business is, for the most part, simpler and safer. For example, there is no

---

[1] William A. Dymsza, "Trends in Multinational Business and Global Environments: A Perspective," *Journal of International Business Studies,* Winter 1984, pp. 25–46; J. A. Young, "Global Competition: The New Reality," *California Management Review,* Spring 1985, pp. 11–25.

FIGURE   21–1   Examples of Various Types of Multinational Corporations

American-Owned MNCs

General Motors	Ford Motor
IBM	Pan Am
General Electric	American Express
F. W. Woolworth	Bank America
Sears, Roebuck	Eastman Kodak
Mobil Oil	Procter & Gamble
ITT	Gulf & Western

Foreign-Owned MNCs

Unilever	Toyota Motors
Royal Dutch/Shell	Sony
Nestlé	Volkswagen
Datsun	Perrier
Honda	Norelco

Nonprofit MNCs

Red Cross (Swiss)
Roman Catholic Church (Italy)
U.S. Army (U.S.)

American Firms Owned by Foreign MNCs

Magnavox	Bantam Books
Gimbel's Department Store	Baskin-Robbins
Libby, McNeill & Libby	Capital Records
Stouffer Foods	Kiwi Shoe Polish
Saks–Fifth Avenue	Lipton

Many organizations are truly multinational in character.

need to alter the firm's products to fit different cultures. Managers need not deal with different currencies or worry about political uncertainties or learn different languages.

Why, then, do so many American business organizations become involved in international business? The major reasons are a desire for growth, a desire to increase efficiency of operations, competitive pressures, environmental pressures, and various incentives. Let us examine each of these:

Desire for growth.   A firm may be forced into international business by weakening opportunities at home: economic growth may decline; taxes may increase; legislation may become too burdensome. Or a firm may be drawn into international business because it sees chances for growth and outstanding opportunities to market its products in other nations while it continues to sell at home. Coca-Cola, for example, markets its products in 155 countries.

Increased efficiency of operations.   The desire to lower overall production costs leads many firms into international business. Increasingly many products such as radios, televisions, stereos, and digital watches are assembled abroad. Other products, such as certain electronics items, are both produced and assembled abroad for American companies. Both of these procedures help lower production expenses, because wages and certain other costs tend to be lower overseas.

Competitive pressures.   Imported products from foreign-owned firms can compete with products produced at home. One way to ensure that a foreign firm does not compete is to own the foreign firm. Also, being first into another country with a product is one way to keep a competitor from establishing itself there.

Environmental pressures.   Some industries viewed as undesirable in one nation are considered desirable by less affluent economies. Considered undesirable because of their impact on the environment and ecology, industries such as steel mills, pulp and paper mills, and cement plants face increasing regulation, the added costs of running cleaner operations, and the costs of helping clean up the environment. Such regulations and expenses have led many organizations to choose multinational operations in countries with fewer restrictions.

Incentives.   Many countries offer tax incentives to attract firms. Different countries tax multinational organizations at different rates. Such tax incentives are crucial in attracting new business firms to a country. Other nations provide certain financial guarantees to foreign firms to establish production and/or marketing facilities on their soil. Such tax and financial incentives are designed to transfer some of the risks of doing business to the host country.

Commitment to International Business

The extent of a firm's involvement in multinational business has great impact on development of its strategic plan. Once a firm decides to go multinational, there are three basic strategies for entering the foreign market. These strategies are illustrated in Figure 21–2, which indicates that the firm's overall strategy is hardly affected when its commitment to multinational business is low. However, as opportunities begin to look more attractive, the firm's involvement takes on a broader scope. Each approach in turn leads to greater involvement and commitment to international business.

Export.   Exporting is the simplest way for a firm to enter a foreign market.[2] Exporting involves little or no change in the basic mission, objectives, and

---

[2] E. Dichtel, M. Leibold, H. G. Koglmayer, and S. Muller, "The Export Decision of Small and Medium-Sized Firms," *International Management Review* 24, no. 2 (1984), pp. 49–60.

FIGURE   21–2   Evolution of a Multinational Corporation.

Export	Foreign activities	Direct investment
Goods are shipped to foreign markets, but no major effort is made toward becoming an MNC. No change in basic mission, objectives, and strategies.	Increased exports lead to justification of foreign activities. They may involve licensing or joint - venture arrangements, hiring or working with nationals in the foreign country.	Commitment made to direct investment. Subsidiary companies may be bought or formed. Mission, objectives, and strategies become international in scope. They become global and the firm is an MNC.

Low commitment   High commitment

Degree of commitment

Most organizations evolve into a multinational corporation rather than becoming one in a short period of time.

strategies of the organization. It continues to produce all of its products at home. The firm also may sell components to another American firm that exports the completed product. Taking another step, the firm can appoint an agent in the foreign market to represent it with the customers in that market.[3]

Foreign activities.   As exports increase in importance to the firm, it may decide that it can justify having its own foreign activities. This decision usually involves joining with nationals in a foreign country to establish production and/or marketing facilities. Some type of association is formed with the local firm or individual. Licensing or joint-venture arrangements usually are involved. Licensing is granting to an outside company the right to produce and/or market the firm's product in another country. Gerber and Coca-Cola have used this arrangement to enter foreign countries. Joint-venture arrangements involve foreign investors forming a group with local investors to begin a local business. Each group shares ownership. Several U.S. banks are owned jointly by both U.S. and foreign interests.

Direct investment.   The strongest commitment to becoming a global enterprise occurs when management decides to begin producing the firm's products abroad. This strategy enables the firm to maintain partial-to-full control

---

[3] E. Kaynak and V. Kothari, "Export Behavior of Small and Medium-Sized Manufacturers: Some Guidelines for International Marketers," *International Management Review* 24, no. 2 (1984), pp. 61–69.

over production, marketing, and other key functions.[4] Toyota made a direct-investment decision when it recently decided to construct an assembly plant in Kentucky.

No matter which entry strategy is utilized, effective international management is required.

THE ENVIRONMENT OF THE MULTINATIONAL MANAGER

Future managers might wonder if multinational enterprises involve unique requirements for effective performance of the managerial functions. Planning, organizing and controlling are required regardless of the business setting. However, the differences between cultures may require multinational managers to learn about special environmental factors and institutions. They also may have to change some of their basic assumptions concerning people, organizations, and the role of the manager.

In the opening section of our book, we discussed the importance of environmental factors in managerial performance. Their importance is magnified many times in an international setting, where effective management requires careful consideration and appreciation of potential differences in culture, economics, politics, and technology.

Culture

In multinational business, culture is a very complex environmental influence. It includes knowledge, beliefs, laws, morals, art, customs, values, and any other capabilities and habits that an individual learns as a member of a society. Cultures vary widely from nation to nation. So if a multinational company is global in nature, its management will be required to adapt managerial practices to the specific and unique aspects of culture in each country.[5]

It is important to remember that cultures influence behavior. Human needs are inherently similar in any country. But the cultural environment determines the relative importance of each need and the means through which needs are satisfied. In different societies, different objects or goals are prized, and behavior that is valued in one society may be frowned upon or forbidden in another.[6]

---

[4] A. Eddy and B. Seifert, "International Benefits of Foreign Acquisitions," *International Management Review* 24, no. 2 (1984), pp. 72–77.

[5] For an excellent example, see E. Beliaev, T. Mullen, and B. J. Prunnett, "Understanding the Cultural Environment: US–USSR Trade Negotiations," *California Management Review,* Winter 1985, pp. 100–112.

[6] R. S. DeFrank, M. T. Matteson, D. M. Schweiger, and J. M. Ivancevich, "The Impact of Culture on the Management Practices of American and Japanese CEODs," *Organizational Dynamics,* Spring 1985, pp. 62–76.

Finally, the attitudes of individuals in various countries differ on such subjects as authority, the importance of work, material possessions, competition, risk taking, profit, time, and introducing change. A manager cannot assume that the attitudes toward these and similar subjects in the company will be consistent in all countries. Hard work, for example, is viewed as good in some areas of the world. But in other areas, it is considered something to be avoided. Authority is seen as a right in some nations—Japan, for instance. But in others, such as the United States, it must be earned by demonstrated ability.[7]

Economics

The economic environment is important anywhere a multinational company does business. Income levels, growth trends, inflation rates, balance of payments, and economic planning strategies vary greatly among nations. The MNC constantly must be aware of a nation's economic stability, as reflected by its rate of inflation and stability of its currency.

Nations are classified as either a developed country or a less developed country (LDC). Many LDCs have strong feelings of nationalism. And in the last 30 years, many LDCs have launched drives for political independence and freedom from foreign dominations. These developing nations have felt the need to consolidate control of their economies by altering their relationships with foreign firms. In some LDCs, extensive government regulations have had the ultimate purpose of limiting the growth of multinational companies. More recently, however, there has been a movement away from this trend. The reasons for the shift are changing attitudes and rising direct investment.[8]

■ *Changing attitudes.*   Charges of exploitation by MNCs still are heard. But changes have taken place in the attitudes of both host governments and multinational companies. And these changes have led to greater mutual understanding and accommodation. Host countries' fears of foreign domination still exist. But they have eased substantially. Apparently there now is an appreciation that a country's relationship with MNCs need not be a no-win situation—it can be one of mutual gain.

■ *Rising direct investment.*   With improved relations, the third entry strategy, direct investment in less developed countries, has doubled since

[7] See W. O. Torrence, "Blending East and West: With Difficulties along the Way," *Organizational Dynamics,* Autumn 1984, pp. 23–34, for an interesting account of a Japanese firm's experience running a plant in Middle America and its experience in adapting to meet the needs and demands of U.S. workers.

[8] A. Desta, "Assessing Political Risk in Less Developed Countries," *Journal of Business Strategy,* Spring 1985, pp. 40–53.

the early 1960s. Apparently many multinational companies believe the possible returns are worth the risks. Also, these direct investments do not reflect the flow of other resources, such as technology and managerial and marketing skills, that may overshadow the monetary contributions.

It is wrong to assume that total agreement has been reached between multinational companies and developing nations. Controversies continue to occur over the issues of exploitation of resources and threats to sovereignty. And a basic difference in perceptions and objectives remains at the heart of these controversies. Multinational companies, for instance, now give greater recognition to their social responsibilities. But they still tend to concentrate on short-run performance criteria. Efficient and profitable operation is regarded as automatically benefiting workers, customers, and suppliers directly. And the host country is viewed as benefiting indirectly through the MNC's payment of taxes. On the other hand, critics in the host country often stress what they feel are undesirable political, social, and economic effects created by multinational companies in developing countries struggling to achieve political and economic autonomy.

Politics

Political differences can greatly affect international management. Nations differ greatly in how their political and legal environments treat imports and direct investment by foreigners. Some governments subsidize multinational companies. Japan, Great Britain, and France actively support exporters with subsidies. On the other hand, some nations penalize political adversaries through economic boycotts and prohibiting trade. For instance, an American MNC could face government-subsidized competitors in Japan, Great Britain, and France and not be able to do business at all with countries (such as Cuba) boycotted by the United States. The impact of politics on the multinational firm is illustrated in the Management Focus on European wine sales.

MANAGEMENT FOCUS
The European Community Blames Japanese Government for Poor Wine Sales

Some people say that if you order a bottle of Japanese wine in Tokyo, you may not get what you think. Japanese law allows a bottler to use any name on any kind of wine. Thus, a bottle of Cabernet Sauvignon in Tokyo might be made of mostly raisins, sugar, and alcohol, with a few Japanese grapes.

MANAGEMENT FOCUS (*continued*)

That Japan calls these products wine and then slaps high tariffs on "real" wine has the European community upset, to say the least. To maintain its strong liquor sales in Japan and to penetrate that country's fast-growing market for wine, the European community has launched a fight against Japan's protected alcoholic-beverage industry. European officials call the dispute a "test case" of Japan's willingness to open its markets.

While brandy is France's largest single export to Japan and Scotch whiskey is Great Britain's, the European community's share of the $24 billion Japanese alcoholic-beverage market is less than 1 percent. The European community says it does badly because Japan puts high tariffs on imports of bottled European wine. They believe that the politics of the tax system also work against bottled whiskey imports.

Source: "The EC Tries to Uncork Japan's Wine Market," *Business Week*, December 2, 1985, pp. 48.

Managers of multinational companies must be sensitive to changing political and legal environments in the nations in which they operate. These changes can influence all of the managerial functions and make the difference between success and failure. When evaluating the political environment of a particular country, managers should consider at least the following three factors: the attitude toward imports and direct investments, the stability of the government, and the efficiency of the government.

■ *Attitudes toward imports and direct investment.* While some nations support and encourage foreign investment, others are very hostile and may force import quotas and heavy taxes on the firm and require that a large portion of top management be nationals. Coca-Cola no longer operates in India for these reasons.

■ *Stability of government.* In many cases where governments have changed, a foreign firm's property has been taken, its money held, or new duties and quotas have been imposed. Unfortunately governments change rapidly and violently in some countries. Holiday Inns lost millions of dollars during the civil war in Lebanon in 1980 and 1981. And some countries with governments that have remained stable for long periods of time suddenly lose that stability through coups, revolutions, or other turmoil. The perceived stability of government can influence many management decisions, from the chosen entry strategy to the scope of operation and the amount of direct investment.

■ *Efficiency of government.*   American businessmen are frequently disillusioned with the inefficient bureaucracies found in many countries. Often little assistance is provided to businessmen; customs procedures are inefficient and burdensome; and market information is nonexistent. Systems of law in each country can be quite different. For example, the United States developed its legal system by means of English common law; American courts are guided by principles derived from previous cases. In much of Europe and Asia, the legal systems are based on civil law. In such systems, judges are less important and the bureaucrat (civil servant) is extremely important. Unfortunately some American managers have found that many inefficiencies and obstacles in local governments tend to disappear once a suitable payment is made to a civil servant. In many nations, such bribes are considered a normal part of doing business.

In 1977, Congress passed the Foreign Corrupt Practices Act. For the first time in U.S. history, it became a crime for corporations to bribe an official of a foreign government in order to obtain or retain business in another country. The law requires publicly held companies to institute internal accounting controls to ensure that all transactions are made with management's specific authorization and are fairly recorded. Meanwhile, in West Germany, France, and Great Britain, payments of bribes abroad remain not only legal but tax deductible. This practice places U.S. companies at an obvious disadvantage in certain areas.[9] The complexity of the relationship between international management and politics was summarized succinctly by Henry Kissinger when he said:

> We have come a long way, and very rapidly, to the . . . proposition that international business depends decisively on international politics. . . . We have come a long way from the 19th century when the United States accounted for very little in the scale of world economies. . . . The future of American business will require the highest degree of sensitivity to the political framework in which it functions and to the great coming changes in the world political process.[10]

Technology

Technology influences productivity, jobs, interpersonal relationships, and the structure of organizations. And it has obvious impacts on multinational companies. A company's technological superiority in multinational operations often is the major reason for its direct foreign investment and commitment

---

[9] Geoffrey Latta, "The International Regulation of Multinational Companies," *Benefits and Compensation International,* May 1985, pp. 8–12.

[10] Henry Kissinger, "The Future of Business and the International Environment," Address to the Future of Business Project for Strategic and International Studies at Georgetown University, Washington, D.C., June 28, 1977.

to multinational business. But some nations have an abundance of technological capacity, while others virtually have none. International managers must determine how the levels of technology in foreign countries might affect their operations and sources of raw materials, energy, and transportation.

MANAGEMENT IN A MULTINATIONAL CORPORATION

The Planning Function

The objectives of a multinational company cannot be the same as if it were operating only in the United States. There is too much potential for conflict between corporate objectives and the economic and political objectives of the countries in which the firm operates.[11] In many nations, the role played by government in planning helps heighten the possibility of conflicts with the MNC. For example, Japan's Ministry of International Trade and Industry plans the nation's economy to the point of specifying five-year percentage growth rates in exports of specific products.

In certain situations, a country may have objectives—such as a favorable balance of payments or an improved standard of living for its citizens—that do not coincide with the corporate objectives of the MNC. A common source of conflict is that in order to achieve a profitable objective, some of the earnings of the foreign subsidiary must be returned to the MNC's headquarters. This outward flow of earnings could have negative impact on the host country's balance of payments. For this reason and similar ones, some nations place restrictions on multinational companies.

Civil servants hold influential positions in foreign bureaucracies. Thus, they often dominate the planning functions of many countries. Managers of multinational companies must become acquainted with the attitudes and practices of these individuals, for an important reason: The civil servants often establish the conditions under which the managers must do their planning.

Figure 21–3 presents some factors that can complicate the planning environment for a multinational manager. The greater the number of differing factors, the more complex the planning environment.

The Organizing Function

After a company decides to go multinational and its planning function is well along, an organization structure must be devised to provide a structure

---

[11] Gary Hamel and C. K. Prahalad, "Do You Really Have a Global Strategy," *Harvard Business Review,* July–August 1985, pp. 139–48.

FIGURE   21–3   The Planning Environment in Domestic versus Global Settings

---

The management function of planning takes on greater complexity in an international environment.

Domestic Setting	Global Setting
Similar culture.	Diverse cultures.
Limited language differences.	Multilingual.
One economic system.	Multiple economic systems.
One political system.	Numerous political systems.
One basic legal system.	Diverse legal approaches.
One monetary system.	Multiple monetary systems.
Similar markets.	Diverse markets.

---

of jobs and authority for achieving the organizational objectives.[12] As with planning in international management, organization structures often must be adapted to local conditions. Organizational effectiveness depends greatly on flows of information. And these flows become more difficult to maintain as geographically dispersed decision centers are established. Consequently an MNC must have an effective worldwide communication system for transmitting information throughout the organization.

Multinational companies usually employ the basic organizational structures discussed in this textbook. Let us briefly examine each one:

■ *Product design:* An MNC following the product-design structure assign to a single unit the operational responsibilities for a product or product line. Product-design structure is widely used in multinational companies with diverse product lines that are being marketed in geographically dispersed areas. Such multinationals as Sperry Rand and Clark Equipment Company use this design, illustrated in Figure 21–4.

■ *Geographic design:* With this design, a multinational company groups all functional and operational responsibilities into specific geographical areas. The geographic design is used widely and by such organizations as International Telephone and Telegraph and Pfizer, which do not have highly diversified product lines. The area managers are given decentralized decision-making authority. And they coordinate practically all of the operations within their geographic areas. The geographic design is illustrated in Figure 21–5.

■ *Functional design:* For an MNC using the functional design, managers at the corporate headquarters, who report to the chief executive, are given global responsibilities for such functions as production, marketing, and financing. Each manager has the authority to plan and control worldwide operations within the function he or she manages. The functional design is

---

[12] Theodore Herbert, "Strategy and Multinational Organization Structure: An Interorganizational Relationships Perspective," *Academy of Management Review,* April 1984, pp. 259–70.

FIGURE   21–4   Product Organization Design

Used when MNCs market diverse product lines in geographically dispersed areas.

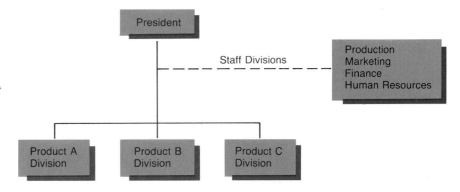

FIGURE   21–5   Geographic Organization Design

Some multinational firms group all functional and operational responsibilities into geographical areas.

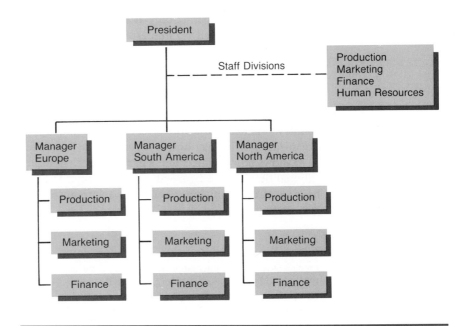

FIGURE   21–6   Functional Organization Design

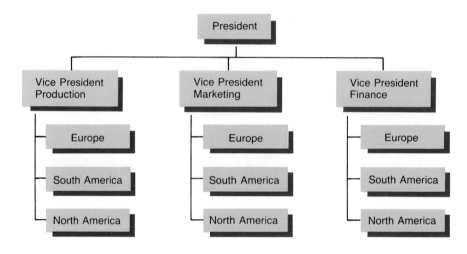

A design popular with both MNCs and domestic firms.

useful for an MNC with a very limited product line, because duplication of effort can be avoided. Extractive industries such as oil and gas often use this design, illustrated in Figure 21–6.

No organization structure is suitable in all cases, for either multinationals or companies that operate only at home. We saw in Chapter 7, that organization design is affected by numerous factors. A multinational company in a high-technology industry probably would not organize around geographic regions. More likely, it would use a functional design. A company with relatively inexperienced managers probably would not use a product design.[13]

Another factor that influences the organizing function of a multinational company is the degree to which management is home-country oriented, host-country oriented, or world oriented. How management views itself and the organization will affect how it organizes the firm in foreign countries.[14] Figure 21–7 shows how management's particular orientation can influence the organizational design. The figure also demonstrates the impact the orientation can have on decision making, control, performance evaluation, communication, and staffing.

---

[13] See J. D. Daniels, R. A. Pitts, and M. J. Tretter, "Organizing for Dual Strategies of Product Diversity and International Expansion," *Strategic Management Journal,* July–September 1985, pp. 223–39, for a study of organizational structures of 37 large U.S. multinationals.

[14] J. D. Daniels, R. A. Pitts, and M. J. Tretter, "Strategy and Structure of U.S. Multinationals: An Exploratory Study," *Academy of Management Journal,* June 1984, pp. 292–307.

FIGURE   21–7   **Management Orientation and Impact on the Organizational Design**

	Orientation		
Organizational Design Factors	*Home Country*	*Host Country*	*World*
Complexity of organization	Complex in home country, simple in subsidiaries.	Varied and independent.	Increasingly complex and interdependent.
Authority; decision making	High in headquarters.	Relatively low in headquarters.	Aim for a collaborative approach between headquarters and subsidiaries.
Evaluation and control	Home standards applied for persons and performance.	Determined locally.	Find standards that are universal and local.
Rewards and punishments; incentives	High in headquarters, low in subsidiaries.	Wide variations; can be high or low rewards for subsidiary performance.	International and local executives rewarded for reaching local and worldwide objectives.
Communication; information flow	High volume to subsidiaries; orders, commands, advice.	Little to and from headquarters, little between subsidiaries.	Both ways and between subsidiaries; heads of subsidiaries part of management team.
Staffing, recruiting, development	Recruit and develop people of home country for key positions everywhere in the world.	Develop people of local nationality for key positions in their own country.	Develop best people everywhere in the world for key positions everywhere in the world.

Source: Adapted from Howard V. Perlmutter, "The Tortuous Evolution of the Multinational Corporation," *Columbia Journal of World Business,* January–February 1969, p. 12.
Management's orientation also affects how a firm is organized in a foreign country.

The Controlling Function

Effective performance of the controlling function is extremely important in a multinational company. The more global the operation, the more difficult effective management control becomes. The concepts of preliminary control, concurrent control, and feedback control also are applicable in controlling multinational companies. However, because of cultural differences, the controlling function may not be used in some countries to the same degree it is used in the United States. For example, such things as performance appraisals and quality controls may have little meaning in certain countries.

Nevertheless, the implementation of control in the international environment requires the same three basic conditions needed domestically: standards, information, and action.

In establishing *standards* for an MNC, consideration must be given both to overall corporate objectives and to local conditions. This often involves bringing local managers into the planning process. As citizens of the country in which they work, the local managers can provide input useful in establishing standards that contribute to organizational objectives without causing intercultural conflicts.

Information must be provided that reports actual performance and permits appraisal of that performance against standards. Problems can occur here that may not appear in domestic organizations. For example, should profitability be measured in local currency or the home currency? The value of different currencies may cause headquarters to arrive at performance measures that differ from those of the local managers. Finally, the long distances between subsidiaries and headquarters can help cause too much information—or too much irrelevant information—to be fed into the MNC's communications system. Decision support systems must be designed or altered to optimize the amount of information necessary for control.

Managerial *action* to correct deviations is the final step of the controlling function. The possible actions range from total centralization of decisions—where all operating decisions are made at corporate headquarters—to a situation where international units are independent and autonomous. In the majority of cases, most actions are taken by international managers with specific guidelines from corporate headquarters. Effective managerial control of a global enterprise is extremely complex but vital to the firm's survival.

MANAGING PEOPLE IN MULTINATIONAL CORPORATIONS

Effectiveness in managing people can vary from nation to nation because motivation incentives and styles of leadership are influenced by a variety of factors. As with domestic organizations, effective management of a multinational company requires managers who understand the needs, values, and expectations of the people in the nations where the firm operates. As we noted earlier, attitudes toward work, competition in the marketplace, and authority vary greatly among cultures. Thus, leadership styles and motivation techniques that might be effective in America, Canada, Great Britain, and parts of Western Europe probably would not be effective in Mexico, Africa, Turkey, Taiwan, or South America. In other words, not only differences among cultures are great but so are the dominant needs of people in different countries.

Thousands of managers are selected each year for international assignments. These selection decisions often are critical to the success of a multinational organization. It has been found that matching environmental variables with the characteristics of individual managers is important. Several studies also have indicated that technical and managerial qualifications, social adaptability, feelings toward foreigners, and a spouse's attitude are key factors when selecting international managers. Finally, the relative importance of international operations to corporate success is an important criterion to take into account when making foreign assignments.[15]

Some multinational firms operating in foreign countries do not place host-country individuals in important managerial jobs. This is particularly true for most Japanese and European multinational companies. Other companies, however, follow a policy of filling executive positions in foreign countries with local nationals.[16] This policy overcomes objections by those who believe that outsiders will be directing the economic development of their nation. It also places in managerial positions individuals who know the local language, politics, economy, customs, and behavior patterns. The Management Focus illustrates Montedison's approach to management selection.

MANAGEMENT FOCUS
Recruiting Foreigners to Rescue Montedison

In a last-ditch effort to avert financial disaster, Italy's hard-pressed chemical giant, Montedison, imported foreign—notably American—managers. During 1982, the company went overseas to fill key jobs from strategic planning to managing the company's pharmaceuticals, dyestuffs, and oil operations—the businesses the firm hoped would bring it profitability in the future. The company's chairman, Mario Schimberni, commented: "I had to change the mentality here to a profit mentality, from one of waiting for the Italian state to bail out the company. This is a provincial welfare mentality that has built up over the past 10 years. I needed proven outside leadership in specific sectors, such as fine chemicals. I couldn't find what I needed in Italy, so I went abroad."

SUMMARY OF KEY POINTS

■ The multinational corporation (MNC) presents a critical challenge to future managers. Specifically that challenge is managing organizations, people, and operations in an international environment.

---

[15] Also see Mark Mendenhall and Gary Oddov, "The Dimensions of Expatriate Acculturation: A Review," *Academy of Management Review,* January 1985, pp. 39–47.

[16] Y. Zeira and M. Bania, "Selection of Expatriate Managers in MNCs: The Host-Environmental Point of View," *International Studies of Management and Organization,* Spring 1985, pp. 33–51.

- Most organizations become MNCs in an evolutionary manner; the decision to become an MNC is very often a gradual sequence of stages. Each stage—exporting, licensing, establishing foreign activity, direct investment—involves greater involvement in and commitment to becoming a multinational company.

- The major reasons behind the decision to become an MNC are the desire for growth, the desire for increased efficiency of operations, competitive pressures, environmental pressures, and tax and/or financial incentives.

- The environment of a multinational manager will differ in many respects from that faced domestically. Among the most important differences are culture, economics, politics, and technology.

- Cultural differences can result in differing attitudes toward the importance of work, authority, competition, introducing change, material possessions, risk taking, and profits. These attitudes can influence the effective performance of the management functions.

- Economic factors such as income levels, growth trends, inflation rates, economic planning, balance of payments, and the stability of the currency and overall economy can vary widely between nations. Each can influence organizational performance.

- It is difficult to separate politics and the MNC. The attitudes in host countries toward imports and direct investment, the stability of government, and the efficiency of government vary widely between nations. Each may change rapidly in those nations where governments change rapidly.

- Technology has affected and will continue to affect multinational companies. Often a company's technological superiority in multinational operations is the major reason for its commitment to multinational business. Technology levels also influence the sources of raw materials, energy, and transportation in a particular area.

- The management function of planning can be more complex in an MNC. The greater the cultural and language differences, the more diverse the economic, political, and legal systems. Also, the greater the number of markets and monetary systems it faces, the more complex the planning environment for an MNC.

- MNCs employ the basic organizational structures of domestic organizations: product design, geographic design, and functional design.

- Effective performance of the controlling function is extremely important in MNCs. The concepts of preliminary control, concurrent control, and feedback control are applicable in controlling MNCs.

- Because of cultural differences, the controlling function may not be used in some countries to the same degree it is used in the United States. Such techniques as performance appraisals and quality control may have little meaning in some cultures. However, the conditions for effective control, standards, information, and action are still required.

- Managing people will vary across nations because styles of leadership and motivation techniques are influenced by the needs, values, and expectations of the people in the nations in which the MNC operates. Thus, leadership styles and motivation techniques that might be effective in America may not be in other parts of the world.

- Some MNCs, especially those in Japan and Europe, follow a policy of placing no host-country individuals in important managerial positions. Others follow a policy of filling all executive positions in foreign countries with local nationals, individuals who know the local language, politics, economy, customs, and behavior patterns. This helps overcome locals' objections to outside control.

DISCUSSION AND REVIEW QUESTIONS

1. The decision to become an MNC usually is influenced by several factors. Discuss each one in detail.

2. "A firm does not become an MNC overnight." Discuss.

3. Discuss the management function of planning in a domestic versus global setting.

4. Culture, economics, politics, and technology are environmental factors that greatly influence managerial performance in an MNC. Briefly discuss the role of each.

5. "How effective an individual is in international management will be determined by how well he or she can adjust to local conditions." Discuss.

6. Do you believe that you would be effective in an overseas assignment? Explain why or why not.

7. Much is being written presently on the differences between Japanese and American approaches to managing people. Consult the business publications in your library and contrast the two approaches.

8. Would the social-responsibility aspects of managerial actions differ between domestic and international managers? Discuss.

ADDITIONAL REFERENCES

Adler, N. "Women Do Not Want International Careers: And Other Myths about International Management." *Organizational Dynamics,* Autumn 1984, pp. 66–79.

Bassing, G. R., and R. H. Dekmejian. "MNCs and the Iranian Revolution: An Empirical Study." *International Management Review* 25, no. 2 (1985), pp. 67–75.

Chang, S. K. C. "American and Chinese Managers in U.S. Companies in Taiwan: A Comparison." *California Management Review,* Summer 1985, pp. 144–56.

Galbraith, J. K. "The Defense of the Multinational Company." *Harvard Business Review,* March 1978, pp. 83–93.

Kelley, L., and R. Worthly. "The Role of Culture in Comparative Management: A Cross-Cultural Perspective." *Academy of Management Journal,* March 1981, pp. 164–73.

Negandhi, A. R; G. S. Eshghi; and E. C. Yuen. "The Management Practices of Japanese Subsidiaries Overseas." *California Management Review,* Summer, 1985, pp. 93–105.

Ouchi, W. *Theory Z: How American Business Can Meet the Japanese Challenge.* Reading, Mass.: Addison-Wesley Publishing, 1981.

Pascale, R. T., and A. G. Athos. *The Art of Japanese Management: Applications for American Executives.* New York: Simon & Schuster, 1981.

Rugman, A. M. "The Strategic Management of Canadian Multinationals: The Pulp and Paper Industry." *Multinational Business,* Spring 1985, pp. 18–26.

Schonberger, R. J. "The Transfer of Japanese Manufacturing Management Approaches to U.S. Industry." *Academy of Management Review,* July 1982, pp. 479–87.

CASES

APPLICATION I

IBM MOVES TO COUNTER THE JAPANESE

In late 1982, International Business Machines Corp. announced it would buy a 12 percent share of Intel Corp. for $250 million in cash. Many observers of the computer and semiconductor industries tried to forecast the long-run implications of the deal.

Many computer and semiconductor experts believe that the IBM–Intel arrangement signals the evolution of a strategy for meeting the Japanese challenge in high technology. They see the pact as the strongest sign yet that the U.S. high-technology sector is abandoning self-centered thinking in favor of an enlightened policy of cooperation. If this is true, the ramifications stretch far beyond the effects on IBM (the world's preeminent computer maker) and Intel (the leading independent semiconductor innovator).

The prevalent opinion is that IBM is moving to block the Japanese before they do to computers what they did to the U.S. television industry. One expert commented, "The Japanese TV makers coordinated an attack on the United States by low-bidding and undermining the structure of the suppliers that supported the industry. The same thing is happening in integrated circuits." Integrated circuits (chips) are the vital components of all computers, and Intel virtually is IBM's only outside source.

Apparently, independent semiconductor companies are running into long-term financing problems. One observer stated, "Innovation isn't paying for itself. The Japanese presence in the worldwide marketplace has upset the economics of the industry permanently." Within six to nine months after a new product is introduced, the Japanese unveil a competitive chip and cut the price. The result is the U.S. chipmakers cannot get their investment back. It appears that Intel has been hit especially hard because its traditional cash cow has been memory chips—the market segment where Japanese competition is keenest.

To forestall the undermining of U.S. chipmakers in general and Intel in particular, IBM has made its feelings known very clearly. IBM believes that semiconductor manufacturing is a key part of its future, and it is trying to ensure that its suppliers are lined up and adequately financed.

Questions for Analysis

1. What do you think of IBM's move? Discuss it in terms of what you have read in this chapter as well as in the chapter on strategic planning.

2. "If the Japanese can do it better and cheaper, it's just a matter of time until someone will buy their output. By placing barriers or enacting laws to protect American manufacturers, you are only putting off the inevitable." Comment on this statement.

APPLICATION II

WICKES GOES MULTINATIONAL

It seems that almost daily, Americans read of instances where foreign organizations take the lead in innovativeness and competitiveness in the world marketplace. This is not the case, however, with the Wickes Corporation.

Wickes is one American corporation that has identified an opportunity abroad and successfully capitalized on it. The California-based retailer has created a huge foreign market for do-it-yourself home remodeling supplies and equipment. Wickes currently has 45 home-improvement centers in England and Western Europe. Each center is very large, selling both hardware and lumber.

The stores represent one of the most successful multinational retailing ventures ever undertaken by an American retailer. In fact, this part of Wickes' business is its most profitable division. The company's 22 other divisions are comprised mostly of low-margin businesses in the United States: furniture retailing, food processing, and over 300 lumberyards and home-improvement centers. The return on investment in the foreign home-improvement centers is twice the average realized at the company's lumberyards and remodeling centers in the United States, which serve mostly contractors and builders.

Obviously Wickes intends to continue expanding into other foreign markets. And, in spite of the fact that Europe rapidly is becoming saturated with home-improvement centers, Wickes plans to construct 15 to 20 new outlets yearly with money borrowed locally. (It costs $1–2 million to open one store.)

Observers believe Wickes' strategy is a good one. Because the remodeling business is recession-proof both in the United States and abroad, the home-improvement part of Wickes' business provides a big cushion for the company's earnings in case future declines in new housing starts hurt their business with contractors.

Questions for Analysis

1. What cultural, economic, political, and technological influences might affect Wickes' business abroad?
2. The European division of Wickes has been self-financed since the early 1980s. In other words, all financing is done locally. Evaluate this policy.
3. Wickes is giving serious consideration to expanding to South America. Do you believe it can be as successful in that part of the world?

22

MANAGEMENT CAREERS

LEARNING OBJECTIVES

After completing Chapter 22, you should be able to:

■ **Define**
career in the context of occupations and professions.

■ **Describe**
the relationship between career stages and career paths.

■ **Discuss**
the concept of career effectiveness and the criteria that determine career effectiveness.

■ **Compare**
the needs of individuals and organizations in career planning.

■ **Identify**
the personal characteristics of individuals who select management as a career.

▢ MANAGEMENT IN ACTION

Does Everyone Need a Mentor to Succeed?*

Mentorship can enhance a person's career progression and development. Derived from Greek mythology, the term implies a relationship between a young adult and an older, more experienced person, or mentor. A mentor supports, guides, and counsels the younger individual learning the ropes in the organization.

One study of adult males suggests that the mentor relationship is the most important relationship in young adulthood. Companies like AT&T, Johnson & Johnson, Merrill Lynch, and Federal Express, as well as the Internal Revenue Service and the U.S. Army have implemented policies to develop mentor programs. In implementing the programs, these firms all seemed to consider five factors before moving ahead:

1. *Who should participate?*   Some of the firms believe that all incoming junior managers should automatically enter the program. Other firms have the incoming managers decide for themselves whether they want to participate.
2. *Matching the mentor and protégé.*   Interviews between the parties involved are used to determine if a match exists.
3. *Length and timing of programs.*   Most of the programs last six months. In these firms, mentors and protégés are encouraged to pursue the relationship beyond the formal six-month period.
4. *Frequency of interaction.*   A minimum of two, three, or four interactions a month are established in most programs. The participants are also encouraged to meet informally as often as they like.
5. *Mentor responsibilities.*   The mentor is expected to introduce the protégé to other key people, to the importance of company policies and programs, and to corporate culture norms and expectations.

The mentor relationship is not necessarily important for career success for all individuals. However, some have reaped major benefits from establishing or being involved in a mentor relationship. As you read this chapter and think about career paths, career planning, and career development, ask yourself whether a mentor relationship could be beneficial to your long-term success.

---

* Source: Adapted from Kathy E. Kram, *Mentoring at Work* (Glenview, Ill.: Scott, Foresman, 1985); Michael G. Zey, "Mentor Programs: Making the Right Moves," *Personnel Journal,* February 1985, pp. 53–57.

The distinction between careers *in* management and management *as* a career is more than a play on words. A career in management implies *descriptions* of *what* constitutes such careers and *where* such careers are acted out. Management as a career implies somewhat more personal issues, such as *why* one should pursue such a career, *who* should attempt such careers, and *how* an individual can increase the odds of having a successful and fulfilling career in management. This chapter explores both careers in management and management as a career.

CAREERS IN MANAGEMENT

The idea of career connotes a profession that requires training and is undertaken for life. It also brings to mind the idea of moving upward in one's chosen line of work: commanding larger salaries, assuming more responsibility, and acquiring more status, prestige, and power.

For our purposes, *"The career is the individually perceived sequence of attitudes and behaviors associated with work-related experiences and activities over the span of the person's life."*[1] This definition implies that (1) a career consists of both attitudes and behaviors, (2) it is an ongoing sequence of work-related activities, and (3) it is clearly work related. Nevertheless, a person's nonwork life and roles play significant parts in it. For example, a midcareer manager, 50 years old, can have quite different attitudes about a job advancement involving greater responsibilities than a manager nearing retirement. A bachelor's reaction to a promotion involving relocation is likely to be different from that of a father of school-age children.

If a career requires someone to neglect nonwork factors, it may be detrimental to the person's health and overall quality of life. The Management Focus on "Careers and Workaholism" raises some concerns that should be evaluated by people making career decisions.

MANAGEMENT FOCUS
Careers and Workaholism: A Relationship of Concern

Marilyn Machlowitz has studied, written about, and consulted in the area of career management. She expresses some interesting ideas in her various books and lectures of the topic. Dr. Machlowitz believes that "none of us have any idea of what career means when we're growing up." After people decide on a career, they

---

[1] Douglas T. Hall, *Careers in Organizations* (Santa Monica, Calif.: Goodyear Publishing, 1976), p. 4.

MANAGEMENT FOCUS (*continued*)

usually spend between six and eight years getting settled in. Once they've reached this stage, they often become apprehensive. There is a lot of anxiety about whether the right career choice was made in the first place.

How people compensate for their career anxieties is an indicator of the amount of control they want over their lives. One way some of us exercise control is by becoming a workaholic. That is, we work long hours, always think about the job, and neglect family, friends, and ourselves in the process. The workaholic is looking for a way to exercise power over career activities.

The notion of workaholism is interesting when it is related to the notion of a career. Is it necessary to be a workaholic to be successful? If the job demands more than you have to give in terms of competence or energy, it may require you to become a workaholic. However, if you focus on the job because of an inner drive, guilt, personal/family problems, and the like, then it is totally within your ability to minimize the tendency to be a workaholic. In the first case, not having the competence may mean that the person is in a position not suited for his or her talents. In the second case, the person is making a conscious effort to be a workaholic.

At this point, we don't know for sure if being a workaholic is hazardous to a person's health. Related research suggests that only focusing on one aspect of life—the job—can result over the long haul in negative emotional, physical, or behavioral reactions. In choosing, assessing, or reviewing a career, it is important to think about what you must give and give up to be successful. To do this effectively, think about what it means to be a workaholic, your strengths, your weaknesses, and your career goals. This kind of self-assessment can help avoid some of the pitfalls of being misplaced in a career not suited for your personality, skills, energy level, and goals.

Source: Adapted from George A. Milite, "Careers," *Management Review,* September 1985, p. 57.

Career Effectiveness

Career effectiveness in organizational settings is judged not only by the individual but by the organization itself. But what is meant by *career effectiveness?* Under what circumstances will individuals state that they have had "successful" or "satisfying" careers? And will the organization share the individuals' views about their careers? Of the numerous criteria of career effectiveness, four are often cited. They are performance, attitude, adaptability, and identity.[2]

Performance.   Salary and position are the usual indicators of career performance. Specifically, the more rapidly one's salary increases and one advances up the hierarchy, the higher the level of career performance. As one advances (is promoted), responsibilities become greater in terms of employees supervised, budget allocated, and revenue generated. The organization is vitally interested in career performance, since it bears a direct relation to goal attainment. That is, salary and position in most instances reflect the extent of an individual's contribution to attainment of the organization's objectives.

Two obstacles sometimes hinder accurate appraisal of career effectiveness. First, an organization may fail to recognize performance fully. Thus, employees may not be rewarded with salary increases and promotions. Second, the organization's expectations for an individual may not match the individual's goals or abilities. The organization may accurately assess the individual's potential for greater performance, yet the individual's noncareer interests, such as family, community, or religion, might prevent optimal job performance. In such instances, the individual may be satisfied with career performance, yet the organization is disappointed. This mismatch results from the individual's *attitudes* toward the career.

Attitudes.   This aspect of career effectiveness refers to the way individuals perceive and evaluate their careers. The more positive these perceptions and evaluations are, the more effective the careers are. Individuals with positive attitudes are more likely to be committed to the organization and interested in their jobs.

Adaptability.   Few professions are stagnant. On the contrary, change and development are much more common in contemporary professions, and change requires new knowledge and skills. For example, medicine and engineering have and will continue to use new information and technology. Individuals unable to *adapt* to these changes and to *adopt* them in their careers run the risk of early obsolescence. Career adaptability, therefore, means application of the latest knowledge, skill, and technology in a career.

Identity.   Two important components comprise career identity: (1) the extent to which individuals are aware of their interests, values, and expectations; (2) the manner in which individuals view their lives, the extent to which they see themselves as extensions of their pasts. The important question is, "What do I want to be, and what do I have to do to become what I want

---

[2] The discussion of these criteria is based on ibid., pp. 93–96.

to be?"[3] Individuals who find satisfactory answers to this question are likely to have effective careers and to make effective contributions to their organizations.

Effective careers in management are likely for individuals with high levels of performance, positive attitudes, adaptiveness, and identity resolution. These criteria are not unique to management. They apply to all careers.

Career Stages

Individuals go through distinct but interrelated stages in their careers. The simplest version would include four stages:

1. Prework stage: attending school.
2. Initial work stage: moving from job to job.
3. Stable work stage: maintaining one job.
4. Retirement stage: leaving active employment.

Most working people prepare for their occupation by undergoing some form of organized education in high school, trade school, vocational school, or college. They take a first job, but chances are they will move to other jobs in the same or other organizations. Eventually they settle into a position in which they remain until retirement. The duration of each stage varies among individuals, but everyone generally goes through them.

Studies have found that needs and expectations change as the individual moves through the career stages.[4] Managers in American Telephone & Telegraph (AT&T) expressed considerable concern for security needs during the first years on their jobs. This stage, called the *establishment* stage, ordinarily lasts during the first five years of employment. Next the *advancement* stage occurs, approximately between age 30 and age 45. During this period, the AT&T managers expressed considerably less concern for security needs satisfaction and more concern for achievement, esteem, and autonomy. Promotions and advancement to jobs with responsibility and opportunity to exercise independent judgment are characteristics of this stage.

After the advancement stage comes the *maintenance* phase, a period marked by efforts to stabilize the gains of the past. In some respects, this stage is a plateau—no new gains are made. Yet it can be a period of creativity, since the individual has satisfied many of the earlier psychological and financial needs. Although individuals and careers vary, esteem and self-actualization

---

[3] Erik H. Erikson, "The Concept of Identity in Race Relations: Notes and Queries," *Daedalus* 95 (1966), p. 148, as cited in Hall, *Careers,* p. 95.

[4] Douglas T. Hall and Khalil Nougaim, "An Examination of Maslow's Need Hierarchy in an Organizational Setting," *Organizational Behavior and Human Performance* 3 (1968), pp. 12–35; Raymond E. Hill and Edwin L. Miller, "Job Change and the Middle Seasons of a Man's Life," *Academy of Management Journal,* March 1981, pp. 114–27.

tend to be the most important needs in the maintenance stage. Many people experience a midcareer crisis during this stage, which signals problems encountered in achieving satisfaction from their work.[5]

The maintenance stage is followed by the *retirement* stage. The individual has completed one career and may move on to another one. A retiree experiences self-actualization through activities that were impossible to pursue while working. Painting, gardening, volunteer service, and quiet reflection are some of the many possibilities. But depending on the individual's financial and health status, the retirement years can be spent satisfying security and physiological needs.

These four career stages are generally applicable and have been studied in a variety of settings. One recent study of "knowledge" workers raised some interesting issues about career stages and career effectiveness.[6]

The fastest growing segment of the work force are knowledge workers—professionals such as accountants, scientists, and engineers. These professionals spend their careers in large, complex organizations after having spent several years obtaining advanced training and degrees. Organizations that employ them expect them to provide the innovativeness and creativity necessary to survive in dynamic and competitive environments. Obviously the performance levels of professional employees must be of the utmost concern for the organizations' leaders.

Effective management of professionals begins with understanding the crucial characteristics of the four stages of professional careers. Professional employees could avoid some disappointments and anxieties if they also understood more about their career stages:

Stage I. Young professionals enter an organization with technical knowledge but not with understanding of the organization's demands and expectations. Consequently they must work closely with more experienced persons. The relationship that develops between the young professionals and their supervisors is an *apprenticeship.* The central activities expected of apprentices include *learning* and *following directions.* To move successfully and effectively through Stage I, professionals must be able to accept the *psychological state of dependence.* Some professionals cannot cope with a situation similar to school; and during apprenticeship, they are directed by an authority figure, just as they were in school. Often people anticipate considerably more freedom

---

[5] Abraham K. Korman, Ursula Wittig-Berman, and Dorothy Lang, "Career Success and Personal Failure: Alienation in Professionals and Managers," *Academy of Management Journal,* June 1981, pp. 342–60; John Veiga, "Plateaued versus Non-Plateaued Managers: Career Patterns, Attitudes and Path Potential," *Academy of Management Journal,* September 1981, pp. 566–78.

[6] The following discussion is primarily based on Gene W. Dalton, Paul H. Thompson, and Raymond L. Price, "The Four Stages of Professional Careers—A New Look at Performance by Professionals," *Organizational Dynamics,* Summer 1977, pp. 19–42.

from their first job. Those who do not cope successfully can compromise their careers.

Stage II.   Once through the dependency of Stage I, the professional employee moves into a stage that calls for working independently. Passage to this stage depends upon proven competence in some specific technical area. The technical expertise may be in a content area such as taxation, product testing, or quality assurance, or it may be in a skill area such as computer applications. The professional's primary activity in Stage II is to be an *independent contributor* of ideas in the chosen area. The professional is expected to rely much less on direction from others. The *psychological state of independence* may pose some problems because it is in such stark contrast to the dependence required in Stage I. Stage II is extremely important for the professional's future career growth. Those who fail do so because they either do not have the requisite technical skill to perform independently or lack the self-confidence to do so.

Stage III.   Professionals in Stage III are expected to become the mentors of those in Stage I. They also tend to broaden their interests and to deal more and more with people outside the organization. Thus, the central activities of professionals in this stage are *training* and *interactions* with others. They assume *responsibility for the work of others,* and this characteristic of the stage can cause considerable psychological stress. An individual who cannot cope with this new and different requirement may decide to shift back to Stage II. Others may be satisfied seeing some of their peers move on to bigger and better jobs. They are content to remain in Stage III until retirement.

As the opening Management In Action suggests, the mentoring relationship has significant potential to enhance the development of individuals. Another area that can enhance the career development of individuals in Stage III is referred to as peer relationship development. Kram and Isabella examined the nature of supportive and significant peer relationships at early, middle, and late career stages in a large manufacturing company.[7] The researchers interviewed 15 male and female managers. The analysis of the interview data indicated that a continuum of peer relationships exists. The relationships were classified as information peer (information sharing), collegial peer (job-related feedback, friendship), and special peer (emotional support, confirmation).

The three types of peer relationships seem to be perceived somewhat differently by individuals at different career stages. For example, concerns about competence and professional identity often characterize the developmental needs of a person such as an engineer or an accountant at the initial, or

---

[7] Kathy E. Kram and Lynn A. Isabella, "Mentoring Alternatives: The Role of Peer Relationships in Career Development," *Academy of Management Journal,* March 1985, pp. 110–32.

establishment, stage. Individuals in their 20s use information peers to learn the ropes on how to get the job done, they use collegial peers to help define their professional role, and they use special peers to acquire a sense of competence and to help manage the stresses and anxieties of work and developing families.

Kram and Isabella's interesting study suggests that peer relationships can be an adjunct to or used instead of a mentor relationship to support individual career development. For individuals without a mentor, peers can be a valuable source of help, support, and encouragement. It would be interesting to examine peer relationships in other than manufacturing settings. Would such relationships be able to mature in rapidly changing environments such as those found in high-tech industries?

Stage IV.   Some professional employees remain in Stage III, while others progress to stage IV that involves *shaping the direction of the organization itself.* Although we usually think of this as the job of one individual (the chief executive), it may in fact be undertaken by many others. For example, key personnel in product development, process manufacturing, or technological research may be Stage IV types. As a consequence of their performance in Stage III of their careers, Stage IV professionals direct their attention to long-range strategic planning. In doing so, they play the roles of manager, entrepreneur, and idea generator. Their primary duties are to *identify* and *sponsor* the careers of their successors and to interact with key people outside the organization. The most significant shift for a person in Stage IV is to accept the decisions of subordinates without second-guessing them. Stage IV professionals must learn to influence (that is, practice leadership) through such indirect methods as idea planning, personnel selection, and organization design. These shifts can be difficult for one who has relied upon direct supervision in the past.

Career Paths

A career path is the sequence of jobs a person holds during a career. To the organization, career paths are important for human resource planning. An organization's future human resource needs depend upon the projected passage of individuals along the paths. From the individual's perspective, a career path is the sequence of jobs that can lead to achieving personal and career goals. It is virtually impossible to integrate completely the needs of both the organization and the individual in the design of career paths, yet systematic career planning has the potential for closing the gap.

In the traditional sense, career paths emphasize upward mobility in a single occupation or functional area. When recruiting personnel, the organization's representative will speak of engineers', accountants', or sales' career paths. In these contexts, the recruiter will describe the different jobs typical individuals will hold as they work progressively upward in an organization. Each job, or rung, is reached when the individual has accumulated the necessary experience and ability and has demonstrated a readiness for promotion.

Implicit in the concept of career paths is the attitude that failure results whenever an individual does not move up. This makes it difficult to use lateral and downward transfers as alternatives for managers who no longer wish to pay the price of upward promotion.

An alternative to traditional career paths is to base career progression on real-world experience and individualized preferences. Such paths would have several characteristics:[8]

1. They would include lateral and downward as well as upward possibilities not tied to "normal" rates of progress.[9]
2. They would be tentative and responsive to changes in an organization's needs.
3. They would be flexible enough to take into account the qualities of individuals.
4. Each job along the path would be specified in terms of acquirable skills, knowledge, and other specific attributes, not merely educational credentials, age, or work experience.

An example of a career path for general management in a telephone company is depicted in Figure 22–1. According to the path, the average duration of a first-level management assignment is four years. It consists of two and a half years as a staff assistant in the home office and one and a half years as the manager of a district office in a small city. By the 14th year, the average manager should have reached the fourth level of management. At this level, the assignment might be that of division manager of the commercial sales and operations division. Obviously, few managers reach the fifth level, much less the seventh (president). The number of openings declines and the number of candidates increases as one nears the top of the organization.

The performance of businesses, universities, hospitals, indeed all organizations depends on the effectiveness of managers. Their careers, similar to those in any occupation, follow the same general stages along appropriate career paths, although there is no single correct path to a successful management career.

The career progression presented in Figure 22–1 indicates that a person steps up the ladder, one rung at a time. In reality, not everyone can step up each rung of the ladder. Thus, it is important to recognize the concept of career plateauing. A plateau is defined as the point in a career when the

---

[8] James W. Walker, "Let's Get Realistic about Career Paths," *Human Resource Management,* Fall 1976, pp. 2–7.

[9] Douglas T. Hall and Lynn A. Isabella, "Downward Movement and Career Development," *Organizational Dynamics,* Summer 1985, pp. 5–23.

FIGURE   22–1   Career Path, General Management

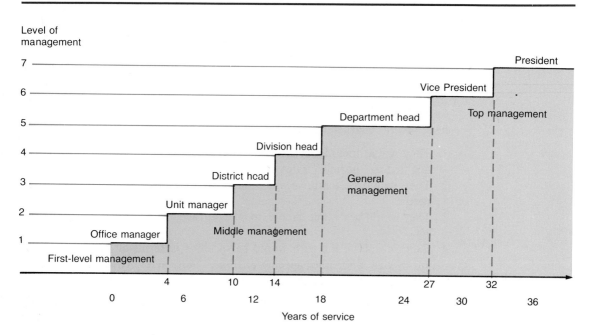

Most jobs are stepping stones to other, more demanding positions.

---

likelihood of further movement up the ladder is very low.[10] It becomes the final point of ascension in a person's career.

Figure 22–2 illustrates four categories of workers. "Comers" are individuals with high potential for advancement. "Stars" are the high performers who are likely to be promoted again and again. The "deadwood" are individuals with limited potential for advancement who are performing below expected norms. "Solid citizens" are high performers who are not likely to be promoted.

A research study of salespersons in two companies examined the issue of career plateaus and how individuals responded to such a situation.[11] It was found that the business strategy of the company had a significant effect on the incidence of plateauing and on the performance of the plateaued salesperson. One firm was in a mature industry and had a modest growth

---

[10] Douglas T. Hall, "Career Plateauing and Subidentity Change in Midcareer," in *Organizational Career Development*, ed. Douglas Hall (San Francisco: Jossey-Bass, 1986).

[11] John W. Slocum, Jr., William L. Cron, Richard W. Hansen, and Sallie Rawlings, "Business Strategy and the Management of Plateaued Employees," *Academy of Management Journal*, March 1985, pp. 133–54.

FIGURE   22-2   A Career Plateau Model

Performance Level	Likelihood of Future Promotion	
	Low	High
High	Solid citizens (effectively plateaued)	Stars (not plateaued)
Low	Deadwood (ineffectively plateaued)	Comers (not plateaued)

Source: Based on T. P. Ference, J. A. Stoner, and K. E. Warren, "Managing the Career Plateau," *Management Review*, October 1977, p. 603.

rate. The other firm was in a declining industry, and management paid attention to improving efficiency. The results indicated significantly more plateaued salespersons in the second company. This study introduces the possibility that the incidence of career plateauing may be significantly linked to the business strategy used by the firm.

MANAGEMENT AS A CAREER

An individual striking out on a career has a vital interest in doing everything possible to make an informed job decision. Initial choices are reversible but not without some costs—lost time being the most obvious.[12] Although it is impossible to know at age 20 or so what one's interests, values, abilities, and needs will be when age 40, there are some things to consider. For example, the reader should have a fair idea at this point of what managers do and are expected to do.

Generally we know that managers are called upon to manage work, people, and operations. They are expected to plan, organize, and control individuals, groups, and organizations. They are expected to motivate people and groups, to provide leadership and to sense, recognize, and provide for change. They are expected to use information to make decisions that either directly or indirectly affect efficient production and operations. Each of these aspects of managerial work has been presented in this book's three approaches to management, reviewed here.

---

[12] Meryl Reis Louis, "Managing Career Transition: A Missing Link in Career Development," *Organizational Dynamics,* Spring 1982, pp. 68–77.

Managing Work and Organizations

The managerial issues associated with managing work and organizations are the focus of the classical approach. Planning, organizing, and controlling organizations were the first issues examined by management theorists and practitioners. Scientific management and classical organization theory made significant contributions that are now taken for granted in management practice, such as the principles of work measurement and simplification, principles of planning and organization, and basic control techniques.

Managing People

The behavioral approach unites the ideas of the social and behavioral sciences and tests their applicability to management. Managing people to achieve effective levels of individual and group performance demands knowledge of individual differences, motivation, leadership, and group dynamics. Managing people is the most challenging and difficult aspect of the manager's job. People are unique; and while theories of motivation may be able to predict the behavior of most of the people most of the time, they cannot be counted on to predict what an individual will do in a specific situation. The art of management is to know the limitations of theory and to modify predictions when necessary.

Managing Production and Operations

All organizations exist to achieve results, whether producing goods or providing services. The process of acquiring and combining the physical and human resources to achieve the intended results is the production and operations function. The management science approach—with the aid of mathematics, statistics, and computers—has made great strides in providing models that achieve effective and efficient performance of the production and operations function.

Management is an applied discipline. Unlike medicine and engineering, there is no science of management per se. Instead management takes theories and concepts from all relevant sciences. Thus, effective managerial performance results from choosing appropriate theory and technique for a particular problem or situation that arises in the manager's job.

Understanding the job of a manager, we can attempt to answer some questions about careers in management. Who should pursue a career in management? What are the characteristics needed to achieve career effectiveness as managers? How does one who has these characteristics plan a management career?

WHO SHOULD PURSUE MANAGEMENT AS A CAREER?

The trait theory of leadership does not provide precise answers to the question of who will become a leader. The same can be said of the question "Who will achieve an effective career in management?"

There is little doubt that the demand for good managers will increase during the next decade. In fact, there is evidence that the demand for good managers will exceed the supply. Many top-paying managerial jobs go unfilled because:

1. During periods of economic recession in the 1970s, companies cut back the number of executive positions and have only recently begun to reopen them.
2. The turnover has increased as executives moved to new positions or left the executive ranks for other pursuits.
3. Additional management positions have been created in response to increasing governmental regulations.
4. Chief executives nearing retirement age believe that the middle-management talent presently on board is not capable of more responsible positions.
5. Few people are willing to assume the personal costs associated with more responsible positions and choose to remain where they are rather than move up the management ladder.
6. Those people who do desire to move up simply do not know how to go about searching for the opportunities.

The disparity between executive openings and available talent has several implications. Organizations must become more proficient in managing the careers of their employees. Personnel planning coupled with career development programs could ease the problem. Equally important, individuals who aspire to reach the executive suite must take greater personal responsibility for planning their own careers. Opportunities for executive positions are available, but they will go to those who prepare for them. Preparation for a management career begins with personal assessment.

In specific situations, the supply of managerial talent can exceed the demand. In periods of economic decline, opportunities for promotion also decline. Organizations confronting these situations must remedy the problems of frustrated ambitions.

Characteristics of Effective Managers

What traits make a manager effective? We cannot make perfect predictions about who will achieve career effectiveness in management, but it is possible to outline some considerations.

The will to manage.   The desire or need to influence the performance of others and the satisfaction derived from doing so is termed the "will to manage."[13] The fundamental characteristic of management is that managers achieve results through other people and that the setting for managerial work is an organization. Those who have studied the will to manage correlate it with several attitudes:[14] favorable attitude toward authority, desire to compete, assertiveness, desire to exercise power, desire to stand out from others in the group, and sense of responsibility.

John Miner devised questionnaires that measure the strength of these attitudes and found that individuals who score relatively high on each item are likely to select management as a career and are likely to achieve career effectiveness. One of his more important findings is that students' will to manage (as measured by the questionnaire) declined throughout the 1970s from the level of the 1960s. Miner predicts that this shift will contribute to the shortage of managerial talent during the 1980s. Thus, if Miner's ideas are correct, an individual who has a strong will to manage should have a competitive edge in pursuing a managerial career.

Some evidence suggests that the will to manage can be strengthened through training. In one study of 116 college leaders at a major university, scores on the will-to-manage questionnaire increased in one group that underwent training. Scores of the comparison group, student leaders who did not take the training courses, remained unchanged during the study.[15] Similar studies of practicing managers also indicate that the will to manage can be developed.[16]

Supervisory ability.   Supervisory ability is an important variable that distinguishes effective and ineffective managers.[17] Effective management involves utilizing the correct supervisory tactics required in a particular situation. The ability to use appropriate supervisory practices implies a contingency orientation toward management. Effective managers recognize and apply the relevant elements from each of the approaches of management, are responsive to changing social and economic conditions, and can motivate people.[18] As we have noted through this text, each approach to management contributes

---

[13] Sterling Livingston, "Myth of the Well-Educated Manager," *Harvard Business Review,* January–February 1971, pp. 79–89; John B. Miner, *The Challenge of Managing* (Philadelphia: W. B. Saunders, 1975), p. 276.

[14] Miner, *Challenge,* pp. 220–23.

[15] Timothy M. Singleton, "Managerial Motivation Development: A Study of College Student Leaders," *Academy of Management Journal,* September 1978, pp. 493–98.

[16] Miner, *Challenge,* p. 296.

[17] Edwin E. Ghiselli, *Exploration in Managerial Talent* (Santa Monica, Calif.: Goodyear Publishing, 1971).

[18] Lawrence A. Armour, ed., *Managing to Succeed: Success Stories from The Wall Street Journal* (Homewood, Ill.: Dow Jones-Irwin, 1979).

to the body of management thought and practice. Effective careers in management are related to the ability to select the appropriate idea for the situation.

Ability to assess potential for effective management career. Individuals can use personal initiative to discern whether they really want and are able to have a career in management. Both Miner and Edwin Ghiselli have devised measurements of will to manage and supervisory ability. With the assistance of a counseling professional, individuals can reach some tentative understanding of their potential. However, our knowledge of which variables predict managerial success is quite incomplete. Moreover, the measurements of those variables are not totally valid.[19] The emphasis should be on *tentative* understanding of whether one *wants* to manage and *has* or *can develop* the ability to manage. The confrontation of these two issues is a first step in career planning.

Career Planning

Career planning involves matching an individual's career aspirations with the opportunities available in an organization. Career pathing is the sequencing of specific jobs associated with those opportunities. The two processes are intertwined. Planning a career requires identifying the activities and experiences needed to accomplish career goals. Career path considerations include the sequence of jobs that results in reaching these career goals. Although still a relatively new practice, many organizations are turning to career planning as a way to *proact* rather than *react* to problems associated with ineffective managerial careers. Some employers are using career planning at the blue-collar level, as the following Management Focus on Lockheed Marine emphasizes.

MANAGEMENT FOCUS
Lockheed Marine Brings Career Planning to Blue-Collar Employees

At Lockheed Marine, a Lockheed Corporation subsidiary located in Seattle, the impetus for designing career planning programs stemmed from a need to improve productivity. The success of career planning for white-collar employees has been well documented, but

---

[19] See Arthur P. Brief, Ramon J. Aldag, and Thomas I. Chacko, "The Miner Sentence Completion Scale: An Appraisal," *Academy of Management Journal,* December 1977, pp. 635–43.

MANAGEMENT FOCUS (*continued*)

little has been written about it for blue-collar employees. At Lockheed, there are 11 unions to which craftworkers belong. Membership assures them of apprenticeship training and a position on seniority lists. A switch in careers, therefore, would require a large personal investment in terms of job security, training, and wages. A second consideration is the well-established career paths that exist within the skilled trades. A typical career ladder might progress from apprenticeship to journeyman and then to leader, supervisor, and superintendent. Variations from this pattern are rare.

Because of lagging productivity, a main objective of Lockheed Marine's career planning program was to match the right person to the right job. A major part of the program involved career/life planning classes that are conducted throughout the year. The classes are open to all employees and are held half on company time and half on employee time. Small-group interaction, personal inventories, films, and lectures typify the classes.

Another component of the program is the career resource center, which contains more than 200 books ranging from technical manuals to occupational literature and time management workbooks. Off-site seminars on personal financial planning and investment, positive parenting, coping with life transitions, and stress management are available for employees and their families. The emphasis here is to make a special effort to help employees improve their self-awareness, self-concept, and knowledge of factors that influence their career progression and satisfaction.

The effectiveness of Lockheed Marine's program has been evaluated in terms of participant morale, satisfaction, and performance. The results indicate overwhelming success. Also, approximately 50 percent of the program participants were promoted to positions of greater responsibility. Lockheed is satisfied that its blue-collar career planning and development investment has paid off in terms of a more motivated and productive work force.

Source: Adapted from Mary Russell, "Career Planning in a Blue-Collar Company," *Training and Development Journal*, January 1984, pp. 87–88.

The career planning and pathing process is described in Figure 22–3. Successful practice places equal responsibility on the individual and the organization. Individuals must identify their aspirations and abilities and, through counseling, recognize the training and development required for a particular career path. Organizations must identify their needs and opportunities and,

FIGURE   22–3   A Career Planning Process

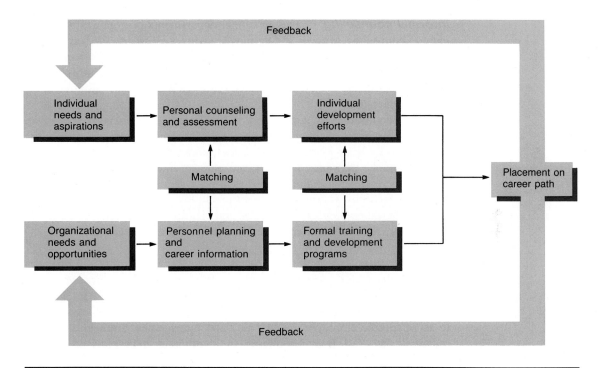

Effective career planning satisfies the needs of both the individual and the organization.

through personnel planning, provide career information and training to their employees. Career planning cannot proceed unless information about career paths, expected vacancies, and position requirements is available to employees.[20]

Companies such as Weyerhaeuser, Nabisco, Gulf Oil, Exxon, and Eaton use career development programs to identify a broad pool of talent available for promotion and transfer opportunities. Career counseling is often restricted to managerial and professional staff, but IBM, General Electric, TRW, and Gulf provide career counseling for blue-collar as well as managerial personnel.

Matching individual and organizational needs can be done through a variety of personnel practices. A recent American Management Association survey revealed that the most widely used practices are (1) informal counseling by the personnel staff and (2) career counseling by supervisors. These two

---

[20] Kenneth B. McRae, "Career-Management Planning: A Boon to Managers and Employees," *Personnel,* May 1985, pp. 56–60.

approaches are often quite informal. Less common, somewhat more formal practices involve workshops, seminars, and self-assessment centers.

Informal counseling.   The personnel departments of organizations often include counseling services for employees who wish to assess their abilities and interests. Counseling that moves into personal matters is acceptable if these matters are important in determining career effectiveness. In this context, organizations tend to view career counseling as a service to employees, but not a primary one.

Career counseling by supervisors is usually included in performance appraisals. The question of where the employee is going in the organization quite naturally arises in this setting. In fact, the inclusion of career information in performance appraisal predates the current interest in career planning. Effective performance evaluation, by definition, lets the employees know how well they have done and what the future holds. Thus, supervisors must be able to counsel employees in terms of organizational needs and opportunities both in a specific department and throughout the organization.

Formal counseling.   Since supervisors usually have limited information about the overall organization, more formal, systematic counseling approaches are often adopted. Workshops, assessment centers, and career development centers are increasingly used. Typically such formal practices are designed to serve specific employee groups. To date, management trainees and "high potential" or "fast track" management candidates have received most of the attention. However, women and minority employees are increasingly benefiting from programs, a trend that reflects organizations' commitment to affirmative action.

An example of how one organization has implemented a formal career planning system is Syntex Corporation's Career Development Center. The center's staff first assesses the individual's strengths and weaknesses in the eight skills Syntex believes are most related to effective management: (1) problem analysis, (2) communication, (3) setting objectives, (4) decision making and handling conflict, (5) selecting, training, and motivating employees, (6) controlling employees, (7) interpersonal competence, and (8) use of time. On the basis of scores in the eight areas, each manager sets career and personal goals with assistance from the center's staff.

Each manager's career planning effort is highlighted by a weeklong seminar. Usually attended by 24 managers, the seminar places each manager in simulated situations that require applications of the eight skill areas. Candidates participate in the simulations, then review their own career plans. The purpose of the seminar is to encourage realistic self-appraisal. Afterward participants meet with their immediate supervisors to set up their career development plans.

There are also professional career counselors outside the organization. The Management Focus on professional counseling discusses this.

MANAGEMENT FOCUS
Getting Professional Career Counseling Help

Life used to be simpler than today. People picked the careers their parents expected them to or went to whatever job was available. Once employed, most people stuck to their careers; in fact, few had the luxury of considering a change. They patiently waited for a few moves up the corporate ladder, supported their families, and collected a gold watch upon retirement. Many people still follow this career course. But for millions of others, life is more complex.

Many people decide that they may be in the wrong career—that they would be better satisfied or more creative in a different one. When people become euphoric at 4 P.M. on Friday and depressed because it's Sunday evening and they have to go to work tomorrow, it says something about their feelings about the job. To help these people, there are professional career counselors who charge fees that can range from less than $100 to several thousand dollars. The career counseling field, because of the demand for the service, has attracted some excellent professionals but has drawn others who have dubious credentials.

People in their 40s become conscious that all of their young dreams are not going to come true. Career counselors seem to be seeing an increasing number of clients in that age that are troubled by what is called "midlife crisis." Some want to confirm that they are in the right field; others believe that a career shift will solve their problems. For any person to try a new career at 30 or 40 is a difficult task. It takes a lot of courage to look at yourself, your career, dreams, and goals and decide to make a shift. It is a lot easier to stay put and do the best you can.

Cindy Erb of Catalyst, a nonprofit career counseling and information agency in New York, states that career counseling is not a magical process where perfect solutions to problems are hatched at every session. Instead she asks clients to remember that career counseling is a guidance process that asks the clients to look at their lives and goals, then to find out how their particular skill strengths fit into accomplishing their goals.

Most qualified professional career counselors use discussions, tests, surveys, life inventories, and other assessment tools to get people to look at themselves and to indicate strengths and weaknesses. Then comes the process of offering interpretation of results, a guiding hand, and support to clients. If individuals prefer to not have management know that they are questioning present career situations, then a reputable outside professional career counselor may be a good idea.

Adapted from Berkeley Rice, "Why Am I in This Job?" *Psychology Today*, January 1985, pp. 54–59.

Other personnel practices.   Organizations can use a variety of personnel practices to facilitate their employees' career plans. One of the oldest, most widely used practices is some form of the *tuition aid program.* Employees can enroll in educational and training courses available at nearby schools, and the organization pays all or part of the tuition. J. I. Case, a Tenneco Company with corporate offices in Racine, Wisconsin, is one of many organizations that provide in-house courses and seminars, plus tuition reimbursement for courses related to the individual's job.

Another practice is *job posting.* The organization publicizes job openings to employees. This requires more than simply placing a notice on the company's bulletin board. At minimum, effective job posting should meet the following conditions:[21]

1. Posting should include promotions and transfers as well as permanent vacancies.
2. Available jobs should be posted at least three to six weeks prior to external recruiting.
3. Eligibility rules should be explicit and straightforward.
4. Standards for selection and bidding instructions should be stated clearly.
5. Vacationing employees should be given the opportunity to apply ahead of time.
6. Employees who apply but are rejected should be notified in writing and a record of the reason should be placed in their personnel files.

Whatever counseling approach is used, the crucial element of its success will be the extent to which *individual and organizational* needs are satisfied.

Career planning benefits.   Career planning is becoming more widespread in organizations. Individuals who wish to make formal career plans should seek out those organizations that have demonstrated a commitment to career planning.

From the organization's perspective, who is most likely to benefit from career planning? Although this question has only been recently raised, it appears that some individuals gain little from the process. Recent studies, for example, indicate that career planning is most effective for people who have relatively high needs for growth and achievement, the skill to carry out their career plans, and a past history of career successes.[22] These results should not be interpreted to mean that career planning is for the select few. Much more needs to be known about the issue before conclusions are drawn.

---

[21] David R. Dahl and Patrick R. Pinto, "Job Posting: An Industry Survey," *Personnel Journal,* January 1977, pp. 40–42.

[22] Sam Gould, "Characteristics of Career Planners in Upwardly Mobile Occupations," *Academy of Management Journal,* September 1979, pp. 539–50; John B. Miner and Donald P. Crane, "Motivation to Manage and the Manifestation of a Managerial Orientation in Career Planning," *Academy of Management Journal,* September 1981, pp. 626–33.

But the findings do indicate that organizations should try to identify people who are most likely to take advantage of career planning programs.[23]

Individuals need not rely on company-sponsored programs, however. Nothing except lack of initiative prevents any of us from using our own resources to answer the key questions:

1. Do I want to be a manager?
2. Do I have the ability to be a manager?
3. How do I go about having an effective career in management?

SUMMARY OF KEY POINTS

- Management can be a challenging, rewarding career for those who have the knowledge, skills, attitudes, values, and opportunity to pursue it. Career effectiveness implies that one's performance, attitude, adaptability, and identity resolution are satisfying to both the organization and the individual.

- As a career, management progresses through stages that are more or less typical of all occupations. Career paths tend to be specific to individual organizations.

- Each career stage involves both career and personal demands. Both opportunities and problems arise when one's career and one's personal life conflict.

- Individuals desiring a career in management should be encouraged to plan their careers. Career plans are tentative by nature, but they force individuals to consider their own strengths and weaknesses.

- Two factors are essential in management: Does one really want to manage (will to manage), and does the person have or can the person develop the ability to manage (supervisory ability).

- More and more organizations are providing some form of career counseling and development to their employees.

- The potential for effective managerial careers is crucial. Failure to recognize and develop managerial talent will almost certainly affect an organization's performance adversely throughout the 1980s.

DISCUSSION AND REVIEW QUESTIONS

1. Define and explain your personal concept of *career.* Is the concept, as you define it, applicable only to those who are gainfully employed? In the explanation, compare your concept of career with the one used in the chapter discussion.

---

[23] Mary Ann Von Glinow, Michael J. Driver, Kenneth Brousseau, J. Bruce Prince, "The Design of a Career-Oriented Human Resource System," *Academy of Management Review,* January 1983, pp. 23–32.

2. Explain the interrelationships between life and career stages. If there are interrelationships, do they imply that we cannot or should not attempt to compartmentalize our lives into career and noncareer purposes and activities? Explain.

3. What information would you like to have if a prospective employer asked you to prepare a brief statement of career aims. What are the sources of such information? Do you presently have this information? Why or why not?

4. How would a person know if his or her career had plateaued?

5. To what extent are you willing to relocate to achieve greater career effectiveness? If you are relatively unwilling to relocate, what personal factors account for that reluctance, and what are the implications for your career goals?

6. How can you discover career paths in a particular organization? Is this the kind of information you would want to receive when you interview for a job? What questions would you ask to get this information?

7. What is the value of a mentor relationship (see the Management in Action) to an organization?

8. What are some of the differences between peer and mentor relationships?

9. If it is true that the will to manage declined among college students during the 1970s, how would you explain the decline?

10. Is it important that the first organization you work for have a career counseling program? Why?

ADDITIONAL REFERENCES

Bass, B. *Leadership and Performance beyond Expectations.* New York: Free Press, 1985.

Buckholz, S., ed. *The Positive Manager.* New York: John Wiley & Sons, 1985.

Clance, P. R. *The Imposter Phenomenon.* New York: Peachtree Publishers, 1985.

"Computerized Career Planning." *Business Week's Guide to Careers,* Winter 1985–1986, pp. 28–32.

Delong, T. J. "Reexamining the Career Anchor Model." *Personnel,* May–June 1982, pp. 50–61.

Driver, M. "Career Concepts and Career Management in Organizations." In *Behavioral Problems in Organizations,* edited by C. L. Cooper. Englewood Cliffs, N.J.: Prentice-Hall, 1979.

Hall, F., and D. T. Hall. *The Two-Career Couple.* Reading, Mass.: Addison-Wesley Publishing, 1979.

Hamner, W. C. *Organizational Shock.* New York: John Wiley & Sons, 1980.

Hauze, W. C. *Career Veer: How to Position Yourself for a Prosperous Future.* New York: McGraw-Hill, 1985.

Kelley, R. E. *The Gold Collar Worker.* Reading, Mass.: Addison-Wesley Publishing, 1985.

Kelly, N. "Zale Corporation's Career Development Program." *Training and Development Journal,* June 1982, pp. 70–75.

Kotter, J.; V. Fuax; and C. McArthur. *Self-Assessment and Career Development.* Englewood Cliffs, N.J.: Prentice-Hall, 1978.

London, M. *Managing Careers.* Reading, Mass.: Addison-Wesley Publishing Co., 1982.

Machlowitz, M. *Whiz Kids: Success at an Early Age.* New York: Arbor House, 1985.

Ritti, R. R., and G. R. Funkhouser. *The Ropes to Know and The Ropes to Skip.* Columbus, Ohio: Grid Publishing Co., 1977.

Sheehy, G. *Passages: Predictable Crises of Adult Life.* New York: E. P. Dutton, 1976.

Willis, R. "Peak Experience: Managers in the Mountains." *Management Review,* December 1985, pp. 18–23.

Zey, M. G. *The Mentor Connection.* Homewood, Ill.: Dow Jones-Irwin, 1984.

CASES

APPLICATION I

CAREER DEVELOPMENT AT THE U.S. GENERAL ACCOUNTING OFFICE*

The U.S. General Accounting Office (GAO) recently devised a career development program whose primary purpose is to help employees make appropriate career decisions. Their experience indicates that an organization must first develop the ability of managers to "do" career development. GAO's managers are no different from those in other organizations. They tend to get caught up in the day-to-day routine and fail to budget time to consider long-run issues such as their subordinates' futures, yet GAO emphasizes career development of subordinates as an important managerial responsibility.

The first step in implementing the program was to assess the needs of managers. The following were identified:

1. Managers need to know more about the theory and practice of career development.
2. Managers need to know about opportunities throughout GAO, not just in that part where they presently work.
3. Managers need access to career development information that exists in both line and staff units.

---

* Source: Adapted from I. Marlene Thorn, Francis X. Fee, and Jane O'Hara Carter, "Career Development: A Collaborative Approach," *Management Review,* September 1982, pp. 27–28, 38–41.

4. Managers need to take a more active role in career counseling and to recognize both nontraditional and traditional career paths.
5. Managers must be assured that top management is committed to organizationwide career development and that time devoted to it is considered worthwhile.

GAO met these needs in a variety of ways, but chief among them was a new workshop called Career Development Orientation for Managers. The workshop consists of three parts: (1) philosophy, concepts, and overview, (2) individual career planning process, and (3) organizational career development process. Each of these parts draws on materials widely available in the career development literature, but the specific circumstances and experiences of GAO are highlighted. For example, Part 1 emphasizes the philosophy of career development at GAO rather than dealing with issues at an abstract level.

Some of the questions raised in Part 1 include:

1. What is career development?
2. Who should be responsible for it?
3. Should career development address individual or organizational needs?
4. Do career development programs raise false expectations?
5. What are the characteristics of individuals who can make effective use of career development programs?

Admittedly these questions are difficult to answer, but GAO believes that they must be addressed before proceeding to the next two parts.

Part 2 informs managers about the content of career counseling exercises provided by GAO's counseling and career development staff. Managers completed the exercise to learn what their subordinates would experience. Exercises consisted of four widely used career counseling steps:

1. Understanding self, including one's values, needs, skills, and abilities.
2. Understanding one's environment, including job options, educational and training options, financial considerations, and projected skill needs.
3. Planning the future course of events related to development of self and taking advantage of opportunities.
4. Life management, including the whole range of nonwork-related events, activities, and experiences of individuals.

The activities of Part 2 are person oriented. Doing them effectively requires expertise and training in psychology. GAO does not ask managers to lead subordinates through all four steps. The manager's role is that of a referral agent who assures that individuals who desire counseling receive it.

Part 3 emphasizes GAO's stake in employee career development. Mirroring Part 2, it consists of four steps:

1. Understanding organizational needs, including identification of specific deficiencies within GAO.

2. Understanding organizational environment, including present and potential job opportunities and career paths within GAO.
3. Organizational action planning, which requires managers to identify the specific steps they will take to implement career development in their own units.
4. Problem recognition and referral, which requires managers to be alert and sensitive to employees' psychological well-being.

Managers' completion of the workshop signaled the implementation of career development in GAO. Management considers the program to be very timely. Since growth at GAO is limited, so are the number of career advancement opportunities. Therefore, matching individual and career needs is especially important.

Questions for Analysis

1. Evaluate the GAO career development program.
2. What would be your answers to the five questions raised in Part 1 of their training program?
3. What should be the policy of organizations in mature and declining industries toward career development?

APPLICATION II

MANAGERS FOR ALL SEASONS?*

Most business people believe that to be an effective manager and enjoy a fulfilling career, an individual need only be competent and have an indepth knowledge of the industry. Lee Iacocca, for example, is a competent and skilled manager who is an expert on the automobile industry. Other observers believe that a manager's unique skills must be related to the life-cycle stage of the product line. They cite the difference between demands placed on entrepreneurs and on managers of established firms. An individual seeking a career in management must consider the pros and cons of these two conflicting theories.

Consider the experience of Robert C. Hazard, Jr., and Gerald W. Petitt. From 1977 to 1980, Hazard was chief executive and Petitt was second in command of Best Western International, Inc. Under their leadership, Best

---

* Source: Adapted from "Matching Managers to a Company's Life Cycle," *Business Week,* February 23, 1981, pp. 62, 67, 70, 74.

Western expanded from 800 to 2,597 hotels, began operations in 19 countries, and set up the industry's premier computerized reservation system. The outward signs of success included an increase in room occupancy from 5 percent in 1974 to 11 percent in 1980, and an increase in pretax profits from 3 percent in 1974 to 15 percent in 1980. Best Western was transformed from a regional chain to an international giant.

The management style that Hazard and Petitt used was "go-go growth." They made and implemented decisions without consultation with the company's board members—a group representing the views of owners and managers of affiliate Best Western motels. Their individual styles were complementary, and they were able to get their ideas accepted on the basis of past successes. They were neither interested nor skilled in persuasion or politics. They had achieved their greatest accomplishments by working toward bottom-line results and avoiding the infighting that often accompanies high-risk decisions.

Eventually Hazard and Petitt were no longer able to perform at Best Western. The apparently unbridled growth began to cause the affiliates some uneasiness. The 1979 gasoline shortage reduced travel and caused depressed profits. Programs to increase growth no longer seemed appealing in the face of declining business. Board members increasingly rejected Hazard and Petitt's proposals, and neither man was adept at obtaining support from the stubborn groups. So in 1980, Hazard and Petitt left Best Western.

Both were hired by Quality Inns because that company's board wanted the Hazard-Petitt entrepreneurial flair. Quality Inns had abundant cash and was ready to take off, but it needed direction and a push. The Hazard-Petitt team announced its growth strategy only two months after it took over: by the mid-1980s, the number of Quality Inns will increase from 345 to 750 and reservations will be handled by a sophisticated computer system. Sound familiar? After three years of bare survival (1975–1977), when growth was the last item on the corporate agenda, Quality Inns is now primed for growth. Enter Hazard and Petitt.

Questions for Analysis

1. Can an individual be an effective top manager and enjoy career success throughout the product life cycle? What does this imply for your own career planning?
2. How can a growth-oriented company provide for top management succession from within its own ranks of managers?
3. Where would you rather be in top management in the years to come? In Best Western? In Quality Inns? Explain.

EXPERIENTIAL EXERCISE

CAREER PLANNING

Purpose

The purpose of this exercise is to provide experience in thinking about what is important in one's life and career.

The Exercise in Class

1. Each student will complete the following steps:
   a. Draw a horizontal line that depicts the past, present and future of your career. On that line, mark an X where you are now.
   b. To the left of the X, on the part of the line that represents your past, identify events in your life that provided real and genuine feelings of fulfillment and satisfaction.
   c. Examine these historical events and determine the specific causes of your feelings. Does a pattern emerge? Write as much as you can about the events and your reactions to them.
   d. To the right of the X, on the part of the line that represents your future, identify career-related events that you expect to provide real and genuine feelings of fulfillment and satisfaction. You should be as explicit as possible when describing these events. If you are only able to write such statements as, "Get a job" or "Get a big raise," your career expectations are probably vaguely defined.
   e. After you have identified future career-related events, rank them from high to low according to how much fulfillment and satisfaction you expect from each.
   f. Now go back to Step c and rank those historical events from high to low according to how much fulfillment and satisfaction each provided. Compare the two sets of ranked events. Are they consistent? Are you expecting the future to be the same or different from the past in terms of sources of feelings of fulfillment and satisfaction? If the future, expected sources are quite different from the past, actual sources, are you being totally realistic about the future and what you want from your career?
2. Each individual should answer the following questions and share answers with others:
   a. Which one of the six steps was most difficult to complete? Why?

b. What are the principal categories of sources of fulfillment and satisfaction? Can all these sources be realized in a career? Which ones are most likely to go unrealized in the career of your choice?

c. Do you desire a career in management? Is your answer based on consideration of the potential sources of fulfillment and satisfaction that you value? Explain.

The Learning Message

This exercise will demonstrate the difficulties of identifying what we want from our careers. Most of us have vague and ill-formed notions of what careers are all about until we actually begin on a career path. Discussions with others about sources of career satisfactions can be very helpful.

23

Chapter

MANAGING IN A CHANGING WORLD

LEARNING OBJECTIVES

After completing Chapter 23, you should be able to:

■ **Define**
work ethic, managerial competencies, and social costs.

■ **Describe**
the widespread trend toward more women and blacks in management.

■ **Discuss**
reasons why management must be concerned about technological advances.

■ **Compare**
the experience of women and blacks in their efforts to become managers in U.S. corporations.

■ **Identify**
some of the new occupations that will become established by 1990.

■ MANAGEMENT IN ACTION

Intrapreneurs Go Public*

The new business rage today is the "intrapreneur," a new breed being hired by forward-looking companies to develop new products and new markets. The term *intrapreneur* was coined by Gifford Pinchot III when he suggested that intracorporate entrepreneurs were a way to combine the advantages of small firms with those of big ones.

Self-starting is one of the characteristics of intrapreneurs. They do not want to be told what to do, taking the initiative to correct problems and make innovations. Pinchot argues the entrepreneur and intrapreneur have similar motivations. Both are pushed by the desire to accomplish something: "What drives the intrapreneur is a deep personal need for achievement." Pinchot believes that companies should try to tap employees' interest by giving them the freedom and the financial backing to chase their ideas.

Some companies have encouraged experimentation, innovation, failures, and working with total freedom. For example, 3M has a policy that allows engineers to use a percentage of their time working on their own projects. Arthur Fry, a 3M chemical engineer, used to get annoyed at how pieces of paper that marked his church hymnal always fell out when he stood up to sing. He knew that Spencer Silver, a scientist at 3M, had accidently discovered an adhesive that had very low sticking power. Normally that would be bad, but for Fry it was good. He figured that markers made with the adhesive might stick lightly to something and would come off easily. 3M allowed Fry 15 percent of his time to work on the project. Fry made samples and then distributed the small yellow pads to company secretaries. They were delighted with the product. This is how Post-its™ were born at 3M. Sales last year were over $200 million.

As you read this chapter and think about the changes that are occurring, give some consideration to intrapreneuring. Is it "old wine in a new bottle" as claimed by Peter Drucker, or is it something that organizations will need to support to remain competitive? The results so far indicate that some large, powerful corporations are willing to experiment with intrapreneurs to improve their competitive positions.

---

* Source: Adapted from Beverly A. Potter, "Intrapreneurs: New Corporate Breed," *Business Week's Careers*, Winter 1985–1986, pp. 69–71; "Here Come the Intrapreneurs," *Business Week,* February 4, 1985, pp. 36–37.

The most exciting, challenging period of history is right now. Never before have societies, organizations, and people changed faster. Managers have inherited a great deal from the pioneers of the field—Frederick W. Taylor, Henri Fayol, Chester Barnard, Douglas McGregor, Elton Mayo, Frank and Lillian Gilbreth. But today's manager, more than ever, faces increasing social responsibilities, government regulations, and participation of women and minority groups in the work force. Managers have to confront change and uncertainty. They must generate performance that will strengthen their organizations and allow them to survive the future.

By tying together all that has been said about management, this chapter attempts to set the stage for the future, based on today's trends that we expect to continue into the 21st century. Management fads will come and go, but the practice of management will continue to be based on solid principles and an ability to work effectively with people.[1]

MANAGING: A DEMANDING JOB IN THE MIDST OF CHANGE

As previous chapters indicate, the manager's job is *not* neat, routine, easygoing, clearly understood, and easy to evaluate. Planning, organizing, and controlling functions are performed in a rather hectic, fragmented, and complicated manner. The evidence, as reported by practicing managers and research indicates that:

1. Managers must often make decisions with incomplete information.
2. Communication in organizations is often unclear and misleading.
3. Individual differences get in the way of neat, orderly institutional programs.
4. Managers need controls, but tight controls often destroy employees' motivation.
5. Top administrators often reject managers' innovative ideas because they threaten philosophies or practices in place for years.
6. Groups have a significant influence on individual behavior, but many managers do not understand the characteristics and processes of groups.

In the next decade, the manager's job probably will undergo more scrutiny by researchers than in any other era. Through better and more thorough research, the manager's job will be made clearer to society, and some highly publicized myths could be debunked. For instance, the old cliche "Workers do, managers tell" will come to be regarded as a silly misconception.[2]

The manager is expected to act out various roles: interpersonal, informative, and decisional. The work requires a high level of energy, intelligence, and determination. Managers must convert technological, social, economic, and political changes into programs that improve the quality of citizens' lives.

---

[1] "Business Fads: What's In—And Out," *Business Week,* January 20, 1986, pp. 52–61.

[2] Leonard R. Sayles, *Leadership* (New York: McGraw-Hill, 1979), p. 21.

FIGURE   23–1   Management Competencies

Some of the skills needed to manage effectively.

Skills	*Why Needed?*
Problem solving.	To attack the problems correctly and effectively.
Good listening.	To learn about problems and to establish relationships with co-workers.
Managing time.	To prevent becoming over-loaded by work and being stressed.
Communicating clearly.	To establish plans, procedures, and programs and to learn about the feelings of others.
Computer literacy.	To provide managers the capacity to use data bases in making decisions.
Rewarding equitably.	To maintain motivation and receive the respect of subordinates.
Providing subordinates with a clear understanding of their jobs.	To create an atmosphere of understanding.
Showing respect for others.	To develop trust, confidence, and loyalty among co-workers.

Managers must *do* and continue to *do* so that acceptable performance is achieved.

To improve the quality of people's lives, managers must possess competencies. A *competence* is a skill or expertise that is applied to particular problems.[3] Some of the skills needed to manage—to implement a plan, reward employees, or organize a new venture—are presented in Figure 23–1. The figure does not present a complete list of required managerial skills. The skills listed can, however, be a basis for improving a manager's overall performance. Being effective also requires that managers understand the *changes* taking place in society. Resisting and ignoring change are not viable strategies for managers.

CHANGES IN THE MANAGER'S WORLD

The past two decades have brought dramatic change to just about every aspect of our society: medicine, technology, economics, and politics. (Figure 23–2 presents some of the more publicized changes.) With these changes have come some significant side effects. Our nation now faces the need for

---

[3] Michael A. O'Neal, "Managerial Skills and Values for Today and Tomorrow," *Personnel,* July 1985, pp. 49–55.

FIGURE   23–2   Changes in the Past Two Decades

Medical

Use of TV network for M.D.s.
Use of cable TV for medical conferences.
Use of computers to diagnose psychiatric problems.
A preventive-medicine orientation instead of a disease orientation.

Technological

Personal home computers.
Diesel passenger cars.
Use of fossil fuels.
Supersonic transportation.
Space exploration.

Economic

Increases in the standard of living.
The development of China.
The use of foreign capital to build new plants in the United States.
The development of Third World nations, Japan, and West Germany.
Increases and decreases in the value of the dollar on international currency exchanges.
A large foreign trade deficit because of an imbalance between imports and exports.

Social

Over 10 million Americans unemployed.
Declining birthrate.
Development of experimental communities.
Increased crowding.
Increased pressure from the Third World for greater share of material goods.
Increased welfare payments by the government.

Political

Equal employment rights.
Turmoil in the Middle East and Central America.
Resignation of a vice president and a president.
Increases in the number of women winning elections.
End of U.S. involvement in Southeast Asian wars.

---

new energy sources, the depletion of crucial natural resources, and increased social activism and consumerism. Demographic patterns are shifting; the number of women and members of minority groups in managerial and professional positions is increasing; government is becoming more involved in business transactions, and international business and business competition are increasing.

Studying trends is a method used by some to forecast the future. The views of two experts, John Naisbitt and Patricia Aburdene, are presented in the Management Focus on "Reinventing the Organization."

MANAGEMENT FOCUS
Reinventing the Organization

The shrinking of the work force and the approaching dominance of the baby boomers within its ranks will facilitate what Naisbitt and Aburdene call a reinvention of the way organizations are structured. These two forecasters present 10 considerations for reshaping company policies and structures:

1. The best and brightest people will gravitate toward those organizations that encourage and support personal growth.
2. The manager's new roles will be those of coach, teacher, and mentor.
3. The best people want ownership in the company.
4. Companies will turn to third-party contractors, shifting from hired labor to contract labor.
5. Authoritarian management is yielding to a networking, people-oriented style of management.
6. Intrapreneurship (entrepreneurship within corporations) is creating new products and new markets and revitalizing companies from inside out.
7. Quality of goods and services will be paramount.
8. Intuition and creativity are challenging the "it's all in the numbers" textbook type of solution.
9. Large corporations are emulating the positive and productive qualities of small business.
10. The dawn of the information economy has fostered a massive shift from concern about details and efficiency to overall quality of life.

The message offered by Naisbitt and Aburdene is that managers will have to become more effective facilitators. Managers in the new Information Age will have to rethink, redo, and reexamine the authoritarian "do it my way" model if they are going to survive the invasion of baby boomers and the ever-present international competitors lined up to serve American markets.

Source: Adapted from Anthony J. Rutigliano, "Re-Inventing the Workplace," *Management Review,* October 1985, pp. 33–35.

Managers in the future, as always, will have to adjust to changes in society. They will have to develop programs and policies that can succeed in a changing, often unpredictable *environment.*

ENVIRONMENTAL FORCES

An organization's external environment plays a major role in determining how successful managers will be in performing their jobs. Throughout this book, we have described the link between the environment and the internal functioning of organizations. Many environmental forces are beyond the control of managers. However, being aware of influential factors assists managers in performing the functions of management. Some environmental factors to consider include natural and human resources, population changes, technology, governmental regulations, and international competition.

Natural Resources

Managing the limited available natural resources has become a very important responsibility in the last 10 years. Business, government, unions, and citizens have a stake in conservation: Inappropriate management will mean lower national productivity, inconveniences, food shortages, and an overall decline in our standard of living.

We are not running out of energy. However, we are running out of cheap oil and gas. We are also running out of money to pay for energy. Some of the energy sources that have been substituted for oil and gas have created a number of problems. For example, nuclear fusion was initially considered by its developers to be a clean source of limitless power. However, the potential problems with nuclear energy were highlighted in the spring 1986 accident at Chernobyl, Russia. Radioactive emissions created a crisis situation and public concern. Furthermore, the use of nuclear energy creates radioactive wastes that are difficult to dispose of safely.

Renewable energy sources—wind, water, direct sunlight—seem to offer some promise. They add no heat to the atmosphere, and they produce no radioactive materials. However, they cannot meet limitless energy demands.

Each of the world's 150 nations has a different plan for conserving and using energy and all other natural resources. Managerial coordination of these differing viewpoints is required. Plans and clearly understood objectives must be established; and managers must plan, organize, and control the use of resources.

Human Resources

Human resources are now and will remain *the* most crucial asset of an organization. Average life expectancy in ancient Greece was about 22 years. Some individuals in that society did live to ripe old ages, but their number was small. Today many of us reach the age of 70 and remain active contributors to organizations. Learning how to use young and old workers effectively presents an ongoing challenge to managers.

Career planning, job enrichment, training, and development are all designed to match jobs and people more optimally. To this end, organizational designs will become more flexible, working hours will be modified to meet personal needs, and technology will be modified to mesh with the talents and skills of operating employees. Retraining for a second career will become more popular with employees no longer challenged by their work.

The era of concern about human resources has arrived, and that concern will become more pronounced in the future. Managers will attempt to create a work environment conducive to personal growth and self-actualization.[4]

Population and Other Demographic Trends

Demographic patterns will change drastically in the future. Most industrialized nations (such as the United States, Great Britain, France, Canada, West Germany, Japan, and Australia) will experience a decline in population growth as a result of decreasing birthrates.

Demographers associate increasing female participation in the work force with a decline in the number of children that families will raise. The reduced amount of time available for parenting in families if the mother works may create a demand for new school services that deal with functions usually learned at home. Schools may need to teach the skills of eating, drinking, dressing, and manners to young children. Table 23–1 shows the declining birth rate, the increasing life expectancy rates, and the aging of our population.

The managerial implications of changing population patterns and parenting behaviors are becoming obvious. Population is one of the main factors affecting the demand for goods and services. Studies of population data will become a more important basis for adjustments in product development and modifications in production. For example, managers examining population data can determine that over 65 percent of the people in the United States are over 21 years old and that approximately 36 percent of these are over 40 years of age. Since many adults already have homes, cars, and appliances, this means that other types of goods may prove more attractive to an older population.

Managers must also consider the shifts in population patterns in locating new employees, talent, plant sites, and markets. Americans are rapidly leaving the northern and eastern metropolitan areas of New York, Philadelphia, Cleveland, and Boston and are heading for the South and West. As a result,

---

[4] Thomas C. Keiser, "The Rules of the Game Have Changed," *Training,* January 1986, pp. 43–47.

TABLE   23–1   Selected Characteristics of U.S. Population, 1960–2000

Characteristic	1960	1970	1980	1990 (projected)	2000 (projected)
Population size	180,671,000	204,878,000	221,651,000	243,004,000	259,869,000
Rate of increase over prior decade	18.5%	13.4%	8.2%	9.6%	6.9%
Number of births	4,257,850	3,731,386*	3,575,000	3,868,000†	3,676,000
Percent males	—	48.7%	48.7%	48.7%	48.6%
Percent females	—	51.3%	51.3%	51.3%	51.4%
Life expectancy (years)					
Males	66.6	67.1	69.4‡	69.7‡	70.0‡
Females	73.1	74.6	77.3‡	77.8	78.3‡
Median age of population	29.4	27.9	30.2	32.8	35.5

* The annual number of births reached a low point in 1973 (3,136,965).

† Based on average annual birth rate for five-year period.

‡ Based on linear interpolation of 1976 and 2050 Bureau of Census estimates.

Source: U.S. Bureau of the Census, *Current Population Reports,* Series P-25 (Washington, D.C.: U.S. Bureau of the Census). Projections are based on Series II assumptions.

the nation's fastest growing region is the Sun Belt, whose northern limits form an arc stretching from southern California to the Carolinas. America's modern-day migrants are searching for new jobs, goods, and services and for lifestyle changes. Managerial plans to meet these needs must be developed and implemented.

Figure 23–3 presents the distribution patterns of U.S. population by geographic regions. Demographic changes are important environmental influences on managerial plans involving staffing, career planning, product development, marketing, and training and development. Dramatic changes in the population mix, income patterns, and geographic locations will continue to be concerns of managers.

Technology

The development of technology is a high-risk, costly, and uncertain activity. Seldom is an organization able to make a technological breakthrough within management's cost estimates. As a result, managers face the ongoing challenge of knowing when to abandon a project that is running up excessive costs. This will require careful planning, organizing, and controlling.

Recently the managers of technological projects have had to consider a new type of costs—*social costs,* such as water, air, and noise pollution. The government aggressively monitors side effects of technological advancements

FIGURE   23–3   Distribution of U.S. Population by Geographic Regions, 1970–2000

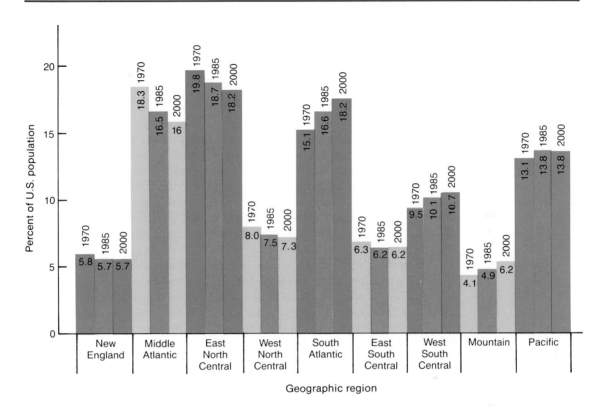

Source: U.S. Bureau of the Census, *Current Population Reports,* Series P-25, No. 460, and Series P-20 No. 324 (Washington, D.C.: U.S. Bureau of the Census). Projections based on Series II assumptions.

and imposes economic and legal sanctions against firms responsible for hazardous conditions in the environment.

Managers in some organizations have faced huge losses because of poor planning and controlling of technology projects. Before selling most of its computer business to Honeywell, General Electric poured $500 million into computers, nuclear power, and commercial jet engines. RCA also had to terminate its computer operations because of poor strategic planning. By contrast, IBM has managed its research efforts along a specific technology and has successfully captured the major share of the world's computer market.

Management of technological change and advancements is not easy. Organizations will have to find a balance between too few and too many risky ventures. This search will be frustrating unless managers comprehend that technology is costly, risky, necessary, and intense.

Government

The American economic system is a form of mixed capitalism shared by private enterprise and government. Private firms produce what consumers demand at a price that allows the firm to earn a satisfactory profit. The government, however, has continued to exert more influence on the economy over the past two decades. Through its power to enact and enforce laws, government influences many managerial decisions.

Since 1960, the U.S. Congress has passed nearly 90 major laws regulating various phases of business. Many of these laws are listed in Figure 23–4. Most of them focus on consumerism, minorities, safety, and the employment of women. The vast majority of managers will continue to comply with these and other new regulations. Effective laws and a better relationship between government, business, and labor can improve the quality of life within society. The development of a better business-government relationship will become an important priority for managers and government administrators. Through more socially responsible behavior by organizations, the relationship can become more harmonious.

Government's role in American enterprise often varies, depending on the political party involved. However, local, state, and federal government will continue to be involved in all of the areas covered by the legislation listed in Figure 23–4. Government's primary role will be to support and encourage business, but it will also continue to be a watch dog. There will probably be more Ralph Naders and more regulation.

International Competition

The American economic system is powerful but not self-sufficient; the United States is becoming increasingly dependent on international trade. In fact, most industrial nations need to exchange goods and services with other nations.

To remain competitive, comprehensive strategies will be needed. As international competition becomes more intense, the planning, organizing, and controlling functions of managers become more complex. Managers must be able to seize on the opportunities available in various world markets. So evaluation of market opportunities in other nations must be a continual process. Also, an organization must comply with the law of the land. For example, U.S. firms selling products in Canada must by law provide packaging information in French and English. Japanese autos sold in America must meet U.S. air pollution standards.

**FIGURE   23–4   Some Significant Post-1960 Legislation
Regulating Business**

---

*Some laws that
managers must deal
with in doing their job.*

Federal Hazardous Substances Labeling
Act of 1960

Fair Labor Standards Amendments of
1961, 1966, and 1974

Federal Water Pollution Control Act
Amendments of 1961

Oil Pollution Act of 1961 and Amendments
of 1973

Air Pollution Control Act of 1962

Drug Amendments of 1962

Clean Air Act of 1963 and Amendments
of 1966 and 1970

Equal Pay Act of 1963

Civil Rights Act of 1964

Automotive Products Trade Act of 1965

Federal Cigarette Labeling and Advertising
Act of 1965

Water Quality Act of 1965

Clean Water Restoration Act of 1966

Fair Packaging and Labeling Act of 1966

Federal Coal Mine Safety Act Amendments
of 1966

Financial Institutions Supervisory Act of
1966

Oil Pollution of the Sea Act of 1966

Age Discrimination in Employment Act of
1967

Air Quality Act of 1967

Agricultural Fair Practices Act of 1968

Consumer Credit Protection Act of 1968

Natural Gas Pipeline Safety Act of 1968

Radiation Control for Health and Safety Act
of 1968

Cigarette Smoking Act of 1969

Child Protection and Toy Safety Act of 1969

Federal Coal Mine Health and Safety Act
of 1969

Natural Environmental Policy Act of 1969

Tax Reform Act of 1969

Investment Company Amendments of 1969

Bank Holding Act Amendments of 1970

Bank Records and Foreign Transactions
Act of 1970

Economic Stabilization Act of 1970 and
Amendments of 1971 and 1973

Environmental Quality Improvement Act of
1970

Fair Credit Reporting Act of 1970

Noise Pollution and Abatement Act of 1970

Occupational Safety and Health Act of 1970

Securities Investor Protection Act of 1970

Water and Environmental Quality Improvement Act of 1970

Export Administration Finance Act of 1971

Consumer Product Safety Act of 1972

Equal Employment Opportunity Act of 1972

Federal Environmental Pesticide Control
Act of 1972

Noise Control Act of 1972

Agriculture and Consumers Protection Act
of 1973

Emergency Petroleum Allocation Act of
1973

Highway Safety Act of 1973

Water Resources Development Act of 1974

Pregnancy Discrimination Act of 1978

Crude Oil Windfall Tax Act of 1979

Energy Security Act of 1980

Depository Institution Deregulation and
Monetary Control Act of 1980

Economic Recovery Tax Act of 1981

Gramm-Rudman Act of 1985

2345671234567

SPECIAL ISSUES FOR MANAGEMENT

Certainly the environmental forces just discussed will continue to affect the management of work and organizations, people, and production and operations. However, a number of specific issues will have to be addressed by effective managers.

Women as Workers and Managers

Fall 1978 was a benchmark for working women. It was then that their labor market participation rate surpassed 50 percent. That is, more than

TABLE 23–2 Civilian Labor Force, by Sex, Age, and Race

(Actual 1975–1984 and middle growth projections to 1995)

	Actual			Projected	
Group	1975	1980	1984	1990	1995
Total, age 16 and over (thousands)	93,775	106,940	113,544	122,653	129,168
Men	56,299	61,453	63,835	67,146	69,282
16–24	12,371	13,606	12,727	11,163	10,540
25–54	34,991	38,712	42,302	48,079	51,200
55 and over	8,938	9,135	8,805	7,904	7,542
Women	37,475	45,487	49,704	55,507	59,886
16–24	10,250	11,696	11,260	10,089	9,623
25–54	21,860	27,888	32,360	39,632	44,519
55 and over	5,365	5,904	6,084	5,786	5,744
White	82,831	93,600	98,492	105,467	110,086
Black	9,263	10,865	12,033	13,602	14,796
Total, age 16 and over (percent)	100.0%	100.0%	100.0%	100.0%	100.0%
Men	60.0	57.5	56.2	54.7	53.6
16–24	13.2	12.7	11.2	9.1	8.2
25–54	37.3	36.2	37.3	39.2	39.2
55 and over	9.5	8.5	7.8	6.4	5.8
Women	40.0	42.5	43.8	45.3	46.4
16–24	10.9	10.9	9.9	8.2	5.8
25–54	23.3	26.1	28.5	32.3	34.5
55 and over	5.7	5.5	5.4	4.7	4.4
White	88.3	87.5	86.7	86.0	85.2
Black	9.9	10.2	10.6	11.1	11.5

Source: *Monthly Labor Review*, November 1985, p. 18.

half of all women 16 years of age and over were in the work force.[5] Table 23–2 projects that their share of the total labor force will increase to over 46 percent by 1995.

Perhaps the most noteworthy increase in the participation of women in the labor force has been among 25- to 34-year-olds. Their participation has increased about 24 percent between 1970 and 1981.[6] In the past, women in this age group typically stopped working when they married or had their first child. Now, many young women continue to work while having a family.

Occupational choice has widened for women. In 1980, 86.3 percent of all working women were employed in 10 occupations, such as domestic workers, laundresses, dressmakers, teachers, and restaurant workers.[7] Today, while over half of all women are still employed in 20 traditional women's jobs, there are some women working in almost every occupation from ironworker to professional baseball umpire to neurosurgeon. By 1985, women represented 16 percent of the lawyers and 16 percent of the doctors in the United States.[8]

Despite the gains, the majority of working women is still employed in only 20 of the 441 jobs listed in the Census Occupational Classification system. Management still hasn't taken advantage of talented women who are needed to work on the type of problems discussed in this book: productivity, managing work and organizations, managing people, and managing production and operations. Figure 23–5 indicates the percentage of women in management.

A study of women officers in the 1,000 largest U.S. industrial companies and 50 leading financial and retailing concerns painted this picture of the women who have crossed the barriers to management: More often than not, the female manager is married, in her 40s, from a low- to middle-income upbringing, holds at least one college degree, and is still very much a minority in American management. Only 6 percent of all working women are counted as managers of any sort; this means that about 3 million women are considered managers. The top half of the organizational hierarchy remains virtually all male.[9]

The study also added to the documentation of unequal pay between men and women. The average female executive earns less than $50,000 a year in cash compensation, compared to over $60,000 earned by her male counterpart. Working women in general earn about 60 percent of what men earn. To close this gap, the accepted concept of equal pay for equal jobs has been expanded to include equal pay for comparable jobs. The Supreme Court,

---

[5] Seymour L. Wolfberg, "Planning for the U.S. Labor Force of the 80s," *National Productivity Review,* Spring 1982, pp. 228–39.

[6] "Job Options for Women in the 80s," Pamphlet 18 (Washington, D.C.: U.S. Department of Labor, Women's Bureau, 1980).

[7] Ibid., p. 1

[8] John Naisbitt, *The Year Ahead: 1986* (New York: Warner Books, 1985), p. 51.

[9] "Women and the Executive Suite," *Newsweek,* September 14, 1981, p. 65.

FIGURE   23–5   Women as a Percentage of Total Employment in Major Occupations, 1969, 1974, and 1980 Era

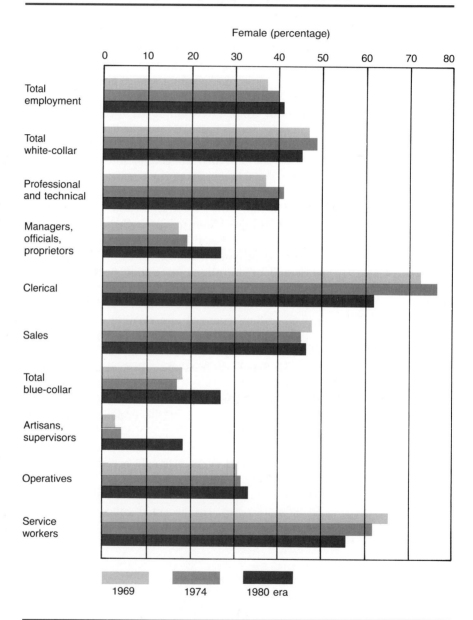

Source: Francine D. Blau, "The Data on Women Workers, Past, Present, and Future," in *Women Working,* ed. Ann H. Stromberg and Shirley Harkness (Palo Alto, Calif.: Mayfield, 1978), p. 56.

on June 9, 1981, ruled that a sex discrimination suit may be brought under the 1964 Civil Rights Act on a basis other than discrimination in "equal or substantially equal work."[10] The ruling came in a suit out of Washington County, Oregon. Prison matrons there alleged sex discrimination because male prison guards, whose jobs were somewhat different, received substantially higher pay. The county had evaluated the men's jobs as having 5 percent more job content than the female jobs and paid the males 35 percent more.

Studies conducted by Hendrick and Struggles, Inc., an executive-search consulting firm, indicated that 6 of every 10 female executive officers in major U.S. corporations earn less than $30,000.[11] On the other hand, male executives earn 35 percent more, on the average, than their female colleagues. Unless this type of discrepancy is corrected, organizations can expect more lawsuits to find their way to court.

Unequal pay is not the only barrier between women and top management jobs. Women who are or are trying to be in management still complain of subtle and overt male hostility directed toward them.[12] Other frequently cited barriers are the "old boy" network, insecure men, and the attitude that a woman cannot be taken seriously.

The double standard is a persisting problem. In many cases, females are expected to outperform male counterparts in comparable jobs or to work flawlessly with no complaints. Even as management hierarchies become more coed, unfair pressures still will be applied to many women.

Some companies, however, are helping female employees balance job and home life because managers realize that two-job families are a fact of life in our society. It is estimated that there are 25 million two-paycheck families in the work force, and couples experience problems with career choices that involve relocation and excessive overtime.[13] Both men and women have had to turn down opportunities to relocate or to work numerous overtime hours because of family responsibilities or career complications for their spouses. Unless organizations are considerate and tolerant of these kinds of refusals, many careers may be thwarted unnecessarily.

Beyond the corporate structure, women are breaking out and starting their own businesses at a far higher rate than men. The Management Focus offers a "Profile of Female Entrepreneurs."

---

[10] Michael F. Carter, "Comparable Work: An Idea Whose Time Has Come?" *Personnel Journal,* October 1981, pp. 792–94.

[11] Frank Allen, "Women Managers Get Paid Far Less than Males, Despite Career Gains," *The Wall Street Journal,* October 7, 1980, pp. 31, 39.

[12] Alma S. Baron and Ken Abrahamsen, "Will He—Or Won't He—Work with a Female Manager?" *Management Review,* November 1981, pp. 48–53.

[13] Mary Bralove, "Keeping Work World Out of Family Life Is Growing Problem for Two-Job Couples," *The Wall Street Journal,* December 7, 1981, p. 27.

MANAGEMENT FOCUS
Profile of Female Entrepreneurs

Since 1977, the number of firms owned by women has jumped 33.4 percent to a 1985 total of 3 million, with some $40 billion in annual revenues. Currently about a third of the new companies launched each year in the United States are started by women.

What have researchers found out about the female entrepreneur? One study concludes that male and female entrepreneurs are much more alike than they are different. They seem to share the same personality traits: determination, a willingness to learn from their experiences, a high energy level, a strong desire to achieve, and the belief that they control their own destinies.

In a study published in the *Journal of Small Business Management*, research on 468 female entrepreneurs found that 51 percent were the first-born children in their families (also true among male entrepreneurs). The majority of the women had grown up in middle- or upper-class families, and 68 percent had attended college and graduate school. A majority of their fathers had been entrepreneurs or self-employed.

Fifty-five percent of the entrepreneurs were married and had children. Most of them married college-educated professional men, stayed home to raise their children, and afterward opened their businesses. Most opened service businesses in areas such as sales, consulting, design, public relations, or advertising. None of the companies was based on a new market. Sixty percent of the businesses had been in operation for four years or less. Only 19 percent of the firms took in annual gross revenues of more than $500,000. Nearly all reported that a major problem in starting their businesses was obtaining loans.

Source: Adapted from Gail Gregg, "Women Entrepreneurs: The Second Generation," *Across the Board,* January 1985, pp. 10–18.

Despite the obstacles, women with ambition, drive, and willingness to take risks have advanced into management. Those women whose careers survive and thrive will undoubtedly be among the most competent, politically astute, and motivated managers in society. Their skills, intelligence, and determination will set a standard for other aspiring managers now entering the work force.

Minorities in Organizations

Until the middle of the 20th century, many organizations specified the desired sex and race when advertising for employees. But recently businesses, as well as many citizens, have tried to minimize discrimination in employment. Although women have problems in organizations, minorities have even more hurdles to overcome. Racial, ethnic, and sexual job discrimination has had a long history.

Fortune once listed 379,000 black managers in American businesses.[14] Integrating more minority managers into the organization mainstream is a continuous task for companies—both in response to government pressures and in voluntary acceptance. As a result, more and more black managers are entering key managerial positions. They are the success stories of the past decade's affirmative action programs; they have moved from entry-level jobs into middle management. Now, along with their white peers, they stand on the brink of senior-level positions.[15] Yet progress has been slow, and pressure on black managers is often intense. Blacks are now waiting to see whether qualified black managers are allowed to enter senior management positions. Organizations will clearly have to show aspiring black managers that reaching the top is possible, if they are to continue to attract black men and women.[16]

Spanish-surnamed people, American Indians, and Orientals make up 5 percent of the population of the United States. All of them have shared the kinds of employment discrimination that blacks have suffered. The education levels of the Spanish-surnamed and American Indians have been lower than the rest of the population, and this has hindered their taking on important, high-skill jobs.[17] But Orientals, who have high educational levels, have moved into an increasing number of white-collar and skilled occupations in the past 25 years. There is still much work to be done. The American Indian is found in labor-type jobs in proportionately greater numbers than whites; blacks hold fewer professional jobs than whites; and blacks hold fewer managerial jobs than whites.

Movement of these minority groups into organizations will be difficult, even with government intervention. Differences in customs, values, and accents will slow down their movement into the mainstream. Managers can, of course, take an active leadership role in overcoming discrimination.

---

[14] Juan Cameron, "Blacks Still Waiting for Full Membership," *Fortune,* April 1975, p. 165.

[15] Robert S. Greenberger, "Many Black Managers Hope to Enter Ranks of Top Management," *The Wall Street Journal,* June 15, 1981, pp. 1, 15.

[16] Effanus Henderson, "Blacks in Corporate America: Is There a Future?" *Personnel Journal,* January 1986, pp. 12–19.

[17] John W. Wright, *The American Almanac of Jobs and Salaries* (New York: Avon, 1982).

The Work Ethic Message

Chapter 3 documented the sagging productivity in the United States. A number of reasons ranging from management inattention to government regulations were cited as contributing factors to the problem. Some people attribute the decline to another cause: the work ethic. If by work ethic—a very elusive term—we mean the desire to do a good job irrespective of financial reward, then research shows that the work ethic in the United States is quite strong. A 1980 Gallup study for the United States Chamber of Commerce showed that an overwhelming 88 percent of all working Americans feel that it is personally important to work hard and do their best on the job. The study concludes that there is widespread commitment among U.S. workers to improve productivity and suggests that there are "large reservoirs of potential upon which management can draw to improve performance and increase productivity."[18]

In a more subtle examination of employee attitudes toward work, a 1982 study for the nonprofit Public Agenda Foundation explored three concepts of what might be called the "unwritten work contract"—the assumptions that each person makes about what he or she will give to the job and will expect in return. The first conception is that people work only to sustain themselves, to survive. The second view regards work as purely an economic transaction. The more money people get, the harder they work. The less money they receive, the less effort people put forth. The third conception views work as carrying a moral imperative to do one's best apart from practical necessity or financial rewards. The study found that nearly four out of five people accept the third concept, aligning themselves with the statement: "I have an inner need to do the very best job I can regardless of pay." Fewer than one out of 10 working Americans embrace the idea of work as a mere economic transaction.

Yet at the same time that the work ethic has remained strong, there is a clear message to managers that most Americans believe people are working less. A 1981 Harris study for Sentry Insurance revealed that:[19]

- Of all working Americans, 78 percent feel that "people take less pride in their work than they did 10 years ago."
- Seventy-three percent believe that "the motivation to work hard is not as strong today as it was a decade ago."
- Sixty-one percent feel that our workmanship is worse than it was.

Although the work ethic remains strong, it appears that managers need to do something about the loss of pride in workmanship and about poor-quality outputs. America has become a land plagued by loose wires, missing

---

[18] Daniel Yankelovich, "The Work Ethic Is Underemployed," *Psychology Today,* May 1982, p. 5.

[19] Ibid., p. 6.

screws, ill-fitting assembly, and things that don't work. Too many examples indicate quality problems:[20]

> Bolts supporting the Civic Center in Hartford, Connecticut, snapped and the entire steel and concrete roof plunged into the 10,000 seat auditorium.
>
> All 273 people on board a DC–10 died when an engine bolt snapped as the plane was taking off from Chicago's O'Hare Airport.
>
> At Three Mile Island, a relief valve stuck in the open position and brought the nuclear core to the brink of a meltdown.
>
> In New York City, Houston, Los Angeles, Atlanta, and Santa Monica, 2,500 brand-new Grumman buses costing $130,000 each developed cracks and sagging rear axles shortly after going into service.

The list goes on and on. It convincingly and sadly shows that major problems exist in the workplace. One researcher suggests that the problem lies in poor managerial implementation of reward systems that must be corrected in the future.[21] The Gallup study asked workers whom they thought would benefit from the improvements in their productivity; only 9 percent felt that they, the workers, would. Most assumed that the beneficiaries would be consumers, management, or stockholders. Management must educate workers about how they benefit from productivity improvements.

In principle, it seems that most Americans are willing to work hard, but they continue to work under reward systems that do not motivate them to do so. Why should workers make a greater effort if they don't have to and if they believe that others, not they, will benefit from such efforts? Managers finally need to realize that workers are responsive to something other than economic rewards. The economic view is an obsolete and inaccurate image of the workforce. Survey after survey shows this to be the case. Management must give the proper encouragement by rewarding good performance, and it must communicate again and again about who benefits from productivity improvements. Managers must also show by their actions that hard work and results will be properly rewarded.

The Unemployment Problem

During the past decade, more than 30 million jobs have been lost as a direct result of plant closings. Communities have been disrupted, workers' security undermined, and productivity reduced. Greater involvement and cooperation between labor, management, and the government are needed to deal not only with unemployment and retraining in a general sense but

---

[20] Marvin Harris, "Why It's Not the Same Old America," *Psychology Today,* August 1981, p. 25.

[21] Yankelovich, "Work Ethic," p. 8.

also with the shuttered factories, displaced workers, and ghost towns.[22] The shifting landscape of jobs is presented in the Management Focus (of course, the available mix of jobs in 1990 can only be estimated at this time).

MANAGEMENT FOCUS
Job Shifting: What's Going and What's Coming

So where will people entering the work force find jobs in the future? No one answer is perfectly accurate. Computers and information technology might replace the auto as the symbolic soul of the economy, but the future is unpredictable, to say the least.

Most experts and job forecasters do agree that the largest job increases will come in two general areas: information and what is termed "conservation." Information will include computers, robotics, biotechnology, and transmission technology such as laser and fiber optics. Conservation will be of both human and ecological natures—from health care to already established conservation efforts such as solar energy, more efficient use of raw materials, and waste disposal. The U.S. Department of Labor has researched job trends for the future. Table 23–3 lists jobs that are going and jobs that are coming.

Worries about unemployment are hardly new in industrialized nations. The 19th-century steel barons thought their businesses would die when all the railroads were built. The railroad barons thought their businesses would die when cars and trucks and airplanes came along. There are still a lot of fears. New jobs like those listed in Table 23–3A (paralegal, computer programmers, and medical assistants) will continue to grow. On the other hand, stenographers and shoe sewing machine operator jobs will decline at a higher rate. And many jobs will disappear completely. It is estimated that there are now 30 million unemployed people in the world.[23] As of 1986, about 9 million of this group are in the United States. Being unemployed has tremendous social, psychological, and economic consequences.[24]

The worker who accepts technology advances (such as robots and computers) and is willing to retrain for the future is far more likely to be employed

---

[22] Barry Bluestone and Bennett Harrison, *The Deindustrialization of America* (New York: Basic Books, 1982).

[23] Marvin Cetron and Thomas O'Toole, *Encounters with the Future: A Forecast of Life into the 21st Century* (New York: McGraw-Hill, 1982).

[24] Arthur Shostak, "The Human Cost of Plant Closings," *AFL–CIO American Federationist,* August 1980, p. 22.

TABLE   23–3   Job Trends, 1984–1995 (000s)

A. Fastest-Growing Occupations

| Occupation | Employment | | Increase | | Percent of Total Job Growth |
	1984	1995	Number	Percent	1984–95
Paralegal personnel	53	104	51	97.5%	.3%
Computer programmers	341	586	245	71.7	1.5
Computer systems analysts, electronic data processing (EDP)	308	520	212	68.7	1.3
Medical assistants	128	207	79	62.0	.5
Data processing equipment repairers	50	78	28	56.2	.2
Electrical and electronics engineers	390	597	206	52.8	1.3
Electrical and electronics technicians and technologists	404	607	202	50.7	1.3
Computer operators, except peripheral equipment	241	353	111	46.1	.7
Peripheral EDP equipment operators	70	102	32	45.0	.2
Travel agents	72	103	32	43.9	.2
Physical therapists	58	83	25	42.2	.2
Physician assistants	25	35	10	40.3	.1
Securities and financial services salesworkers	81	113	32	39.1	.2
Mechanical engineering technicians and technologists	55	75	20	36.6	.1
Lawyers	490	665	174	35.5	1.1
Correction officers and jailers	130	175	45	34.9	.3
Accountants and auditors	882	1,189	307	34.8	1.9
Mechanical engineers	237	317	81	34.0	.5
Registered nurses	1,377	1,829	452	32.8	2.8
Employment interviewers, private or public employment service	72	95	23	31.7	.1

TABLE   23-3   *(continued)*

B. Fastest-Declining Occupations

Occupation	Employment		Percent Decline
	1984	*1995*	
Stenographers	239	143	−40.3%
Shoe sewing machine operators and tenders	33	22	−31.5
Railroad brake, signal, and switch operators	48	35	−26.4
Railcar repairers	27	21	−22.3
Furnace, kiln, or kettle operators and tenders	63	50	−20.9
Shoe and leather workers and repairers, precision	43	35	−18.6
Private household workers	993	811	−18.3
Station installers and repairers, telephone	111	92	−17.4
Sewing machine operators, garment	676	563	−16.7
Textile machine operators, tenders, setters, and setup operators, winding	279	235	−15.7
Machinery maintenance mechanics, textile machines	26	22	−14.8
Statistical clerks	93	81	−12.7
Industrial truck and tractor operators	389	342	−11.9
Central office operators	77	68	−11.5
Farm workers	1,079	958	−11.2
College and university faculty	731	654	−10.6
Farm and home management advisers	27	24	−9.6
Extruding and drawing machine setters and setup operators, metal and plastic	28	25	−9.1
Pressing machine operators and tenders, textile, garment and related	116	106	−8.8
Postal service clerks	317	290	−8.5

Source: *Monthly Labor Review,* November 1985, p. 52–53.

than the worker who resists. There will be hardships along the way. More and more employees will have to change old habits, learn new skills, and move to new locations. Management must understand that some outstanding performers will openly resist technological change. A study of 300 executives at 15 companies concluded that 10 percent of the managers would refuse to accept electronic workstations. The study predicted that 10 percent would lose their jobs without even understanding why they lost them.[25]

Americans have come to view being unemployed as a failure of the economic system rather than of the individual. More and more, citizens look to government to solve the problems of idle workers. As a result, unemployment's cost to the government is now staggering. For every percentage point the jobless rate increases, the cost to the federal government goes up $25 billion from the combination of lost tax revenue and unemployment benefits paid.

THE FUNCTIONS OF MANAGEMENT

Environmental forces are significant and unpredictable, as are the special issues just discussed. Few, if any, principles of management apply in all situations or for all the issues described. If one message has been emphasized in this book, it is that there are no perfect solutions to management problems. To be an effective manager in the future, one must understand the dimensions that make each situation unique, so that one's analysis and decision making can be adjusted accordingly. The performance of the functions of management—planning, organizing, and controlling—will be influenced by each unique situation.

Planning

Although systematic and careful planning and decision making are associated with better performance, there are different degrees of planning and different approaches to decision making. In some situations, rigid and well-structured plans are preferred; in other situations, flexibility and more general plans are suitable. The same is true in decision making. Being able to adjust plans and decision processes will be needed more than ever before because of the frequency and the intensity of the changes that managers face. Change requires that managers be flexible enough to apply what is needed before and during the occurrence of events.

---

[25] Cetrou and O'Toole, *Encounters with the Future,* p. 268.

Organizing

There is no one best design for all organizations. What works for Metropolitan Life Insurance may have little applicability to General Mills, Textron, or IBM. The appropriate organization design must depend on the objectives, technology, environment, managerial styles, and employees. In fact, the same organization may have different design arrangements for various departments. Instead of searching for ideal designs, the manager in the future will use multiple and changing designs.

Controlling

The amount and the type of control used by an organization depend on the degree to which control is required to accomplish goals. Weighing the costs and benefits of various control procedures will probably become a more widely used analytic procedure in the future. For example, analyzing the costs and benefits of contemporary performance evaluation methods may reveal problem areas that management will have to correct. The manager of the future will be performing the functions of planning, organizing, and controlling in order to manage work and organizations, people, and production and operations more effectively. Managing is not an easy job. A career in management is for the person who likes to face challenges and gain the benefits of being successful.

SUMMARY OF KEY POINTS

- Managing is complicated, challenging, and vital to the success of organizations.
- The manager of the future must possess competencies, or skills, that can be applied to particular problems. The required competencies include problem solving, listening, communication, computer literacy, and interpersonal skills.
- Environmental forces that managers must cope with in the future will include natural-resource shortages, population changes, technological advances, government regulations, and increased international competition.
- Increasing numbers of women in the work force as entrepreneurs and in the management ranks present special issues of managerial interest. Even today, obstacles such as pay discrepancies and hostility plague many women. These problems have to be corrected to attract more qualified women into organizations.
- Black managers in growing numbers are finally at the point of moving into key senior managerial positions. Blacks are watching closely to determine if the barriers to discrimination have actually been removed.

- Management has to convince employees, who possess a strong work ethic, that they will benefit from productivity improvements. At this time, many workers do not believe that their efforts to improve productivity will be equitably recognized or rewarded.
- Unemployment is likely to continue. However, managers can attack unemployment, plant closings, and community disruptions if they join with the government and organized labor to retrain, relocate, and reeducate workers. The federal government will not be able to solve the unemployment problem without the expertise, resources, and involvement of labor leaders and management.

DISCUSSION AND REVIEW QUESTIONS

1. Why has computer literacy become an important competency requirement for management?
2. The Japanese work ethic appears to be strong (see Chapter 3). Why haven't people acknowledged that the American work ethic is also quite strong?
3. Why would Drucker criticize the idea of intrapreneurs as being "old wine in a new bottle"?
4. Government regulations since 1960 have addressed a number of areas. Which regulation has, in your opinion, had the greatest positive impact on the quality of life?
5. How serious is the energy shortage in industrialized nations such as the United States, Canada, and Australia?
6. As we move to a society less blue-collar oriented, some believe that the talents of women will become more evident. Why?
7. There are still some staunch advocates of the position that business organizations exist to provide goods and services and to earn a profit. It is claimed that because of its economic orientation, business is not prepared to be socially responsible. Do you agree with this position?
8. Why would some people believe that male and female entrepreneurs have different personal characteristics?
9. What signals are blacks looking for to determine whether they are accepted in management circles?
10. How can a student of management acquire the skills needed to be a success in management?

ADDITIONAL REFERENCES

Archer, F. "Charting a Career Course." *Personnel Journal,* June 1984, pp. 60–64.

Brandt, S. C. *Entrepreneuring in Established Companies.* New York: Dow Jones-Irwin, 1986.

"Challenges Future Bosses Will Face." *U.S. News & World Report,* December 23, 1985, p. 46.

Gallese, L. R. *Women like Us.* New York: Morrow, 1985.

Harriman, A. *Women/Men Management.* New York: Praeger Publishers, 1985.

Harris, P. R. *Management in Transition.* San Francisco: Jossey-Bass, 1985.

Humple, C. S., and M. Lyons. *Management and the Older Workforce.* New York: American Management Association, 1983.

Ingle, S. *In Search of Perfection.* Englewood Cliffs, N.J.: Prentice-Hall, 1985.

Keirnan, T. *The Road to Colossus.* New York: Morrow, 1985.

Linbroth, J. "How to Beat the Coming Labor Shortage." *Personnel Journal,* April 1982, pp. 268–72.

Lublin, J. S. "Women Hard-Hats Losing Ground as Slump, Budget Cuts Take Toll." *The Wall Street Journal,* April 15, 1982, p. 31.

Naisbitt, John. *Megatrends.* New York: Warner Books, 1982.

Ohmae, K. "Foresighted Management Decision Making: See the Options before Planning Strategy." *Management Review,* May 1982, pp. 46–55.

Rowan, R. "America's Most Wanted Managers." *Fortune,* February 3, 1986, pp. 18–25.

Schmidt, W. H., and B. Z. Posner. *Management Values and Expectations.* New York: American Management Association, 1982.

Stone, R. *The Push Button Manager.* New York: McGraw-Hill, 1985.

Strassman, P. A. *Information Payoff.* New York: Free Press, 1985.

Tarkington, C. "Losing Job Means Shattered Dreams, Broken Traditions." *APA Monitor,* January 1983, p. 8.

Wild, R. *How to Manage.* New York: Facts on File Publications, 1985.

CASES

APPLICATION I

THE FACTORY OF THE FUTURE*

In Walt Bohland's vision of tomorrow's auto factories, people don't get their hands dirty. Robots do the greasy work, the grunt work. Camera-holding computers replace most human inspectors. Repair stations don't exist, because cars are built right the first time.

"It's going to be clean, quiet, virtually all automated and safe," says Boh-

---

* Source: Doug Carroll, "Big 3 Plan to Eliminate the Grunt Work," *USA Today,* January 17, 1986, pp. 1–2.

land, executive engineer at Ford Motor Co.'s robotics and automation testing center.

"Ultimately the factory of the future is going to be a computer with a factory on the end of it," says Ford engineer Todd Cleaver.

In the Detroit suburbs where Henry Ford invented the mass-produced automobile nearly 80 years ago, people like Bohland and Cleaver are reinventing the assembly line. Traditional automaking is being overhauled in high-tech think tanks at each of the Big Three automakers. At Ford, it's called Alpha; at General Motors, Saturn; and at Chrysler, Liberty.

In bits and pieces, the future is taking shape today in prototype factories with lasers used for welding, robots for assembling, and computers keeping the line running. Unskilled labor is history.

And there is an attitude change, too. From white-collar boardrooms to blue-collar lunchrooms, teamwork and quality are more than buzzwords. "We sit down and talk through the way people do their job, what you feel can be done better, what you think you need to do it better, things we're doing to increase your progress. Before, we'd say, 'Shut up and do what I tell you,'" says Frederick Herr, Ford's vice president of manufacturing and engineering.

At the heart of the revolution is the need to cut costs while increasing quality. The University of Michigan's Transportation Research Institute says U.S. carmakers spend twice as many labor-hours making small cars as Japanese companies spend. Result: Japanese cars cost $1,500 to $2,000 less to make.

Detroit also wants to get cars off of drawing boards and into showrooms faster. That process takes as much as five years. "Ideally, it should be about 10 months," Herr says. Computer-aided design—where designers "draw" cars on computer screens instead of drafting boards—combined with computer-assisted engineering and manufacturing are slashing thousands of labor-hours and millions of dollars. GM's AUTOCHIP software cuts from as much as two years to a few months the time needed to design custom-integrated circuits for cars' electronic systems.

For consumers, this is good news. "You're going to get more car for your money," says industry analyst Thomas O'Grady of Integrated Automotive Resources, Inc.

Glimpses of the future:

- Ford's Livonia, Michigan, transmission plant, 80 percent automated with the latest in high-tech equipment. Machines do the "gofer" jobs here: Computers on the lines hail automated, unmanned vehicles that glide across the factory floor, bringing parts to where they are needed.
- GM's Saginaw Division in Saginaw, Michigan, where a $52 million "Factory of the Future" is being set up to make front-wheel drive axles starting in 1987. "We think many of the technologies emerging from the Factory of the Future will significantly change the way

we manufacture components for automobiles," says Thomas Angiers, division director of manufacturing engineering.

■ Chrysler's showpiece Sterling Heights, Michigan, assembly plant. More than 100 robots give 4,300 workers the ability to turn out 60 LeBaron GTSs and Dodge Lancers every two hours.

One obstacle to the Factory of the Future is getting all the computers, made by competing manufacturers, to talk to each other. "On the desks of some supervisors, you have four or five computer systems. They call up information from one and put it into another," says Mark Cocroft, a GM spokesman. "We are literally being buried in cables at our plant."

GM's solution: Manufacturing Automation Protocol (MAP), a manufacturers' standard for computer hardware and software that still is being developed. At the Factory of the Future, MAP will cut from weeks to minutes the time needed to change from making one axle to another on the assembly line.

The plant will be totally automated with no direct human labor. Instead, more than 50 robots and computer-controlled machinery will produce axles. It also will be a "paperless" plant: Everything from work schedules to inventory reports will be on computers.

Reductions in labor are estimated at between 30 percent and 40 percent from the current work force. One shift will be staffed by only two supervisors, who watch over machines.

To get ready for this project, about 70 GM hourly and salaried employees have been taking courses for almost a year to learn how to operate computers, robots, and the other equipment. They've also been taking courses in personal relations to prepare for jobs that will stress teamwork more than ever.

"One of our goals is to run the factory on a participatory management type of philosophy. We envision being able to run operations in the Factory of the Future without a salaried supervisor like we have today," explains Robert Zeilinger, manager of GM's Factory of the Future.

What's happening at Saginaw, say executives and union leaders, is a harbinger of what's coming in the industry. Unskilled labor will be replaced with better educated workers who have a stronger voice in decision making. "Young entry people will have to understand computer systems, vision systems, and probably have some understanding of physics and chemistry, depending on the plant you're in," says Herr, a 29-year Ford veteran.

Ford autoworker Bob McCallum, who came into the industry 22 years ago when he was 25, saw the handwriting on the wall and hit the books—hard. He signed up for a Ford training program for its newly automated Livonia transmission plant. After completing 360 hours of advanced instruction in robotics, metrics, and other subjects over 12 weeks, McCallum helps train others in the same subjects.

"With this training, our chances of keeping the doors open on this building

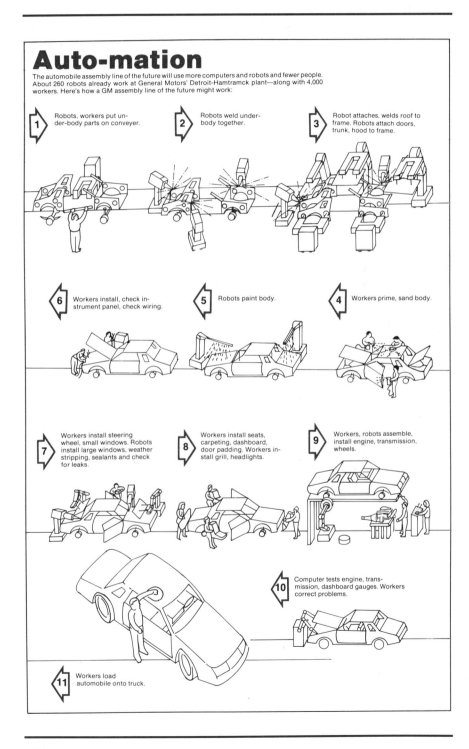

Auto-mation

The automobile assembly line of the future will use more computers and robots and fewer people. About 260 robots already work at General Motors' Detroit-Hamtramck plant—along with 4,000 workers. Here's how a GM assembly line of the future might work:

1 Robots, workers put under-body parts on conveyer.

2 Robots weld under-body together.

3 Robot attaches, welds roof to frame. Robots attach doors, trunk, hood to frame.

6 Workers install, check instrument panel, check wiring.

5 Robots paint body.

4 Workers prime, sand body.

7 Workers install steering wheel, small windows. Robots install large windows, weather stripping, sealants and check for leaks.

8 Workers install seats, carpeting, dashboard, door padding. Workers install grill, headlights.

9 Workers, robots assemble, install engine, transmission, wheels.

10 Computer tests engine, transmission, dashboard gauges. Workers correct problems.

11 Workers load automobile onto truck.

are 100 percent better. If my sons want a job in the auto industry, at least Livonia will still be here."

Questions for Analysis

1. Will participatory management in the auto industry result in more or fewer jobs?
2. In the factory of the future, there is no room for unskilled labor. Why?
3. Why is computer literacy becoming more important in the auto industry?

APPLICATION II

BLACK & DECKER DECLARES WAR ON INTERNATIONAL COMPETITORS*

International competition is now a fact of life in organizations and will remain so in the foreseeable future. Some firms, like Black & Decker Mfg. Co., view this competition as a "war to survive" and contend that managers play a significant role in whether survival is achieved. Unlike many American firms, Black & Decker has decided to meet international competition, especially that from Japan, head-on.

A lot of companies have thrown up their hands and cried that they can't compete on price or quality with the Japanese. Instead, Black & Decker has decided to do battle with Japanese competitors in the professional power tool market. This market represents only 21 percent of Black & Decker's sales, but it has been the most profitable part of the company's business. Black & Decker fears that if the Japanese gain in the professional power tool market, they will also be able to make major inroads in the consumer market.

In the past five years, Makita Electric Works, Ltd. and other Japanese tool companies have captured up to 20 percent of the worldwide professional tool market. Now they are burrowing into U.S. markets at prices that have made Black & Decker's professional tool business less profitable. To meet the Japanese competition, Black & Decker has had to match their production costs. This has forced Black & Decker to close some plants, build and implement robots, reduce its staff by 20 percent, and improve its distribution system.

Black & Decker has also copied features of Japanese competitors' products

---

* Source: Adapted from Betsy Morris, "Black & Decker Meets Japan's Push Head-On in Power Tool Market," *The Wall Street Journal,* February 18, 1983, pp. 1, 8.

and has taken steps to increase worker productivity while reducing prices. In addition, the company has spent $256.2 million to modernize plants.

At least one domestic competitor questions Black & Decker's wisdom. The competitor isn't sure that Black & Decker can hold the line on their price cuts.

Despite Black & Decker's difficulties, it has several advantages over other domestic industries, such as steel and autos, that have fought the battles of the imports. The company is nonunion and, with operations in 55 countries, is truly an international firm. This gives management a global attitude and a knowledge of how to compete in world markets. Also, it is a company that reacts to competition early instead of waiting until competitors gain a toehold on a market.

The tool market in Japan ranks among the world's largest markets, behind the United States and West Germany. However, Black & Decker has not set up operations in Japan, a fact some experts consider an error. In the 1960s, Black & Decker attempted manufacturing and sales in Japan but failed to penetrate Japan's distribution system. Today the company would like another opportunity. It does have brand recognition and a widespread distribution system. It also understands the Japanese market better today than in the 1960s.

The jury is still out on whether the Black & Decker competition with Japan will succeed. However, instead of seeking government aid to meet international competitors, Black & Decker decided to push out on its own. It is indeed a brave effort.

Questions for Analysis

1. Why would being nonunion be considered an advantage for Black & Decker when engaged in international competition?

2. Why would experts feel that it is a mistake for Black & Decker not to have established operations in Japan when they are challenging Japanese competition?

3. One expert considers Black & Decker tough enough to compete with the Japanese. He put it this way: "They haven't spent all their life in some nice soft pussycat market like the United States. They know what the real world is like." What does he mean?

EXPERIENTIAL EXERCISE

ATTITUDE MEASURE OF WOMEN AS MANAGERS

Purpose

The purpose of this exercise is to assess attitudes people have about women in business.

The Exercise in Class

1. Each student should complete the Women-as-Managers Scale (WAMS) in Exhibit 1. The best answer to each statement is your *personal opinion*. The statements cover many different and opposing points of view; you may find yourself agreeing strongly with some of the statements, disagreeing just as strongly with others, and perhaps uncertain about others. Whether you agree or disagree with any statement, you can be sure that many people feel the same way you do.

    Using the numbers from 1 to 7 on the rating scale below, mark your personal opinion about each statement in the blank that immediately precedes it. Remember, give your *personal opinion* according to how much you agree or disagree with each item. Please respond to all 21 items.

1—strongly disagree   5—slightly agree
2—disagree   6—agree
3—slightly disagree   7—strongly agree
4—neither disagree nor agree

2. Receive the scoring instructions from your instructor.
3. After students have scored their individual forms, set up groups of five to six students. (Try to have men and women in each group.) The group discussion should focus on the individual scores.

The Learning Message

The scores on the WAMS will provide some indication of how comfortable a person is with women in managerial positions. Since women are entering management in greater numbers, attitudes about them as managers are important and should be understood.

EXHIBIT   1   Women-as-Managers Scale

_____ 1. It is less desirable for women than men to have a job that requires responsibility.

_____ 2. Women have the objectivity required to evaluate business situations properly.

_____ 3. Challenging work is more important to men than it is to women.

_____ 4. Men and women should be given equal opportunity for participation in management training programs.

_____ 5. Women have the capability to acquire the necessary skills to be successful managers.

_____ 6. On the average, women managers are less capable of contributing to an organization's overall goals than are men.

_____ 7. It is not acceptable for women to assume leadership roles as often as men.

_____ 8. The business community should someday accept women in key managerial positions.

_____ 9. Society should regard work by female managers to be as valuable as work by male managers.

_____ 10. It is acceptable for women to compete with men for top executive positions.

_____ 11. The possibility of pregnancy does not make women less desirable employees than men.

_____ 12. Women would no more allow their emotions to influence their managerial behavior than would men.

_____ 13. Problems associated with menstruation should not make women less desirable than men as employees.

_____ 14. To be a successful executive, a woman does not have to sacrifice some of her femininity.

_____ 15. On the average, a woman who stays at home all the time with her children is a better mother than a woman who works outside the home at least half time.

_____ 16. Women are less capable of learning mathematical and mechanical skills than are men.

_____ 17. Women are not ambitious enough to be successful in the business world.

_____ 18. Women cannot be assertive in business situations that demand it.

_____ 19. Women possess the self-confidence required of a good leader.

_____ 20. Women are not competitive enough to be successful in the business world.

_____ 21. Women cannot be aggressive in business situations that demand it.

Source: James R. Terborg, Lawrence H. Peters, Daniel R. Ilgen, and Frank Smith, "Organizational and Personal Correlates of Attitudes toward Women as Managers," _Academy of Management Journal,_ March 1977, p. 93. With permission.

■ **INTEGRATIVE CASE I**

Southern Federal Savings and Loan Association*

Southern Federal Savings and Loan Association's offices were gearing up to offer consumer loans, NOW accounts, and renegotiable rate mortgages (RRMs) which were allowed by the Depository Institutions Deregulation and Monetary Control Act of 1980. By July 1980, steps to introduce these new products were well under way. Mr. Knight, the chief executive officer, explained:

> We'll get into consumer loans as early as September 1st or 15th—whenever we can gear up and get in. We're trying hard to get in just as soon as possible because we know it will affect all our branch offices—all branch managers and at least one other person have got to be trained and familiar with them. That's a big job. But we need to get on with it just as quickly as possible because NOW accounts are coming January 1st, and we don't want two things of this magnitude slapping us at the same time. If we can get into consumer lending in September, then we'll have a little bit of time to get feeling comfortable with that before starting to feel uncomfortable when NOW accounts go.

Southern Federal's Management

Mr. Knight was in his 16th year as president of Southern Federal. He had not grown up in this business but had become president of Southern Federal after selling his poultry business. In describing how he became involved, Knight explained:

> I sold out my interests in the poultry business on February 1, 1962, became mayor of the city on January 1, 1964, and came over here in December 1964. My predecessor had reached retirement age, but they didn't give him until the first of January as was customary. There was some internal conflict. I replaced him on the 11th of December. That didn't set well with him, but I didn't have anything to do with it.
>
> I didn't seek the job and didn't particularly want it, but one of the directors came by and asked me if I'd consider filling in for an interim time. I assumed he was talking from January on. I said, "Well, I hadn't thought about it, but I might be interested," because the position as mayor was supposed to be a part-time job. After that, four directors fell in behind me; they said, "We'd just like to have you fill in." So I've been filling in since 1964, but my filling-in time is about up, because I turned 65 on June 17. I don't know what my relationship will be after January 1.

* Source: This case was prepared by William R. Boulton and James A Verbrugge, University of Georgia. Permission to publish granted by the authors and the Case Research Association.

James Redding, Southern Federal's second in command, also came from the outside in 1960. Prior to joining Southern Federal, he had been in the real estate and insurance business and had been helping the association part-time. He explained:

> I was helping them out part time with problems they were having in the appraising and construction end of the business and decided to try it full-time. I did the appraising and developed inspection sheets for builders to use in drawing money for construction loans. I worked on that end of it and later just sort of became general flunky around here.

Knight commented on the development of the organization:

> There was no organization 16 years ago. We were small by comparison. But we are a whole lot larger, so we have had to departmentalize. We had to gear up for that. We had to employ people. Besides Redding and Billings, assistant in mortgage loans, I've employed everyone in frontline management. They are more or less the type of people that I like on my side.

In discussing the actual structure of Southern Federal, Knight continued:

> The direct line is myself, James Redding, and Jack Pope. After that you break down into various departments. Bob Thompson is mortgage loan officer. Jim Heart is controller.
>
> I'm the managing officer and the president and the chairman of the board. But after January 1, if I stay, I'd probably like to take a little different role—back off just a little bit—and let James and Jack and those folks really run the association, and I would act more in a policy and advisory capacity. If the board is willing to do that, I'd like to do it, because I'm not a retirement-type person.

A copy of Southern Federal's current organizational structure was not readily available to Vice President Jack Pope, the one to develop such charts. He explained:

> I've done some sketches of the organization chart but passed them on to Redding and didn't keep a copy. We've talked about it. We know how it works, or at least the department heads know.

Exhibit 1 shows the organization chart which Pope drafted.

With regard to the key positions at Southern Federal, Jack Pope explained the concept:

> I took an ideal S&L organization chart and tried to compare it to what we once had. I think that may have assisted in the decision to reorganize our loan department and put someone in control. The loan department had been split up between Thompson, Billings, and Heart into loan originations, loan processing, and taxes and insurance. . . . Now Bob Thompson is department head. Harold Billings is responsible for closings and handling loans in process.
>
> Jim Heart was put in charge of accounting. Elizabeth Smith had reported to me in accounting. Jim didn't have any training as controller, but it was

EXHIBIT 1 **Southern Federal Savings and Loan Association Organization Chart—August 4, 1980**

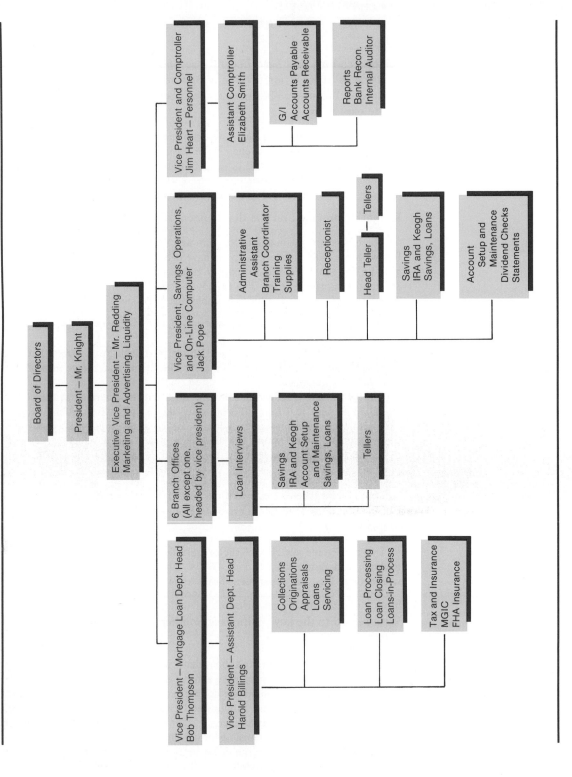

felt he could do the job, and he has. I didn't think Elizabeth was particularly pleased at first, but it has worked out well. Jim is also responsible for new employee and personnel interviews and keeps EEOC and affirmative action records in order. He has little to do with daily personnel operations except in his own department.

My duties are in operations. I have responsibility for tellers and savings counselors. I have a branch coordinator working for me now. I'm responsible for the on-line computer service, so I write the procedures or make any changes when we change the system. Supplies and purchases also come under my jurisdiction. Someone else is responsible for custodial services.

The new branch coordinator position has responsibility for branch communication and training. Knight explained the branch coordinator's role:

We just promoted one of the girls who has a lot of talent and ability to branch coordinator. From that respect, she has no supervisory jurisdiction over a branch manager, but she is really coordinating personnel. If someone doesn't show and the manager doesn't think he can operate, he calls her and we get somebody on the road to help out. The same for supplies. When you get six branches, you just can't do it from your hip pocket. You have to have some plan of handling things.

The Board of Directors

Southern Federal's board of directors significantly changed since Knight joined the association. He explained the early structure:

When I came over here, the average age of the board was about 70. We had one that was 90. Another that was 80. Several were in their 70s—they were the young guys. I was just a babe in the woods. That had to be changed. You may think that's no trouble, but it is.

We set limits of 70. When I reach 70, I'm off the board, and that's the way it ought to be. We finally agreed that if they served three years from the time we made that agreement, that was fair, and they would become emeritus members and leave the board. It just takes time to do those things.

In describing the current membership of the board, Knight continued:

We have the director of campus planning, who has been here a long time. The university football coach also represents another area of thinking as a director. We also have the owner of a downtown retail men's store and a fine doctor and surgeon who has a good financial mind. We have the controller for a local textile plant and an ex-government official that now heads up the university research lab. We then have myself, Redding, the president of North County S&L, and one of our retired executives that knows the business.

Southern Federal's board of directors holds meetings on the second Tuesday of every month. Knight explained the role of his board members:

We have an agenda which includes basic items that are required, then gets into new business and things that need to be brought to the board's attention.

Two of the members, Redding and myself, serve as members of the Loan Committee. We provide a written report from the loan committee, and the board acts on that. The director of campus planning is a good board member who takes the time to read the information we send him. So I usually ask if he has any comments on the Loan Committee's minutes. If he sees one he doesn't understand, he'll ask a question. We may give our reasons for that particular loan and the interest rate charged, or whatever attracted his attention.

The controller over at the textile mill has a real good financial mind. I usually ask him for comments on the financial statement that's prepared by Jim Heart. He's sharp enough that if he sees an unusual figure, it flags him and he'll put a circle around it. So we get into things that he doesn't understand or that need clarification. Sometimes he'll understand it, but he'll do it for the benefit of the other board members. That kind of takes care of the nuts and bolts.

Redding commented further on their board's involvement:

Our board is made up of a pretty knowledgeable group of folks here in town. They set the policy and the tone of what we're going to do. For what services we offer, I think they take most of the recommendations that management makes.

They turned us down on a logo one time. We've got to get us a logo. I was talking to our advertising man the other day about getting one. We had about three logos and they turned them all down. You have to get some uniformity in advertising as you get bigger. We're working on that in sort of a hit-and-miss way.

They were quite active in designing and planning the North Highway branch. Quite active. But they're not like down at South Bank and Trust—they're down there all the time. Of course, South Bank and Trust almost lost all the money they had down there, too.

They weren't active in the North County merger but, of course, participated in some group meetings and gave the green light to see if we could go ahead and effect it. That was a chore, and we don't have all the strings tied together yet.

They had a discussion of consumer loans last meeting. Bob Thompson was also at the last meeting talking about the rollover rate mortgage, explaining that. We had one meeting on NOW accounts; they said go ahead on those two things.

Southern Federal's Management Philosophy

Southern Federal has become a leading institution in the community. This has not always been the case, as Knight explained:

When I came here, we had several problems that I perceived. One was that we were really an organization that survived or prospered or declined based on its participation in the community. If you don't participate in the community, I don't know how the community is going to participate with you. The way that they participate with us is to put their savings and their loans here. But the association was really just withdrawn. It wasn't outgoing. It took no real part, for instance, in the United Way or in supporting those things that make a good community. It did not suggest that the officers of the association join the civic clubs and take part. These are things that I believe you've got to do if you're going to be successful in your operation and have the name and image out there all the time.

We gave just a little token to financial drives. Today we are the largest financial institution in South County, given the fact that Republic is a branch and the chain could swallow us up many times; but one on one, we're larger. We try to give a leading gift. I think we have to.

Besides attempting to have a meaningful leadership role in the community, Southern Federal also attempts to maintain a good working environment for its employees, as Jack Pope explained:

We have a good working environment—somewhat relaxed. We don't push people. We assign a job and expect it to be completed in a reasonable period of time. Most people like that.

This atmosphere does not mean that employees live a "life of ease," as Knight pointed out:

One thing that Jack Pope places a lot of emphasis on is encouraging employees to take advantage of the courses that we pay for, which are furnished by the U.S. League's financial education section. They are constantly involved in courses.

This is part of our merit program—to be qualified for a position, you must have passed satisfactorily those courses to make you qualified for that position. Now if it comes down to two people going for the same position, the one who had qualified his or herself in the best manner—and, if it came down to a fine line, had the best grades—would probably be the one to get that position, everything else being equal. Most of these people will make As and A+s. When these girls go after something, they usually work at it and do a good job.

Southern Federal also has been able to attract and keep good people. With regard to their low employee turnover, Knight explained:

Generally speaking, we don't have much turnover. We have always had a great esprit de corps. We have tried to encourage that with fringe benefits, uniforms, family get-togethers, etc. So far we've screened our employees pretty darn good. We've been lucky. We've had some misfits, but I think they realized they were and eventually worked out.

Now, First National Bank works on a different concept. They employ a lot of students and have a lot of turnover. They kind of accept that turnover, and I think it costs them, too. We'd rather have continuity and have you see the same person when you come in here—if it's possible.

Commenting on the loss of several employees earlier in the year, Knight explained:

Gosh, we took a siege here about three months ago, and we lost them, bam, bam, bam, just like that. And we're losing another next Tuesday. You just can't help it—she used to work for this dentist in another town. That joker is now going to also have an office here; he remembered her and made an offer she couldn't turn down. He offered her $2,500 more than we are paying here. She's a good employee, and we hate to lose her; but there is no way we can keep her without destroying the whole scale. You lose some like that, reluctantly.

Redding also expressed his feelings about the recent turnover:

We had the quitting bug come through here about a year ago, and everyone got to quitting. And then we'll have the baby bug come by here, and it'll bite a bunch of them.

Employee Compensation and Incentives

Along with having a good work environment, Southern Federal has also attempted to provide competitive salary and benefits for its employees. Pope explained:

We try to be competitive on salary with the banks around here, and benefits are on top of that. We have not had a great deal of turnover except for earlier this year. Usually the bank people come to us for jobs because they hear good things about us.

All employees who have been with the company at least six months participate in Southern Federal's profit sharing. Knight explained the system:

We have profit sharing—I guess you would call it that. There is no setting aside and waiting 10 years. We have a little formula—Redding works it up—that for the last two years has, generally speaking, amounted to between 10 and 14 percent of salary. How long you have been here and how much you are making is all tied into it. If you've been here less than six months, you're gonna get a ham. If you've been here over six months, you're gonna get your pro rata.

We take a fixed percentage of income which we're adding to net worth. It's about a 50 percent deal. I believe it behooves us to treat the employees well and try to have people who are willing and ready to wait on people when they come through our doors, and make the person want to come back. Most of our people go out of their way.

Southern Federal also provides employee uniforms and other benefits, as Redding explained:

Many years ago, we put in a dress code. We give the ladies dresses. They got to squabbling about the thing here the other day; so we put it to a vote, and they voted 34 to 4 to keep the dresses.

We also furnish meals here. We have a dining room downstairs. The branch personnel get $1.75 a day to buy their cokes and soup. Here, it's free cokes, free coffee, free doughnuts, free lunch, free uniforms. Whether we should put that in a paycheck and forget about it, I don't know; but I like it this way.

We provide hospital insurance, retirement, all of that—but not for the dependents—we have life insurance tied in with their retirement and hospitalization.

Southern Federal's Management Control and Information Systems

Southern Federal does not set formal goals and objectives for itself. Knight explained about the absence of objectives:

We just haven't set any objective over here that we're trying to reach. I'll tell you, we would have missed them so far. I told the board at the first of the year that we would be lucky if we were in the black for the year. Well, we made so much money in the first four months on penalties that they said, "What are you talking about?" I said, "Just wait. It's coming." It came, but now, again, we're turning it back the other way. Our projections don't look all that bad for the rest of the year, if we can hold it. It's very upsetting. There is no real way to keep up with it.

There just doesn't seem to be any way to cope with some of the things we encounter. Suppose that last January we had set up some goals and objectives. We would have missed them for various reasons. We would have missed it on income for four months. We had the best income we've ever had because we were collecting penalties. I wasn't smart enough to look ahead and say we were going to collect penalties, because I didn't even know we were going to be levying penalties. It's not from lack of thought or desire to do it that way; it just seems beyond our control. Everybody else seems to be controlling what you can do. The only thing we can do is operate as best we can with what they give us to operate with and try to better our performance. This is what we tell our employees, "We have to do better than we did last year," and we try to tell them various ways to do it.

No, we don't set goals, except that we try to do better each year than we did the year before. It's a relative thing. We're working against ourselves to do better. I don't know how you can set goals with the Federal Home Loan Board and with policies, now, of the DIDC committee. You could set some goals, but you don't have the ability to meet them. They're changing things so fast. Now, if they ever settle down, it may be different.

Redding commented further:

We don't have any formal goals. We don't belong to the Rotary Club. I guess subconsciously we'd like to be the biggest one in the state, try to build up our deposits, get savings. We look at it and, if it looks like the loan volume is off and we got money and feel the economy is better, we'll have our advertising man go after the loans, start working with the real estate people, try to be competitive with rates, and scheme as best we can. We would like to get one percent net, but we haven't done it. We're on profit sharing here, and everyone participates—it's not going to be as good a year as it has been.

Southern Federal's savings operations have been installed on NCR's time-sharing system, which allows management to trace savings throughout the day. Jack Pope explained:

> When we first started using the NCR system, Redding used to come in every hour to find out how savings and withdrawals were coming. We found that you couldn't tell how you were doing until late afternoon because it fluctuates so much from hour to hour.

Besides tracking their savings operations, management also tracks the firm's overall performance. Knight, as he picked up a summary of branch profit performance, explained:

> I can show you expenses and income from each branch. Of course, some of it's hard to come by exactly, but we can come within sight of it, and that's all you really need to know. The total accounting picture is accurate. River County, for instance, has a little branch out there. It's not a profitable situation. It's slowly growing.
>
> We keep strict accounting on each branch. We separate them so I can look at my records and tell you how each one of them is doing. I can look at my daily record and tell you what each one of them is doing in savings. It is good to know how much you're receiving. You certainly don't want to put more money into an area than you're taking in. It varies, This month, Lakeview's having a real good month on savings. North Highway is the leading branch on savings and has been ever since Mary Defoe went out there. That's the way I knew it would happen, because she really has a good rapport with people that save with us.

Redding further explained:

> We have an annual budget—keep up with it and track variances monthly. It's done by hand. We have a Wang upstairs but don't use it. The damn thing takes a chauffeur, and we don't have one.

Jack Pope commented on the reason Southern Federal has the Wang computer:

> We bought the Wang because we were going to put our loan-processing records on the computer. We bought that system because we thought it would be easy to adapt the software—but then we got our lawyers involved and we couldn't decide what format was legal, etc. It's been a year and a half, and we still don't use it.

Management had also planned to have a more extensive computer facility in the future. Knight explained:

> I was ready to buy a computer about two years ago, but Jack Pope, the operations officer, and Jim Heart, the controller, both felt like it would be money that could be better spent somewhere else. They felt we could stay on NCR until we reached about $250 million. Well, with NOW accounts coming in, I think that timetable is going to be changed.

The North Highway office was designed—the floor, wiring, and everything is ready to go—to set the computer and everything that goes with it in there. That will go into the basement out there—it's a good place because the temperature won't change as much and it's easy to keep it cool, which is better for the computer.

Pope also commented on their planning system:

We have looked at several models, but haven't decided on one yet. We do some hand calculations, or what-ifs, of existing figures. But it isn't done with much depth.

With regard to keeping in touch with the critical operations of the association, Redding looked at the papers covering his desk and responded:

Gosh, I don't know. You see how tidy my desk is! I guess Knight and I talk, and we talk with the other people in the departments, listen to all sorts of rumors, talk to other people in the business—other associations. We watch our profit picture—it looks gloomy right now though. The money market rates being what they are, it'll be October before we really get rid of the bad stuff.

I think we've done a pretty good job in spite of the fact that we're not organized. We're not highly structured. I'm just now getting around, after 20 years, to getting some little plan for the janitor. This has become a problem, now, on how to keep the darn branches cleaned up. That thing out on North Highway has weeds everywhere. We have about three acres out there. We ought to have had better sense. We had to paint the Eastside Mall Branch because it wasn't quite so clear—you see we throw a little competition in there. Get them competing with each other. South Rim and Lakeview, they're about the same size—I pick on them to ask them why they're not doing so well.

With Southern Federal's first priority being entrance into the consumer loan business, there is a need to recruit a new manager. James Redding, executive vice president, is concerned about the kind of person they are going to need. He explained:

Now facing us is the consumer loan, which we'll be getting into by September. That will entail adding someone who is knowledgeable of consumer lending, which will include automobile loans, signature loans, 90-day loans, or anything oriented to family financing. We want someone who will charge enough. We might get someone from one of these short-loan places. I used to be in the short-loan business. I'm the secretary and treasurer for Equitable's loan company. We took it over. We had a manager, and I supervised it from afar. Our motto was "Consolidate all your little bills into one huge staggering debt." That's from the lending end.

With the rapid introduction of consumer lending activities, Southern Federal also has to prepare employees to handle them. Redding continued:

That's a problem in going into consumer lending. You're going to have to do it in the branches, and what do they know about consumer lending? Nothing! So you're going to have to get them trained. Whether they do one automobile a day, a week, or an hour, we're going to have to give them responsibility and work from there. Jack Pope is reviewing that.

Of course, with consumer lending, you're going to have to be able to give customers answers in 10 minutes or an hour—so we're also going to have to change our approval process.

Questions for Analysis

1. In response to environmental and competitive pressures, Southern Federal's management made several changes in the organizational structure. Describe and evaluate these changes.
2. Evaluate the management philosophy at Southern Federal. What are the central ideas of the philosophy? Are these central ideas consistent with the demands of the business?
3. Evaluate Southern Federal's planning and controlling methods and practices. What could be done to improve them?
4. What seems to be the prevalent leadership style at Southern Federal? Is this style appropriate for the situation? Explain.
5. What operations management methods appear useful in managing savings and loan companies? Are there, for example, applications of PERT, linear programming, and inventory control that Southern Federal's management should investigate?

▧ INTEGRATIVE CASE II

National Motor Parts Company*

The National Motor Parts Company is one of the five largest firms in the basic auto parts industry. It has nine operating divisions and a total work force of over 80,000 employees. Its extensive staff organization provides specialized skills at the corporate, divisional, and plant level. At each of these levels, the cost accounting and industrial engineering groups exert a considerable amount of interest over the development and execution of corporate policy. Though individual divisions are operationally autonomous, division officials generally follow the policy suggestions made by the cost accounting and industrial engineering staffs. A partial organization chart is shown in Exhibit 1.

---

* Copyright 1977, by John G. Hutchinson and Charles E. Summer.

EXHIBIT   1   Partial Organization Chart

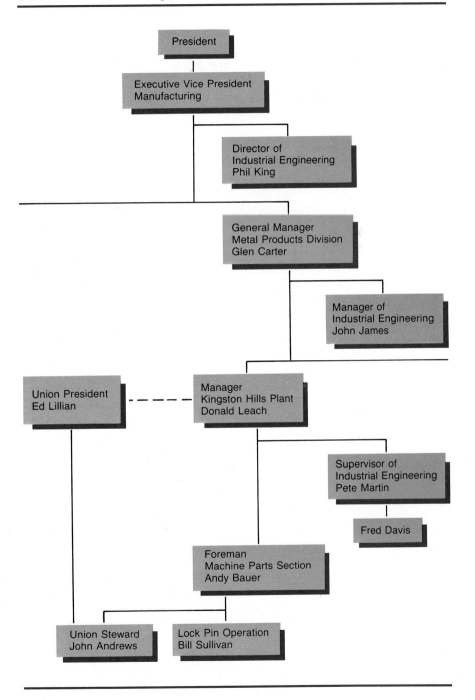

One program recently advocated by Phil King, corporate director of industrial engineering, was a review of work standards on all jobs which had not been checked or audited within the previous two years. King's request arose from the fact that he had seen several instances of what appeared to him to be goldbricking during a tour of plants in several of National's operating divisions. Upon his return to the central office, King met with two of his staff engineers, and after careful deliberation, an audit plan was drawn up. This plan was subsequently approved by the executive vice president in charge of manufacturing operations.

The audit plan suggested by King used a technique known as work sampling to check on the idle time present in individual job standards. In essence, the approach taken relied on the fact that a series of short, random observations, if taken often enough over an appropriate time period, could give an accurate picture of the operations performed in each job. The work-sampling results would be used to determine which jobs were not requiring the employees to work for an entire day to meet their stated output standards. By the same token, those jobs which were demanding a full day's work to meet existing standards would also be recognized. Though work sampling was to be used to identify standards which were loose (i.e., standards which did not require a full day's work to meet output requirements for that day), King's proposal included the further suggestion that looseness, when detected, should be checked in detail by the use of stopwatch time study and a thorough motion study of the job in question.

To launch his program, King held a series of meetings with the heads of divisional industrial engineering groups. Though objections were raised about the cost and time considerations inherent in the proposal, the division engineering managers agreed that the plan was technically sound and agreed to put it into effect as soon as possible.

One of the more receptive listeners to King's audit procedure was John James, manager of industrial engineering in National's Metal Products Division. This division employs 21,000 people in five plants. James, who holds degrees in both industrial engineering and mathematics, thought that King's plan was both technically sound and eminently practical. He returned to division headquarters in Kingston, Michigan, and drew up procedures to implement the plan in the Metal Products Division's five plants.

Within a month after the corporate staff meeting, James offered his own version of the audit plan to Glenn Carter, the division manager. Carter, who had come to respect James's technical ability and practical know-how, accepted the plan readily and agreed to present it at the next weekly meeting of his plant managers. Carter suggested that he should merely outline the plan to his plant managers and that James should be available to fill in details and to answer questions.

In the subsequent meeting, each of the plant managers agreed that such an audit was sound, and each in turn suggested that James contact the heads of their plant industrial engineering departments to explain the details of his plan. Three plant managers who had formerly been in charge of industrial engineering groups in the National hierarchy offered to provide additional clerical and engineering help on a temporary basis in order to get the program moving quickly.

After gaining the support of Carter and the five plant managers, James met with the heads of industrial engineering in each of the division's five plants. Though the familiar objections were raised about the time and cost of such a program, all five men stated that the audit procedure was practical, and they agreed to put it into effect immediately. Within this group, the plan was embraced most enthusiastically by Pete Martin, the industrial engineer in charge of the Kingston Hills plant.

The Kingston Hills plant shares the same plot of land as the headquarters of the Metal Products Division. It employs more than 5,000 workers and is generally considered to be the most modern and most efficient of the division's plants. Donald Leach, the plant manager, is one of the three men in the division who rose to his present position from a supervisory job in the industrial engineering hierarchy. Leach's plant is equipped with the latest advances in automated equipment; and it is, according to division records, the most profitable plant in the division. Leach prides himself on his ability to attract and retain good managerial talent, and he is particularly proud of the work done by Pete Martin in developing new methods of work and in adapting mathematical techniques and procedures to fit the needs of the operations at the Kingston Hills plant. Thus, when Martin suggested the adoption of an audit program, Leach agreed readily and offered Martin additional clerical help to work on the details of setting up the program.

Pete Martin went to work on the program immediately, and within a week the first audit reports were completed. After one month, audits had been completed on 17 operations. Sixteen of these audits indicated that very little idle time was evident in the operations studied, but the audit performed on one job, the production of a tiny metal lock pin used in automatic transmission units, seemed to show an unusual amount of idle time. The job in question was performed by Bill Sullivan, an experienced, long-service employee. Sullivan set up, tended, and performed certain minor maintenance tasks on an automatic screw machine. Because the products he worked on were varied, the original standards had been measured quite carefully.[1] Since the time when the original standards were set, changes had occurred which caused the standards to become loose. Materials changes, changes in tolerance limits on the various machined parts, the time and methods used to set up the various runs, the actual length of machine runs, and the adoption of a more standardized parts line had all occurred in recent years; and since several of these changes had apparently not been reflected in adjustments

---

[1] Sullivan's standard at this time was .33734 minutes per piece, or approximately 180 units of output per hour.

in the affected output standards, it was a rare day when Sullivan failed to obtain his expected or standard output.

The looseness of Sullivan's standards was no revelation to several of his immediate co-workers. One worker, for example, when conversing with Pete Martin about the audit, stated, "If your audit doesn't pick up that soft touch Sullivan's got, you'd better toss the whole thing down the drain." Few of the workers were bitter about Sullivan's "gravy train" job, however, since the looseness of his standards gave him no wage advantages over his fellow workers. In other National plants where payment is tied directly to output through the use of incentive payment plans, the relative looseness of standards had frequently caused bitter disputes because of the wage inequities it generated. In the Kingston Hills Plant, the failure of management to detect a loose standard means that workers accrue leisure-time benefits, not higher wages. Though workers objected to such unfair workloads, no grievance had ever been filed to ask management to correct such inequities.

The second phase of the audit procedure entailed a review of Sullivan's job by Fred Davis, one of Martin's most competent engineers. In this study, Davis compared the previously set standard with the newly calculated time required to perform the operation under changed conditions. This, in turn, showed a tentative idle time of four hours per shift.[2] Davis's stopwatch time study of the screw-machine operation confirmed the results of the initial audit, and a detailed methods study of the job turned up substantial changes in the original working conditions, including changes in materials and methods of operation. Leach, when confronted with this information by Martin and Davis, ordered them to take steps to correct what he believed was an inequity in the basic workload structure.

After several weeks of study, Davis devised a plan where, with certain layout changes and some methods improvements, Sullivan would operate not one, but two machines. Davis's methods study showed that the time allowances were adequate enough to allow Sullivan to complete the requirements of the revised job if he worked a full eight-hour day. Davis showed his plan to Pete Martin, and together they presented it to Leach. Leach approved the plan and directed the Purchasing Department to acquire another automatic screw machine. He thereupon called in Andy Bauer, Sullivan's immediate supervisor and informed him that Sullivan should be told of the impending change.[3] Bauer, who had worked with Davis on the methods study, agreed to tell Sullivan that management intended to exercise its contractual right "to make changes in methods, equipment, materials, and conditions

---

[2] Though a four-hour idle time may seem to be so high as to be almost unbelievable, engineering studies performed elsewhere in National Motors uncovered similar looseness. Experts in the industrial engineering field concede that this situation can arise in even the best-managed plants.

[3] The new standard called for a time of .1664 minutes per piece, or approximately 360 units per hour.

of work in order to obtain greater efficiency and to adjust existing work standards to reflect such changes." The labor contract further stated that "in case of such methods change, only those elements of the standard will be changed which are affected by the change in methods, etc." One other section of the contract spelled out the fact that "standards will be set on the basis of fairness and equity and that they shall be consistent with the quality of workmanship, efficiency of operation, and reasonable working capacities of normal operations." In the National Motors contract, as in most others in the basic auto industry, the resolution of work-standards disputes can be solved only by dealings between management and the labor union. Arbitration is specifically prohibited as a means of settling disputes over work standards.

Two months later, the new machine was installed at the workplace along with several minor changes in layout and work flow. Foreman Bauer instructed Sullivan in his new duties, and Sullivan, though he was unhappy about the new layout, started to work with the two machines. During the day, John Andrews, the union steward, stopped by to check on the new job.[4] Sullivan complained violently that he was the victim of a "speedup." Andrews, after listening to the details of the shift from one to two machines, suggested that Sullivan file a grievance.

That evening Sullivan wrote a grievance and, shortly before starting work the next morning, turned it over to John Andrews. Andrews, following the normal procedure for processing such grievances, presented it to Andy Bauer for discussion and possible solution. Because of the technical nature of the grievance, Bauer called upon Pete Martin and Fred Davis to explain the nature of the change to Andrews. When Martin and Davis showed their detailed methods studies to Andrews, he stated, "What you guys have done here is to blow up a big smoke screen to hide the fact that you're pulling a speedup on Sullivan's job." The net result of the meeting was that the grievance, still unsettled, moved to the second step in grievance procedure. This step involved discussion between the head of the local union, Ed Lillian, and Donald Leach, the plant manager.

Leach, when presented with Bill Sullivan's grievance, immediately called Pete Martin into his office to discuss the problem. Together they reviewed the methods study and the subsequent standards revisions. The approaches and the figures shown by Martin seemed correct and reasonable to Leach, and he believed that the contractual clause allowing him "to make changes in methods, equipment, materials, and conditions of work in order to obtain greater efficiency and to adjust existing work standards to reflect such changes" justified the introduction of the second machine. He stated, "It's

---

[4] One of the main duties of a union steward is to represent the worker in presenting grievances to management. This person is usually elected to this office by fellow workers. Stewards hold regular jobs in the plants where they perform their duties, and they receive no extra pay for their union activities.

my duty to my work force to maintain an efficient operation so that the job security of all the workers will be protected." Leach also said, "The only way we can continue to grow and prosper and provide steady employment for our workers is to push for more efficiency in all of our plant activities." In his upcoming meeting with Ed Lillian, Leach planned to use this reasoning as the basis for his insistence on the introduction of the second machine. He also intended to allow Lillian to review any and all of the data used as the basis of changes made on the disputed job.

Ed Lillian, on the other hand, expected to rely heavily on John Andrews to present the union side of the dispute. Lillian told Andrews that he would support him fully if the company's actions were in violation of the labor contract.

The feelings of the parties prior to the grievance meeting are summarized below:

Bill Sullivan: All of a sudden I'm expected to turn out 3,000 pieces per day where I used to have to do 1,400.[5] If this isn't a speedup, I don't know what the hell it is. I've got rights, and I expect the union to protect them.

John Andrews: The company hasn't done a thing to change methods here. They've just come in and made changes to correct their mistakes from the past. Their actions violate the fairness and equity clauses relating to revision of work standards which exist in the labor contract.

Pete Martin: We've made good studies of Sullivan's job, and we know that the lock-pin standard is loose. It's not unfair to ask him to put in a fair day's work in order to earn a fair day's pay.

Ed Lillian: Even though Don Leach is sometimes tough in his dealings with us, he's been fair and consistent. On this issue, however, I'm not sure he's really right.

Donald Leach: I believe that I'm both contractually and economically correct when I take the stand that the second machine should be maintained on this operation. After all, if we don't have efficiency in this plant, the workers won't have any job security.

Glenn Carter: The real issue here is whether or not managers have the right to run their own plants. If we have to subsidize inefficiency in our operations, we won't be in business very long.

The grievance meeting scheduled to resolve this dispute was affected by at least two other factors:

1. Strikes over production standards are legal during the life of the labor contract. Though other issues (wages, hours, working conditions, etc.) can be grieved, no strikes can be called legally on these matters until the existing contract expires.

2. Though one more step remained in the division's grievance procedure,

---

[5] In actuality, Sullivan was required to turn out 1,440 pieces per day before the audit. After the methods change and subsequent standards revision, Sullivan's quota rose to 2,880.

Carter had written a note to Ed Lillian which stated that he "would not, under any circumstances, alter the stand taken by Leach in the plant-level negotiations." Since the dispute cannot be arbitrated, the parties are faced with the problem of devising some other strategy to solve (or to "win") the disagreement.

In a front-page editorial on the day before the grievance meeting, the local *Kingston Daily Record* asked the disputants to act with "caution and care." The *Record's* editorial recalled that "the steel industry became embroiled in a similar issue which evolved into a strike lasting six months."

Questions for Analysis

1. Each of the parties to the disagreement has feelings about the causes of the dispute. Analyze the bases for each person's feelings in terms of unstated assumptions and values.

2. Which people appear to be analyzing the causes of the dispute in terms of *work-related,* as distinct from *person-related,* management activities? Explain.

3. What, in your judgment, are the underlying causes of this dispute? What do you believe should be the solution to the dispute? How can similar disputes be avoided in the future?

4. What solution would a manager propose who understands principles and methods of only classical and management science approaches? What solution would be proposed by a manager who understands only behavioral approach principles and methods?

5. Analyze the dispute in terms of the causes of intergroup conflict. What would be the appropriate strategy for managing the conflict during the grievance meeting?

Glossary

Acceptance Theory of Authority   A theory of authority that Barnard proposed, according to which the ultimate source of authority is the decision of the subordinate to accept the superior's orders.

Accountability   The process by which a subordinate reports the use of assigned resources to a designated superior.

Activity   The work necessary to complete a particular event in a PERT network. An activity consumes time, which is the paramount variable in a PERT system. In PERT networks, three time estimates are used for each activity: an optimistic time, a pessimistic time, and a most likely time.

Administrative Duties   The 16 guidelines that Fayol believed should direct the manager in carrying out the organizing function. There is considerable overlap between his 16 administrative duties and his 14 management principles.

Affective Attitude   The part of attitude that involves a person's emotions or feelings.

Affirmative Action Program   A program in which an employer specifies how the company plans to increase the number of minority and female employees.

Allocation Models   This type of management science model is used in a situation where several possible candidates or activities are all competing for limited resources. It enables the user to allocate scarce resources in order to maximize some predetermined objective.

Altruism   An ethical standard which places highest value on behavior that is pleasurable and rewarding to society.

Anthropology   Examines all the behaviors of man that have been learned. This includes social, technical, and family behaviors. It is often defined as the study of man and his works.

Attitude   A person's tendency to feel and behave toward some object in some way.

Attribution   An inference made about one's own feelings or another person's feelings based on observed behavior.

Authority   The legitimate right to use assigned resources to accomplish a delegated task or objective; the right to give orders and to exact obedience. The legal bases for formal authority are private property, the state, or a Supreme Being.

Behavior   Any observable response given by a person.

Behavioral Approach to Management A body of literature characterized by its concern for human behavior in the work environment. The school's primary means for acquiring knowledge is the scientific method with emphasis upon research. The behavioral approach to management thought followed the classical approach. Its first phase may be identified as "human relations" theory. This phase became popular in the 1940s and early 1950s. Its second phase was the "behavioral science" approach which came into popular use in the early 1950s.

Behavioral Approach to Organizational Design A design approach that emphasizes people and how the structure of an organization affects their behavior and performance. The advocates of a people orientation to design believe that the classical approach suppresses personal development because it is so rigid and restrictive.

Behavioral Change Planned change in the attitudes, skills, and knowledge of organizational personnel.

Behaviorally Anchored Rating Scales (BARS) A set of rating scales developed by raters and/or ratees that uses critical behavioral incidents as interval anchors on each scale. About 6 to 10 scales with behavioral incidents are used to derive the evaluation.

Behavioral Motivation Theory The behavioral approach to management advocates the pluralistic view of motivation that emphasizes that many different types of needs influence behavior and that man is motivated by the desire to satisfy many needs.

Behavioral Science Approach This approach to the study of management can be thought of as the study of observable and verifiable human behavior in organizations, using scientific procedures. It draws especially from psychology, sociology, and anthropology.

Behavior Modification An approach to motivation that uses operant conditioning: operant behavior is learned on the basis of consequences. In management, if a behavior causes a desired outcome (for managers), then it is reinforced (positively rewarded), and because of its consequences, it is likely to be repeated. Thus, behavior is conditioned by adjusting its consequences.

Benefits Financial payments (e.g., insurance premiums) made by an employer over and above the base wages and salary.

Bill of Materials A document which details the required components of each subassembly and finished good. The "demand" for components is derived from the demand for the subassemblies and finished goods.

Biofeedback A technique, usually involving the use of some kind of instrumentation, in which the user attempts to learn to control various bodily functions such as heart rate and blood pressure.

Bureaucracy An organizational design that relies on specialization of labor, a specific authority hierarchy, a formal set of rules and procedures, and rigid promotion and selection criteria.

Career   An individually perceived sequence of attitudes and behaviors associated with work-related experiences and activities over the span of a person's life.

Career Path   The sequence of jobs associated with a particular initial job that leads to promotion and advancement.

Career Planning   The process of systematically matching an individual's career aspirations with opportunities for achieving them.

Career Stages   Distinct but interrelated steps or phases of a career, including the prework stage, the initial work stage, the stable work stage, and the retirement stage.

Carrying Costs   These are the costs incurred by carrying an inventory. They include such costs as the taxes and insurance on the goods in inventory, interest on money invested in inventory and storage space, and the costs incurred because of the obsolescence of the inventory.

Case Study   This type of research design attempts to examine numerous characteristics of a person or group over an extended period of time. Since the results achieved by a case study are usually based on a sample of one, the user cannot be certain as to their generality. Most cases studies raise questions for future research.

Categorical Imperative   An ethical standard that judges behavior in terms of its consistency with the principle: "Act as if the maxim of your action were to become a general law binding on everyone."

Central Tendency Errors   The appraiser tends to rate appraisees around the midpoint, in essence indicating that every subordinate is about average.

Certainty Decision   A decision in which the manager is certain about the state of nature or competitor action that will occur. Thus, the probability that a particular event will occur is 1.00.

Civil Rights Act of 1964   An act that makes various forms of discrimination illegal. Title VII of the act spells out the forms of illegal discrimination.

Classical Approach to Management   A body of literature that represents the earliest attempts to define and describe the field of management. The approach's main focus is on formally prescribed relationships. Its primary means for acquiring knowledge are personal observation and case studies.

Classical Approach to Organizational Design   Relies on such management principles as unity of command, a balance between authority and responsibility, division of labor, and delegation to establish relationships between managers and subordinates.

Classical Management Motivation Theory   The classical approach to motivation emphasized monetary incentives as prime means for motivating the individual. This approach was undoubtedly strongly influenced by the classical economists who emphasized man's rational pursuit of economic objectives.

Closed System An approach that generally ignores environmental forces and conditions.

Coercive Power The power of a leader that is derived from fear. The follower perceives the leader as a person who can punish deviant behavior and actions.

Cognitive Attitude The part of attitude that involves a person's perceptions, beliefs, and ideas.

Cognitive Dissonance A state in which there is a discrepancy between a person's attitude and behavior.

Command Group The group shown on an organization chart that consists of employees who report to a single manager.

Communication The transmission of information and understanding through the use of common symbols.

Conceptual Management Skill The ability to coordinate and integrate ideas, concepts, and practices. Such skill is most important to top-level managers.

Concurrent Control The techniques and methods that focus on the actual, ongoing activity of the organization.

Conditions of Certainty A situation in which a person facing a decision has enough information to know what the outcome of each alternative will be.

Conditions of Risk A situation in which a person facing a decision can estimate the likelihood (probability) of a particular outcome.

Conditions of Uncertainty A situation in which the decision maker has absolutely no idea of the probabilities associated with the various alternatives being considered. In such a situation, the intuition, judgment, and personality of the decision maker can play an important role.

Consideration Acts by a leader that imply supportive concern for the followers in a group.

Contingency Management An approach that considers an organization's objectives, organizational and job design, human resources, environment, and managerial skills as interacting and affecting the type of management decisions made about planning, decision making, organizing, leading, and controlling.

Contingency Organizational Design This is the view that the internal functioning of organizations must be consistent with the demands of their task, technology, and external environment, and the needs of their members if the organization is to be effective. Contingency design focuses on what is best for a particular organization.

Continuous Reinforcement A reinforcement schedule that involves administering a reward each time a desired behavior occurs.

Controlling Function All managerial activity that is undertaken to assure that actual operations go according to plan.

Core Job Dimensions   As proposed by Hackman and others, there are five core job dimensions which, if present, provide enrichment for jobs. The dimensions are variety, task identity, task significance, autonomy, and feedback.

Cost/Benefit Analysis   A technique for evaluating individual projects and deciding among alternatives. This technique is being adapted to the needs of public sector organizations to aid them in improving their performance.

Criterion   A way of identifying success in an activity.

Critical Incident Method   The appraiser uses a log of positive and negative critical incidents to assess the performance of appraisees.

Critical Path   The longest path in a PERT network, from the network beginning event to the network ending event.

Culture   Culture is a very complex environmental influence that includes knowledge, beliefs, law, morals, art, customs, and any other habits and capabilities an individual acquires as a member of society. It is important to be aware that cultures are *learned,* cultures *vary,* and culture *influences behavior.*

Decentralization   The pushing downward of the appropriate amount of decision-making authority. All organizations practice a certain degree of decentralization.

Decision Making   The process of thought and deliberation that results in a decision. Decisions, the output of the decision-making process, are means through which a manager seeks to achieve some desired state.

Decoding   The mental procedure that the receiver of a message uses to decipher the message.

Defensive Behavior   Behavior such as aggression, withdrawal, and repression, which is resorted to by an individual when blocked in attempts to satisfy needs.

Delegation   The process by which authority is distributed downward in an organization.

Departmentalization   The process of grouping jobs together on the basis of some common characteristic, such as product, client, location, or function.

Descriptive Model   This type of model describes how a system works. It describes things as they are and makes no value judgments about the particular thing being studied. It may display the alternative choices available to the decision maker, but it does not select the best alternative.

Determinants of Personality   The formation of the human personality is influenced by the mutual interaction of many factors. Four general classifications of factors must be considered: constitutional determinants, group-membership determinants, role determinants, and situational determinants.

Deterministic Model The word *deterministic* refers to the type of variables included in the model. A model is deterministic when the law of chance plays no role. All the factors taken into account in the model are assumed to be exact or determinate quantities.

Diagnosis The use of data collected by interviews, surveys, observations, and records to learn about people or organizations.

Direct Investment Entry Strategy The strongest commitment to becoming an MNC is when management decides to begin producing the firm's products abroad. This strategy enables the firm to maintain partial to full control over production, marketing, and other key functions.

Direction A method of concurrent control which refers to the manager's act of interpreting orders to a subordinate.

Discounted Rate of Return The rate of return that equates future cash proceeds with the initial cost of an investment.

Distinctive Competence A factor that gives the organization an advantage over similar organizations. Distinctive competences are what the organization does well.

Downward Communication Communication that flows from individuals at higher levels of an organization structure to individuals at lower levels. The most common type of downward communication is job instructions transmitted from the superior to the subordinate.

Dual Careers A situation in which both the husband and the wife are pursuing careers.

Egoism An ethical standard which places highest value on behavior that is pleasurable and rewarding to the individual.

Emergent Leader A person from within the group who comes to lead or influence its members.

Encoding The converting of a communication into an understandable message by a communicator.

EOQ Model The economic order quantity model, which is used to resolve problems regarding the size of orders. A manager concerned with minimizing inventory costs could utilize the model to study the relationships between carrying costs, ordering costs, and usage.

Equal Employment Opportunity Act of 1972 A law that has specific provisions about equal opportunities for employment.

Equal Employment Opportunity Commission A governmental commission that enforces laws that attempt to provide equal opportunities for employment without regard to race, religion, age, creed, sex, national origin, or disability.

Esteem Needs The awareness of the importance of others and of the regard accorded by others.

Event An accomplishment at a particular point in time on a PERT network. An event consumes no time.

Expectancy Motivation Model   Views motivation as a process governing choices. In this model, a person who has a goal weighs the likelihood that various behaviors will achieve that goal and is likely to select the behavior he or she expects to be most successful.

Expected Time *(t$_e$)*   A time estimate for each activity that is calculated by using the formula:

$$t_e = \frac{a + 4m + b}{6}$$

where a = optimistic time, m = most likely time, and b = pessimistic time.

Expected Value   The average return of a particular decision in the long run if the decision maker makes the same decision in the same situation over and over again. The expected value is found by taking the value of an outcome if it should occur and multiplying that value by the probability that the outcome will occur.

Experiment   This type of research design contains two key elements: manipulation of some variable by the researcher and observation or measurement of the results.

Expert Power   The power that individuals possess because followers perceive them to have special skills, special knowledge, or special expertise.

Export Entry Strategy   The simplest way for a firm to enter a foreign market is by exporting. This strategy involves little or no change in the basic mission, objectives, and strategies of the organization, since it continues to produce all of its products at home. The firm will usually secure an *agent* in the particular foreign market who facilitates the transactions with foreign buyers.

External Change Forces   Forces for change outside the organization, such as the pricing strategies of competitors, the available supply of resources, and government regulations.

Feedback Control   Techniques and methods which analyze historical data to correct future events.

Final Performance Review   The last step in the MBO process, a final meeting between the manager and the subordinate which focuses on performance over an entire period. The final performance review must accomplish two important purposes: (1) an evaluation of the objectives achieved and the relating of these accomplishments to rewards such as salary increments and promotion and (2) an evaluation of performance, intended to aid the subordinate in self-development and to set the stage for the next period.

First-Line Management   The lowest level of the hierarchy. A manager at this level coordinates the work of nonmanagers but reports to a manager.

Forecasting   An important element of the planning function which must make these two basic determinations: (1) what level of activity can be expected during the planning period and (2) what level of resources will be available to support the projected activity. In a business organization, the critical forecast is the sales forecast.

Foreign Activities Entry Strategy   As exports increase in importance to the firm, it may decide that it can justify its own foreign activities. This decision usually involves joining with nationals in the foreign country to establish product and/or marketing facilities. It differs from direct investment in that some type of association is formed with a local firm or individual. This type of association usually takes the form of licensing or joint-venture arrangements. *Licensing* is granting the right to produce and/or market the firm's product in another country to an outside firm. *Joint-venture* arrangements involve foreign investors forming a group with local investors to begin a local business with each group sharing ownership.

Formal Groups   The established departments, units, and teams created by the managers in an organization.

Friendship Group   An informal group that evolves because of some common characteristic such as age, political sentiment, or background.

Frustration   This occurs when individuals are unable to satisfy their needs. Frustration may result in constructive problem-solving behavior or defensive behavior.

Generativity   An individual's concern for actions and achievements that will benefit future generations.

Goal Participation   The amount of involvement a person has in setting task and personal development goals.

Grapevine   An informal communication network in organizations that short-circuits the formal channels.

Graphic Rating Scales   Appraiser uses a printed form with various job dimensions and is asked to provide a rating for each appraisee.

Grid Training   A leadership development method proposed by Blake and Mouton that emphasizes the necessary balance between production orientation and person orientation.

Group Assets   The advantages derived from the increase in knowledge that is brought to bear on a problem when a group examines it.

Group Cohesiveness   The attraction of individual members to a group in terms of the strength of the forces that impel them to remain active in the group and to resist leaving it.

Group Development   The phases or sequences through which a group passes: mutual acceptance, decision making, motivation, and control.

Group Liabilities   The negative features of groups, such as the group pressure that is expected to bring dissident members into line, the take-over by a dominant member, and the reduced creativity that results from the embarrassment of members about expressing themselves.

Group Norm   Agreement among a group's members about how they should behave.

Group Politics   The use of self-serving tactics to improve a group's position relative to that of other groups.

Group Think   A phenomenon that occurs when a group believes that it is invincible, turns off criticism, attempts to bring noncomplying members into line, and feels that everyone is in agreement.

Halo Effects   The forming of general impressions (positive or negative) about a person based on an impression formed from performance in one area.

Halo Error   A positive or negative aura around a ratee that influences a rater's evaluation.

Hawthorne Effect   The tendency of people who are being observed or involved in a research effort to react differently than they would otherwise.

Hawthorne Studies   Management studies conducted at the Western Electric Hawthorne plant in a suburb of Chicago. The most famous studies that have ever been conducted in the field of management.

Hierarchy of Needs   A widely adopted pluralistic framework of motivation. Developed by psychologist A. H. Maslow, the theory stresses two ideas: (1) Only needs not yet satisfied can influence behavior; and (2) human needs are arranged in a hierarchy of importance. When one level has been satisfied, a higher-level need emerges and demands satisfaction. Maslow distinguishes five general classes of needs: physiological, safety, social, esteem, and self-actualization.

Horizontal Communication   Occurs when the communicator and the receiver are at the same level in the organization.

Horizontal Specialization of Management   The process by which the natural sequence of a task is broken down into specialized subgroups and a manager is assigned the authority and responsibility for coordinating the subgroups.

Human Management Skill   The ability to work with, motivate, and counsel people who need help and guidance. Most important to middle-level managers.

Human Relations Approach   This approach to management emphasized the important role that individuals play in determining the success or failure of an organization. It embarked on the critical task of compensating for some of the deficiencies in classical theory. Basically, it took the premises of the Classical Approach as given. However, it showed how these premises were modified as a result of individual behavior and the influence of the work group.

Human Resource Management The process of accomplishing organizational objectives by acquiring, retaining, terminating, developing, and properly using the human resources in an organization.

Human Resource Planning The steps taken in estimating the size and makeup of the future work force.

Immediate Performance Measures Measures of results that are monitored over short periods of time, such as a day, a week, a month, or a year. These include measures of output, quality, time, cost, and profit. Immediate performance measures are not always easy to obtain.

Incremental Influence This concept refers to the influence of a leader over and above the influence base best owed by position in the organization.

Informal Groups Natural groupings of people in response to some need.

Initiating Structure Leadership acts that develop job tasks and responsibilities for followers.

Inputs Used in calculating productivity ratios. Labor, cost, materials, and miscellaneous goods and services are typically used to calculate inputs.

Insufficient-Reason Criterion If a manager is operating under conditions of uncertainty, it is assumed that there is an equal probability that each of the possible states of nature or competitive actions may occur.

Integration The degree to which members of various departments work together effectively.

Intelligence Information Data on elements of the organization's operating environment, such as clients, competitors, suppliers, creditors, and the government, for use in short-run planning, and data on developments in the economic environment, such as consumer income trends and spending patterns, and in the social and cultural environment, for use in long-run strategic planning.

Interest Group A group formed to achieve some job-related but personal objective.

Intergroup Conflict The disagreements, hostile emotions, and problems that exist among groups. These conflicts emerge because of limited resources, communication problems, differences in perceptions and attitudes, and a lack of clarity.

Intermediate Performance Reviews In the MBO process, periodic reviews of performance that monitor progress toward achieving the objectives that have been established and the action plans that have been developed. These reviews are an important element of control in management by objectives.

Intermittent Reinforcement A reinforcement schedule that involves rewarding desired behavior only periodically.

Internal Change Forces   Forces for change that occur within the organization, such as communication problems, morale problems, and decision-making breakdowns.

Inventory Models   A type of production control model which answers two questions relating to inventory management. "How much?" and "When?" An inventory model tells the manager when goods should be reordered and what quantity should be purchased.

Job Analysis   The procedures for determining the tasks that make up a job, and the skills, abilities, and responsibilities an employee needs to do the job.

Job Depth   The relative freedom that a jobholder has in the performance of assigned duties.

Job Description   A statement that furnishes information about a job's duties, technology, conditions, and hazards. Data for preparing the description come from the job and analysis.

Job Enlargement   A form of despecialization in that the number of tasks performed by the employees is increased. The increase in tasks theoretically makes the job more interesting and challenging. Consequently work becomes more psychologically rewarding.

Job Enrichment   Suggested formally by Herzberg, this involves building into individual jobs greater scope for personal achievement, recognition, and responsibility. It is concerned with strengthening the motivational factors and only incidentally with maintenance.

Job Evaluation   Attaching a dollar value to a job so that comparisons of jobs on the basis of value can be made.

Job Evaluation System   A process used to determine the relative value of jobs within the organization.

Job Rotation   The procedure of moving a worker from one work station to another to minimize boredom.

Job Scope   The relative complexity of the assigned task as reflected by its cycle time.

Job Specification   A statement derived from the job analysis about the human qualifications needed to perform the job.

Just-in-Time (JIT) Inventory Control   A refined application of MRP which results in components becoming available at the precise moment in time when they are required. The effect of JIT is to reduce to a minimum the carrying cost of component parts.

Leader-Member Relations   In the Fiedler situational model of leadership, a factor that refers to the degree of confidence, trust, and respect that followers have in the leader.

Leadership   In the context of management theory, the ability of a person to influence the activities of followers in an organizational setting. Management theory emphasizes that a leader must interact with the followers in order to be influential.

Lead Time   The length of time between ordering and receiving an item of inventory. Inventory on hand must be sufficient to meet demand during the lead-time period.

Legitimate Power   The power that rank gives to a leader in the managerial hierarchy. For example, the department manager possesses more legitimate power than the supervisor because the department manager is ranked higher than the supervisor.

Less Developed Country (LDC)   An LDC has a very low gross national product, very little industry or a vastly unequal distribution of income, with a very large number of poor.

Linear Programming   A production planning technique with widespread applicability in organizations that produce repetitive and routine products and services. The technique enables management to make the optimal allocation of resources to alternative products and services.

Line Functions   Activities that contribute directly to the creation of the organization's output. In manufacturing, the line functions are production, marketing, and finance.

Macro-Organizational Design   The design of an organization or a department.

Maintenance Factors   Distinguished by Herzberg in his "two-factor" theory of motivation. Maintenance factors are those conditions of the job which operate primarily to dissatisfy employees when they are not present. However, their presence does not build strong motivation among employees. Herzberg distinguished 16 of these factors (for example, salary, job security, work conditions).

Management by Objectives (MBO)   A planning and controlling method which comprises these major elements: (1) the superior and the subordinate meet to discuss goals and to jointly establish attainable goals for the subordinate; (2) the superior and the subordinate meet again afterward to evaluate the subordinate's performance in terms of the goals that have been set.

Management Development   The process of educating and developing selected personnel so that they have the knowledge, skills, attitudes, and understanding needed to manage in the future.

Management Science Approach   A body of literature characterized by its use of mathematical and statistical techniques to build models for the solution of production and operations problems. The approach's primary means for acquiring knowledge is mathematical deduction.

Managerial Roles   The organized sets of behavior that belong to the manager's job. The three main types of managerial roles discovered by such researchers as Mintzberg are interpersonal, informational, and decisional roles.

Master Production Schedule A document which details the planned production of all finished goods for a particular time period. The master production schedule is based upon the strategic plan and the production plan.

Material-Requirements Planning (MRP) An inventory planning and controlling technique that involves identifying each component and subassembly of a complete product and then coordinating the ordering and delivering of those components and subassemblies. The technique usually requires a computer to deal with the mass of required information.

Matrix Organizational Design A design in which a project-type structure is superimposed on a functional structure.

Maximax Criterion The optimistic manager believes that only the most favorable result will occur and decides to maximize the maximum payoff.

Maximin Criterion The pessimistic manager believes that only the least favorable result will occur and therefore decides to maximize the minimum payoff.

Mechanistic System An organizational design in which there is differentiation of job tasks, rigid rules, and a reliance on top-management objectives.

Mentor A relationship that exists when an older employee helps a younger person learn the job, the systems procedures, and the rituals of the organization.

Micro-Organizational Design The design of a job.

Midcareer Plateau The point or stage of a career at which the individual has no opportunity for further promotion or advancement.

Middle Management The middle level of an administrative hierarchy. Managers at this level coordinate the work of managers and report to a manager.

Minimax Criterion The manager believes that once a decision is made and an outcome occurs, there will be some regret and selects that strategy which results in the least regret.

Mission A long-term vision of what an organization is trying to become. The mission is the unique aim that differentiates an organization from similar organizations. The basic questions that must be answered in order to determine an organization's mission are, "What is our business? What should it be?"

Motion Study The process of analyzing work in order to determine the most efficient motions for performing tasks. Motion study, a major contribution of scientific management, was developed principally through the efforts of Frederick Taylor and Frank and Lillian Gilbreth.

Motivation The inner strivings that initiate a person's actions.

Motivational Factors Distinguished by Herzberg in his two-factor theory of motivation. Motivational factors are those job conditions that, if present, operate to build high levels of motivation and job satisfaction. However, their absence does not prove highly dissatisfying. Herzberg distinguished six of these factors (for example, achievement, recognition, advancement).

Multinational Company (MNC)   An MNC is a business firm doing business in two or more countries.

Negative Reinforcement   Removing a disliked event immediately after response occurs in order to bring about an increase in the response's frequency.

Noise   Any interference with the flow of a message from a sender to a receiver.

Nonprogrammed Decisions   Decisions for novel and unstructured problems or for complex or extremely important problems. Nonprogrammed decisions deserve special attention of top management.

Normative Model   This type of model is specifically constructed to select from among alternatives the best one based on some previously determined criteria, which are also included in the model. It tells how the system should be in order to achieve a particular objective.

Norms   An agreement among the group members as to how members should behave.

Occupational Safety and Health Act (OSHA)   An act to protect the health of employees. Employers must furnish workplaces free from recognized hazards to life and health.

Operating Management   Manages the implementation of programs and projects in each area of performance, measures and evaluates results, and compares results with objectives.

Operations   A broad term that is used to describe the activities and flow of work, resources, and materials in goods- or service-producing organizations.

Order Cost   An element in inventory control models that comprises clerical, administrative, and labor costs; a major cost component that is considered in inventory control decisions. Each time a firm orders items for inventory, some clerical and administrative work is usually required to place the order and some labor is required to put the items in inventory.

Organic System   An organizational design with a behavioral orientation, participation from all employees, and communication flowing in all directions.

Organizational Change   The intentional attempt by management to improve the overall performance of individuals, groups, and the organization as a whole by altering the organization's structure, behavior, and technology.

Organizational Communications   Information that flows outward from the organization to the various components of its external operating environment. Whatever the type of organization, the content of this information flow is controlled by the organization (e.g., advertising).

Organizational Objectives   The broad continuing aims that serve as guides for action and as the starting point for more specific and detailed operating objectives at lower levels in the organization. This book classifies organizatinal objectives into four categories: profitability, competitiveness, efficiency, and flexibility.

Organizational Performance   The extent to which an organization achieves the results that society expects of it. Organizational performance is affected in part by managerial performance.

Organizational Psychology   The study of behavior and attitudes within an organization, including the effect of the organization upon the individual and the individual's effect upon the organization.

Organizational Strategies   The general approaches that are utilized by the organization to achieve its organizational objectives. These approaches include market penetration, market development, product development, and diversification strategies.

Organizational Structure   The formally defined framework of task and authority relationships. The organization structure is analogous to the biological concept of the skeleton.

Organizing Function   All managerial activity that results in the design of a formal structure of tasks and authority.

Outputs   Used in calculating productivity ratios. The output of a firm usually is expressed in a volume amount. Outputs also are considered for group and individual productivity ratios.

Participative Approach   A technique advocated by behavioralists that stresses the idea that employees throughout the firm should be allowed to participate in decision making.

Path-Goal Leadership   An approach to leadership in which the leader indicates to followers the "paths" to accomplish their goals.

Payback Period   The length of time that it takes for an investment to pay for itself out of future funds.

Peer Relationship   A relationship between peers that provides support, feedback, infomation, and/or friendship.

Perception   The process by which individuals organize and interpret their impressions of the environment around them.

Performance Appraisal   A procedure used by managers to asess performance and inform the employee of their expectations and opinions.

Performance Evaluation   A postcontrol technique which focuses on the extent to which employees have achieved expected levels of work during a specified time period.

Personal-Behavioral Leadership Theories A group of theories that are based primarily on the personal and behavioral characteristics of leaders. These theories focus on *what* leaders do and/or *how* leaders behave in carrying out the leadership function.

Personality The sum of an individual's traits or characteristics. These traits interact to create personality patterns.

Physiological (Basic) Needs Consist of needs of the human body, such as food, water, and sex.

Planning Function All managerial activities which lead to the definition of objectives and to the determination of appropriate means to achieve those objectives.

Policies Guidelines for managerial action that must be adhered to at all times. Policymaking is an important management planning element for assuring that action is oriented toward objectives. The purpose of policies is to achieve consistency and direction and to protect the reputation of the organization.

Position Power A factor in the Fiedler theory of leadership that refers to the power inherent in the leadership position.

Positive Reinforcement A response is followed by a positive reinforcer, resulting in an increase in the frequency of the response.

Power The ability to influence another person's behavior.

Preliminary Control Techniques and methods which attempt to maintain the quality and quantity of resources.

Prescriptive Management Discovering and reporting how managers should perform their functions.

Principle of Management A generally accepted tenet which guides the thinking and on-the-job practices of managers.

Private Sector Organizations Profit-making organizations in the U.S. economy.

Probabilistic Model Model based on the mathematics of statistics. Conditions of uncertainty are introduced in the model, often based on observations of real-world events.

Production A term that is used to address manufacturing technology and the flow of materials in a manufacturing facility.

Productivity Any ratio of output to one or more corresponding units.

Profitability Measures Profitability measures include the ratio of net profit to capital, to total assets, and to sales.

Program Evaluation and Review Technique (PERT) A production planning technique with widespread applicability in organizations that produce large-scale, nonroutine products. The technique enables management to make the optimal allocation of resources to the activities that lead to completion of the product.

Programmed Decisions   Responses to repetitive and routine problems, which are handled by a standard procedure that has been developed by management.

Projection   The tendency of people to attribute to others traits which they feel are negative aspects of their own personality.

Punishment   The introduction of something disliked or the removal of something liked following a particular response in order to decrease the frequency of that response.

Quality Circles   A small group from the work unit, ranging in size from 4 to 15, who voluntarily meet on a regular basis to study quality-control and productivity improvement techniques and to identify and solve work problems.

Realistic Job Previews (RJP)   The practice of providing realistic information to new employees. The recruiter tells it like it is to avoid creating expectations that cannot be realized.

Recency of Events Error   The tendency to make biased ratings because of the excessive influence of recent events.

Recruitment   Steps taken to staff an organization with the best-qualified people.

Recycling   The process by which one MBO cycle gives way to another. The final for performance evaluation session of one MBO leads directly into the establishment of objectives for the next cycle. Divisional or departmental objectives are established, individual objective-setting sessions are conducted, and the MBO process recycles.

Referent Power   The power of a leader that is based on the leader's attractiveness. The leader is admired because of certain personal qualities, and the follower identifies closely with those qualities.

Resource-Requirements Planning (RRP)   An advanced application of MRP which includes all the resources required to produce a product or service. Bills of resources identify required materials and labor, machines, capital, cash, and any and all other resources.

Reward Power   The power generated by followers' perception that compliance with the wishes of leaders can lead to positive rewards (for example, promotion).

Risk Decisions   Decision situations in which managers do not know for certain the probability of occurrence of the state of nature or competitive actions. However, they have some past experience and/or data upon which they can rely to develop probabilities. These probabilities are used with conditional values to determine expected values.

Robot A reprogrammable multifunctional manipulator designed to move material, parts, tools, or specialized devices through programmed motions.

Safety Stock The quantity of materials that management decides is necessary to have on hand at all times to guard against stock-outs due to unforeseen circumstances.

Salaries Compensation based on time. The unit of time is a week, a month, or longer.

Sample Survey Collection of data from a limited number of units which are assumed to be representative of the entire group.

Scalar Chain The graded chain of authority through which all organizational communications flow.

Scientific Management The practices introduced by Frederick W. Taylor to accomplish the management job. Taylor advocated the use of scientific procedures to find the one best way to do a job.

Self-Actualization Needs The need to fully realize one's potential.

Self-Fulfilling Prophecy The notion that what a leader expects of someone else and the way the leader treats the other person will result in the expectation coming true. For example, if a manager treats a subordinate as if he or she is lazy, the subordinate will behave in a manner to support the treatment.

Sensitivity Training An organizational change approach that focuses on the emotions and processes of interacting with people.

Services Nonmonetary programs provided by companies to employees (e.g., gymnasium facilities).

Simulation Model A mode which replicates some aspect of the firm's operation. By performing step-by-step computations with the model, one duplicates the manner in which the actual system might perform.

Situational Favorableness This is the degree to which a (work) situation enables a leader to exert influence over a group. This concept is associated with Fiedler's theory of leadership.

Situational Theory of Leadership An approach that advocates that leaders understand their own behavior, the behavior of their subordinates, and the situation before they utilize a particular leadership style. The application of this approach requires the leader to have diagnostic skills in human behavior.

Social Loafing The tendency of a member in a group to not work hard or carry a fair share of the work, by hiding within the group structure.

Social Needs Needs for social interaction and companionship.

Social Psychology Branch of psychology dealing with the behavior of individuals as they relate to other individuals.

Span of Control   The number of subordinates who report to a superior. The span of control is a factor that affects the shape and height of an organization structure.

Stable External Environment   An environment in which there is little unpredictable change.

Staff Functions   Activities which contribute indirectly to the creation of the organization's output. Ordinarily, staff personnel advise line personnel.

Staffing   A process that includes the forecasting of personnel needs and the recruitment, selection, placement, and training and development of employees.

Status Consensus   The agreement of group members about the relative status of members of the group.

Status Hierarchy   The ranking of group members within the group; that is, the prestige rank order of group members.

Stereotyping   The attribution of a whole set of traits to persons on the basis of their membership in particular groups.

Strategic Business Units (SBUs)   A division or product line of an organization that can be considered a "business"; an important part of the organization's portfolio plan in the strategic planning process. Management must decide which business to build, maintain, or eliminate.

Strategic Management   Develops the mission, objectives, and strategies of the entire organization; the top-level decision makers in the organization.

Strategic Planning   A planning process that deals with long-range goals, selection of activities to achieve those goals, and the allocation of resources to those activities.

Stress   The consequence of the interaction between an event or situation and the individual as modified by individual differences.

Strictness or Leniency Rater Errors   Ratings that are lower or higher than the average ratings usually given because of the strictness or the leniency of the rater.

Structural Change   A planned change of the formally prescribed task and authority relationships in an organization's design.

Supervision   A subfunction of control that refers to the oversight of subordinates' work activity.

Supportive Relations   The consideration and interest displayed by a manager toward subordinates.

System 4   Likert's people-oriented organization design, which emphasized open communication, supportiveness, inputs from employees to managers, and general supervision. The opposite extreme of System 4 is System 1 organization design.

Tall Pyramid Structure A structure which fosters narrow spans of control, a large number of management levels, and more centralized decision making.

Task Group A formal group of individuals working as a unit to complete a task.

Task Structure The degree of structure imposed on a job. The job may be routine or nonroutine. If the job is routine it will be spelled out in detail. An inspector on the assembly line has a structured task, while the job of the research scientist has relatively little task structure.

Team Building A change technique that focuses on the interaction within a group to identify and solve problems and implement changes.

Technical Management Skill The skill of working with the resources and knowledge in a specific area. Such skill is most important to first-level managers.

Technological Change A planned change in the machinery, equipment, or techniques that are used to accomplish organizational goals.

Technology The types and patterns of activity, equipment, and material, and knowledge or experience used to perform tasks. Technology is an important contingency variable in organization design theory.

Theory X and Theory Y McGregor's theory that behind every management decision is a set of assumptions that a manager makes about human behavior. The Theory X manager assumes that people are lazy, dislike work, want no responsibility, and prefer to be closely directed. The Theory Y manager assumes that people seek responsibility, like to work, and are committed to doing good work if rewards are received for achievement.

Time Series Analysis A statistical technique for analyzing the relationship between a specified variable and time.

Time Study The process of determining the appropriate elapsed time for the completion of a task or job. This process was developed as part of Frederick W. Taylor's effort to determine a fair day's work.

Top Management The top level of an administrative hierarchy. Managers at this level coordinate the work of other managers but do not report to a manager.

Training A continual process of helping employees to perform at a high level. Training may occur on the job or at a special training facility.

Trait Theory Attempts to specify which personal characteristics (physical, personality, mental) are associated with leadership effectiveness. Trait theory relies on research that relates various traits to effectiveness criteria.

Transactional Analysis A behavioral change approach designed to give individuals insight into their impact on others and their interpersonal communication style.

Uncertainty Decisions   Decision situations in which no past experiences or historical data are available. Any one of a number of criteria are employed depending upon the personality of the manager.

Unity of Command   A management principle which states that each subordinate should report to only one superior.

Unity of Direction   The process of grouping all related activities under one superior.

Unsatisfied Need   The starting point in the process of motivation. It is a deficiency of something within the individual that provides the spark that leads to behavior.

Upward Communication   Upward communication flows from individuals at lower levels of an organization structure to those at higher levels. Some of the most common upward communication flows are suggestion boxes, group meetings, and appeal or grievance procedures.

Value Set   A lasting set of convictions that are held by a person, an accompanying mode of conduct, and the importance of the convictions to the person.

Variable Budgeting   A form of budgeting that targets expected costs at various potential output levels.

Variable Costs   Costs that vary closely with changes in production. For example, as the number of units produced increases, the amount of material used also increases. Thus the cost of material used to produce a product would be an example of variable costs.

Vertical Specialization of Management   The process by which the right to command is delegated downward so as to create a hierarchy of positions graded by degrees of assigned authority.

Vroom-Yetton Theory   A situational theory of leadership that attempts to identify the appropriate leadership style for a given set of circumstances or situations. The leadership styles are defined in terms of the extent to which the subordinates participate in decision making.

Wages   Compensations based on the time an employee works or number of units produced.

Waiting-Line Models   Waiting-line models enable the manager to reach optimal decisions in facilities planning. They help in striking a balance between the cost of additional facilities and some other factor such as idle time or customer ill will.

Weighted Checklist   A rating system consisting of statements that describe various types and levels of behavior for a particular job. Each of the statements is weighted according to its importance.

Work Overload   There are two types of overload: *quantitative*—when a person has too many different things to do or an insufficient amount of time to do the job; *qualitative*—when a person feels a lack of ability to do a part of the job.

NAME INDEX

SUBJECT INDEX

Repetitive production, 582–91
Research and development, 202–3
Resource-allocator, 31
Resource requirements planning, 629
Resources
  budgeting, 106–8
  forecasting, 105–6
  in planning, 105–8
Return-on-investment method of capital control, 215–16
Reward power, 374–75
Rewards, 312
Reverse performance review, 376
Risk conditions, 540–43
Robotics Institute of America, 472
Robots, 472–74, 754–58
Routine technology; see Mass production
Rumors, 436–38
  reasons for, 437

S

Safety and health standards, 265–66
Safety needs, 295
Safety stock of goods, 617
  determination of, 626–27
Salaries, 262
  of women, 741–43
Sales volume forecasting, 104–5
Sample survey, 287
Sampling, in quality review, 518
Satisfaction-reward preference loop, 312
Sayama, Japan, 45
SBU; see Strategic business units
Scheduling of production, 511
Scientific management
  basis of, 79
  early proponents, 78
  labor-management disputes, 79–80
Scientific subenvironment, 193
Scope of change, 479
Screening; see Employee selection and placement
Selective perception, 429
Self-actualization need, 297–98
Self-appraisals, 256, 271–72
Self-interest, 449
Semantic problems, 431
Sensitivity training, 467–69
Service
  definition, 508
  quality control, 207

Sex discrimination suit, 743
Sherman Antitrust Act, 661
Short-circuiting of communication, 432
Short-range unit plans, 114–15
Situational favorableness, 391
Situational theories of leadership, 289–98
Situation demands, 185
Social loafing, 352
Social needs, 295–96
Social psychology, 285
Social responsibility
  activities, 655–60
  at American Express, 649–40
  at Apple Computer, 658
  areas of social concern, 655
  at Atlantic Richfield, 647
  beneficiaries of, 655–56
  changing expectations, 660–63
  classification of activities, 654
  contemporary expectations, 663
  continuum, 653–54
  to customers, 656–57
  to employees, 657–58
  external beneficiaries, 659–60
  general social issues, 660
  at Hasbro Company, 647
  history of, 661–63
  internal beneficiaries, 656–59
  managerial ethics, 663–67
  and managers, 650–51
  minimum legal requirements, 651
  3M Company, 647
  multinational companies, 682
  at R. J. Reynolds, 652–53
  as social obligation, 649–51
  as social reaction, 651–52
  as social responsiveness, 652–53
  to stockholders, 658–59
  at Union Carbide, 647
Social responsiveness, 652–53
Sociology, 285
Sociotechnical systems, 464–65
Solvency measure, 220
Source credibility, 430–31
Southern Christian Leadership Conference, 672
Spans of control, 161–62
Specialization of labor, 150–53
Spokesperson role, 30
Staff personnel, 166–67
Staff specialist, 167
Standard cost analysis, 221–22
Standardization, 168–69

Standard labor/materials costs, 221
Standards
  definition, 208
  of multinationals, 690
  performance appraisal, 255
  of quality, 517–18
  quality of raw materials, 213–14
  safety and health, 265–66
Stars, 133
State of nature, 537
Statistical quality control, 223
Statistical sampling of raw materials, 213–14
Stereotyping, 429
Stockholders, 658–59
Strategic business units (SBUs)
  business portfolio matrix, 133–34
  cash cows, 133–34
  cash traps, 134
  characteristics, 132
  question marks, 134
  stars, 133
  strategic choices, 134–36
Strategic level of management, 25
Strategic planning
  company mission, 122–23
  definition, 121
  diversification, 143–44
  Family Store, 144–46
  growth of, 120–23
  mission statement, 123–28
  multinationals, 678–80
  organizational mission, 123–28
  organizational objectives, 128–29
  organizational strategies, 129–31
  and operational plans, 137
  poor, 737
  process, 123–39
  by strategic business units, 132–36
  at 3M Company, 136–37
Strategy
  Chandler's view, 197–99
  cost leadership, 196–97
  in decision making, 537
  differentiation, 197
  diversification, 131
  focus, 197
  for growth, 198
  market development, 131
  market penetration, 130–31
  at Porsche, 196
  Porter's view, 196–97
  product development, 131
  role and achievement, 129–30

COMPANY INDEX

This book has been set VideoComp in 10 and 9 point Times Roman, leaded 2 points. Part titles are 16 point and chapter titles are 14 point Helvetica Bold. The size of the type area is 35 by 47½ picas.